AF605792

Myth and the Creative Process

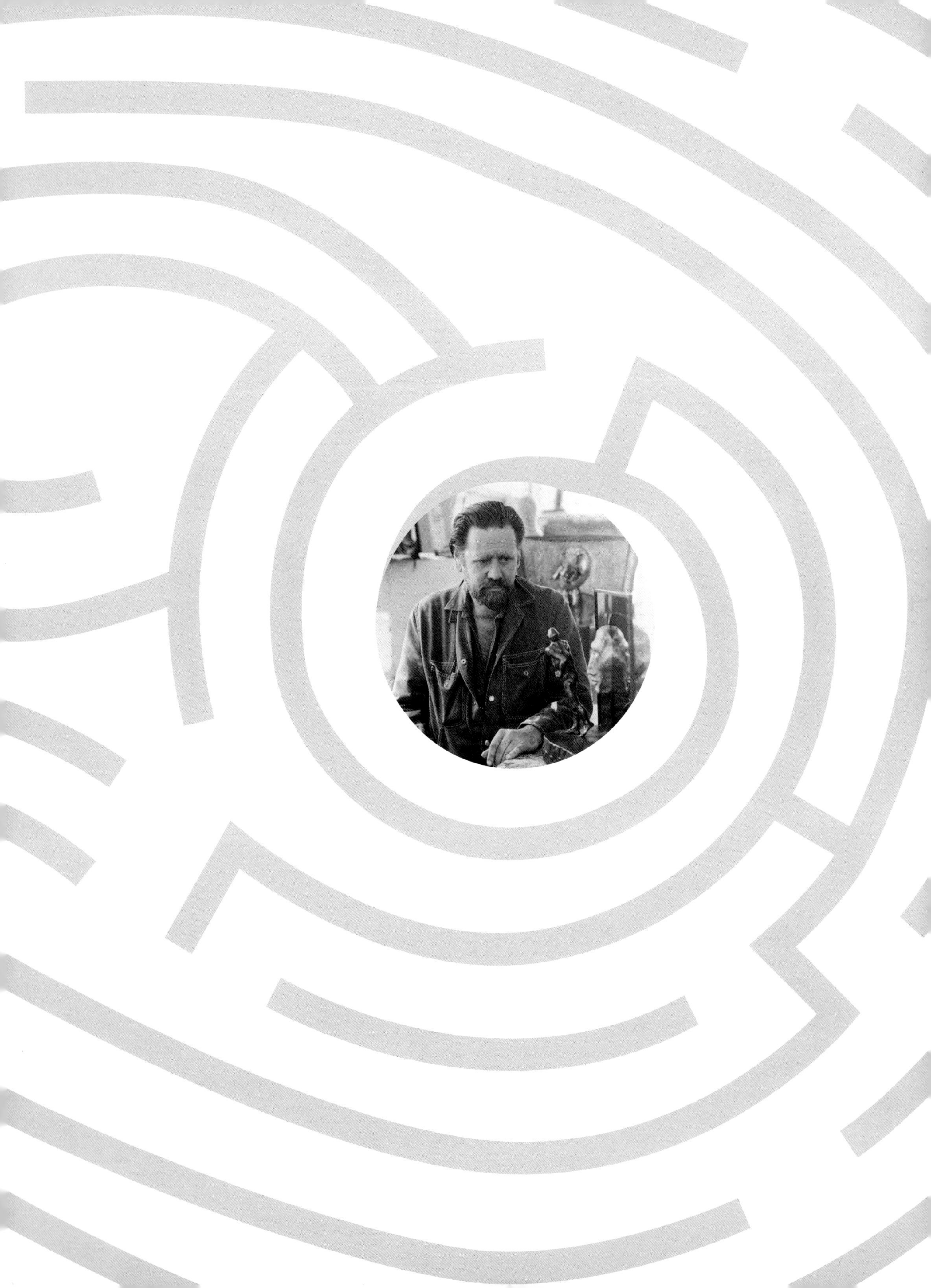

Myth and the Creative Process

Michael Ayrton and the Myth of Daedalus, the Maze Maker

Jacob E. Nyenhuis

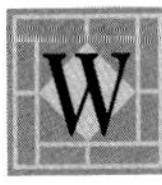

WAYNE STATE UNIVERSITY PRESS / DETROIT

Published by Wayne State University Press,
Detroit, Michigan 48201.
Manufactured in the United States of America.
07 06 05 04 03 5 4 3 2 1

Library of Congress Cataloging-in-Publication Data

Nyenhuis, Jacob E., 1935–
Myth and the creative process : Michael Ayrton and the myth of Daedalus, the maze maker / Jacob E. Nyenhuis.
p. cm.
Includes bibliographical references and index.
ISBN 0-8143-3002-9 ((cloth) : alk. paper)
1. Ayrton, Michael, 1921–1975. 2. Daedalus (Greek mythology)—Art.
I. Title.
N6797.A98 A4 2003
709'.2—dc21
2002007159

∞ The paper used in this publication meets the minimum requirements of the American National Standard for Information Sciences—Permanence of Paper for Printed Library Materials, ANSI Z39.48-1984.

To Leona,
whose patience, encouragement,
and love have sustained me during
my long journey into this labyrinth

Contents

Illustrations

COLOR PLATES

HALFTONES

Acknowledgments

My debt of gratitude extends over several decades, since my initial foray into this project began with a commissioned article on classical myth in twentieth-century art and literature, published in Wayne State University's *Graduate Comment* in December 1967. I am indebted first, therefore, to Professor Ernest J. Ament, the guest editor of that issue, for inviting me to write the article. I am likewise indebted to the late Professor H. D. F. Kitto for introducing me to Michael Ayrton when we three were all visiting professors at University of California, Santa Barbara, in the fall of 1967.

Research and writing were facilitated by grants and a sabbatical from both Wayne State University and Hope College, by visiting professorships at UCSB, Ohio State University, and the American School of Classical Studies at Athens, by a short-term fellowship at the University of Chicago through the generosity of the Mellon Foundation and under the aegis of the Midwest Faculty Seminar Program, and an appointment as visiting scholar at Green College, Oxford. I am grateful to faculty and adminstrators at these institutions and to my students in undergraduate and graduate seminars in which I first tested my ideas about myth and the creative process. I especially offer my gratitude to President Emeritus John H. Jacobson and President James E. Bultman of Hope College for their support and encouragement. I am also grateful to Dr. Elton J. Bruins, Director of the Van Raalte Institute at Hope College, for my post-retirement appointment as the A. C. Van Raalte Senior Research Fellow and for the fine research office and research support that this appointment has provided.

Publication of this book has been made possible by a subvention provided by generous gifts to Hope College for this purpose. Deserving of very special appreciation are dear friends Roger and Connie Brummel, who were the first to come forward with a donation for this project. I also express my deep appreciation to Hope College Trustee Arnold Van Zanten and President Bultman for their generous support of this project.

Many galleries and their staff provided valuable information and assistance. Chief among them were Richard B. Findley of Sears Vincent Price Gallery, Chicago, R. Stanley Johnson of R. S. Johnson-International Gallery, Chicago, Christopher Hull Gallery, London, and Michael le Marchant of Bruton Gallery, Somerset. Librarians at Wayne State University, the University of Michigan, the University of Chicago, and the Bodleian in Oxford, as well as Lisa Hodgins of Conde Nast-UK and Van Wylen Library faculty at Hope College—particularly Mark Christel, Kelly Gordon-Jacobsma, David Jensen, and David O'Brien—provided invaluable assistance at key points in my research. Secretarial assistance was provided early on by Carol Bartley, Penelope Majeske, and Marijo Powder at Wayne State University, and later, at Hope College, by Lannette Carson, Ann W. Farley, Susan Feldkamp, Barbara Masselink, and Barbara Westrate, especially by handling the extensive correspondence required to communicate with galleries, museums, photographers, publishers, and collectors.

Permission to publish photographs and excerpts from books and journals is gratefully acknowledged. The photographic credits are listed separately, but appreciation for the right to publish copyrighted material from the following sources is hereby acknowledged:

The estate of Michael Ayrton for permission to quote from *The Maze Maker* (Longmans, Green, 1967; and Holt, Rinehart & Winston, 1967) and *The Testament of Daedalus* (Methuen, 1962).

"The Fall of Icarus *(From Brueghel's Painting)*" by Charles F. Madden, copyright 1960. Used by permission of *Northwest Review*.

"Landscape with the Fall of Icarus" by William Carlos Williams, from *Collected Poems 1939–1962: Volume II*, copyright © 1953 by William Carlos Williams. Reprinted by permission of New Directions Publishing Corp. Used by permission of New Directions Publishing Corporation.

"Museé des Beaux Arts," copyright 1940 and renewed 1968 by W. H. Auden, from *W. H. Auden: The Collected Poems* by W. H. Auden. Used by permission of Random House, Inc. Used in the U.K. by permission of Faber and Faber.

"Ars Poetica*: in memoriam Michael Ayrton, sculptor*," by Donald Davie. Used by permission of Mrs. Doreen Davie.

A Portrait of the Artist as a Young Man by James Joyce, copyright 1916 by B.W. Huebsch, copyright 1944 by Nora Joyce, copyright © 1964 by the Estate of James Joyce. Used by Permission of Viking Penguin, a division of Penguin Putnam Inc.

Several colleagues read drafts of my manuscript, offered valuable insights, and spared me a number of errors and omissions. Charles A. Huttar and John Montgomery Wilson, now professors emeriti of Hope College, deserve special appreciation. Professor John Betts, University of Bristol and editor of Bristol Classical Texts, gave much needed encouragement after he reviewed the penultimate draft. Finally, two unidentified readers for Wayne State University Press and a member of the Press's editorial board also provided advice and insights that led to further improvements in my manuscript. The editorial support provided by WSU Press has been exceptional. It has been a pleasure to work with copy editor Sandra Williamson and managing editor Kathryn Wildfong, as well as with associate director Alice Nigoghosian and director Arthur B. Evans. The unfailing support and encouragement by Arthur Evans over more than a decade warrant my enduring gratitude.

Without the consistent support and cooperation of Michael and Elisabeth Ayrton right up to their deaths in 1975 and 1991, and since then of Elisabeth's daughter, Prudence Hopkins, and granddaughter, Justine Hopkins, I could not have produced such a complete catalogue nor such an extensive treatment of Michael's work. They provided me with catalogues of Michael's exhibitions, many of his publications, and access to and copies of many sketch books and numerous files of reviews, press cuttings, and drafts of manuscripts. Michael readily and patiently answered my endless questions during my visits to Bradfields from 1971 to 1974 and through frequent correspondence. Elisabeth continued to do the same for me after his death. Both of them read an initial draft of my manuscript in 1974 and Elisabeth read part of the revised draft in 1989. Their positive comments on my insights into Michael's art gave me great pleasure and strong encouragement to persevere in my daunting task.

No one, however, has borne the cost of this long and arduous task more than my beloved wife Leona. She endured my absences while I traveled to England and to research libraries in the United States. She tolerated my endless hours spent in writing and revising my manuscript, as I stole time from nights, weekends, holiday recesses, and vacations to make room for sustaining my scholarly efforts while I discharged my full-time administrative and teaching responsibilities. She helped me type the first draft while we were living in Athens and she read and critiqued more than one version of this book. Through my long peregrinations in this scholarly labyrinth, Leona has sustained me with her deep and abiding love. My debt of gratitude to her far exceeds my ability to express it. By dedicating this book to her, I publicly honor and thank a most remarkable woman—my wife, my best friend, and my one true love.

Abbreviations

Abbreviated names of ancient authors and works follow the systems used in the standard Greek and Latin dictionaries (LSJ = Liddell-Scott-Jones, i.e., H. G. Liddell and R. Scott, *A Greek-English Lexicon,* rev. H. S. Jones; OLD = *Oxford Latin Dictionary,* ed. P. G. W. Glare) consulted by classicists. The following abbreviations are used in the text, notes, catalogue, and bibliography.

CLASSICAL AUTHORS

Apollod.	Apollodorus, *Bibliotheca* (*The Library*)
Apollod., *Epit.*	Apollodorus, *Epitome* (summary of last part of *Bibliotheca*)
Apollonius, *Argon.*	Apollonius of Rhodes, *Argonautica*
Arist.	Aristotle
Arist., *Mir.*	Aristotle, *Mirabilia*
Bacch., *Dith.*	Bacchylides, *Dithyrambs*
Dion. Hal.	Dionysius of Halicarnassus
D.S.	Diodorus Siculus
Herod.	Herodotus
Hes., *Th.*	Hesiod, *Theogony*
Homer, *Il.*	Homer, *Iliad*
Homer, *Od.*	Homer, *Odyssey*
Hyginus, *Fab.*	Hyginus, *Fabulae*
Lact., *Inst.*	Lactantius, *Divinae Institutiones* (*Divine Institutes*)
Ovid, *A.A.*	Ovid, *Ars Amatoria* (*The Art of Love*)
Ovid, *Met.*	Ovid, *Metamorphoses*
Paus.	Pausanias, *Description of Greece*
Petronius, *Sat.*	Petronius, *Satyricon*
Plato, *Alc.*	Plato, *Alcibiades*
Plato, *Resp.*	Plato, *Respublica* (*The Republic*)
Pliny, *N.H.*	Pliny (the Elder), *Naturalis Historia* (*Natural History*)
Plut., *Thes.*	Plutarch, *Theseus*
Sophocles, *O.C.*	Sophocles, *Oedipus Coloneus*
Virgil, *Aen.*	Virgil, *Aeneid*
Zenobius	Zenobius, *Proverbs*

JOURNALS AND REFERENCE WORKS

AJA	*American Journal of Archaeology*
Arch. Zeitung	*Archaeologische Zeitung*
BSR	*Annual of the British School of Archaeology at Rome*
EAA	*Enciclopedia dell'Arte Antica*
EWA	*Encyclopaedia of World Art*
JHS	*Journal of Hellenic Studies*
LIMC	*Lexicon Iconographicum Mythologiae Classicae*
MDAI(R)	*Mitteilungen des deutschen archaeologischen Instituts (roemische Abteilung)*
RE	Pauly-Wissowa, *Real-Encyclopaedie der klassischen Altertumswissenschaft*

Introduction

The power of myth to inspire artists and captivate generation after generation of children and adults lies deep within the human psyche. Through the centuries, myths of the Greeks and Romans have had special power over artists and writers and, through them, over much of Western civilization. What is the source of their power? Why does one myth have special appeal to a particular artist or a particular era, whereas a very different myth inspires other artists and other times? Is it true that "in every culture and every age ... [the] cultural canon is determined by unconscious images, symbols, and archetypes"?[1]

My own interest in these overarching questions led me to write this book. To understand the broader questions, I have elected to focus on a single cycle of myth associated primarily with the island of Crete, although it is also linked to Athens and southern Italy, among other places. The myth of Daedalus and Icarus, of the Minotaur and his prison—the labyrinth at Knossos, on Crete, devised by Daedalus to house the monstrous offspring of the wife of King Minos and Poseidon's bull—and of Theseus, who came from Athens to break the destructive power of the Minotaur, is a richly complex story of captivity and escape, ingenuity and creativity, flight and fall, success and failure. It is a myth with universal significance, yet replete with great personal meaning for the individual human being.

Although the myth of Daedalus and Icarus has inspired artists at many different points in history, it has had a special attraction for twentieth-century writers and artists who recognized its implications for this era of airplane and spaceship travel.[2] There was also a heightened interest, especially in the latter half of the twentieth century, in mazes and labyrinths, whether as puzzle mazes, hedge mazes, or turf mazes, as symbols in art and literature, or as vehicles for religious meditation and spiritual renewal. I have selected this particular cycle of myth for these reasons, but also because one artist in this century made the myth peculiarly his own.

My chance encounter with British sculptor Michael Ayrton (1921–1975) many years ago opened up to me new insights and a new avenue of research. As I began to explore Ayrton's works of art and his writings, I discovered he had plumbed deeply the many aspects of this richly evocative myth. His interpretation of the myth of Daedalus enlarges and enriches a long and varied tradition of literary and artistic engagement with this myth. By focusing on Ayrton's entanglement with this myth for most of the last twenty years of his life, it is possible to gain insight into the creative process itself and to learn how myth both shapes and is shaped by the creative imagination of a talented artist.

Michael Ayrton had an impressively diverse talent. Equally at home in drawing, painting, sculpting, and writing, he also designed costumes for ballet and theater, illustrated books, wrote art criticism, taught art in both England and America, and even entered successfully into filmmaking. He moved effortlessly from word to image, from image to word. The BBC made him something of a celebrity through his frequent appearances on both radio and television. His immense knowledge and ready wit made him a stimulating conversationalist, a welcome companion on almost any occasion.

Michael Ayrton also was a man of deep passion. He pursued these with obsessive devotion, whether the object of this devotion was myth, metaphor, or music. He mined the classical myth of Daedalus and Icarus, of the Minotaur and his labyrinthine prison, to depths unrecognized or untapped by his predecessors, enlarging and enriching the myth by his words and images. His "passion amounting to mania"[3] and his "singular obsession" for the music of Hector Berlioz resulted in drawings, paintings, and sculpture of unusual intensity. For the centenary of the death of Berlioz in 1969, Ayrton "wrote, narrated, chose the music, and provided paintings, drawings, sculptures and costume designs for a television programme on Berlioz" and subsequently paid homage to Berlioz with a gallery exhibition in London, exhibiting works produced over two decades.[4]

Michael Ayrton also possessed powerful ambition and great courage. Perhaps it was a combination of ambition, courage, and youthful bravado that led him at age twenty-three to challenge Picasso, whose dominance of the art world threatened to smother Ayrton's own creativity. Even in his mature years, Ayrton continued his critical challenge to Picasso, with further essays, all of which have been reprinted in *The Rudiments of Paradise* (217–48), and a roman à clef about Picasso: *The Midas Consequence* has as its main character a famous artist named Capisco, a name created by rearranging the letters of Picasso's name (with one slight substitution).[5] A mixture of ambition and passion led Ayrton finally to identify himself with Daedalus, the archetypal craftsman of classical mythology, whose renown as an artisan led Homer (*Iliad* 18) to compare the craft-god Hephaestus to him, rather than vice versa.

When I first met Michael, we were both visiting professors at the University of California, Santa Barbara. It was the fall term, 1967–1968. While researching an article on the Daedalus-Icarus myth in twentieth-century art and literature, I came across two photographs of works by Michael Ayrton. In the course of a conversation with a fellow visiting professor in classics, H. D. F. Kitto, I mentioned these works by an artist who was unfamiliar to me. He replied, "A chap in the art department rang me up the other day to say that there was this chap Ayrton in his department whom I ought to meet. Perhaps he's the same chap. Why don't you ring him up and find out?" I did, and he was.

During our telephone conversation, Michael Ayrton informed me that he had in fact completed several hundred more images of Daedalus and Icarus, plus a recently published novel, *The Maze Maker.* He invited me to come by to see photographs of his work and borrow a copy of the novel. I was fascinated by the tremendous diversity of the images and, as I read the novel, was intrigued both by the reconstruction of the myth and by the myth making interwoven with the retelling of the story.

Although Ayrton concluded his formal education when barely in his teens, such was his erudition that at UC-Santa Barbara he was teaching not only a graduate seminar on painting but also a graduate seminar in literature. A voracious reader, he had a phenomenal visual memory and a remarkable gift for presenting his learning in an interesting, provocative manner. Perhaps because he was largely self-educated, he frequently offered insights and interpretations that ran contrary to traditional scholarship on a subject, but he also often proved that he was familiar with these sources and that he had good reason for disagreeing with conventional interpretations. He therefore could be at once refreshing and frustrating to critics.

A few years after the publication of my first article on the myth ("Daedalus and Icarus: A Symbol for our Time?"), I undertook preliminary research for a book that would trace the myth through the centuries, exploring its manifestation in art and literature. It soon became apparent to me that no other artist had so fully understood or contributed so much to the interpretation and extension of the myth as had Michael Ayrton. With his assurances of cooperation, I therefore began research for a book devoted to Ayrton's Daedalian images, paying annual visits to Bradfields, his home in Essex, until the year before his death.

Ayrton's extensive and well-organized files and his sketch books were freely open to me. Throughout my visits and through correspondence between visits, Michael generously and patiently responded to my every question, whether it concerned a large philosophical issue or a minor discrepancy between two exhibition catalogues. Conversations over dinner or around the fireplace at Bradfields gave further insight into the man and his work. Michael also read a first draft of this manuscript (which then carried the title, "Journey Through a Labyrinth: Michael Ayrton and the Myth of Daedalus") during the year preceding his death, despite his ill health, and responded with enthusiasm to its understanding of his progressive involvement with the cycle of myth surrounding Daedalus. Later, less than two years before her death, his wife Elisabeth read several chapters of a revised draft and offered strong encouragement to complete my renewed efforts.

Ayrton's work merits study solely because of his demonstrated ability as writer and artist, but close study is also warranted to gain insight into the role of myth in the creative process of a twentieth-century artist. He was admittedly unconventional for his time, finding his sources to a large extent in the ancient Greek world or in its renaissance in Italy. Both this unconventionality and his obsessive involvement with Greek myth first attracted me to study the work of Michael Ayrton, but it is the emotive power of his art, the extraordinary handling of myth, and the depth of his insight into the human condition that have sustained my interest throughout the years.

In an essay written in 1966, "The Path to Daedalus," Ayrton helps us somewhat to understand his approach to myth and ancient art:

> I tend to seek in the art of the past as I tend to find in places long inhabited, a certain intensity, a double life relevant to its own period and to my own which centres upon the interpretation and extension of myth. I do not feel myth to be material for a poetic or aesthetic exercise to be played with as it came to be played with after the fifth century B.C. on the one hand, or during the late fifteenth century A.D. on the other. I must be seized with a belief in the validity of the myth in a sense comparable, however minimally, to Virgil's "belief" in the myth contained in the Aeneid, or perhaps it would be more accurate to suggest that the reality of my belief is not totally dissimilar to the reality contained in myth for those who, before Herodotus, identified myth with history as being the "Truth." I am not being disingenuous when I write this. I am well aware of the distinction between history and myth. . . . [W]hat I do is driven through me by a force of myth which is nothing to do with aesthetic or allegorical conceit. Therefore I did not choose to spend ten years of my life with Daedalus in order to polish and augment dramatic fiction, rather I became, on May 11th, 1956, the dedicated chronicler of a myth.(181)

The structure of this book is fundamentally chronological, but it is impossible to do full justice to an artist as complex and as diversely talented as Michael Ayrton with a purely chronological account. The themes that inspired him and which he pursued with an obsessive devotion are interwoven throughout his work. The web of ideas translated into images or conveyed powerfully in language intricately encompasses his entire life. At times, therefore, the interpretation of his work must necessarily also abandon strict chronology to get to the essence of his artistry. Throughout this process, I have attempted not only to offer insights into how an artist could derive inspiration for nearly two decades from a single, interrelated cycle of myths, but also to demonstrate the ways in which these myths have been enriched and enlarged by Ayrton's creative genius.

The central theme of the labyrinth or maze provides coherence to the mature stage of Ayrton's life as an artist. From the time of his arrival on 11 May 1956 at Cumae, on the Bay of Naples, he began his journey into the labyrinth, which was for him first of all a place, but became for him a compelling image of life. It was at Cumae that Daedalus ended his airborne flight from Crete. It was here that he built a temple to Apollo, in which he hung his wings as a dedication to the god whose blazing intensity killed his son, Icarus. It was also here that Aeneas first landed on his journey from

Carthage to found the nation of Rome, here that Virgil in *Aeneid* VI has Aeneas discover the story of Daedalus hammered out in relief on the bronze doors of the temple. And Cumae was the home of the Cumaean Sibyl, who told Apollo's prophecies from within the labyrinthine passageways that honeycomb the rock beneath the acropolis on which the temple was built. As Ayrton journeyed into the metaphorical labyrinth, he eventually came to identify himself with the archetypal craftsman Daedalus, creator of the Cretan labyrinth, but he also discovered that the inhabitant of the maze, the Minotaur, that monstrous offspring of Pasiphaë and the bull, was likewise part of himself, the bestial nature hidden within all of us.

In Greek myth the labyrinth is not only a testament of the artistic skill of Daedalus, not only the prison of the Minotaur, not only a monument to the unnatural lust of Pasiphaë. It is also an arena symbolizing the complexities of life and death, particularly for Theseus, who threaded the labyrinth with the assistance of Ariadne, daughter of Minos and Pasiphaë and half-sister to the Minotaur. Through succeeding centuries, literature has elaborated every aspect of this structure, using it to symbolize the tortuous, confusing path through life, or into the self, the psyche, or a text or narrative. Some writers and critics use *labyrinth* and *maze* interchangeably; others would distinguish between these terms.[6] Ayrton belongs, in a sense, in the former group, but his history of mazes in "The Making of a Maze" and other writings and his works of art show a much greater understanding of the metaphor and the reality than do most creative writers and artists. Moreover, by creating a new visual syntax, particularly through his use of mirrors, Ayrton extended the meaning of the labyrinth beyond the maze in disturbing but significant ways.

The more deeply Ayrton penetrated the maze, the more confident he became of his creative abilities, the more skillfully he moved from word to image and back again, merging literary and visual images so dynamically that they seem almost inseparable. It is daunting to take on the task of interpreting his works in bronze and paint, on the inked page and drawn in ink, for he was extraordinarily articulate in an age when artists are too often assumed to be inarticulate. Like Michelangelo and Leonardo, whom he understood deeply and admired greatly, or like his own compatriot Blake, he could move with complete ease from one medium to the other, between word and image. And he wrote so much about his own work that it may seem almost foolhardy to try to say something new. Nevertheless, his work warrants careful study and invites comparisons drawn by someone looking at the writings and the visual images from the outside.

On 9 June 1949, when Ayrton was only twenty-eight, Wyndham Lewis wrote in a review: "Michael Ayrton is one of the two or three young artists destined to shape the future of British art."[7] Yet, when Ayrton died on 16 November 1975 at the relatively young age of fifty-four, after a quarter century of ostracism by the art establishment, his passing was "almost unmarked. The *Times* offered a sour obituary."[8]

How does one account for such lack of recognition? Is it attributable to the alleged English disdain for a polymath and their greater scorn of a polymorph?[9] The answers may be found, at least in part, in the life of Ayrton himself. No biography can fully capture his protean vitality nor plumb the depths of people's motives; nonetheless, a study of the life of Michael Ayrton will reveal some of the many dimensions of this multifaceted, talented artist. With the opening chapters as both background and context, we can move more easily to the analysis of his progressive involvement with the cycle of myth surrounding Daedalus, Icarus, the Minotaur, and the labyrinth. As we journey into Michael Ayrton's own personal labyrinth, we can put to the test his assertion that another man's maze almost invariably will not appear terribly intricate, but "to the maze-maker himself his maze is an all-absorbing thing compounded of confusion, achievement, frustration and reverence, which continually grows in complexity."[10]

A Portrait of the Artist

1

Michael Ayrton created many self-portraits during his life. Some were in the form of drawings or paintings, and even sculpture, whereas others were created by verbal images. The tributes to Michael after his death, published in a special issue of *Labrys* (3 [October 1978]), provide many additional insights into who he was as a person and as an artist. *Michael Ayrton: A Biography* by Dr. Justine Hopkins, his step-granddaughter, provides a comprehensive account of his life. It offers the interested reader a much more expansive treatment than is warranted for our purposes.

The present study seeks to gain a deeper understanding of the human condition through close analysis of the interplay of myth and creativity in Michael Ayrton's artistry, but the very process of studying his work will reveal insights into the artist as well as opening up the multiple dimensions of the created works. Nonetheless, an introduction to the artist's life should contribute to that understanding by disclosing formative influences upon his art.

Michael Ayrton was born 20 February 1921 to Gerald Gould and Barbara Bodichon Ayrton Gould. He was their only child and was given the hyphenated name Ayrton-Gould to preserve the heritage of both his parents. When barely adult, however, and as a fledgling artist, he dropped the hyphen and his father's name, demonstrating both his independence and his desire for artistic recognition. He said that he chose to use his mother's name rather than his father's since "A" is at the beginning of the alphabet and his name would therefore appear at or near the beginning of any list of artists in a group exhibition.[1] Between his birth and that act of self-assertion lay many experiences that would shape his development as a person and as an artist. To understand him and his work, therefore, one needs to know something of his heritage and his education, both formal and informal.

Gerald Gould (1885–1936), a graduate of Magdalen College and a fellow of Merton College, Oxford, was a Georgian poet with many published volumes of verse, but also a novelist, essayist, and literary critic. When Gould's *The Journey: Odes and Sonnets* (New Haven: Yale Univ. Press, 1921) was published, one reviewer described him as "that rare thing in our age, a purely metaphysical poet. . . . [E]ach of his poems is a struggle to grasp at truth, and in each one he is baffled, defeated, still a searcher for the final vision which ever eludes him."[2] Gould is known, however, not only for his poetry. His numerous prose works include criticism on both poetry and fiction (*Essay on the Nature of Lyric*, 1909, and *The English Novel of Today*, 1924), as well as a novel and collections of essays and literary parodies.

Gould reviewed novels for both the *Observer* and the *News-Chronicle* and served consecutively as lead writer (1915–1919) and associate editor (1919–1922) of the leftist *Daily Herald.* Although Gould flourished in the intellectual environment of the university, his wife and their shared ardor for socialism drew him away from the haven of the university and into a politically active life, which eventually strained his scholarly constitution. As a consequence, severe ill health, exacerbated by his alcoholism, forced his withdrawal from social engagements during the last few years of his life.[3] Hopkins offers this succinct summary of his end: "Then, on 2 November 1936, Gerald Gould died at home at Hamilton Terrace, at the age of fifty-one. Cirrhosis of the liver and associated diabetes mellitus, exacerbated by bronchial pneumonia, finally proved too great a strain for his heart" (1994, 26).

Gould died when Michael was only fifteen, but his tremendous erudition was at once a cause for admiration and a source of frustration to his son throughout his life. On one occasion, Ayrton claimed that his father could "quote the whole of the *Iliad* in Greek" (*Listener,* 16 April 1970, 512, col. 1). After Ayrton's own death, one of his friends reported that Michael "wondered whether all his *writing* was not a homage, an apology, in the Platonic sense, to his father, whose surname he dropped since he said no-one could be a famous artist and possess the hyphenate name Ayrton-Gould, wished on him by the conjunction of his parents."[4] Gould provided his son the example of a man passionately committed to the rights of women, but no "commitment to conventional morality," for Gould was an adulterer who brazenly included his son in some of his visits to his mistresses (Hopkins 1994, 11–12).

Ayrton's ambivalent relationship with his father and the fact that Michael during his formative years had to deal with his father's illness and death may help explain the way he interpreted the myth of Daedalus and Icarus. The tension between father and son, the son's decision to go his own way, to pursue his own vision, and the son's desire to rise higher than his father are all part of the psychological underpinnings of Ayrton's view of the myth. Yet in *The Maze Maker* as elsewhere (see chapters 5 and 6), he identifies more closely with Daedalus than with Icarus, so the psychology of his art is more complex than a simple Freudian interpretation of a father-son rivalry, more than a love-hate relationship. It hardly needs saying, of course, that the identification with Daedalus is a reasonable one for a sculptor, although many artists through the centuries (see chapter 3) have identified themselves with the Icarian striving toward new heights.

Although Michael Ayrton wrote a great deal about his own art and shaped his official biography found in various of his publications and exhibition catalogues, it is important to remember, as Northrop Frye maintains, that the artist is not the "definitive interpreter of himself."[5] Ayrton may not have fully recognized or acknowledged the childhood influences that shaped him, but those influences are present in his art and his writings. It is our task to attempt to identify and clarify the impact of those influences, to attempt to provide "a contextualized account of the artist viewed from outside the borders of self-knowledge."[6] This is no easy task when dealing with an artist, since "the artist is endowed with a very high sensitivity of perception—self-perception and perception of others—and an inborn capacity, sometimes with high degrees of versatility, to communicate in various media of expression."[7]

Barbara Bodichon Ayrton (1890–1950)[8] began a lifelong career in politics while she was still in her teens, when she and her mother joined the Women's Social and Political Union in the summer of 1906.[9] By late summer 1908, because of her involvement in the suffrage movement and her father's severe illness, she left her studies at University College, London. In January 1909 she became an organizer for the Women's Social and Political Union. Following her marriage to Gerald Gould in July 1910, she interrupted her work only long enough to take a honeymoon, and she was never deterred from a vigorous pursuit of equality for women, even though her militant suffragist activity resulted in a brief incarceration in 1912.

Mrs. Ayrton Gould's determination and strength of character also were evident in her repeated candidacy for Parliament, from 1922 until her election as M.P. for North Hendon in 1945. In the interval between initial candidacy and election twenty-three years later, she became an executive member of the Labour Party (1929), its vice chairman (1938) and its chairman (1939–1940). She served on numerous committees and commissions, including the Arts Council and the British Council, of which she was vice chairman. Her active participation in politics throughout her adult life may well have been influenced by the example of her mother, one of the early women scientists.

Barbara Bodichon Ayrton was the only daughter of Hertha Marks Ayrton, M.I.E.E. (1854–1923), and Professor William Edward Ayrton, F.R.S. (1847–1908).[10] A native of London and a graduate of University College, London, William Edward Ayrton was professor of physics at the Technical College, Finsbury, when Miss Hertha Marks began her scientific studies with him in 1884.[11] The author of numerous technical papers, especially on electrical subjects, Professor Ayrton is perhaps best remembered for his invention, frequently in association with Professor John Perry, of electrical measuring instruments such as the electrodynamometer wattmeter and the transmission dynamometer (*Encyclopedia Britannica,* 1952, 7, 815, and 12, 442). In recognition of his achievements, the Royal Society awarded him the Gold Medal in 1901. After Professor Ayrton married Hertha Marks in 1885, their scientific careers became somewhat intertwined, like the careers of their friends the Curies, although Mrs. Ayrton also achieved independent fame for her work on the electric arc. Her book, *The Electric Arc* (1902), culminated nearly two decades of work on the subject. In 1906 she was the first woman to receive the Hughes medal from the Royal Society, for her "experimental investigations on the electric arc, and also upon sand ripples."[12] Hertha Marks Ayrton was active in the suffrage movement until 1914, when she returned to the laboratory to invent the Ayrton anti-gas fan; the fans were first employed at the front in France in May 1916 (*Encyclopedia Britannica,* 1952, 2, 823). A woman of exceptional talent, energy, and perseverance, Hertha Ayrton took great joy in the final two years of her life in Barbara's infant son, Michael, who was to manifest similar traits.

Barbara Ayrton interrupted her public career barely long enough to give birth, and she "never made any attempt to disguise the fact that her son took second place, at least in practical terms, to her work" (Hopkins 1994, 24). As a result, Michael was brought up largely by others. For the first two years of his life, he was given much of his care by his grandmother, whom he scarcely remembered, but who "had given to the beginning of his life a warmth and security which he would certainly never have got, and indeed was never to get, from his mother" (Hopkins 1994, 9). During this time, Hertha Ayrton corresponded regularly with her stepdaughter, Edith Zangwill, about child rearing, revealing herself "as an early advocate of a sensitive and liberal approach to children" (Hopkins 1994, 9). It is not surprising that after Hertha's death, Michael also spent considerable time at Far End, the home of his aunt, Edith Zangwill. Hopkins attributes to this household certain influences upon Michael that carried over into his adult life, particularly an "expectation of women as ministering to their menfolk" that was taken for granted, "although [the women were] perfectly free to lead their own lives" (1994, 11).

Michael Ayrton's childhood included such notable experiences as being read to sleep by the poet William Butler Yeats. Years later Ayrton confided that he had been terrified by Yeats's imposing figure and booming voice. Ayrton also recalled overhearing a violent quarrel between his father and Mr. Yeats, who had developed extreme right-wing, fascist political views; the intensity of this quarrel and the loud shouts of these two important writers made a lasting impression upon young Michael. Since Michael's father was on the fringes of the Bloomsbury group, Michael at an early age also had contact with other prominent literary figures, such as Bertrand Russell, H. G. Wells, and George Bernard Shaw.

Besides the advantages of this literary and intellectual environment, Ayrton benefited from an unusually liberal and permissive family environment. He once said to me, as we traveled by automobile from London to his home in Essex, that he felt that his parents treated him more as a friend and an equal than as a child. Moreover, their demanding careers precluded close parental supervision, so he developed an independent spirit and matured at an early age. After receiving an education at preparatory schools in London and in the country, Michael was sent off to boarding school at twelve, as was customary for the children of the circle of friends to which his parents belonged. He reported having spent two unhappy and frequently sickly years at the Beeches, Greater Felcourt, Sussex.[13]

Ayrton's formal education was abruptly terminated when he was fourteen. Official biographies attribute his termination of studies to ill health and a newly discovered passion for art, but an alternative version offers a more interesting explanation. In an interview conducted by Joan Bakewell in the BBC's "Line Up" program, Ayrton recounted this story: while Michael was enrolled in a coeducational boarding school in Surrey, his father came down one Sunday for a visit and forthrightly explained the facts of life to him; after Michael unsuccessfully tried to apply his father's teachings to an equally inexperienced girlfriend, she summoned an older girl, who would "know because she's 17." The seventeen-year old did indeed "know," but the headmistress and an elderly guest discovered the trio emerging from the hayrick, whereupon all three students were summarily expelled from school. Then, said Ayrton, "I said to my father: 'Look, what you told me has got me fired [expelled].' He was so overcome with laughter that I never got sent back to school again so I left school at 14."[14]

In more serious moments, Michael made it clear that he terminated his education by his own decision to become an artist. Although his parents encouraged his amateurish artistic efforts when he was at boarding school, they did not welcome his decision to become an artist. His father, in particular, had envisioned Michael following in his footsteps at Oxford and did little to conceal his disappointment at Michael's choice, "which Michael bitterly resented" (Hopkins 1994, 21). He also strongly "resented [his parents'] assumption of the inferiority of the artist to the writer or politician" (ibid.). One cannot help but wonder whether Michael's decision to use his mother's name rather than his father's had any connection to his resentment at his father's reaction to his decision to become a painter. On the other hand, one could also compare this decision to Picasso's earlier adoption of his mother's name instead of Ruiz, his father's name: one psychoanalyst has interpreted Picasso's choice as a reflection of an oedipal reaction against the brutality of the sexual act between his father and his "tender mother," such as Picasso expressed in his *Minotauromachy,* which is full of "*reduplication symbols* portraying varying aspects of the sexual act as it might be conceived by a child."[15]

Following his departure from school, Michael briefly but unsuccessfully attended various art schools, commencing with Heatherley's and, in autumn 1937, St. John's Wood Art School, "where his contemporaries remember him as a boy—not even a youth—of amazing precocity."[16] When home for the Easter holidays in 1935, Michael met Richard Gorer, a close friend at Cambridge of Michael's second cousin, Oliver Zangwill; despite the difference in age between them, Gorer took an interest in this bright young fourteen-year old, whom he invited on several occasions to his home in Kent. Gorer gave Michael his first commission, in 1936: he was asked to design a label for apple boxes for the apples grown on Gorer's estate (Hopkins 1994, 19–20). At Heatherley's Michael met and became friends with Michael Middleton, whom he asked to help with the design of a poster for one of his father's friends, Francis Meynell, because he lacked the confidence to do it alone (Hopkins 1994, 28). Another important friendship also developed when he was enrolled at St. John's Wood Art School, for it was here that Michael first met John Minton, who subsequently became a particularly close friend and erstwhile collaborator.

In early 1937 Michael made a secret trip from Paris to Barcelona,[17] purportedly intending to support the government of Spain against the rebel forces of Francisco Franco, but his mother somehow learned of his whereabouts and promptly summoned him home (Hopkins 1994, 28–29). Shortly after his return to London, Barbara sent him to Vienna to live with his octogenarian cousin, Amelia (Millie) Levetus. He resided there for about six weeks, in May and June, 1937, although one of his official biographies describes it as "a prolonged visit to Vienna." While living there, Michael was introduced to "all the foremost intellectuals and literati of the day," including Sigmund Freud, according to Michael's claims (Hopkins 1994, 30). In Vienna, he also "copied old-master drawings in the Albertina Museum for six hours every day and spent his pocket money on woodcuts by Dürer and the minor German masters of the early sixteenth century."[18] Years later, in 1960, he wrote about the value of copying the works of the old masters; he saw copying as a means to understanding the original: "[T]he copyist, acting intuitively, will bring out those aspects of the work he studies which touch him most nearly, but he will also be thinking himself into the mind of the master whose secrets he hopes will be revealed to him, by copying" ("The Translated Image," 1971, 155f). In an even more emphatic statement, he declared: "This penetration and comprehension of a master's work can only be achieved by copying it" (ibid. 161). Forty years earlier, in 1897, also at age sixteen, Picasso had devoted his attention to copying the old masters in the Prado, rather than attending classes at the Royal Academy in Madrid.[19]

In London during 1937, Ayrton became quite well acquainted with Henry Moore, who lived nearby. Ayrton and Moore "shared the same frame-maker in Haverstock Hill," and they were brought together by their engagement in anti-fascist activity (letter to the author, 19 June 1973). Ayrton reported that he was a frequent visitor to Moore's home and that he even "bought two drawings from him at £2 each (framed)" (ibid.). Many years later, when Ayrton was learning to sculpt, he sought advice from Moore, visiting him at his studio at Hoglands, Much Hadham (see below).

From 1937 to 1939 Ayrton spent much of his time in France and, to a lesser extent, in the Netherlands, returning periodically to London. In April 1939 Michael and his friend John Minton moved into a studio on the Avenue de Saxe in Paris, where they spent their days either working in their studio or visiting art galleries and museums and their evenings at "Le Dôme, on the Boulevard Montparnasse" (Hopkins 1994, 40–41). Around the middle of May, accompanied by Michael Middleton, another friend from art school, they left for Les Baux, where they remained, for the most part, until mid-July. Just before their departure for Les Baux, they made their final visit to the ballet, "to see Serge Lifar dance in the ballet *Icare* at the Opéra, a performance which inspired Michael to a painting, *Icarus*" (Hopkins 1994, 42; see chapter 4, for a discussion of this painting). While at Les Baux, the trio traveled to Nîmes, where they observed bullfighting with Spanish bulls (Hopkins 1994, 43). Watching the bulls and the matadors influenced Michael's painting, in both form and content, not only at the time but also much later in his life. Although he did not identify these experiences in Paris and Nîmes in 1939 as foundational for his obsession with Icarus and the Minotaur during the last twenty years of his life, they undoubtedly were part of his artistic and intellectual memory when he began his peregrinations in the myth of Daedalus and Icarus in May 1956.

Michael returned to London shortly after the outbreak of World War II. That autumn, according to his official biography, "he exhibited for the first time at the Zwemmer Gallery a group of small figure compositions influenced by Tchelitchew, Berman and the French Neo-Romantics" (1962a, 13). Ayrton's own master record book, however, in which he listed all the exhibitions of his work, records this exhibition as the fifth occasion on which his work was publicly shown (see appendix A).[20] While in Paris, both Minton and Ayrton worked under Pavel Tchelitchev, Eugène Berman, and Christian Berard: Peter Cannon-Brookes declares that the tradition represented by this trio "constitutes an important though little-studied element in the European Neo-Romanticism which was blossoming before the outbreak of the war."[21]

Ayrton's work attracted the attention of Sir Hugh Walpole, who was the first to purchase his paintings. Introduced by his new patron to John Gielgud, Ayrton at age nineteen, in late 1940 or early 1941, received his first major commission, the design of costumes and scenery for a production of *Macbeth*.[22] He sought and received approval to have John Minton collaborate with him on this ambitious project; they had already collaborated "on a series of designs for a hypothetical production of Purcell's *Dido and Aeneas*."[23] Shortly after they completed their preliminary designs, on 9 October 1941, Ayrton was conscripted into the Royal Air Force as A/C2 Gould, M.A., and John Minton was called up soon thereafter, on 10 December 1941. As a consequence, they had to carry out most of their work on the set designs during two-day leaves from military service.

Ayrton's military career was short-lived. He had been in ill health much of the year prior to his induction, and military life did nothing to improve his condition. Although he was "a young man who from childhood had dreamed of flight, who had passionately studied early and contemporary aircraft and spent his money on *Popular Flying* and other aeronautical magazines" (Hopkins 1994, 60), his poor health and strong will toward independence and self-determination made him physically and psychologically unfit for military service. In one of his letters to his mother, he declared, "Like most people here I would sell my soul for a discharge, and if I don't get one I shall have no mind or soul left to sell" (Hopkins 1994, 61). He sought by every means imaginable, including a threat to his mother that he would go on a hunger strike, to obtain his release from what seemed to him both intolerable and impossible, until a worsening of his health led to the granting of a leave on 10 December 1941, "awaiting formal Discharge Certificate; Free to take up Civil Employment (has permission to wear plain clothes)" and, on 4 May 1942, the surrender of his "identity card" (Hopkins 1994, 62f.).

During the winter and spring of 1942 Ayrton continued work on the Gielgud production of *Macbeth,* which was fraught with turmoil and heated exchanges between Ayrton and Gielgud, who accused the former of "ungraciousness of manner and lack of charm and generosity towards the work of people in every department" and appealed to him to "appear more modest" (letter quoted by Hopkins 1994, 65). Despite the repeated conflict between designer and director, the play opened in Manchester, toured to five other cities, and opened in July at the Piccadilly Theatre in London.

Near the end of the staging in London Ayrton entered into an intimate relationship with Joan Walsh that lasted more than six years. While "surrounded by an animated group of friends" at the Players Theatre Club, where Joan, who was "estranged from her husband, the theatre designer Henry Locke, worked behind the bar at the club on an occasional basis," Michael caught her attention and aroused her interest; they spent the evening dancing, the night at her flat, and the next day observing his paintings at the Leicester Gallery (Hopkins 1994, 71f.). It was not long before she joined him at his mother's flat at 76 Belsize Gardens. After living there for a brief period, they moved in the spring of 1943 into a large studio next to the BBC on All Souls Place, where they lived together until 1949, when their relationship ended.[24]

A joint exhibition of the collaborators' paintings and their designs for *Macbeth,* held in October 1942 at the Leicester Galleries, led to Ayrton's appointment to teach life drawing and theater design at the Camberwell School of Art.[25] He held this post from 1942 to 1944, during a time when the cultural isolation resulting from the war gave rise to a revival of English Romanticism and a more provincial prejudice in art. Graham Sutherland, whose indebtedness to William Blake and Samuel Palmer provided a link with the past of British art, was the acknowledged leader of a group of landscape painters that included not only Ayrton and Minton, but also John Craxton, Lucian Freud, and Keith Vaughan. In the mid-1940s Ayrton spent a considerable amount of time at Dale in Pembrokeshire. In 1945 and 1946 he was "in fairly frequent contact with Sutherland who spent months in the neighbouring hamlet of Sandy Haven" (letter to the author dated 19 June 1973). The influence of Paul Nash upon this group of painters and upon Ayrton in particular—who first met Nash in 1944—was also significant.[26] Midway through this period at Camberwell, Ayrton had his first one-man show, an exhibition at the Redfern Gallery entitled "The Temptation of St. Anthony. Paintings and Drawings." These works (one of which is in the Tate Gallery collection) showed the influence of some of the old masters whose works he had copied in Vienna, especially the works of Dürer, Grünewald, and Pieter Brueghel the Elder.

His representations of St. Anthony also gave expression to the extreme turmoil of Ayrton's own life, for it was at this time that Minton declared his love for Michael in a letter. Michael wrestled mightily with his own feelings about Minton and his fear of homosexuality. Some of those feelings and fears were poured out in a letter of response to Minton written in the early spring of 1943:

> I have been in love with you for about four years fighting—I couldn't just put it plainly then, or try to live it

> physically because deep down in me is this virulent calvanist [*sic*] hatred or if you like fear of homosexuality which even now fills me with terror and horror when I contemplate it physically. . . . Maybe you thought I believed as I tried to, all the things I said to give you the impression it was all a beautiful brother-like friendship as far as I was concerned. But I couldn't have it any other way . . . because I seem to be a sort of double pervert.[27]

After the vehement expressions of feeling between them, and Michael's rejection of giving physical expression to those feelings, there was a permanent rupture in their formerly close relationship. Michael survived the emotional trauma, at least in part, because of the compassion and understanding of both Joan and his mother. His struggles against homosexual feelings come out later in some of his art, but only as a theme in a minor key.

During this same time, Ayrton also began to illustrate books, the first of several dozen that he would illustrate in his lifetime. In 1944 he designed scenery and costumes for the Sadler's Wells Ballet Company's production of Albert Roussel's *Le Festin de l'Araignée* (choreography by Andrée Howard), launched his writing career with articles in a variety of journals, and succeeded John Piper as art critic for the *Spectator.* He attracted considerable attention, gained a degree of notoriety, and aroused intense hostility with the first of his several critical essays on Picasso, "The Master of Pastiche" (1944), which was presented in 1945 as a broadcast on the BBC.[28] Despite his harsh criticism of Picasso in 1944, the following year he wrote in a letter to John Arlott, who was writing a commissioned article on Ayrton: "My most important influences are as follows: —1st and foremost & forever my roots lie in the Gothic tradition of Flanders and early England: Mathias Grunewald, Breughel etc. Blake of course and Palmer, and at one time and another, Pavel Tchelitchew, Rouault, Sutherland *and of course Picasso.*" (Hopkins 1994, 116) The extent of Picasso's influence upon him appears most strongly later on, when he takes up his treatment of the Minotaur, Picasso's signature creature drawn from Greek myth, but one finds various instances where Ayrton has drawn upon or responded to work by Picasso.

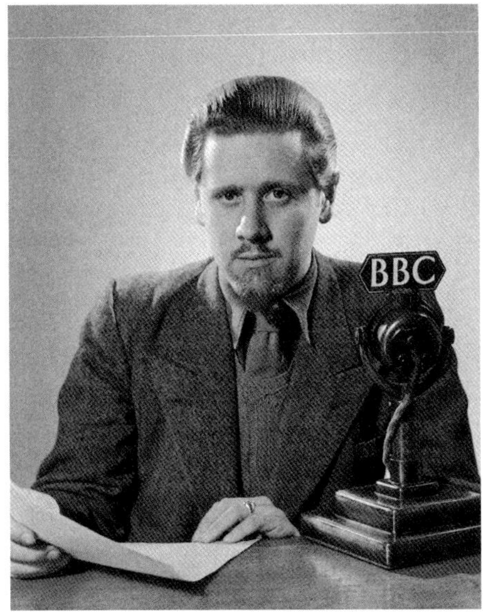

Figure 1. **MICHAEL AYRTON IN 1946: AS BBC BROADCASTER.** BBC Information and Archives.

In 1945 Ayrton met Wyndham Lewis, who was then in his early sixties. Despite the disparity in age and the polarity of their political views, Lewis and Ayrton developed such artistic and intellectual affinities that Ayrton would later successfully re-complete a Lewis drawing of Ezra Pound that had been partially destroyed. Ayrton also became Lewis's artistic alter ego, designing book jackets and illustrating texts for Lewis when blindness forced him to discontinue drawing.[29]

Although it is difficult to single out one year as the most important in the rapidly expanding career of this young artist, 1946 was clearly a pivotal year for him. Because of his selection as a regular member of the BBC "Brains Trust," Ayrton became a radio celebrity and probably one of the best known of the young British painters, although his visibility to the public apparently had little effect on his reputation as a painter. More important, however, was his decision to give up his post as art critic for the *Spectator* to concentrate on painting (Michael Middleton was chosen as his successor in this post). Also during 1946 Ayrton saw the publication of his first book, *British Drawings,* which he had written two years earlier, and he collaborated on the production of

Purcell's *The Fairy Queen.* This seventeenth-century adaptation of *A Midsummer Night's Dream* was presented at the Royal Opera House at Covent Garden. Ayrton's collaborator was his close friend and neighbor at All Souls Place, the composer-conductor Constant Lambert, an expert on Purcell. Composer Humphrey Searle, in a tribute to Michael Ayrton after his death, contended that Ayrton got into trouble with the management of Covent Garden for rallying support for the choice of Constant Lambert over the Austrian-born conductor Karl Rankl; as a result, he asserted, Ayrton was never again invited to design scenery and costumes for Covent Garden.[30]

At all events, this was his last venture into theater design, although the production was revived and partly redesigned by Ayrton in 1951, not long before Lambert's death. Of the original production, it was said that there was unanimous agreement about the beauty of the scenery and costumes designed by Ayrton; some of his drawings for this production are included in the theatrical collections of the Victoria and Albert Museum. Ayrton readily acknowledged the influences upon his work: "[H]e based himself firmly upon the Inigo Jones drawings preserved in the library at Chatsworth, and upon Italian sources which Jones himself had drawn upon, notably the work of the great Alfonso Parigi."[31] He exhibited infrequently in 1946. The largest exhibition was a small collection of drawings, consisting mostly of Welsh landscapes.[32]

In his official biography in *Drawings and Sculpture* (1962a), Ayrton identified 1946 as the year of his first trip to Italy, although Hopkins, relying upon dated correspondence, places that first trip in 1947.[33] Regardless of when it occurred, Ayrton described his first visit to Italy as "one of the two most important visual experiences of his life" (1962a, 14). One can readily understand the impact of the art of the Italian Renaissance upon an artist who had been deprived of such visual stimuli throughout the six years of the war, when the collections of the National Gallery and the Victoria and Albert Museum were in storage. During this and subsequent yearly visits to Italy, Ayrton came under the influence of such early Renaissance painters as Masaccio and Piero della Francesca. His fascination with their visual images and his intense intellectual curiosity compelled him to embark upon a study of the Renaissance that would significantly affect the course of his artistic career. The following year Ayrton returned to Italy, to the new source of his inspiration, to the artists of the Renaissance, as he would annually until 1952 and frequently thereafter. From the end of July 1947, Michael and Joan resided for some months at Ischia, where they were joined by Constant Lambert. When their visas were about to expire, Michael and Joan traveled to Genoa to renew them, then spent a month in Florence. During this stay in Italy, Ayrton's study of Renaissance art led him to the sculpture of Giotto's proto-Renaissance contemporary, Giovanni Pisano, which was to have a profound and enduring influence upon him. Not only would he begin sculpting six years later under Pisano's spell, he would also continue his careful examination of Pisano's sculpture, with the eventual publication in 1970 of his comprehensive analysis of the sculptor and his work, *Giovanni Pisano: Sculptor.*

In 1947 the Grey Walls Press, London, published *Paintings by Michael Ayrton,* with an introduction by James Laver, then keeper of the department of prints and drawings at the Victoria and Albert Museum. Included were plates of forty paintings, covering the period from August 1939 to February 1947. Since this collection understandably excludes paintings inspired by Ayrton's first visit to Italy, Laver could declare that "the foundations of Ayrton's 'poetic, mystical and organic art'" lay in Matthias Grünewald's "Isenheim polyptych now at Colmar" and in "Peter Brueghel and the 'Gothic' painters generally" (9).[34] Laver's observations (11) about recurring themes and "*obsessional* themes" such as *The Temptation of St. Anthony* and *The Agony in the Garden* proved prophetic, when viewed nearly thirty years later from the end of Ayrton's obsessional involvement with the myth of Daedalus and Icarus.

Although Ayrton's discovery of Renaissance and proto-Renaissance sculpture did not immediately transform him into a sculptor, it had a direct effect upon his painting: "The imagery of his paintings . . . became less linear and more sculptural as he moved from the northern Gothic tradition, to which he had given his first allegiance, towards a southern classicism, the achievement of which, impossible though it may be to an artist of his temperament, became his goal" (Ayrton 1962a, 15).

The extent of Ayrton's identification with the artists of the Renaissance and the degree of his rejection of contemporary fashions in art were clearly and compellingly expressed in a statement written two years later for the catalogue of a retrospective exhibition at the Wakefield City Art Gallery (1949):

> I am not really gifted with "painterliness" in the French sense, a shortcoming which critics have not been slow to point out. Paint texture and handling of the material interests me no more than it interested Hugo van de Goes or Antonello da Messina and indeed the overriding influence upon my recent work of artists who were primarily concerned with fresco . . . has inevitably reduced my interest in "handling" to a minimum. . . . The work of sculptors was the most potent single influence on painting during the formative years of the Renaissance; Giotto owed much to the Pisani, Masaccio much to Donatello, and Leonardo's master was Verrocchio. Sculptural form realised pictorially by drawing was at the centre of the Renaissance and is the significant factor in the 19th century art of Ingres, Degas and Seurat and in the 20th century art of Juan Gris and Wyndham Lewis. It is also the chief virtue of the Cubists. Herein my main interest lies. I would go further and maintain that this astringent form of art is needed to-day to balance the powerful influence which Impressionism, Expressionism, Neo-Impressionism and so on, still combine to exercise upon contemporary painting. . . . I aim, rashly enough, at the creation of monumental images as timeless, as impersonal and yet as human as those of Piero della Francesca and Giovanni Pisano, as filled with secret communication and unspecified drama as those of Masaccio. This grandiose ambition will fail, probably in every particular, but it is to me preferable to the current and general desire of painters to express an original opinion about the critical situation in which the artist finds himself to-day, and which painters often tend to express by loading their canvas with the bloated flesh of emotionalism. ([8–9])

Because Ayrton rejected many of the trends in contemporary art, there are relatively few contemporary artists with whom one might compare him. An American figurative sculptor, Leonard Baskin (15 August 1922–3 June 2000), is a notable exception. His opinions about art and his inspiration by artists of an earlier era strongly resemble Ayrton's views and his work. It is not surprising, therefore, that Baskin came to know, admire, and collect the work of Ayrton. Nor is it surprising that Baskin once wrote a brief review of Ayrton's work or that Ayrton soon thereafter wrote a critique of Baskin's sculpture (1962–1963).

Just as Michael Ayrton went to Italy and discovered a source of inspiration in the proto-Renaissance sculptor Giovanni Pisano, so also Leonard Baskin went there a few years later (in early 1951) and found inspiration for his sculpture, in the works of Tino di Camaino (ca. 1285–1337), the erstwhile pupil of Giovanni Pisano. There Baskin came to realize that, "for him, the critical issue of sculpture was its monumentality. This was the clue he needed, the opening word in the dialogue he would take up with the past. He was to discover in Tino the partner with whom to begin to explore the essential problem of form in art. And Baskin's dialogue with the past pointed his future direction."[35]

Baskin's visit to Pisa occurred rather by accident, since he had planned a visit to Siena instead, but having missed that bus, he took the next one, which was headed for Pisa. There he stumbled upon Tino's work, whose "archaizing quality" was due to the retention of "certain Byzantinizing features" that set him apart from his master. Not only did Tino's monumental figures in strictly confined space capture the attention of Baskin, they also stood at the beginning of a stylistic tradition reaching across the centuries to Maillol, Lehmbruck, and Barlach, and, through them, to Baskin, a tradition marked by an archaizing classicism blended with expressionism.[36]

A critic's statement about Baskin applies equally well to Ayrton: "Leonard Baskin is one of those anomalies of contemporary art, though more complex than most. He belongs to the 20th century, to a certain extent is of it, yet repudiates it. He has not received the recognition he deserves, simply because he is not and does not want to be in the so-called mainstream of modern art. It is hard to say whether the neglect of this major artist is due to his own intransigence or to the myopia of art critics and art historians."[37] It must be said, however, that Baskin received much more critical attention than Ayrton did during his lifetime. Some of the hostility toward Ayrton arose from his arrogance toward other artists and his scathing reviews of their work, but the erudition of both Ayrton and Baskin, as well as their repudiation of much of modern art, has caused both of them to receive less than their due recognition.

For Ayrton, it can be said, as it was for Baskin, that "the human being is still at the center of the only universe we can know and so . . . he [Baskin] has explored . . . the landscape of man—the human figure" and in maintaining his focus on the human figure, he [Baskin] has "maintained an aesthetic position uncompromisingly . . . opposed to all modernist styles: to abstraction . . . to Pop, Neo-Realism, and Photo-Realism."[38] Like Ayrton among British artists, Baskin stood virtually alone among American sculptors of his generation "in his rejection of abstract and non-objective imagery, technological innovation, the use of synthetic plastic media, open form, and imagery drawn from everyday life."[39]

Shortly before the Wakefield Gallery retrospective exhibition, the composer Hector Berlioz became another one of Ayrton's obsessions. After hearing two performances of Berlioz's *Les Troyens* conducted by Sir Thomas Beecham in 1947, Ayrton began to draw and paint Berlioz. Ayrton's first drawings of Berlioz were made in 1948, but the obsession would continue for more than twenty years, culminating in 1969 in a television program and book in honor of Berlioz. An interesting parallel occurred at a similar juncture in the life of Leonard Baskin, who reported that, while at Yale, he discovered Gustav Mahler, whose music thereafter "touched him with special power,"[40] just as Berlioz did for Ayrton.

An anecdote about Michael Ayrton concerning an event that occurred around this time reveals further insights into both Ayrton's humor and his supreme self-confidence. On the occasion of an opening of an exhibition of works by John Craxton ca. 1948, Ayrton remarked to Craxton, "There's a touch of Picasso in these drawings." To which Craxton replied, "Certainly he can draw." Whereupon Ayrton roared, "Picasso draw?!? I can draw ten times better!"[41]

Ayrton's youthful self-confidence in the face of the towering presence of Picasso resembles Baskin's description of himself and his supreme self-confidence as a youth: "I was brash and arrogant and quite horrendous, I think. But with total conviction of my own future greatness. I have always thought it an absolute necessity for anyone who aspires to be an artist to have a conviction of his own greatness—otherwise how can you carry on, in the face of all the grandeur that's preceded you?"[42]

Ayrton's return to Italy for six weeks early in 1949, in the company of Nigel and Elisabeth Balchin, resulted in a major change in his personal life.[43] Events of the previous year laid the foundation for this change, although matters had begun quite simply with a literary dispute at the Savile Club between Michael and Nigel, a very successful novelist. A friendship built on mutual respect developed, and Michael was subsequently invited to spend a weekend at the Balchin home, Leigh Barton, in Kent. Before long, Michael became attracted to Elisabeth, Nigel dallied for a time with Joan, and the four spent a week together in Paris in February 1949. Not long thereafter, Michael, Nigel and Elisabeth departed for Italy on a trip that proved fateful for the Balchins' marriage and altered Michael's life forever. Joan moved out of the flat at All Souls Place in May 1949, but it would be nearly a year before Elisabeth would join Michael there, since her separation from Nigel was neither simple nor easy, with the divorce not final until November 1951. She and her youngest daughter Freja ("Missie"), aged five, lived there with Michael from spring 1950 until shortly before Christmas 1952. No doubt it was also personally significant for Ayrton that his mother's "final illness coincided with the break-up of his relationship with Joan";[44] Barbara Ayrton died of cancer in October 1950.

Ayrton's fortunes as an artist began to change in 1949, when the larger of his Italian paintings were exhibited at the Redfern Gallery: "for the first time an exhibition of his pictures was greeted by an almost unanimously enthusiastic press."[45] The *Observer's* Nevile Wallis noted that Ayrton had

> interpreted in his own fashion . . . those Italian Renaissance painters who shared Giotto's feeling for tactile values, and

> endowed their works with a spiritual significance which gives the highest import to the scenes and figures they depicted. . . . The result is an array of . . . strangely compelling peasant groups and portraits, which should persuade some of the artist's young contemporaries that there were masters at work before 1910 (*Observer*, 5 June 1949).

Wyndham Lewis, who wrote an introduction to the catalogue for the show, also wrote an understandably favorable review in the *Listener.* Noting Ayrton's unmistakable stamina, "the air of stability possessed by his work," its "classic serenity," and his "emphasis on subject matter" he had discovered in Italy, Lewis pointed to Ayrton's potential as a bridge for young British artists back "into a more literary world"; in this review Lewis also made his sadly mistaken prediction, "Michael Ayrton is one of the two or three young artists destined to shape the future of British art."[46]

Ayrton's first retrospective show, held at the Wakefield City Art Gallery in August–September 1949, was his first one-man show in the provinces. It toured to Harrogate, Halifax, and Hull. The comprehensive catalogue contained various essays, including one by Philip Hendy, then director of the National Gallery. Hendy detected influences of Wyndham Lewis, Paul Nash, and Graham Sutherland upon the youthful Ayrton's work, but he concluded that the most dominant influence was that of Ayrton's teacher in Paris, Eugène Berman: "It is from Berman that comes the classicism that Lewis has rightly pointed out as the essence of Ayrton's art" (1949, [3]). In a subsequent review of the exhibition, Hendy went further in his analysis of Ayrton's move toward classicism:

> [Ayrton's] recent work . . . is both more personal and more decisive, and certainly more characteristic of his cool and rather satirical mind than the revived English romantic style which he affected during and after the isolation of the war. He has turned . . . back to . . . Eugène Berman. . . . Berman has helped him, no doubt, towards his new classicism; but most of all it must be Italy herself. . . . The relation between man and nature is the classical, Mediterranean relationship. His landscape exists for human beings to occupy, as it has not done for a long time in British painting.[47]

During 1950 and 1951 Ayrton was engaged in projects for the Festival of Britain, for which he designed *The Elements as Sources of Power* for photographic enlargement into a vast mural. At the same time he worked on the revision of the theater design for Purcell's *The Fairy Queen,* which was revived at Covent Garden in 1951.[48] Ayrton also turned his talents in a new direction in 1951, when he collaborated with Basil Wright to produce a color film, "The Drawings of Leonardo da Vinci." Ayrton selected the material for this film, arranged the sequence of its presentation, and wrote the script and commentary.[49]

Among the several solo exhibitions Ayrton had in 1951, the one at Redfern Gallery, London, elicited particularly favorable reviews. Eric Westerbrook, writing a review entitled "One of the Few" (*Art News* [2 June 1951]), assessed Ayrton's uniqueness in these words: "Only a few artists now aim at a deeper and more powerful statement and Michael Ayrton is of this honourable band. . . . [H]ere is a painter who is unafraid of his skill in drawing. . . . To this he adds a classically conceived design . . . to discuss nature and humanity." G. S. Whittet, in his "London Commentary" in *Studio* (August 1951), likewise took note of Ayrton's interest in humanity, which he describes as

> the mainspring of his art. But his sitters are arch-types of humanity rather than individuals, and one recognizes a universal image in the sombre faces of a Dominican monk or a playing boy. . . . With each successive showing, Michael Ayrton impresses with his deliberate and thoughtful pictorial inventiveness. Influenced by Italian drawing, of which one can detect the shadow of Raphael, the artist is refining and perfecting a rare ability to impose his personal vision on the common subject—mankind. (90)

A few years later and across the Atlantic, Leonard Baskin in 1959 defended his own commitment to figurative sculpture:

> The human figure is the image of all men and of one man. It contains all and it can express all. Man has always created the human figure in his own image . . . . To discover these marvels, to search the *maze* [italics mine] of man's physicality, to wander the body's magnitudes is to search for the image of man. And in the act of discovery lies the act of communication. . . . [Man] has made of Arden a landscape of death. In this garden I dwell, and in limning its horror, the degradation and the filth, I hold the cracked mirror up to man. All previous art makes this course inevitable.[50]

Ayrton's personal life took on new dimensions with his marriage in November 1952 to Elisabeth Balchin (née Walshe) and his concurrent acquisition of three stepdaughters: Prudence (Mrs. Prudence Hopkins, now of Rockhampton, Gloucestershire, mother of Dr. Justine Hopkins and the late Marlin Jonathan Hopkins), Penelope (Dr. Penelope Leach of London, wife of Gerald Leach and mother of Melissa and Matthew Leach), and Freja (a.k.a. Missie, formerly Mrs. Richard Gregory of Bristol, now of Rockhampton, Gloucestershire, and mother of Alexander). Shortly before Christmas 1952, Ayrton and his new family left London to settle in North Essex, at Bradfields, just outside the village of Toppesfield near Halstead. The splendid large house at Bradfields, the major parts of which were constructed at various times between the thirteenth and eighteenth centuries, continued as home and drawing/writing studio for Ayrton until his death twenty-three years later. A large barn on the estate was converted into Ayrton's sculpture studio, and the once again well-kept gardens became the temporary home of many of his sculptures.[51] The marriage to Elisabeth, the acquisition of a family, and the move to the country all contributed to Ayrton's stability and growing maturity as an individual and as artist.[52]

During 1953 Ayrton was deeply affected by the death of Dylan Thomas (1914–1953), although the death of his closest friend, Constant Lambert, two years earlier, was more painful for him. Dylan was one of a group of friends, including Edith Sitwell, Humphrey Searle, and many others, who frequented the flat at All Souls Place. Ayrton's homage to Dylan Thomas, published in 1953, demonstrates the impact Dylan had on him:

> It occurred to me when Dylan died that all the time I had wasted hanging about in pubs was very nearly the time I had not wasted in my life except perhaps for the time I had spent following my trade or sullen craft. It occurred to me then that those few people whose deaths had most diminished me were like Dylan in that they took time to be either historical or opening or closing.
>
> I seldom met Dylan by appointment but I met him many times by chance and each time I felt I had won something in a lottery. The prize varied, but it was always larger than life and funnier and death had no dominion. Nor was this less the case when I sought him out, which was seldom for I seldom knew where exactly to seek and I was not an intimate friend of Dylan's—although he was an intimate friend of mine. So I found it preferable to let chance determine our meetings, which it did, and these meetings would last an hour or a couple of days, with never a moment's doubt and Dylan mixed the time, three parts farce and one part glory. All that is left now is the glory and this must do to be going on and on with.[53]

His painting, *Portrait of Dylan,* completed in 1949, also conveys the warmth of his friendship for Dylan.

Leonard Baskin was similarly devastated by the death in 1964 of his very close personal and professional friend Rico Lebrun. When they had met some seven years earlier, they found that their aesthetic interests corresponded perfectly. Ben Shahn and Lebrun were among Baskin's few professional friends, because he had largely been isolated from his own generation of artists. It is therefore entirely understandable that Baskin would describe Lebrun's untimely death as "a savage stroke levelled at American art [which] deprived me of my greatest ally in the struggle for figurative art."[54]

Another pivotal development in Ayrton's life occurred during 1953, for he made his first venture into sculpture. In *Drawings and Sculpture* he tells us that he had "hung about on the brink of making sculpture for several uncomfortable years," during which time his "painting became a substitute for sculpture, which did it no good. It was clear to me that I must start, but it seemed to require a lot of nerve" (1962a, 25). He gained inspiration for the move into sculpture from observing a blind woman in a London gallery during a Manzu show, at a time when they were the only two people in the gallery. She "felt her way from bronze to bronze, reading the work with her finger-tips. The sight of her fingers on the bronze, the sensation of her touch, as much as anything pushed me into starting to work in the round, but of course I painted her first, whoever she was" (1962a, 25, above pl. 1). Ayrton has described his initial attempt at this new medium and identified some of the influences upon his sculpture in *Drawings and Sculpture* (above pl. 17):

> I began, like most people, by making mud pies with clay. I couldn't do anything with it and produced nothing worth keeping. At this point Henry Moore came to the rescue. He showed me how to work direct in plaster on iron armatures which I welded myself, but what gave me the most powerful impulse was the wax he used for certain small *maquettes*. This wax, which is cast direct, remains my favorite medium for small sculpture.
>
> My first bronzes gave me such a lift when they came from the foundry that I incorporated them in the long series of still-lifes that I was painting at that time. I put them on tables with the other paraphernalia, the skulls, wineglasses and so on, from which I was painting these very literal pictures. From this juxtaposition I learned that relationship of bone forms with sculpture which has played a considerable part in what I have since done in bronze.
>
> Apart from Moore's example, it was the bronzes of Pollaiuolo, Donatello, and Degas, and the stone carvings of Giovanni Pisano and thereafter the Greek sculpture of the sixth century B.C. which meant and still mean most to me.

Elsewhere in *Drawings and Sculpture* (1962a, 16) he adds the name of Rodin to the list of masters whose work he passionately studied as he moved into sculpture. Both Ayrton and Baskin admitted to being influenced by Rodin. The human figure and humanistic values are central to the work of both artists, as they were to Rodin and sculptors for centuries before him, looking back toward Renaissance Italy and classical Greece. It can be said of both Ayrton and Baskin that a number of their sculptures resemble Rodin's bronzes, with "the same malleability of material, the sensuousness of moulding of garments."[55] For Baskin, Rodin's *Balzac* represented "the guardian of realism, the repudiator of romanticism."[56] The link between this sculpture and works by Baskin and Ayrton will be explored in depth later (see chapter 5; for other examples of Baskin's works, see chapter 3). One can also see the influence of Giacometti in Ayrton's work—both in the way the wax is worked and in the composition of some of his sculptures. This influence is hardly surprising, for it was a visit by Michael and Elisabeth to Giacometti's studio in 1950 that gave Michael encouragement to advance beyond his "until then vague moves toward sculpture."[57] Giacometti's influence is especially evident in the composition of *Icarus Rising, Variant I* (1964; Cat. No. 413), in which the elevation of Icarus evokes the elongated forms of Giacometti, such as *Man Pointing*, which appears in *Fabrications* (1972) in "A Problem of Space" (10–17).

The single event in 1954 that Ayrton considered significant enough to record in biographical sketches was his first visit to America, when he introduced the 1951 film, *The Drawings of Leonardo da Vinci*, at an international seminar at Harvard University. The following year was distinguished by a retrospective exhibition of his work from 1945 to 1955, held September–October 1955 at the Whitechapel Art Gallery, London. In the preface to the exhibition catalogue, gallery director Bryan Robertson declared that "the extra-ordinary measure of [Ayrton's] accomplishment with its wide range of expression and mastery of many techniques is clearly evident. The expanding sureness of his imagery and his powers of draughtsmanship, unique among his generation, are by any standards deeply impressive" (5). In his review of Ayrton's artistic progression, Robertson discovered "a compelling record of the development and consolidation of a highly personal vision. Interspersing this sequence, are a series of portraits which show consistent authority and perception and culminate in the new and very moving portrait of Wyndham Lewis"; all this leads him to describe Ayrton as "one of the most gifted artists of his generation" (ibid.).

Assembling this retrospective show also gave the artist an opportunity to assess his own development. In "Notes by the Artist" published in the catalogue (6–7), Ayrton conceded that he was for the first time clearly aware that in his painting he had been "consistently compressing elements which were predominant" in his earlier works, perhaps in order to generate within his pictures pressure that would "set up tensions of maximum intensity." In the course of the compression, the "most insidious temptations—melodrama, the grandiose, romantic expressiveness" are "shut in and pressed down and down, to emerge controlled by a dispassion in direct ratio to the initial passion which gave impetus to the act of painting." He described this "curiously puritanical attitude" as "characteristic of the natural romantic moving with determination toward a classical art." Looking back over this decade of trying to control his painting, which included the construction of pictures according to fifteenth-century Florentine geometric principles, Ayrton concluded that it was "an attempt to build up a structure strong enough to hold the restless actions and emotions of the human protagonists whose personal relationships would seem to be my perennial obsession."

In another note, on sculpture (7–8), Ayrton viewed his sculpture as a logical extension of his drawing. Again he stressed the importance of tension:

> The quality of tension at which I aimed in these little bronzes is a muscular tension but it is, I think, closely related in a sense to the tension which seems to me continually to be set up by human beings in relation to one another. . . . [I]t is the link between my sculpture and much of my painting. Tension is to me the quality which excites me most in a work of art. . . . It has nothing to do with undesirable nervous strain. That is why a Matisse still-life can be tranquil as a result of the perfect interplay of tensions. It is not a paradox.

In yet another note in the catalogue, this time on drawing, Ayrton spoke of drawing as "the centre," as "the central activity from which both painting and sculpture stem," and as "the core of visual experience" (8). Through retrospection, he became convinced "that sculpture was crucial to him" and that he could release his drawing and painting only by making sculpture (1962a, 15).

By 1956, Ayrton had progressed in his annual travels through Italy to the region of Magna Graecia, to Cumae on the Bay of Naples. Whereas in 1962 Ayrton described his first visit to Italy ("in 1946") as "one of the two most important visual experiences of his life" and his first visit to Greece (in 1957) as "the second great visual experience of Ayrton's life" (1962a, 14 and 16), in 1971 he accorded the greatest significance to his first visit to Cumae:

> His chance arrival at Cumae, north of Naples on May 11th 1956 was undoubtedly the most important single occurrence in his working life. The site of Daedalus' landing after his winged flight from Crete, the site of Aeneas' first landfall in Italy recorded by Virgil in Book VI of the *Aeneid*, and the rock from the core of which the Cumaean Sibyl spoke her oracles were here combined for Ayrton in the culminative work of Berlioz, the music drama *Les Troyens* which ends in the departure of Aeneas from Carthage to find Italy in this very place (Cumae). In this sudden fusion of narratives and in this numinous landscape, Ayrton found the starting point for almost all his subsequent work. (Rosenthal 1971, 42).

In many respects, this view of his arrival at Cumae is an accurate statement of its implications for his artistic career, particularly in terms of its profound spiritual and emotional impression on him. The inspiration of the place and the description in Virgil's *Aeneid* of Daedalus at Cumae would dramatically alter the course of Ayrton's life and art, for here he began to be drawn ineluctably into the myth that would dominate his work for most of the next two decades.

Ayrton exhibited rarely during this highly consequential year, and then only a few works, but the following year he exhibited fairly frequently, showing his Cumaean work for the first time in the summer of 1957, in London. He also exhibited his work for the first time in both the Soviet Union and the United States. A collection of essays, *Golden Sections,* was also published in 1957. For it Wyndham Lewis wrote the foreword—the last piece he ever wrote.

The following year Ayrton made an extended visit to Greece, which further enhanced and enlarged "the second great visual experience of Ayrton's life" (Ayrton 1962a, 16). Part of his six-month sojourn in Greece was devoted to advising Basil Wright on his production of the film *The Immortal Land.* That project had a significant by-product, since Ayrton and Wright codirected a second film, *Greek Sculpture.* In the process of making this prize-winning film, Ayrton studied sculpture with extraordinary care to achieve the most effective angles and perspectives for the camera. Wright attributes to Ayrton an "almost instantaneous grasp of what film could do to analyse and clarify works of art" and credits him with the fact that

> when filming in Greece . . . revelations, sometimes really breath-taking, came about, as, for instance in our filming of the Moscophoros and Delphi Charioteer. These revelations were due not only to Michael's ability unerringly to plunge *in medias res* but also to the humility with which he always approached great art. Out of this humility emerged a greater understanding, and out of that understanding he drew from his own genius the indestructible will power through which, for example, he met the challenge to construct Daedalus' maze.[58]

The impact of these experiences upon his art in general and upon his sculpture in particular was dramatic and immediate. Not only did he later declare that the greatest stimulus to his sculpture was "unquestionably his first visit to Greece," he even asserted that "from that time forward the landscape, the myths, and the sculpture of Greece became his primary source of inspiration" (Ayrton 1962a, 16).

Further recognition came to Ayrton during this year through his inclusion in both the Guggenheim Award Exhibition at the Whitechapel Art Gallery and the Contemporary Art Society Exhibition at the Tate Gallery. Over the next two years he continued his travels—to Mexico, twice to Greece, and twice to the United States—and he continued to exhibit his work. At St. George's Gallery, London, in 1959 he exhibited a group of Cretan drawings and a series of six color lithographs, called *The Greek Suite,* which significantly advanced Ayrton's representations of the myth and its geographical setting.

Nevertheless, the full impact of the myth upon his art would not become apparent until the exhibition at the Matthiesen Gallery, London, in October 1961. This solo exhibition, entitled "The Icarus Theme," was devoted exclusively to the products of his mythological inspiration. Included were numerous landscape paintings, especially of Crete and the Cyclades, stucco reliefs depicting the flight and fall of Icarus, several drawings of Icarus, and over a dozen bronzes, most of them concerned with Icarus.

While Ayrton was creating these drawings and paintings during his first extended stay in Greece and on Crete during 1958, he was overcome by "an unexpected compulsion to write scraps of verse" concerned with Icarus (1962d, 64). Early in 1960 he assembled these bits of poetry and began to write a narrative about Daedalus around them, also rewriting the inchoate verse into "Songs of Icarus" (1978d). The prose and poetry were combined with a series of drawings into *The Testament of Daedalus,* published in 1962.

In a postscript to the *Testament,* written in May 1962 on the eve of his return to Crete, as well as through the narrative itself, Ayrton reveals how completely he had entered into the myth during the six years since his arrival at Cumae. He says, "The legend grew in me, forced itself upon me and emerged in the form of reliefs, bronzes, drawings and paintings in various media" (1962c, 64). He speaks of "a time when the Greek landscape possessed me. Delos especially exercised upon me an intense compulsion" (ibid.). As he traveled by boat to the islands and by plane within Greece and between Greece and Italy, conscious of the preparations of "the fledgling astronaut" for travel into space, he "became entangled in this particular myth. Perhaps it is because the flight of Daedalus and Icarus has a relevance to the twentieth century more piercing even than most myths which, being universal, are always relevant at any time to man's existence. I say I became entangled in this myth because I did not choose it consciously as a good subject. That is not how I work" (Ayrton 1962c, 65).

The key words "forced," "possessed," "compulsion," and "entangled" offer a telling insight into how Ayrton worked, as if he were in the grip of a force greater than himself that was the source of his inspiration as an artist. He also speculates on the psychology of his increasing obsession with the myth of Daedalus and Icarus: "I have always had recurring dreams of flight. When I was a schoolboy I had a passion for early aeronautics.

My father was a classicist who used to tell me about the Greeks and the Homeric legends in my early childhood. I don't know how much or how little these things have to do with it" (Ayrton 1962c, 65). A psychoanalyst in the Freudian tradition would offer a very different explanation for these recurring dreams. In the 1911 edition of *The Interpretation of Dreams,* Freud acknowledges that he was rather late in coming to appreciate fully the significance of dream symbolism; in the 1914 (fourth) edition, he added a special section on the subject. In one of his lectures on psychoanalysis, "Symbolism in Dreams," Freud offers a psychoanalytic interpretation of dreams of flying: "dreams of flying, so familiar and often so delightful, have to be interpreted as dreams of general sexual excitement, as erection-dreams."[59]

Acknowledging that "we live by myth, inventing it when necessary, returning to it with satisfaction when it seems useful," Ayrton equated Icarus with pilots whom he "envied in general and found intolerable in particular" while he was in the R.A.F. He wondered whether Icarus was "the perpetual hero" and described Daedalus, "the *polytechnos,* the 'maker of things,'" as the "greatest mythical progenitor, after Prometheus, of . . . the artist" and as "the cunning man, creator and trickster" (1962a, 65–66). Classical mythology also was a major source of inspiration for Baskin, and both artists drew upon biblical stories, although Baskin drew much more heavily upon this source than Ayrton did (his series on St. Anthony being one of the more notable examples of such reliance upon biblical tradition).

Although operating under very different aesthetic principles from Ayrton, abstract artist Mark Rothko also acknowledged the role of myth in his work. Like many of his fellow abstractionists, Rothko was influenced by Carl Jung's concept of the archetype to draw upon the myths of Greece and other early cultures. They believed that "it was possible through the language of color and biomorphic form to transmute the emotions of their private experience into universally understood images."[60] Rothko reverted to myths of antiquity because, he said, "they are the eternal symbols upon which we must fall back to express basic psychological ideas. They are the symbols of man's primitive fears and motivations . . . changing only in detail but never in substance, be they Greek, Aztec, Icelandic or Egyptian. And our modern psychology finds them persisting still in our dreams, our vernacular and our art, for all the changes in the outward conditions of life."[61]

The *Testament* is itself more an example of mythmaking than it is a retelling of the myth as it exists in the fragments of literature from which we reconstruct it. Ayrton admits as much in the postscript when he says he realized that he had to explain for himself "the relationship between Daedalus and his son and the passion Icarus had for Apollo," but he also offers an insight into how word and image intertwined as he spun out his own version of the myth: "Those images in which I came to portray Icarus at the climax of his flight, in suicidal contact with the sun itself, are the result of the narrative. The narrative, on the other hand, is the result of many previous images, the reliefs, bronzes, drawings and paintings out of which it grew" (Ayrton 1962c, 67).

The concluding observation of the postscript expresses a desire that Ayrton would articulate a number of times in succeeding years:

> I wish I was sure that I am free of Icarus and that I have enough of that part of Daedalus in me to make good images. The artist, "the maker of things," seeks to represent some part of what he thinks man is, and was, in order to discover himself in the process: or so I believe. Perhaps he also hopes to extend man's experience of himself—by strapping some kind of wings on him—but this would be a fortunate chance and is not the crux of the matter. (1962c, 70)

One of Ayrton's friends and collectors declared after his death: "Ayrton's remarkable *The Testament of Daedalus* does not explain his work, but reveals the passion that has inspired it and throws light on artistic creation in general. . . . To understand Ayrton this is the book to read, but to understand his work it is only necessary to see it."[62]

The public was given greater opportunity to see Ayrton's work in 1962 with the publication of *Drawings and Sculpture.* Almost half of the 139 illustrations were of works produced from 1956 to 1962; most of these were linked directly or indirectly to myth, particularly to the myths associated with Cumae and Crete. Four years later a second edition was published with sixty-seven additional illustrations, showing how much more deeply Ayrton had become entangled in the myth. In between these two editions, Ayrton's work derived from the myth was exhibited to a far-flung audience: from London to Johannesburg; from Sussex to Buffalo, New York; from Leeds to Quebec and other Canadian provinces; and from Athens to Nairobi.

In April–May 1964 the Grosvenor Gallery, London, exhibited eighty works from the brief period 1962–1964, including bronzes, paintings, collages, and drawings, all variously related to the myth of Daedalus. The oracle in her various manifestations, the sentinel Talos, the Minotaur, and the paintings of landscapes that these mythical figures inhabit all demonstrate at once Ayrton's artistic versatility and at the same time the inexhaustible riches of the myth that had become his obsessive concern. In the introduction to the catalogue for this show, T. G. Rosenthal observes in Ayrton's work "an almost unique combination of cerebral and sensual elements so that . . . Ayrton's physical versatility and sensitivity are controlled by a restlessly seeking intellect." He also concludes that Ayrton "has successfully combined his twin obsessions with antiquity and the human figure to a remarkable degree. By doing this he has rationalized and justified his own journey through the labyrinth of the twentieth century and his own pursuit of a non-circular truth. . . . [I]t is a measure of Ayrton's strength as an artist that, starting with classical themes, he has created works which are wholly of our time and unquestionably and relevantly modern."[63]

From 1964 to 1966 Ayrton moved into his maze-making phase as he continued to penetrate deeper into the seemingly bottomless well of inspiration provided by the myth. In these works Daedalus became for Ayrton "a being at once more general and more personal. He has become any man who, during his life, builds in and around himself a maze of circumstances and experiences. . . ." (1962a, above pls. 140 and 141). Concurrent with the creation of these drawings, paintings, and sculptures, Ayrton was writing a new book under the inspiration of the myth. Published in 1967, *The Maze Maker* was called a novel by its publishers, but Ayrton termed it the "autobiography" of Daedalus, leaving one with the clear conclusion that Ayrton now had come fully to identify with the archetypal craftsman. He claimed that he wrote it to try to get himself out of the myth, but once again he found himself only deeper in it.

The Maze Maker won the Royal Society of Literature's Heinemann Award for 1967.[64] As a result of the great technical detail of Ayrton's descriptions in the book of Daedalus's wondrous inventions, he received two major commissions: to design a giant maze in New York's Catskill Mountains and recreate for a New Zealander the Golden Honeycomb Daedalus made for Aphrodite on Mt. Eryx. The former commission especially was responsible for drawing Ayrton still more deeply into the myth, with all its potential for new and profound insights into the human condition, for he made new discoveries in the process of completing the *Arkville Maze* (Cat. No. 673).

In 1969 Ayrton had two important retrospective shows, one at Hamet Gallery, London, the other at the Reading Museum Art Gallery. Outstanding events of the year for Ayrton included the completion of the *Arkville Maze* in New York and the presentation of the BBC color television program on Berlioz (9 March 1969, repeated 30 November 1969): "Berlioz, A Singular Obsession," Ayrton's personal tribute for the centenary of the composer's death, was subsequently also published by BBC Publications.[65]

After the completion of the maze, there was a slight hiatus in Ayrton's artistic production. He believed that he had exhausted the potential of the Daedalus myth, and he was awaiting some new source of inspiration to take hold of him. Never one to sit idle, however, he occupied his time with writing short stories, which later were published in a collection entitled *Fabrications* (1973). The year 1970 was also marked by the publication of *Giovanni Pisano, Sculptor.* Thus, during 1969–1970, two of his major obsessions—Daedalus and Hector Berlioz—and one of his major art historical projects, on an artist who had a profound influence upon his sculpture, had seemingly come to an end. This coincidence of events brought

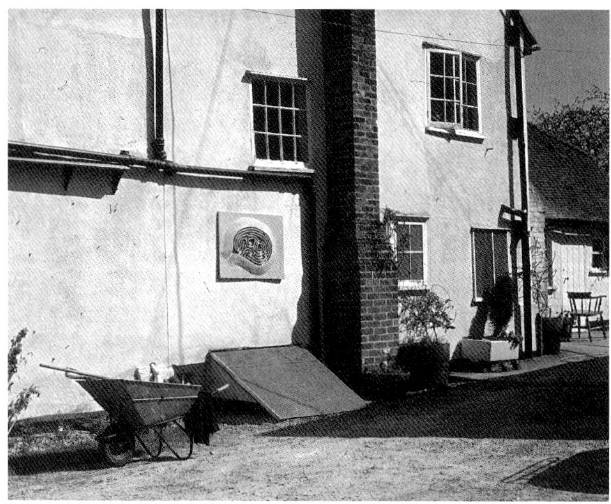

Figure 2. **MICHAEL AYRTON'S HOME, "BRADFIELDS,"** near Halstead, Essex, 1972. *Arkville Maze Maquette* (Cat. No. 641) attached to wall.

Ayrton to a crucial turning point in his career just when he appeared to be at his prime as an artist. Fortunately, however, his discovery of the implications of mirrors and other reflective surfaces for extending the symbolism of the maze provided the necessary impetus for him to resume his creation of works of art (see chapter 7). This new development was a natural extension of his use of bronze mirrors in one of the chambers of the *Arkville Maze*. There also was perhaps a degree of atavism in the use of mirrors or, at the very least, a splendid coincidence, for Ayrton's grandfather, Professor William Ayrton, "had produced during his time in Tokyo three papers on the oriental 'magic mirror.' These publications—together with the pair of bronze mirrors which he had brought back with him and which passed eventually . . . to Michael—were to play a catalytic role in the obsession with reflections and engimatic metaphors which informed a large part of the latter's artistic production" (Hopkins 1994, 2).

Writing and publication continued apace, with the publication in 1971 of *The Rudiments of Paradise,* a collection of essays on art and music. The National Book League's "Word and Image" series, launched that same year with an exhibition (actually expanded into two exhibitions with a single catalogue) of work by Ayrton and Wyndham Lewis, illustrated convincingly that Ayrton had achieved impressive mastery of both image and word, and that he moved effortlessly from one to the other.

In 1972 Ayrton completed his largest sculpture to date, *Corporate Head* or *Reflective Head* (Cat. No. 772), which was commissioned for the international headquarters of the S. S. Kresge Corporation (later renamed the Kmart Corporation), located in Troy, Michigan. This bronze and glass sculpture rises more than twenty-one feet from the terrace at the entrance to the large, labyrinthine office building (see chapter 7). The Daedalus I Gallery of Birmingham, Michigan, organized an exhibition, "The Maze and Beyond" (September–October 1972), to accompany the dedication of the sculpture.[66] A solo retrospective exhibition, structured around the maze theme, opened in Chicago the following month, and, early in 1973, a touring exhibition, "Maze and Minotaur," opened at the Portsmouth City Art Gallery, traveling subsequently to Southampton, Bath, Exeter, and Rye. In May, 1973, the Museum of Art at Pennsylvania State University presented a solo exhibition of Ayrton's work, in collaboration with the university's Institute for the Arts and Humanities Studies, on the occasion of Ayrton's residence as visiting fellow of the institute.

A variation on the bronze *Icarus III* (Cat. No. 136), entitled *Icarus III, Variant I* (Cat. No. 756), was presented in 1973 to the Corporation of London and erected on a special pedestal, designed by Ayrton, in Old Change Court, near St. Paul's Cathedral.[67] Not long thereafter, in late summer, while he was at work designing a turf maze for a second cast of the *Arkville Minotaur* (Cat. No. 663) to inhabit Postman's Park, London, Ayrton fell ill. His condition continued to worsen, until it was properly diagnosed as a rare form of diabetes and treatment was begun. For almost a year, therefore, Ayrton was too sick to accomplish any significant work, but in 1975 he completed a number of animal drawings, based upon his visit to East Africa as part of his convalescence. He intended to transfer these ink and wash drawings into etchings, but he completed only one etching.

"The impulse to create images is fundamental to us. It is an act of power resulting from our act of worship"

He turned his attention to research and writing for a projected series of fourteen television programs entitled, *A Question of Mirrors.*[68] Each program was given a single word as its title. The script for the first one, "*Metaphor*," provides further insight into Ayrton's development as an artist, revealing that he became as involved with the conception of the mirror as he had with his earlier obsessions. In it he says,

> Isn't the function of people who practice any art largely this: to produce reflections of facts in metaphor; to show the form and pressure of the time? I make images and the visual arts, whether sculpture or painting, no less than poetry and prose, come to exist because they are, or use images as *metaphor*—or complexes of metaphors, layer upon layer, an onion skin of metaphor comparable to the construction of the lens of the human eye itself. . . . I work visually, paint, draw, make sculpture, write and *think* visually so it's not surprising that I take Leonardo da Vinci very seriously and follow him when he tells us (in mirror writing, naturally—as was his custom) that "the mirror, above all is our master." . . . But perhaps Leonardo demonstrated, more clearly than anyone, the paradox that truth and error may coexist in metaphor in a single image. . . . I make sculpture with mirrors—turning mirrors—and they reflect "in a glass darkly." The mirrors are translucent and they play strange games(1978b, 38 and 41).

In the script for the seventh program, "Fragments," Ayrton tells how he began the use of mirrors with the *Arkville Maze* (Cat. No. 673):

> I began exploring mirrors by putting a fragmented fractured one in the coil of a maze. I wanted to fragment Icarus as he began his tragic flight towards the sun, by breaking up his image as reflected in sunlight, so that his end might appear in his beginning. . . . It is perhaps by the jigsaw of fragments that we can endure some reality. To face it may be to risk facing a greater "truth" than most of us can manage. As the philosopher A. N. Whitehead put it, it is those who believe they have the whole truth who do the damage. (1978b, 48)

To mind comes this trenchant observation by Baskin: "[Man] has made of Arden a landscape of death. In this garden I dwell, and in limning its horror, the degradation and the filth, *I hold the cracked mirror up to man* [italics mine]. All previous art makes this course inevitable."[69]

The script for the final program, "Darkly," starts with an anecdote that reveals Ayrton's humor and his attitude toward religion: "I remember when I was first a conscript early in World War II, I was filling out a form — name, occupation, etc. etc. Religion? I didn't have one, so I wrote down *Gnostic.* It was pure swank and in the hope of ducking church parades. 'Gnostic'? said the weary corporal, gathering up our papers '*So you think you know?*' Gnosis is a Greek word for knowledge. The corporal crossed out Gnostic and put in C of E."[70]

He did, of course, have a religion, as we all do, but it was a complex one, with Greek myth as a dominant strain. In "The Translated Image" he writes: "The impulse to create images is fundamental to us. It is an act of power resulting from our act of worship" (1971, 154). In his introduction to *Rudiments,* he declares: "I have not . . . been a zealous advocate of passive obedience to a Zeitgeist. . . . I do not therefore expect to find myself buried in Westminster Abbey. . . nor . . . entombed in the contemporary equivalent which, in my trade, is an inevitable if simple entry in the recently widely expanded sepulchre called art-history" (1971, 9). Despite all his disclaimers, it is evident that Christianity played an essential part in Ayrton's mythic understanding, and "his pantheism passed beyond the confines of any single pantheon; he experienced the world as numinous in the broadest possible sense, and strange beyond imagining."[71] From his obsession with St. Anthony in the early forties to his "Christian" paintings of the late forties, there is an evident empathy for Christianity that is clarified by this statement in a BBC broadcast in 1967:

> I am not a Christian and cannot raise a flicker about Christian Greece, and yet the Christian civilisation of Italy and the West, from which inevitably I depend for the tradition in painting and sculpture which formed me, are important and creative to me. Perhaps in an absurd way, in my split-time sense, there is a certain logic in this.

> When . . . Byzantium fell, the West reaped the scattered fruits of the ancient Greek world and the Renaissance flowered from its seeds. I am Western and those are the two worlds which have given me the means to make what I make.[72]

In his identification with Daedalus he entered into the ancient Greek mind in an extraordinary way, absorbing some of the ancient Greek religion along with it, as well as embracing the essential humanism of that civilization.

While Ayrton was at work on his major undertaking on mirrors, he was also pursuing another keen interest, the poetry of Archilochus, who lived in the seventh century B.C.E and was the first personal poet of the Greeks. Archilochus also was one of Gerald Gould's acknowledged lyric ancestors (Hopkins 1994, 406), so this interest could reflect a subconscious attempt to win his father's approval, an attempt to reconcile himself with his father's memory. The poetry of Archilochus has been preserved only in scraps, but Ayrton tried to understand the poet, portraying the poetry both in his own translation and through visual images to accompany the text. With the assistance of his stepdaughter, Prue Hopkins, he set up an etching studio at Bradfields and made sixteen plates, which were ready for printing by November 1975. In one of the scripts for the program on mirrors, Ayrton says: "Archilochos . . . is imprinted on me and I went looking for his ghost, on the islands of Paros and Thasos where he had lived, in order to exorcise him by making etchings to illustrate his poems" (1978b, 55). In April 1975 he and Elisabeth spent a week in Greece, much of it devoted to tracing the life and the spirit of Archilochus, who had "emerged as an alter-ego for Michael" (Hopkins 1994, 405–6).

Archilochus proved to be Ayrton's final exorcism. After completing his superbly executed and highly evocative series of Archilochos etchings, Ayrton directed his attention to refining his translations of the text, relying on classical scholars from Cambridge University to assist him. On Friday, 14 November 1975, therefore, Professors G. S. Kirk, Moses Finley and others dined with Michael and Elisabeth at Bradfields, spending "the whole evening discussing fine points" (Hopkins 1994, 414). The following Sunday, 16 November, the Ayrtons planned to drive down to London, since Michael had an early appointment on the 17th with Karl Sabbagh for continuing consultation on the BBC series on mirrors.[73] An unexpected call from an old friend, Norman Hammond, resulted in entertaining him for lunch in their usual style; immediately thereafter, Elisabeth and Michael drove down to London (Hopkins 1994, 415). That evening, in their flat on Eton Road, Michael suffered a massive heart attack. Within minutes after arriving at the Royal Free Hospital, he entered "the maze which leads to death."

For a special edition of *Labrys* devoted to the memory of Michael Ayrton, novelist Frederic Raphael—friend, collector and admirer—wrote a moving commentary, "On the Recent Death of an Artist." In it he declares,

> I lament the loss of Michael in two rather distinct ways: I lament what I have lost and I lament what you have lost, and you I divide into two groups, the innocent and the guilty. The innocent are those who never knew Michael and scarcely knew his work . . . ; the guilty are those who, in a position to know better (and often claiming to know better), never bothered to reward him with their attention or to do themselves the favour, to put it crudely, of recognising what was there for the taking, and the treasuring. The death of an artist is a terrible thing. (66).

Later he writes, "The greatness of the man lay not only in his work, . . . but also in the spread of his ambition, in the noble sense. . . . What was great in him was his great use for greatness, his insistence on surrounding himself with it, honouring it, on living as though it were possible" (69–70).

Professor Donald Davie, another friend and admirer of Ayrton, wrote a poetic tribute, "Ars Poetica: *In Memoriam Michael Ayrton, Sculptor*":

> Walk quietly around in
> A space cleared for the purpose.
>
> Most poems, or the best,
> Describe their own birth, and this
> Is what they are—a space
> Cleared to walk around in.

Their various symmetries are
Guarantees that the space has
Boundaries, and beyond them
The turbulence it was cleared from.

Small clearances, small poems;
Unlikely now the enormous
Louring, resonant spaces
Carved out by a Virgil.

The old man likes to sit
Here, in his black-tiled *loggia*
A patch of sun, and to muse
On Pasternak, Michael Ayrton.

Ayrton, he remembers:
Soon after reading his
Obituary, behold!
A vision of him:

The bearded, heavy-shouldered
London clubman, smiling
Against a *quattrocento*
View of the upper Arno.

This was in answer to prayer:
A pledge, a sufficient solace.
Poor rhyme, and are you there?
Bless Michael with your promise.[74]

Through his alter ego in *The Maze Maker* Ayrton told us: "[T]he topology of my labyrinth remains ambiguous. Its materials are at once dense, impenetrable, translucent and illusory. Such a total maze each man makes around himself and each is different from each other, for each contains the length, breadth, height and depth of his own life. I, Daedalus, maze maker, shall take this that I have written . . . and dedicate it at the entrance to the maze which leads to death" (1967, 282). For those of us who mourned his departure—and even for those who were unaware of him or who were not grieved at his passing—he has left a rich legacy in word and image. Through his richly evocative works he still speaks to us—and will speak to generations yet to come. As we explore his progressive involvement with Daedalus, Icarus, and other figures of Greek myth, the coils of his labyrinth will unwind to reveal an artist with a driving ambition to rival the great artists of past and present, such as Michelangelo and Picasso; an artist whose striving to rise to the heights of Icarus and rival the prototypical sculptor Daedalus led him to enrich and enlarge the myth that was his obsessive concern for the final twenty years of his life.

The Mythical Context for Ayrton's Words and Images

2

To understand Michael Ayrton's contributions to the richly evocative cycle of myths associated with the island of Crete, it is necessary to know the basic stories concerning the various mythical characters who were either central or tangential to his work.[1] His understanding and appreciation of the myth of Daedalus, in all its dimensions, cannot be fully recognized without an awareness of the context in which he created his works in ink, paint, wax, chalk, bronze, and other media. Although Ayrton claims not to have read the *Aeneid* until age thirty-five (see chapter 4), once he became involved with the myth of Daedalus, he read voraciously and eclectically, as he did with his study of the Renaissance and proto-Renaissance artists. His *Rudiments of Paradise* and *Fabrications* reveal him as a widely read and knowledgeable man, although he claimed to have been anything but a scholar. He did, however, frequently consult classical scholars at Oxford, Cambridge, and the British Museum. They directed him to many of the ancient sources cited in this chapter. *The Maze Maker* reveals how extensive his knowledge was, showing his familiarity with most, if not all, of the sources used for this summary. In one of his several essays on Picasso, Ayrton reveals indirectly the scope of his own reading of the classical sources of the myth when he declares (1971, 246): "I do not suggest that Picasso is learned in the writings of Plutarch, or Bacchylides, or Diodorus Siculus or has steeped himself in Virgil, or Catullus, or Apollodorus, or Hyginus, or Pausanias. He has however had a look at Ovid and who knows what else? Maybe Euripides is familiar to him." *Fabrications* adds Josephus to his list of ancient authors (1973, 26ff.), along with novelists as diverse as Stendahl, Dostoevsky, André Breton, and Victor Hugo (34ff.), the philosopher Kierkegaard (60ff.), and many arcane works (50, 95, and bibliography, 224). From my conversations with him over the years, I know that he also was well versed in James Joyce, André Gide, and many other writers of the nineteenth and twentieth centuries, as well as writers and artists of the previous centuries.

The major extant literary sources for the myth derive from a period extending from the second century B.C.E. to the second century C.E. In approximate chronological order they are: Apollodorus *Bibliotheca,* Diodorus Siculus *Bibliotheca,* Virgil *Aeneid,* Ovid *Ars Amatoria* 2 and *Metamorphoses* 8, Plutarch *Theseus,* Pausanias *Description of Greece,* and Hyginus *Fabulae.*[2] It is indeed regrettable that fifth- and fourth-century dramas based on the myth have all been lost, save usually for occasional lines of verse and a few words taken out of context. The *Daedalus* of Sophocles and his *Camici* would prove invaluable additions; the *Cretans* (presently more complete than most) and *Theseus* of Euripides likewise would be a great boon, as would the *Cocalus* and *Daedalus* of Aristophanes, the *Daedalus* of Plato (the comic poet), and comedies by lesser known poets.[3] But unless new papyri miraculously bring these dramas to light, we must continue to rely primarily upon summaries of historians and mythographers, dubious reconstructions of lost plays, and paradigmatic allusions by classical authors.

VIRGIL'S STORY OF DAEDALUS

Michael Ayrton first encountered the myth of Daedalus through the opening lines of the sixth book of Virgil's *Aeneid.* The following translation of that crucial passage (*Aeneid* 6.1–44, translated by Beryl Ament specifically for this book) offers an appropriate introduction to this fascinating myth.

> He spoke with tears in his eyes and spurred on the fleet until at long last they glided onto the shores of Euboean Cumae. They turned their prows to the open sea, then the anchors began to stay the fleet with their iron grip and the curved sterns fringed the shore. Eagerly the young men leaped onto the Western soil. Some of them sought out the source of fire concealed in stones of flint, while others stripped the woods where wild animals had their overgrown dens and pointed out where they had found streams.
>
> But Aeneas did not forget his duty and went in search of the pinnacles where mighty Apollo is lord and the huge cave a little way off which is the retreat of the awe-inspiring Sibyl. Apollo, the prophetic god of Delos, inspires her great mind and being, and for her he lays open the future. And now they came to the groves and golden roofs of Diana, the goddess of the crossroads.
>
> Daedalus, so the legend says, in his flight from the rule of King Minos had the effrontery to entrust himself to the heavens on swift wings and soared to the icy North on his bizarre journey. At length he lighted effortlessly on the peak of Cumae. On this spot where he was first restored to land he consecrated to you, Apollo, his feathered oars and constructed a mighty shrine. On one door he depicted the death of Androgeos; nearby, the Athenians, cruelly commanded to hand over as compensation seven youths each year. The urn is standing there. The lots have been drawn. On the other door the land of Crete is shown rising out of the sea. Here is displayed Pasiphaë and her obscene passion for a bull, which led her to mate with him through a ruse, and their hybrid progeny, the Minotaur, offspring neither man nor beast, but the evidence of an unspeakable love. Here is the palace and the insoluble maze, the result of Daedalus' celebrated labor. But Daedalus himself took pity on the all-consuming love of Ariadne and solved for her the confusing contortions of the structure, guiding her groping footsteps with a thread. Icarus, what a large role you would have played in that ambitious undertaking had you not been the source of your father's grief. Twice he had tried to portray his son's tragedy in gold; twice the father's hands had failed.
>
> The Trojans would have surveyed the details endlessly, but soon Achates, who had been sent ahead, was at their side and with him the priestess of Apollo and Diana, Deiphobe, the daughter of Glaucus. She spoke to the king: "This is no time for sight-seeing. Now you would do better to sacrifice seven bullocks from a herd as yet unyoked and seven ritually chosen sheep." When she had finished addressing Aeneas the priestess summoned the Trojans into the lofty temple, and they did not delay carrying out the sacrifices she had ordered.
>
> The side of the cliff at Cumae is hollowed out into a huge cave. There are countless wide entrances and countless passages, and from every orifice hurtled voices, the responses of the Sibyl.

Into this short account Virgil has compressed the central core of the myth, using a technique somewhat reminiscent of Homer's description of the shield of Achilles (*Iliad* 18.478ff.). The poet's purpose required this compression, but the artist who found in this account a rich and compelling source of inspiration required its expansion. The deeper his penetration into the myth, the greater was Ayrton's need to know its every aspect, to trace its literary and artistic expression. To understand Ayrton's almost countless interpretations of the myth, it is therefore essential that one be familiar with the fullest description of the myth that can be derived from extant ancient sources. Although Ayrton himself reconstructed the myth in *The Maze Maker,* he also expanded and interpreted it in the process, just as he did with his sculpture, drawings, and paintings. The following reconstruction of the story not only of Daedalus and Icarus, but also of related mythical figures, does not attempt to follow the course of Ayrton's discovery of the many different aspects of the myth. Rather, this summary offers a frame of reference for studying Ayrton's work.

DAEDALUS: FROM BIRTH TO BANISHMENT

The myth of Daedalus is no exception to the rule that each myth, each legend, has one or more variants. There is no agreement about the parentage of Daedalus. Our earliest authority, Pherecydes, identifies Metion, son of the Athenian king Erechtheus, and Iphinoë as the artisan's parents. Apollodorus, however, and most other sources make him grandson to Metion, naming Eupalamus and Alcippe as his parents (Apollod. 3.15.8).[4] Eupalamus, i.e., "Skillful," would of course seem an appropriate name for a mythmaker to give to the father of the first craftsman, which might therefore lend greater credence to Metion as his true father.[5] Among these sources, however, there is no disagreement that Daedalus was by birth an Athenian of the Erechtheid clan. He belonged to the "younger branch of the royal family of Athens, and is descended, through Erichthonius, from Hephaestus and—almost—from Athena."[6] The names for his parents and grandparents clearly imply that in Daedalus there is combined the manual dexterity and the intellectual capacity required to make him stand out as a brilliant artisan. The following brief account offers confirmation of this view.

He by far excelled other men in the art of building, in making statues and in stone carving; he also was known as an inventor whose many devices greatly advanced the development of art (D. S. 4.76.1). Hyginus says that he reputedly received his professional skill (*fabricam*) from Athena and that he was the first to make statues of the gods (*Fab.* 39 and 274). Apollodorus describes him as the finest master-builder and the first inventor of sculpture (Apollod. 3.15.8), but Diodorus credits him instead with highly significant advances in the art of sculpture. By contrast with his predecessors, who carved statues with closed eyes and with arms and hands hanging attached to their sides, Daedalus fashioned statues with open eyes, separated legs, and extended arms and hands, causing subsequent generations to invent the story that Daedalus's statues were so lifelike that they could see and walk, and seemed to be living beings capable of every bodily function (D. S. 4.76.2–3).

Although he won great fame as an artisan in his native Athens, Daedalus was banished from his homeland for the alleged murder of his apprentice, his young nephew Talos (Latin "Talus"), son of his sister Perdix (Apollod. 3.15.8). Some sources, however, name him Calos; others identify him as Perdix.[7] Fear that his reputation would be eclipsed as his nephew's fame rose motivated the murder, says Apollodorus, although the only evidence he offers of the youth's talents was that he employed a snake's jawbone to saw a thin stick. Diodorus appreciably expands the story of Talos's prowess, attributing to him the invention of an iron saw modeled after the snake's jawbone, the potter's wheel, and the compass (D. S. 4.76.5–6).[8] The murder was accomplished by hurling the youth from the acropolis, but the corpse was discovered (Apollod. 3.15.8) or Daedalus was apprehended in the process of burying what he said was a snake (D. S. 4.76.6), whereupon he was tried and condemned by the court of the Areopagus. Daedalus then fled to one of the other Attic demes and thence to Crete, leaving behind the Daedalidae ("descendants of Daedalus") as his legacy (D. S. 4.76.7–4.77.1), or made his way directly to the kingdom of Minos (Apollod. 3.15.8).[9] Minos was the son of Zeus and Europa, whom Zeus—in bull form—had carried across the sea to Crete, where he mated with her.

DAEDALUS ON CRETE

The craftsman's outstanding reputation won for him the friendship of King Minos (D. S. 4.77.1). He made images for Minos and his daughters ("as Homer also revealed in the *Iliad,*" says Pausanias) and won for the Cretans an enduring reputation for making *xoana* (carved wooden images or statues of a deity) (Paus. 7.4.5 and 8.53.8).[10] It was, however, his assistance of the queen, Pasiphaë, which gave rise to the fabulous inventions associated with his name in Crete. Prior to this time Minos made an annual sacrifice to Poseidon of the best bull born into his herd, but when a bull of exceptional beauty was born, Minos substituted an inferior one, thereby arousing the anger of Poseidon, who therefore inflicted Pasiphaë with an unnatural passion for this bull (D. S. 4.77.1–2). Through the ingenuity of Daedalus, who fashioned a wooden cow for her, she gratified her lust, had intercourse with the bull, and gave birth to the Minotaur (D. S. 4.77.1–3), whose name was Asterius (Apollod. 3.1.4) or Asterion (Paus. 2.31.1). This biform creature was said to have either a bull's face or head and neck, but the rest of him was human.[11]

Daedalus subsequently constructed a labyrinth to house this disgraceful hybrid monster, perhaps at Minos's command, since an oracle had instructed Minos to shut up the Minotaur (Apollod. 3.1.4). The labyrinth had innumerable passageways winding back upon themselves as confusingly as the course of the Meander River in Phrygia; these passageways so deceived the eye that even Daedalus, says Ovid, was scarcely able to find his way back to the entrance (*Met.* 8.155–68), although Diodorus merely says that it was difficult for one unfamiliar with the winding passageways to find his way out (D. S. 4.77.4).[12] The sacred books of the priests of Egypt purportedly recorded a visit by Daedalus (D. S. 1.96.2), who there saw a king's tomb called the Labyrinth remarkable for its ingenious design, which made egress difficult without a guide; Daedalus admired the skill of this tomb's construction and built a similar one in Crete for Minos as a residence for the Minotaur (D. S. 1.61.2–4 and 1.97.5). Diodorus reported that in his day the Egyptian labyrinth was still standing, but Daedalus's Cretan creation had entirely disappeared (D. S. 1.61.4).

Some time earlier Androgeos, son of Minos, had gone to Athens to participate in the games held during the Panathenaic festival. Although he was a victor in the games, he paid a high price for his victory: he was murdered either by jealous competitors or by the treachery of Aegeus, king of Athens, who feared that Androgeos's friendship with his political rivals constituted a threat to his power.[13] When Minos demanded satisfaction for his son's death but received none, he declared war on the Athenians. Since the war was not reaching a speedy conclusion, Minos enlisted divine aid, calling on his father, Zeus, to avenge him on the Athenians, whereupon the entire province was afflicted with pestilence and famine. Upon seeking oracular advice about relief from their misfortunes, the Athenians were told to pay whatever penalty Minos demanded in satisfaction for the murder of Androgeos. He demanded that the Athenians surrender seven youths and seven young maidens every nine years as food for the Minotaur, as long as it lived.[14] When they complied with his order, the plague was broken.

Nine years later, when Minos again came to exact payment, Theseus, son of Aegeus, was among the sacrificial troop, either voluntarily or chosen by lot.[15] Upon arrival in Crete the handsome Theseus aroused the passion of one of the daughters of Minos, Ariadne, who agreed to assist him in the conquest of the Minotaur and the escape from the labyrinth if he would swear an oath to take her back to Athens as his wife (Apollod. *Epit.* 1.8 and D. S. 4.61.4). When Theseus agreed to her terms, she sought the assistance of Daedalus, who disclosed the following means of escape: Ariadne gave Theseus a ball of red thread, which he fastened to the entrance of the labyrinth; he was to unwind the skein as he made his way to the central chamber that housed the Minotaur, then rewind it as his guide out of the maze after slaying the Minotaur.[16] He slew the Minotaur with his fists (or with a sword),[17] retraced his steps with the aid of the thread, and escaped with Ariadne and his young companions. The rest of the story of both Theseus and Ariadne, although mythologically interesting, is irrelevant to the present study.[18]

IMPRISONMENT, FLIGHT, AND FALL

When Minos learned of the escape of Theseus and his comrades, the king imprisoned Daedalus in the labyrinth, along with his son Icarus, who had been born to him by Naucrate, a slave of Minos.[19] According to an alternate version, Daedalus remained in hiding on Crete through Pasiphaë's help and was unable to escape because Minos had every boat searched and also posted a reward for his capture. Whatever the circumstances,

Daedalus could not escape either by land or sea, so he constructed wings for himself and his son. The most complete and best-known ancient version of the flight is found in Ovid's *Metamorphoses* (8.183–235), which is used as the primary source for the following account.

Imprisoned on the island by Minos because of his craft, Daedalus longed to escape, and his homesickness offered a new challenge to his inventiveness. Realizing that only the sky was outside Minos's dominion, he decided to employ it as his escape route. He directed his attention to unknown, untried skills, attempting to change the course of nature. Fastening together carefully selected feathers with thread and wax, he skillfully formed them in the shape of birds' wings. Meanwhile his son watched and meddled in his father's work, little realizing that he was handling potentially destructive materials. When the task was finished, the father tested his invention, then instructed his son in the newly discovered art of flying: "I warn you, Icarus, to follow a route midway between heaven and earth, lest the water weigh down your wings if you fly too low or the sun scorch them if you fly too high. Fly between both. . . . [A]nd follow my lead" (*Metamorphoses* 8.203–8).

Meanwhile Daedalus was also affixing the untested wings to his son's shoulders. As he worked at this task and gave warnings to his son, the old man's cheeks were wet with tears and his hands trembled. He kissed his son (for the last time, but he didn't know it), then took the lead in flying, fearing for his companion like a bird who has launched her fledglings from a high-perched nest into thin air. Urging his son to follow his lead, he instructs him in an art that would prove fatal; as he moves his own wings he looks back to check on his son's progress in flight. A fisherman catches sight of them, and his rod quivers; a shepherd steadies himself with his staff, and a farmer leans on his plough handle, all dumbfounded at the sight, believing that these aerial navigators must be gods.

They had already passed Delos and Paros, Juno's sacred island Samos lay on the left, and Lebinthus and honey-rich Calymne were on the right, when the boy began to fly more recklessly and found that he liked it. Led on by lust for the open sky, he left his guide and soared higher and higher; as he neared the sun, its intensity melted the fragrant wax that held his wings together. He flaps his bare arms, but without the wings they catch no breezes. Calling his father's name, he plunges into the deep blue waters, which later were named the Icarian Sea in his memory. His unhappy father, bereft of his son and thus of fatherhood, cries out, "Icarus! Icarus! Where are you? Where shall I look for you?" While he was still calling "Icarus!" he spied the feathers floating on the water and cursed his craft. He buried his son in a tomb, and the land, like the sea, was renamed for the youth.[20]

Already in antiquity the myth of the aerial flight was rationalized as an escape by ship. In the version recorded by Diodorus, Pasiphaë provided Daedalus with the escape vessel and Icarus met his death when he fell into the sea as he recklessly disembarked from the ship at an island subsequently renamed Icaria (D. S. 4.77.5–6). Pausanias, however, reports that Daedalus constructed small ships for himself and his son, equipping them with newly invented sails that enabled them to outdistance Minos's oar-equipped ships, but Icarus's ship overturned because he was a clumsy helmsman (Paus. 9.11.4–5).

DAEDALUS AT CUMAE AND ON SICILY

After his son's death, Daedalus safely made his way to Cumae, where he built a temple to Apollo (Virgil *Aen.* 6.14–19),[21] or to Sicily, where he was hospitably received by King Cocalus. Daedalus remained a rather long time with Cocalus and the Sicanians, since he was highly regarded for his craftsmanship. During his residence on the island of Sicily his benefactions to his hosts were considerable. Near Megaris he built a flood-control reservoir (*kolumbethra*) from which the Alabon river flowed into the nearby sea. In the territory of Acragas, on the Camicus river, he built on a rock the strongest city in Sicily, which was made completely impregnable by reason of a narrow, winding ascent; so ingenious was this approach to the city that only three or four men were needed to defend it. Cocalus therefore built his royal palace in this city and stored his treasures there. In the territory of Selinus, Daedalus so successfully regulated the steam emitted from a fire within a cave that people were able to receive a pleasurable cure from physical ailments.

At Eryx, where a temple of Aphrodite was built in a narrow space on a precipitous rock, Daedalus constructed a wall on the crag itself, thus extending its overhanging ledge beyond expectation. He also crafted for Aphrodite of Mt. Eryx a golden honeycomb so well wrought that it perfectly resembled an actual honeycomb.[22] Although Daedalus was said to have constructed numerous other works in Sicily, they had perished by Diodorus's time (D. S. 4.78).

Diodorus reports that Minos, upon learning of Daedalus's flight to Sicily, undertook a campaign against it (D. S. 4.79.1), but Apollodorus and Zenobius record a more intriguing story. To each country where his search carried him in pursuit of Daedalus, Minos brought a shellfish with a spiral shell, promising a handsome reward to anyone capable of threading it, for he thought that in this manner he would find Daedalus. When he came to Camicus and the court of Cocalus where Daedalus was hidden, he again displayed the spiral shell. Cocalus accepted it and declared that he would thread it, then gave it to Daedalus, who fastened a thread to an ant, bored a hole in the shell, and let the ant pass through it. When Minos received the threaded shell, he realized that Daedalus was there and demanded his immediate surrender. Cocalus promised to comply with the request and offered hospitality to Minos. But Minos was killed by the daughters of Cocalus, who either scalded him in his bath or poured boiling pitch over him.[23] Some say that Cocalus delivered the corpse of Minos to the Cretans after killing him in a hot bath, with the explanation that Minos slipped in the bath and died from his fall into hot water. Whereupon the Cretans ceremoniously buried their king underground in an elaborate tomb, whose upper level served as a temple to Aphrodite; they then established various Cretan settlements on the island (D. S. 4.79; cf. 16.9.4).

LATER WANDERINGS OF DAEDALUS

The subsequent fate of Daedalus is cloaked in obscurity, although he is linked to works at several other sites. Aristotle records the story of two statues in the Electrides Islands (in the Adriatic Sea) attributed to Daedalus. One was made of tin, the other of bronze, and they reflected archaic workmanship. It was said that each of the islands possessed a statue of either Daedalus or Icarus that had been set up as a memorial when he arrived from Sicily and Crete in his flight from Minos. Later on Daedalus fled from these islands to the island of Icarus when the Pelasgians sailed there after being banished from Argos (Arist. *Mir.* 836a and b). In a variant story of Daedalus's wanderings, he was said to have gone to Sardinia from Sicily: Iolaus, the companion of Heracles, colonized the island with the fifty sons of Heracles begotten on the daughters of Thespius, a son of Erechtheus; he then summoned Daedalus from Sicily and commissioned many great works that were still standing in Diodorus's time and bore the name "Daedaleia" after their builder (D. S. 4.30.11).[24]

After recounting the story that Daedalus copied the Egyptian Labyrinth (above), Diodorus next compares the statues of Daedalus to those of ancient Egypt: the proportions of Egyptian statues were correlate with those of Daedalus among the Greeks. He then adds that the very beautiful propylon of the Hephaesteion in Memphis was built by Daedalus. Because of the people's admiration for Daedalus, a wooden self-portrait was set up in the temple, and his fame achieved such heights because of his native skill and his many other discoveries that he was accorded divine honors. On one of the islands near Memphis a temple of Daedalus was still receiving local homage in the time of Diodorus (D. S. 1.97.6). How or where Daedalus met his end is not recorded, although Ovid has Daedalus request permission from Minos to return to Athens that he may die there (*A.A.* 2.25–28), and Hyginus records the myth that Theseus, after slaying the Minotaur, brought Daedalus back with him to his native Athens (*Fab.* 40).

CATALOGUE OF OTHER CREATIONS ATTRIBUTED TO DAEDALUS

The ancient myths and legends surrounding the archetypal craftsman presumably do not catalogue all his wondrous creations, but some of the ancient writers seem to attempt such a catalogue. Perhaps it therefore would not be inappropriate to note here those works attributed to Daedalus that I have not already described.

As one might expect of Baedeker's illustrious precursor, Pausanias is our major source for this kind of information. At Athens, in the temple of Athena Polias (the Erechtheion), there was among the votive offerings a portable folding chair made by Daedalus (Paus. 1.27.1). When Pausanias came to Corinth he saw a nude *xoanon* of Heracles, purportedly the work of Daedalus, near the temple of Athena Chalinitis ("of the Bridle"), which was close to the theater. At this point he offers a succinct artistic appraisal of the works of Daedalus, observing that all of them looked rather strange but yet conveyed a sense of divine inspiration (Paus. 2.4.5). The Heracleion at Thebes housed an archaic *xoanon* presumed by the Thebans (a presumption accepted by Pausanias) to have been carved by Daedalus, who dedicated it to Heracles as a token of gratitude for the burial of Icarus (Paus. 9.11.4–5). Elsewhere, however, Pausanias expresses the opinion that the *xoanon* made by Daedalus for Heracles stood on the boundary between Messenia and Arcadia (Paus. 8.35.2).[25] Another statue in Boeotia alleged to have been made by Daedalus was set up in the grove of Trophonius, across the river Hercyna from Lebadeia, where the oracle of Trophonius was located on the mountain beyond the grove. Visitors to the oracle—who alone are shown the statue—followed a carefully prescribed ritual that began with a viewing of this image (Paus. 9.39.8).

Besides these two works of Daedalus in Boeotia—the *xoana* for Heracles in Thebes and Trophonius near Lebadeia—there were known to Pausanias works in both Crete and Delos: in Crete there were *xoana* of Britomartis at Olus and Athena at Knossos (Pausanias reminds the reader that at Knossos there also was a white marble relief carved by Daedalus, *The Dance of Ariadne*, which Homer mentions in the *Iliad*). On Delos there was a small *xoanon* of Aphrodite with its right hand damaged by the passage of time and ending at the base in a square block rather than feet. Pausanias surmised that Ariadne received the latter statue from Daedalus and took it along when she followed Theseus, who, the Delians say, dedicated the statue of the goddess to Delian Apollo lest it serve as a constant painful reminder of his lost love if he were to take it home with him (Paus. 9.40.3–4).

Although these works conclude Pausanias's catalogue of extant works by Daedalus, it should be noted that among notable artistic thefts in antiquity he also included a statue by Daedalus carried off to newly founded Gela from Omphace, a Sicanian town, when the Dorians were migrating to Sicily (Paus. 8.46.2). On a promontory at Soloeis in Sicily stood a magnificent altar of Poseidon attributed to Daedalus, on which were carved men, women, lions, and dolphins.[26]

In these diverse myths that grew up around Daedalus, we find contradictions and inconsistencies. One source credits him with making the first statues, whereas another attributes to him a significant advancement in the art of sculpture whereby statues became lifelike. Although archaic *xoana* comprise most of the works ascribed to him, he is also associated with stone sculpture, architecture, the invention of craftsmen's tools, and even working in gold. His name is linked not only with Athens and the Attic craftsmen known as Daedalidae, but especially with the fabulous civilization of Minoan Crete and with western colonies founded centuries later in Magna Graecia (e.g., Cumae), Sicily, and Sardinia.

The decipherment of the Linear B script has added new evidence to link Daedalus with Crete at a very early date. The very first clay tablet found at Knossos by Sir Arthur Evans, at the beginning of the season in 1900, contains an inscription which purportedly records an offering "to the Daedaleion."[27] Ventris and Chadwick, whose decipherment of the Knossos Tablets has greatly expanded our knowledge of the Mycenaean period, comment on this discovery: "The Daedaleion seems an appropriate name for a shrine at Knossos. At Pylos we find Iphimedeia, a semi-mythical figure in Homer, apparently receiving divine honors."[28] They also accept the view that the eleven tablets in the *Fp*-series record the distribution of olive oil and that "the series forms part of a ritual calendar, specifying or recording offerings sent to a limited number of places, priests and divinities."[29] It seems remarkable that this tablet records in the month of Deukios an offering to the Daedaleion which is twice as large as that for Dictaean Zeus and is surpassed only by the offering "To all the gods."[30] Although one can only conjecture, the probable implication of this fact is that the sanctuary of Daedalus was larger and more important than those of Dictaean Zeus and a number of other divinities who received offerings during that month.

With these tablets were found seventeen tablets of the *Fs*-series, "an undated record of an offering or ration of five to six commodities in fixed order and in more or less constant amounts": barley, figs, flour, oil, wine, and honey.[31] The name Daedaleion purportedly occurred on one tablet which is now missing and possibly on another.[32] Another intriguing tablet in a fragmentary series appears to record the offering of an amphora of honey to "The Mistress of the Labyrinth": if this reading proves acceptable, it will require further reconsideration of cult practices on Crete.[33] One tentative conclusion that can be drawn from the offerings to the Daedaleion is that there was a shrine established to honor the palace builder, Daedalus, at some time after its completion.[34]

Given the time span between the Minoan civilization on Crete and the archaic period of Greek sculpture, the safest way to resolve the contradictions and temporal implausibilities in the myth would be to make a clear distinction between the Minoan or Cretan Daedalus and the Daedalus of the archaic period to whom the beginnings of Greek sculpture are attributed.[35] But to do so would be to ignore the mythic process. Moreover, since the name of Daedalus is closely related to both a verb and an adjective that Homer used to describe works that were artfully or skillfully wrought, it is frequently argued that his name was derived from this verb.[36] Whatever the source of Daedalus's name, Homer's comparison of the work of the divine artisan Hephaestus to that of Daedalus (*Il.* 18.590ff.) clearly suggests that by Homer's time the mythical reputation of Daedalus was well established. The dancing floor so artfully wrought by Hephaestus on the shield of Achilles and so vividly described by the poet merits comparison only with "the one that once Daedalus artfully wrought in broad Knossos for Ariadne of the lovely tresses" (*Il.* 18.591–92).

DESCENDANTS AND PUPILS OF DAEDALUS

Later writers, however, link Daedalus with more historical figures. Indeed, much of the work attributed to him cannot antedate the seventh century, and he is named as the teacher of artists who flourished during the sixth century. Dipoenus and Scyllis, who were born in Crete around the fiftieth Olympiad (580 B.C.E.) and subsequently migrated to Sicyon in the Peloponnese and from there to Aetolia (Pliny *N.H.* 36.9), were said to be either students of Daedalus or his sons by a woman of Gortyn (Paus. 2.15.1);[37] Pliny also identifies them as the first to win a reputation for sculpting in marble. Among the works attributed to them were a statue of Athena in her temple at Cleonae in the Argolid and a group of ebony images in the temple of the Dioscuri (at Argos) representing the Dioscuri with their sons, Anaxis and Mnasinous, accompanied by their mothers, Hilaeira and Phoebe (Paus. 2.15.1 and 2.22.5). Clearchus of Rhegium was said to have been a pupil of either Daedalus himself or Dipoenus and Scyllis; Pausanias declares that his bronze statue of Zeus Hypatus ("Most High") next to the temple of Athena in Sparta was the oldest of all bronze statues: it was not cast whole, but the separately wrought limbs were fitted together with nails (Paus. 3.17.6). Another pupil of Daedalus was the Athenian Endoeus, probably a slightly older contemporary of Clearchus (both were active in the latter half of the sixth century); he followed his exiled master to Crete after the death of Calos (Talos/Talus); included among his creations was a seated statue of Athena bearing an inscription which said that Callias dedicated it but Endoeus made it (Paus. 1.26.4).[38]

CUMAEAN SIBYL AND TALOS

There remain two mythical figures who are connected with Daedalus and whose stories relate to Ayrton's exploration of myth: the Cumaean Sibyl, who became for him more generalized, and the bronze man Talos (Talus), whom he identified with Daedalus's nephew. Aside from the Pythia at Delphi, the Cumaean Sibyl is undoubtedly the best known of numerous oracular females described by this generic term. Originally viewed as a single prophetic figure whose wanderings accounted for localized legends, the sibyl multiplied in number until she became identified in Varro's canonical list with at least ten different regions, from Asia Minor to Italy.[39] In addition to their geographical epithets, some sibyls were further distinguished by personal names.

Virgil names the Cumaean Sibyl Deiphobe (*Aen.* 6.36), although she also was called Amalthea, Demophile, and Herophile. He also describes the ecstatic nature of her prophetic utterance. Her appearance and color suddenly change, her hair comes loose, her breast heaves, and her heart swells in wild frenzy. Inspired by the breath and divine power of the approaching god, she looms larger than life, and her voice acquires a divine resonance. She speaks, then falls silent, chilling Aeneas and his comrades (*Aen.* 6.46–55). Before she becomes fully subject to Apollo, the prophetess wildly, with giant frenzy, storms about her cave, in hopes of dislodging the mighty god from her breast, but he wearies her foaming mouth all the more, taming her wild heart, and by constraint he molds her to his will. The hundred doors of her house open spontaneously, and through them float the words of the prophetess, now fully under the god's power (6.77–82). From her sacred shrine the Cumaean Sibyl prophesies shuddering riddles, and her cave echoes and reechoes as she wraps truth in mystery. Thus does Apollo violently shake the reins and twist the goads into her breast as she rages under his inspiration; then her frenzy passes and her raving lips grow quiet (6.98–102). This same sibyl, freed from the god's possession, guides Aeneas into and through the realms of the dead, mingling Roman prophecy with her instructions to the hero.

It was around this Cumaean Sybil that a vast body of Roman legend arose, including the famous story of her offer of the Sibylline Books to the legendary king Tarquinius Priscus. The Cumaean Sibyl created nine books of prophecy predicting the future of the new city of Rome, which was rising to the north; she offered them for a price to the king, who rejected the offer, considering the cost too high. The nine books were deliberately reduced by fire to six, then to three; the remaining three, bought at the price originally demanded for the nine, were entrusted to a special college of priests and were to be consulted only by senatorial decree, unlike the free access granted to the prophecies of the other sibyls.[40]

Ovid records another famous story about her gift of eternal life from Apollo, which proved a curse, since she neglected to request perpetual youth before denying him her love; with the passing centuries she increasingly shriveled up until only her voice remained (*Met.* 14.130–53). Petronius adds that she finally grew so old that she hung in a bottle; when asked what she wished, she replied that all she wanted was to die (*Sat.* 48.8). In one version of the story, Apollo, when banishing her from her native Erythrae in Lydia, prophesied that her long-postponed death would not come until she again looked upon her native earth. In her 990th year, the people of Erythrae sent to her at Cumae a question on a clay tablet. When she looked upon this solid form of her native land, she died.

Plato in his *Minos* speaks of Talos as the guardian of the laws for all of Crete outside the royal city. Thrice yearly Talos went around to the villages with bronze tablets on which the laws were inscribed, thus preserving the laws in the villages; from this activity he received the epithet "Brazen" (*Minos* ca. 320). Apollonius of Rhodes in his *Argonautica* records the following expanded version of the story of Talos as the bronze man of Crete. Talos was the sole remaining survivor of the bronze race[41] and was given to Europa by Zeus to guard Crete by circling the island on his bronze feet three times a day. The rest of his body was also bronze and invulnerable, but he had a blood vein at his ankle beneath his sinew, with only thin skin covering this vital spot. In his role as guardian of Crete he drove off approaching ships by throwing large rocks at them. When he dealt thus with the Argo, Medea successfully bewitched him and caused him to graze his ankle on a sharp rock; the life blood flowed out of him like melted lead and, though he stood a while swaying to and fro, he soon toppled to the ground like a mighty pine tree (*Argon.* 4.1638–88). Apollodorus, drawing upon other sources, provides a number of variants: Talos was a gift to Minos from Hephaestus and was said by some to be a bull, rather than a bronze man; he had a single vein stretching from his neck to his ankles where a bronze plug stopped the end of the vein; Medea either drugged him into insanity or deceived him with a promise of immortality and drew out the plug so all his life blood drained out, causing his death; others say, however, that Poeas shot him in his ankle with an arrow and thus killed him (Apollod. 1.9.26).[42] Still other versions of the myth report that he warded off strangers from

Crete either by burning them or by heating himself red-hot before clasping them in his arms, meanwhile displaying a sardonic grin.[43]

DEMETER AND PERSEPHONE

Although Demeter and Persephone were not linked in Greek myth directly with the myth of Daedalus and Icarus, Ayrton made such a linkage in his own conception of mythology. It is necessary, therefore, to provide a limited amount of information about them as well. The Homeric *Hymn to Demeter* and Theocritus *Idyll VII* are two of the major sources of information about this important pair of deities.

Demeter, whose name may mean either "Earth-Mother" or "Grain-Mother," was the goddess of vegetation springing from the earth, but particularly of grain (as is suggested by her Roman name, Ceres). Her representations in art usually include a profusion of grain, fruit, or flowers. She was honored, with her daughter Persephone, at the national festival of the Thesmophoria. This festival of and for women was concerned with the civilizing power of agriculture and the giving of laws for agriculture. The Eleusinian Mysteries included secret initiatory rites in honor of Demeter and Persephone.

Persephone (Latin Proserpina) was often called "Kore" (Maiden), since she was the only child of Demeter (in most versions of the myth). While Demeter was attending a banquet of the gods, Persephone and some companions gathered flowers in Sicily. After wandering away from her comrades, Persephone came upon a beautiful narcissus plant with a hundred blooms and roots extending deep into the earth. When she tried to pull the plant from the ground, a great chasm opened up and out came Hades (Pluto), the lord of the underworld, riding in a chariot. He snatched her up and carried her back to the realm of the dead. As he did so, she screamed in fright, but she was heard only by Hecate in her subterranean cave and seen only by the sun, Helius. Soon thereafter, Demeter came searching for her daughter. On the tenth day of wandering, she came upon Hecate, who informed her that her daughter had been carried off by some god, although she had not seen who it was, but had only heard her cries. The next day Demeter accosted Helius, who confirmed that it was Hades, Demeter's brother, who had carried off Persephone. In grief and anger, Demeter caused all the crops to fail by parching the seeds. Demeter rejected all appeals from the Olympians that she relinquish her claim on her daughter, so eventually Zeus yielded to her demands and sent Hermes down to inform Hades that he was to release Persephone to her mother, but before he did so, he gave her pomegranate seeds to allay her hunger, thus tricking her into having to live in the underworld. A bargain was struck, however, and Persephone was allowed to spend two-thirds of the year on earth and required to return to the realm of Hades for the other third. This story serves as etiology for the cycle of the seasons, and the mother and daughter are often referred to as the seasonal goddesses.

THE SIGNIFICANCE OF THE MYTH OF DAEDALUS

Daedalus was a mortal, celebrated as much for his wit as for his skill, like the divine Athena and, to a lesser degree, the craft god Hephaestus. Pausanias tells us that Daedalus was "famous throughout the whole world for his talent, but also for his wanderings and misfortunes" (Paus. 7.4.5). The stories recounted above reveal much of the richness of the character and adventures of this archetypal craftsman. The legend of Daedalus includes a number of themes common to myths of the artisan in other cultures, but the narrative reveals the distinctively Greek perception of the artisan-artist and his techniques:[44] he is "an ambiguous and disconcerting person." By inventing statues of the gods, the "sculptor renders the invisible visible," but by "having opened the eyes of the statues," Daedalus gave them sight, i.e., his statues both see and are seen. By hiding Pasiphaë, the Minotaur, even himself, Daedalus also "renders the visible invisible." On the one hand, he gives his statues life, on the other, he is directly or indirectly responsible for killing Talos, Icarus, the Minotaur, and Minos. The "creator of form is the maker of illusion," e.g., in the form of the false cow that hides Pasiphaë and deceives the bull into coupling with her. Master of technique, Daedalus reflects the opposition "between the notions of straightness and circularity or sinuosity," demonstrating the former in his carpentry and in his flying, the latter in his design of the labyrinth. He uses his technical skill for the benefit of others, but he also employs it to bring harm and destruction. Finally, the labyrinth Daedalus designed is an "enigmatic place, . . . the spatial representation of the notion of *aporia*. . . . [T]he very image of the mind that conceived it, tortuous, sinuous, and infinite in its changes of direction."[45]

The retelling of the cycle of myths that grew around Daedalus and the civilization of ancient Crete reveals both the complexity and the elasticity of Greek myth, apparent throughout the centuries since the myths first took root in the Greek consciousness. Succeeding chapters will demonstrate the multiplicity of interpretations and reinterpretations evoked by this fascinating tale of extraordinary inventiveness, unnatural passion, labyrinthine prisons, superhuman daring, youthful recklessness, and remarkable achievements. Especially evocative throughout the years has been the labyrinth, a symbol of complexity, confusion, frustration, and ambiguity. Demonstrating at once order and chaos—the order created by the intellect of the designer and the experience of chaos for the maze inhabitant or maze treader—the labyrinth also establishes a variety of other contrasts and paradoxes, such as security and risk, imprisonment and freedom, linearity and circularity, suspense and anticipation, clarity and confusion, obscurity and insight, and, ultimately, life and death. The pattern and the path of the labyrinth, in both literature and art, can be either unicursal or multicursal, leading either to redemption or destruction.

Is it any wonder this concept became such an intriguing and compelling metaphor?

The Artistic Context for Ayrton's Words and Images

3

Michael Ayrton's interpretation of the myth of Daedalus enlarges and enriches a long and varied tradition of literary and artistic engagement with this myth. To understand his unique contributions, as well as to extend the foundation for a study of the role of myth in the creative process, it is both desirable and necessary to trace this myth through centuries—even millennia—of creative adaptations and interpretations.

Ayrton was aware of many of his predecessors and their contributions to the understanding of this richly evocative cycle of myth. He did not, however, engage in a systematic, scholarly exploration of that tradition. After he began his wanderings in the myth at Cumae, without the intention of making it a focus for his artistic expression (see chapter 4), he read a variety of sources as he tunneled deeper into the recesses of this complex story. He also drew upon a vast storehouse of literary and visual treasures that he had accumulated over the first thirty-five years of his life. The extent of his knowledge of classical literature has already been noted at the beginning of chapter 2.

We can safely assume Ayrton's familiarity with many, but not all, of the treatments of the myth in classical art described below and in appendix C. Through his extensive travels in Italy (chapter 1), he would have seen the wall paintings of the fall of Icarus, of Daedalus and Pasiphaë, among others, and of course Giotto's Daedalus on the Campanile in Florence. His friends and acquaintances at the British Museum introduced him to various illustrations of the myth found in the collection there—from wall paintings to bronze to pottery to seal stones. His travels in Greece and Crete gave him opportunity to view other representations of the myth. Although I cannot aver that he saw all the works cited here—for surely he did not see every one of them—I can confidently assert that his knowledge of the treatment of the myth was extensive. He also owned a copy of W. H. Matthews's book on labyrinths (which he brought to my attention), was very conversant with the works of W. F. Jackson Knight, and wrote a history of mazes and a history of bronze making, for which he did extensive research in his own distinctive way. What he learned, he expressed in his books and articles, but also in his drawings and sculpture.

For inspiration he drew upon his vast visual memory—developed from weeks spent copying the old masters in Vienna at age sixteen, from his teachers Tchelitchew and Berman, from studying Greek sculpture to produce a film with Basil Wright, from his study of artists about whom he wrote: from Pisano to Picasso, from Giotto to Giacometti, from Michelangelo to Moore, from Barna da Siena to Baskin. Some influences

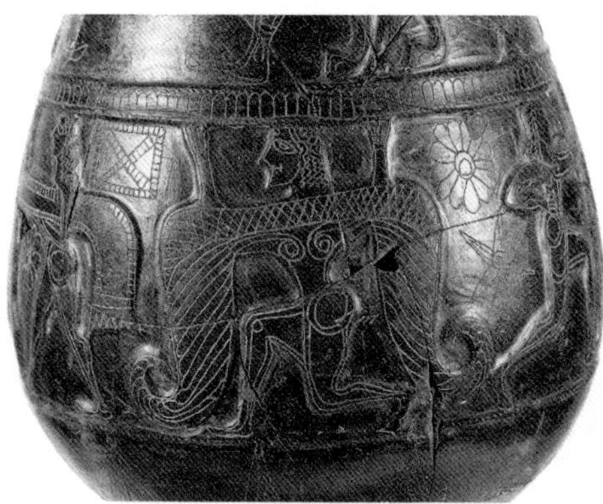

Figure 3. **DAEDALUS: BUCCHERO OLPE FROM CERVETERI** (3rd quarter of 7th c. B.C.E.). Marina Martelli, Rome.

were very subtle, others more obvious. Unlike Picasso, whom he criticized for plundering previous art works, he paid homage to his artistic ancestors as he incorporated their influences into his art.

The current survey of this tradition is not intended to be exhaustive[1] but to provide insight into the various implications and applications of this myth and establish a context for Ayrton's obsessive involvement with the multiple dimensions of a myth with particular relevance to the twentieth century. A more extensive catalogue of artistic expression of the myth is provided in appendix C.

The first section of this synopsis will focus on artistic renderings of the myth in classical antiquity, since chapter 2 gives a full account of the presentation of the myth in classical literature. Later sections will draw upon both art and literature to provide an overview of creative expressions of the myth. Appendix C includes a selection of representations either excluded from the following survey or presented in condensed form here.

IN CLASSICAL ANTIQUITY

The iconographic history of Daedalus and Icarus in classical antiquity is extensively treated in my essay, "Daidalos et Ikaros," published in *Lexicon Iconographicum Mythologiae Classicae* (*LIMC*), volume III.[2] That catalogue contains over sixty representations of Daedalus and Icarus and makes reference to almost thirty others, yet this number is scarcely half of those identified by Brommer in *Denkmälerlisten.*[3]

A *bucchero olpe* (see Figure 3) excavated in 1988 from a grave at Cerveteri (Caere) forces a reconsideration of some of the statements I made in this article in *LIMC*, since this newly discovered vase predates by some fifty years previously known works.[4] The olpe "comes from a local workshop of the third quarter of the seventh century B.C." and includes the image of "a winged man moving to the left in *Knielauf* formula with upraised arms," who is "labelled TAITALE, the early Etruscan name for Daidalos."[5] From the same period comes an Archaic (Laconian?) ivory relief of a winged, bearded Daedalus, now housed in the British Museum.[6]

In the sixth century B.C.E., both Daedalus and Icarus appear on Greek vases. Daedalus appears first, on a Boeotian Corinthianizing alabastron now in Bonn and dated ca. 570: he is shown winged and carrying a double axe and a bucket.[7] Icarus appears for the first time on a fragment of a vase dated 560, other fragments of which also include the birth of Athena, with Hephaestus. This fragment of a black-figure hydria (see Figure 4) was found on the Acropolis of Athens (*LIMC* no. 14); inscribed "Ikaros" and depicting a running figure with winged boots and a short chiton, this vase fragment antedates by at least a century the earliest extant literary reference to Icarus, found in the *Cretans* of Euripides.[8] The appearance of Icarus alone is rare and early.[9]

The reconstruction of a black-figure neck amphora, dated about 550, provides the earliest known iconographic association of father and son (*LIMC* no. 31). On it, two bearded figures fly to the right. The first figure's torso and wings are oblique, as if ascending, the second one's are horizontal; the former carries two rods, which may represent a single instrument, the latter carries an axe in his right hand, a saw and a curved tool in his left. The iconography clearly fits Icarus and Daedalus, respectively. The two also appear together on an unusual work, a gold Etruscan bulla dated 475–450 (*LIMC* no. 32). This inscribed bulla, which was "used as a perfume flask" and "formed a part of a necklace," depicts two winged figures who are identified by the inscriptions as Daedalus (*Taitle*) and Icarus (*Vikare*); the former "carries a saw in his left hand and an adze in his right, while his companion is equipped with a double axe and a square."[10]

One of the early representations of Daedalus alone also bears his name in Etruscan and is closely related to the gold bulla.[11] Almost all the earliest representations of Daedalus alone are found in Etruscan art from the fifth or fourth century. They depict him as a craftsman, showing him winged and using or carrying an adze and a saw; others add an axe or hammer (*LIMC* nos. 1, 12, 31, and 11a, respectively). In Etruscan art, Daedalus is sometimes bearded, sometimes beardless, and sometimes nude, and always young, whereas in Roman representations he is bearded and usually half-draped (cf. *LIMC*).[12]

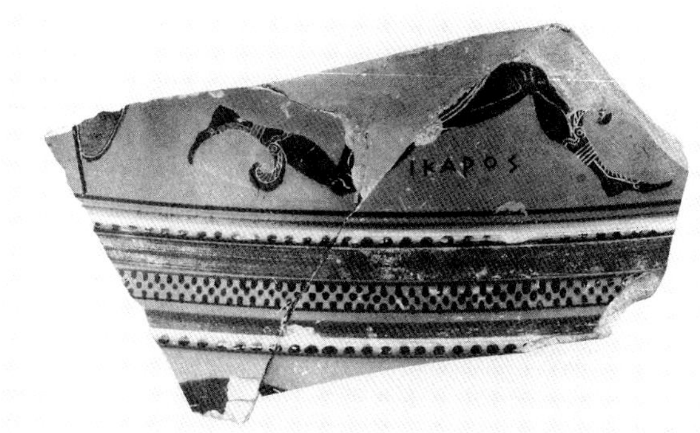

Figure 4. **ICARUS: FRAGMENT OF A BLACK-FIGURE HYDRIA** (560 B.C.E.). National Archaeological Museum, Athens.

South Italian vases of the late fifth and fourth centuries introduce a new association between Daedalus and Icarus. Around 420–400, a red figure skyphos fragment reveals Daedalus attaching wings to Icarus, as does a volute-krater from the end of the fourth century (*LIMC* nos. 19 and 20). This theme reappears in the first and second centuries C.E. on Roman stucco and marble reliefs and on sarcophagi (*LIMC* nos. 22–24). It continues on gems and cameos well into the Imperial period (*LIMC* nos. 25–30)[13] and on coins from Galatia dated 211–217 (*LIMC* no. 51).

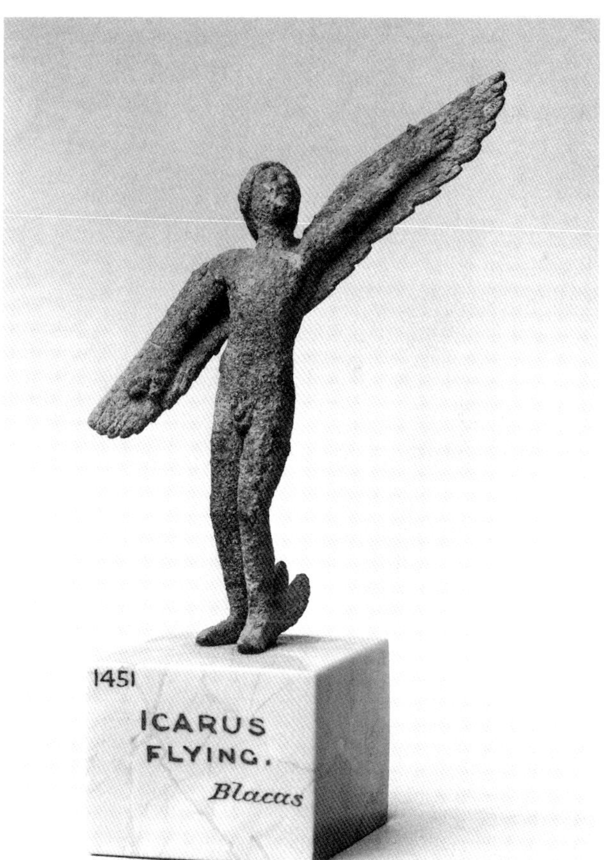

Figure 5. **FLIGHT OF ICARUS: BRONZE STATUETTE** (430 B.C.E.). British Museum.

The flight of Icarus is portrayed in two bronze statuettes of him included in the British Museum collection and one bronze statue from Smyrna: BM 1451 is a Greek work dated about 430 B.C.E. (see Figure 5); the statue from Smyrna is also Greek, probably from the fourth century, and BM 1452 is Imperial, the work of Greek artists in Italy (*LIMC* nos. 15, 16, 18).[14]

Particularly during the Roman Imperial times, however, artists were especially intrigued by the consequences of the flight from Crete. The fall of Icarus therefore is a common theme in Roman wall paintings (*LIMC* nos. 36–43).[15] Illustrative of this genre is a painting in the British Museum (Plate 1) from a period known as the Fourth Style (BM P 28 = *LIMC* no. 42). This painting contains a very full scene: a walled city with amphitheater, an elaborate temple, sketchy buildings; Icarus, seen from the rear with winged arms outstretched, plummets toward the sea; a winged Daedalus flies toward a rocky crag on which recline two draped women; on the sea is a boat with two oarsmen; on the shore are a gesticulating goatherd and his goats; scrawled across the middle of the painting is a name, DONATOS.

The dramatic accounts in Virgil, *Aeneid* 6.9–44, and Ovid, *Metamorphoses* 8.183–235, may well have inspired artists and their patrons to select this theme. It is one of the four most common mythological themes in Roman wall painting, occuring at least ten times among the approximately eighty paintings currently known to us. All ten paintings in Pompeii of the fall of Icarus derive from a lost Hellenistic original, possibly through a lost Roman original painted not later than the last decade of the first century B.C.E.[16] Perhaps Daedalus's special connection with both Cumae and Sicily made him a desirable subject for artists from Magna Graecia, who shaped landscape painting in Hellenistic and Roman times.[17] But one must look to other contemporary interests to explain the surprising frequency of this motif during the Imperial period. Engineers and builders would likely have been interested in Daedalus as craftsman, but that would not fully explain the interest in the fall of Icarus. Perhaps familiarity with the accounts in Ovid also contributed to the choice of this story as an illustration in the landscape paintings that were of such great interest to the Romans. The presence of accessory figures—various onlookers, including the fishermen on the shore or in a boat—clearly suggests an acquaintance with the story in Ovid's *Metamorphoses* 8, and two of the paintings (*LIMC* nos. 37 and 43) reflect an awareness of Ovid's *Ars Amatoria* 2.77–78.

Drawing upon the poetry of both Ovid and Horace, the wall painters of the Third Style developed a new or at least more suggestive interpretation of the old myths than did the earlier painters. Horace, in his *Odes* and *Epodes,* often juxtaposes mythological figures to illustrate a moral point he wishes to make. His influence is particularly evident in the moralizing juxtaposition of the fall of Icarus with Perseus rescuing Andromeda, and in similar juxtapositions of heroes and criminals, with the intent of contrasting the reward of the hero with the punishment of the offender.[18] It is noteworthy that the falling or fallen Icarus also appears in a panel near other audacious offenders against the gods, such as Actaeon and Marsyas.

Despite the frequency with which the flight and fall are represented in Roman wall painting,[19] the story that Daedalus made the false and hollow cow for Pasiphaë (Plates 2 and 3) appears to be even more common, occurring in at least sixteen instances.[20] One of the best known paintings on this theme, *Daedalus Showing Pasiphaë the Wooden Cow,* is found in the House of the Vettii in Pompeii, in the northeast room off the lovely central garden. Daedalus is shown pointing out to Pasiphaë and her attendant the means for entering the false and hollow cow he contrived for her to satisfy her unnatural passion for the white bull sent from the sea by Poseidon. In the foreground is a child, presumably Icarus, playing with his father's tools. On the other walls are two panels, *Ixion Bound to the Wheel by Hephaestus* and *Dionysus Surprising the Sleeping Ariadne.* The former one offers a reminder of the consequences for Ixion of desiring an inappropriate union with a goddess (Hera), whereas the latter panel foreshadows what will follow for Pasiphaë's daughter, who will be abandoned on Naxos by Theseus following their flight from Crete after he slew the Minotaur with the aid of Ariadne's red thread of escape.

Given the popularity of the Theseus legend and the interest in his conquest of the Minotaur, it is not surprising that this feat was frequently portrayed in ancient art. In the British Museum alone one finds over twenty ancient works of art (mostly vases, but also sculpture and terra-cotta) depicting the Minotaur, usually being slain by Theseus (see appendix C).[21] The theme of Theseus and the Minotaur is frequently treated in every medium, from gold jewelry and coins to vases, funerary urns, wall paintings, bronzes, and marble (e.g., on a metope of the Hephaesteion in Athens): indeed too frequently to permit more than a sweeping generalization, particularly since Michael Ayrton was singularly uninterested in Theseus, although he certainly showed a great interest in the Minotaur.[22]

As a transition from classical antiquity to the Middle Ages, it is important to take note also of the Minotaur's prison, the labyrinth designed by Daedalus at the command of Minos. The metaphor of the labyrinth takes on special meaning for many writers in the medieval period. It therefore is necessary to be aware of the widespread dispersion of the depictions of the labyrinth, as well as of its literary heritage.

Visual representations of the labyrinth occur far and wide in antiquity. They are found "on prehistoric rock carvings . . . , on a Linear B tablet from Pylos, on sixth-century Egyptian seals, on the Tragliatella pitcher [Etruscan, seventh century B.C.] . . . , on Hellenistic coins, on gems, in a graffito on a house in Pompeii [see Figure 6], and on Roman floor mosaics all over Europe and North Africa."[23] Some have notations added (e.g., "Labyrinthus, hic habitat Minotaurus [Labyrinth, here lives the Minotaur]," which is carved into a pillar in a house in Pompeii, or "Truia [Troy]," which is engraved on the Tragliatella wine jar), many include a portrayal of the battle of Theseus with the Minotaur or other scenes from the myth. Some are square, as on the Pylos tablet and on the pillar of a house in Pompeii, whereas many others are curvilinear. Both square and circular designs preserve the classical seven-ring labyrinth design, as can be seen on Cretan coins or on the examples just cited.

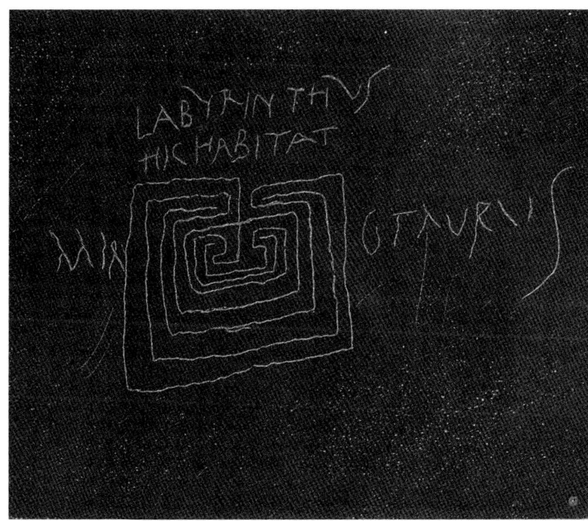

Figure 6. **POMPEII: GRAFFITO**
("Labyrinthus hic habitat Minotaurus" [Labyrinth: Here dwells the Minotaur], early 1st c. C.E.). Replica, Maze Museum.

Almost all these depictions are strictly two-dimensional, and all but two are unicursal, i.e., the only choice the maze-wanderer would appear to have would be whether to enter the maze or labyrinth in the first place.[24] In a unicursal maze the wanderer may not realize that the way leads inevitably to the center, because the meanderings of the maze may be so confusing and tiring that he or she might grow weary before reaching the center, whereas in a multicursal maze she or he might be overwhelmed by the choices that have to be made at every decision point. In the former instance, arrival at the center is assured, provided that the wanderer perseveres in following the winding path of the maze. In the latter case, arrival depends upon the choices he or she makes along the way. At the center of the Cretan labyrinth, of course, was the Minotaur, but other mazes might have symbolized safety and protection against an invader or entrance into Mother Earth (i.e., to death and the grave) or rebirth and renewal.

Virgil, in *Aeneid* 6, describes the bronze doors on the temple of Apollo at Cumae, both the temple and the doors having been created by Daedalus after he descended there from his airborne flight from Crete. It was here, Virgil tells us, that Daedalus dedicated to Apollo the wings that made escape from Minos possible. Brooks Otis interprets the description of the temple doors as symbolic not only of "the underworld, the Kingdom of the Dead, and the terrible and guilty secrets hidden within it," but also of "the labyrinthine past and its hidden contents," specifically of Aeneas's erotic past.[25] The labyrinth design of the doors is seen by another scholar, Penelope Reed Doob, as the pattern of the *Aeneid* itself:

> The *Aeneid*, one of the most influential works of western literature, is the earliest major example of truly labyrinthine literature: it includes explicit images of the maze and references to its myth, employs a labyrinthine narrative structure, and embodies themes associated with the idea of the labyrinth. . . . [T]he idea of the labyrinth constitutes a major if sometimes covert thread in the elaborate *textus* of the *Aeneid*, providing structural pattern and thematic leitmotif.[26]

Although visual renderings of the labyrinth are almost universally unicursal, the literary representations are most frequently multicursal. Doob sees in this fact a clash of paradigms, but a clash that occurs only "to post-Renaissance minds [to whom] a maze is either multicursal or not really a maze at all," although both Pliny and Boccaccio distinguished between historical and artistic labyrinths.[27] An investigation of the development of the myth during the Middle Ages will illustrate these points more clearly.

FROM THE MIDDLE AGES THROUGH THE RENAISSANCE

Throughout most of the art and literature of the Middle Ages there is hardly a mention of Daedalus or Icarus, although the symbol of the labyrinth figures prominently in both Boethius and Dante. One explanation may lie in the concern, especially in the early Middle Ages, with reconciling the paganism of classical antiquity with the fundamental teachings of Christianity. The myths told in Ovid were subjected to allegorization during much of this period. Toward the end of the Middle Ages, however, changes in intellectual culture opened the way for renewed interest in myth without the attendant allegorizing. During the Renaissance, particularly the Spanish Renaissance, the figure of Icarus emerges at center stage.

Standing on the cusp between classical antiquity and the Middle Ages, Boethius (ca. 480–524) serves as a bridge between paganism and Christianity. He took the high degree of labyrinthine artistry bequeathed by Virgil and combined it with the tradition of Christianity, following the example of some earlier Christian writers, but he infused Virgil's pessimism with "an optimistic theodicy demonstrating that what appears to be a labyrinthine world of random confusion and injustice is in fact, with the proper perspective, a manifestation of the cosmic order created by divine providence."[28] Boethius's *Consolation* shows in its structure, content, and imagery a "labyrinthicity . . . not as marked as that of the *Aeneid*," but it clearly "not only involves labyrinths and labyrinthine matters but also reflects labyrinthine epistemology and aesthetics."[29] It is noteworthy that "illuminations of mazes accompanied five medieval manuscripts of the *Consolation*."[30]

The *Aeneid* may have provided a model for the journey of Boethius, but his journey differs dramatically from that of Aeneas. The Christian worldview suffusing the *Consolation* includes not only a constant guide leading toward a clearer vision of heaven but also an unshakable faith in the divine order of the universe and, with that faith, a firm belief that God rules the world with justice, even if human perception is at times blinded to it. As he constructs his Christian worldview, Boethius borrows from his Christian and pagan ancestors:

> In seeing the world as an apparently impenetrable labyrinth that is really divinely ordered artistry, he echoes Gregory of Nazianzus and Jerome; in comparing the quest for false felicity to a multicursal journey into dead ends, he reflects Gregory of Nyssa, Ambrose, and Prudentius; in emphasizing an elevated, comprehensive point of view as a remedy for labyrinthine blindness, he reiterates Gregory Thaumaturgus; in seeing fallen man's labyrinthine mind and passions as a cause for blindness, he concurs with Prosper of Aquitaine. Surer labyrinthine debts, perhaps, accrue to Macrobius, Plato, and Sidonius, for whom labyrinths of words can be supremely deceptive. . . . Yet finally Boethius's view of labyrinthine logic resembles Augustine's in the *De magistro:* learning is necessarily circuitous, a protracted and repetitive tracing of *ambages* to arrive by memory at what one already knows. . . . Appropriately enough, as a devotee of classical philosophy and a would-be reconciler of Plato and Aristotle, Boethius redeems pagan philosophy and labyrinth alike.[31]

To achieve his goal, Boethius uses both devices prescribed by mythology for escape from the maze. With the help of a thread (Daedalus's gift to Ariadne), he retraces his steps (Books 1–3); and by flight (Book 4), he rises to a higher vantage point (using Daedalus's own means of escape): "And I shall give you wings to your mind which can carry you aloft, so that, without further anxiety, you may return safely to your own country under my direction, along my path, and by my means" (4p1.9). Thus it is clear that "Philosophy is both Ariadne and Daedalus."[32]

Both Dante and Chaucer, as well as the makers of mazes for cathedral floors, may well have been influenced by Boethius. If so, it would likely be because Boethius uses philosophy to disclose the labyrinth's "ability to signify both confusion and artistic order depending on whether the perceiver struggles within or looks on from above," as he proceeds to reveal the divine architect of the ordered cosmos, leading the perceiver out and up to God.[33]

Between Boethius and Dante, the myth often finds expression in illuminated manuscripts, such as the five manuscripts of Boethius's *Consolation of Philosophy* that were illustrated with labyrinthine drawings. These illustrations serve as a bridge between these two major representatives of the literary tradition in which the myth enters into the very fabric of the narrative, as well as appearing explicitly at various points. The labyrinth metaphor continues to wind its way through the centuries, imitating the meander pattern of the Greek key design that persists through the centuries.

In the twelfth century, the image of Icarus reappears in Provence in a love poem by Rigaud de Barbezieux, but "in a context that makes the effort to fly not only arrogant but sacrilegious."[34] The troubadour expresses the hope "that Cupid will forgive him if, like Icarus, he flies too high, for his lover's pride is innocent," establishing a theme that would recur through succeeding centuries, comparing the boldness of the lover with the flight of Icarus.[35]

Dante (1265–1321) borrowed from the Cretan cycle of myth, both for the labyrinths in the *Comedy* and for its dramatis personae. In his hands, however, these figures were most often transformed by his Christian vision into new and symbolically richer people. Dante's choice of Virgil's *Aeneid* as a model for his *Comedy* and of Virgil himself as the pilgrim's guide through a portion of his labyrinthine journey is a commonplace of criticism. It is less common, however, to identify the labyrinth, as Penelope Reed Doob does, as both "a recurrent theme in the *Comedy*" and "the best visual model for the narrative structure of the poem," or to argue "that the idea and myth of the labyrinth participate in the shaping of the text and illuminate our reading of it, regardless of Dante's conscious intentions or subconscious memories."[36] Doob also asserts: "The *Comedy* deals only obliquely with the labyrinth of *this* life, the labyrinth Aeneas and Boethius's narrator never really transcend, and it emphasizes instead the anagogical labyrinths that reward and punish the choices made in the multicursal labyrinth of the living."[37]

There are, of course, frequent allusions in the *Comedy* to various figures of the Cretan myths and legends, as well as to the Cretan labyrinth itself. A few illustrations should suffice in this context: Dante's disorientation at the beginning of the *Comedy* and his experience of hell, where he wanders circuitously and hesitantly, clearly evoke the emotions of being trapped in a maze; Minos is a judge in hell (as he was in Virgil's Hades), with virtual omnipotence over the damned, assigning them their place in hell (*Inferno,* passim); Dante and his guide in the *Inferno* found the entrance to the seventh circle of Hell occupied by the Minotaur, the "infamy of Crete, / Which was conceived in the false cow" (*Inferno* 12.12–13); and the wooden cow created by Daedalus for Pasiphaë is mentioned a second time in *Purgatory* 26.87.[38] Dante used Icarus to illustrate the extent of his terror when, in *Inferno* 17.109–14, he describes being carried through the air on Geryon's back. What greater fear was there than this? Not Phaëthon's,

> Nor was poor Icarus' fear, when he perceived
> His back unfeathered by the melted wax
> (His father shouted "No! That's not the way!"),
> Greater than mine when I beheld myself
> Surrounded by the air on every hand
> And nothing visible except the beast.[39]

Two other figures in the *Comedy* warrant greater attention—Theseus and Ariadne. Scholars have frequently noted that, for Dante, Theseus clearly and unquestionably represents the Christ. Theseus is the means by which the reader is expected to see Christ, who was victorious over hell, conquering the forces of evil and the hybrid rulers of hell every bit as fully as Theseus overcame the Minotaur of Crete. In this treatment, Dante echoes the theme of the harrowing of hell, which is a commonplace in the early medieval period. The role of Ariadne, which for Dante is even greater than that of Theseus, is

> played chiefly by Beatrice, whose loving cords, footsteps, and counsel lead Dante from all threatening labyrinths. . . . Christ-Theseus may open the paths, but Beatrice-Ariadne sees to it that they are followed. . . . Her discourse . . . provides the thread that guides him to knowledge of himself and God. . . . To ensure his escape from sin and worldliness, she augments Ariadne's guidance with Daedalian wings, accompanying Dante on his flight through paradise and guiding his wings (25.49–50). Whatever Beatrice may signify . . . she *acts* as Ariadne.[40]

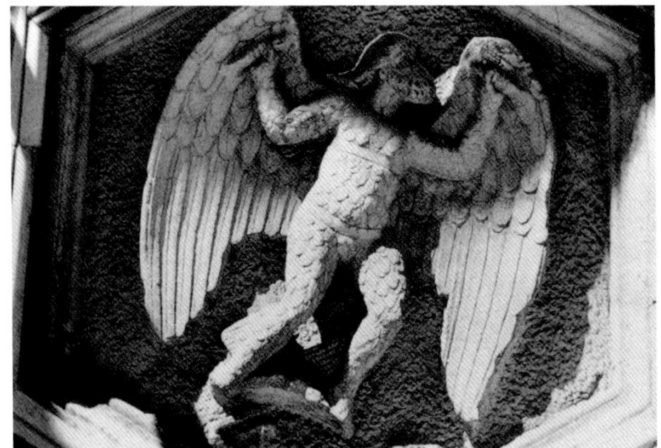

Figure 7. Giotto di Bondone, **BAS-RELIEF OF DAEDALUS** on the Campanile in Florence (ca. 1337).

When Beatrice no longer suffices as his guide, she is replaced by Mary, the mother of Christ.

The impact of Dante on succeeding generations was very strong, for he, perhaps even more than Boethius, infused Virgil's artistic vision with a Christian worldview. The influence of Virgil on the Middle Ages has been well documented by Domenico Comparetti, who saw Dante as a Christian Virgil. Daedalus, Theseus, the Minotaur, and Ariadne all persist in literature after Dante, in part because of the way in which he transformed them through his blending of mythology with Christian imagery.

Giotto di Bondone (ca. 1277–1337)[41] oversaw the construction of the Campanile of the Duomo in Florence, which was begun in 1334.[42] Hexagonal white marble panels on the Campanile contained relief sculpture worked by various artists according to Giotto's plans. The panels begin with the creation of humankind and progress to various pioneers; they show the liberal arts, various trades, the planets, and selected other themes. A bas-relief of Daedalus fills one of the panels on Giotto's Campanile (see Figure 7). Daedalus is winged, and his entire body is covered with feathers, making him a bird-man. Giotto thus extends the myth with this further transformation of the figure of Daedalus. By focusing on the fabled artificer, Giotto both simplified the sculptor's task and emphasized that aspect of the prototypical artisan's inventiveness which fit with the themes on many of the other panels. By selecting the protypical artisan, moreover, Giotto may well have intended to underscore his artistic vision, a vision that looked outward to the visible world, the world of sight and sense, the world of nature, the world viewed from above by reason of the cleverness of Daedalus.[43] If Giotto consciously chose Daedalus as a symbol of his own artistic vision, a vision that looked outward rather than inward, he was making a powerful statement to his contemporaries and his successors, inviting them to follow him on Daedalian wings into the realm of imagination, creativity, and reason.[44]

Boccaccio (1313–1375) testified to the extensive influence of Giotto, but he also contributed to the perpetuation of myth by using it allegorically. In *Genealogy of the Gods,* he allegorizes Pasiphaë as both the soul and the true Sun, Minos as human reason, the bull as sensual delights, and the Minotaur as the vice of bestiality produced by the union of the soul with mundane pleasures. In this respect, he provides a transition from Giotto's symbolic and paradigmatic use of Daedalus to Chaucer's contributions to the perpetuation and reshaping of the myth. Boccaccio also contributed a link between earlier literary artists and Chaucer through his distinction between artistic and historical labyrinths.[45]

Geoffrey Chaucer (ca. 1340–1400) demonstrated a thorough knowledge of classical literature, but particularly of Virgil and Ovid, who had a profound influence upon the Middle Ages and the Renaissance. In *The House of Fame* (212 ff.),[46] for example, Chaucer imitates the device used by Virgil in *Aeneid* 6.20–33 (see chapter 2) when he describes a temple of Venus engraved with scenes depicting incidents from the *Aeneid.* He also shows his acquaintance with Ovid's account of the story of Daedalus and Icarus.[47] In the second book of *The House of Fame,* Chaucer uses Icarus to illustrate height. Carried aloft by the eagle of Jupiter, Chaucer finds that he can no longer make out details on earth. It is no wonder, says the eagle, for no one else has risen half as high, neither Alexander nor Scipio,

> Ne eke the wrechche Dedalus
> Ne his child, nyce Ykarus,
> That fleigh so highe that the hete
> Hys wynges malt, and he fel wete

In myd the see, and there he dreynte,
For whom was maked moch compleynte.
(The House of Fame 919–24)

Chaucer also compares the House of Rumor to the labyrinth of Daedalus, finding the former far more intricate, perhaps as a clever reversal of Homer's comparison of the work of Hephaestus to that of Daedalus (*Iliad* 18.590ff.):

Tho saugh y stonde in a valeye,
Under the castel, faste by,
An hous, that Domus Dedaly,
That Laboryntus cleped ys,
Nas mad so wonderlych, ywis,
Ne half so queyntelych ywrought.
And ever mo, as swyft as thought,
This queynte hous aboute wente,
That never mo hyt stille stente.
(The House of Fame 1918–26)

These brief citations do not do justice, however, to the contributions Chaucer made to the perpetuation of the myth, and particularly to the conception of the labyrinth. In a brilliant analysis of *The House of Fame,* Penelope Reed Doob demonstrates effectively the extent of Chaucer's grasp and reshaping of the tradition of the labyrinth, revealing that Chaucer wove "his own elaborate variations on the theme, ingeniously blending literary, intellectual, metaphorical, visual, and popular labyrinth traditions."[48] Having persuasively argued that Chaucer was likely well acquainted with both visual and verbal labyrinth traditions, Doob proceeds to explore and illustrate "the controlling image of the labyrinth, which becomes the work's iconographic center and a *signum sequendi* through the poem's complexities."[49] Chaucer not only names but also quotes Virgil, Ovid, Boethius, and Dante, all of whom wrote labyrinthine works. Although Chaucer also imitates them, he does so with "a radical shift in perspective," says Doob, by "turning its primary focus away from the moral tradition stressed by its models" and by making "errors . . . not moral but epistemological":[50]

The functional inseparability of truth and falsehood caused by our imperfect perspective and perceptions is the central epistemological theme of *The House of Fame*, and it is explored through the vehicle of the labyrinth, which becomes an emblem of the limitations of knowledge in this world, where all we can finally do is meditate on *labor intus.* If this sounds profoundly depressing, oddly enough it is not; so let us follow Geoffrey, who is neither Boethius nor Dante, on his bewildering peregrinations through one disorienting labyrinth after another until he reaches the chaotic "domus Dedaly" (1920) in which the poem ends so anticlimactically.[51]

Doob sees the poem itself as a multicursal labyrinth, with many confusing twists and turns, and containing numerous labyrinths within it. Unlike his illustrious predecessors, Chaucer provides neither a guide nor wings to escape the maze which he creates, although the poem does include "an avuncular golden-feathered philosopher-eagle" who soars in circuitous spirals and fails to fly high enough to grant Geoffrey the necessary transcendent perspective.[52] Doob judges the poem to be "deeply skeptical" (333), but "not finally a pessimistic poem" (336), nor would despair ever "occur to Geoffrey, whose dream, after all, is wonderful: if these be labyrinths, they are enchanting ones, as full of delight as of frustration" (337).

Chaucer, says Doob, "declares and celebrates a labyrinthine poetic of Daedalian artistry"; his "need to accept the inextricability of the maze was both philosophical and artistic, . . . and he converted that necessity into a great virtue": "This labyrinthine aesthetic is fully if circuitously enunciated in *The House of Fame* with its mazed narrator, settings and structure; here Chaucer reconstructs, rather than transcends, the complexity of the many labyrinths in which we live and write—labyrinths we cannot, and perhaps do not even wish to, escape."[53] Doob's comprehensive and penetrating analysis of Chaucer and the medieval mind lays a solid foundation for the consideration of succeeding interpretations of the myth, but especially the work of Michael Ayrton.

In the sixteenth century, the Daedalus/Icarus theme appears at least a half dozen times in paintings and engravings, in addition to book illustrations. Most of these illustrations of the myth merely keep it alive in public consciousness without further enriching or extending the myth (see appendix C). One sixteenth-century artist, however, made a significant contribution to the understanding and perpetuation of the myth. Pieter Brueghel the Elder (ca. 1525–1569; Plate 4) painted his familiar *Landscape with the Fall of Icarus* around 1555 to 1558, when he was just over thirty years old. In it we can see his remarkable "ability to make his criticism of life implicit rather than explicit. He begins with proverbs and allegories, in which landscape is a setting and an accessory; he evolves to the great landscapes in which the accidents of human life are one with the weather and the seasons."[54]

Critics have often remarked that the main theme of this picture, like many other landscapes, is not located in the visual center of the painting. It is in fact obscured from the casual observer. Most critics note Brueghel's debt to Ovid, since Brueghel includes a fisherman with his rod, a shepherd with his staff, and a plowman with his plow, but they often overlook the fundamental alterations of the Ovidian story. In Ovid all three observers stare in absolute amazement at the flying figures, but the death of Icarus occurs far away, out of their sight. In Brueghel, however, the focus of attention shifts from the fliers to the spectators, who could have seen him plunge to his death but look away from Icarus, whose falling feathers and submerging torso with flailing legs are barely discernible in the corner of the picture.

Perhaps it is valid to see this painting as an allegory, as it was already in the sixteenth century, soon after it was painted. This landscape was interpreted as a contrast between the solid value of the toiling peasant's life and the futility of Icarus's venture. The plowman dominates the entire painting; not only is he in the foreground, the bright red shirt under his tunic represents the most noticeable use of color, thus attracting the viewer's attention. As he plows the field, he seems oblivious to anything except his physically demanding task. The painting may well be intended, in part, to illustrate the familiar Flemish proverb: "No plough stops for a man who dies."

Virgil's *Georgics* rather than Ovid's *Metamorphoses* has been proposed as the inspiration for this change in the myth, emphasizing the virtue of *labor,* hard work.[55] The creative process is often complex, and an artist may blend together elements from multiple sources, rather than following a single literary or visual source. The basic themes of the *Georgics* would certainly have been compatible with the life experience and worldview of a sixteenth-century artist, so this thesis is plausible.

The painting is rich in symbolism for the attentive observer. One finds, for example, a bleached corpse under the hedge at the far end of the field. It balances and underscores the death of Icarus in another quadrant of the painting, but it also offers a reminder of the brevity of life for the toiling peasant as well as for the rash youth who dared fly too high. There is, moreover, a generally overlooked message in the painting. The fact that all three of the Ovidian figures who stared in amazement at Daedalus and Icarus are shown here so intent on their own private tasks that each is oblivious to Icarus's private tragedy should not be ignored. Brueghel uses the myth here to indict his own peasant contemporaries and humankind in general for their inability to share in, or sympathize with, the misfortunes of a fellow human being.

Another artist, using a different medium nearly four centuries later, captured the essence of that message. In "Musée des Beaux Arts," W. H. Auden[56] enriches our appreciation of this and a number of other Brueghel landscapes:

About suffering they were never wrong,
The Old Masters: how well they understood
Its human position; how it takes place
While someone else is eating or opening a window
    or just walking dully along;
How, when the aged are reverently, passionately waiting
For the miraculous birth, there always must be
Children who did not specially want it to happen, skating
On a pond at the edge of the wood:
They never forgot
That even the dreadful martyrdom must run its course
Anyhow in a corner, some untidy spot
Where the dogs go on with their doggy life and the
    torturer's horse
Scratches its innocent behind on a tree.

In Brueghel's Icarus, for instance: how everything
turns away
Quite leisurely from the disaster; the ploughman may
Have heard the splash, the forsaken cry,
But for him it was not an important failure; the sun shone
As it had to on the white legs disappearing into the green
Water; and the expensive delicate ship that must have seen
Something amazing, a boy falling out of the sky,
Had somewhere to get to and sailed calmly on.

Auden's statement, "what interests me most about a painting is its iconography,"[57] takes on new meaning when this poem itself is subjected to iconographic analysis. Between the opening generalization and the concluding stanza about Brueghel's *Icarus* Auden offers seemingly casual examples to illustrate the isolation of sufferers caused by the indifference of fellow human beings, but these examples are actually derived from a number of Brueghel's Christian paintings.[58] The juxtaposition of visual images drawn from paintings centered around the suffering and death of Christ with images depicting the lonely suffering of Icarus further universalizes the experience. Auden also "alludes obliquely to the historical agony of mankind as it was working itself out in the 1930's," and his poem stands as "a lasting and powerful example of tragic irony skillfully strung on the deceptive tensions of a lyric poem."[59] Beneath the surface irony of this poem lie a deep sense of rage and a serious concern for the seeming irreconcilability of the ideal and real worlds.

Among the numerous poems inspired either by the myth directly or through Brueghel's painting, two poems published twenty years after Auden's provide sufficient contrast to illustrate the rich diversity of interpretation and creative expression. The one emulates the ironic tone of Auden's poem, although conveying a different mood, whereas the other is highly impressionistic. The former, "The Fall of Icarus (*From Brueghel's Painting*)" by Charles F. Madden,[60] attributes the indifference of the sailors, farmer, and shepherd to their selfish preoccupation with their individual tasks, whereas Auden suggests that they may have seen the fall but turned away, ignoring Icarus's plunge to his death.

The bulging sails by a riotous wind caught
pull the ships and their rigging nets toward shore
to be emptied. The sailors quickly will calm their floors
and their houses in the evening light will melt
into the mountains.
And on the hill with one foot planted in the earth
his plowing almost done; his eyes cast down
and fully shielded
from the sun which now is growing shadow, the farmer
turns in soil and toil the final circles of the day.
Below him a quiet pastoral: on lichen bearing rocks
the feeding sheep, the quiet watching dog,
the silent shepherd
so stalking with his eyes the homing flights of birds
that neither he nor the intent fisherman closer
to the shore,
none had seen the silent fall of Icarus
through the riotous wind and the shadows
of the coming evening light,
nor do they hear his sigh, both of pity and delight
of his remembered waxed and winged flight.

The other poem, "Pictures from Brueghel II: Landscape with the Fall of Icarus," by William Carlos Williams,[61] is as visual and sensuous as it is brief. Williams, in this offering of one of his "rubbings of reality,"[62] recreates Brueghel's painting through a sensitive but subjectively Romantic observation of another artistic medium.

According to Brueghel
when Icarus fell
it was spring

a farmer was ploughing
his field
the whole pageantry

of the year was
awake tingling
near

the edge of the sea
concerned
with itself

sweating in the sun
that melted
the wings' wax

unsignificantly
off the coast
there was

a splash quite unnoticed
this was
Icarus drowning

There is a terrible irony in the way in which Williams sees this painting. By noting that the fall of Icarus occurred in the spring, when things normally come to life under a beneficent sun, and by the sweat of those who work beneath its penetrating rays, Williams makes the death of Icarus seem totally unnecessary and contrary to everything happening in nature. For Brueghel, he seems to say, the private tragedy of Icarus goes quite unnoticed, and it is not significant that the same sun that brings the plant world to fruition melts away the life of Icarus. And yet, by calling attention to the contrast evident in the painting, Williams conveys both Brueghel's message and his own. In this lean, sparse little poem, Williams universalizes the death of Icarus, reminding us that we, like the ploughman and the shepherd, are no longer aware of the terrible significance of death; that we, in our egocentricity, have lost concern and compassion for our fellow human beings.

Icarus also served as an important symbol in Spain during the century following Brueghel's painting. The vital role of Icarus in the Spanish Golden Age (1550–1650) has been attributed to two Neapolitan poets, Jacopo Sannazaro (1458–1530) and Luigi Tansillo (1510–1568). An admirer of Petrarch, Sannazaro wrote a sonnet that had a profound influence upon numerous poets in Italy and elsewhere, but especially in Spain, since Spain held control over Naples from 1503 until about 1700. This famous sonnet "conveys something of the audacity, the defiance of human limitations, the sheer *joie de vivre,* which we associate with the Renaissance. At the same time it reminds us of the myth's elemental power, which we first learned of in Horace: spirit soars above earth into air, is consumed by fire, and drops into water to achieve lasting glory"[63]:

Here Icarus fell; these waves beheld his fate,
which drew the daring wings to their embrace;
here the flight ended; here the event took place,
which those unborn will yearn to emulate.
Thrilling and welcome was his sorrow's weight,
since dying he achieved immortal praise;
happy that, since he died above disgrace,
so fair a prize his loss should compensate.
With such a fall well may he be content,
if, soaring to the sky dove-like and brave,
he with too fierce a flame was burnt and spent;
his name now echoes loud in every wave,
across the sea, throughout an element;
who ever in the world gained such a grave?

The influence of both Sannazaro and Tansillo came about through Garcilaso de la Vega, who met Tansillo in Naples during the 1530s.[64] The influence of Tansillo's sonnet, "Poi che spiegate ho l'ale al bel desio [Now that my wings are spread to my desire],"[65] is clearly evident upon Sonnet XII ("Si para refrenar este desseo") of Garcilaso de la Vega, which represents the first instance in which Icarus appears in Spanish lyric poetry; this sonnet was written in 1535, when Garcilaso was in Naples with Tansillo.[66]

During the sixteenth century, awareness of the riches of classical antiquity expanded greatly with the publication of numerous editions of classical authors, translations and commentaries on these authors, and compendia of classical mythology. It has been argued, however, that the lyric poets of the Spanish Renaissance drew their knowledge and inspiration not so much from these sources as from other poets. Nonetheless, one cannot overlook the fact that Ovid's *Metamorphoses* was already well known and very popular long before the first printed translation in Spanish appeared around 1541. The translation was far from literal, for whole stories were transposed from one part of the *Metamorphoses* to another. The Icarus story, moreover, like many others, is more a paraphrase than a translation. The next half century produced many more translations, all of which continued to contribute to the increasing popularization of mythology. Some of the translations also included commentaries and allegorical interpretations of the myths, which were frequently incorporated into the poetic treatments of myth. The allegories often repeated allegories and rationalizations of myth by writers from antiquity, as well as those of moralizers like Bersuire (see appendix C). Examples of the allegorizing of the myth of Icarus include: Daedalus discovered the use of the sail, and the flight of the father and son was merely a metaphor for great speed, with Icarus's death caused by his inexperience as a sailor; Icarus is simply a moralistic model, setting an example to be avoided by all who would escape misfortune; Icarus symbolized the vanity of excessive ambition; by assaulting the "holy heavens" Icarus committed sacrilege; Daedalus was gradually transformed from a positive example of one who avoided the extremes, unlike his rash son, into a negative model of one who defied natural law.[67]

Whereas in fifteenth-century Spanish poetry Daedalus is occasionally present as the archetype of the artist but Icarus is scarcely mentioned, in the sixteenth century Icarus takes center stage. Following the example of Tansillo's "Amor m'impenna l'ale e tanto in alto," poets of the Spanish Renaissance often identify with Icarus, using his story to express their feelings of love, fear, and ambition. The lover in these poems finds consolation in the realization that if he, like Icarus, dies because he flies too high, he will also be immortalized for his attempts to scale the heights of love. In the sonnets of Garcilaso de la Vega, the influence of Tansillo is evident, for example in the parallelism between the poet/lover and both Icarus and Phaëthon, but Garcilaso does not follow him precisely, whereas Gutierre de Cetina closely imitates Tansillo.

For many of the poets, including Manuel de Portugal and Francisco de Aldana, Icarus becomes the symbol for the lover's thoughts led on by an irresistible attraction to the heat or flame that will ultimately destroy him. The beloved becomes identified with the sun, into whose burning eyes the lover has the audacity to look, risking his life in the process.

Fernando de Herrera employs the myth in several sonnets, in which he combines the theme of heroic love with the image of the beloved as an irresistible attraction offering at once both delight and danger. The poetry of Herrera expresses key images closely related to the myth of Icarus, which he also blends with the myth of Phaëthon: in the images of "the lover soaring toward the source of the light of his life" and the "irresistible consuming fire of love," the two mythical heroes appear both directly and by allusion.[68] Herrera uses the same imagery for his own poetry, i.e., "the daring flight, the fear, the self-renewing energy that attracts and repels."[69] The lover and the poet who gives expression to the lover's feelings thus merge together in the imagery of the myth. The feeling of inadequacy on the part of the poet to achieve the heights to which he aspires is expressed through the evocation of the flight of Icarus and its disastrous consequences.

With all these poets, the aspirations of the lover and the poet are portrayed as noble, as he "sets out to transcend his humanity and gain immortality in an act of supreme daring."[70] In subsequent treatments of the myth, however, Icarus is portrayed less as hero and more as misguided, overly self-confident, and proud. During the Counter-Reformation, Icarus became the object of ridicule, censured for his excessive ambition and pride.

FROM THE ELIZABETHANS THROUGH THE NINETEENTH CENTURY

In 1567, Arthur Golding published his translation of Ovid's *Metamorphoses* in England. Written in iambic couplets of fourteen syllables and with allegorical comments added, this translation was used by Shakespeare and his contemporaries.

Christopher Marlowe (1564–1593) drew heavily upon Ovid, whom he also translated (the *Amores* was published after Marlowe's death under the title *Elegies*) and who spoke to Marlowe and the Elizabethans in new and direct ways. Having abandoned the moralizing of Ovid that occurred during the Middle Ages, Marlowe embraced his forthright eroticism, creating a "mood of enticement"[71] in *Dido* and other dramas, but it was the towering ambition of Icarus that infused many of the Marlovian tragedies. The symbol of Icarus as the over-reacher is the dominant image for the protagonists in the tragedies: "His protagonist is never Everyman but always *l'uomo singolare,* the exceptional man who becomes king because he is a hero, not hero because he is a king; the private individual who remains captain of his fate, at least until his ambition overleaps itself; the overreacher whose tragedy is more of an action than a passion, rather an assertion of man's will than an acceptance of God's."[72]

Marlowe's tragedies are grounded in the Greek humanism that shaped Renaissance thought. Whereas medieval thought was grounded in morality and the pursuit of virtue, under the confidence that all of life was guided by divine Providence, Renaissance thought gave expression to the freedom of will and the power of the individual to control his own destiny. Imbued with this spirit and striving to go beyond it, Marlowe bequeathed to succeeding ages a world-and-life view that contradicted the Christian values that undergirded previous generations.

Harry Levin's study of Marlowe, *The Overreacher,* demonstrates the true significance of the Icarian imagery in the tragedies:

> Tragedy is grounded upon mortality; and in obscuring the prospect of a hereafter, it enhances the perception of here and now. Moreover, in exalting the individual to heroic stature, it frees him to act. . . . Orthodox Christianity . . . had preached contempt for "all that is in the world, the lust of the flesh, the lust of the eyes, and the pride of life." But concupiscence, curiosity, and vainglory—temptations which men become saints by resisting—are leading motives of humanistic drama, which—in more affirmative terms—would be inconceivable without fullness of life, freedom of will, and the inevitability of death. The unholy trinity of Marlowe's heresies, violating the taboos of medieval orthodoxy, was an affirmation of the strongest drives that animated the Renaissance and have shaped our modern outlook.[73]

Icarus is a controlling image for the heroes in Marlowe's tragedies, including *Tamburlaine* and *Dr. Faustus,* in which he embodies the "paradoxical condition of the Renaissance hero—a modern, secular hero in a still-medieval as well as Christian universe."[74] He is also employed by critics to describe Marlowe himself. Levin draws upon clinical psychology, borrowing a phrase from Dr. Henry A. Murray, when he diagnoses Marlowe as suffering from an "Icarus complex."[75] The "Icarus complex" involves the "disposition to isolate one's self on a higher plane while attracting the admiration of others"; narcissism; and the dread of falling as the "chief anxiety."[76] Levin saw Icarus as "the archetype of the overreacher" and Marlowe, "by temperament a tragedian," justifying these conclusions by the explicit acknowledgment of the prologue attributing "Faustus' downfall to waxen wings which mount beyond his reach" and by Dido's words to Aeneas:

> Ile frame me wings of wax like Icarus,
> And ore his ships will soare vnto the Sunne,
> That they may melt and I may fall in his armes:
> Or els Ile make a prayer vnto the waues.[77]

Marlowe himself was scarcely more than a youth when he died at age twenty-nine, and his poetry, like his life, epitomizes the exuberance, the exhilaration, the excess of Icarus. He was driven by the "most damnable appetite of all, which . . . wholly possessed the ego," the urge to excel, i.e., that which "Pascal's Jansenist masters termed *libido excellendi,*" says Levin, who adds: "What could characterize Marlowe more succinctly, or better sum up his Icarian desire for flight?"[78] Like the heroes of his tragedies, Marlowe himself was a tragic overreacher.

By exalting the individual and casting his tragic heroes as overreachers, Marlowe converted the image of Icarus from a negative to a positive one, and he recreated him as a symbol of human aspiration and achievement. Ever since Marlowe, moreover, Icarus has served as a symbol for the poet who challenges accepted norms and aspires to new heights of expression. Marlowe's contribution to the perpetuation and extension of the myth is therefore of fundamental significance. He transformed the symbol of Icarus, reshaping the way in which successive generations would view his flight beyond human limitations. Hereafter, there is an evident dualism in the representation of Icarus, a dualism that continues to the present day.

At the beginning of the seventeenth century, there was a reaction against the gods and heroes of classical mythology. Icarus became a negative model, an example of impetuous youth and misguided ambition to be repudiated and avoided. He was mocked and parodied, ridiculed and rejected. With changing moral values, Icarus came to symbolize the worst of the erotic literary tradition that had undermined traditional moral values. In this climate, Icarus became the image of the derivative, plagiarizing artist. In the seventeenth century, moreover, the poets' sympathies lay with the father, so Daedalus was treated more positively, while Icarus was criticized and condemned for his pride, disobedience, vanity, and violation of natural law. Daedalus was also condemned during this era for his failure to accept the constraints of natural law. In one sense, the moralizing approach to myth brought Icarus full circle, back to allegory, although there were different nuances in the seventeenth century than in the Middle Ages.

During the Baroque era (ca. 1600–1750), Daedalus and Icarus are featured in wall paintings at the Galleria Farnese in Rome, in landscape paintings on copper, in portraiture, in decorations of a hunting lodge near Madrid for King Philip IV, in small gouaches and pen drawings, and in book illustrations. Studying these many treatments of the myth, we can observe the progression from the early baroque of Carracci and Carravaggio, with naturalism as its expression, to the High Baroque realized in the "sensuousness and colourism of Rubens" and the "third or classicistic phase, in which the opulent and emotional qualities of the 'High Baroque' were supplanted by a more rigorous order, clarity and composure," with Andrea Sacchi and Poussin as leading representatives.[79]

Baroque artists gradually reshaped the myth as they gave it visual expression. Domenico Zampieri, Carracci's assistant who is better known as Domenichino (1581–1641), depicts the fisherman in the boat and a semi-recumbent shepherd, following Ovid; but contrary to Ovid, he shows them startled out of their customary tasks not merely by the sight of two humans in flight, but specifically and frighteningly by the fall itself. Like Brueghel a half century earlier, Domenichino was responding to the evocative power of the myth but changed it to fit his artistic vision. In his choice of subject, however, Domenichino clearly expresses the Baroque spirit.

Carlo Sareceni Veneziano (ca. 1580–1620) perpetuates this interpretation in a series of three landscape paintings, but he gives it contemporary relevance by adding a noble, mounted on his horse, gesturing toward the falling Icarus, and by also depicting the burial of Icarus.

Sir Anthony Van Dyck (1599–1641) directs attention to a subject rarely treated in classical antiquity, the actual fastening of wings on Icarus (see Figure 8). (This subject was also treated by two of his contemporaries, Andrea Sacchi and Jakob Jordaens [see appendix C]). Well known for his portraiture of British royalty, Van Dyck presented Daedalus and Icarus as portraits. He twice painted their portraits, with Icarus in one painting presented as "a self-portrait of the artist . . . posed with his hand on his father's head."[80] It is not uncommon for an artist to use self-portraiture in her or his depiction of a subject, particularly a subject taken from myth or literature. In this regard, it is important to note that both Michael Ayrton and Leonard Baskin expressed the view that all painting is a self-portrait and that both presented their self-portraits in depictions of Daedalus.[81] Van Dyck's own identification of himself with Icarus should not be overlooked, particularly in view of Marlowe's identification with Icarus, which contributed to subsequent literary and artistic developments in which Icarus became a symbol for the aspiring artist. Perhaps Van Dyck is hinting here at his own aspirations as an artist, his own desire to excel, to rise to heights not previously attained.

Two paintings by Peter Paul Rubens (1577–1640) of the *Fall of Icarus* accentuate the fall (see Figure 9). Rubens completed two sketches for a painting to be included in a series of mythological subjects used to decorate a hunting lodge, Torre de la Parada, near Madrid for King Philip IV.[82] In the version now in Philadelphia (completed ca. 1636–1638), Icarus's pink loincloth represents the only vivid color in the painting. Behind the figures of Daedalus and Icarus golden sun rays break through the clouds. Reminders of the cause of Icarus's fall, the rays of the sun also contribute to the emotional experience of this painting, adding to the intensity of feeling.

The large version of the painting for the hunting lodge was executed by Jacob Peter Gowy after the sketch

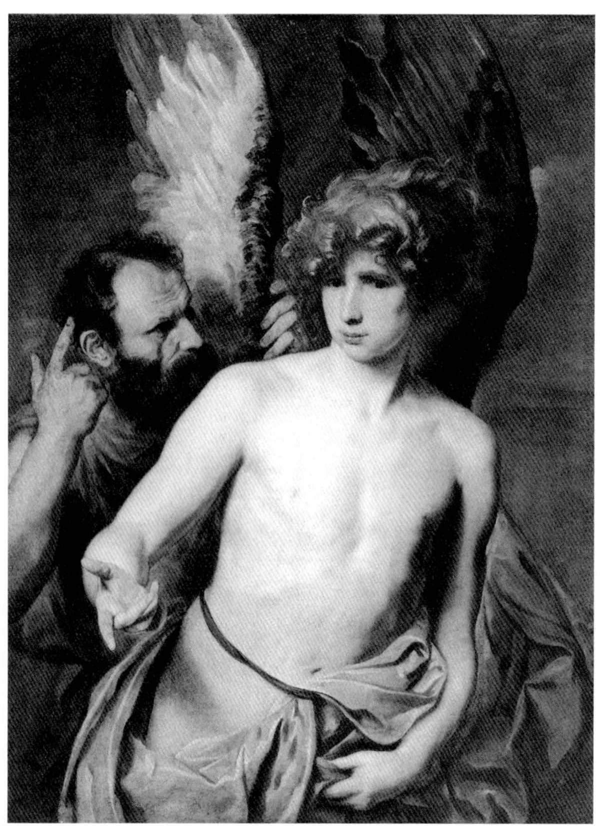

Figure 8. Sir Anthony Van Dyck, **DAEDALUS FASTENING WINGS ON ICARUS** (1620s). Ontario Art Gallery, Canada.

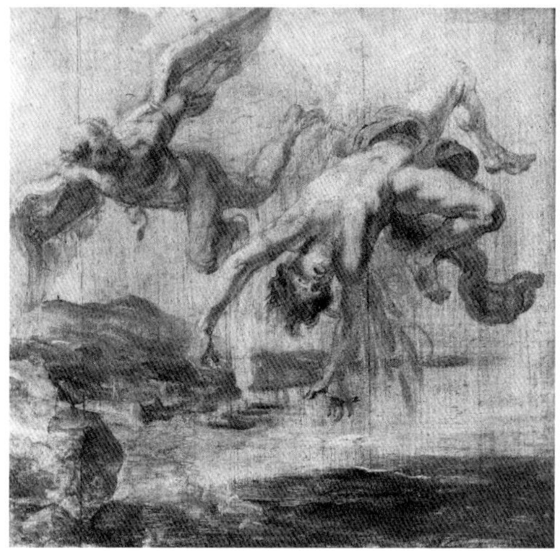

Figure 9. Peter Paul Rubens, **FALL OF ICARUS** (ca. 1636–1638). Musées royaux des Beaux-Arts de Belgique, Brussels.

now in Brussels.[83] A crimson drapery, rather than a pink loincloth, partially covers the nude body of Icarus, and in the background there is a luminous sky, as in the sketches. Icarus somersaults backward, with only a vestige of a wing on his right arm, while Daedalus flies alongside, turning toward him in horror. As in his paintings of death and martyrdom, such as *The Raising of the Cross* (1610–1611) and *The Martyrdom of St. Lieven* (ca. 1633), Rubens conveys tremendous emotional power in these depictions of the fall of Icarus. The helplessness of both the father and the son draws forth from the spectator a profound emotional response. The father's shock and horror evoke the pain of losing a child, whereas the son's vain attempts to forestall the inevitable consequence of his hubristic flight evoke the fright of falling to one's death. The agony of suspense at the fall of Icarus heightens the emotive force of these powerful renderings of the myth. The touch of color in these two paintings draws one's attention to the plummeting figure of Icarus, pulling the viewer into the experience of pain, grief and loss. The baroque theme of death is also strongly present in other representations (see appendix C).

In the last quarter of the eighteenth century, Antonio Canova (1757–1822),[84] bridged the baroque and the neoclassical eras with two sculptural treatments of the Cretan cycle of myth. Moving beyond early sculptures of *Eurydice* and *Orpheus* in the neoclassical tradition of ornamental sculptures for Italian gardens,[85] he created in 1777–1779 a marble sculpture of *Daedalus and Icarus* (see Figure 10).[86] The success of *Daedalus and Icarus* led to an important commission on a related theme, *Theseus and the Minotaur* (1781–1783; see Figure 11). Although the two works are close in time, their styles are significantly different, revealing Canova's adaptability to direction from his mentors. The former manifests "his natural inclination toward expressive vivacity," still under the influence of baroque artistic standards, whereas the latter offers evidence that he had "modulated his style in accordance with the new doctrine of tranquil grandeur" influenced by the critical views of Winckelmann and his followers.[87]

Daedalus and Icarus is slightly over life size (86-5/8″ x 37-3/8″ x 38-1/4″), with the two figures in a "contrapposto stance . . . that is thoroughly conditioned by the traditional baroque devices of active and passive legs, spiral torsion in the trunk, and counterbalanced position of the arms," although the composition of the group is judged to be rather unconventional, and the "sensitive interpretation of the subject and the energetic realism of the two protagonists" are deemed "novel and highly personal."[88] They are linked together not only by the placement of Daedalus's right arm around the left shoulder and back of Icarus, but also by the thread that stretches taut across the front of the sculpture, from the wing over the right arm of Icarus across the belly of Daedalus to his clenched left fist, below which the looped cord dangles like a noose.

The contrast in age between father and son is exaggerated especially in the portrait of Daedalus, who is portrayed with a deeply furrowed brow, aging flesh, and the suggestion of sagging stomach muscles. Noting the similarity of this sculptural portrait's "ruthlessness in its description of decrepitude" to that found in "Pigalle's nude portrait of Voltaire," Fred Licht (who joined with photographer David Finn to capture the distinctive power of Canova's sculptures) elaborates on the contrast between the portrayal of the adolescent Icarus and the aging Daedalus:

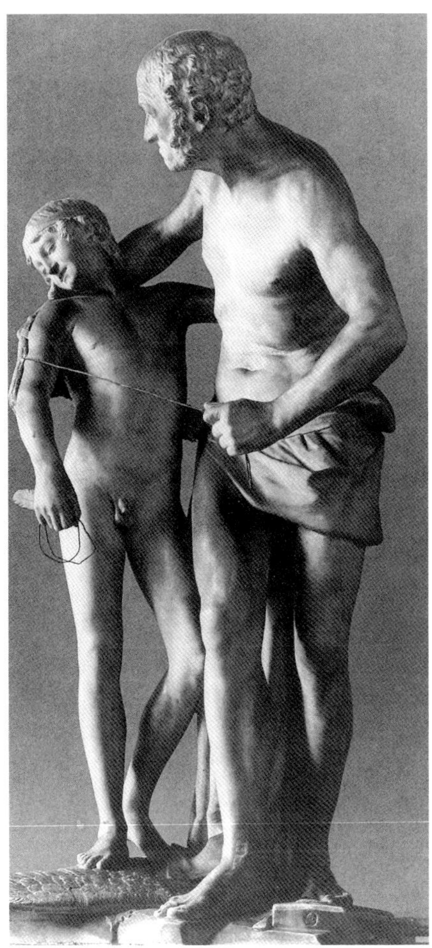

Figure 10. Antonio Canova, **DAEDALUS AND ICARUS** (1777–1779). Museo Correr, Venice.

> Canova's contrast between youth and age is abetted by a psychological interpretation expressed in highly differentiated gestures. Icarus is portrayed in a moment of self-satisfied delight at the prospect of adventure. He stands in a pose that reflects his slightly fatuous mood. Daedalus, on the other hand, is interpreted as the wise artificer putting his fantastic contraption to the test; simultaneously he is also the father, solicitous of his son's safety. His pose is active, unlike that of Icarus, directed to an exterior goal. Such interplay of reciprocal relationships is typical of the Baroque, as is the inclusion of large volumes of space into the mass of the composition. It is only the astringent realism that sets this sculpture apart from all that was being done in Venice, or in Italy, at this time.[89]

In this sculpture, Canova expresses the emotive duality of the myth. The tools of the sculptor's trade—the mallet and the chisel—lie at the feet of Daedalus, the artificer, but the iconography of Icarus includes the wing, the vehicle of escape from the constraints of life, the limits of humanity. It is this very duality that Ayrton would express in his *Daedalus-Icarus Matrix* (Cat. No. 640) for the *Arkville Maze* (Cat. No. 673) two centuries later (see chapter 6), expressing in wax and bronze the figurative tradition represented so eloquently by Canova. The symbolism of Icarus includes "the great wing that will allow the dreamer to soar, risking everything in an attempt to realize mankind's ancient dream of attaining the unattainable—as do all true artists."[90] Canova thus may be

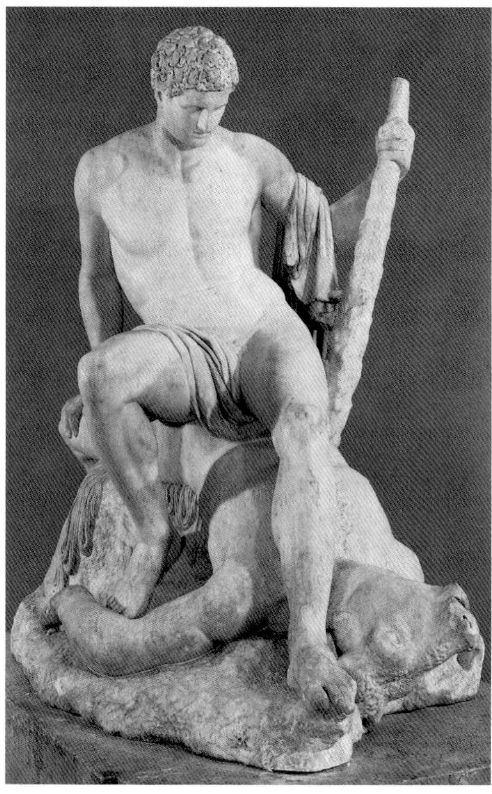

Figure 11. Antonio Canova, **THESEUS AND THE MINOTAUR** (1881–1883). Victoria and Albert Museum.

expressing his rejection of the artistic standards of eighteenth-century Venice and his desire to identify with Icarus, who symbolizes the preference to "transcend the limitations set by craftsmanship at the risk of failure."[91] In the twentieth century, Michael Ayrton also rejected contemporary artistic standards, but he chose to identify more closely with the artificer, the prototypical sculptor, as he sought to expand the limits set by craftsmanship.

In Canova's *Theseus and the Minotaur* we see the first large-scale neoclassical sculpture, which represents a "milestone in the history of modern sculpture."[92] Influenced by his mentors, Gavin Hamilton and his circle, Canova turned from the more common theme of the slaying to that which was depicted by the Codrus painter in his red-figure kylix (appendix C), i.e. the moment after the death of the Minotaur. A nude, partially draped Theseus sits astride the belly of the Minotaur's corpse, looking down upon his victim, while grasping a club (the presumed tool of conquest) in a slightly raised left hand. The other, larger end of the club rests on the defeated Minotaur, whose carcass is draped over a rock, with his pitiable head rolled back in death.[93] Ariadne's thread coils over the rock, under the Minotaur's leg, reminding the viewer that she had aided Theseus in his victory over her monstrous half-brother. Canova therefore portrays not the ferocity and the uncertainty of the outcome of the struggle, but rather the moment of truth that follows the killing of the hybrid creature. Portraying the "theme of human courage triumphing over monstrous strength," Canova "presents not the exultant victor but the young man contemplating the consequences of his acts, sunk in melancholy awareness that victory is attended by a loss of innocence. Perhaps this foreknowledge of the obligations that victory brings reflects Canova's own condition at this moment of his career."[94]

Although Canova may well have identified in certain respects with Icarus, as did poets of the Spanish Renaissance, it has been argued that the identification of Icarus with the artist is "peculiar to Romanticism."[95] Because Michael Ayrton was devoted to, even obsessed with, the music of Hector Berlioz and because he also associated with British Romanticism during the isolationistic years of World War II, it is important to try to understand the link between Romanticism and the symbolism of Icarus for this nineteenth-century artistic movement.[96]

The identification of the artist with Icarus appears to have been particularly strong for French Romanticism:

> The French Romantics, then, actually reenacted the full myth of Icarus, the flight in the ambitions and experiments of the first Romantic generation—that of Hugo and Balzac, of Berlioz and Michelet—and the fall in the minds, if not in the works, of the second and third generations, who saw a social decline in the Second Empire and a moral decadence in the state of mind of their contemporaries. If for no other reasons than the self-conscious exhibitionism of the Romantics and their awareness of the full pattern of their age, the myth of Icarus seems especially appropriate for the nineteenth century.[97]

For the Romantics, Icarus represented not only political freedom but especially an "unrestrained aesthetic imagination."[98] Romanticism, in its reaction against neoclassicism, emphasized both the imagination and the emotions, glorified both lack of moderation and a passion for greatness, and expressed a profound love of nature. Also evident in the development of Romanticism was a strain of pessimism, which found its expression in a predilection for melancholy, the longing for death, the contemplation of suicide, and the glorification of suicide.[99] This moral malady, the *mal du siècle,* expressed the dark side of the myth of Icarus.

It may not always be immediately evident that the Romantics, particularly the French Romantics, identified themselves with Icarus, for they assumed a variety of masks. Victor Hugo might reenact the myth of Orpheus; Balzac might characterize the poet as "a demiurge, a man who shaped or changed and so ruled the world,"[100] and identify him with Prometheus,;[101] Vigny might give voice to the Parnassian ideal.[102] Nonetheless: "Behind all the masks assumed by the authors of the nineteenth century was the archetype of Icarus. Even when the mask was that of an Orpheus or a Prometheus, a Satan or a Narcissus, the face behind the mask was the face of Icarus, the Romantic artist as Romantic artist."[103]

The roots of Romanticism can be observed in Rousseau (1712–1778), more so in the *Confessions* than in *Narcissus,* although the latter—his first work—anticipated the Romantics' self-absorption. It is, however, the exhibitionism which complements narcissism that characterizes Romanticism, and Icarus is the "true archetype of the Romantic artist" in the view of the nineteenth-century historian of Romanticism, Théophile Gautier (1811–1872): "The fate of Icarus frightened no one. Wings! wings! wings! they cried from all sides, even if we should fall into the sea. To fall from the sky, one must climb there, even for but a moment, and that is more beautiful than to spend one's whole life crawling on the earth."[104]

The shadow of Victor Hugo (1802–1885) looms large over the nineteenth century and over Romanticism, for he was a self-conscious and ambitious Icarian Romantic. His literary personality dominated the age, and his writings and his public presence promoted his personal vision. In 1880 he wrote: "Every man who writes writes a book; this book is himself."[105] Nearly fifty years earlier, in 1833, he had written of his belief that he was fulfilling a mission, expressing the divine order behind the seeming "chaos of history, nature, and mysterious universal forces," and his works reveal that "the conviction that he was inspired by God to perform a task set by God grew steadily throughout the rest of his life."[106] His literary and political ideals had fused together by 1830, with "liberty" as the ideal for both the artist and society.

Honoré de Balzac (1799–1850) gave expression to the same titanic will evident in Hugo, and he shared Hugo's Romantic view of the poet, although Balzac differed from Hugo on the subject of the poet's divine inspiration. Balzac's novels often portray artists and poets who deviate from the Romantic ideal rather than embodying it. One of his disciples, Charles de Bernard, published a novel, *Les Ailes d'Icare,* while Balzac was at work on *Illusions perdues.* Bernard's novel recounts the story of an ambitious young artist from the provinces who epitomizes Icarus, flying high but falling far. In the title and in the novel, Bernard captures much of the essence of French Romanticism and its Icarian character.

Romantic satanism was present but muted in Hugo and Balzac. By identifying Satan with Prometheus, Balzac appeared to sanction revolt. Charles Pierre Baudelaire (1821–1867) gave expression to the satanism of the *Jeunes-France* and offered petty insults to the bourgeoisie. In Baudelaire is combined the narcissistic contemplation of self and Icarian exhibitionism, but he "reversed the process. He allowed the reader to catch him in the very act of self-confession or self-contemplation."[107] Baudelaire saw the artist as double, as Narcissus and his own reflection, with the actual poet inferior to the ideal he saw in the mirror. He portrayed himself "as a worshipper of Satan, so that he might be rejected by society, for the ironic analysis of the self led to the realization that the self was detestable."[108] The self-torturing Narcissus reflected in the poetry of Baudelaire offers a different perspective on the Icarian ideal of Romanticism. Although Baudelaire portrayed himself as Icarus, he found that in an age of decadence he could express only a sense of failure and nostalgia for flight; the apex of Romanticism was past. His "Plaintes d'un Icare" cannot celebrate a strong-willed, titanic, exhibitionist Icarus, but only a weak and inadequate failure. He has regressed from Icarus to Narcissus, from towering ambition to abject self-pity and self-absorption. In a real sense, Baudelaire represents the nadir of Romanticism's ideal of the artist as Icarus, for he glorifies the fall, whereas in early Romanticism the flight and the fall were kept in a kind of equipoise, and in the Renaissance the flight was glorified and the fall minimized.[109]

However one reads Romanticism, whether as a literary and artistic movement or as a shift in paradigms, "from a static and mechanic to a dynamic and organic world view,"[110] or any other way, it is clear that it is difficult to reduce it to a neat and tidy definition. In both intellectual and political history, the nineteenth century was a period of change and complexity. Romanticism, coming on the heels of and giving expression to many of the ideals of revolution, was itself "an age of exacerbated polarities: the cult of reason and of the irrational, of inspiration and of learning, of pessimism and a belief in progress, a religious renewal and a radical questioning of religion, and so on."[111] The myth of Icarus, which embodies the polarities of flight and fall, optimism and pessimism, freedom and imprisonment, achievement and failure, life and death, is therefore an appropriate symbol for Romanticism, particularly since so many French Romantics evoked his memory in their writings and in their lives.

At the end of the nineteenth century, Icarus appeared along with other heroes of the Pre-Raphaelites and Symbolists, radiant in his fallen beauty. A bridge between the Romantics and the twentieth century was provided by British artist Herbert J. Draper (1864–1920). In 1898 Draper painted a very large (72″ x 61-1/4″) oil on canvas, *The Lament for Icarus.*[112] In this painting, Icarus lies sprawled across a rock in the midst of a green-blue sea, surrounded by nymphs who weep for his fall. Showing no signs of the disastrous plunge, his body manifests his natural beauty. His wings likewise are "still perfect, of multi-coloured feathers (painted by Draper from the real wings of Birds of Paradise, suitably enlarged)."[113] It is true, however, that his skin appears dark, particularly in comparison to the white radiance of the nymphs, which may suggest the consequences of getting too close to the sun.

Commenting on this painting, Dr. Justine Hopkins declares that Draper identifies Icarus "with the other heroes of the Pre-Raphaelites and Symbolists (Wallis' *Chatterton* is a good example), who, like James Dean half a century later, manage to *live fast, die young and leave a beautiful corpse*—the aim is the creation of wonder and melancholy, and demonstrates the potency of Icarus as a symbol of the turn-of-the-century aesthetes, as well as the more robust interpreters who came before and after."[114] And so it is that Icarus again is resuscitated as a symbol for the artist who strives for a moment of youthful glory and an eternity of fame.

IN THE TWENTIETH CENTURY

The history of art in the twentieth century encompasses many different and often overlapping trends. Impressionism gave way to Postimpressionism in the 1880s, which in turn gave way to other movements, such as Cubism and Expressionism.[115] These movements were manifested in both painting and sculpture. Among the major sculptors of the twentieth century, Maillol experimented with continual variations on the image of the nude, Giacometti played with elongated, emaciated figures, Henry Moore with the reclining nude and the eternal feminine, and Brancusi with variations on the ovoid form. Jacques Lipchitz (1891–1973), on the other hand, resembled Rodin with his infinite variety of themes and forms. His works range from Cubism to Abstract Expressionism to portraiture and figurative sculpture. His themes encompass stories from the Bible, both Old and New Testament, and from classical mythology, as well as arising out of personal experience. A major obsession was the Prometheus theme (1931–1953), but he also drew upon the Cretan cycle of myth, with versions of the *Rape of Europa,* and *Theseus and the Minotaur.* He employed these classical myths to express his horror at what Hitler and the Nazis were doing to Europe and the Jews in the 1930s and 1940s. Lipchitz has said that for him, "from the beginning, the subject of Prometheus was that of the victory of light over darkness, of struggling mankind over the gods who wished to keep them in ignorance,"[116] but as he worked on various versions, he conceived of the topic "as a struggle, not a simple conquest, in which light, education, science were struggling against darkness and ignorance, which had not yet been conquered," and he made it into a "political sculpture, propaganda for democracy."[117] In the face of the changing political environment in Germany, his *Europa and the Bull* (1938–1941) evolved from the theme of "tender and erotic love," with the bull "caressing Europa with his tongue," into a theme of conflict and terror: he now used "the Europa as a symbol for Europe and the bull as Hitler, with Europe killing Hitler with a dagger."[118]

In similar fashion, Lipchitz used his *Theseus and the Minotaur* (1942) to comment on the war. In preliminary drawings, he focused on escape and rescue because of his concern for the safety of his family and himself. As the idea evolved, however, his focus changed. He says that he came to identify the Minotaur with Hitler and Theseus with General Charles De Gaulle, but he made an important discovery once he completed the sculpture: "When I finished the sculpture, I realized that the monster is also a part of Theseus, as though there were a Hitler in each of us whom we must destroy. Theseus is killing part of himself."[119] From this brief elaboration on the work of Lipchitz, we gain another glimpse into how myth both shapes an artist's perceptions and is shaped by the artist, but we can also gain a deeper understanding of the creative process itself.

In the course of the twentieth century there were many other movements, such as fauvism, dadaism, De Stijl, constructivism, kitsch, surrealism, pop art, op art, realism, and neorealism. It is not my intention to give equal treatment to every movement, nor even to comment on every development in the art of the century. Ayrton was well aware of the various trends of the first three quarters of the century, following most of the developments with disdain right up to his death in 1975.

Three individuals cast long shadows across the twentieth century, and all had an influence upon Michael Ayrton. Sigmund Freud (1856–1939) changed the way people understand the operations of the mind and the emotions of an individual, but he also had a profound effect upon the creation and the interpretation of art, by introducing psychoanalytic theory into the study of art. James Joyce (1882–1941) altered the structure of literature with his use of stream of consciousness techniques, particularly in his later works. And Pablo Picasso (1881–1973) so dominated the art world with his prolific, constantly changing creation of works of art in multiple media—from drawing to painting to sculpture to etching —that many artists, including Ayrton, felt almost suffocated by his overpowering influence. As he mined the art of the past, voraciously appropriating its riches, Picasso reshaped our perception of it. No artist working in the twentieth century could ignore the impact of these three dominant figures. Even as he railed against Picasso, Ayrton acknowledged his indebtedness to him. His novel, *The Maze Maker* (see chapter 5), reveals the influence of Freud and his protégé, Carl G. Jung (1875–1961), who adapted and revised Freud's conception of the unconscious with his theory of the collective unconscious.

Joseph Campbell identifies this period directly after the end of World War I as a time when "there appeared a spectacular series of historical, anthropological, literary, and psychological works, in which the archetypes of myth were recognized . . . as fundamental to the structuring of human life and, in that sense, prophetic of the future as well as remedial of the present and eloquent of the past," offering the following examples to drive home his point:

> T. S. Eliot's poem, *The Waste Land*, Carl Jung's *Psychological Types*, and Leo Frobenius' *Paideuma* appeared in 1921; James Joyce's *Ulysses* in 1922; Oswald Spengler's *Decline of the West* in 1923; and Thomas Mann's *The Magic Mountain* in 1924. It was very much as though, at a crucial juncture in the course of the growth of our civilization, a company of sages, masters of the wisdom that arises from the depths of being, had spoken from their hermitages to give warning and redirection. However, what men of deeds have ever listened to sages? . . . Thus the nations learn in sweat, blood, and tears what might have been taught them in peace, and as Joyce's hero in *A Portrait* states, what those so-called thoughts and their protagonists represent are not the ways and guides to freedom, but the very nets, and the wielders of those nets, by which the seeker of freedom is snared, entrapped, and hauled back into the labyrinth.[120]

Freud's structural model of the psyche, or the psychical apparatus, appears derivative from Plato's tripartite psychology. In the *Phaedrus,* the soul (psyche) is represented as a chariot drawn by two poorly matched horses —one dark, lustful, rapacious, the other light, spirited, and modest—who are held in check by a charioteer holding the reins; the charioteer represents the rational power in the soul. In Freud's sketch of the psyche, made in 1933, one sees a vertical oval containing the unconscious id at the bottom, the ego in the middle, and the superego off to the side, spanning the ego and the id; there is a preconscious region near the top, along with the drawing of an eye to represent the conscious perception.[121] Freud's model has been reconstructed by psychologist David G. Myers, who shows the mind or soul as an iceberg: the tip of the iceberg is the ego, functioning as "executive mediator" between the deeply submerged id ("unconscious psychic energy") and the partially submerged superego ("internalized ideals"); the conscious mind rises above the surface of the water; the preconscious mind lies just below the surface, accessible but outside awareness; and the unconscious mind is far below the surface.[122]

In *An Outline of Psycho-Analysis,* Freud summarizes his key theories. The id contains everything that is inherited, but above all the instincts. The ego serves as the intermediary between the id and the external world, i.e., reality. The superego constitutes a third power, which the ego must take into account: a precipitate from childhood, it includes influences of family, racial and national traditions, and the immediate social milieu.[123] Freud posits that there are only two basic instincts: Eros, or the love instinct; and Thanatos, or the death (destructive) instinct. The aim of Eros is "to establish ever greater unities," to bind things together, whereas the aim of Thanatos is "to undo connections and so to destroy things."[124] Into his understanding of Icarus, Michael Ayrton incorporated both Eros and Thanatos, as is evident in *The Maze Maker* (see chapter 5).

Not long before his death in 1961, Jung declared: "Thus far, nobody can say anything against Freud's theory of repression and wish fulfillment as apparent causes of dream symbolism."[125] Jung chose, however, to abandon Freud's use of "free association" in connection with dreams and focus on the dream itself, in which "man produces symbols unconsciously and spontaneously."[126] He also rejected Freud's notion that messages from dreams are limited to sexual allegory.[127] In his development of Freud's concept of the unconscious, Jung discovered that part of "the unconscious consists of a multitude of temporarily obscured thoughts, impressions, and images that, in spite of being lost, continue to influence our conscious minds" and that "the unconscious is no mere depository of the past, but it is also full of germs of future psychic situations and ideas."[128]

Joseph L. Henderson, a Jungian, links the story of Icarus to the hero myth of the Winnebago Indians of North America. The fourth and final stage of the hero myth is represented by the Twins. This is the stage of late adolescence when the ego is able to triumph by mastering and assimilating the shadow. In the "bloom of youth, attractive, full of energy and idealism," the hero offers himself as a sacrifice because the driving idealism of youth "is bound to lead to overconfidence: the human ego can be exalted to experience godlike attributes, but only at the cost of over-reaching itself and falling to disaster."[129] This, says Henderson, "is the meaning of the story of Icarus, the youth who is carried up to heaven on his fragile, humanly contrived wings, but who flies too close to the sun and plunges to his doom."[130] It is necessary for the youthful ego to take this risk of overreaching in order to move from adolescence into maturity.

In a related interpretation of the Cretan cycle of myth, Henderson notes parallels between the slaying of the Gorgon Medusa by Perseus and the slaying of the Minotaur by Theseus. Both of them, he says, "had to overcome their fear of unconscious maternal demonic powers and had to liberate from these powers a single youthful feminine figure" [Perseus rescued Andromeda, Theseus Ariadne], and he suggests that the Minotaur may symbolize "the unhealthy decadence of matriarchal Crete."[131] He contends, moreover, that "in all cultures, the labyrinth has the meaning of an entangling and confusing representation of the world of matriarchal consciousness; it can be traversed only by those who are ready for a special initiation into the mysterious world of the collective unconscious."[132] Theseus's rescue of Ariadne "symbolizes

In classical antiquity and throughout much of Western tradition, the power to create was believed to originate outside the self.

the liberation of the anima figure from the devouring aspect of the mother image. Not until this is accomplished can a man achieve his first true capacity for relatedness to women."[133]

Jung uses the term "process of individuation" to describe the pattern of psychic growth reflected in the dreams he interpreted for his patients. In many dreams, the dreamer finds himself wandering in a "maze of strange passages, chambers, and unlocked exits" below the ground. These patterns are reminiscent of "the seven doors of the Egyptian underworld, itself seen as a maze." For Jung and his followers, "corridors, labyrinths, and mazes" are often taken to symbolize the unconscious.[134]

In classical antiquity and throughout much of Western tradition, the power to create was believed to originate outside the self. Homer and Hesiod invoked the Muses to assist them in their creative tasks, and such invocations persist through the centuries at least up to and including Dante. Plato in the *Phaedrus* speaks of "the madness of those who are possessed by the Muses," thus reinforcing the notion that poets derive their creative power from a divine madness. Even in modern times, poets and artists are sometimes described in such terms. For Plato, however, this "divine madness" did not extend to other classes of artists, for he labeled sculptors and painters craftsmen. They therefore had to "make existence visible," and they carried out their creative tasks "in the full sunlight of reason."[135] In the eighteenth century, however, the Romantics combined plastic, literary, and musical arts and attributed to all of them an irrational creative process. This view persisted until Freud and Jung offered their insights into the creative process. Freud saw creativity as "a refinement of biological productivity" and its motivation as the satisfaction of basic instincts, of basic sexual needs. Jung, on the other hand, identified cognition as the "original impulse of creativity" and developed his theory of archetypes as the foundation for humankind's "symbolic activity," i.e., the creative process.[136] For Freud, the creative process originated in the unconscious, whereas Jung posited the collective unconscious as the source of archetypal images that appear in the work of artists and writers.[137]

As one studies art and literature of the twentieth century, one cannot ignore these theories about creativity nor the contributions of psychoanalysis to both the creation and the interpretation of art. Evidence of the preoccupation with the myth of Daedalus and Icarus in the twentieth century is found in the fact that the number of significant treatments or usages of the myth surpassed the productivity of the preceding nineteen centuries.[138] James Joyce, Bertrand Russell, W. H. Auden, William Carlos Williams, André Gide, Leonard Baskin, and Henri Matisse are some of the key figures, in addition to Michael Ayrton, who focused attention on the myth and these mythic figures, with their compelling attraction in an age in which human flight was achieved on a grand scale.

The labyrinth and its fabled prisoner also have had considerable appeal in this century. Whereas Picasso brought the Minotaur into sharp focus especially for artists, art historians, and the cognoscenti, the labyrinth or maze entered public consciousness much more extensively, particularly in the latter half of the century, when maze building in England, the United States, Japan, and elsewhere multiplied in public and private spaces, creating tourist attractions and engendering reflection on the mystical power of this ancient symbol. Meanwhile, writers such as Jorge Luis Borges and literary critics began to explore the multiple levels of meaning found in this potent symbol.

James Joyce (1882–1941) ushered in the twentieth century's concern with Daedalus and Icarus in 1914–1915 when *A Portrait of the Artist as a Young Man,* with Stephen Dedalus as the novel's hero, was published in serial form in the *Egoist. Portrait,* a drastically condensed and revised version of the previously unpublishable *Stephen Hero,* displays a greater sense of the symbolic significance of the hero's name (Stephen Daedalus in *Stephen Hero*) than did the earlier conflated novel, although the choice of the name for the hero in the original novel represented a deliberate fusing of Christian and pagan traditions to underscore the internal conflict in the hero's mind. The name Stephen was selected to recall the first Christian martyr;[139] the surname, Daedalus, was intended to evoke the illustrious and artful pagan artificer. Thus, "Stephen would be a saint of literature, and like Dedalus [*sic*] would invent wings to soar beyond his compatriots, and a labyrinth, a mysterious art based on great cunning."[140] As a result of Joyce's increased awareness of the symbolic potential of his hero's surname, the bird imagery and related motifs are much more fully developed in *Portrait* than they had been in *Stephen Hero.*[141]

From "he was baby tuckoo" on the first page to the invocation of Daedalus on the last, birds function as one of the controlling images of flight in *Portrait.*[142] At times the references to Daedalus are direct and unequivocal, at times there are only subtle hints, but the reader is never permitted to forget for long the symbol of the hero's namesake. Directly after the baby tuckoo comes the imagery of the Promethean eagle, followed by a youthful exchange that evinces curiosity about the hero's name. The full implications of the name, however, do not come until much later:

> He heard a confused music within him as of memories and names . . . and from each receding trail of nebulous music there fell always one longdrawn calling note, piercing like a star the dusk of silence. Again! Again! Again! A voice beyond the world was calling.
> —Hello, Stephanos!
> —Here comes the Daedalus! (167)

With the mood set for reverie and otherworldly communication, with the reality of the presence of friends who are calling him also impinging on his consciousness, Stephen is now prepared to acknowledge the growing sense of the full import of his name:

> —Stephanos Dedalos! Bous Stephanoumenos! Bous Stephaneforos![143]
>
> Their banter was not new to him and now it flattered his mild proud sovereignty. Now, as never before, his strange name seemed to him a prophecy. . . .
>
> Now, at the name of the fabulous artificer, he seemed to hear the noise of the dim waves and to see a winged form flying above the waves and slowly climbing the air. What did it mean? Was it a quaint device opening a page of some medieval book of prophecies and symbols, a hawklike man flying sunward above the sea, a prophecy of the end he had been born to serve and had been following through the mists of childhood and boyhood, a symbol of the artist forging anew in his workshop out of the sluggish matter of the earth a new soaring impalpable imperishable being?. . .
>
> His heart trembled; his breath came faster and a wild spirit passed over his limbs as though he were soaring sunward. His heart trembled in an ecstasy of fear and his soul was in flight. His soul was soaring in an air beyond the world and the body he knew was purified in a breath and delivered of incertitude and made radiant and commingled with the element of the spirit. An ecstasy of flight made radiant his eyes and wild his breath and tremulous and wild and radiant his windswept limbs. (168–69)

Overwhelmed by his sudden self-discovery, he is in ecstasy, an "ecstasy of fear" and an "ecstasy of flight." The emotional sensation of flight aroused by his spiritual union with his namesake contributes to the frequently recurring images of flight and of birds and of flying, both in this passage and immediately following it: "His throat ached with a desire to cry aloud, the cry of a hawk or eagle on high, to cry piercingly of his deliverance to the winds" (169).

This sublime experience produces a new self-consciousness and a new resolve: "He would create proudly out of the freedom and power of his soul, as the great artificer whose name he bore, a living thing, new and soaring and beautiful, impalpable, imperishable" (170). Out of and immediately after this experience he sees the vision of a girl, who is eloquently described almost entirely in bird imagery. Although the bird imagery might seem to evoke his namesake, it is clear that Icarus is the dominant force behind the vision:

> Her image had passed into his soul forever and no word had broken the holy silence of his ecstasy. Her eyes had called him and his soul had leaped at the call. To live, to err, to fall, to triumph, to recreate life out of life! A wild angel had appeared to him, the angel of mortal youth and beauty, an envoy from the fair courts of life, to throw open before him in an instant of ecstasy the gates of all the ways of error and glory. On and on and on and on! (172)

Slightly earlier Icarus also had been symbolized, following Stephen's rejection of the priesthood for which he had been preparing:

> His destiny was to be elusive of social or religious orders. . . . He was destined to learn his own wisdom apart from others or to learn the wisdom of others himself wandering among the snares of the world.
>
> The snares of the world were its ways of sin. He would fall. He had not yet fallen but he would fall silently, in an instant. Not to fall was too hard, too hard: and he felt the silent lapse of his soul, as it would be at some instant to come, falling, falling but not yet fallen, still unfallen but about to fall. (162)

The rich symbolism of this passage recalls, of course, Lucifer's fall from grace, but the symbol of Icarus is perhaps even stronger.[144] The expectation of the fall, the realization of its possible consequences, the determination to make mistakes, possibly even a great one with eternal consequences, the rejection of all authority and authority figures evoke Icarus on his fatal flight, soaring ever nearer to the sun, contrary to his father's earlier strong admonitions. Stephen Dedalus, a portrait of the young artist, James Joyce, blended with fictional invention, represents a merging of the Christian and pagan elements in the artist's mind and soul. He is both Daedalus and Icarus, a composite of success and failure, of creation and destruction, life and death, the fundamental human cycle. *Portrait* concludes with Stephen's optimistic invocation of his mythological namesake: "Old father, old artificer, stand me now and ever in good stead." Imbedded in this appeal is the fond hope that the old artificer will help him escape the labyrinth of family, religion, native land, and the rest of his confining environment, but the hope is tinged with the remembrance of the fate of Icarus, producing an attendant apprehension.

There is, however, a fundamental difference between Stephen and his namesake, for whereas Stephen longs for wings to go into exile, Daedalus constructed wings to escape his place of exile. That Stephen's (and Joyce's) flight to Paris is temporary and unsuccessful becomes immediately clear in *Ulysses.* The interrelation of the two novels is a commonplace of Joycean criticism, as is the Daedalian frame of reference in *Ulysses.*[145]

Whereas *Portrait* shows us the awakening intellectual and aesthetic consciousness of the artist from early youth to age twenty, when, full of hope and anticipation, Stephen leaves for Paris to escape the web of conformity, *Ulysses* portrays the consequences of his dashed hopes, frustrations, and disappointments. The abandonment of his natural father for his mythical namesake in *Portrait* adds poignancy to the relationship of Stephen and Bloom in *Ulysses,* and the isolation and progressive alienation of Stephen from society in *Portrait* is intensified in *Ulysses* because of the failure of the self-imposed exile to achieve any resolution of the self/society polarity, but the problem achieves more cosmic, more universal proportions in *Ulysses.*

One brief quotation from *Ulysses* illustrates Stephen's identification with Icarus, in this exchange about Stephen's return from Paris in response to his father's telegram that his mother is dying:

> Your own name is strange enough. I suppose it explains your fantastical humour.
>
> Me, Magee and Mulligan.
>
> Fabulous artificer, the hawklike man. You flew. Whereto? Newhaven-Dieppe, steerage passenger, Paris and back. Lapwing. Icarus. Pater, ait. Seabedabbled, fallen, weltering. Lapwing you are. Lapwing he. (208)[146]

There is in this allusion an implication that Stephen also is identified with Daedalus. This kind of multiple identification occurs as well in the work of Michael Ayrton.

Although a careful analysis of *Ulysses* is beyond the scope of this book, it is important to observe that Joyce, as a modern-day Daedalus, set out to construct his own labyrinth with *Ulysses* and later (in 1939) with *Finnegan's Wake.* Both novels are intricate literary and philosophical labyrinths. Recent criticism, calling attention to the labyrinth as a fundamental element of the structure of the novel, notes that in *Ulysses* and several other twentieth-century novels, "in addition to encountering the labyrinths *in* the texts, we confront the labyrinths *of* the texts."[147]

Pablo Picasso (1881–1973), whose artistic shadow covered the twentieth century, received some of his artistic education by copying old masters in the Prado in Madrid, and he was deeply influenced in his youth by Henri de Toulouse-Lautrec. In 1900 he painted his *Le Moulin de la Galette,* reworking an 1889 painting on the same subject by Toulouse-Lautrec, whose painting was a reworking of one done by Renoir in 1876. It has been said, however, that "Picasso was not merely imitating. He also tried to reconceive the originals he copied."[148] When Picasso took up etching, he sought to establish himself as the rightful successor to Rembrandt, who was not only an acknowledged master of this medium but also "in Picasso's time was considered the greatest artist of all time."[149] In so doing, Picasso was declaring himself the preeminent artist of the twentieth century.

Picasso mined countless sources for his inspiration, including Greek myth. Picasso's new brand of classicism was shaped not by Winckelmann but by Nietzsche, who, in *The Birth of Tragedy* (1872), challenged Winckelmann's notion of the "serenity" at the center of Greek art, arguing that the "Apollonian" ideal was a sublimation of the "procreative lust" of Dionysos. It is indeed the Dionysiac "intoxication" and the "procreative lust" that underlie the interpretations of the Minotaur by Picasso. Picasso's minotaurs are a far cry from *The Minotaur* (1877–1886) of the symbolist painter George Frederick Watts (1817–1904). Watts was more concerned to "paint ideas, not things," and his Minotaur stares passively out across the sea into a colorful, cloud-filled sky. Whereas Watts stated that his intention was "less to paint works that are pleasing to the eye than to suggest great thoughts which will speak to the imagination and the heart and will arouse all that is noblest and best in man,"[150] Picasso gave dynamic expression to basic sexual urges in his treatment of this hybrid creature.

The Minotaur became Picasso's iconographic symbol, particularly during the 1930s, when the bestiality within humanity was emerging more clearly on the world stage. Although Picasso had periodically depicted bullfights since his childhood, he completed his first *Minotaur* (Zervos VII, 135), a very large collage consisting of charcoal and pasted paper on canvas, on 1 January 1928.[151] In the next decade, however, minotaurs, bulls, and bullfights dominated his oeuvre. In 1930 he received the commission and completed the illustrations for the Skira edition of Ovid's *Metamorphoses.* In June 1933 his collage of the Minotaur graced the cover of the first issue of a new magazine of the surrealists, *Minotaure,* published in June 1933 by Albert Skira. The completion of that collage in May 1933 inspired him to produce, within the next year or so, a series of eleven etchings and various drawings of the Minotaur, showing the Minotaur in extraordinary situations—embracing or raping nude women, participating in a bacchanal, drinking with artists, wounded, and blinded, with a little girl as his guide. In spring 1935 he completed his most ambitious etching up to that time, the *Minotauromachy,* in which he intermingled the previously separate themes of the Minotaur and bullfights; and in May–June 1937 he painted the vast canvas *Guernica,*[152] which is arguably the best-known work of art of the twentieth century. In these drawings and etchings of the Minotaur, one sees a broad range of symbols, from savage force to pathos, from passion to ambivalence.

In 1938, at age seventeen, Michael Ayrton published his very first piece on any subject, which he later described as "a short and badly written panegyric on the *Guernica* when it was shown in London during that year" (1971, 240). In each of the next three decades (in 1944, 1956, and 1969) Ayrton would write a piece on Picasso, all generally critical, yet with more than a hint of respect. There are also some surprising parallels between Ayrton and Picasso, although Ayrton may not have been aware of them. At age sixteen, Picasso copied the old masters in the Prado in Madrid, and at age sixteen Ayrton copied the old masters in the Albertina Museum in Vienna. Like Picasso, Ayrton chose to use his mother's name over his father's. Ayrton's most direct challenge to Picasso can be seen in his recurring images of the Minotaur, beginning in 1962 (see chapter 5).

An insight into Picasso's fascination, even obsession, and identification with the Minotaur theme is found in these words of one of his critics: "The inexhaustible sexuality of the Minotaur particularly fascinated Picasso, and many of the drawings and etchings show the Minotaur making love to a woman with such violent

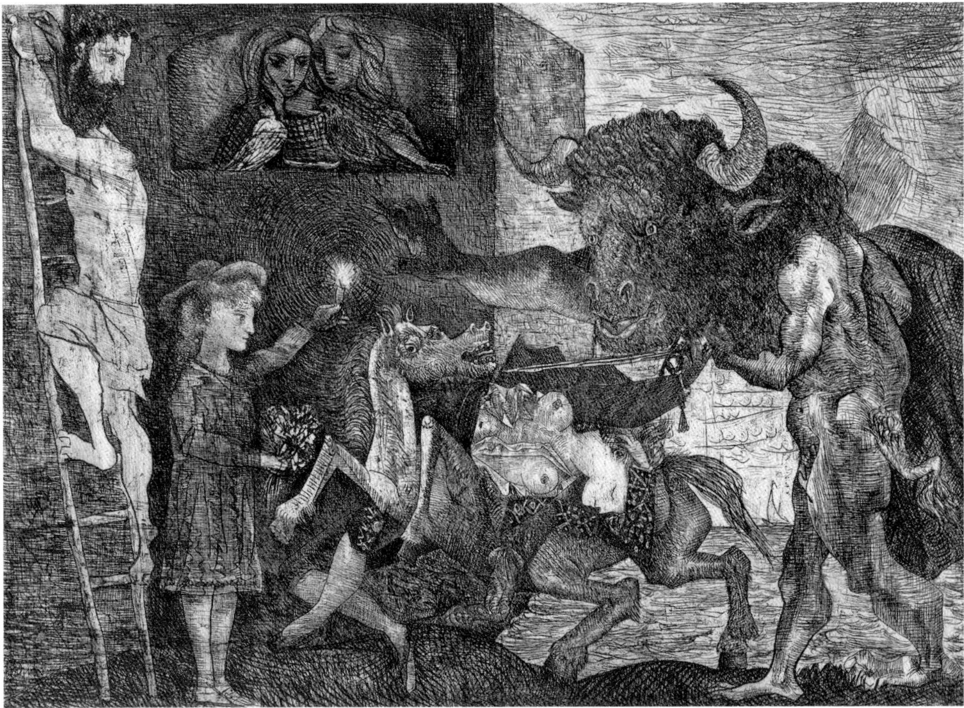

Figure 12. Pablo Picasso, **MINOTAUROMACHY** (1935).

urgency that it is indistinguishable from rape, just as her ecstasy is indistinguishable from pain."[153] In comments on Picasso's monumental *Minotaur and Nude* (1933; ink and wash on paper), the same critic notes the eroticism also present in Picasso's contemporary paintings of bull-fights and observes that these works "turn on exactly the same theme of the intimate relationship between love and death, passion and violence"; the woman to whom the Minotaur makes love is said to resemble Marie-Thérèse Walter, his mistress.[154] It is also significant that a small pencil drawing of another hybrid, the centaur, completed in 1920, adumbrates his treatment of the Minotaur. *Nessus and Dejanira* (12 September 1920)[155] expresses lust in the face of the centaur and, by the way that Nessus grips the nude wife of Heracles, implies his intention of raping her.

Picasso's *Minotauromachy* etching (Bloch 288; see Figure 12) gave forceful expression to his feelings about political events occuring in Europe at the time. On the right, the Minotaur rises out of the sea and proceeds inland. He is depicted as a man with a disproportionately large head and neck of a bull or bison, growing on and extending far forward from his shoulders. In his path are a female matador and her horse, which the Minotaur has disemboweled. He reaches past them toward a girl with a candle and a flower. Behind her a man flees in terror, climbing a ladder, but looking back at the scene of destruction. Above the girl, at a window, are two women, apparently observing two doves on the window ledge, who seem oblivious to the actual and impending destruction. The Minotaur stands out as a symbol of brutality in the midst of weaker symbols of hope and light, represented by the young girl with the candle and flowers.

It was tempting for critics to interpret this etching in explicit terms. Did the Minotaur represent Hitler? Did the little girl represent the naïveté of France and Russia trying to pacify Nazi Germany? Did the women in the window represent the United States and the Allies?

In response to the temptation to interpret this and other Minotaur etchings as representing specific historical events, Herbert Read declared:

> It would not be appropriate to discuss on this occasion the psychological significance of the imagery proliferated by Picasso in this phase of his work. . . . But one may say quite briefly that the imagery is archetypal—that it is an iconography of sex and fertility, of birth and death, of love and violence, such as we find in all great epochs of art. To reveal the significance of the symbols is not a useful activity: they remain most potent in their secret integrity. They come from the unconscious and speak to the unconscious. We unrobe them at our peril.[156]

There can be no doubt, however, that *Guernica* (Zervos IX, 65; see Figure 13) is a reaction to a horrible event of the Spanish Civil War. This large oil was painted in direct and immediate response to the report of the bombing of the Basque town of Guernica by German bombers on 28 April 1937. The similarities in execution to the *Minotauromachy* are readily apparent, although it has been suggested—wrongly, I believe—that the recurrence of the archetypal symbols of the bull, the horse, and an individual holding up a light may have been more unconscious than deliberate.[157] It has also been argued that Picasso combined in *Guernica* his classical linear style with "surreal recordings of the subconscious" and that "his contouring, the use of detail motifs, and the perspective" all were determined by "the basic idiom of children's drawings," which was, for Picasso, "evidently a completely new discovery."[158]

Commenting on *Guernica,* Read interprets Picasso's choice of symbols in psychoanalytic terms:

> It is a picture so rich in symbolic significance, that one is almost persuaded that Picasso has at some time made a study of Jung and Kerényi! In addition to the figure of the Wise Man . . . we have the Minotaur, representing the dark powers of the labyrinthine unconscious; the sacrificial horse, bearing on its back the overpowered libido; and confronting them the divine child, the culture bearer, the bringer of light, the child-hero who fearlessly confronts the powers of darkness, the bearer of a higher consciousness.[159]

Although Read questions whether the use of these symbols is deliberate manipulation by "a man of culture who reads voraciously" or simply the product of Picasso's unconscious, nevertheless he implies that they are the spontaneous expression of the artist's unconscious: "Artistic creation, to the same degree and in the same manner as effective symbols, implies spontaneity: the artistically valid symbols are those which rise, fully armed by the libido, from the depths of the unconscious."[160]

Because *Guernica* is a work of such power and complexity, critical analyses abound on every aspect of the painting, as well as of the painting as a whole. Rudolf Arnheim's *Picasso's Guernica* is a groundbreaking piece of criticism of this work. Arnheim analyzes the preparatory drawings in relation to the final canvas, deducing decisions Picasso made along the way and the probable reasons for these choices. To provide a context for his analysis, Arnheim presents his introductory "Notes on Creativity." He traces the history of attempts to understand and explain the creative powers of humankind, in a broad sweep from the Greeks to Determinism, Freud, and Jung. In contrast to Herbert Read's elevation of spontaneity to preeminence in the creative process, Arnheim argues that artists ought not succumb to "spontaneous impulses," which tend to be chaotic, but should use them as "raw material for invention," remembering that spontaneity differs "in kind from those sudden happy solutions that are the fruit of much selective observing, sifting, and molding, both conscious and unconscious" (1962, 8). A creative person's "visionary attitude" consists in "visual thinking," which takes the perceived objects literally and, at the same time, symbolically, in much the same way that we engage in abstract thinking.[161] In his interpretation of *Guernica,* Arnheim (1962, 10–11) employs the "elements of a grammar for visual thinking" developed by Freud in the sixth chapter of his *Interpretation of Dreams.*

Although Arnheim affirms Herbert Read's interpretation of the *Minotauromachy* in terms of Jungian archetypes, he finds such an interpretation inadequate for *Guernica* because of its very obvious linkage to a specific, brutal, military assault upon the town (1962, 16). Through a careful analysis of *Guernica*'s evolution, studying both Picasso's preliminary drawings and photographs taken by

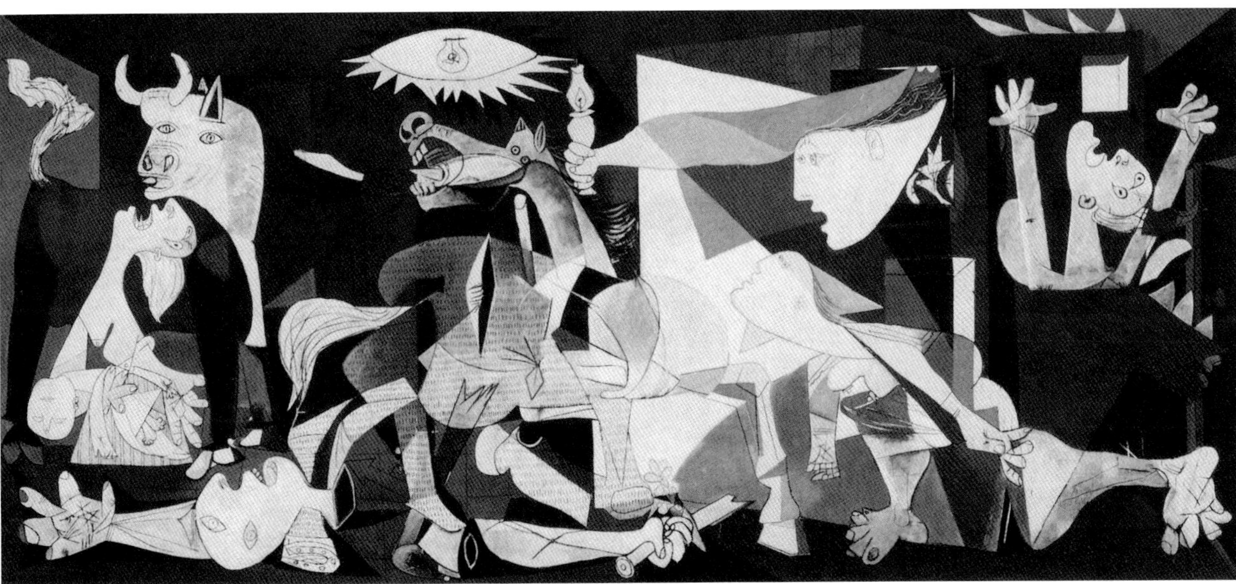

Figure 13. Pablo Picasso, **GUERNICA** (1937).
Museo Nacional Centro de Arte Reina Sofia, Madrid. © 2002 Estate of Pablo Picasso/Artists Rights Society.

Dora Maar of each step of the process, Arnheim sought to determine the visual thinking that led Picasso from his initial concept for the work to the finished painting. Tracing the visual thinking that led to the alteration or substitution of one motif for another, or the discarding of yet another motif, helps one better to understand not only how Picasso worked but even the creative process in general (1962, 16). Similarly, the study of Michael Ayrton's treatment of the myth of Daedalus is intended to provide insight not merely into Ayrton's visual thinking but also and especially to demonstrate the vital role of myth in the creative process.

At its most elementary level, *Guernica* is a painting completed in fulfillment of a commission awarded to Picasso in January 1937 by the Spanish government in exile. Picasso's mural for their building at the World's Fair in Paris was not begun, however, until 1 May 1937, less than a week after Hitler's massive assault upon Guernica. The commission required that Picasso "convey in one image the sense of the drama of his fatherland ravished by the Fascists." This was no easy task, but the bombing of Guernica on 26 April 1937, "acted as the catalyst for the creative invention" (Arnheim 1962, 17).

In order to achieve the desired reality level, Picasso had to create a distance from the "actual Basque town," but he also had to "dematerialize each object and break up the continuity of physical space" (Arnheim 1962, 21):

> In other words, the search for the proper style, which, as the sketches will show, was a principal concern of Picasso's, cannot be considered a matter of whim or taste. Since the reality level required by the meaning of the picture strictly determined the amount and kind of deviation from realism he could introduce, he had to find for his shapes the style that corresponded to the appropriate ratio between the faithful portrayal of a historic episode and the expression of certain ideas. His ways of drawing an eye or hand anywhere in the picture determined whether the bull would appear as a domestic animal in a Spanish town, as an apparition, a miracle, an allegory, or as one of a number of figures intended to depict suffering and hope through a war episode.

Arnheim quite rightly contends that a proper comparison of the *Minotauromachy* and *Guernica* "would show to what an astonishing extent an artist's images are independent of the meaning he makes them carry in any particular instance, and would help to keep us from assuming automatically that the same pictorial motif represents the same meaning in different contexts" (1962, 21). Arnheim demonstrates his point forcefully by focusing on the bull, which appears in both works but cannot carry the same meaning in *Guernica* as in the *Minotauromachy.*

In *Guernica* the bull presents an "extreme of stability" in symmetry with the falling woman, who "presents the extreme lack of support": "the falling woman's isolation is that of the final catastrophe. The bull is outside that catastrophe, appealed to, but unaffected. . . . *Guernica* is not victory but defeat—a sprawling chaos, shown as temporary by its dynamic appeal to the dominant, timeless figure of the kingly beast" (Arnheim 1962, 23). Viewing the bull as the enemy, says Arnheim, would do violence to the purpose of the commission, to Marxist thought, and to the "indomitable spirit of Spain," whereas his own interpretation broadens the "philosophical and religious concept, from suffering as the state of man to suffering as a contingent affliction of the indestructible human soul" (1962, 23–24). Furthermore, viewing Picasso's oeuvre demonstrates that this "powerful animal is identified with Picasso himself, with the creative artist, the lusty, overpowering male" and the "Minotaur . . . is an impersonation" (Arnheim 1962, 27).

A very different interpretation of the bull was advanced by Carla Gottlieb a few years after Arnheim's study was published. She contends that the image of the bull is best suited to the French Republic, that the horse represents "specific victims: the massacred civilian population of the Basque town," that the woman at the right stands for Russia, and that the other women are allegorical symbols, "i.e. the embodiment of an abstract idea."[162] Yet another avenue of exploration is pursued by William Darr, who gives a thoroughly Freudian interpretation, which takes as its starting point Françoise Gilot's recounting of "Picasso's story of the wrestling match that took place between Marie Thérèse Walter and Dora Maar in his Rue des Grands-Augustins studio while he was painting Guernica."[163] Darr contends that *Guernica* is to be understood in the context of Freud's *Civilization and its Discontents* (1929) and Freud's "thesis of a death affirming principle, Thanatos, paralleling the life affirming principle, Eros."[164] The structure of the frame or room is seen as "Picasso's metaphor of *Guernica* as the world of the mind paralleling Freud's analogy of Rome as a city of the mind."[165] Central to Darr's thesis is the interpretation of the "strange harlequin diamond that breaks across the horse's body" as the "image of the female genitalia . . . with its clear Freudian implications of sex displaced and repressed, unrecognized female death wish that parallels the phallic spear."[166] By means of the condensation of images, Picasso fills the foreground of this painting "with overlapping death and life elements related to Freudian concepts,"[167] and these elements reflect not only the larger themes of war and bullfights but also the very personal circumstances of Picasso's life:

> Françoise Gilot says that Marie Thérèse was the woman with the light for Picasso, and that Dora Maar was already the weeping woman that figures again and again in the paintings of the following years as Dora Maar's sanity eroded away. Picasso seems to see the civil war of Spain with its international overtones as the extension of an even more fundamental disturbance within the self, that the crises in his own life and in the lives of those he loved and who loved him were in their own meaning parallel catastrophes that provided him with the powerful images and metaphors that would make a universal statement because they were personal, terribly individual, but above all, human.[168]

As for the meaning of these symbols in *Guernica,* Picasso himself declared: "the bull is not fascism, but it is brutality and darkness. . . . [T]he horse represents the people. . . . [T]he Guernica mural is symbolic . . . allegoric. That's the reason I use the bull, the horse, and so on. The mural is for the definite expression and solution of a problem and that is why I used symbolism."[169] Although one should not discount these assertions, neither should one assume that the meaning of the painting is limited to the artist's conscious awareness of the ideas that emerged from his unconscious.

Picasso's social conscience was revealed not only in this powerful mural, but also in public statements such as this: "What do you think an artist is? An imbecile who

"Icarus was, before his birth, and remains after his death, the image of man's disquiet, of the impulse to discovery, the soaring flight of poetry—the things of which, during his short life, he was the incarnation."

has only his eyes if he is a painter. . . ? On the contrary, he's at the same time a political being, constantly alive to heartrending, fiery or happy events, to which he responds in every way. . . . No, painting is not done to decorate apartments. It is an instrument of war for attack and defence against the enemy."[170]

Picasso also offered an insight into the creative process with his comments on how a picture changes during its creation: "A picture is not thought out and settled beforehand. While it is being done it changes as one's thoughts change. And when it is finished, it still goes on changing, according to the state of mind of whoever is looking at it. A picture lives a life like a living creature, undergoing the changes imposed on us by our life from day to day. This is natural enough, as the picture lives only through the man who is looking at it."[171] Picasso's opinion that pictures continue to change with each viewing adumbrates the reader-response criticism that flourished around the time of his death.

With word and image Picasso constantly challenged his contemporaries. His great versatility and prolific creativity compel us to consider and compare his work to his predecessors, his contemporaries and his successors.

In September 1919, André Gide (1869–1951) published an essay in *La Nouvelle Revue Françaises,* entitled "Considérations sur la mythologie grecque." In it he describes the continuing relevance of Greek myths and attributes this relevance to his belief that they reify universal expressions of the human psyche. It is not surprising, therefore, that Gide himself drew upon Greek myth in his own work.

Gide's *Theseus,* first published in 1946, was his last work, but the idea of rewriting this legend was formed more than thirty years earlier. Both Daedalus and Icarus figure in this semi-autobiographical, philosophical novella, but they, like Theseus, differ greatly from their ancient representations. In Gide's work, for example, Daedalus tells Theseus that he constructed the labyrinth in such a way that a prisoner *would not* want to escape from it, rather than constructing it so that he *could not* escape. He accomplished this by burning in ever-lit stoves certain plants that emitted semi-narcotic vapors as they burned; the pleasurable intoxication induced by the inhalation of these vapors led each prisoner to lose himself in "a labyrinth of his own devising," which resulted from the "complexities implicit in his own mind."[172] The complexities of Icarus's mind are metaphysical, and he appears briefly, at his father's request, soliloquizing about the nature of God and the relation of man to the divine, although Daedalus tells Theseus that the poor boy is in fact dead, having already fallen into the sea.[173] The idea that the labyrinth is within oneself, rather than external, was later to be accepted and much more fully developed by Michael Ayrton.

Gide's description of Icarus is a powerful interpretation and adaptation of myth: "Icarus was, before his birth, and remains after his death, the image of man's disquiet, of the impulse to discovery, the soaring flight of poetry—the things of which, during his short life, he was the incarnation. He played out his hand, as he owed it to himself to do; but he didn't end there. What happens, in the case of a hero, is this: his mark endures. Poetry and the arts reanimate it, and it becomes an enduring symbol."[174] Implicit in Gide's description of Icarus is Sartre's belief that the desire to be godlike lies behind all human striving. Pride, for Sartre and for Gide, is the quality that makes one human. Icarus as the symbol of that pride has been a recurring theme through the centuries, although the belief system of an age (and of the artist as its interpreter) shapes the way in which Icarus is portrayed. The idealization of the spirit is concomitant for Sartre with the death of God.[175] Gide's view of the labyrinth as a metaphorical complexity of the mind stands in sharp contrast to the visualization of the labyrinth in the work of the Lithuanian-born American artist, Ben Shahn (1898–1969).

The labyrinth, a central symbol of the Daedalus myth, is the title and focus of a 1952 tempera painting by Shahn. In *Labyrinth* (Plate 6) Shahn continues his use of

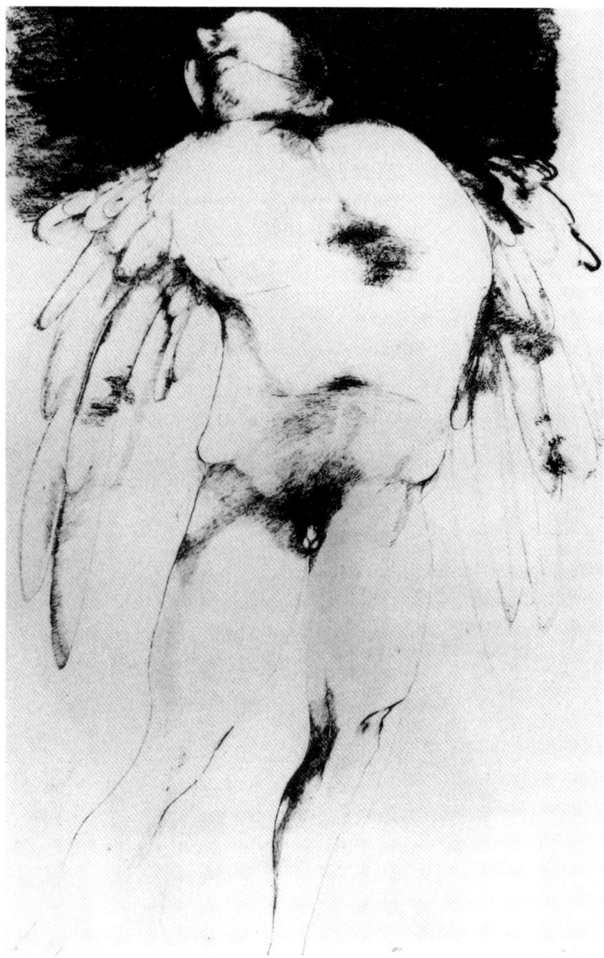

Figure 14. Leonard Baskin, **ICARUS, 1967**.

allegory and classical allusion that he began years earlier. Icarus plunges headfirst toward the rectangular maze in the lower right of the painting. The blazing shades of red and orange evoke the sun; bird imagery and an impressionistic blue sky recall the flight. These bright colors dominate the upper half of the painting, but so powerful are the ghostlike face of Icarus and the black and grey labyrinth that they command the viewer's attention more than the brilliant hues above them. The suggestion of Icarus's return in flight to the labyrinth, equipped with his wings, reminds one of Gide's *Theseus,* with Icarus and Daedalus as post-flight occupants of the maze. The labyrinth here, however, must surely also symbolize the final maze of death, as the somber tones of the lower portion suggest.

The maze or labyrinth is an inherently abstract creation, whether etched on a wall or stone in antiquity or employed as an organizing principle for modern literature. Given Ayrton's dedication to figurative sculpture over against abstraction, it may seem surprising that this abstract concept should play such a large role in Ayrton's art. At the same time, because the labyrinth was a fundamental element of the Daedalus myth, it would have seemed extremely odd for him to ignore it. In his treatment of the labyrinth, Ayrton was influenced by contemporary writers such as the Argentine short-story writer, Jorge Luis Borges (1899–1986), whose *Labyrinths* (1962) is filled with imaginary and symbolic worlds, with the labyrinth as their organizing principle. It was said that Borges had "read everything" and that his "erudition is not profound . . . but it is vast."[176] Borges's short stories are masterful creations of a labyrinth of the imagination, with a city where things become duplicated, with the dreamer who is dreamed, with a garden of forking paths, with a book which itself is a labyrinth, and with endlessly recurring patterns. In "The Garden of the Forking Paths," the narrator says, "I thought of a labyrinth of labyrinths, one sinuous spreading labyrinth that would encompass the past and the future and in some way involve the stars" (1962, 48). The circular repetition of history and the idea of endless recurrence are themes that flow through his stories, reflecting the endless variability of human thought and imagination. As André Maurois says in his preface to

Borges's *Labyrinths,* "Any great and lasting book must be ambiguous, says Borges; it is a mirror that makes the reader's features known" (1962, 10). By its very nature, a labyrinth or maze is ambiguous. Ayrton repeatedly and very effectively illustrated this point in both word and image, as will become clear in subsequent chapters. And he held up to his reader and to the viewer of his sculptures a mirror that makes one's features known, drawing us into a deepening awareness of ourselves as we seek to plumb the depth of this richly evocative archetype.

Leonard Baskin (1922–2000), an artist who was connected with both Shahn and Ayrton (see chapter 1), created several representations of Daedalus and Icarus at the same time that Ayrton was well into his obsession with the myth. Baskin also created numerous birds, bird-men (bronze, aluminum; seated, standing; 1961– 1964), and other figures, such as the *Sibyl* and *Seated Fat Man,* a number of which resonate with or even resemble Ayrton's work, leading one to conclude that there may have been some mutual influence. At times, in fact, the similarities are so strong that one cannot conclude otherwise, whether or not either artist was aware of being influenced by the other.

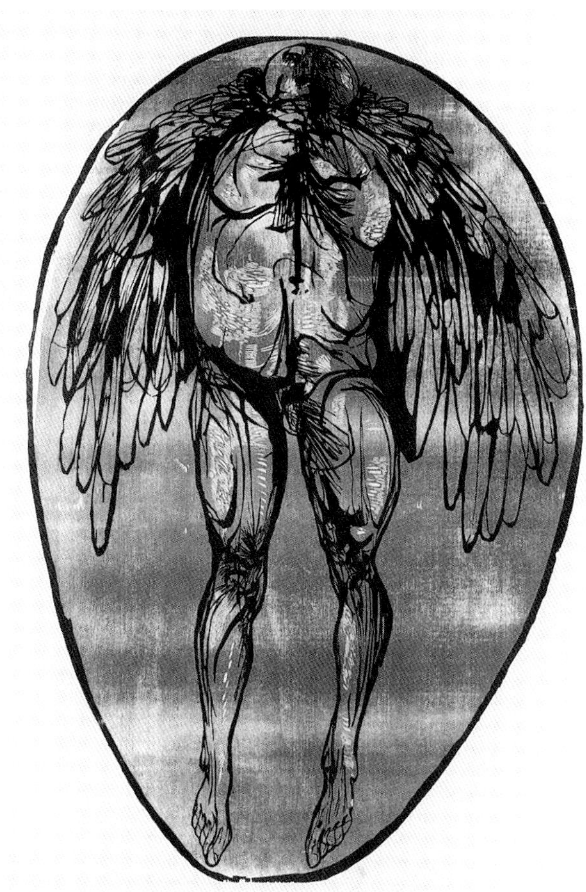

Figure 15. Leonard Baskin, **ICARUS** (1967).
© Estate of Leonard Baskin.
Courtesy of the Library of Congress.

Baskin's *Icarus, 1967*[177] (see Figure 14) is an ink drawing of a nude male with bird's feathers in place of arms. His head is thrown back and his chest thrust out in a manner suggestive of Ayrton's *Icarus Rising* (1961; Cat. No. 206), although the two works are otherwise quite dissimilar. A colorful woodcut of the same year and same title, *Icarus, 1967*[178] (see Figure 15), expands and extends the mass of feathers growing out of the shoulders, but Icarus appears suspended, dangling from an imaginary cord, with his musculature accentuated. Icarus's head resembles the heads of some of Ayrton's figures from the myth. Baskin's *Daedalus,* a 41-inch bronze of the same year, is clearly a self-portrait (see Figure 16).[179] Earlier Baskin took up the theme of the archetypal artist with his nearly life-size bronze of *Hephaestus* (1963)—the divine artisan who created the armor of Achilles and whom Homer compared to Daedalus in *Iliad* 18—which was likewise a self-portrait, as was his bronze of the seer *Teiresias* (1963).[180] The fact that Baskin illustrated the *Iliad* a year earlier has been suggested as the stimulus for his *Hephaestus.*[181] It is also possible, however, to see these

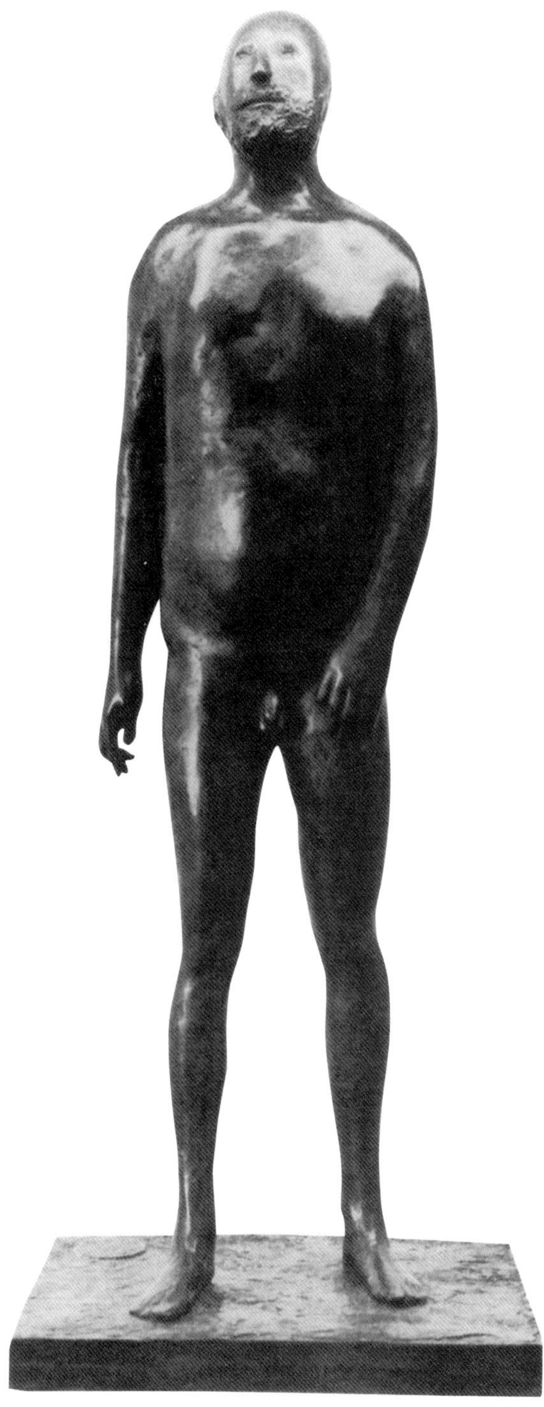

Figure 16. Leonard Baskin, **DAEDALUS** (1967).

works as further evidence of the role of myth in the creative process and to see in Baskin's choice of both Hephaestus and Daedalus as reflections of the aspirations of a sculptor. Ayrton's personal identification with Daedalus clearly reflects such aspirations, as subsequent chapters will reveal. Already before 1949, Baskin took up the myth of Prometheus, the giver of the civilizing arts to humankind and archetypal ceramist who created the human race from clay.[182] All three figures—Hephaestus, Prometheus, and Daedalus—are associated with the creation of art; all are natural inspirations for artists and craftspeople. In 1969, the year in which he also created a small bronze relief of the *Minotaur* and a 38-inch bronze of *Theseus,* Baskin returned to the theme of Icarus, with a small bronze relief of the winged youth, bearing the simple title *Icarus.*[183] His repeated treatment of this myth is related to a significant number of other works (e.g., Abraham and Isaac) that deal with the relationship between father and son, a theme that reflects his own struggles in his relationship with his father, a rabbi, as well as reflecting a fundamental human source of both tension and strength. Like so many other artists, Baskin repeatedly uses myth to provide the psychic distance necessary to handle personal struggles, personal conflicts and tensions, personal fears and anxieties.

CONCLUSION

This survey of artistic treatments of the myth of Daedalus and some of the attendant figures encompassed within the cycle of myth surrounding him illustrates the continuing vitality of myth throughout the centuries. The foregoing selection of artistic interpretations and evocative employment of these myths offers compelling evidence of the significant role that myth plays in the creative process.[184] It is apparent that Malinowski's description of "myth in a primitive society . . . [as] not a mere tale told but a reality lived"[185] could apply equally well to a number of twentieth-century artists, although it will become particularly clear in the ensuing description of Michael Ayrton's progressive involvement with this cycle of myth. For him, and for many other writers and visual artists, "myths are the instruments by which we continually struggle to make our experience intelligible to ourselves."[186]

The close relationship between word and image, between literary and artistic creation, demonstrates the need to take myth seriously. As poet Archibald MacLeish reminds us most forcefully:

> A world ends when its metaphor has died. . . .
> It perishes when those images, though seen,
> No longer mean.[187]

Myth clearly is, for numerous poets, writers, and visual artists, "the matrix out of which [art and] literature [emerge], both historically and psychologically."[188] Although many of our contemporaries consider myth an anachronism in an age dominated by science and technology, the Mexican poet Octavio Paz has rightly observed, in his *Labyrinth of Solitude:* "Contemporary man has rationalized the myths, but he has not been able to destroy them."[189] Such is the dynamism, the vitality, of the Greek myths that they have not disappeared, although they have been adapted, modified, analyzed, psychologized, rationalized, and even radically transformed over the centuries. Mirroring and enlarging human experience, they are at once universal and particular, relevant to an entire society and to a single individual.

Through the Cumaean Gate

"The greatest leaps forward, which appear at intervals to lend credence to the notion of progress in the arts, all tend to arise from withdrawing further into the past than is the current practice at the time. The principle of *recueiller pour mieux sauter* is the instinct of genius. . . ." wrote Michael Ayrton in 1960 when commenting on Georges Seurat's "Une Baignade, Asnières" (1971, 74).

Throughout much of his career, Ayrton himself was engaged in "withdrawing further into the past." In Vienna, when he was only fifteen, he devoted himself to copying the old masters, and, ten years later, when he made his first trip to Italy, he began burrowing even more deeply into the past. But in 1956 he went really deeply into an earlier time. From that point onward his art and his writings reached across the centuries all the way back to classical antiquity, building a bridge to the past while remaining firmly anchored in the present epoch.

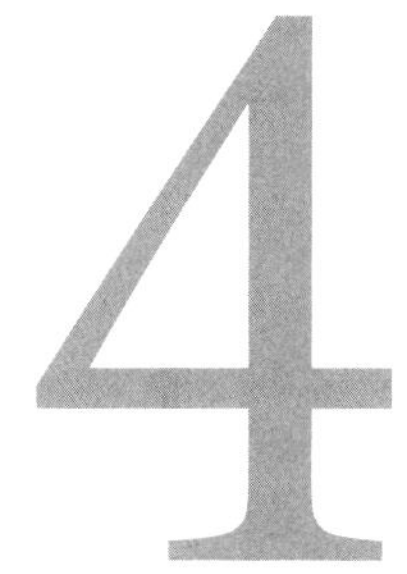

At the age of thirty-five Ayrton began his travels into antiquity, into a world of myth, art, and literature. On that day in May 1956 when he arrived at Cumae, on the Bay of Naples, he was first attracted to the myth of Daedalus. He did not consciously decide to use the myth as a focus for his art, nor did he begin at its beginning. Instead he came upon it near its end, at the point where Daedalus ended his winged flight from Crete. Although he later looked back upon his arrival at Cumae as an act guided by destiny, much as Virgil's Aeneas arrived there driven by a sense of destiny, nevertheless Ayrton's motivation for his visit to Cumae had no apparent relationship to the myth of Daedalus, except only in the most oblique and circuitous manner.

It was, however, Ayrton's first obsession that led him into his second, more enduring one. The music of Hector Berlioz had for a decade held a strong attraction for Ayrton when, in 1947, he heard for the first time a performance of Berlioz's opera, *Les Troyens.*[1] Moved by this "greatest of all nineteenth century music drama" perhaps as deeply as Berlioz had been stirred by Virgil's *Aeneid,* Ayrton made his first extended visit to Italy in 1947 with the opera still resounding in his head. But it was nearly a decade and many visits later before he finally arrived at Cumae, where Virgil's Aeneas landed in search of his father's ghost. It was here, said Ayrton, that he first confronted Virgil's epic poem directly, rather than through Berlioz's opera, and it was as a result of this place that he, at age thirty-five, read the *Aeneid* for the first time (1969, 176f.).

Although some of his writings, such as "The Path to Daedalus," would seem to imply that Ayrton went to Italy because of Berlioz, he admitted that it was merely coincidental that he heard *Les Troyens* before his first lengthy visit to Italy. He was planning to travel to Italy at the first opportunity after the defeat of Mussolini and the Fascists in order to complete his artistic education. Nonetheless, this coincidence haunted his involvement with the myth of Daedalus, for he was a man who saw deeper meaning in such coincidences.[2]

Ayrton's first visit to Italy centered on northern Italy, the Italy of the Renaissance. The way he usually worked was to delve deeply into a subject or an era, reading extensively and studying the art of an epoch very thoroughly. In this instance, his reading focused upon Masaccio and Piero della Francesca, and he "made pilgrimage through the landscape to every relevant church and museum in Lombardy, Tuscany and Umbria" (Ayrton 1969, 178). His attention next turned to the precursors of the Renaissance, Giotto and the Pisani. In each successive annual visit to Italy, he sought to penetrate to the heart of another era, another stratum in the history of art and society. He therefore "traveled" through medieval Italy and the Etruscans, working his way counter-chronologically down to Greek Italy, to Magna Graecia, a region settled in the eighth century B.C.E. by Greeks from Euboean Chalcis.

When Ayrton reached Cumae, he therefore arrived with an exceptional literary and art historical background, but not one that included the Daedalus myth, except in the most rudimentary form. He had done one pen and watercolor of Icarus in early 1940 (Cat. No. 1), probably under the influence of one of his early teachers, Pavel Tchelitchev, "whose work in the early 40s included oblique references to classical myth and particularly to the myths of Daedalus and Icarus."[3] Since this early treatment of Icarus never came up in any of his accounts of his involvement with the myth, Ayrton either was not conscious of this work, or (more likely) he conveniently ignored it. Nonetheless, this work is recorded in his master record book for 1940, and it was exhibited during that year at Leicester Galleries. At the very least, then, Icarus was part of his subconscious world. Dr. Justine Hopkins, who asserts that Ayrton, John Minton, and Michael Middleton delayed their departure from Paris for a summer in Les Baux in order to "see Serge Lifar dance in the ballet *Icare* at the Opéra, a performance which inspired Michael to a painting, *Icarus*,"[4] sees in this work an adumbration of Ayrton's later engagement with the myth: "in intensity, if not in style, this picture foreshadows that obsession."[5]

Hopkins describes this *Icarus* as follows:

> Against a star-spangled sky a tiny winged figure soars upward above a landscape of jutting rocks and strewn boulders; Hell's valley rendered in the idiom of the theatre. The foreground is dominated by three enigmatic figures, a bearded man, a woman and a child of indeterminate sex garlanded with flowers, who stares out of the picture space as from a stage. All three are drawn in starkly distorted pen line and hatching. . . . The colour is muted, a blued monochrome deepening towards the darkness of the distant sea, lit to sinister pallor at the horizon. The mood evoked is one of mysterious melancholy; it is also obscurely disquieting.[6]

She suggests that its "theatricality and distorted perspective recall Berman and Tchelitchew."[7]

Ayrton may not have recalled his early rendition of Icarus, but he did remember having read in Plato's *The Greater Hippias* how Daedalus found himself "dismissed as outdated by Plato's connoisseurs" (1969, 178).[8] And he knew the Cumaean Sibyl, Virgil's Deiphobe, "only as Michelangelo had shown her to me on the Sistine Chapel ceiling" (1969, 180), but she was his first subject after his arrival. She appeared first as a Cumaean peasant woman but later came to be identified by the artist with the legendary Sibyl herself (Cat. Nos. 5–9).

Despite the dramatic coincidence that brought Ayrton to the spot on Monte di Procida overlooking the causeway at the end of which rose the acropolis of Cumae, it was neither the music of Berlioz, the art of Michelangelo, nor the rich literary and mythical heritage of Cumae that captured him. Rather, it was the site itself:

> The place flung a net over me. Places do. It is invariably a place, a landscape, a building, even a heap of stones marking the site of long habitation which starts in me the need to make the objects in bronze or paint, or even verse and prose, upon which my time is spent. The landscape at Cumae is numinous. It accepts every blemish and every indignity put upon it by twentieth century man. He has made a slum of its setting, but its power is not reduced by the railway lines, tumbledown beach houses and squalid bungalows he has caused to crowd about the isthmus. (1969, 179)

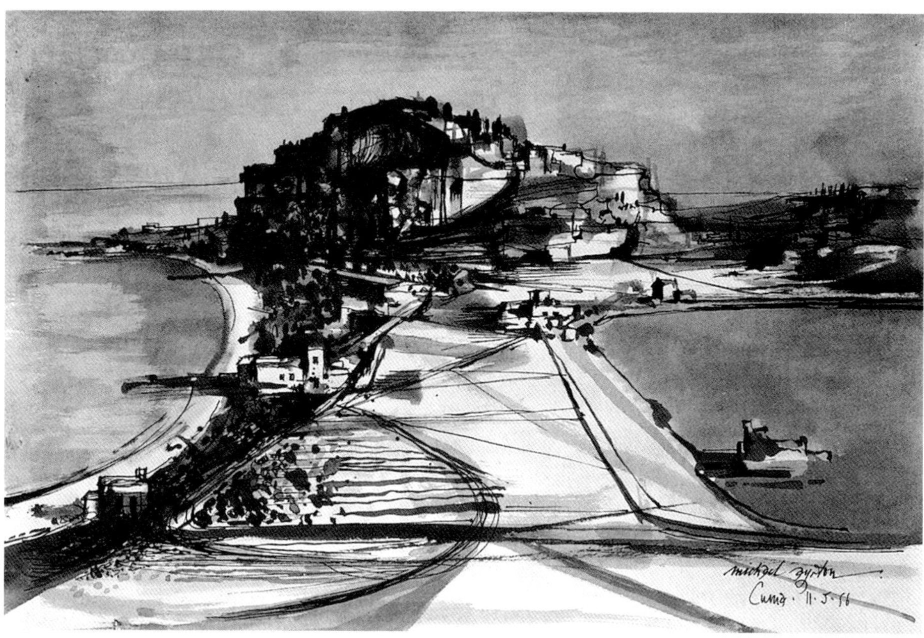

Figure 17. **CUMA** (Cat. No. 10; 11 May 1956).

With his initial interest sparked by the site itself, he innocently began his wanderings in the myth of Daedalus on 11 May 1956. On that day of great moment for him, Ayrton made a wash drawing of the acropolis of Cumae (Cat. No. 10, *Cuma*; Figure 17), trying to record it literally. As one observes the drawing, one has a sense of standing with the artist below the crest of the hill, Monte di Procida, above the bay and looking out along the causeway that separates the lagoon (or "the pallid lake" as Ayrton called it, 1967, 151)[9] from the Bay of Naples and then juts sharply upward into an imposing acropolis. The foreshortening of the causeway accentuates the heavily shadowed rock, whereas the third drawing of the acropolis (Cat. No. 12), which Ayrton sketched the following day, achieves its dramatic effect through an elongation of the causeway and a transference of the deep shadows to the two bodies of water. In this drawing perhaps it is the approach to this intriguing rock as much as the acropolis itself that the artist wished to emphasize. Several paintings followed (Cat. Nos. 13–15; 1956), later giving rise to a print (Cat. No. 16; 1957), all depicting the jutting rock capped with ruins of a temple to Apollo and ventilated by numerous entrances to the Sibyl's subterranean labyrinth.

After sketching the rock from a distance, he walked along the isthmus to approach the place that had fired his imagination. When he got there, he found and entered "the labyrinth of passages that honeycomb the great rock," and he sensed the numinous quality of the place, he felt its spiritual power. He answered its silent command, responding to the call of a myth that "lengthens and thickens, coiling like a labyrinth around itself."[10] This "numinous" rock provided the stimulus for an inter mingling of the music, art, literature, and myth that comprised Ayrton's life.

Along the path at the top of the acropolis he made a discovery that further sparked his curiosity and began to draw him into the myth itself. He discovered some inscribed stone slabs, on which were recorded the Latin text of Virgil's *Aeneid* 6.9–44 (see chapter 2). With difficulty he read the eloquent but subtle Virgilian compression of the myth of Daedalus, but its effect transcended the barriers of language, as his own description reveals:

> As I sat gazing at the inscription and at the overgrown escarpment shining in the afternoon sun, a fragment of Michelangelo's verse came into my mind. It is a mysterious

"When I am nailed by the gods and my insides are drawn into the intestinal maze of Daedalus, my feet remain firmly in the present and I am aware of what is around me."

> expostulation and reads: "This is the way Daedalus rose. This is the way the sun rejects the shadow." In that to me fateful moment, I was conscious of being possessed and the acropolis of Cumae with its "hundred mouthways" cut to make audible the subterranean Sibyls [*sic*] mantic utterances, came to haunt me, as it has done ever since. (1969, 178)

These words are part of an elaboration on his debt to Virgil, in which he declared that "for ten years a single page from Book VI of the Aeneid has been central to my work in sculpture, painting, drawing and writing" (1969, 176). One should not conclude, however, from Ayrton's Virgilian compression of the story about his involvement with the myth that he used only this passage as his source of information or as the stimulus for his creativity.

When Ayrton was drawn to a theme, a symbol, a metaphor, an artist, or a period of art history, a seemingly insatiable thirst for knowledge and insight would impel him to penetrate deeper and deeper into his subject. When he succumbed to the Renaissance, he pursued it single-mindedly. When Giovanni Pisano attracted his attention, he devoted all his energies and attention to him and his age. His concentration on a single period resulted, he said, from the fact that he could not "trot round and through the centuries in a morning like a tourist, but must move, as it were, through time and shut out the future of an age or its past where that is not clearly germane" (1969, 179). Therefore, when he got to Greek Italy, and especially to Cumae, the place and then the myth became his exclusive, obsessive concern.

It would be a distortion of Ayrton's life and art to suggest that his progressive involvement with this myth shut him off from observing and interacting with his environment. Quite the contrary. Elisabeth described Michael as "enhanced and enchanted" by Cumae and as beginning to become "enmeshed" with Daedalus, but at the same time, in her description of their initial visit to Cumae, she speaks of Michael's easy and pleasurable association with the children and adults of the place and notes that the "only hotel anywhere near Cumae . . . turned out to be a sort of brothel or, rather, a house of assignation."[11] Hopkins also calls attention to the importance of the "close identification which Michael saw, and which was vital for him, of the modern and the mythological dimensions." She observes that the "fact that they stayed in a hotel which doubled as a brothel, and that the main Naples sewer releases into the bay below Monte di Procida were facts which wound themselves into his appreciation of the durability of myth—because as well as despite the abuses of civilisation, he felt the power of the numinous shining through."[12] Ayrton himself made this point in a BBC radio program, "A Silence Filled With Greek" (1978c, 12):

> I'm not, by the way, a sober and scholarly figure nervously divorced from my own time or in love with the past. I like street noises. I am as much committed to twentieth-century politics as Pericles insisted Athenians should be in the fifth century. Furthermore, the two parts—or the many parts—of my illusions are indivisible. When I am nailed by the gods and my insides are drawn into the intestinal maze of Daedalus, my feet remain firmly in the present and I am aware of what is around me.

In one of his descriptions of himself, during this same program, Ayrton called himself "a sort of human truffle-hound nosing for some hidden or disguised meaning in landscape long inhabited. I don't mean that I am an archaeologist or a historian, but rather I am a sort of trawling tourist, equipped with an echo-sounder" (1978c, 9). Later, he declared that when he arrived at Cumae, his echo-sounder "oscillated wildly" (1978c, 10). Whenever that happened to him, he said, he would delve ever more deeply into the place until he felt he had exhausted its creative potential for him. It was obvious to him therefore that he would not escape from Cumae with only an afternoon's visit. He was stuck there for the duration. Little did he realize how long would be the duration of his "trawling" in myth-filled Cumae.

This account of Ayrton's early engagement with the myth of Daedalus and Icarus offers glimpses into the role of myth in the creative process. While still in his teens and scarcely four years after he ended his formal education, Ayrton first painted Icarus. This painting was inspired by a ballet performed in Paris by Serge Lifar. The ballet itself drew upon an age-old myth that had been preserved by its retelling in art and literature through the ages. The evocative power of this myth inspired artist after artist to recreate or reinterpret it, because the myth expresses basic human desires and aspirations.

In like manner, the legend of Troy settled deeply into Ayrton's psyche through the emotive power of music, the music of Berlioz's opera, *Les Troyens.* Therefore, when Ayrton arrived at Cumae, there was imbedded in his subconscious mind (or, in Freudian terms, his "unconscious") an awareness of certain dimensions of several mythical traditions linked with this site. As he responded to his environs, the unconscious emerged into consciousness. In Jungian terms, the collective unconscious—represented by myth, the dreams of an entire race—merged into Ayrton's individual unconscious and emerged as symbols in the form of people and places he sketched and painted. As he gave expression to the images arising from his unconscious, he was bringing forth the collective dream of flight, the dream of escaping the tyranny of the maze of circumstances that entrap us and hold us in their power.[13]

John Freeman, in his introduction to Jung's *Man and his Symbols,* contends that Jung and his colleagues did not limit themselves to formal logic but used a "dialectical method [that] is itself symbolic and often devious": "they convince not by means of the narrowly focused spotlight of the syllogism, but by skirting, by repetition, by presenting a recurring view of the same subject seen each time from a slightly different angle—until suddenly the reader who has never been aware of a single, conclusive moment of proof finds that he has unknowingly embraced and taken into himself some wider truth" (14). As we trace Ayrton's progressive involvement with the myth of Daedalus in all its complexity and variability, we will find ourselves similarly presented with a "recurring view of the same subject seen each time from a slightly different angle" and we will find ourselves the possessors of "some wider truth." Such is the power of myth. Such is the power of Ayrton's appropriation and reformulation of this still-relevant myth.

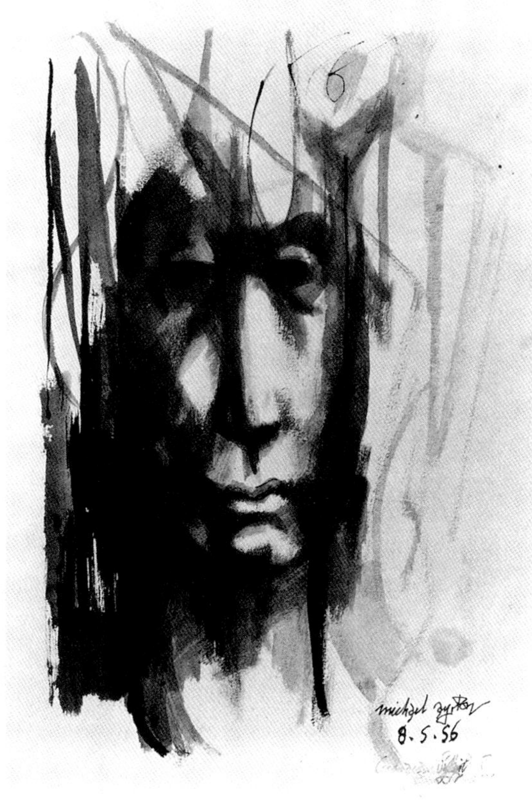

Figure 18. **CUMAEAN SYBIL V** (Cat. No. 9; 8 May 1956).

Ayrton's first two paintings of the acropolis of Cumae (Cat. Nos. 13–14; Plate 10) followed his first drawing by only a few days. Like that wash drawing, the oil attempted a literal representation of the site. He knew little of the implications of that place, but the knowledge would come later. Twelve years later, however, he claimed that from the moment he first saw the rock of Cumae from the vineyard on Monte di Procida he knew he "had reached a moment and a place of the greatest importance to [his] own life" (1969, 180).

Although Ayrton himself identified 11 May 1956 as the pivotal moment when his "echo-sounder" made him keenly aware of Cumae and the acropolis, it was hardly

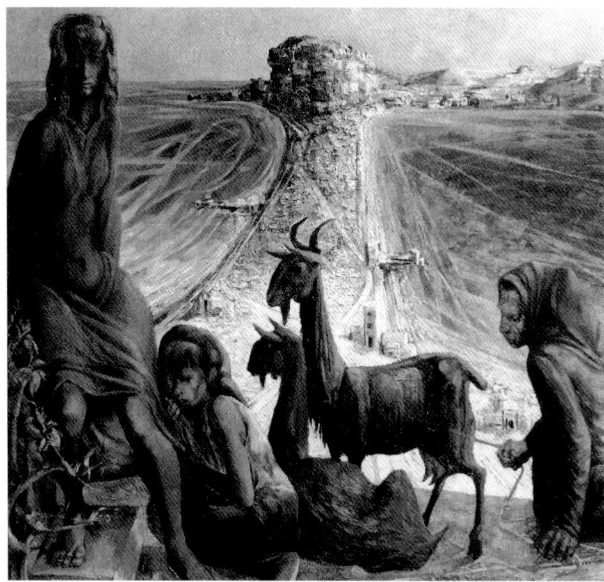

Figure 19. **'CUMEAN SYBIL'** (Cat. No. 17; 1957).

his first day at Cumae. In fact, on 3 April 1956 he first sketched a peasant woman at Cumae, in a pen and sepia wash entitled *Cumaean Sibyl* (Cat. No. 5).[14] Moreover, *Cumaean Sibyl (IV)* and *Cumaean Sybil V* (Cat. Nos. 8–9; Figure 18) were dated 7 and 8 May 1956, respectively, i.e., several days prior to Ayrton's "pivotal moment." These and other sketches were studies for the large oil painting *'Cumean Sybil'* (Cat. No. 17; 1957; Figure 19), but the figure of a woman in the first drawing (Cat. No. 5) "was drawn *before* the conception of the painting and simply represents a Cumaean peasant woman. Her identification with the Sibyl was *post hoc.*"[15]

This large oil depicts the three stages in the evolution of the Sibyl. She is shown as child, as woman, as crone. Ayrton eventually returned to this theme, exploring the rich vein of myth surrounding her and other oracles of Apollo (see chapter 5). Years later Ayrton also showed the evolution of the Minotaur, both in bronze and in a series of ten etchings. As will become clearer in ensuing discussions, these atypical or extra-human figures are presented in Ayrton's art in more stages of development than were other characters of myth who attracted his attention. This oil painting of the Sibyl and a print, *Acropolis at Cumae* (Cat. No. 16; 1957), which was partially derived from it, present a different perspective than do the first drawings of the acropolis (Cat. Nos. 10–12), for they give the appearance of looking down upon the causeway and the acropolis.

The effect of Cumae on Ayrton was described, during the above-mentioned BBC radio program, by his wife Elisabeth, who shared fully in his involvement with the myth and the landscape in which it is set. Recalling their time together at Cumae, she declared, with somewhat overblown rhetoric:

> He was mad; it was the prelude to a madness that has lasted ten years; he was god-struck: the god was Apollo, whose temple, traditionally built by Daedalus, crowns the acropolis at Cumae. Michael, in fact, began here to become entangled with Daedalus, enmeshed is a better word. He didn't realize it at the time, it was just another strange fact about the whole magical peninsula, that Daedalus had landed under the Acropolis and buried his wings on the shore. Michael at Cumae was not so much mad, really, as enhanced and enchanted. (1978c, 10)

From the landscape of Cumae and a seminal portrayal of the Sibyl, Ayrton's interest spread to the landscape of Greece and the Greek islands. During his travels in Greece with Elisabeth, he found inspiration at Delphi, the awesome site of Apollo's most important sanctuary in Greece, where the god also spoke through his oracle (Cat. Nos. 20–21; 1957). And he was inspired by the sacred island of Delos, where Apollo was born, "the island which once floated invisible and now was anchored to the sea bed," and upon which Daedalus, in flight, looked down "as the island waked, passing from silver into the god's gold" (1962c, 43).

Although Daedalus flew from Crete to Cumae and had migrated thence to Sicily, Ayrton reached Crete with Cumae as prologue. Nonetheless, he did not yet fully realize the significance of Cumae or of Daedalus. That realization would illumine him on Crete when he discovered how inextricably he was becoming entangled in the labyrinthine world of the archetypal craftsman. Elisabeth Ayrton, who wrote a novel, *The Cretan,* as a result of their shared experience on Crete, described for BBC radio how that experience began:

> Crete was the beginning of pre-Greek and proto-Greek civilisation and for Michael it was the beginning of Greece too, as it was for me. We went there first when we had been only a few days in Athens and nowhere else in Greece at all. My own background is more directly archaeological than Michael's, and on Crete, as in many other places in Greece, we sparked each other off, starting a fire that has gone on burning ever since. I was consumed with excitement about the extraordinary phenomenon of the Minoan civilisation and the fact that I could walk about in the ruins of the palaces and find shards of ancient pottery and loom weights in the open fields. Michael saw, with the peculiar intensity he has of seeing, the whole landscape in its burnt summer colours in relation to the ruins and, after a time, to the myth of Daedalus and Icarus. You have to go to Crete to see the workmanship of the objects in the museum at Heraklion, to realise why the myth of the archetypal craftsman started in Minoan Crete. When Michael was at Cumae, the landing of Daedalus was just part of a myth, but when he was on Crete he began to know more and more about Daedalus, more than we are told in any earlier version of the myth. (1978c, 12–13)

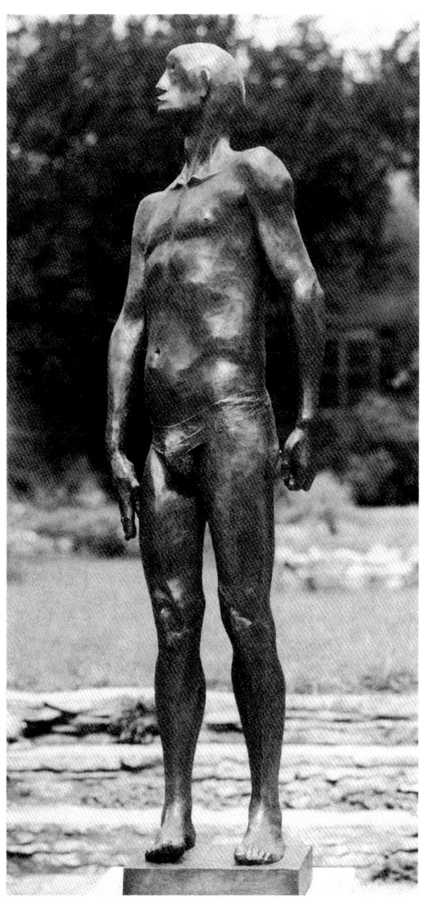

Figure 20. **FALCON WATCHER** (Cat. No. 763; 1956–72). Henry Morgan, Somerset.

The Cretan landscapes that Ayrton painted in 1957 (Cat. Nos. 22–24) were intermingled with falconer and falcon landscape paintings (*Falconer I & II,* Cat. Nos. 18–19; and *Falcon Landscape I* & II, Cat. Nos. 26–27), suggesting that the imagery of flight central to the myth was beginning to take shape in the artist's mind. In 1956 Ayrton began work on a sculpture that was not completed until 1972, a larger-than-life bronze *Falcon Watcher* (Cat. No. 763; Figure 20). This bronze is closely linked with these landscapes of falcons and falconers, but also to a small bronze *Figure in Landscape* (Cat. No. 30; 1957), to a pen drawing *Figures Watching a Bird in Flight* (Cat. No. 108; 21 March 1960), and to a scene in *The Maze Maker.* In this scene near Gortyna at the home of Cameira, mother of one of Daedalus's pupils, Daedalus climbed the hill behind her home: "I watched the hawks flying, until gradually I found a pattern, a key to the labyrinth of the sky through which these birds wandered with such ease" (Ayrton 1967, 103). Both *Figure in Landscape* (Cat. No. 30; 1957) and *Minoan Landscape* (Cat. No. 42; 1958) are part of a sequence of bronzes that used "bones embodied in the plaster before casting": as the bone is metamorphosed into bronze, "the skeleton of a bird can become the bare trees of a mysterious landscape," wrote Ayrton in *Drawings and Sculpture* (below pl. 50 and 51). The use of found objects in sculpture had long been exploited by artists, as he well knew, but their metamorphosis brought him new insight and introduced new possibilities.

In 1958 Ayrton also began a brief experiment with wax and bone reliefs, using found objects as part of the construction. Of the dozen reliefs, only three are directly related to the Daedalus myth (Cat. Nos. 45–47), although most titles in the series indicate an origin in either the Bible or classical mythology. Two of the three reliefs depict

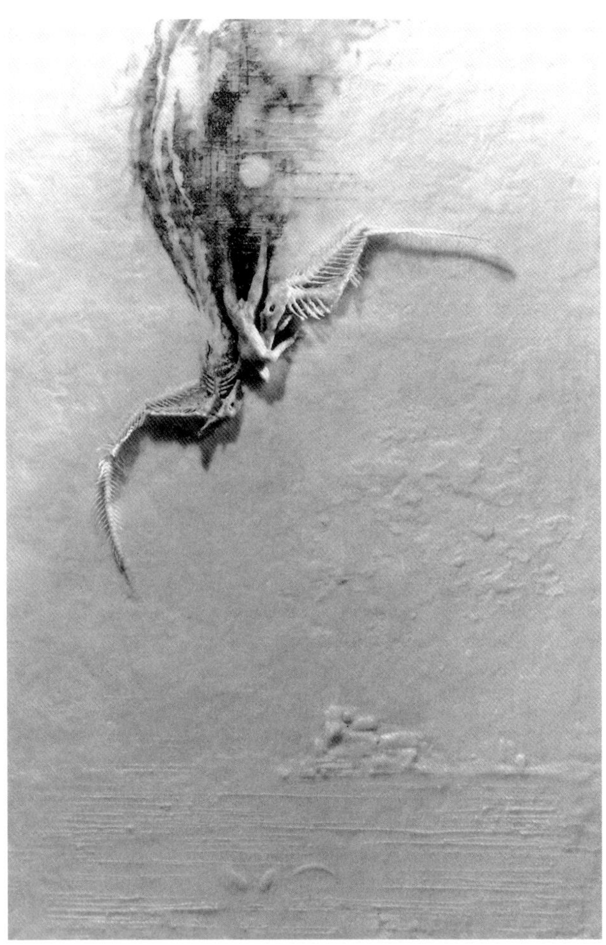

Figure 21. **ICARUS FALLS I**
(Cat. No. 47; 1958–59). John Vickers, London.

different aspects of the fate of Icarus, whom Ayrton had just recently represented in a drawing, *Icarus Suspended* (Cat. No. 44), the first representation of Icarus by Ayrton since his youthful drawing in 1940.

To create these reliefs, Ayrton employed an acetylene torch to melt Cerasina Alb, a white wax, onto hardboard. He then impressed into the wax a variety of materials, including seaweed, broken plate glass, sea urchin shells, bones, a bird's skull, and even a blown goose egg. While the wax was still malleable, he would sometimes draw in it with the tip of the blowtorch or turn off the oxygen for the torch to create a dense smoke, which would impregnate the porous wax. At other times he would tilt the board to let the wax run in different directions. The hardened wax, which varies in depth from one-eighth to one-quarter inch, achieves a high degree of permanence despite its original pliability. Ayrton's methods of creating these reliefs were related to a technique used previously not only by Cellini and Michelangelo but even by the ancient Egyptians, who used encaustic to make mummy portraits. Nonetheless, his experiments did not win general public approval, and only three of the reliefs entered private collections.[16]

Icarus Falls I (Cat. No. 47; Figure 21) is perhaps the most effective and striking relief in this entire series. The two dried fish spines used for Icarus's wings were "found on the beach at Matala, south of Phaestos." The relief dramatically records the story of the fall: Icarus, trailing smoke, plunges in a blaze of defeat, with the victorious sun in the background. His wings, still intact but now merely skeletal, provide no apparatus for slowing or halting his descent. Stripped bare of all protection, his nude figure is strikingly immediate as it calls to mind photographs or movies of plummeting war planes shot down by the enemy. His stark form is momentarily yet eternally suspended in its ignominious hurtling toward the sea, which will engulf him in its vastness as it quenches the flames. And the artist's brilliant success in the use of melted wax to depict a failure caused, as the myth tells us, by melting wax, crowns this work with irony.

Icarus Drowns (Cat. No. 46; Figure 22) likewise achieves its effect through the use of smoke and fish bones, but it differs sharply from the *Icarus Falls I* relief.

The skeletal wings are less distinct but still trail smoke against the sun, which nevertheless is scarcely blurred, and there is a faint image of where the body had been during the descent. The very literal corpse, with his left arm draped around still another fish spine, is heaped upon a small mound of bones, perhaps to accentuate his fate and suggest that Icarus has become a part of the flotsam and jetsam cast upon the shore.

Ayrton's choice of found objects for these reliefs and for the bronze landscapes illustrates the unconscious role of myth in the creative process. The use of the skeleton of a bird in the landscapes hints at the flight of Daedalus and Icarus on wings created from feathers, but it can also imply the fall of Icarus. Similarly, the use of dried fish spines to create wings for Icarus in the two wax and bone reliefs evokes the saw that Daedalus's nephew Talos created by casting a fish spine in bronze. Nevertheless, Ayrton asserted that he did not discover this aspect of the myth until two years later (1969, 184f.).[17] Obviously moved by this discovery and by the fact that he had earlier cast two bronze heads of the Cretan Talos (Cat. Nos. 3 and 32; 1954–1956 and 1957), Ayrton declared: "From these mysterious coincidences I received much pleasure and in some sort a feeling that my activity was ordained" (1969, 185).

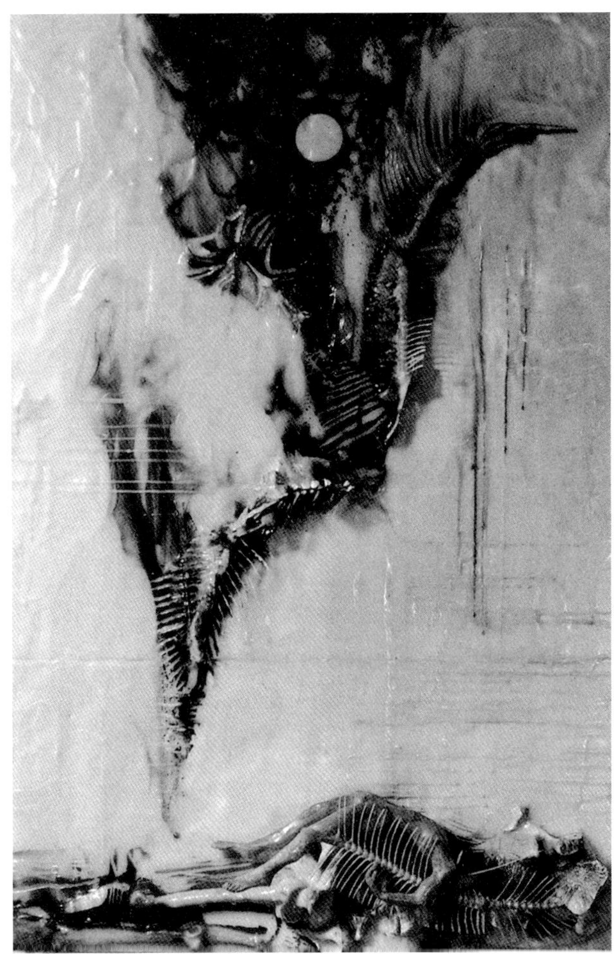

Figure 22. **ICARUS DROWNS** (Cat. No. 46; 1958). John Vickers, London.

The unconscious functioning of myth can also be seen in *The Feather* (Cat. No. 101; 1960; Figure 23). Ayrton said that for no logical reason he had always identified this woman with a feather as Pasiphaë (see catalogue), but his own words in *Testament* offer the obvious answer: "Without Pasiphaë there would have been no flight from Crete, no simulacrum of a dappled cow and no Minotaur in the centre of the labyrinth" (1962c, 31). In her hand she holds the feather, symbol of flight and the inspiration for Daedalus's own flight. One variant of the myth even credits Pasiphaë with providing the means for Daedalus's escape from imprisonment in the labyrinth (see chapter 2). One can reasonably see in these connections a psychological explanation for the identification of this woman as Pasiphaë.

In literature, as in art, myth often functions unconsciously. Poets and storytellers may begin with an idea about human aspiration or human failure but then will draw unconsciously on the myth of Icarus to evoke a

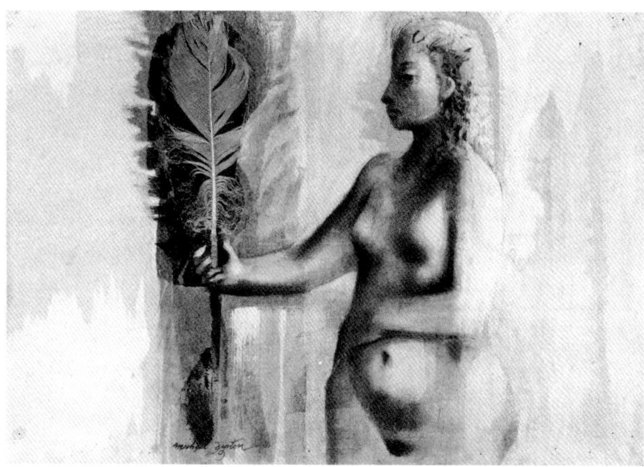

Figure 23. **THE FEATHER**
(Cat. No. 101; 1960).

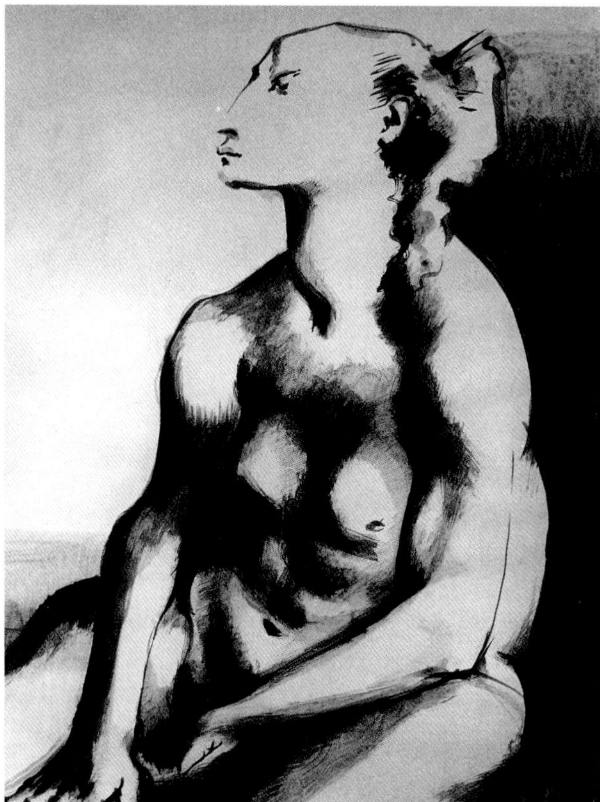

Figure 24. **PASIPHAË I**
(Cat. No. 480; 15 January 1965). J. S. Lewinski, London.

deeper awareness of heroic achievement or of foolhardy striving, depending on how they choose to interpret the myth. The linkages between the myth and the creative idea may be tenuous or substantial, obvious or obscure, but careful analysis will often reveal the evocative power of myth in the creative process. The creative thrust from the unconscious comes under the mastery of the conscious; cognition gives order to the intuitive responses to experience. The artist transforms the ideas arising from the unconscious into vital, dynamic images and literary works of art.

Ever since the day of his discovery of the Virgilian account of the myth of Daedalus at Cumae, Ayrton had been "wandering" in the myth, but the mythical Daedalus did not become a specific entity for Ayrton until his sojourn on Crete. Until that time and, to some extent, during his time on Crete, his interest had focused instead on the landscape and on Daedalus's ill-fated son, Icarus. The wax and bone reliefs depicted both the fall and the drowning of Icarus, but Ayrton obviously found the flight and the fall more evocative than the end result. Several drawings of the fall (Cat. Nos. 52, 53, 70, 71, and 72; 1959; see Figures 25 and 26) served largely as studies for a number of large oil paintings that continued to explore the subject (Cat. Nos. 55, 57, 59, 60, and 87–89; 1959).

One painting, *Icarus Falls IV* (Cat. No. 87; 1959; Plate 13), is in some ways close to the wax and bone relief (Cat. No. 47) in which the wings are reminiscent of Ovid's description, but certain features of this painting suggest abstract expressionism. A remarkable parallel can be found in a painting by American artist Jimmy Ernst, *Icarus III* (Plate 14), which was completed four years later, in 1963.[18] The configuration at the bottom of both paintings appears to be an abstraction of the impact of the plummeting Icarus upon the earth. In Ayrton's painting, as the contorted form of Icarus hurtles earthward, it carries with it an implicit warning to airplane pilots and astronauts, reminding them of the disastrous consequences of Icarian rashness. *The Testament of Daedalus* (see below), which is written as if Ayrton were Daedalus himself writing it several millennia ago, makes clear that the author-artist identifies contemporary pilots with Icarus:

> Icarus, my son, bore different names at the time when men first fought each other in the sky. He has been multiplied and died in squadrons. He has been called many names when they seemed relevant to particular situations, but this testament is not history. . . .
>
> If you must see this story in time, look only at the gap which spans the millennia between our days of flight and the moment in which you live, the moment yesterday when Icarus leaped into the sky again and fought two wars, spilling death on whole cities. In this time he returned to Crete and conquered it from the air and this was the first land ever to be so conquered. That is the kind of irony the gods enjoy, since it is stained with blood and may be interpreted as long-postponed revenge. As you read this testament he leaps further towards his antagonist, beyond the envelope which is your present, which to you is now.
>
> It will be in your mind, like the little wings pinned on the breast, or the crew-cut crew, rubber-faced under the pressure of velocity, in the cramped womb cluttered with dials. Perhaps these are numerous and specific people to you. To me they remain single and specific. They remain Icarus. (1962c, 12–13).

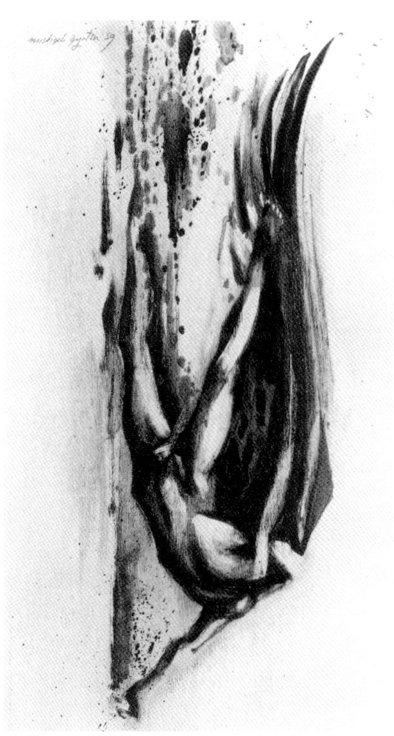

Figure 25. **ICARUS FALLS** (Cat. No. 52; 1959).

The initial drawings, paintings, and relief of the fall of Icarus all reveal a clearly human form falling, with replicas of wings still attached. The skeletal wings of these works also form the basis for Ayrton's earliest bronze on the subject, *Icarus I* (Cat. No. 50; Figure 27), cast in 1959, the year in which most of the works involving Icarus were completed. Its bony, well-ventilated wings, however, are meant to suggest not the fall but the ascent, as is apparent from the slightly crouched position, the swelling of the chest as the lungs fill with air, and the head thrown backward to look up toward the destination of the flight. To one's mind comes a fragment of Daedalus's words in *Testament:* "I saw him lift his spread of wings impatiently so that they clattered" (1962c, 21).

By the following year both the paintings and the bronzes indicate a heightened awareness of who Icarus was and what his motivations and experiences must have been. For example, when one views the bronze *Icarus III* (Cat. No. 136; 1960; Figure 29) from the rear, one sees the head thrown defiantly backward, as his face and the

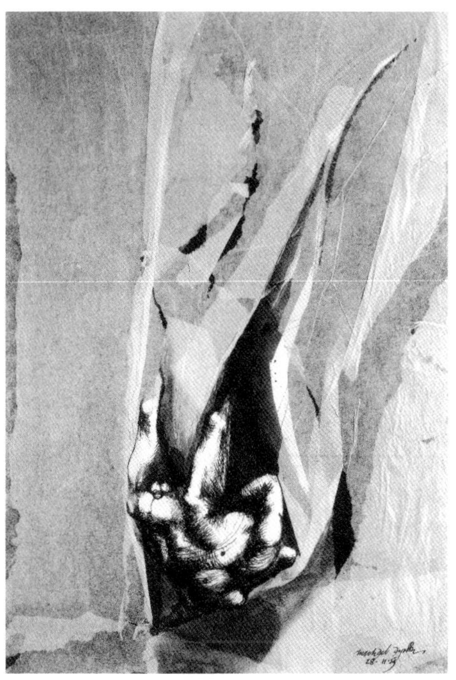

Figure 26. **ICARUS FALLS (STUDY)** (Cat. No. 71; 28 November 1959).

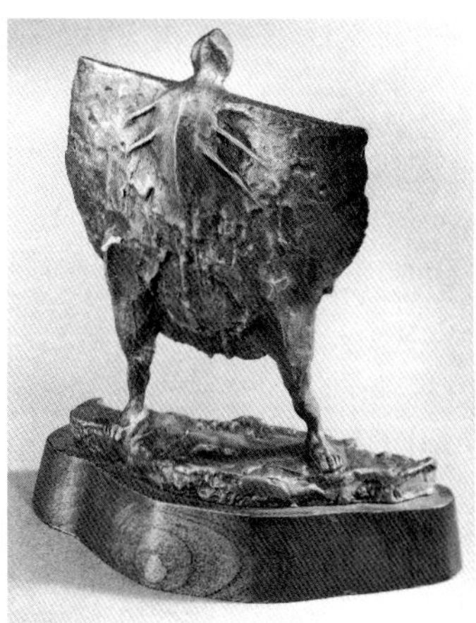

Figure 28. **ICARUS II** (Cat. No. 51; 1959). Henry Morgan, Somerset.

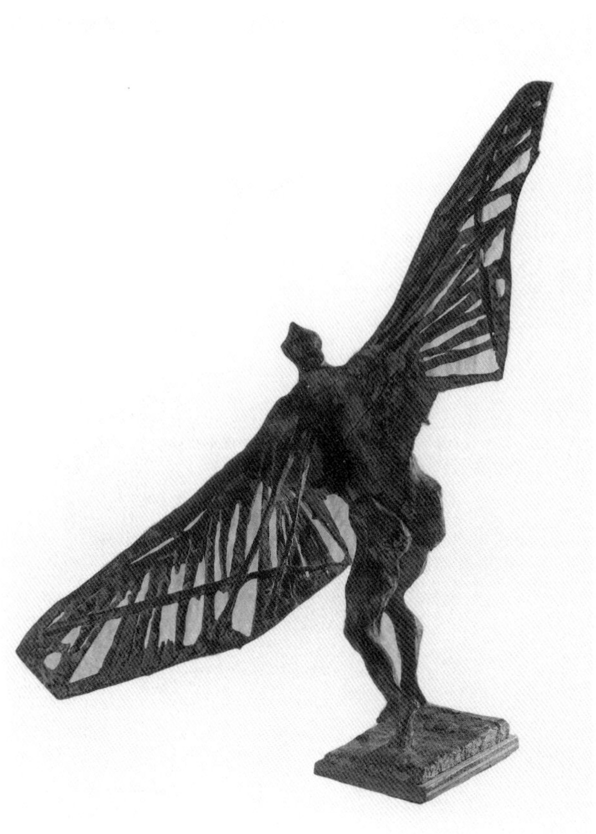

Figure 27. **ICARUS I** (Cat. No. 50; 1959). Eaden Lilley, Cambridge.

winged extensions of his arms are thrust upward in anticipation of the flight. Ayrton's description in *Testament* of Icarus's preparations for the flight must have been inspired by this view of this strongly evocative bronze: "I saw the crest of his shoulders rise and his back took up the tension of his wings. He breathed quickly and heavily. His thighs stretched to take up the pull and they were grooved with the power building in him to thrust" (1962c, 23). When viewed from the side, this work offers new insights, new revelations. Icarus's head seems to have disappeared, and his wings appear to be an integral part of his upwardly straining torso; they have become an outgrowth of his arms, calling to mind the transformation of Daphne into the laurel tree, as shown in paintings and sculpture.[19] His arms have become wings, ready to raise him aloft, to give him the freedom to soar higher and higher to challenge the sun. A frontal view of a variant of this bronze, *Icarus III, Variant I* (Cat. No. 756; 1972; Figure 30, Plate 12), demonstrates this point even more clearly as it rises from its plinth in Old Change Court, London. With his figure silhouetted against St. Paul's Cathedral or against a neighboring patch of the late afternoon sky, Icarus's upswept wings reveal how completely they have become extensions of his body poised for flight.

The wingspan of *Icarus I* and his height are both approximately twenty inches, whereas the wings of *Icarus III* comprise more than half of that sixty-seven-inch-high

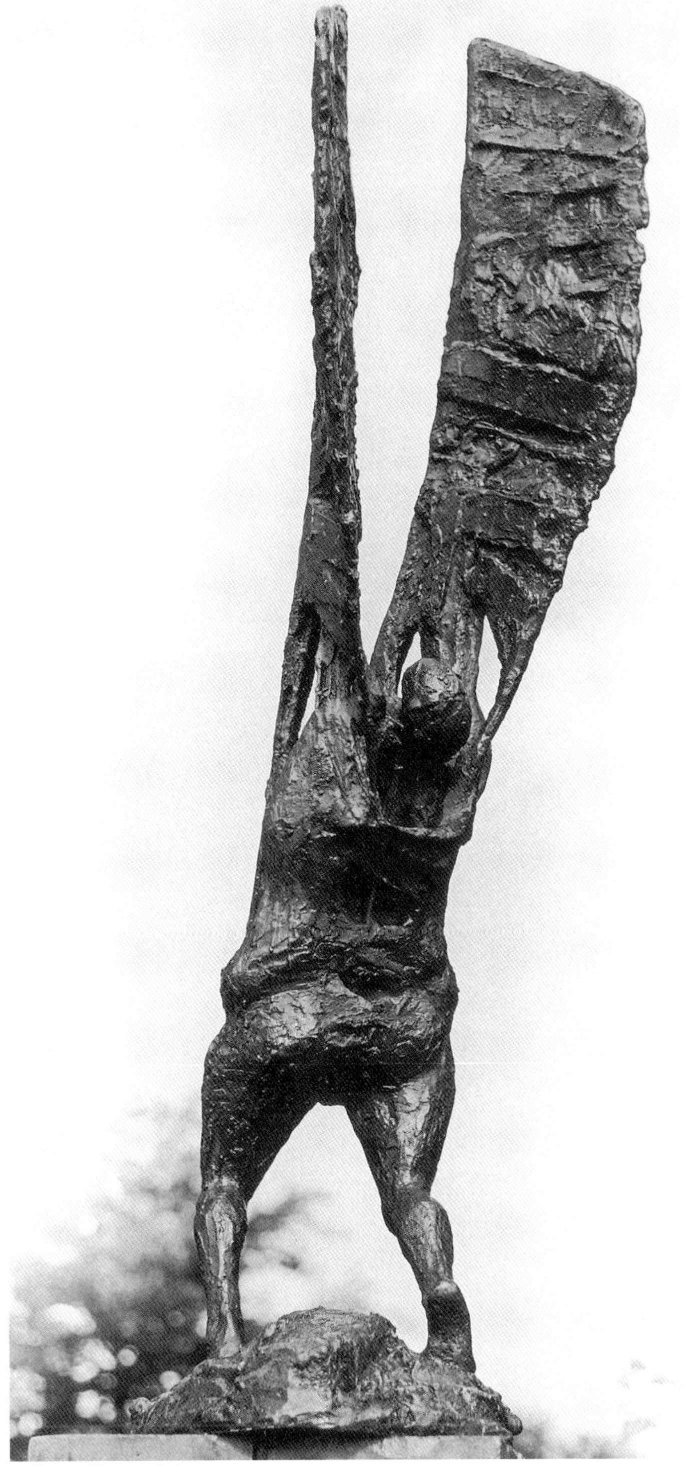

Figure 29. **ICARUS III** (Cat. No. 136; 1960).

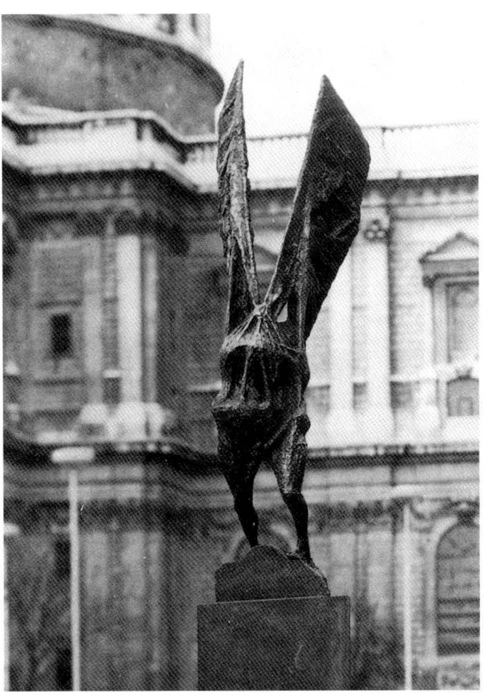

Figure 30. **ICARUS III**, Variant I (Cat. No. 756; 1972). Broseley Studio.

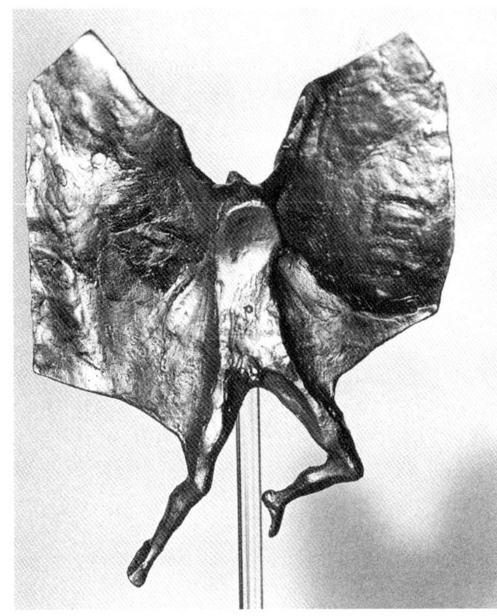

Figure 31. **ICARUS ASCENDANT**, Version II (Cat. No. 321; 1963).

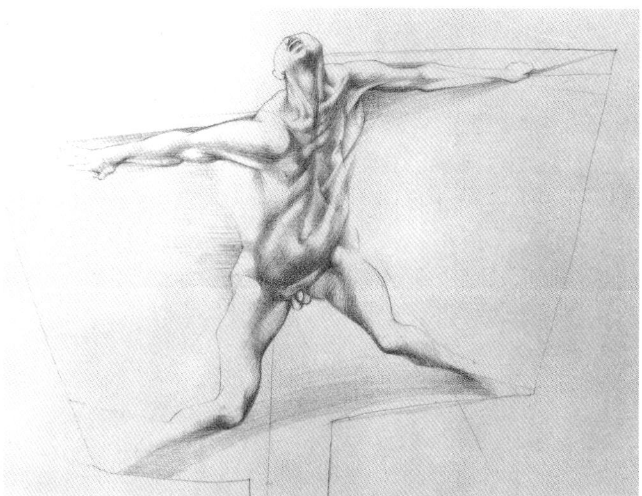

Figure 32. **STUDY FOR ICARUS RISING** (Cat. No. 201; 4 July 1961).

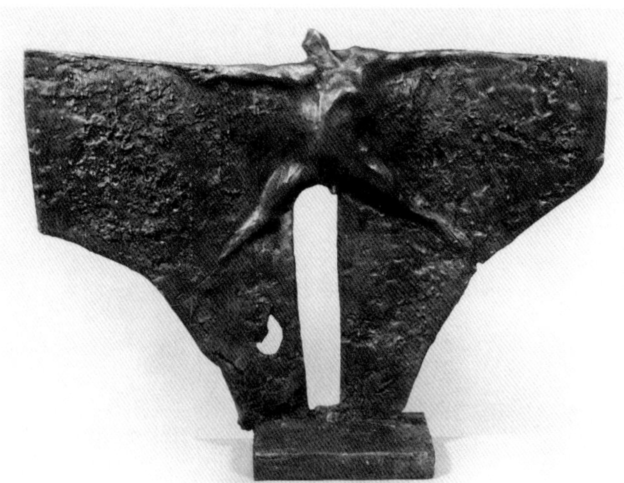

Figure 33. **ICARUS RISING** (Cat. No. 206; 1961).

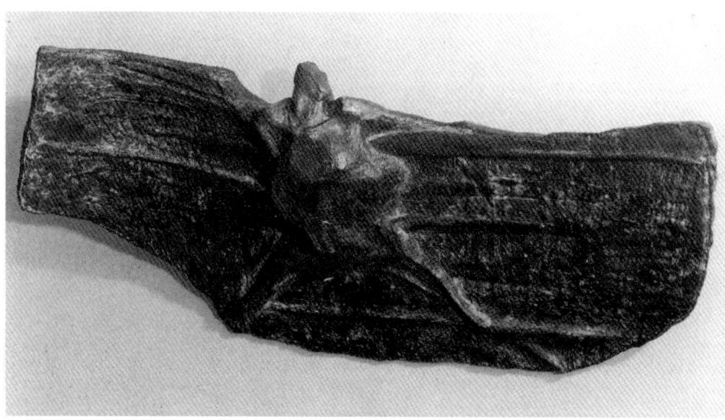

Figure 34. **ICARUS RISING II** (Cat. No. 254; 1962).

bronze. In a further progression in the development of the wings toward believability, the wings on a small gilt bronze cast in 1960 in the form of a plastron, *Icarus Ascendant* (Cat. No. 137; cf. Cat. No. 321, *Version II;* 1963; Figure 31), resemble the wings of a bat. This sculpture must have inspired this passage from *Testament,* in which Daedalus watches Icarus begin his flight: "The wind took him and threw him up on the current and he held himself rigid, stretched like a bat, like the bats whose flight I had studied in the long night in the Labyrinth, whilst I made the wings" (1962c, 23). With the ratio of wings to body significantly increased, this sculpture makes it easier to imagine that such a creature *could* take flight.

The evolution of the Icarus figure into a more realistically aerial personage was attended by a concurrent development of his heroic personality in Ayrton's writings. At about this time he wrote:

> The myth of Daedalus and Icarus has haunted me for four years. . . . I find myself involved in this legend and strangely aware of the relationship between the creative Daedalus and his son, who, lacking his father's talent, compensated for this lack in one superb and pathetic moment of suicidal action. I do not believe that Icarus died by accident, but, in jealous rejection of his father, and in his love for the god Apollo, he flew against the sun itself. This he did in a vainglorious attempt to conquer the god and return to him.[20]

Ayrton's emphasis upon Icarus's lack of the talent enjoyed by his creative father and the "jealous rejection" by Icarus of his father could be drawn from elaborations of the myth through the centuries, but it takes on deeper meaning when viewed in more personal terms. Ayrton revealed a great deal about his relationship to his own father in the dedication to his book, *Golden Sections:* "To the memory of my father, who quietly disguised his disappointment when I failed to follow in his footsteps" (1957b, 5).

A psychoanalytic interpretation of Ayrton's art and his writings would undoubtedly unveil many other examples of the uneasy relationship Ayrton had with his father.[21] A psychoanalyst in the Freudian tra-

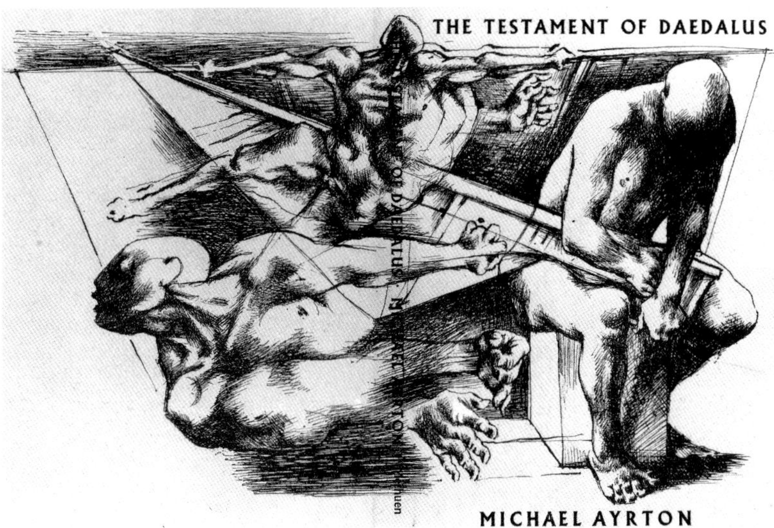

Figure 35. **JACKET OF THE TESTAMENT OF DAEDALUS** (Cat. No. 258; 1962).

dition would likely deduce unresolved oedipal intonations in Ayrton's dedication and in his handling of the myth of Daedalus and Icarus. The son's failure to identify with his father and his jealous rejection of him is expressed more fully in *The Maze Maker,* published five years later (see chapter 5):

> I do not think I was an easy father for Icarus to have. I watched him too closely, hoping passionately to find in him my own particular virtues and have him surpass me in them. I was hard on him, trying to make him in my image when I should have known that the image he would make would be his own. I never understood him while he lived. Perhaps it was not possible. Only his death explained the nature of his life.
>
> How much does a man make his own son? How much does he show himself to his child? Did he in his infancy, when I had lived in despair believing my powers drained out of me, sense my mortality, my inferiority to a god, and despise me even then? And when I was myself again and gave him reason to be proud of me among men, why did he never show me cause to be proud of him until he died? Why did he break what he touched? I never knew him. Perhaps when I have written this all out I shall understand where I failed. Sometimes I think nothing I could have been or could have done would have altered him. (Ayrton 1967, 63–64)

The point illustrated in miniature by *Icarus Ascendant,* with his swollen chest, is more fully expressed in a large bronze cast the following year, but both of them help to illumine these statements by Ayrton. *Icarus Rising* (Cat. No. 206; 1961; Figure 33, Plate 11 [Cat. No. 513]) blends body and wings into a single expression of anticipated ecstasy. The vertical structure of the sculpture aims Icarus at his target, which lies at the zenith of his orbit. His chest is swollen with pride and energy, his muscles strain for the upward thrust, and his open, outstretched right hand grasps for conquest of the god. All this, combined with the thrown-back head, expertly captures both Icarus's jubilance at his exhilarating ascent and his defiance of the sun-god toward whom he soars recklessly. The use of the double axe, a potent Minoan symbol, for the wings gives added depth of meaning to this highly evocative bronze ("He looked like a double-axe suspended" [(Ayrton 1962c, 27]).

Early in 1960 Ayrton assembled bits of poetry associated with Icarus which he had written at various times over the preceding two years. At the same he began to write a narrative to provide a context for the verse. *The Testament of Daedalus* was published in 1962, with a postscript relating the myth to contemporary events and offering insights into Ayrton's development as artist and mythmaker (see chapter 1). Although *Testament* purports to be a reconstruction of the myth, it is in fact mythopoeia, for Ayrton expands the story far beyond any existing literary documents from antiquity. As he himself said in the postscript, "In the course of writing this narrative, while rewriting and extending the verse, the extended sequence of events—or my conception of events, which is permissible *when mythmaking* [italics mine]—came into being" (1962c, 67).

Why did he undertake mythmaking? In part, he admits in the postscript, because he felt a need to explain for himself "the relationship between Daedalus and his son and the passion Icarus had for Apollo" (1962c, 67). In part, undoubtedly, because he was a raconteur who liked to tell a good story. But surely an explanation can also be found in the way Ayrton worked, for example, as an illustrator or portraitist: he would project himself into the illustrations and portraits, almost becoming a part of the portrait himself.[22] Similarly, as he wrote this verbal portrait of Daedalus and Icarus, a portrait shaped by the images he had already made in ink, paint, wax, and bronze, he empathized himself into the character of Daedalus. In the act of creation, therefore, his imagination filled in the many blanks in the story, but it also influenced him to reject some of the earlier versions of the myth, to rewrite aspects of it.

Thus, we find Daedalus introducing himself in these words:

> I am impatient of aesthetic pretension. I make things cunningly and with skill and if they are beautiful I am not displeased. What there is in me of *poesis* rests in my finger tips and in my eyes, but because the poem exists in the thing I make, when I make it, and not in me, it comes to me in the act of discovery. . . . In the making of things and especially in the making of images, lies an act of conquest which is sufficient exercise of power for a proper man. That is my view. I seek order. I seek a measured harmony. I seek balance. (Ayrton 1962c, 13)

For Ayrton, Icarus is the opposite of his father; he is, moreover, opposed to what his father stands for and what his father does. In other words, he is the stereotypical rebellious teenager, but with more than ordinary desire for fame and an extraordinary love for the god Apollo:

> Icarus is more famous than I am, although he had no particular skill and could not be described as a maker of anything, except his own death, which he contrived in a vainglorious and very poetic manner. He is, however, more famous than I am and perhaps I resent that. . . .
>
> The bones of the legend which grew out of our flight and the death, if death it was, of Icarus are bare bones and bleached. . . . The common story goes that Icarus flew too near the sun and caused the waxen parts of his wings to melt and thus fell into the sea and was drowned. This kind of partial truth, like wax, is malleable and is the stuff of legend, but in fact, as you will presently read, Icarus would have burned and fallen no matter how I had contrived his wings. Had they been iron they would have melted. If they had been stone they would have cindered in the stare of the god and streamed like lava down the sky. (Ayrton 1962c, 14–15)

In Ayrton's view, Icarus did not love his father, but he both loved and resented the god Apollo. "Resentment made him a hero," says Daedalus, "for this is how heroes are made and undoubtedly he was a hero of sorts. What else could he be? He was my son and he had no talent. Icarus had no love for order and was clumsy with his hands" (Ayrton 1962c, 15). Here Ayrton provides a characterization of Icarus based upon Freud's theory of two basic instincts, Eros and Thanatos, the one affirming life, the other destroying it. The Freudian principles underlying Ayrton's portrayal of Daedalus and Icarus are more fully developed in *The Maze Maker* (see chapter 5).

In reshaping the myth, Ayrton took great liberties with the story as it is recorded in extant literature (see chapter 2). The following examples illustrate his revisions. Ayrton identifies Daedalus's nephew with the bronze-man Talos whom Medea slew on Crete; in a bit of political commentary, Ayrton has Daedalus say of Talos, "Having become bronze and simple he became a military man and the guardian of Crete" (1962c, 17). He attributes to Minos the accusation that Daedalus was guilty of adultery with the queen, a charge which Icarus believed, so that he thought the Minotaur his half-brother (1962c, 19). Through the words of Daedalus, Ayrton denies that Daedalus warned Icarus not to fly too near the sun because of the destructive power of its heat: "I never thought of such a chance. I warned him of stress in the dive and to fly smoothly to cover the distance" (1962c, 20). Also, Icarus flies far ahead of his father and plunges to his scorching death far from Icaria, the traditional location for his death and burial, "for that island lay far off my course" (1962c, 53). As a child, Icarus broke the shell of a nautilus given him by his father, both as a clumsy act of impatience "to find the sea hidden in its heart" and as an early act of defiance against his father; as a youth, he "defied the god and broke my wings, testing them against the sun. It was the wings I made that the sun threw down broken, but the heart of Icarus broke first, because he was clumsy with his love" (1962c, 30). Naucrate, the wife of Daedalus and mother of Icarus, is said to have been loved by Pasiphaë, implying a lesbian relationship (1962c, 30). And another motivation for Icarus's assault of the sun was his desire "to stay the sun's journey" because of his inordinate fear of darkness (1962c, 33).

This brief recitation of modifications and expansion of the myth illustrates the extent to which Ayrton took possession of the myth fully as much as it possessed and drove him. It also makes clear that myth is not static, but dynamic, that it lives on in the creations of artists not merely as an interesting story cast in bronze or painted on a canvas, but especially as both conscious and unconscious inspiration, breathing vitality into the creative act and into the creation itself. One perceptive reviewer of the book declared:

> To read [this book] is to be given an insight into the tensions and perils and splendour of the creative mind. Daedalic prose and haunting Icarian verse complement each other, and both find fresh visual dimension through the pen drawings. . . . In one sense . . . [it] is his personal artistic *cri de coeur*, autobiography expressed in mythic terms. But it is much, much more: a probing to the roots of all creation, an upward flight that embraces every high and doomed endeavour.[23]

Already at this stage in Ayrton's lengthy entrapment in this myth, he was beginning to reshape the myth to fit his own conception of the world, his own view of reality. His literary and visual creations demonstrate the validity of his wife's assertion that "when he was on Crete he began

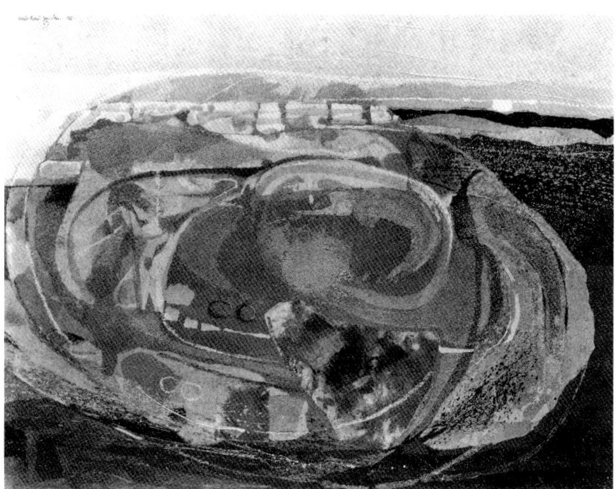

Figure 36. **LANDSCAPE IN THE KESTREL'S EYE** (Cat. No. 277; 1962).

to become part of the legend himself. He began to know more and more about Daedalus, more than we are told in any earlier version of the myth" (Ayrton 1978c, 13).

The telling of the story or, rather, the expanded retelling of the story not only was influenced by the works of art Ayrton produced during the preceding four years; it also influenced the creation of new works. The interweaving of word and image would subsequently increase as Ayrton gained ever deeper insights into the myth, with word and image "sparking each other off."[24] Particularly illustrative of this close connection between word and image is the influence of the painting *Delos, Morning. II* (Cat. No. 38; Figure 37) upon this passage in *Testament*, where Daedalus declares: "The island shone. I swung over it, caught in a combat of currents in the air. All swayed and rippled. From Delos, Aphrodite's doves flew up and scattered like paper torn and thrown into the air. That morning was a great and simple joy and Icarus shouted and sang of it" (Ayrton 1962c, 43).

In the narrative Daedalus says that Icarus came back into his sight just "after midday, beyond Delos" (Ayrton 1962c, 48). Later in his flight he recalls Delos ("In my mind Delos shone") and the story of Apollo's birth there (Ayrton 1962c, 54). In his postscript to *Testament* Ayrton asserts: "Delos especially exercised upon me an intense

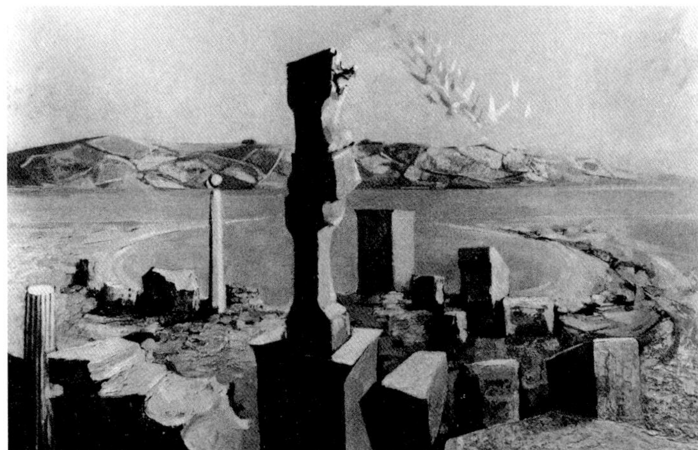

Figure 37. **DELOS, MORNING. II.** (Cat. No. 38; 1958). John Vickers, London.

compulsion" (Ayrton 1962c, 64). The extent and nature of that compulsion is shown in his drawings and paintings of Delos. His first visit to Delos resulted in several paintings, but he came back a number of times to draw it in ink (Cat. Nos. 184–185, 188–190; April–May 1961) and to paint it (e.g., Cat. Nos. 322, 402–403; 1963–1964). The titles of a number of paintings reveal that the island was a sacred place for him, e.g., *Sacred Place* (Cat. No. 36; January 1958), *Delos. Sacred Port* (Cat. No. 402), and *Sacred Place. Delos* (Cat. No. 403).

Just as the images of Delos inspired the description in *Testament,* so also the text inspired new images. In particular, said Ayrton, the portrayal of Icarus "at the climax of his flight [was] the result of the narrative" (1962c, 67). Following Daedalus's assertion that Icarus came back into his sight just "after midday, beyond Delos," Ayrton modified his statement with the declaration:

> I experienced the apex of the flight of Icarus although I did not, could not, have seen it. I do not see how I could have seen it.
>
> At his tip of time, at his apex, he moved upon the sun and joined the god. At this summit, his moving mass changed its form. His trunk splayed outwards, expanding, and the jointed projections of his limbs, disordered in the fission of his body, became the vectors of an energy beyond mortal strength. His proportions altered and his structure was transformed. The cage of ribs passed through the ribs of each wing, each performing an identical function, affirming the ascent implicit in the descent. The wings of his pelvis spread from the spine and in their bowl the duration of his flight was contained like a liquid. At maximum velocity, the sequence of modifications, to which Icarus was subject, appeared simultaneous. A compact projectile and yet spread across the sky, he evolved in that instant a sequence of related anatomies, each designed to succeed and doomed to fail. In these anatomies, the embryo co-existed with the fish, the lizard with the bird and the disintegration of ultimate fatigue moved with the impulse toward birth. (1962c, 48–49)

A series of painted stucco reliefs, as well as some of the oil paintings, demonstrates vividly Ayrton's creative progression from print to visual image. Especially through this new medium he was able to express his conception of the effect of flight upon the human form, particularly flight at high velocity. These reliefs move toward abstract expressionism, but stop short. In *Icarus in Flight* (Cat. No. 124; 1960; Figure 38), for example, Ayrton graphically conveys the anatomical dislocations and distortions described above. The original title, "Icarus modified" (see catalogue), when considered in this context and in the light of related writings, reveals that Ayrton's primary concern lay with the modifications of the human body in flight.

Among the many other studies implied in this passage are two painted stucco reliefs, *Icarus at the Climax*

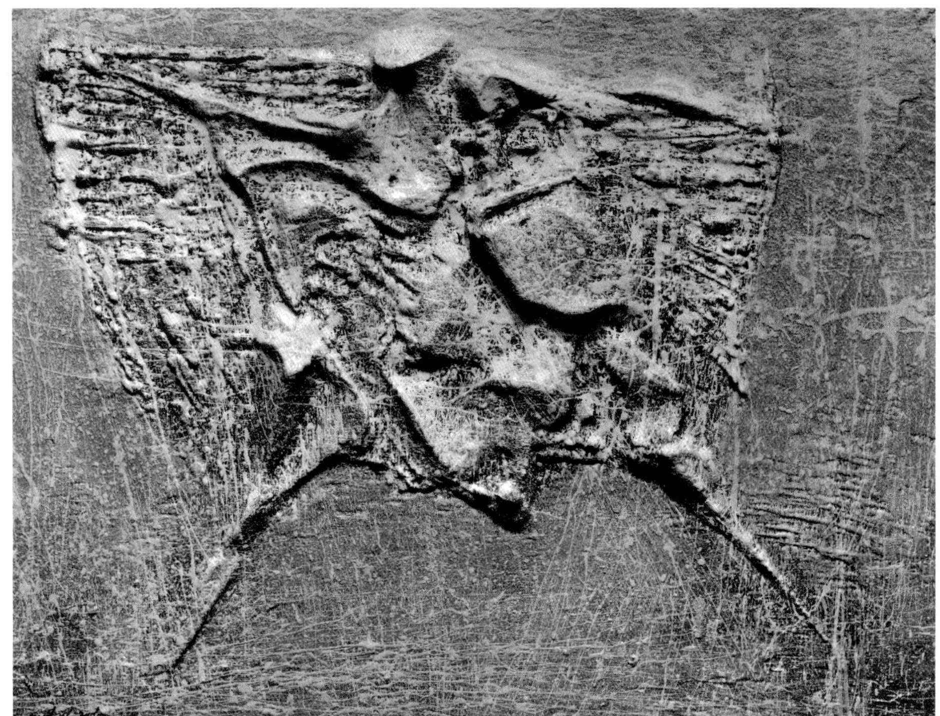

Figure 38. **ICARUS IN FLIGHT (RELIEF I)** (Cat. No. 124; 1960). John Webb, FRPS/Brompton Studios.

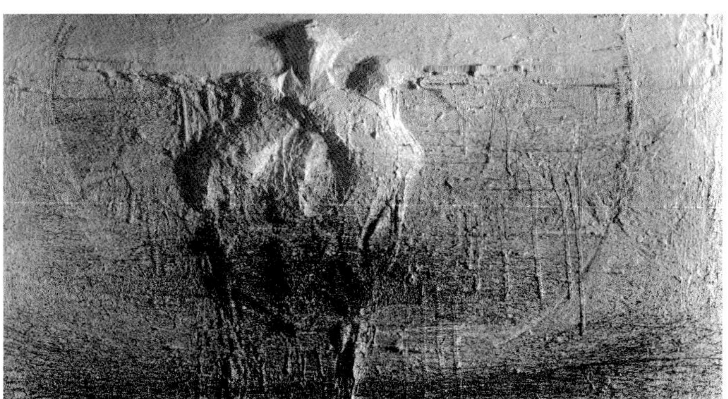

Figure 39. **ICARUS AT THE CLIMAX** (Cat. No. 126; 1960). Eaden Lilley, Cambridge.

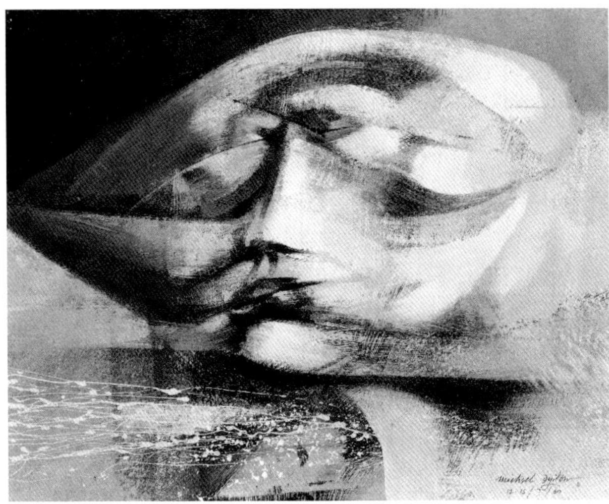

Figure 40. **ICARUS HEAD III** (Cat. No. 127; 12–15 July 1960).

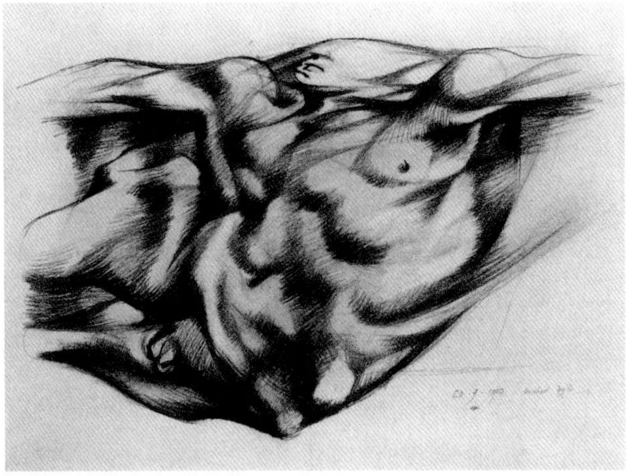

Figure 41. **ICARUS TORSO** (Cat. No. 139; 20 September 1960).

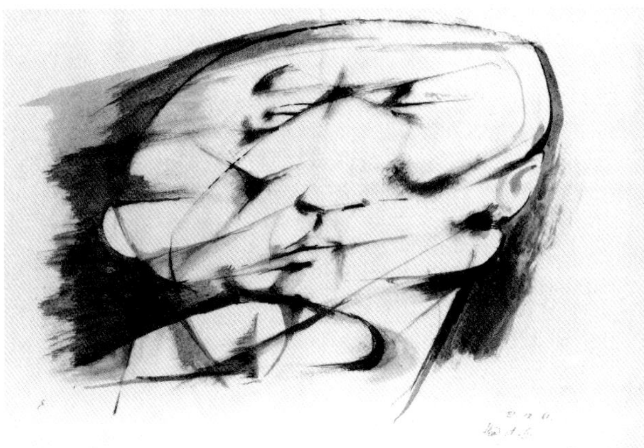

Figure 42. **HEAD AT G** (Cat. No. 231; 31 December 1961).

(Cat. No. 126; 1960; Figure 39) and *Icarus Head at G* (Cat. No. 128; 1960). In the former, Ayrton employed a graduated stippling of color—red, yellow, and black—against a white background. In this image of the climax of the flight, when time is momentarily stopped, both the soaring aspiration of the flight and the inevitable defeat and fall of Icarus are simultaneously and powerfully suggested. Likewise inspired by these words were several oils of the modification of Icarus's head (Cat. Nos. 116, 117, 127; 1960; See Figure 40) and a work in charcoal and collage, *Icarus Suspended* (Cat. No. 138; 1960).

Further verification of this interpretation comes from an essay by Ayrton in *Shell Aviation News:*

> At the apex of his climb, because mass is modified by velocity, Icarus changed his form and the anatomy of this transformation obsesses me. The image I seek is a paraphrase of the human body, adapted to those unknown areas of physical experience which it will presently enter. Daedalus the technician has risen to supremacy in this century and men have become Icarus. Photographs of potential astronauts undergoing tests simulating high velocities have been, for me, one point of departure. The re-shaping of their flesh, under intense pressure, appears at once awe-inspiring and a little absurd, just as the ambition which led both to the triumph and the fall of Icarus is both heroic and ridiculous.[25]

In *Testament,* Ayrton noted that for him the "vital problem . . . has been the figure of Icarus at the time-stopped climax of his flight and what happened when he coupled with the sun. I had to evolve his shape as he rose and then combine in a single image the aspiration and the disaster, the triumph and defeat and the paradox of motionlessness at high velocity" (1962c, 68). In a later retelling of the myth, *The Maze Maker* (see chapter 5), Daedalus declares, in a prophecy to our time:

> Icarus . . . had pride, such pride that the god himself could scarcely match it and when Icarus flew to rape the sun and throw him down, the god spurned him as you would expect. Yet before you dismiss what I saw as folly, mark that Icarus died in orgasm and that Apollo's responding orgasm, long retarded, still took place. Man has taken the god's seed and

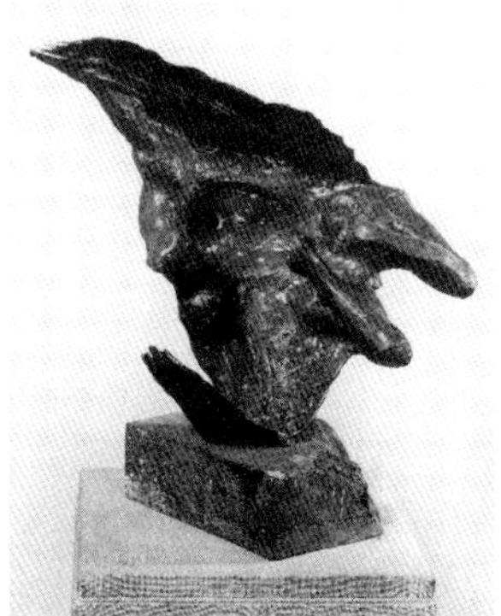

Figure 43. **ICARUS FALLEN** (Cat. No. 152; 1960). John Webb, FRPS/Brompton Studios.

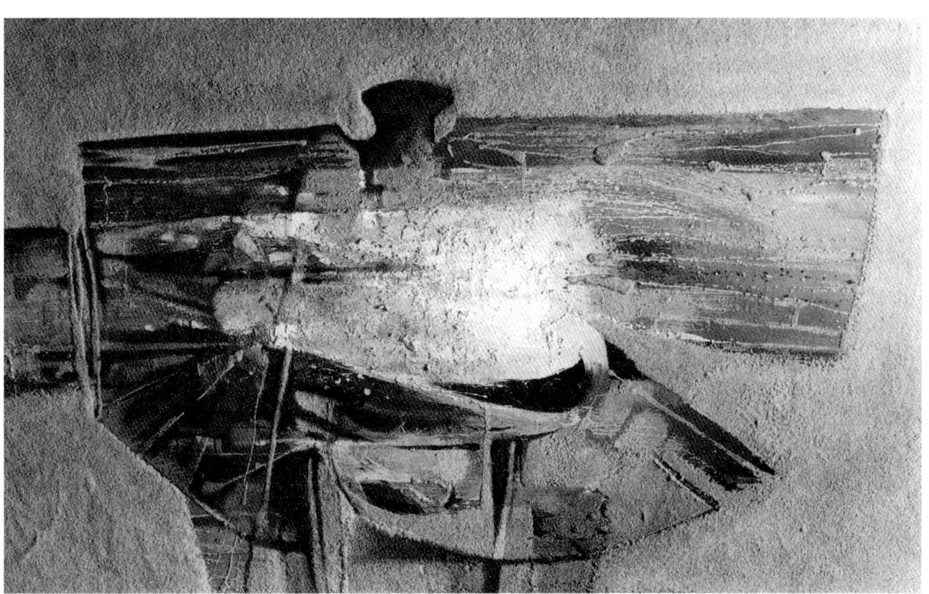

Figure 44. **ICARUS IMPRINT** (Cat. No. 158; 1960). Eaden Lilley, Cambridge.

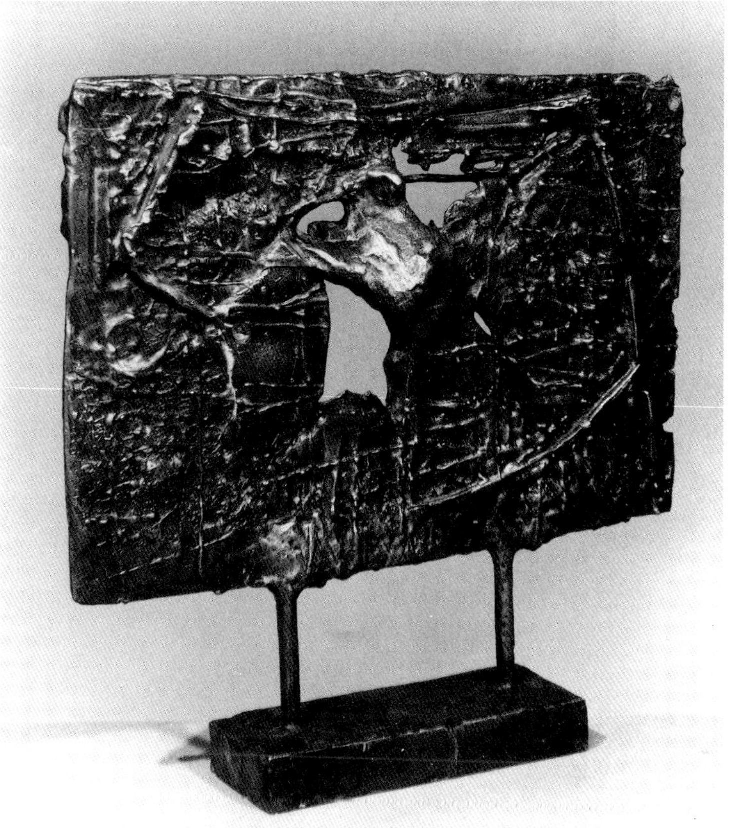

Figure 45. **ICARUS, PIERCED RELIEF** (Cat. No. 205; 1961): front.

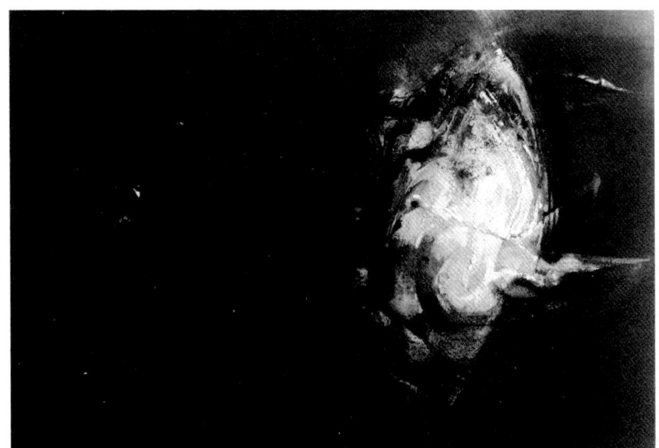

Figure 46. **ICARUS IN CONTACT** (Cat. No. 215; 1961).

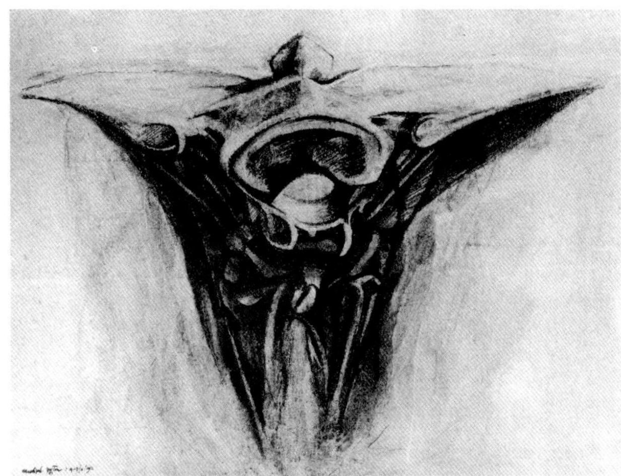

Figure 47. **ICARUS TRANSFORMED** (Cat. No. 199; 4–7 June 1961). Stearn & Sons Ltd., Cambridge.

> you now live in terror that with this semen the world itself may yet be cindered. Mark that when you may be tempted to dismiss a myth. (1967, 134)

Two of the last three paintings in the series of *Icarus Falls* (*V,* Cat. No. 88, and *VI,* Cat. No. 89; 1960; Plate 15) not only are related to the above quotations from the postscript of *Testament* (1962c, 67 and 68), but also seem likely to have inspired the conflated narrative in *Maze Maker.* In both of these paintings a sunburst Icarus appears to explode as he reaches the climax of the ascent and simultaneously begins his plunge toward earth. Suggestive of the splitting of the atom and the atomic bomb, which Ayrton called "Apollo's responding orgasm," these paintings are a far cry from both the Ovidian description of the fall and Brueghel's "Landscape with the Fall of Icarus," which reveals the delicate white legs of Icarus disappearing into the water while a few feathers flutter after them (see chapter 3).

Another oil, *Icarus in Contact* (Cat. No. 215; 1961; Figure 46), with its unusual dark green sky, represented for Ayrton his most complete version of the kind of orgasm—the explosion of the sun—which Icarus experienced. Ayrton completed eleven drawings of *Icarus at the Climax* for this painting, of which one (Cat. No. 143; 1960) was closely linked as well to the large sunburst *Icarus Falls* (Cat. No. 89; above). In the artist's mind it was also closely related to the bronze *Icarus Transformed I* (Cat. No. 216; 1961; Figure 48) now in the Tate Gallery.[26]

The "anatomy of this transformation" which obsessed Ayrton during this period led to two more bronzes of the same title (*II* and *III;* Cat. Nos. 217 and 218; 1961; see Figure 49). Observing these and related sculptures from this period, critic Bryan Robertson offered this assessment: "What Ayrton has done is to try to make sculpture which embodies movement, pressure, and what might come from the inter-action between matter and velocity. All this in formal terms which reinterpret many of the outer characteristics of ancient forms in Greek sculpture but are freshly charged by a general sculptural sensibility which could only spring from this particular moment."[27] Another critic was presumably commenting on both *Icarus Transformed I* and *III* (Cat. Nos. 216 and 218; Figures 48 and 49) when he wrote the following comments, but they also have broader relevance to Ayrton's work: "Mr. Ayrton is one of our most thoughtful artists and . . . he is fascinated by antiquity but . . . he has not bypassed abstraction. *Icarus Transformed* (by the velocity of his fall) is a brilliant conception, the figure half a man and half a lump of unrecognizable, material essence that offers us the secondary pleasure of abstract shapes and pure texture, but always within the clear and comforting

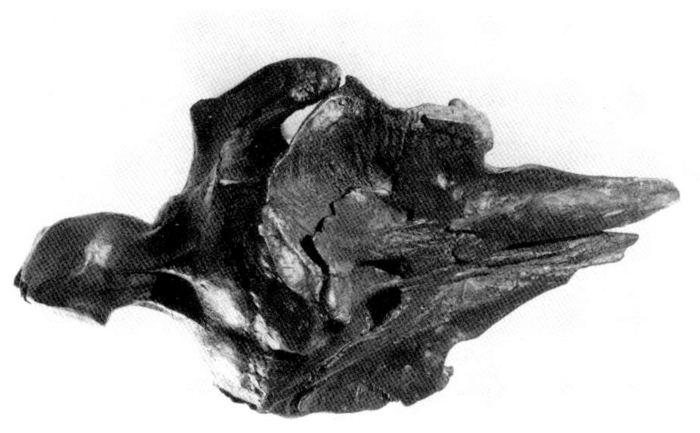

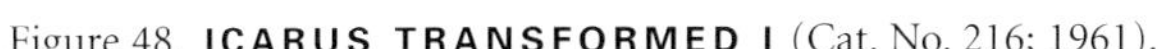

Figure 48. **ICARUS TRANSFORMED I** (Cat. No. 216; 1961).

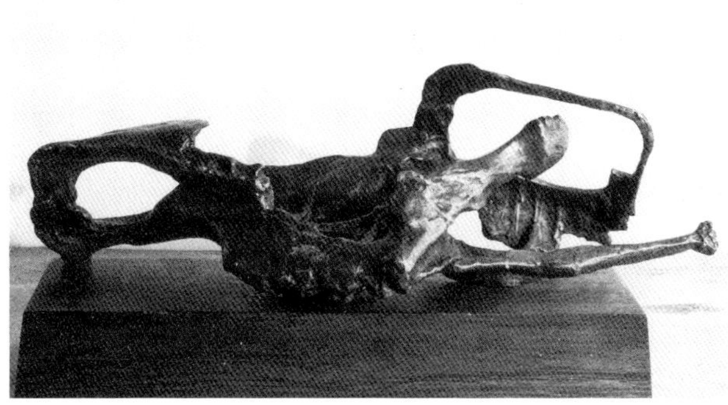

Figure 49. **ICARUS TRANSFORMED III** (Cat. No. 218; 1961).

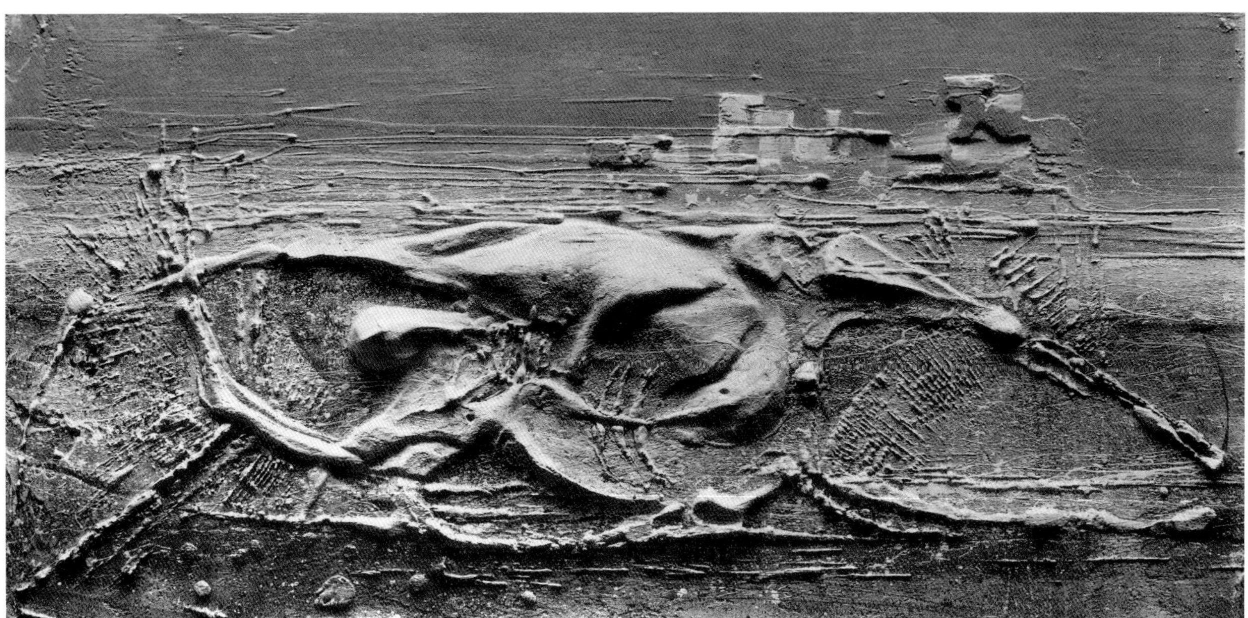

Figure 50. **ICARUS DROWNED** (Cat. No. 125; June-July 1960). John Webb, FRPS/Brompton Studios.

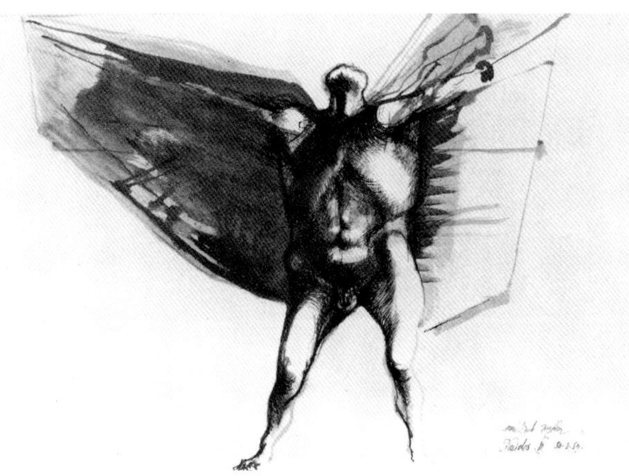

Figure 51. **DAEDALUS III** (Cat. No. 74; 30 November 1959).

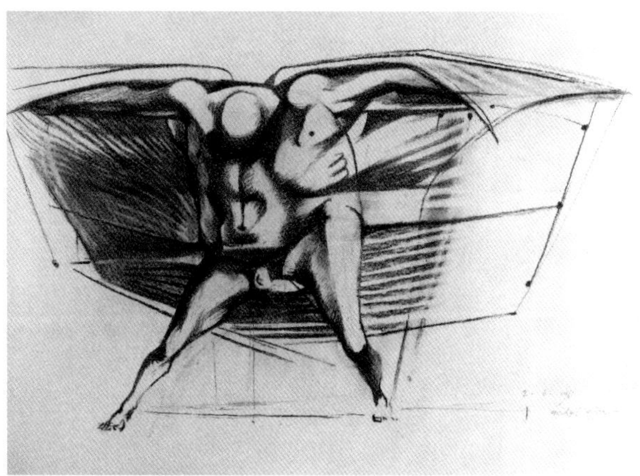

Figure 53. **DAEDALUS WINGED** (Cat. No. 195; 2 June 1961). Eaden Lilley, Cambridge.

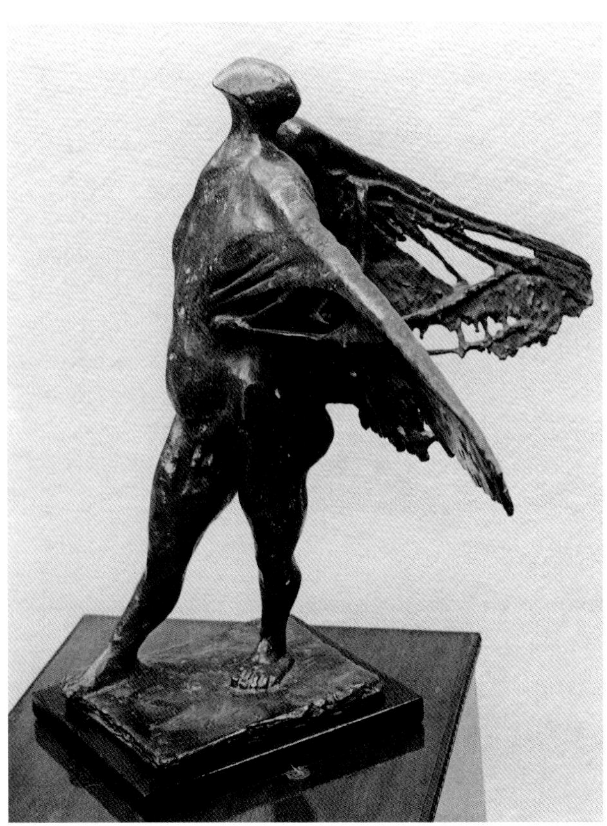

Figure 52. **DAEDALUS WINGED** (Cat. No. 77; 1959–60).

framework of mythology."[28] In these bronzes, Ayrton departs from figurative sculpture into a fairly high degree of abstraction, although the upper torso and head are still distinctly human. As one studies these bronzes alongside the painted stucco relief of *Icarus at the Climax* (Cat. No. 126; 1960; Figure 39), to mind comes this description by the poet Ted Hughes of Leonard Baskin's sculpture: "Humanoid, emerging . . . out of a cauldron of atoms—like a projectile from space, flayed and half-molten, some sort of cry arrested before it reaches the paralysed lips."[29]

Like the first bronze, *Icarus Transformed II & III* explore the impact of gravitational pull on a human figure hurtling away from the earth at an extremely high velocity. Although on the surface they illustrate what might have happened to Icarus if he really flew high enough to challenge and rape the sun, they also are clearly intended by the artist to suggest the probable effect on an astronaut of a sudden loss of pressurization. These bronze studies therefore make at once a dramatic and a frightening statement. The implications of the myth for contemporary society were made increasingly clear by Ayrton as he shaped and reshaped it in various media.

The "paraphrase of the human body" which Ayrton expressed in the many studies of the flight and fall was also carried forward into two works in which he returned

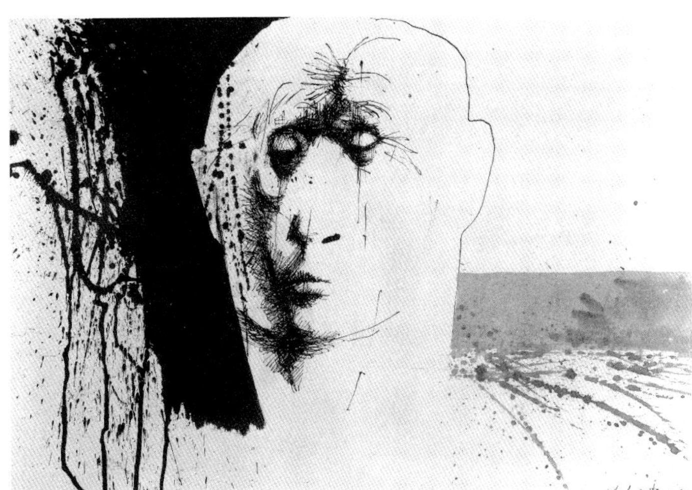

Figure 54. **MEDITATIVE HEAD (DAEDALUS)** (Cat. No. 83; 1959).

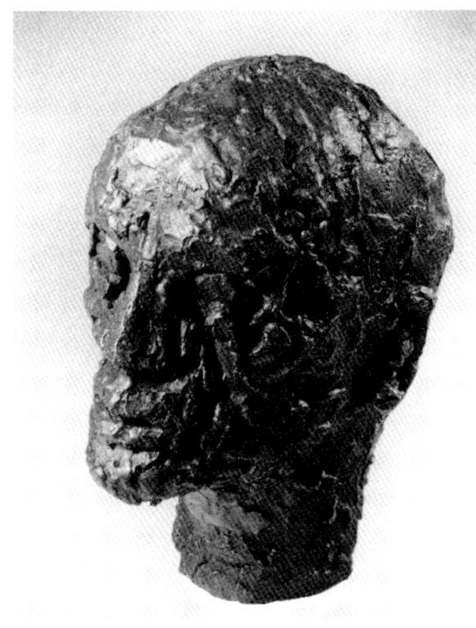

Figure 55. **DAEDALUS HEAD** (Cat. No. 75; 1959–60).

to a theme only briefly touched in 1958, in the wax and bone relief of the drowning of Icarus (Cat. No. 46). In mid-1960 Ayrton created a painted stucco relief, *Icarus Drowned* (Cat. No. 125; Figure 50), and a year later he completed a red and black ink wash of the same title (Cat. No. 226). In both the relief and the wash drawing he applied the conceptual framework of the bronzes of *Icarus Transformed.*

Despite the fact that Icarus dominated Ayrton's work during the years 1959–1961, he did not completely overshadow his inventor-father, who had made possible his one heroic exploit. Although Daedalus became a specific entity for Ayrton on Crete in 1958, as noted above, Ayrton did not attempt to give visual reality to him until near the end of 1959. A pen and wash drawing, *Daedalus III* (Cat. No. 74; 30 November 1959; Figure 51), is the first catalogued representation of Daedalus, even though its title indicates that it must have been preceded by two sketches which the artist did not release. A study for the bronze *Daedalus Winged* (Cat. No. 77; 1959–1960; Figure 52), this drawing blends realism and surrealism; the right wing appears fairly literal and stationary, whereas the left one simulates motion, as if it were successive frames in a moving picture.

Another sketch completed the following day, *Daedalus Winged* (Cat. No. 76), resembles the previous drawing, but there is greater symmetry of the wings; they are swept back, as in the bronze, although the positioning differs from that of the bronze. In the drawing they are spread full, and the outstretched arms reach as far back and as high as humanly possible, but in the bronze the wings are barely at the midpoint of expansion. Ayrton's early hesitancy to depict Daedalus, combined with his initial uncertainty whether this drawing depicted Daedalus or Icarus (see catalogue), imply that he was reluctant to give visual representation to the archetypal craftsman while he himself was still a relative novice in the art of sculpture.

Although one other sketch, the charcoal *Daedalus Winged* (Cat. No. 195; 2 June 1961; Figure 53), also shows Daedalus wearing wings, this aspect of the myth clearly assumed a subordinate role in Ayrton's creative imagination. Whereas the flight was central to the role of Icarus, the inventiveness which made the flight possible dominates Ayrton's portrayals of Daedalus. He thus follows artists from classical antiquity, who frequently depicted Daedalus with the tools of his trade (see chapter 3), thereby emphasizing his inventiveness, his creative abilities. Several of Ayrton's works feature only the head of Daedalus, suggesting the importance of his brain, his creative imagination.

Two drawings of *Meditative Head (Daedalus)* (Cat. Nos. 83 and 95; 1959 and 1960; Figure 54) were studies for the bronze *Daedalus Head* (Cat. No. 75; 1959–1960;

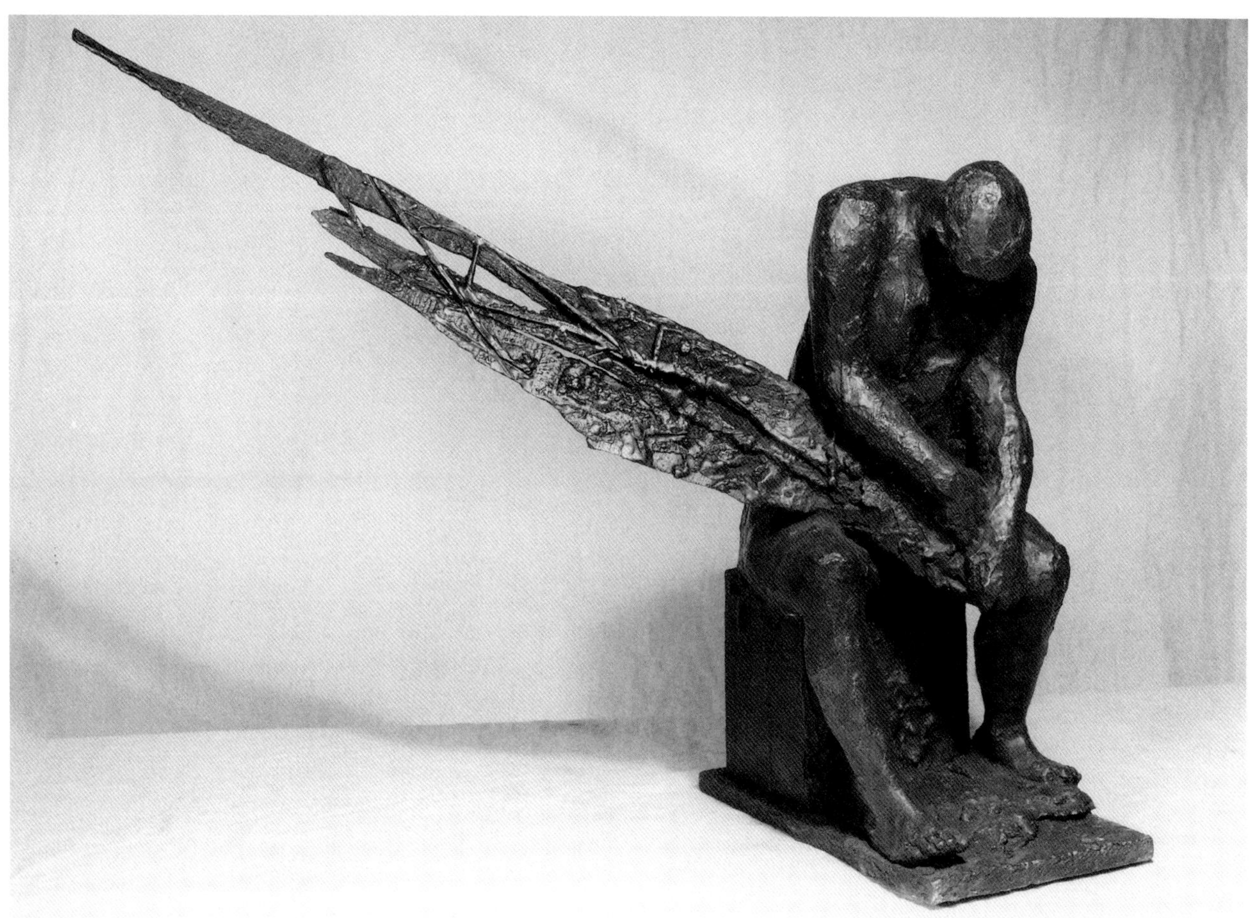

Figure 56. **DAEDALUS WINGMAKER** (Cat. No. 107; 1960).

Figure 55). The titles of the drawings reflect the qualities Ayrton associated with the inventor-artist, but they also offer a clue to Ayrton's own nature, thus hinting at his increasing self-identification with the creative Daedalus. The second of the drawings is reproduced on the first page of *Testament,* undoubtedly a deliberate choice, for Ayrton was never casual in his selection of works to illustrate a narrative, or vice versa. The narrator of *Testament*—Daedalus, of course—is deliberate, deductive, meditative, reflective. At one point he contrasts himself to "poets and other sacred persons" who are blinded by revelation: "I suspect that, since deduction and experiment have been my methods of gaining experience, I am no worse off and better instructed in these matters than many poets. Certainly I am better off than any hero, since I am not beset by my own personality. Cognition I prefer to revelation. . . . Honour lasts longer if it is gained by patient discovery rather than by brief nobility of action" (1962c, 41f.).

Ayrton portrayed not only the cognitive and imaginative qualities of Daedalus, but also that aspect which is crucial to success for a sculptor, the ability of one's hands to execute the ideas conceived in the head. In *Testament,* Daedalus declares, in a statement particularly relevant at this time to Ayrton: "What there is in me of *poesis* rests in my finger tips and in my eyes, but . . . it comes to me in the act of discovery. I make votives of one sort and another and celebrate possibilities in gold and bronze and other materials. . . . I take pleasure in combat with intractable substances and difficult circumstances and I compel them to quiet between my hands" (1962c, 13f.). This passage clearly was inspired by *Daedalus Wingmaker* (Cat. No. 107; 1960; Figure 56). This eighteen-inch bronze reveals the craftsman hunched over in concentration on the task of creating wings, wings that would enable him and his son to achieve a feat no human being had ever accomplished. The strength of the arms, the controlled energy of the hands shaping the wings, the skillfulness of the artisan, and the sense of impending success are all dramatically expressed in this key sculpture. Art critic Nevile Wallis had high praise for this "Rodinesque" sculpture, when he said in his review of *Drawings and Sculpture:* "Now and then he achieves sculptural form as satisfying and compact of muscular energy as his seated Daedalus fashioning a wing."[30] The influence of Rodin is indeed reflected in this bronze, which provides as much aesthetic appeal and emotive power as any of Rodin's finest works. In it, Ayrton demonstrates a level of mastery of material and technique equal to that of sculptors whom he admired and emulated. He achieved a new degree of confidence in his craft even as he gave visual reality to the archetypal craftsman famed for his creative power and his powerful creations.

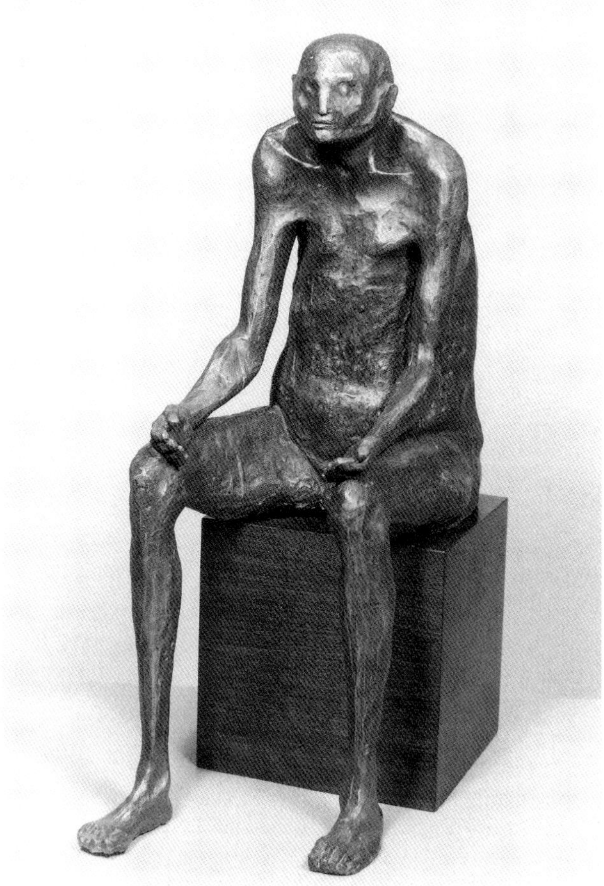

Figure 57. **DAEDALUS AT CUMAE** (Cat. No. 204; 1961).

The following year Ayrton cast his *Daedalus at Cumae* (Cat. No. 204; 1961; Figure 57) after completing two studies (Cat. Nos. 202–203; July 1961) for what he apparently thought would be his final bronze inspired by the myth.

The final paragraph of *Testament* either was shaped by this bronze or the prose was transmogrified into the bronze: "Grief is coming in upon me slowly. It finds its way through the cracks and fissures in the mould in which I am cast and I feel it coat the clay. I am perplexed and I shall say nothing more here" (1962c, 60). This bronze poignantly reveals the mythical first astronaut as a dejected inventor and an exhausted, grief-stricken father. It also captures the physical toll that was taken by the building of the temple to Apollo at Cumae and the aging of Daedalus that occurred during his toiling in the labyrinth beneath the acropolis.

Daedalus at Cumae, moreover, conveys Ayrton's own sense of fatigue after hundreds of attempts to discover and interpret Daedalus to himself and others. As is true for any good work of art, there is more than one inherent meaning. Aside from seeing this work as an expression of physical weariness, one can also view it as an expression of both a sense of completion with the myth and the artist's feeling of insecurity in his use of the craft of Daedalus. Ayrton's own statements in two separate books published a year or so later lend credence to viewing this sculpture in this way. In the one he says, "Daedalus having worked his miracle, must become still" (1962a, following pl. 116). In the other he declares: "I wish I was sure that I am free of Icarus and that I have enough of that part of Daedalus in me to make good images. The artist, 'the maker of things,' seeks to represent some part of what he thinks man is, and was, in order to discover himself in the process: or so I believe" (postscript, 1962c, written May 1962). In this declaration one can discern echoes of the uncertainty about his talent Ayrton had ascribed to Daedalus following the death of Icarus (1962c, 53ff.).

Although Ayrton's extensive treatment of the flight and fall, of the inventor and his exceptional invention, already offered convincing evidence that he was imbued with Daedalian inventiveness, his subsequent creations demonstrate that he had by no means freed himself from his mythical progenitor. He had entered through the Cumaean Gate, he had flown to Crete, had traversed the islands and mainland of Greece, and had finally returned to Cumae, but Ayrton could no more abandon Daedalus at Cumae by casting him in bronze than myth can be prevented from shaping and reshaping itself as it rises up in humankind's individual and collective dreams.

In *Testament* the artist declares that "the liquid which contains legend suspended . . . cannot be plumbed nor can its boundaries be charted" (1962c, 10). One reviewer of the book, recognizing that "we must approach this book as we do Blake's books," asserted that "any interpretation of Mr. Ayrton's poem can be no more than one of many possibilities, for it is polyvalent"; he concluded that "Ayrton's primary concern is . . . with man as creator—the artist, who is both the seer and the maker, Icarus and Daedalus. The Daedalian artist flies low and doubts himself. . . . The Icarian artist risks all. . . . [B]ut each, Daedalus and Icarus, is in varying degrees, necessary to the other."[31]

After completing numerous landscapes, from Cumae to Crete, from Delphi to Delos, and numerous representations exploring the implications of Icarus for our times, Ayrton hesitatingly created images of the archetypal craftsman whose skill he sought to inherit or at least emulate. Over this period of six years of intensive activity, Daedalus entered into Ayrton's psyche to a remarkable extent, but Ayrton was not fully confident that Daedalus had endowed him with his fabled talent. When Ayrton finished *Testament,* he hoped that he had said all that needed to be said about the myth. He must have perceived, however, if only subconsciously, that he could neither plumb the depths nor chart the boundaries of the myth. And when he sought to escape by the gate through which he entered the myth, did he not know that the Cumaean Gate is not single but multiple?

Journey into a Labyrinth

5

"I am sure that all things are ordered and I shall presently grasp the design of these things which concern us here. I shall leave all this that I have written, burying it under the rock."

Thus concludes *The Testament of Daedalus.* A reproduction of the second drawing of "the rock," *Cumae* (Cat. No. 11; 11 May 1956), seals the narrative. By the time this testament was read by the public in 1962, the Daedalus residing within Ayrton had emerged from the Cumaean Gate with a new artistic inspiration. Rather, he had discovered new significance in the Sibyl who briefly attracted his attention at the very beginning of his wandering into the myth. Drawing fresh insight and a new burst of creative energy from the numinous rock and its legendary occupant, he began to draw, sculpt, and paint the oracle. Heraclitus reminds us of the history of the Sibyl (see chapter 2): "The Sibyl, with raving mouth, uttering her unlaughing, unadorned words, reaches us over a thousand years with her voice—through the inspiration of the god."

In her manifestation as the Cumaean Sibyl, the oracle was also known as Deiphobe, daughter of Glaucus. Deiphobe was the one who welcomed Aeneas to Cumae, and it was she who led him down into the underworld to meet the ghost of his father, Anchises. The Cumaean Sibyl, or Deiphobe, lived within the labyrinthine rock at Cumae, and at its center she received the god and uttered his prophecies. The hundred passages honeycombing the rock carried her prophetic voice to whoever was there to hear them.

At Delphi Apollo's mantic oracle was Pythia. She delivered her prophetic utterances while crouching over her sacred tripod, which was set over the fissure in the rock below the temple of Apollo. Breathing the smoke of laurel leaves, Pythia entered into a trance before delivering her ambiguous prophecies. Like Deiphobe and the many other oracles, Pythia spoke when filled with the god. It is a paradox that although the sun god traveled daily across the heavens in full view of humanity, his mouthpieces usually delivered his oracular pronouncements from caverns deep within the earth.

Dr. Anthony Storr, a physician and psychiatrist, once offered this analysis of the oracle:

> The function of the oracle is twofold. On the one hand, she increases consciousness. By her very equivocation, she confronts us with ourselves, and because her answers are indirect, she makes us discover ourselves.
>
> On the other hand, she puts the questioner in touch with his own hidden resources of intuition and inspiration: and this is undoubtedly why she is here portrayed as female. For it is by means of his relation to the feminine, whether this be a real woman in the external world,

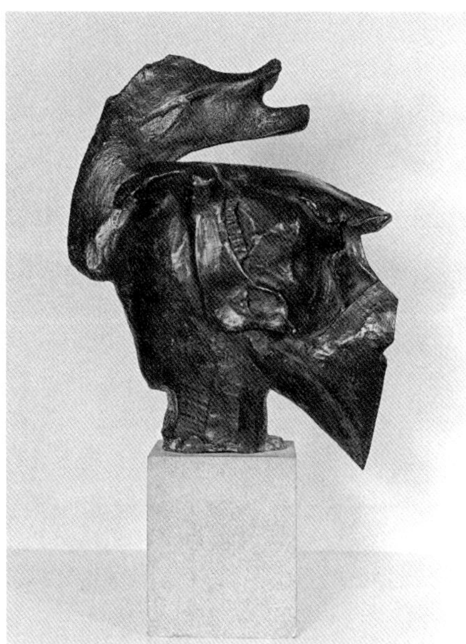

Figure 58. **TALOS ARMED HEAD I** (Cat. No. 3; 1954–56).

> or the feminine part of himself, that a man can become fully aware of his own creative potentialities. In this sense the oracle is the opposite of the Minotaur, and each reaches out to the artist who, as man, is poised between them.[1]

During the time Ayrton was preoccupied with making images of the oracle, he came to understand the oracle of Apollo to a much greater extent than when he first encountered the Cumaean Sibyl in 1956. As he looked back at that first encounter, however, some eight years later, he declared: "When I first came to this long inhabited place, I seemed to breathe a smoke coming from deep in the ground and became drunk with it."[2] During the intervening years, moreover, "ever anxious to establish the archaeological background to his intuitions," Michael consulted Sybille Haynes at the British Museum on the subject of both oracles and tripods, "adding scholarly underpinning to what, in the *hallucinated truth in split time* out of which he worked, he already 'knew.'"[3]

The oracle, however, was not the sole subject of Ayrton's creativity at this time. The Minotaur, another solitary inhabitant of a labyrinth (indeed, of *the* Labyrinth) also began to appear in Ayrton's oeuvre during this period. Linked inextricably with them in Ayrton's art was a third figure—a sentinel, symbol of the blind authority that imprisons and confines victims, such as the socially unacceptable Minotaur. This sentinel bore the name Talos. Ayrton's own entrapment in the labyrinth of myth was foreshadowed in his early bronze sculpture, *Talos Armed Head I* (Cat. No. 3; 1954–1956; Figure 58), whom Ayrton derived from the bronze guardian of Crete. In Ayrton's mind and in his art, this Talos began to merge in identity with Daedalus's own nephew Talos, just as in the narrative in *Testament.*[4] In the process, Daedalus's nephew was reduced from an attractive, inventive youth to an empty-headed, even insane, guardian of Crete who wandered around the island, believing he was made of bronze, but in actuality he was simply garbed in a bronze suit of armor devised by Talos himself (Ayrton 1967, 105–13).

All three figures have relevance to contemporary society, and all are used by the artist to convey a message, even several messages. One critic, Robert Wraight, in his review of an exhibition of Ayrton's work at a London gallery, offered this concise summary of their relevance: "The headless, puffed-up or hollow bronze *Sentinels* are the military powers; the *Minotaur* is the helpless mass of the world's people who believe the modern Talos can defend them; the *Oracle* is (unless I have misunderstood) the embodiment of all our modern prophets, false and otherwise, whose advice is never fully understood until it is too late either to heed or ignore it."[5] Although Wraight's comments provide a starting point for understanding Ayrton's work during this period, he fails to do justice to Ayrton's intelligence or the complexity of Ayrton's imagery. Later in the review, however, he displays an appreciation for the evocative power of Ayrton's sculpture, declaring that one can "approach almost any piece of his sculpture without any knowledge of his intentions, theories or source of inspiration, and it will 'speak' to you in its own language, the language of sculpture."[6]

Nevile Wallis, on the other hand, when reviewing the same exhibition, showed great respect for Ayrton's intelligence, but he limited his praise for Ayrton's art to just a few works in the show:

> Mr. Michael Ayrton's acute and calculating intelligence may remind one of the late Paul Nash's. Both have sought

> to reconcile contrary elements in their work. In both artists a reverence for the imaginative tradition, literary inspiration and an independent mind have combined to produce imagery which has never flowed naturally, yet in inspired moments can attain a certain poetical solemnity of imagination. Nash, of course, was a key figure in his time, a painter and prophet whose presence continues to be felt. Mr. Ayrton today is an uncomfortable isolationist.[7]

The implication of the final statement in this quotation is that Ayrton was out of step with the times. It is true that he was out of harmony with the prevailing trend in art. A careful study of Ayrton's work over the last two decades of his life, however, reveals that he was a prophet speaking out of an imaginative tradition in art and literature that spans centuries, yet he always spoke with a contemporary voice. Ayrton was isolated from the herd because he had a message that expressionism and abstraction could not adequately convey. He followed a largely figurative tradition, rooting himself in the work of the old masters, from whom he learned so much in his formative youth and in the equally formative years just after the war.

During the first stage of Ayrton's journey into the labyrinth, from 1962 to 1964, his prophecies came through the three mythical figures who partook of humanity but were not fully or solely human. The oracle, the sentinel, and the Minotaur dominated Ayrton's creative expression at this time, especially in his drawing. Of the drawings catalogued between 3 February 1962, the date of *Oracle I* (Cat. No. 242), and 23 July 1964, when *Sybil on Blue* (Cat. No. 454) ended this period of creative activity, only a few did not involve this unusual trio (there were, however, some drawings during this time that were unrelated to myth, as was generally true throughout his involvement with mythical themes and subjects). The first painting of the oracle, *Oracle I (August 10)* (Cat. No. 279; Figure 59), did not come until August 1962, and there were just over ten oracle paintings, ending with *Oracle* (Cat. No. 412; February 1964). Ayrton never painted the Minotaur, and there are only two paintings of sentinels (Cat. No. 270; 1962; Cat. No. 358; 13 August 1963; Figures 60 and 61), and one of these paintings, *Sentinel* (Cat. No. 270), approaches bronze, for its red and gold colors create a

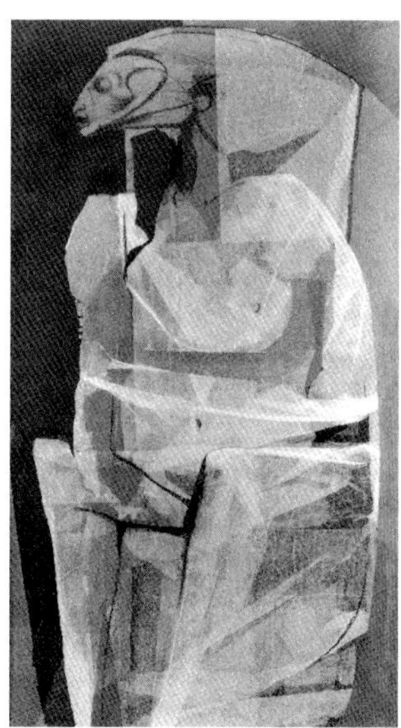

Figure 59. **ORACLE I (AUGUST 10)** (Cat. No. 279; 1962).

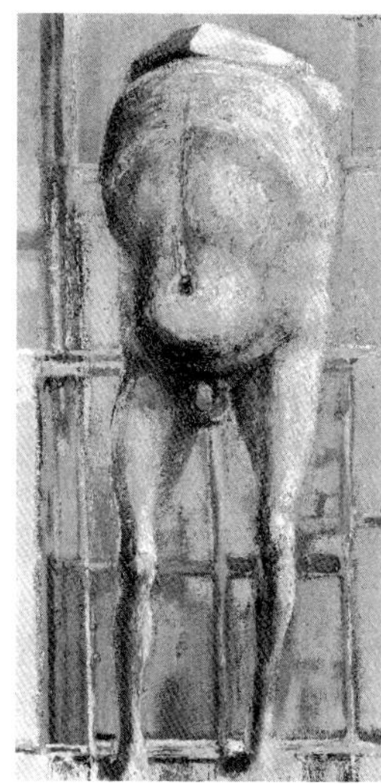

Figure 60. **SENTINEL** (Cat. No. 270; 1962).

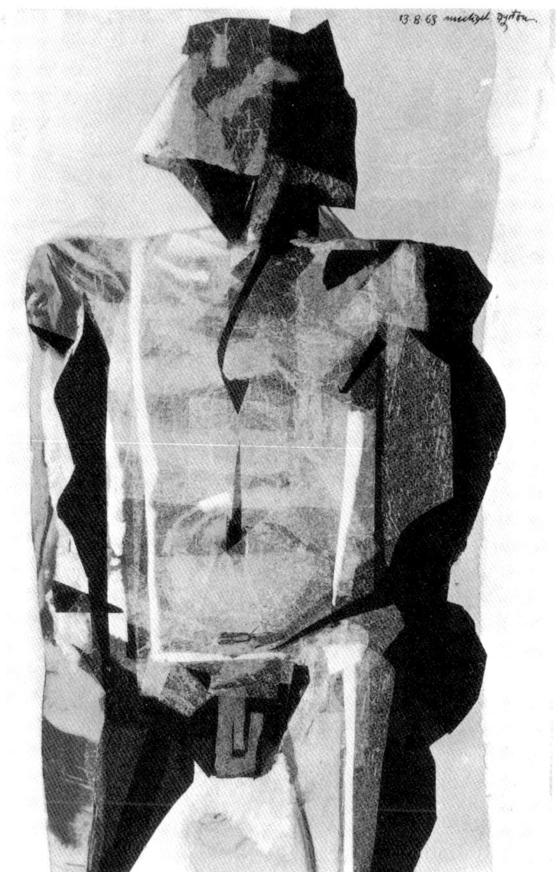

Figure 61. **TALOS** (Cat. No. 358; 13 August 1963).

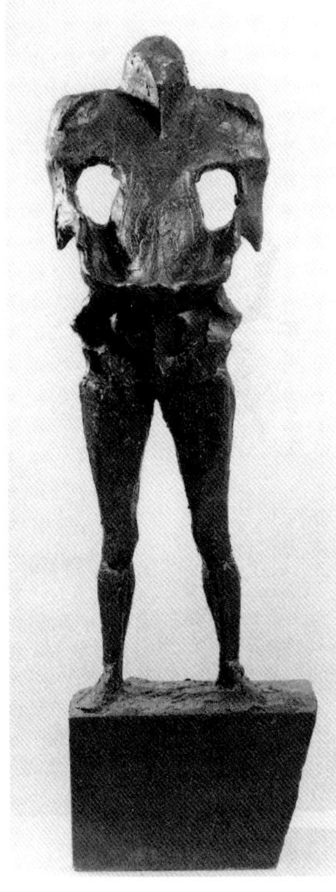

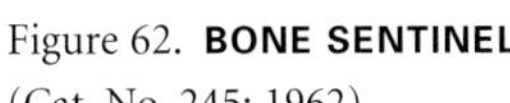

Figure 62. **BONE SENTINEL** (Cat. No. 245; 1962).

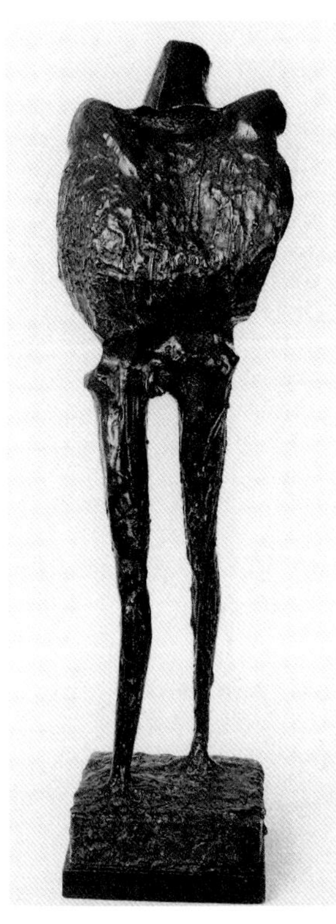

Figure 63. **SLENDER SENTINEL** (Cat. No. 252; 1962).

hot, brazen effect. Ayrton himself saw this painting as "the only instance where the sculpture clearly crossed the board."[8] Although there were only a dozen or so paintings of all three figures combined, they were each cast in bronze in seven to ten different forms during the years 1962–1964.

Ayrton's concern with sentinel images, spanning well under two years from first drawing to last bronze, was more short-lived than his interest in the oracle and the Minotaur. The earliest catalogued drawing, *Sentinel II* (Cat. No. 227; 24 December 1961), was a study for the bronze *Bone Sentinel* (Cat. No. 245; 1962). As in many of Ayrton's sculptures, a bone forms the carapace for this bronze. Ayrton called bone "the carapace of the vitals" (1962a, below pl. 50 and 51), although the chicken bone cast in this bronze provides only a very slender and fragile carapace. Whether Ayrton chose the chicken bone to suggest a "chickenly" cowardice on the part of the sentinel is uncertain, but it would be consistent with Ayrtonian irony to use the chicken bone to convey such an idea. Regardless, one can agree with the critic who observed that "in the *Oracle* and *Sentinel* figures the armature of bone structure is spare and elegant."[9]

Of the seven sentinel bronzes, six were cast in 1962 (Cat. Nos. 245, 250–253, 284) and the other in 1963 (Cat. No. 381). Only the first and last sentinel bronzes are more than two feet tall, but the last one, *Talos (Large version)* (Cat. No. 381; Figure 65), is a life-sized sixty-eight inches tall. Except for *Bone Sentinel* (Cat. No. 245; Figure 62), which appears to have arms because of the shape of the chicken bone, all the sentinels are armless. They are also faceless, and deliberately so. Although *Bone Sentinel* and *Small Sentinel* (Cat. No. 253; 1962) strongly resemble visored, helmeted medieval knights, none of the sentinels is construed by Ayrton as having brains. The guardianship of Crete by Talos, said Ayrton, "is, of course, a fiction, but he is believed capable of defending the place and people take comfort from him. A certain tranquillity lies in his stupid presence, a certain comfort. He has no brains and no arms, but looks very powerful" (1962a, below pl. 117).

The puffed out chest of *Small Sentinel* (Cat. No. 253), when viewed from the side, especially creates this impression of power, but more than a hint of vanity is also expressed in his stance. When viewed full face, however, his head seems to shrink in proportion to the rest of his body, and deep cavities are evident in his armor. *Talos Maquette* (Cat. No. 284; 1962; Figure 64) began a process of squaring and expanding the chest, which was completed in the *Talos (Large version)* (Cat. No. 381; 1963; Figure 65). Talos's box-like torso, supported by the muscular, wide-set legs, enhances his appearance of power, but Ayrton himself destroyed that impression with these words written a few years later: "and Talos the inventor, having been banged idly on the bench of his madness, was flattened and squared off by the impact, to make the shield-shaped warrior he had become when he found me on Crete" (1967, 191–92). Upon viewing this bronze in relation to the text, one readily discovers the interplay of word and image, as is often true with Ayrton's creative expressions. Here he is obviously describing the sculpture of Talos, although an uninformed reader would be totally oblivious to the connection and yet could still appreciate the description, just as the uninformed viewer could appreciate

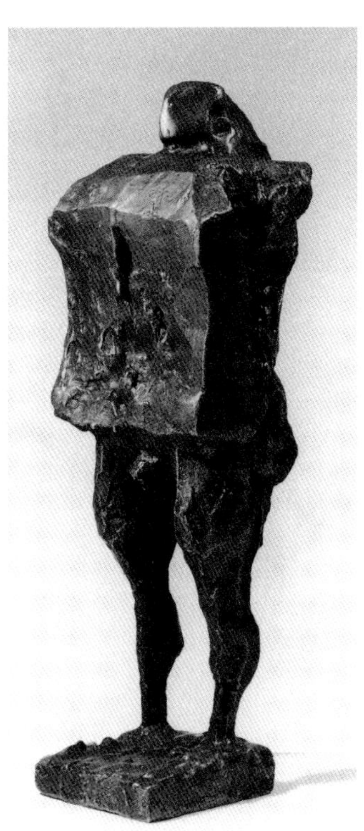

Figure 64. **TALOS. MAQUETTE** (Cat. No. 284; 1962). Eaden Lilley, Cambridge.

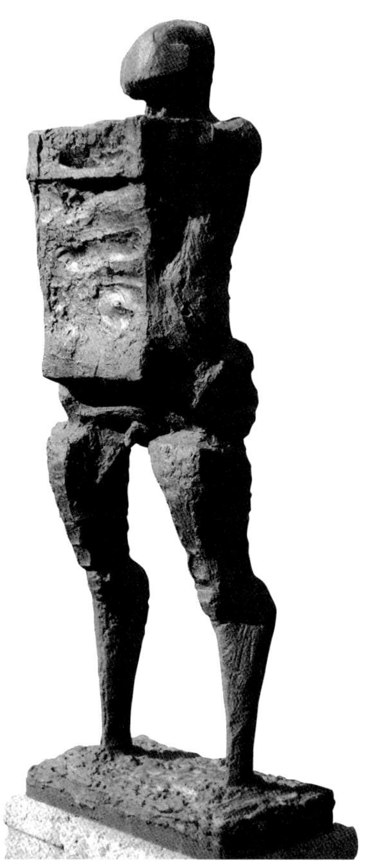

Figure 65. **TALOS** (Large version) (Cat. No. 381; 1963).

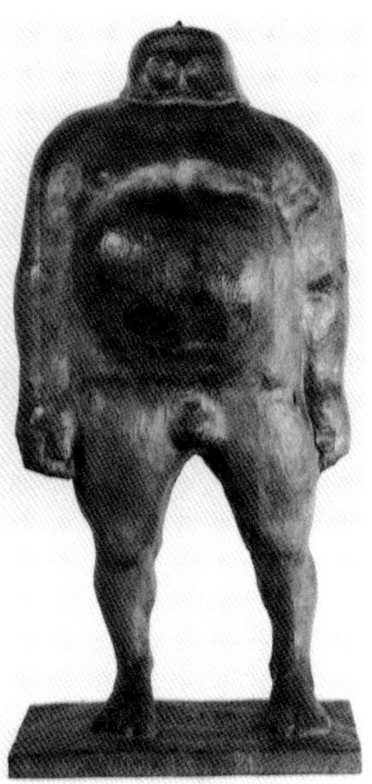

Figure 66. Leonard Baskin, **ARMORED MAN** (1962). © Estate of Leonard Baskin. Manyi Wong, New York.

the sculpture without the text. The word does not require the image, nor does the image need the description to achieve its full power. Nonetheless, being aware of the connection enriches the appreciation and enlarges the myth. Ayrton's alteration of the myth, moreover, would not be readily apparent from simply viewing the sculpture. In that respect, therefore, the word enhances the image.

Earlier in the same "novel" (1967, 108), Ayrton first introduced Talos as the bronze guardian of Crete with this graphic description:

> [T]here, as if on fire beneath the lowering sun, stood an armoured figure like a bronze fortress. It limped stiffly toward us, bellowing. . . . Half its body was hidden by a tower-shield bossed with the image of a partridge. The top of this shield was curved upward to guard the face, while the base of it scraped the ground. What I could see of the figure's legs and feet was booted and clothed in leather. . . . It wore a slashing sword and dagger of bronze suspended from a bronze belt, a bronze plastron high in the neck and a helmet crested with two curved bronze horns pointing forward. This helmet had long cheekpieces tied below the red-bearded chin and between these, a beaten bronze mask covered the rest of the face above the lips.

This frightening bronze man, however, wore a grin that looked so ridiculous Daedalus was reduced to tears by his laughter at this caricature of military might (Ayrton 1967, 109). The subsequent unmasking of this bronze idiot elicited sadness in Daedalus (Ayrton 1967, 110), just as one is saddened to realize that all the mighty army of a superpower is powerless against guerilla warfare in the jungles of Vietnam, against hostage-takers in Iran, in the bombing of embassies and the World Trade Center

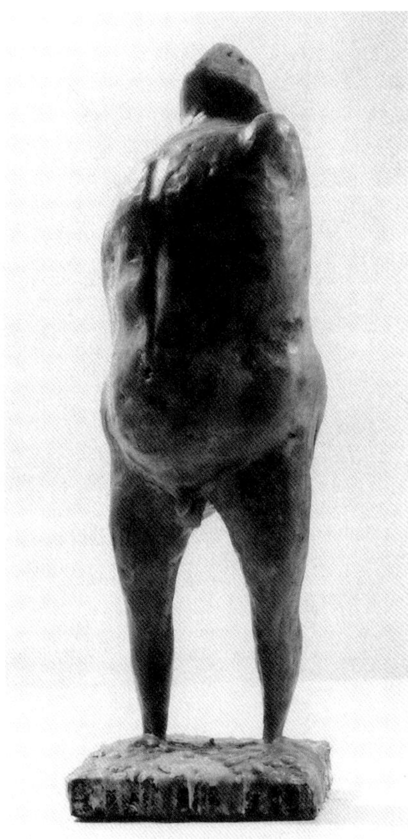

Figure 67. **FAT SENTINEL** (Cat. No. 250; 1962). Stearn & Sons Ltd., Cambridge.

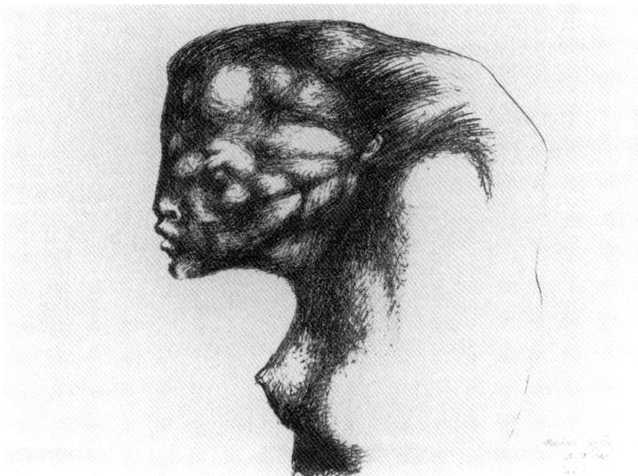

Figure 68. **ORACLE III** (Cat. No. 247; 22 February 1962). Eaden Lilley, Cambridge.

in New York City, or of a ship in the harbor in Yemen. And even when the army of the so-called People's Republic of China or of Romania crushes the defenseless people who want only freedom, that victory is as hollow as Ayrton's sentinel figures and the country's leadership as mindless as the maddened, bronzed Talos. Talos, "the sentinel armless and equipped only with a rudimentary head," said T. G. Rosenthal, "does service for our equivalent figures who need not be named here—the sturdy, the magnificently exteriored who are yet mindless and hollow. Ayrton's Talos is a peculiarly telling image of some of our upper echelons."[10] As a commentary on military might, the weapons race, or the hollow-mindedness of some leaders, the Talos sequence, like the Icarus series, has an immediacy that is paradoxically timeless because of its mythic dimension.

Oracle and Minotaur images overlapped with the Talos or sentinel images, rather than developing sequentially. It therefore is hardly surprising to discover that *Study for Sentinel (Talos)* (Cat. No. 244; 12 February 1962) takes on a new life a fortnight later in two Minotaur studies, *Fat Man I* (Cat. No. 248; 27 February 1962) and *The Fat Man, Half Length* (Cat. No. 249; 27 February 1962),[11] or that the contours of *Oracle II* (Cat. No. 246; 12 February 1962), *Oracle III* (Cat. No. 247; 22 February 1962) and *Oracle* (Cat. No. 259; 23 April 1962) more than just vaguely echo the Talos bronzes. The *Fat Man* studies may have been unconsciously influenced by Leonard Baskin, for there are strong resemblances to Baskin's *Seated Fat Man,* a small 1956 bronze (Jaffe, fig. 31), and a bronze *Seated Birdman* (1961; Jaffe, fig. 90). *Armored Man* (1962; birch; Jaffe, fig. 68) also resembles *Fat Sentinel* (Cat. No. 250; 1962) (see Figures 66 and 67), although the close proximity of dates makes direct influence somewhat doubtful. It is conceivable, of course, that Ayrton influenced Baskin's *Armored Man,* although I have not ascertained a link between them at this particular time. The iconography of Baskin's *Seated Fat Man* is not connected to Greek mythology, but the imagery probably derives from Isaiah 28:1–6 (Jaffe, 62).

The artist's earlier concern with the effect of stress upon the human body, particularly apparent in the Icarus sequence, also revealed itself in *Oracle III* (Cat. No. 247; Figure 68), albeit in a new frame of reference. Here the artist examines how the oracle's head begins to break up under the stress of receiving the god's message. Shown at the point just before utterance, the oracle is represented as having the words forced through her lips. There is a consequent distension of the face and head, rather than a contortion of their muscles.[12] The distortion of the head of the oracle in the third collage on this subject, *Oracle III (August 12 '62)* (Cat. No. 281; Figure 69), also is reminiscent of heads under stress, but this figure's blind-eyed oracular appearance creates a new effect, which the later bronze *Maze Head* (Cat. No. 522; 1965) repeats in another context (see below). The idea of stress is carried even further in *Tattered Oracle* (Cat. No. 323; 25 February 1963); having lasted the thrust of Apollo longer than she could physically endure it, she begins to disintegrate, in orgasm, as Icarus did. It is understandable why Daedalus would have said, in *Testament* (Ayrton 1962c, 41), "Cognition I prefer to revelation," for with revelation one risks being unable to contain the god. The god who was the oracle's source of inspiration is brought clearly to mind by the imagery of a related tissue-paper collage, *Figure with Laurel Leaves* (Cat. No. 394; December 1963; Figure 70). Suggesting both Daphne and the price of Apollo's unfulfilled love for her, the laurel leaves in the oracle's clenched fist command one's attention, for they are set in profile against a lighter background. The god-induced disintegration expressed in *Tattered Oracle* is evident here, but the profile head also illustrates the distortion before the oracular utterance conveyed in the *Oracle III* drawing (Cat. No. 247).

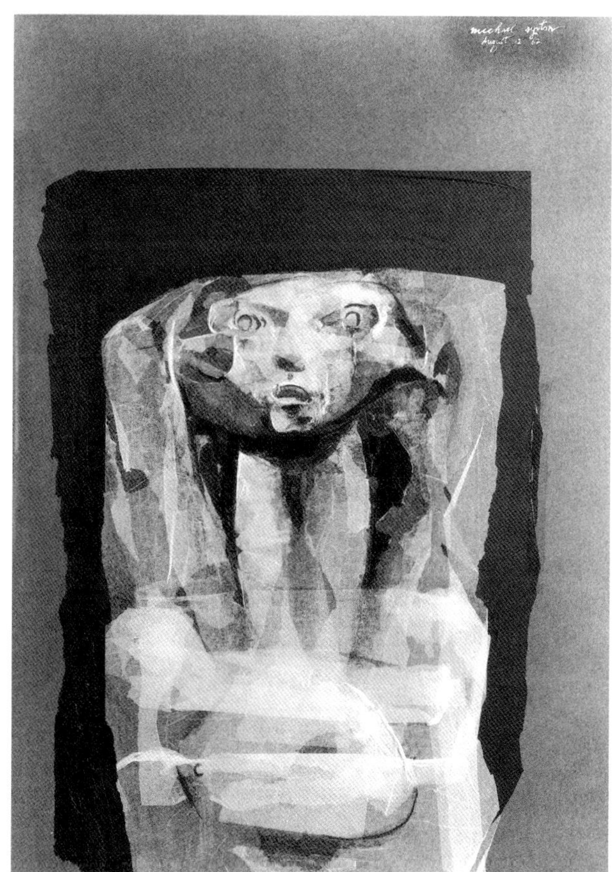

Figure 69. **ORACLE III (AUGUST 12 '62)** (Cat. No. 281).

Like Proteus in the hands of Aristaeus, the oracle constantly reshaped herself in Ayrton's hands. As she did so, Ayrton placed increasing emphasis on the idea of sexual union between Apollo and his oracle. Ayrton made explicit, in drawing and bronze, the orgasmic union with Apollo that Deiphobe described to Daedalus in *The Maze Maker* (1967, 215):

> This tripod and its cauldron are my marriage bed. Here the god takes me and when he does I speak, if I do speak, not as I speak now but in orgasm. What I say then I do not know, for it is not my voice but Apollo's and I am charged with his divinity. His semen jets through me and

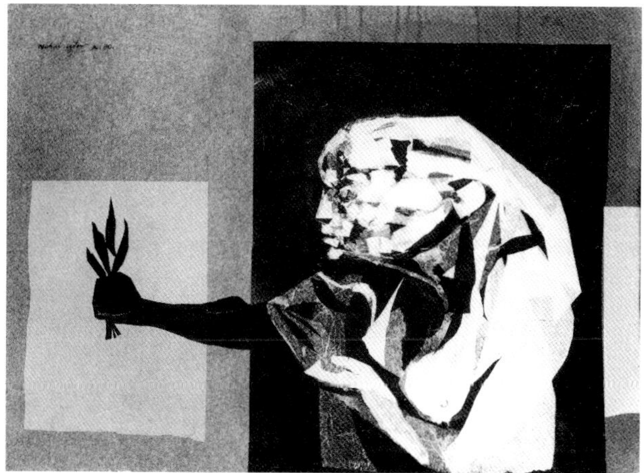

Figure 70. **FIGURE WITH LAUREL LEAVES** (Cat. No. 394; December 1963). Stearn & Sons Ltd., Cambridge.

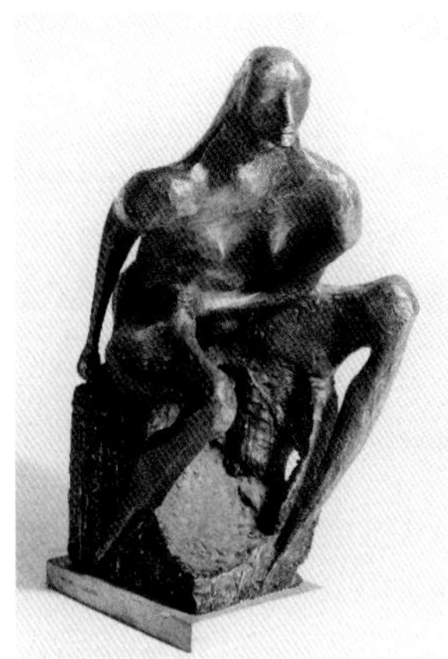

Figure 71. **ORACLE I**
(Cat. No. 296; 1962).
Stearn & Sons Ltd., Cambridge.

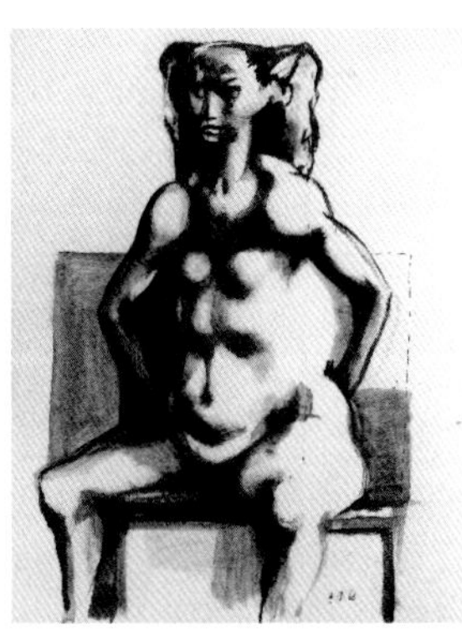

Figure 72. **ORACLE, ASTRIDE**
(Cat. No. 327; 4 March 1963).
Stearn & Sons Ltd., Cambridge.

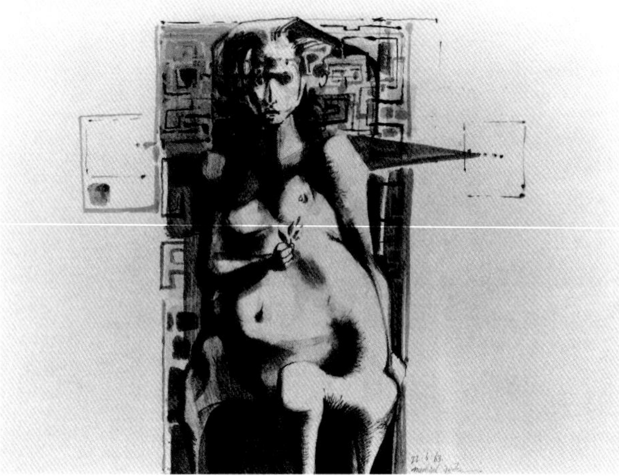

Figure 73. **THE ORACLE AS KEY FIGURE**
(Cat. No. 338; 22 June 1963).

> his ejaculation makes me cry to his rhythm. In this cauldron my apotheosis manifests. In its boiling bowl my flesh is consumed and flows downward. In the steam lies whatever prophecy may be found and when that steam condenses into words you will learn what you already know and be confirmed in it. The condensation takes a little time. All will be over before you hear words.

These words were written several years after Ayrton evolved his ideas about the oracle, and that evolution began in the course of his studies for the first bronze sculpture, *Oracle I* (Cat. No. 296; 1962; Figure 71). Three studies, a black ink wash (Cat. No. 259; 23 April 1962), a wash (Cat. No. 273; 12 July 1962), and a pencil and wash drawing (Cat. No. 274; 16 July 1962), all simply entitled *Oracle,* show the oracle seated, although the two later drawings are closer in conception to the bronze. The similarity between drawing and sculpture is particularly evident in the placement of the arms and the general shape of the upper torso, but the treatment of the lower torso is markedly different in the bronze. The change is at once startling and dramatic, for her thighs are spread to receive the god, and the base has become concave, suggesting that the god's power has already exploded within her. Similar treatments occur in *Pythia* (Cat. No. 379; 1963), *Maquette for Large Oracle I* (Cat. No. 386; 1963), and *Oracle (Large Version)* (Cat. No. 397; 1963–1964; see Figures 76, 79 and 80).

Whereas in Ayrton's version of the Icarus myth, Icarus's love for Apollo is frustrated, in the ancient myths it is usually Apollo who finds his love thwarted, whether his object is male or female. By giving a strongly sexual interpretation to the oracle's relation to Apollo, Ayrton not only rewrites the myth, but also gives the god a satisfaction commonly denied him. The influence of Freud here seems to have invaded the creative process itself, since both Eros and Thanatos are present as forces in Ayrton's presentation of the myth.

Although Ayrton appears to have moved through successive stages in his mining of the rich resources of myth, his development of the oracle series cannot be traced in purely chronological terms, for there is greater fluidity in his portrayal of her than in that of any other of his major thematic figures. Ayrton's own words reveal how protean the oracle was in his grasp. In *The Maze Maker* he described her varied manifestations in a poetic catalogue of the multiple, nonsequential transformations she underwent in his hands as she inspired him to draw, paint, and sculpt her:

> The chamber beyond the door was not large and its walls were as smooth and faultless as the door had been. It was a room shaped like a cauldron and furnished solely with a hearth, a pitted boulder identical with that which I had imagined I had seen after my contest with the Minotaur, and a bronze tripod-cauldron so shallow as to form a stool. The stone duplicated that upon which the horned god had sat. Upon the tripod sat a woman. She was naked and she held in her right hand a branch of laurel. Smoke from the hearth gushed about her. The light was thick as if it were being filtered through the cast skin of a snake.
>
> The woman did not speak, she changed. She passed through a series of transformations not in any sequence but capriciously as if to demonstrate her variety, so that she bloomed, withered, extended and contracted, rose and subsided, died, disintegrated and took shape again, a curled foetus in a placenta of smoke. Her age passed before me, not logically from youth to senility, but abruptly, in disorder. Her presence seemed to flicker in a broken rhythm. She was a child, huge eyed and slender, a kore with tip tilted breasts, a woman full of the child kicking in her belly, a matron ripe as autumn, a child again, clutching bay shoots sticky in her hand, a crone twisted and wizened as a dead shrub and again a maiden. Fragments of her persona were shown to me falling as wayward as leaves so that I could not see her whole, nor did she cease to alter.
>
> The woman turned to bronze, each limb flattened and pulled to marry with her tripod. She shaped herself to a fetish, lost her humanity and became an implacable idol. Her features slipped from her face and she was visored. Her arms clove to her and joined into her sides. She became a snake and reared coiling from the bowl of the tripod.
>
> Then again her hands sprang out from her and became a girl's, her arms lifted like greenstick twigs, Daphne athwart the sun, and this metamorphosis opened to permit the woman to re-emerge from the laurel. She withered so that her skin was rough as bark and wrinkled as dried fruit. She filled with sap and opened her thighs to the smoke licking her belly. She closed them and became legless as a serpent. Her disorder was dazzling. If she had gone through a gamut of changes which had any ordered ritual to explain it, I think I should have grasped the meaning, but there was none. Her disintegrations and re-integrations were totally haphazard and continued until I could no longer watch them and hid my head in my hands. (1967, 208–9)

From among the many transformations suggested in this torrent of images, a representative sample reveals recurring patterns and themes, with frequent subtle but important variations. The positioning of the oracle's legs in *Oracle, Astride* (Cat. No. 327; 4 March 1963; Figure 72) subsequently moves into a depiction of her as tripod in *The Oracle as Key Figure* (Cat. No. 338; 22 June 1963; Figure 73). Although the first sculpture (Cat. No. 296, above) suggested the beginning of a union of the oracle with her base, her legs still remained distinctly her own. All the other sculptures, however, emphasize the marriage of the oracle with her tripod. Either her legs form two of the three legs of the tripod or, conversely, the tripod's legs are also her supports. In *Seated Tripod Figure* (Cat. No. 314; 1962–1963), for example, her legs melt into the solid bronze seat and emerge below it as "spare and elegant" supports. Above, her elongated neck accentuates her role as the voice of Apollo, and her face links this sculpture with votive art of the ancient island cultures of the southern Aegean Sea, for it resembles the familiar faces of small marble Cycladic goddesses of the second or third millennium B.C.E. (also recalled in Ayrton's Cycladic landscapes, Cat. Nos. 86, 91–94; see Figure 74). At the same time, this work has a very contemporary look, since Giacometti and Moore, among others, also evoked these antique images in their sculpture. The influence of both sculptors upon Ayrton has already been noted, but their influence is often somewhat oblique and subtle, as here. Nonetheless, their effect upon Ayrton's visual memory must never be overlooked nor underestimated. Moore may also have had an influence upon the oracle's union with her base: his bronze *Mother and Child* (1953) uses the mother's closed legs to form the third leg of a tripod. If so, Ayrton reversed the arrangement to open the legs, but it is also noteworthy that many of Moore's reclining

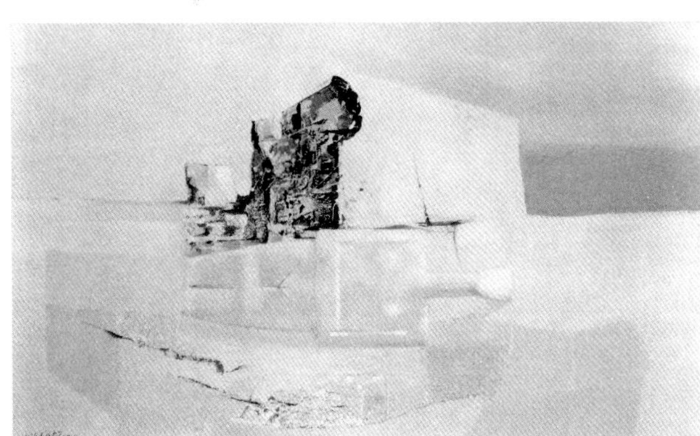

Figure 74. **LARGE CYCLADIC I** (Cat. No. 86; 1959–60).

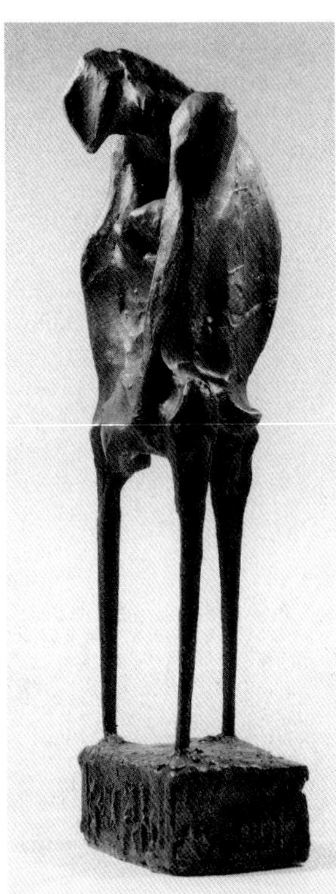

Figure 75. **TRIPOD ORACLE** (Cat. No. 315; 1962–63). Stearn & Sons Ltd., Cambridge.

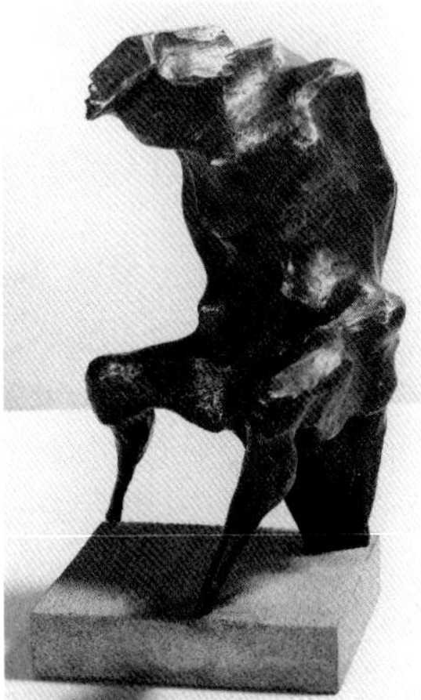

Figure 76. **PYTHIA** (Cat. No. 379; 1963). Stearn & Sons Ltd., Cambridge.

sculptures of the eternal feminine or primordial mother also open their thighs.[13]

Tripod Oracle (Cat. No. 315; 1962–1963; Figure 75) takes on a serpentine shape, although she is mounted on three stilt-like legs, the legs of the tripod itself. The shape of this bronze oracle, of course, calls to mind the battle of Apollo with the earth mother's serpent, Python. Ayrton described this bronze in *The Maze Maker,* following his account of the union of Apollo and Deiphobe:

> In the basin of the cauldron there was no woman. There was a brazen, extended throat rising from a drum which had become part of the tripod cauldron. It was an entity, boneless as a snake but rigid as metal standing upright on tripod tangs. This image, topped by a head as featureless as an axeblade, spoke in words condensed from scalding steam. Each word came sibilant. The pythoness was whispering. Then her speech thickened and the words stuck mollusc in the mass of sound. Words came from her that rang, others that fell plummeting like stones, and through it all the serpent hissing breathed through the sense. (1967, 219)[14]

Ayrton followed this description with an oracular utterance so filled with sibilants that it virtually hisses and so utterly incomprehensible that it is worthy of the most obscure oracle. The oracle who merged into the tripod, moreover, he called a "strange configuration of humanity, divinity, metal and serpent" (1967, 220).

Pythia (Cat. No. 379; 1963; Figure 76), who sits on "a bronze tripod-cauldron so shallow as to form a stool" (208), bears a striking resemblance to a 1961 sculpture by Henry Moore, *Standing Figure: Knife Edge,* which is in the Walker Art Center in Minneapolis. The split-thigh base of *Pythia* may not have been directly influenced by Moore, but the two bronzes appear to rise out of similar artistic sensibilities. Like *Seated Tripod Figure* (Cat. No. 314, above), *Pythia* has a Cycladic-like face, but her body exquisitely captures the sense of a pulsating, undulating, flowing possession by the god. Her distended neck expresses the heaviness, the pregnancy of her god-inhabited voice box. The same idea is readily apparent in a closely related black ink wash, *Oracle, Mantic Head* (Cat. No. 374; 6 October 1963; Figure 77). In the oil *Mantic Head* (Cat. No. 311; 1962–1964) the forward thrust of her jaw and lips likewise combines with her accentuated throat to create the impression that she is in the act of prophesying. A praying mantis may have inspired the bronze *Mantic Figure* (Cat. No. 334; 1963; Figure 78), but the most noticeable feature of the raised head is the open mouth and the distended throat, further developing the oracular theme.

In his final sculptural statement on this subject, *Oracle (Large Version)* (Cat. No. 397; 1963–1964; Figure 79), Ayrton combined a number of earlier motifs to create an imposing, enigmatic figure. The elongation of the neck and the shape of the head give her a serpentine quality, reminding one of Apollo's epithet "Pythian" and the victory at Delphi over the serpent, Python, which won him the title. As noted earlier, the slight reminiscence of Cycladic figurines in the shape of the face and head calls to mind the heads of a number of Henry Moore's sculptures. The Cycladic evocation is also a subtle reminder of Apollo's birthplace on the island of Delos in the Aegean Sea. But the tripod base particularly seizes one's attention. Her legs, spread wide, merge below the knees into the base, which appears to be exploding with the force of Apollo's coupling with her, for the tautened "flesh" is randomly ripped to create apertures for the god's radiance to escape; the swelling of her abdomen, moreover, implies that the union has already occurred, suggesting both the explosive force of the god's sexual assault and its consequences.

In early 1964, when this large final bronze in the oracle series was in progress, Ayrton completed a major oracle picture, a collage on canvas. *Key Figure* (Cat. No. 411; February 1964; Figure 82) summarizes key concepts developed in the course of the oracle's numerous transformations in Ayrton's hands. The laurel leaves in her outstretched hand recall not only the collage *Figure with Laurel Leaves* (Cat. No. 394; above) but also a number of drawings in which she either inhales the leaves, as in *Oracle with Bay Leaves II* (Cat. No. 328; 8 March 1963; Figure 83), or clutches them in her hand, as in *Oracle as Key Figure* (Cat. No. 338; 22 June 1963) and in *The Oracle as Pythia* (Cat. No. 408; 16 February 1964), which is close to the *Pythia* bronze (Cat. No. 379; above). The laurel leaves are placed above a maze configuration, which especially symbolizes Cumae, thus reminding one of her confinement by the god whose symbol is the sun, which rises above her extended right arm. The symbolism of the maze, however, also extends to Knossos and any other subter-

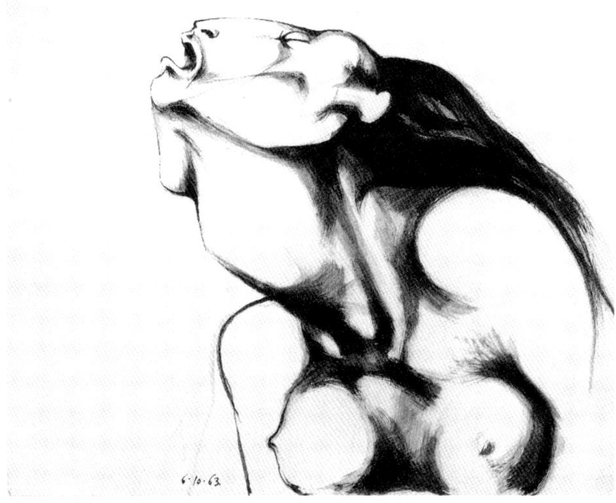

Figure 77. **ORACLE, MANTIC HEAD**
(Cat. No. 374; 6 October 1963). Stearn & Sons Ltd., Cambridge.

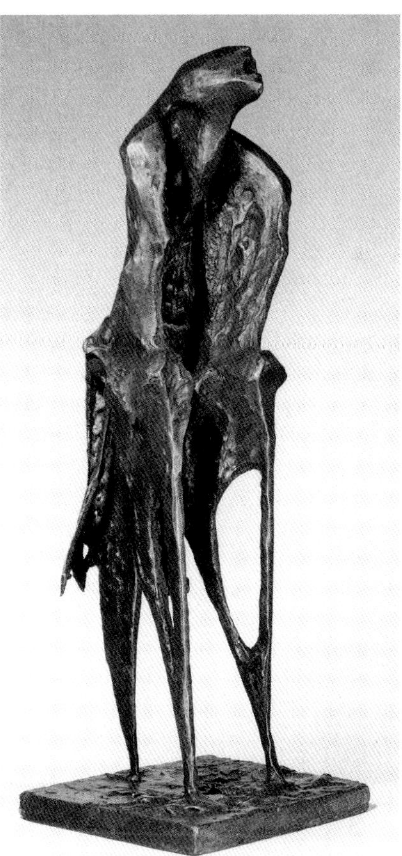

Figure 78. **MANTIC FIGURE**
(Cat. No. 334; 1963). Stearn & Sons Ltd., Cambridge.

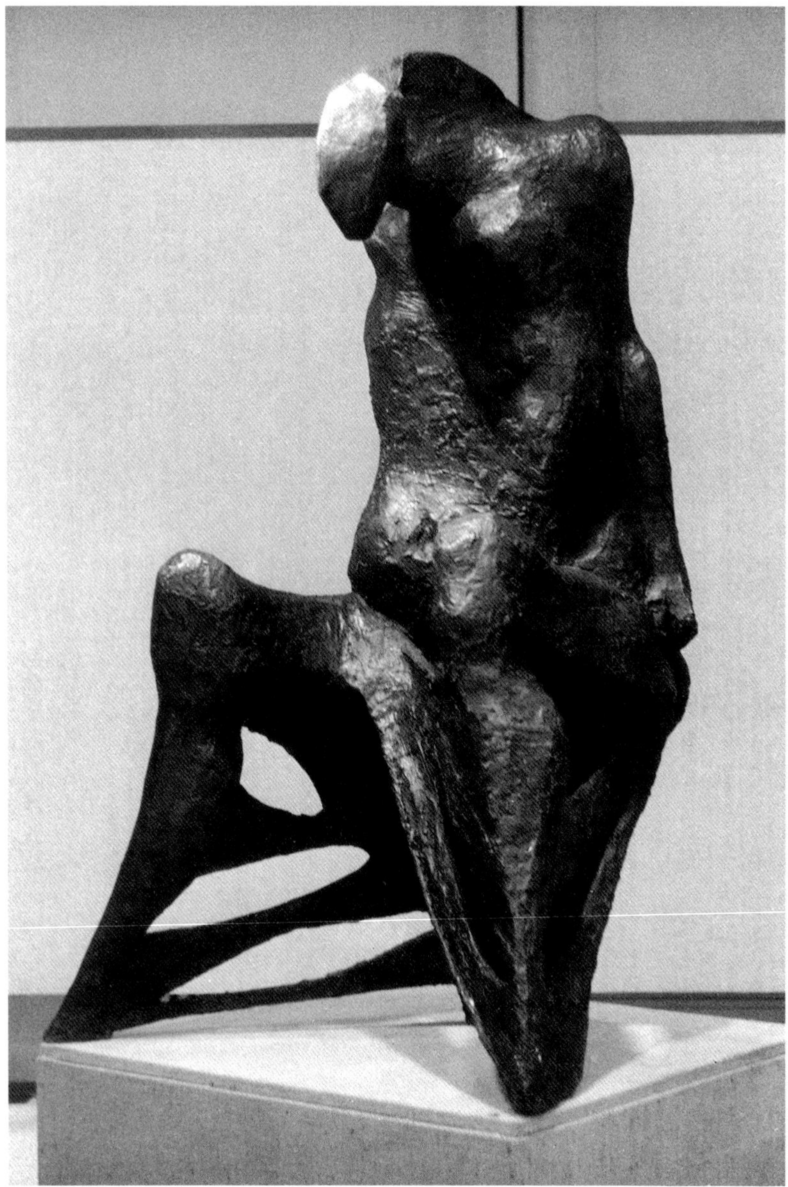

Figure 79. **ORACLE** (Large version) (Cat. No. 397; 1963–64).

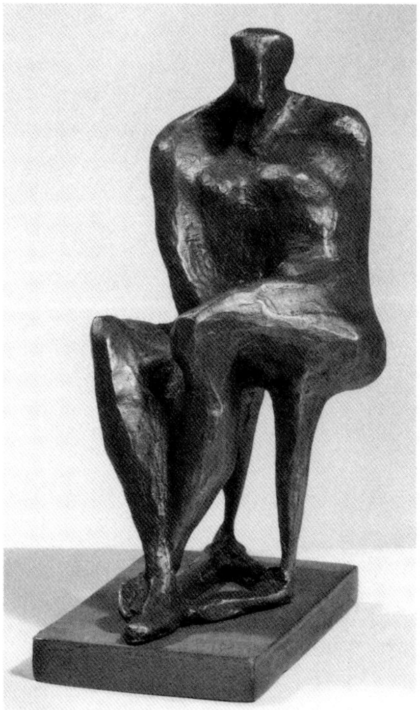

Figure 80. **MAQUETTE FOR LARGE ORACLE I** (Cat. No. 386; 1963). Stearn & Sons Ltd., Cambridge.

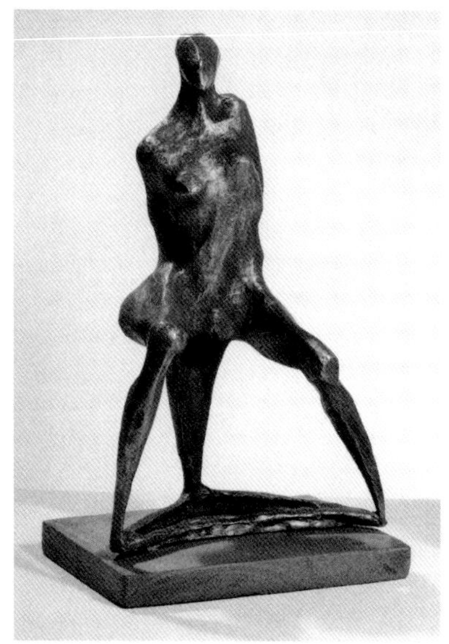

Figure 81. **MAQUETTE FOR LARGE ORACLE II** (Cat. No. 387; 1963). Stearn & Sons Ltd., Cambridge.

ranean place where the victims of a god's favor or anger hide. The maze pattern also recalls such earlier drawings as *Seated Oracle as Kore* (Cat. No. 326; 4 March 1963) and *The Oracle as Key Figure* (Cat. No. 338). The eyes in *Key Figure,* moreover, have the blind, vacant look characteristic of several other versions, such as *Oracle III (August 12 '62)* (Cat. No. 281); we are thus reminded that she functions not as vision but as voice of the god. Her apparently advanced age and her closed mouth further suggest that her energy is spent, that her task for the god is completed, at least for the moment.

For Ayrton, too, the task of interpreting the oracle was nearing completion. His final drawings of the oracle were completed on 23 July 1964. One of these, *Cumaean Sybil* (Cat. No. 453), closely resembles both *Pythia* (Cat. No. 379) and the final bronze *Oracle* (Cat. No. 397). Her serpentine head recalls the latter bronze, as does her heavy womb, but the swollen throat and extended neck also parallel *Pythia.* One can also see the influence of *Deiphobe (Cumaean Sybil)* (Cat. No. 405; 9 February 1964; Figure 84), in which the neck is so exaggerated that it seems almost to exist independent of the body, suspended perpendicular to it, as in *Oracle I (August 10)* (Cat. No. 279), a 1962 collage that served as a study for the bronze *Oracle (Large Version)* (Cat. No. 397; see catalogue).

While Ayrton was portraying the oracle in her various manifestations as the Cumaean Sibyl, Deiphobe, and Pythia, he also came to see her in another mythical figure, Kore or Persephone, the daughter of Demeter, even though the Greek myths do not link the seasonal goddess to the oracle.[15] In March 1963 he introduced this new aspect of his oracles with a wash drawing, *Seated Oracle as Kore* (Cat. No. 326), and a charcoal sketch, *The Oracle as Kore* (Cat. No. 331). There is no clear explanation for Ayrton's elision of Persephone with the Sibyl, but it is conceivable that it happened because the Cumaean Sibyl led Virgil's Aeneas into the realm of the underworld, where Persephone traditionally spent part of each year with her abductor-husband Hades. It is also probable that W. F. Jackson Knight's *Cumaean Gates* contributed, on a subconscious level, to Ayrton's linkage of Persephone and the oracle: in a memorial tribute to Jackson Knight, Ayrton acknowledged that this book profoundly influenced him, so Jackson Knight's discussion of the theory that the

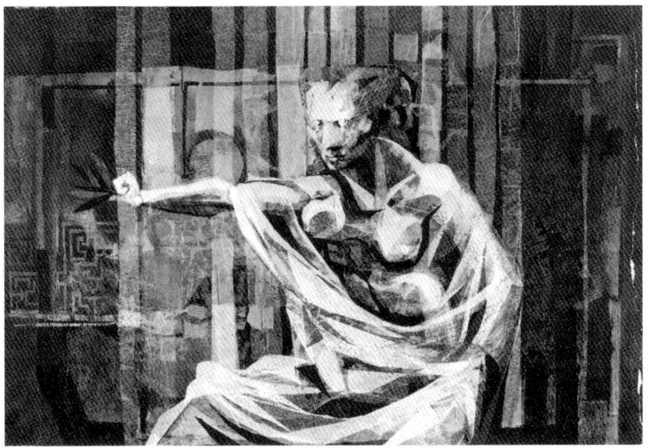

Figure 82. **KEY FIGURE** (Cat. No. 411; February 1964). Stearn & Sons Ltd., Cambridge.

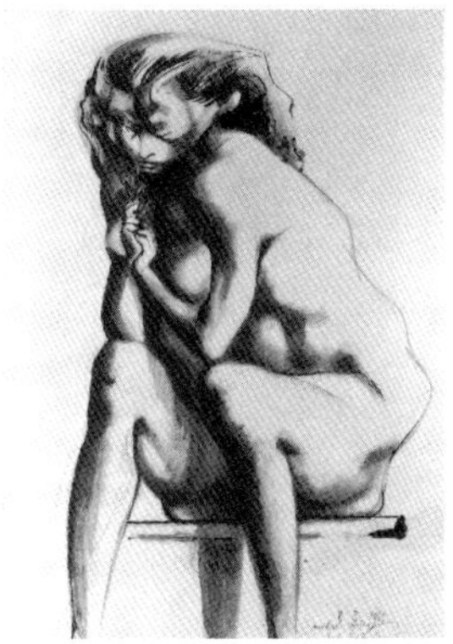

Figure 83. **ORACLE WITH BAY LEAVES II** (Cat. No. 328; 8 March 1963).

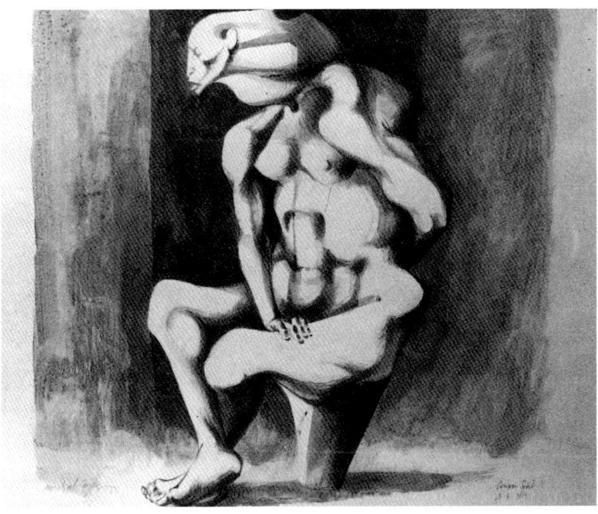

Figure 84. **DEIPHOBE (CUMAEAN SYBIL)** (Cat. No. 405; 9 February 1964). J. S. Lewinski, London.

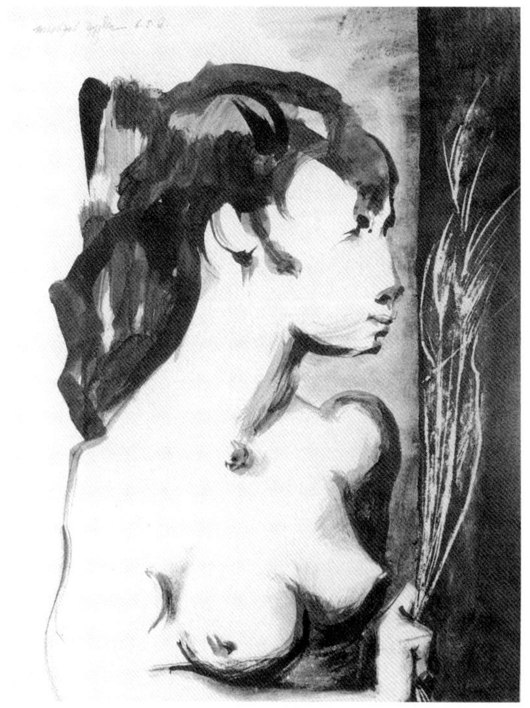

Figure 85. **PERSEPHONE WITH BARLEY STALKS** (Cat. No. 572; 6 March 1966). Brad Iverson, Detroit.

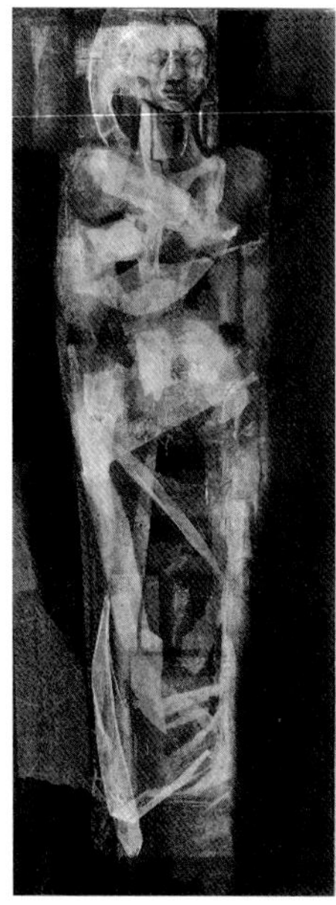

Figure 86. **WINTER DEMETER** (Cat. No. 295; 30 September 1962).

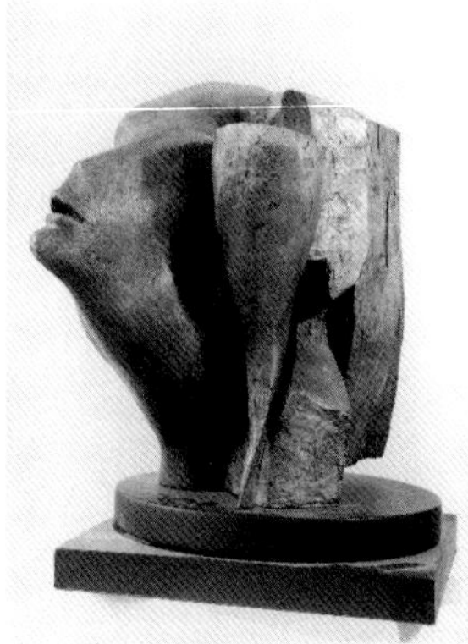

Figure 87. **KORE, HEAD** (Cat. No. 498; 1965): side view.

Eleusinian Mysteries "were in some sense recalled in the Sixth *Aeneid*"[16] may have caused Ayrton to make this association.

Whether one or both of these explanations accounts for Ayrton's creative fusion of the Sibyl and Kore/Persephone, or whether Jung's theory of archetypes is invoked to explain it as the artist's personalization of myth in his dreams and through his acts of creation, it is incontrovertible that Ayrton saw both Persephone and Demeter as further manifestations of the oracle. A collage originally entitled "Shrouded Oracle," dated 30 September 1962, was re-titled as *Winter Demeter* (Cat. No. 295; see catalogue). This figure, with its almost mummified appearance (see Figure 86), relates to a 1967 bronze also entitled *Winter Demeter* (Cat. No. 623). In both style and technique, moreover, this collage also resembles the series of oracle collages completed a month earlier (Cat. Nos. 279–281). The idea of the seasons is likewise present in the oil *Corn and Vine* (Cat. No. 298; 1962, repainted February 1963).[17]

Despite these initial identifications of Demeter and Kore/Persephone with the oracle, neither of them figured prominently in Ayrton's work until after his completion of the oracle series. Virtually all the drawings and paintings of the seasonal goddesses, as well as three of the six bronzes on this theme, were completed during 1965, but the remaining three bronzes were completed during 1966 and 1967 (Cat. Nos. 584, 622, and 623). The first bronze was *Kore, Head* (Cat. No. 498; 1965; Figure 87), after which Demeter was twice cast in bronze with her daughter in *Demeter and Kore I* and *II* (Cat. Nos. 496 and 497; 1965; Figure 89). The acknowledged influence of Henry Moore upon Ayrton's sculpture is evident in these groupings of mother and child, although they retain their distinctly Ayrtonian character and spirit.

One series of pencil drawings, *The Seasons of Demeter,*[18] depicts the revolution of the seasons by changing the shape of the woman's body (see Figures 90–93). In *Spring* (Cat. No. 486; 4 February 1965) her breasts begin to bloom, demanding support, and her body starts to fill out. In *Summer* (Cat. No. 485; 29 January 1965) the increasing fullness of her body, and particularly of her breasts, no longer permits her to sit erect, so she leans on her left

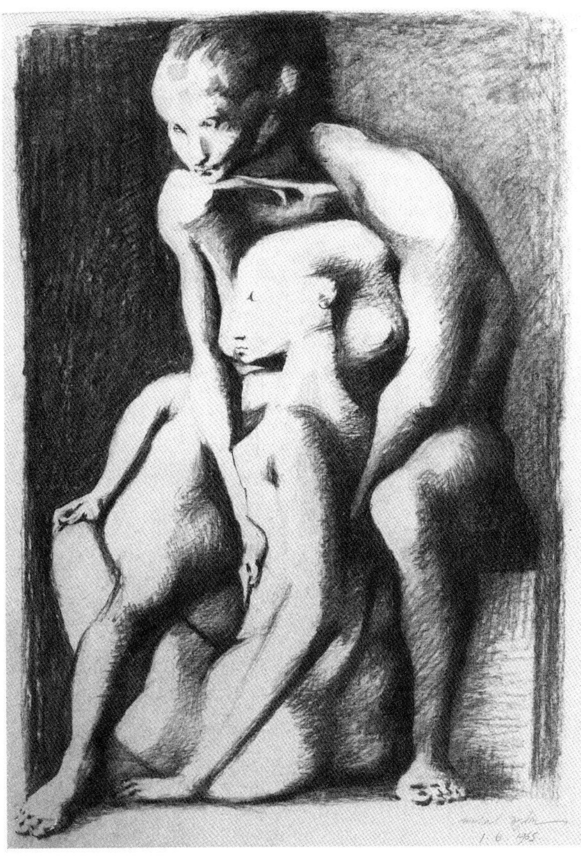

Figure 88. **DEMETER AND KORE**
(Cat. No. 517; 1 June 1965). J. S. Lewinski, London.

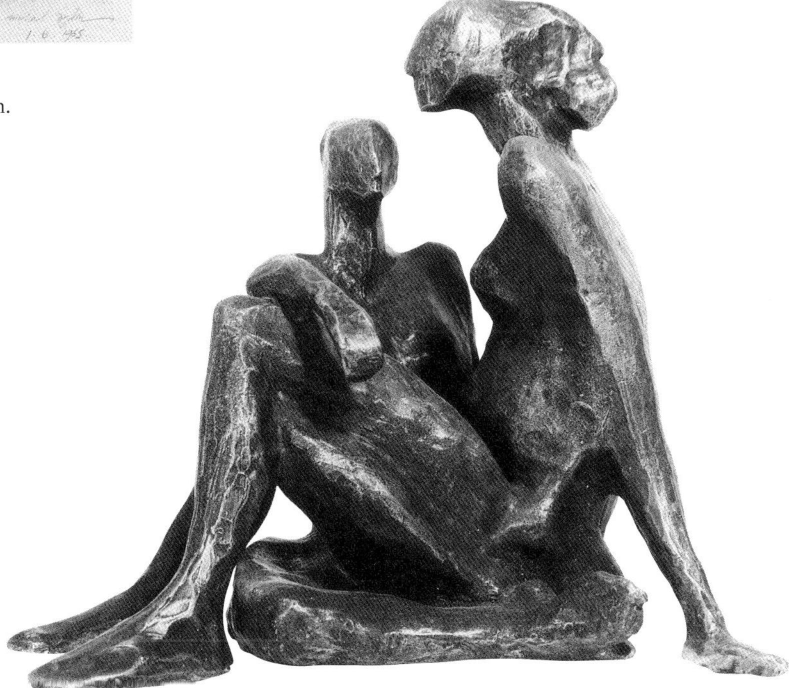

Figure 89. **DEMETER AND KORE II** (Cat. No. 497; 1965). J. S. Lewinski, London.

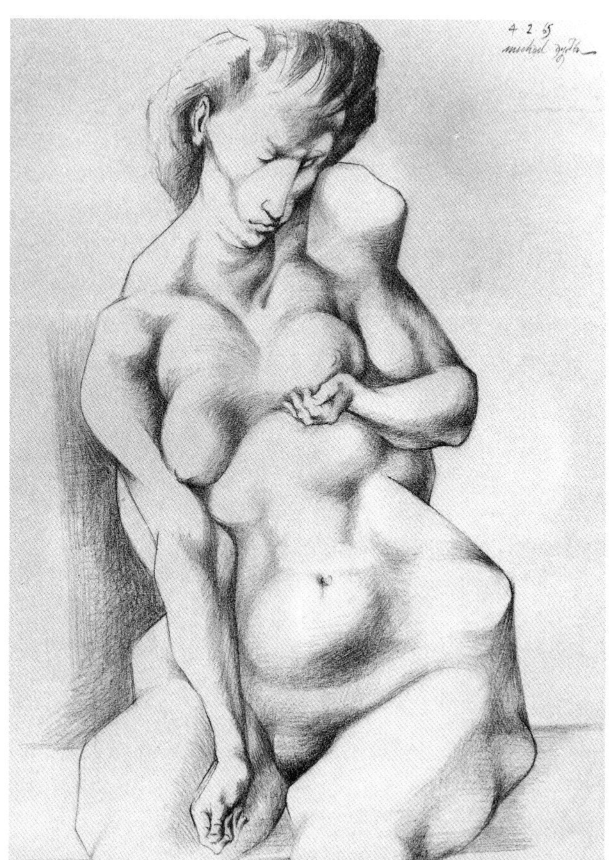

Figure 90. **SEASONS OF DEMETER I. SPRING** (Cat. No. 486; 4 February 1965). J. S. Lewinski, London.

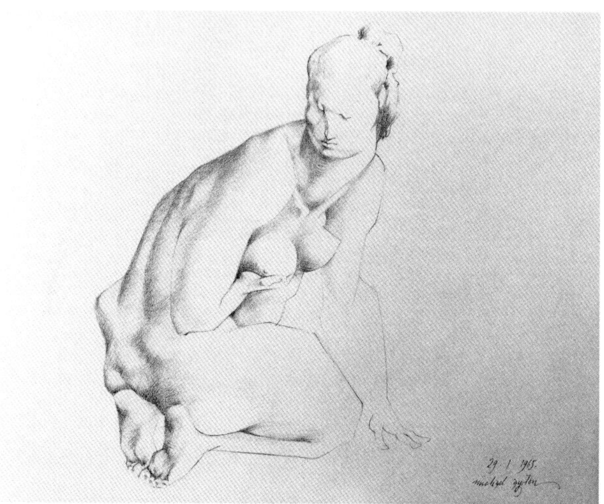

Figure 91. **SEASONS OF DEMETER II. SUMMER** (Cat. No. 485; 29 January 1965). J. S. Lewinski, London.

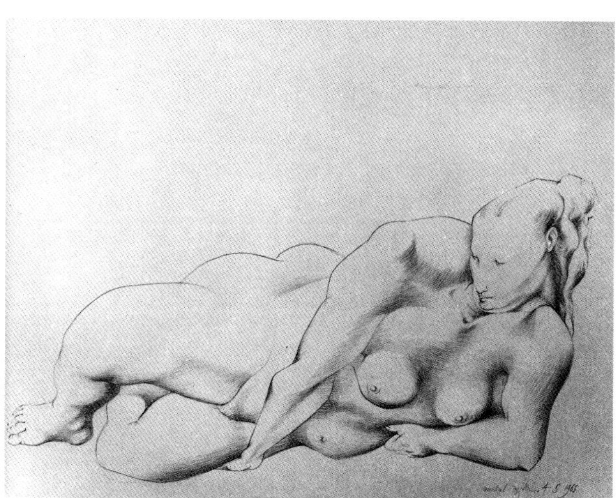

Figure 92. **SEASONS OF DEMETER III. AUTUMN** (Cat. No. 510; 4 May 1965).

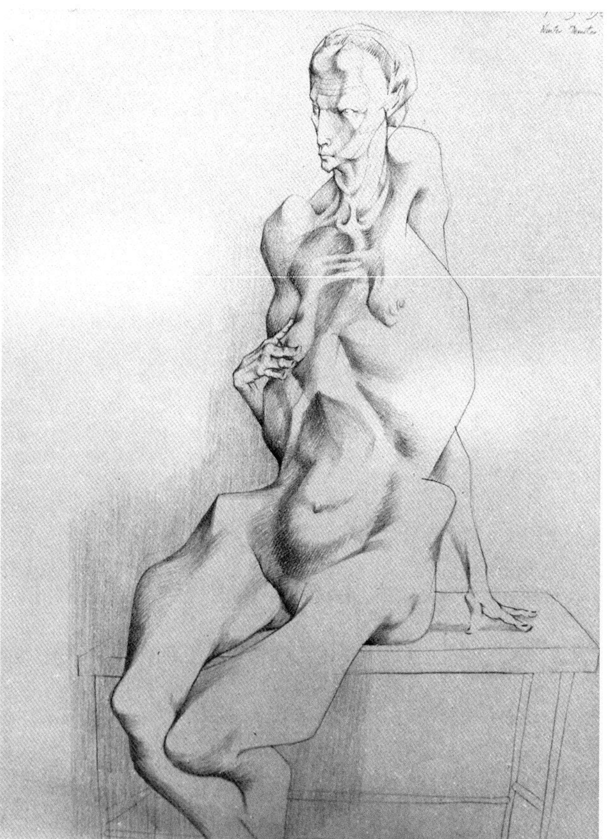

Figure 93. **SEASONS OF DEMETER IV. WINTER** (Cat. No. 511; 4 May 1965).

hand to support her weight. In *Autumn* (Cat. No. 510; 4 May 1965) she is recumbent with the heaviness of her endowments. But as the seasons complete their course in *Winter* (Cat. No. 511; 4 May 1965), she becomes lean, emaciated, almost skeletal; her shrunken breast is further accentuated by the bony fingers that grasp at a mere vestige of what she once possessed.[19]

This richly evocative series of drawings perfectly complements three bronzes of Demeter. *Demeter Pregnant* (Cat. No. 584; 1966; Figure 94) sinks heavily onto a block of wood, steadying and supporting herself with hands that also seem to clench her seat, as if she were already in labor. In this position she evokes not only the drawing of *Summer* (Cat. No. 485) but also two black ink washes, *Pregnant Oracle* (Cat. No. 361; 19 August 1963) and *Oracle, Astride* (Cat. No. 327; 4 March 1963). In *Winter Demeter* (Cat. No. 623; 1967) the drawing is translated into bronze, but with at once subtle and dramatic differences. Her boniness graphically evident, this gaunt figure is so stripped of flesh that her elongated neck seems to float in the socket of her shoulders. Her obviously barren womb and the bone metamorphosed into hair further underscore her leanness. If ever bronze could make this myth come alive, and it can, then this one unquestionably does.

Equally effective but markedly different is the bronze *Summer Demeter* (Cat. No. 622; 1967; Figure 95). Like the *Autumn* drawing (Cat. No. 510), this recumbent Demeter has all the fullness of a Renoir nude. Her fleshy thigh, ripe for eating, complements an accentuated vulva, ripe for taking. Her neck has shortened and thickened to a natural shape, whereas her well-coifed hair further enhances the sensuousness conveyed by her entire body. It is therefore not at all surprising to discover that the female nude in *Waking Figures* (Cat. No. 621; 1967), with all its sensuality, strongly resembles her. Although the Renoir nudes first come to mind when viewing Ayrton's *The Seasons of Demeter: Autumn* and similar works, these richly sensuous portraits of women also evoke Cezanne's bathers, specifically *Bather* (1874–1875), *Three Bathers* (1879–1882), *Five Bathers* (1885–1887), and *The Large Bathers* (1894–1905 and 1906). At times, Ayrton's depiction of Demeter is also strongly evocative of Cezanne's portraits of Madame Cezanne.

In the collages and paintings the goddesses become more abstract and figurative than in the drawings and bronzes. Demeter's presence is felt, for example, in *Barley Flight I* (Cat. No. 518; July 1965) and *II* (Cat. No. 569; 1966), where she is symbolized by barley stalks. In *Barley Matrix* (Cat. No. 530; August 1965), however, it is Persephone who is evoked by the barley stalks, which are intended to convey "an idea about corn hidden underground in winter which Persephone will bring up in the Spring."[20] Closely related to this collage is *Corn Stele* (Cat. No. 538; 1965; Figure 96), which expresses Persephone's descent into the underworld and her survival as a grave stele in the upper world until spring.[21] Regarding this work one critic perceptively remarked: "In his recent work Ayrton has concentrated on Daedalus . . . the master craftsman, the archetype of the experimenter using the materials that come to hand and, by his peculiar genius, turning them, transforming them into works of art by a single stroke of the imagination; such a man evokes a natural response in Ayrton, who can take ears of corn and not simply incorporate them into a painting like [*Corn*]*Stele,* but make them an integral part of the picture."[22] These observations could be applied equally well to any number of these collages, including *The Future Wheat* (Cat. No. 521; 1965), in which a hand print comes to signify "the hand of Kore bringing the harvest back into existence."[23]

All the while Ayrton was creating these highly evocative images of oracles and the seasonal goddesses, he also was engrossed in another central figure of the Daedalus myth—the Minotaur. The "Work in Progress" section that concluded the 1962 edition of *Drawings and Sculpture* stated: "I am concerned at the moment with three figures. . . . One is the *Minotaur,* dangerous ground, for at least one great living artist has been there first" (1962a, below pl. 117). On the surface, this statement can be accepted as a tribute to Picasso's greatness and an admission of trepidation on Ayrton's part. But when considered in the context of the critical essays on Picasso's art that Ayrton wrote at various intervals, beginning in his youth (see chapter 1), it can surely also be seen as a challenge to Picasso, a declaration of intent to rival and surpass the genius whose shadow covered so much of twentieth-century art. At the same time, one must acknowledge that

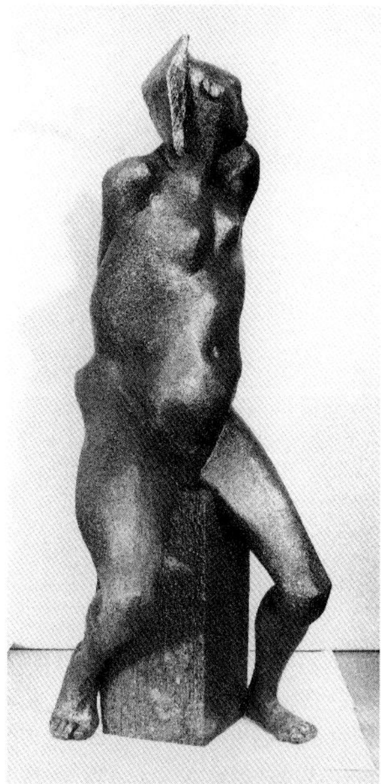

Figure 94. **DEMETER PREGNANT**
(Cat. No. 584; 1966): front view. J. S. Lewinski, London.

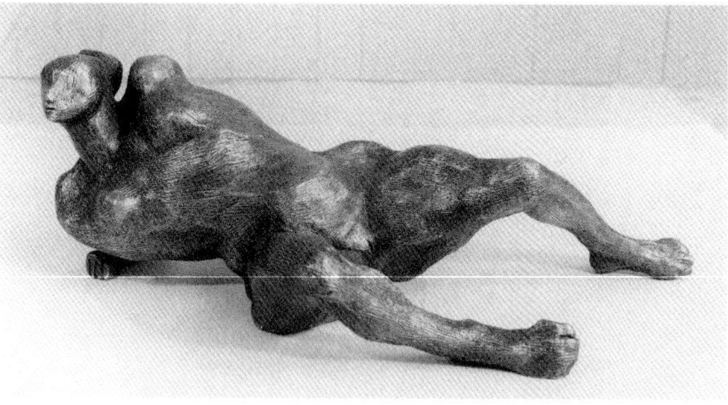

Figure 95. **SUMMER DEMETER**
(Cat. No. 622; 1967). J. S. Lewinski, London.

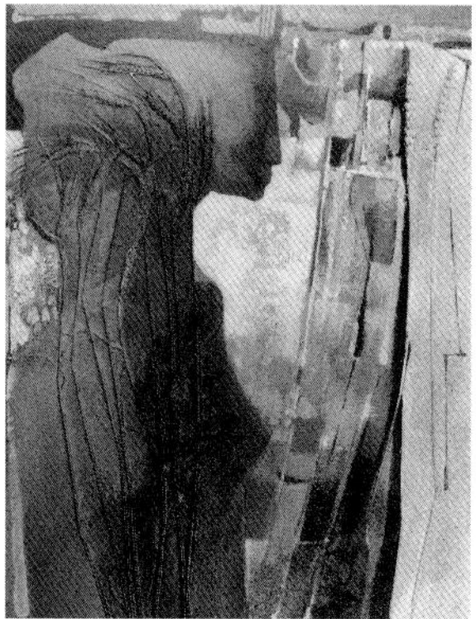

Figure 96. **CORN STELE**
(Cat. No. 538; 1965). J. S. Lewinski, London.

some of Ayrton's drawings of the Minotaur's body resemble a number of Picasso's drawings, particularly in the way in which he drew the limbs, even though Ayrton would have been loathe to concede that Picasso influenced his drawing, unless it was to demonstrate his superior draftsmanship (see chapter 1).

Although Ayrton elsewhere stated, "The Minotaur came sharply into my foreground in 1962" (1970b, 58), the primary evidence of his concern dates from the following year. The only drawings in 1962 were the two *Fat Man* studies for the Minotaur (Cat. Nos. 248 and 249; 27 February 1962) previously discussed in relation to the *Sentinel* figure (above), but there were also two bronzes produced: the small *Seated Minotaur, Version I* (Cat. No. 283; Figure 97) and the almost life-sized *Minotaur I* (Cat. No. 282; Figure 98). The artist's description of the Minotaur as "a brainless, bewildered creature" and as "a monstrous sacrifice, powerful and yet helpless" (1962a, below pl. 117) is particularly suited to the *Minotaur I* bronze. Incapable of action and therefore inert, this grotesque and distorted monster with a human frame conveys both brute strength and childish helplessness. He stood for many years on his plinth near the entrance to the Ayrtons' country estate, Bradfields, at once welcoming and warning visitors, reminding them of his creator's declaration: "How he came to exist is my fault and yours" (1962a, below pl. 117).

The first direct Minotaur drawing, *Seated Minotaur* (Cat. No. 339; 24 June 1963; Figure 99), came more than a year after the *Fat Man* drawings (Cat. Nos. 248 and 249; 27 February 1962). It is, however, related to another 1962 drawing, *Minos Masked* (Cat. No. 256; derived from Cat. No. 123 [see Figure 100], which has the same title and was completed 21 June 1960), which first appeared as a line illustration in *The Testament of Daedalus* (Ayrton 1962c, 32).[24] The influence of the bronze *Seated Minotaur, Version I* (Cat. No. 283; 1962) is also apparent, making this drawing a blend of these two prior expressions, but it also represents another step for Ayrton in the process of trying to understand who or what the Minotaur is. During 1963 the artist made more than a dozen drawings of the Minotaur evolving toward a more human condition. In these drawings one can clearly see "that the most profound experience transmitted to the spectator through the drawing is the same revelation as the artist has made himself," and, further, one recognizes these studies as the means used by the artist "to crystallize thought as to appearances."[25] Viewing *Minos Masked* may encourage one to examine Picasso's sketches for *Guernica,* such as *Head of Bull-Man* (20 May 1937), *Head of Bull-Man with Studies of Eyes* (20 May 1937), and *Head of Man with Bull's Horns* (10 May 1937), but there is very little resemblance between these works of the two artists. Picasso preserved humanity in the heads of the Minotaur/Bull-Man, whereas Ayrton chose to make the mask of *Minos Masked* entirely animal, except for the apertures through which Minos's eyes are visible.

Thus the vacant, animal stare of *Seated Minotaur* (Cat. No. 339) is replaced in *Minotaur Alarmed* (Cat. No. 347; 23 July 1963; Figure 102) with a look of surprise and fright, which is moving toward the expression of human emotions. By November 1963 the head itself approached humanity in *Minotaur, Head Evolving* (Cat. No. 382; 27 November 1963; Figure 103); for the first time the artist conceived of him as actually capable of evolution into human form (see catalogue). In fact, the Minotaur's head in this drawing strongly resembles some of the *Fat Man* heads of other drawings (e.g., Cat. No. 399; 3 January 1964). Two closely related drawings, *Minotaur in Anguish* (Cat. No. 389; 22 December 1963; Figure 104) and *Minotaur Evolved* (Cat. No. 390; 24 December 1963), advance the emotional evolution of Ayrton's Minotaur. His tortured, anguished, piercing screams can almost be heard in one's imagination, as that part of him which is human seeks to strip off the "cattle-brute mask of his head," as Ayrton described it in *The Maze Maker* (1967, 194). The conventional notion of the stomach as the seat of the emotions makes this evolution possible, for the "Minotaur begins in the loins and grows into a bull at the shoulders, but he is human in his belly," said Ayrton.[26]

The second edition of *Drawings and Sculptures,* published in 1966, included a new section of work in progress. In it Ayrton looked back upon his minotaurs and oracles: "The *Minotaur* evolved towards a human condition, the *Oracle* moved away from it towards a series of inhuman images in which her being became concen-

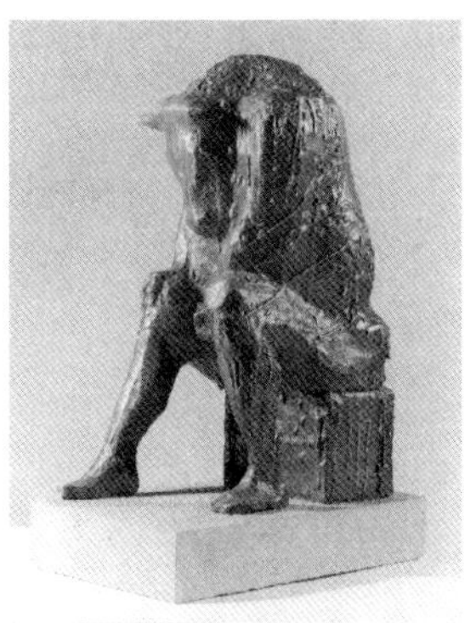

Figure 97. **SEATED MINOTAUR, VERSION I** (Small Minotaur) (Cat. No. 283; 1962). Eaden Lilley, Cambridge.

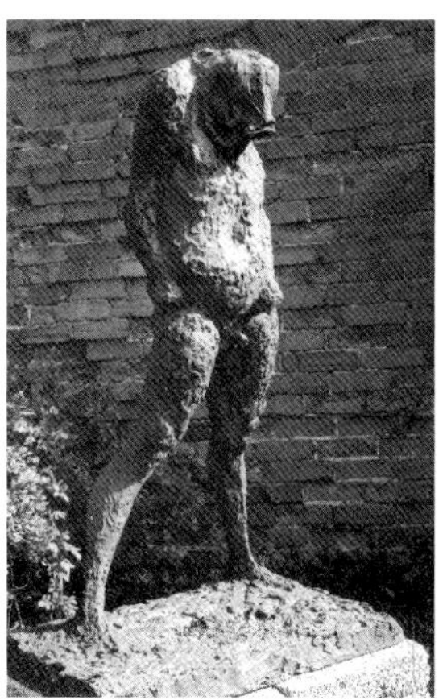

Figure 98. **MINOTAUR I** (Cat. No. 282; 1962).

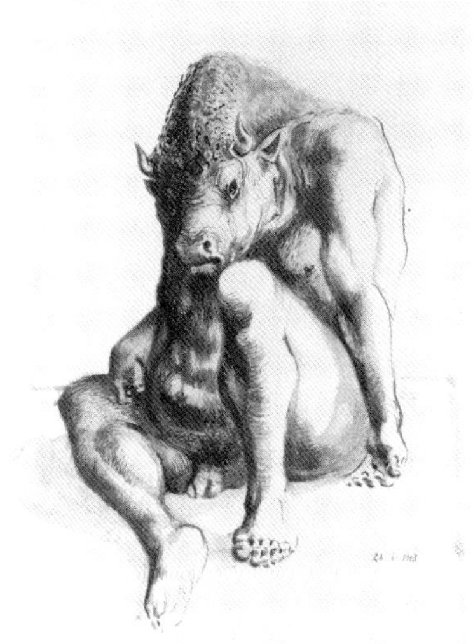

Figure 99. **SEATED MINOTAUR** (Cat. No. 339; 24 June 1963).

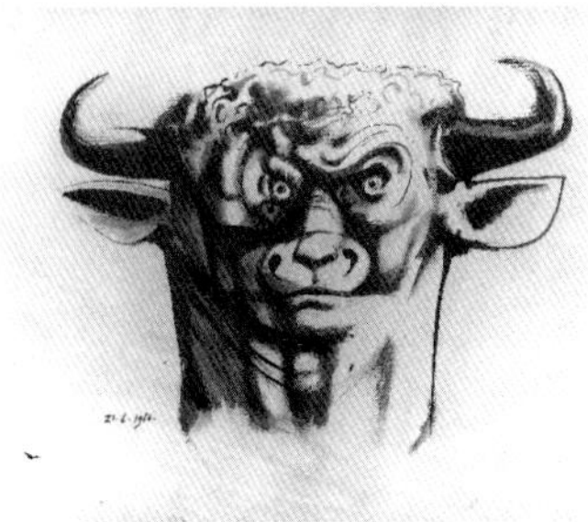

Figure 100. **MINOS MASKED**
(Cat. No. 123; 21 June 1960). Eaden Lilley, Cambridge.

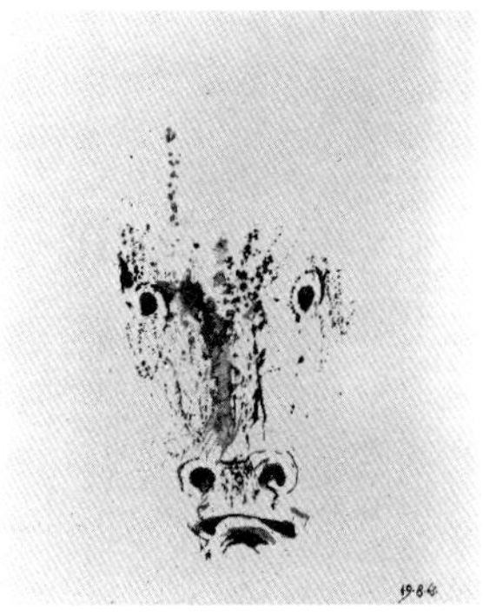

Figure 101. **MINOTAUR MASK**
(Cat. No. 362; 19 August 1963).

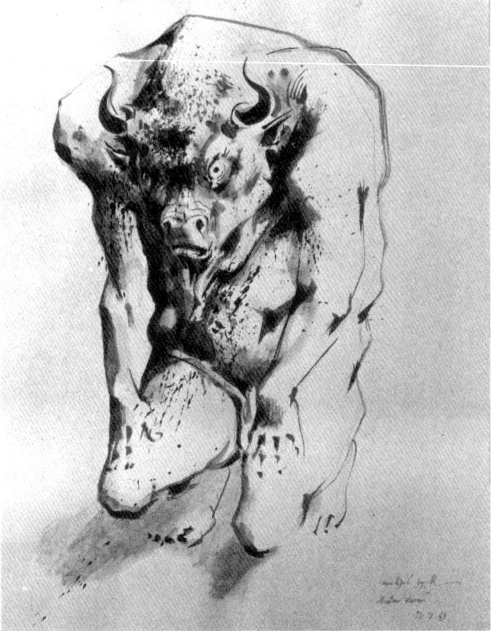

Figure 102. **MINOTAUR ALARMED**
(Cat. No. 347; 23 July 1963). J. S. Lewinski, London.

trated upon containing the prophetic voice of the god" (above pl. 140 and 141). As these two figures met or passed each other in the plane of being which conceptually must lie between the human and inhuman spheres, they momentarily seem to blend together, merge into one, and then emerge transmogrified in the artist's mind and in his hands. Thus two 1963 bronzes, *Pythia* (Cat. No. 379) and the maquette for *Evolution of the Minotaur* (Cat. No. 384; Figure 105), possess markedly similar qualities of texture and shape. The pulsating, expanding throat of *Pythia* more than vaguely resembles the Minotaur's throat or, more precisely, the "wattled folds of hide [which] sag from the chops, a cloak of hide to hide the man" (Ayrton 1964, 51).

The Minotaur, although he may hide man within him, is still a hybrid, still part beast. As the *Restless Minotaur* (Cat. No. 351; 1963; Figure 106) sits, in nearly human fashion, he is betrayed by his head: "The front carries the stigma, the impediment of birth, a bone pitchfork grappled to the brow. It weighs him down" (Ayrton 1964, 50). And from his taurine head, spittle from the cud courses down onto his human knee, an unremitting reminder of his dual nature. In *Crouched Minotaur* (Cat. No. 346; 1963; Figure 107) he seems almost completely to have lost his humanity as the weight of the sinewed hump upon his shoulders weighs down his bull's head. It sags down upon his knee, and the leg below the knee extends not to a human foot, as previously, but to a cloven hoof. The arm that braces him from falling likewise terminates in a hoof. He has reverted to beast, with but faint reminders of his former share in humanity.

The animality of the Minotaur is most complete in *Minotaur Revealed* (Cat. No. 352; 1963; Figure 109). The bone forms, although metamorphosed into a new reality in bronze, are nonetheless unquestionably animal. The ox skull is a stunning but brutal reinforcement of the truth of the Minotaur's existence and, by artistic extension, of the human condition as Ayrton saw it. By raising this Minotaur aloft on a dowel to reveal his bestiality, Ayrton also reminds us of that which is bestial in us, for the dowel calls to mind the Dionysian thyrsus, upon which the Bacchantes impaled their victims. Because of Euripides' *Bacchae,* Agave is the best-known example of a woman under the spell of Dionysus. She held aloft the bloodied head of her son, Pentheus, believing that the head impaled upon her thyrsus was the head of an animal until her horrified father, Cadmus, drew her out of her trance. It is important in this context to remember that Dionysus, the symbol of irrationality in fifth-century Greece, sometimes took the form of a bull; Ayrton later gave visual expression to this manifestation of the god in his drawing, *Dionysus in Bull Form and Crouched Minotaur* (Cat. No. 509; 25 April 1965).

Ancient wall paintings show Minos turning away in horror and revulsion from the monstrous offspring of his wife and the white bull from the sea. Through some of his Minotaur drawings and bronzes Ayrton arouses in the spectator a similar sense of dread and revulsion, for their emotive power operates at a visceral level when Ayrton is most successful in giving visual reality to the idea of the man-beast, as in *Minotaur Revealed* or in his full-sized bronze, *Evolution of the Minotaur* (Cat. No. 385; 1963–1964; Figure 110). In the latter work the residual bestiality of the Minotaur is somewhat diminished from that of *Minotaur Revealed,* but it is nonetheless inescapable. The progression away from the dominance of bestiality continued in the smaller bronze *Minotaur in Jeopardy* (Cat. No. 471; 1964; Figure 111), which resembles *Seated Minotaur* (Cat. No. 283) but yet expresses a deeper sense of the human aspect of the Minotaur. As he sits with his hands over his head, he appears to be trying to shield himself from an external threat, just as a human being instinctively would do.

T. G. Rosenthal, in his introduction to the catalogue of the exhibition at the Grosvenor Gallery in 1964, captured the significance of Ayrton's Minotaur images in these words:

> This strange sense of struggle, humanly inarticulate and yet with the intellectual impotence of the animal comes over in several of Ayrton's finest drawings and in the life-size bronze sculptures which show the Minotaur in his attempts to slough off his hide, hooves and horns and become wholly human, shedding the beast to become sensate man. The rough texture of his body is surmounted by an increasingly sentient face and we can read into this

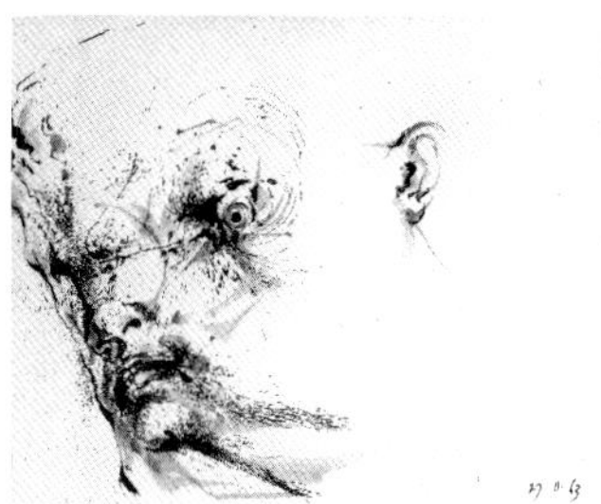

Figure 103. **MINOTAUR, HEAD EVOLVING** (Cat. No. 382; 27 November 1963). Stearn & Sons Ltd., Cambridge.

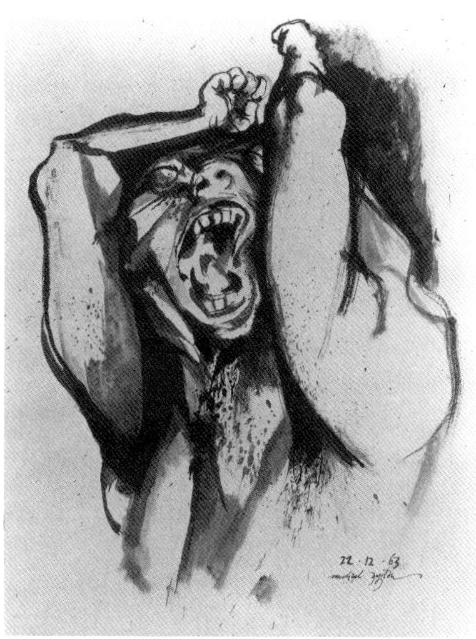

Figure 104. **MINOTAUR IN ANGUISH** (Cat. No. 389; 22 December 1963).

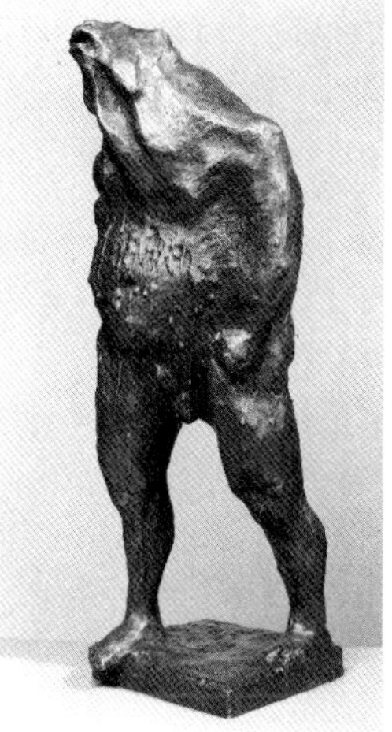

Figure 105. **EVOLUTION OF THE MINOTAUR** (Maquette) (Cat. No. 384; 1963).

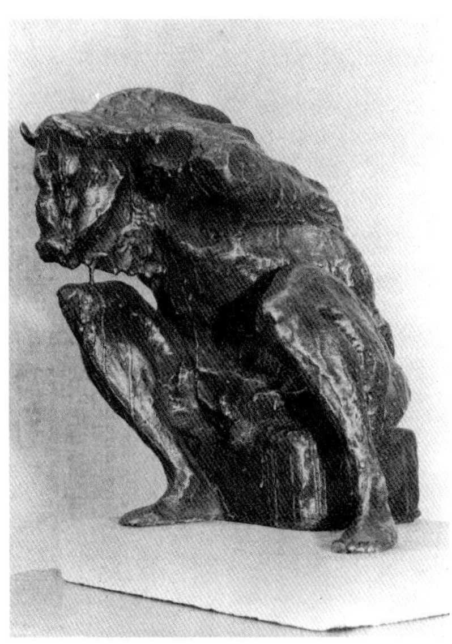

Figure 106. **RESTLESS MINOTAUR** (Cat. No. 351; 1963).

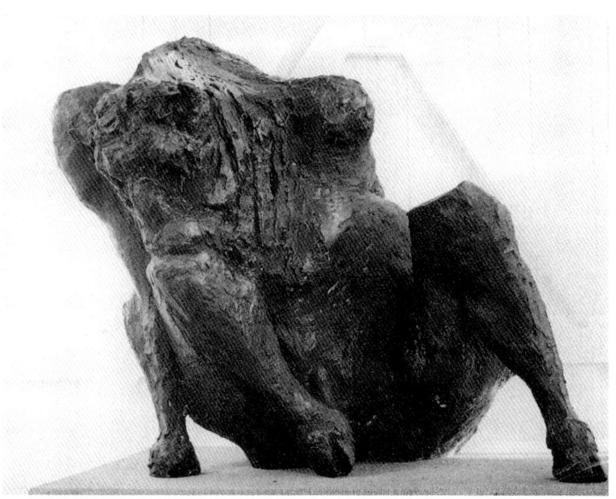

Figure 107. **CROUCHED MINOTAUR** (Cat. No. 346; 1963). J. S. Lewinski, London.

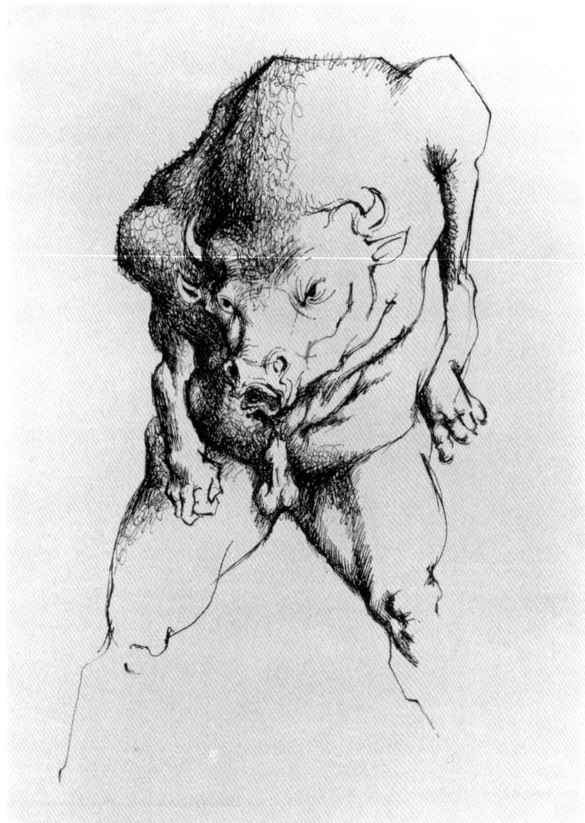

Figure 108. **MINOTAUR AT BAY** (Cat. No. 420; March 1964?).

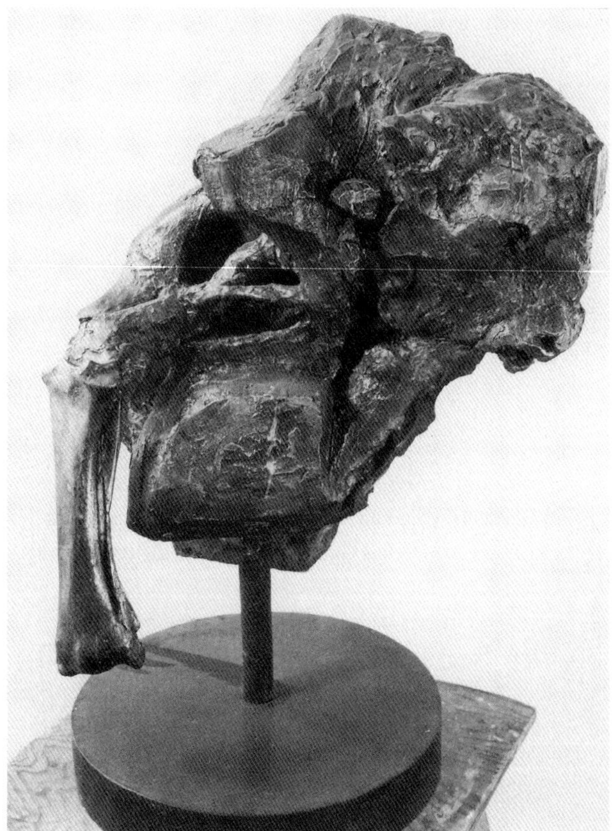

Figure 109. **MINOTAUR REVEALED** (Cat. No. 352; 1963).

> whatever allegory we like, from the ritual slaughter of a Spanish Sunday to modern man trying to rid himself of the violence, both without and within, which will always menace and try to control us. ([5–6])

After completing *Evolution of the Minotaur* and *Minotaur in Jeopardy,* Ayrton abandoned the Minotaur for about a year. When he returned to this subject, he introduced another aspect of the Minotaur with his charcoal and collage, *Mazed Minotaur* (Cat. No. 499; 4 April 1965; Figure 112). In this almost cubist collage, Ayrton graphically illustrates the Minotaur's twisting and turning in his attempts to escape the labyrinthine prison that Daedalus, at Minos's bidding, created to conceal Pasiphaë's outrageous progeny.

This is the first work in which Ayrton linked the Minotaur and the maze, but he had by no means ignored the Minotaur's prison while he was wrestling with the challenge of depicting the prisoner. Although Ayrton claimed to have known nothing of the long history of mazes until he began to write his "autobiography" of Daedalus, which was published in 1967 as *The Maze Maker,* he eventually "became entangled in the long, complicated, and curious history, prehistory, and meaning of mazes, which begins at least five thousand years ago" (Ayrton 1970b, 59). Before that happened, however, his intuition led him to a view of the labyrinth described in this essay written several years later:

> but perhaps because, like every human being, I contained a maze, I found that I wrote of the labyrinth below the rock of Cumae as the entrails of the Earth and believed, as Daedalus would have done, that the Earth was female. Her name in Greek is Gaia. The whole of the central part of the book takes place below the rock of Cumae, and in writing it, the idea came to me that the maze, which is a natural place of terror, a convolution of dark caves and buried passages, must have originated inside the belly of man and his animal prey. As a symbol, in its most profound and ancient form, the inexplicable yards of intertwining intestine that man first revealed when he inserted his flint knife into his victim were the source of his awe and the potency of the image. The complex of guts would have

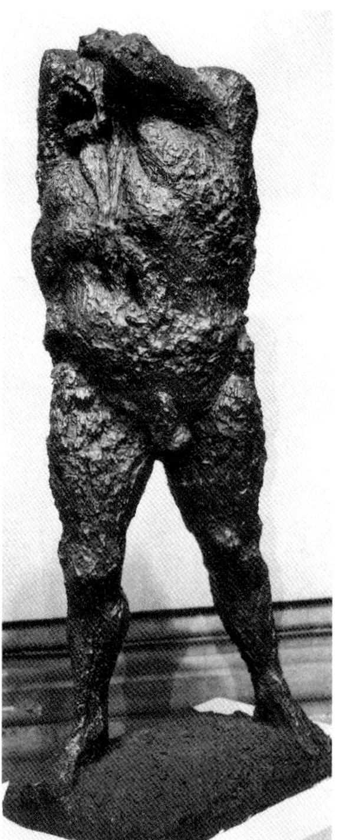

Figure 110. **EVOLUTION OF THE MINOTAUR** (Cat. No. 385; 1963–64).

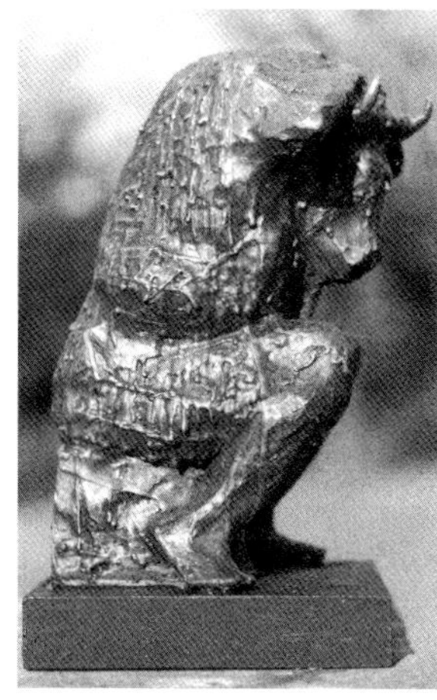

Figure 111. **MINOTAUR IN JEOPARDY** (Cat. No. 471; 1964).

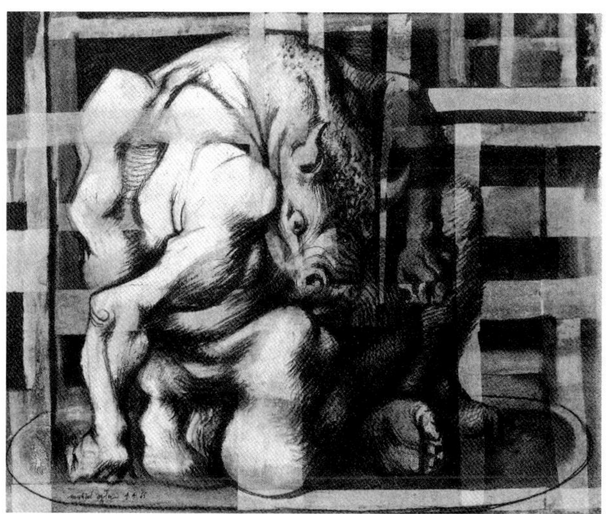

Figure 112. **MAZED MINOTAUR** (Cat. No. 499; 4 April 1965).

> been inexplicable, and that his children were formed somewhere in the passages and chambers within the female body would have been part of the mystery. When a child was born from his woman, it was joined to her by a red thread, by Ariadne's red thread. This I divined; the evidence of Sumerian divination and other recondite matters, I learned later. (Ayrton 1970b, 63)

The symbol of the labyrinth had already appeared in a number of oracle drawings and paintings (above), but the maze itself was also the subject of a number of independent works. *Labyrinth* (Cat. No. 310; late 1962; Figure 113) represents the first total labyrinth picture, although the labyrinth was variously suggested in such earlier paintings as *Minoan Landscape* (Cat. No. 181; March 1961; Figure 114) and *Bleached Landscape* (Cat. No. 212; 1960–1962). In *Labyrinth* the artist is attempting to convey a general sense of the maze underground. Since he did not conceive of the maze in this instance as being viewed from above, the maze was not precisely diagrammed; in this conception, one enters the labyrinth and exits from it in three dimensions.[27] The configuration of the labyrinth in this painting suggests the womb, an appropriate symbol, particularly in view of the already noted significance that Ayrton attached to Gaia, Mother Earth. But it also suggests the brain, a suitable symbol for the artificer, Daedalus, whose fabled intellect lay behind the complexities of the Cretan labyrinth.

Through Jung and his followers, we are reminded that the Egyptian underworld with its seven doors was seen as a maze and that it is "a well-known symbol of the unconscious with its unknown possibilities" (1964, 170–71). The maze or labyrinth is interpreted as "an entangling and confusing representation of the world of matriarchal consciousness" (Jung 1964, 125). Thus when Ayrton began to develop labyrinth paintings and various other representations of the maze, he was entering a realm well mined by the psychoanalysts. As he gave expression to these ideas and images arising from his personal unconscious, he also drew upon the collective unconscious of the human race and the rich myth of the labyrinth at Knossos. In the process of creating images, Ayrton derived from the story of the fearful Cretan labyrinth the mythic inspiration that would enable him to express the anxieties of humankind engaged in the frightening process of individuation, the process of separation from the mother to develop an independent personality. Through Ayrton's labyrinth drawings, paintings, and sculpture, we are given a vehicle for our own individual and collective experience of this reality.

Two collages of the same period as *Labyrinth, Night Labrys* (Cat. No. 312; December 1962), and *Labrys* (Cat. No. 316; early 1963; Figure 115), were closely related in thought if not in expression.[28] *Night Labrys* depends on deep blue colors to develop the imagery of the double axe, an important symbol in Minoan art and religion that is generally believed to explain the derivation of the word labyrinth in the Greek language. Rosenthal attached great significance to this painting:

> In a painting like *Night Labrys* we see at first an abstraction composed largely of blues of great lustre; then when we come nearer we see that it is in fact a landscape, inspired by Cumae in southern Italy, the 8th century B.C. Greek settlement that for eight years has cast its spell on Ayrton; a landscape that reveals its labyrinthine complexity both in the outlines of his painting and in the layer upon layer of paper of which the painting is composed. And then, distancing oneself again, one sees that the main outline of the picture is the shape of a double headed axe, the "labrys." . . . Thus mythology and form are fused into a work of art and the scholasticism—even the antiquarianism—of which Ayrton has been accused in the past show themselves to be not adjuncts of an intellectual and hence inadequate art but the essential concomitants and the invaluable tools of his enormously fertile mind.
>
> Visually, despite its relatively small size and scale, this particular painting is a work of considerable splendour and great sensual power with colours of glowing subtlety. This painting—or, more properly, paper collage—and the other recent landscapes of Crete and the Cycladic islands, done in the same medium, show a new maturity in Ayrton's work as a painter. This is, in a sense, a second maturity because one tends to forget the excellence of some of his early paintings from the end of the nineteen-forties when he was one of the group containing Sutherland, Piper, Vaughan and Minton which dominated English painting at that time. (1964, [4])

The companion piece, *Labrys,* evokes the image of the maze in the double axe through the use of warm earth colors and tissue paper collage.

Although both these collages achieve highly evocative effects through the maze configuration imposed upon the shape of the *labrys,* Ayrton's pivotal *Cumaean Gate* (Cat. No. 365; 1963), painted soon afterward, reverts to the conception of the underground maze he first explored in *Labyrinth.* In *Cumaean Gate* the implications of the subterranean maze are made at once more specific and more general. The complex, multidimensional passageways that honeycomb the rock at Cumae dominate the left half of the painting, with the outline of a hill capping the multiple maze images. The right half of the painting opens up into two large, gaping, dark openings, which suggest the entrance to the underworld. Here are recalled the underground connections between Cumae and Avernus described in Virgil's *Aeneid;* thus it also symbolizes the tomb, adding yet another layer of meaning to the symbols of the womb and the brain in *Labyrinth,* making this an even more compelling painting.[29]

With the painting *Maze Head* (Cat. No. 457; 1964; Figure 116) a new development occurs in the conception of the maze. As one studies the canvas, which at first appears to be little more than a magnified section of *Labyrinth* (Cat. No. 310), suddenly a human face materializes in the labyrinth. The head is in the maze and the maze is in the head, both conceptually and in the form of the brain. Here the head is that of a contemplative man, calling to mind Ayrton's literary image of Daedalus in *The Testament of Daedalus* (see chapter 4) and the contemplative, reflective heads of Daedalus. Some of the other *Maze Head* figures, however, depict struggle within the mind. These figures surely suggest Daedalus, but they could equally well represent Everyman.

The artist's own description of this period in his life, i.e., from early 1964 to 1966, casts considerable light not only on this painting, but also on his entire maze maker phase:

> But finally Daedalus came to dominate the Maze, and by then I had identified myself with him so compulsively that the myth began to reshape itself, expanding in my mind,

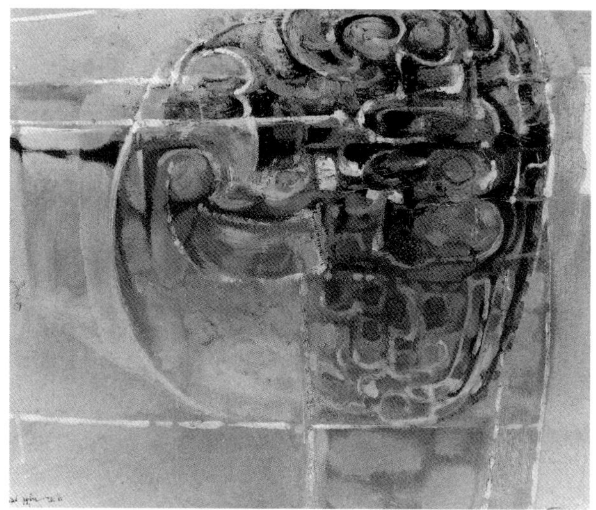

Figure 113. **LABYRINTH** (Cat. No. 310; December 1962). Eaden Lilley, Cambridge.

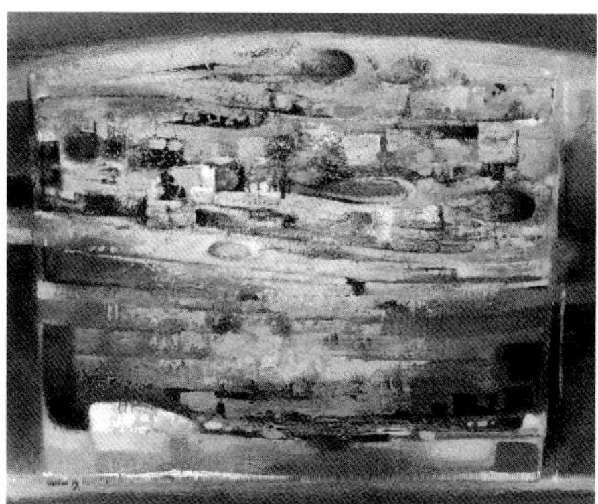

Figure 114. **MINOAN LANDSCAPE** (Cat. No. 181; 1961). Eaden Lilley, Cambridge.

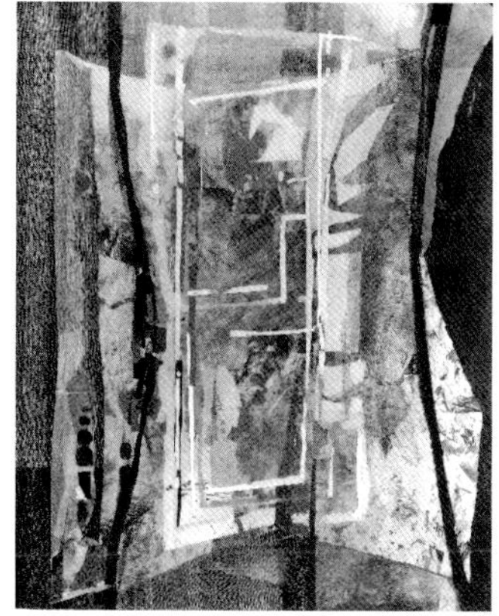

Figure 115. **LABRYS** (Cat. No. 316; 1963).

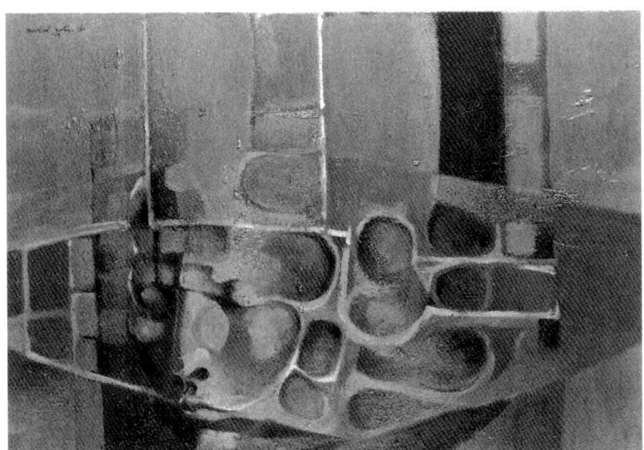

Figure 116. **MAZE HEAD** (Cat. No. 457; 1964).

and without any warning I found myself writing a further narrative, a transposed autobiography.

I did this to complete a jigsaw, or rather, to find a way out of the myth itself. I believed that if I could add to the sum of all the images I had made a narrative that would place them, would assemble the mass of fragments that all my work in painting and sculpture seemed to be, I might see the Labyrinth of Daedalus clearly and escape from it. I took two years to write *The Maze Maker*, and the publishers called it a novel. During all that time I made drawings, paintings, and sculptures on the theme of the *Maze Maker*. It was no use: I was not out, I was deeper in. I had written the whole "autobiography" of Daedalus to rid myself of him, and I had produced in fact the exact reverse of an illustrated book, for all the images preceded it or continued to emerge while I was writing, and the text did no more for me than explain what I was doing in there. (1970b, 59)

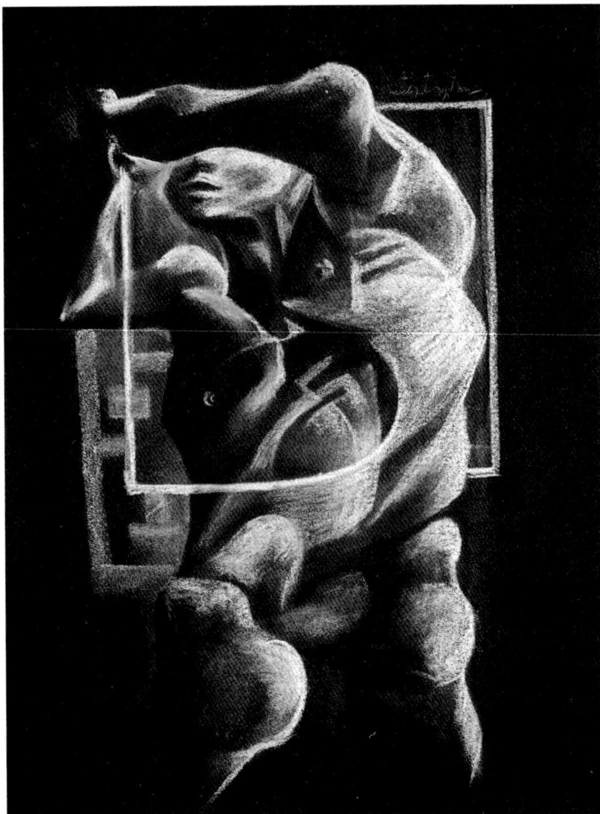

Figure 117. **DAEDALUS, MAZE MAKER** (Cat. No. 503; 20 April 1965). Brad Iverson, Detroit.

The earliest drawing of a Maze Figure, *Study for Nautilus Maze Figure* (Cat. No. 407), was completed on 15 February 1964. During June and July 1964 Ayrton produced most of his *Aspects of Gaia* (Cat. Nos. 421–452; Plate 20), a series of small landscapes closely related to the narrative in the second part of *The Maze Maker* (see catalogue). *Cumaean Section* (Cat. No. 424; 22 June 1964) recalls the painting *Cumaean Gate* (Cat. No. 365), for it conveys a similar idea about the underground maze, although more abstractly. By Ayrton's own admission, the best images in this series seem to deal with the brain and the omphalos, or navel, which is of course irrefutable evidence of the umbilical cord that once linked us to our mother. In *Omphalos I* (Cat. No. 431; 13 July 1964) this basic idea of the Earth Mother, or Mother Earth, emerges as a landscape metaphor and as the omphalos of humankind.[30]

By August 1964 Ayrton had become inextricably entangled in his maze-making phase described in the passage quoted above. Even the most cursory examination of the catalogue of drawings between August 1964 and April 1966 (between Cat. Nos. 455 and 572) will reveal how extensively the maze maker came to dominate Ayrton's creative imagination during this period. Beginning with *Maze Maker I* (Cat. No. 460; Figure 118) in late 1964, Ayrton began to translate many of his maze-maker

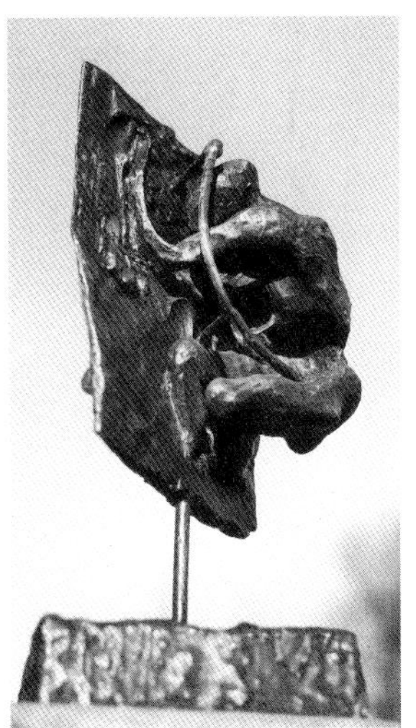

Figure 118. **MAZE MAKER I** (Cat. No. 460; 1964): front view.

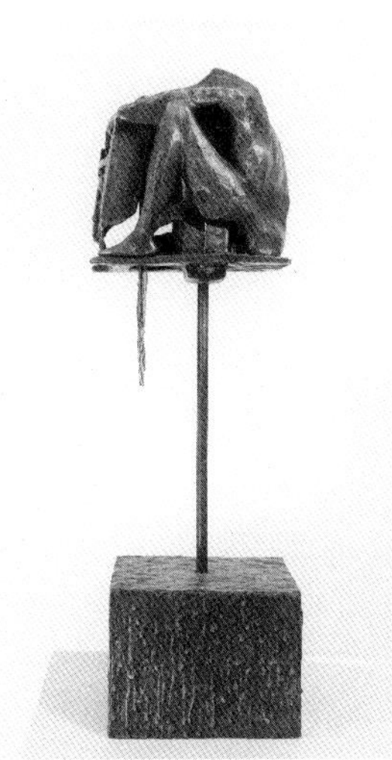

Figure 119. **BLADE MAZE FIGURE** (Cat. No. 514; 3 May 1965).

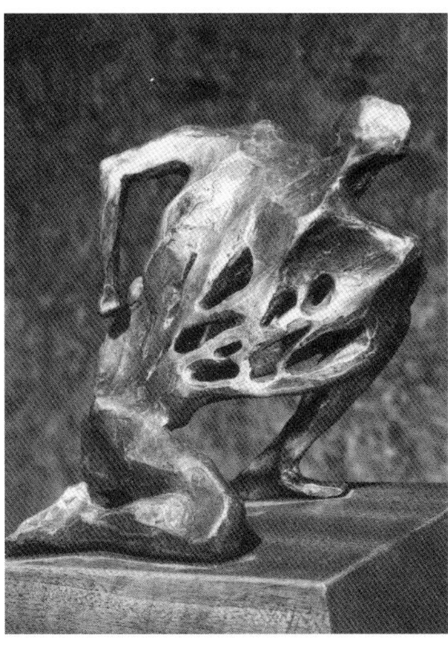

Figure 120. **KNEELING MAZE FIGURE** (Cat. No. 515; 1965).

drawings into bronze, producing a similar profusion of intriguing, provocative, and forceful images. In this maze-making stage Ayrton explored a wide range of ideas, from the maze maker struggling to control the maze he is making, to the maze player trying to bring musical harmony out of the dissonance of his life, to the entrapment of the maze maker in the tangled web of his thoughts, emotions, or experiences. In the process, Ayrton discovered that the more the maze maker tries to escape from the maze, the more deeply he becomes entangled and trapped in it.

In Ayrton's explorations of this theme, the archetypal bronzesmith and maze maker has "become at once more general and more personal. He has become any man who, during his life, builds in and around himself a maze of circumstances and experiences" and this, said Ayrton, we all do: this personal labyrinth "has two inevitably linked functions. It excludes to protect and contains to imprison" (1962a, above pl. 140 and 141).

At the same time Ayrton was attempting to lay bare the invisible structures of other people's labyrinths of fear and hope, he was also creating and exposing his own labyrinth of hopes and fears. Joseph Rykwert's description of Daedalus is equally relevant to Ayrton himself: "Daedalus develops the labyrinth from the lobes of his brain, from the convolutions of his gut. Its complexity is Daedalus's own attempt to order the chaos of sensation and idea, to master and imprison the pain in his body and the menace in his mind, of which the Knossan maze is an exposition and therefore an attempt at its resolution."[31] The narrator of *The Maze Maker,* who is both Daedalus and Ayrton, reinforces this notion with his declaration, "I write to unwind my own labyrinth" (1967, 13). Writing, drawing, painting, and sculpting were all part and parcel of Ayrton's own labyrinth and his "attempt at its resolution."

Maze Maker (large version) (Cat. No. 544; 1965; Figure 121, Plate 19) followed several earlier sculptures of the same name. When compared with the first two of these, *Maze Maker I* (Cat. No. 460) and *Maze Maker II* (Cat. No. 523; Plate 18), this sculpture is seen to be both more complex and more enigmatic. In it, the metaphor of the individual's attachment to and dependence upon his own labyrinth is made explicit by the umbilical cord that ties him to "the framework of material events." In it, moreover,

> the element of struggle is made explicit, expressing Ayrton's attachment to Greek art as well as Greek myth. In so much of Greek statuary and vase painting the possibility of movement is implicit. The specific question posed by the large *Maze Maker* is the nature of the struggle. Ayrton is not trying to suggest that the figure, which does not in this case refer specifically to Daedalus, is trying to escape from the maze . . . perhaps the truth is that he is trying to

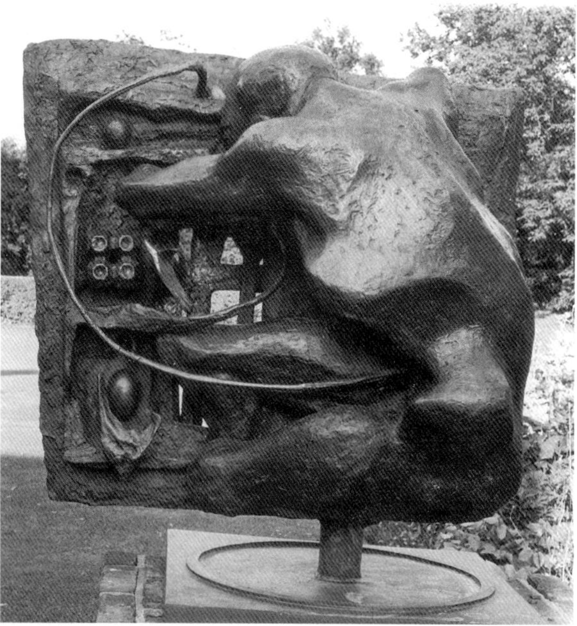

Figure 121. **MAZE MAKER** (Large version) (Cat. No. 544; 1965): front view.

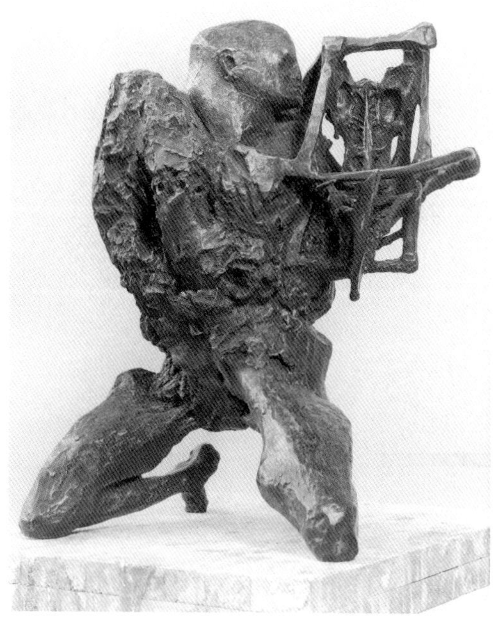

Figure 123. **MAZE PLAYER** (Cat. No. 551; 1965).

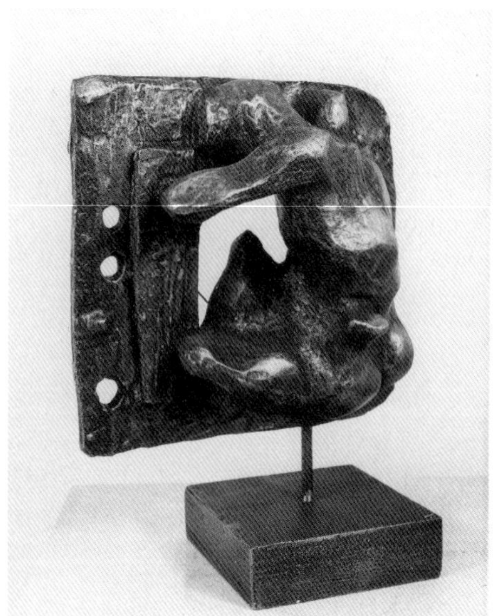

Figure 122. **MAZE MAKER III** (Cat. No. 524; 1965).

> get control of the maze, and in that way to dominate his environment.[32]

One can see Ayrton's classicism in this sculpture, both in its evocation of the narrative style of relief sculpture and in the "central position taken by man."[33]

In *Maze Player* (Cat. No. 551; 1965; Figure 123) the artist views the maze made by each individual as a musical instrument upon which people play their own tunes, which presumably represent both the harmony and the dissonance that comprise one's life. Ayrton himself said that in this work he had "strung the labyrinth like a lyre and the strings wind out from the maker's guts and nerves to supplant the navel cord."[34] This seemingly simple presentation of an idea permits the spectator readily to understand it and perhaps to see it as an expression of her or his own life. Yet it is also important to see this work in the context of a lengthy iconographic and literary tradition, as recent as Salvador Dali's painting, *An Average Atmospherocephalic Bureaucrat in the Act of Milking a Cranial Harp* (1933), and going back as far as the Middle Ages and the Renaissance.

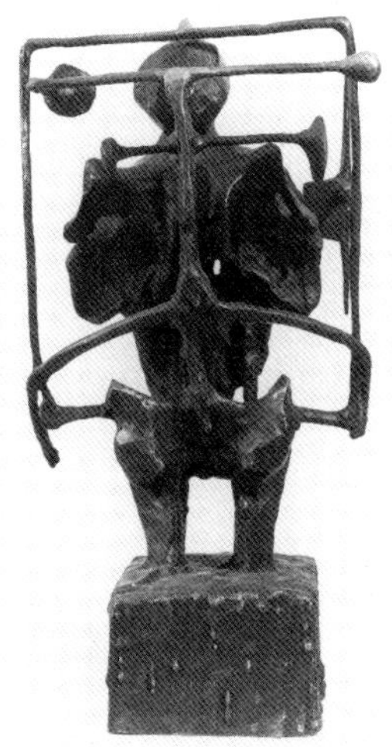

Figure 124. **MAZE TORSO** (Cat. No. 552; 1965): back view.

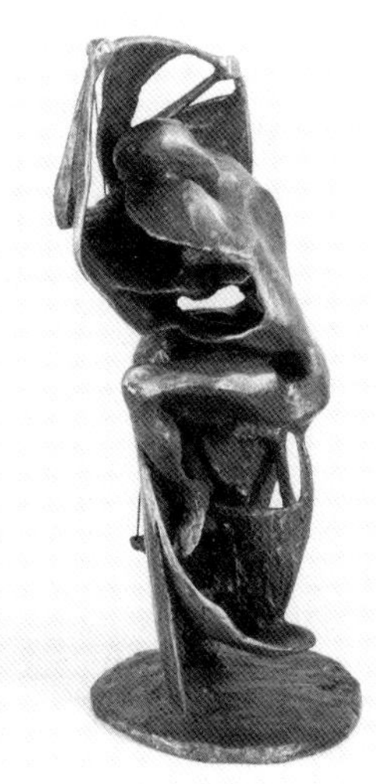

Figure 125. **NAUTILUS MAZE FIGURE (UPRIGHT)** (Cat. No. 553; 1965). J. S. Lewinski, London.

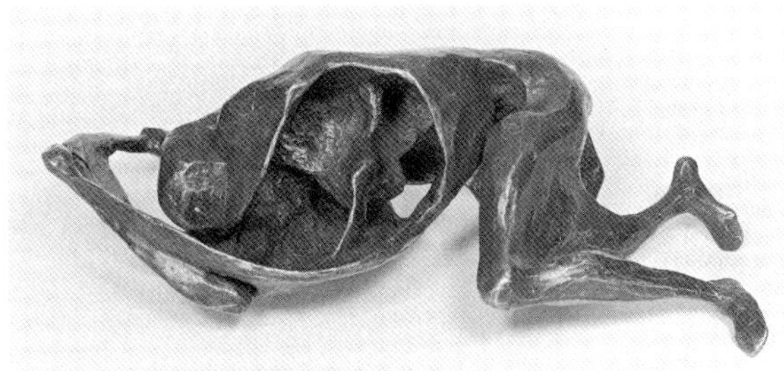

Figure 126. **NAUTILUS MAZE FIGURE (PRONE)** (Cat. No. 554; 1965).

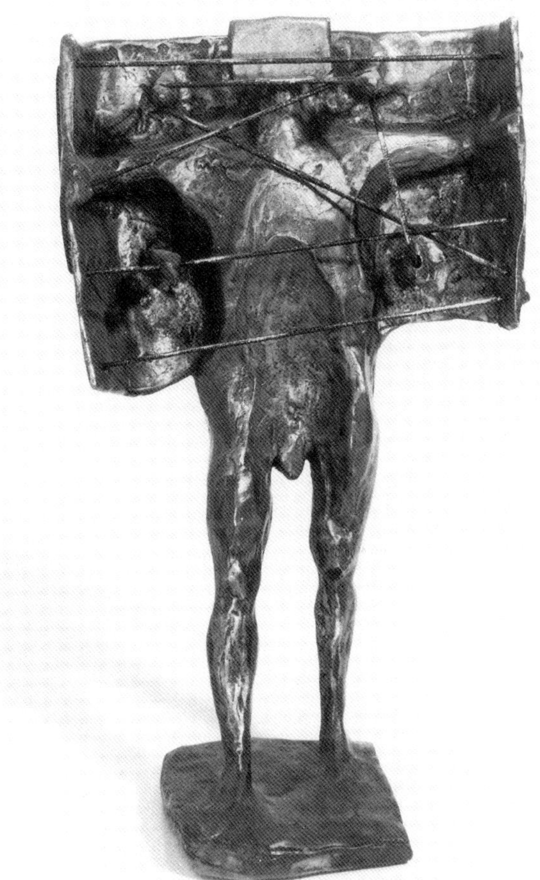

Figure 127. **SMALL STANDING MAZE FIGURE** (Cat. No. 558; 1965).

The use of metaphor and symbol pervaded medieval poetry and devotional books, but it also continued on into the Renaissance, partly because certain popular books, such as *Biblia pauperum* and the *Speculum humanae salvationis,* fixed the images in the visual memory and established them as part of a mental habit. Metaphysical poets such as George Herbert and John Donne were directly in the stream of tradition that flowed from the Middle Ages through Spenser and the sixteenth century. Writers in this tradition saw the world as a complex of meanings or values—seen pure, in their essence, as we see the "meaning" in metaphors, apprehended and appreciated rather than demonstrated and utilized; writing in this tradition shows this world in images.[35]

The conceit or motif of the musical instrument formed from a human's inner being, whether from entrails or brain, is part of this tradition and is to be found, for example, in the poetry of both Donne and Herbert. For them the image "is that of man as God's music, his sinews or heart-strings stretched like those of an instrument so that God's music may be played upon him."[36] Elisabeth Ayrton was "especially passionate about the Metaphysical poets, and Herbert in particular, so it is extremely likely that she introduced Michael" to Herbert's usage of this image and even to the poem which I find to be most aptly linked to the symbolism of man as God's music.[37]

Among the many examples in Herbert's poetry is this excerpt from "Easter" (lines 7–14, italics mine)[38]:

> Awake, my lute, and struggle for thy part
> With all thy art.
> The cross taught all wood to resound His name
> Who bore the same.
> *His stretch'd sinews taught all strings what key*
> *Is best to celebrate this most high day.*
> Consort both heart and lute, and twist a song
> Pleasant and long.

Regarding this passage, Rosemond Tuve declares: "The basic 'concept' of the 'conceit' quoted is the crucified Christ as a lyre, Love as music. . . . The whole conceit is simply a specifically musical form, in more Christian phrasing, of the great metaphor which we are so familiar with (in Spenser and other poets) in neo-Platonic or cosmological phrasing, i.e. Love as concord and harmony between dissimilars."[39]

Although Ayrton almost certainly did not intend a religious meaning for *Maze Player,* it lends itself to such an interpretation, for it is rich in symbolism. And given Ayrton's erudition, he may well have been aware of the tradition and some of the iconography of the conceit. Whatever his intentions, moreover, it is legitimate for the viewer of his work to read one's own meaning into it, as well as try to understand the message Ayrton intended to convey. Surely he would have realized that this motif conveys varied meanings, such as creativity, harmony, tension, and suffering, as well as the obvious meanings suggested above. And when he said that the strings of this lyre labyrinth "supplant the navel cord," he must have intended us to consider this work in relation to *Maze*

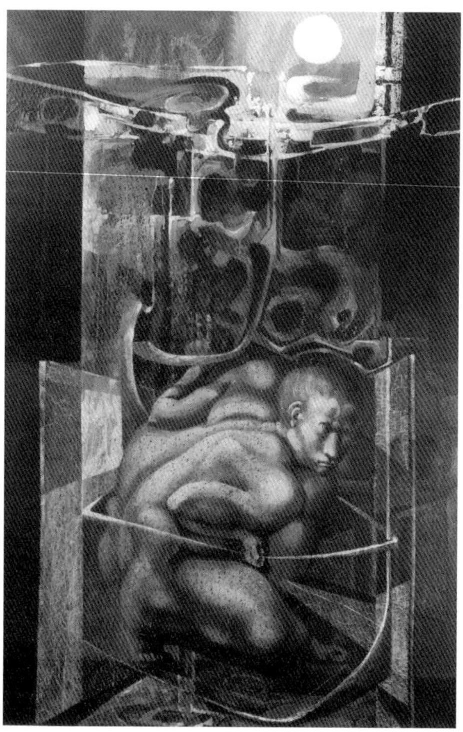

Figure 128. **MAZE MAKER II** (Cat. No. 593; 1966). J. S. Lewinski, London.

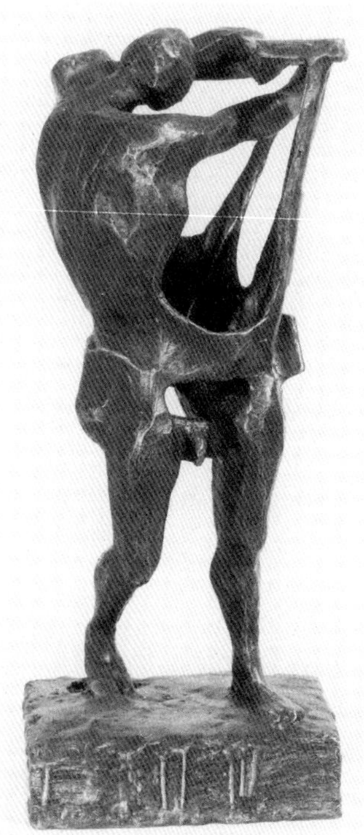

Figure 129. **TURNING MAZE FIGURE** (Cat. No. 598; 1966). J. S. Lewinski, London.

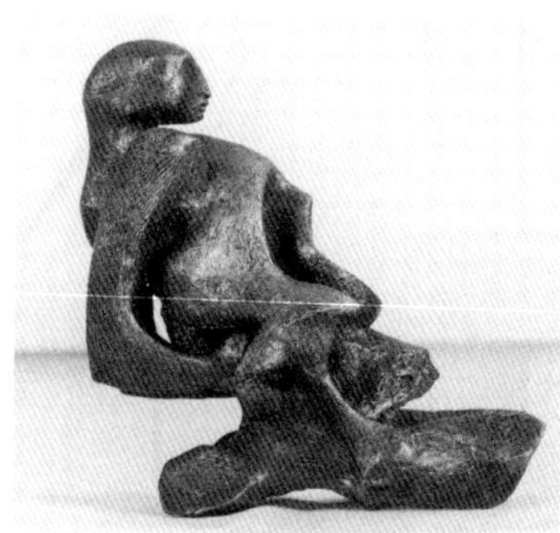

Figure 130. **BONE MAZE FIGURE** (Cat. No. 606; 1967). J. S. Lewinski, London.

Maker (large version) (Cat. No. 544; Figure 121, Plate 19), where the umbilical cord plays such an obvious function.

Another related work, *Nautilus Maze Figure (Upright)* (Cat. No. 553; 1965; Figure 125), and its variant, *Nautilus Maze Figure (Prone)* (Cat. No. 554; 1965; Figure 126), extend the concept of the maze maker, as a critic has noted:

> [O]ne is intrigued by the intricacy of the forms as the human figure struggles to free himself from the maze-like complexities of the shell while at the same time it appears to be making the shell and creating his own maze. The shell/maze becomes both a protection and a prison, the creation of man and that from which he most wants to escape. And as both prison and place of refuge it becomes that which man fears and loves most—himself. Yet no matter how hard he searches, to what extent he escapes from the world of his own making, or hides deep within it, as in the episode between Tros and Icarus on the voyage to Crete in Ayrton's novel "The Maze Maker" the centre of the maze is never totally revealed.
>
> That is to say that Ayrton's work is paradoxical rather than ambiguous. The various possibilities of explanation, of understanding, exist at the same time and do not present a choice. The multiple imagery presents simultaneous interpretations.[40]

In the passage from *The Maze Maker* (1967, 65) cited above, Tros broke the nautilus shell that Daedalus gave to three-year old Icarus, but the innermost chamber of the shell remained unbroken; there was still a further mystery hidden from him.

That point could also be made about *Maze Head* (Cat. No. 522; 1965; Figure 131; Plates 16 and 17). The blind-eyed oracular appearance of this sculpture recalls an oracle collage (Cat. No. 281; Figure 69), but it also must be considered in relation to the *Maze Head* painting (Cat. No. 457; see above) and drawings (e.g., Cat. Nos. 455 and 459, 461–462; see Figure 132). The jumble of thoughts and images, represented by the "apparently disconnected elements" within this head, may appear simple and obvious to an onlooker who is given a glimpse into someone else's maze. But this bronze conveys a truth about human experience worthy of any oracle. Another person's maze—whether he be James Joyce describing his inner struggles in *A Portrait of the Artist as a Young Man,*

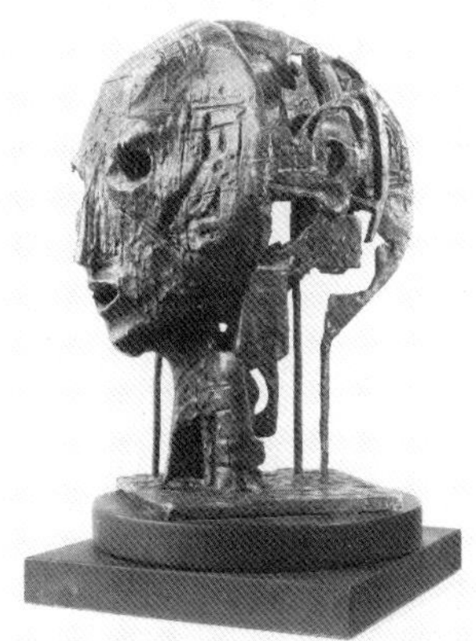

Figure 131. **MAZE HEAD** (Cat. No. 522; 1965).

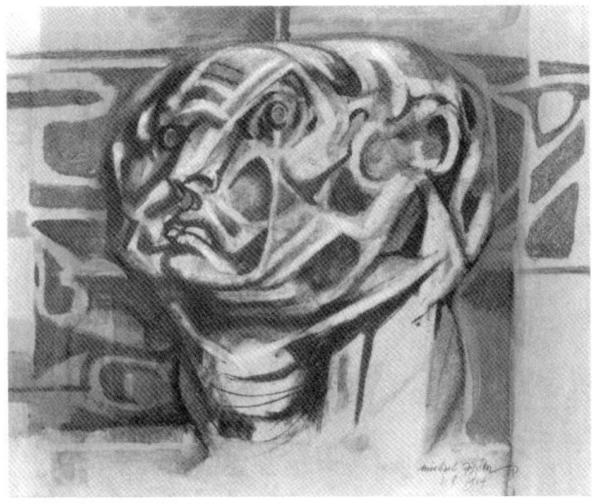

Figure 132. **MAZE HEAD I** (Cat. No. 455; 1 August 1964).

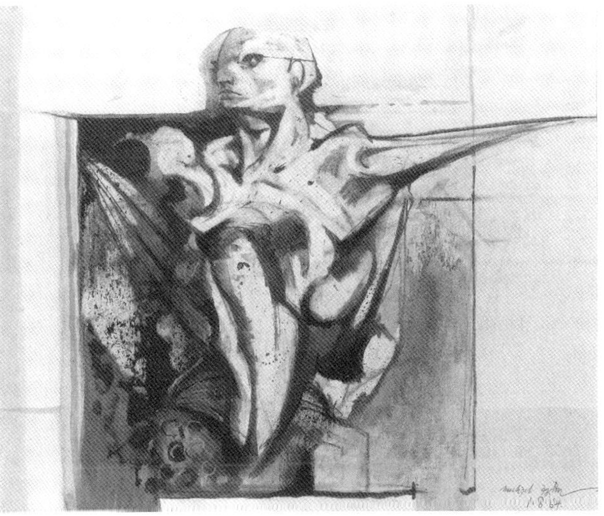

Figure 133. **ANATOMY OF DAEDALUS** (Cat. No. 456; 1 August 1964).

a Michael Ayrton trapped in a myth, or any other human being, male or female, young or old, simple or complex—almost invariably will not appear terribly intricate, but, said Ayrton, "to the maze-maker himself his maze is an all-absorbing thing compounded of confusion, achievement, frustration and reverence, which continually grows in complexity."[41]

Fifteen years earlier, in 1950, Henry Moore had produced two bronze heads, *Openwork Head* and *Head* (Neumann, figs. 69 and 70). The latter is more than twice as tall as the former (15.5″ vs. 7″), whereas Ayrton's *Maze Head,* at ten inches, falls between them in size. In both of Moore's bronzes, the head is conceived as a hollow shell, with all but the mask-like face aerated by openings between strips of metal. Although I would not suggest that Ayrton simply copied his idea from Moore, I do find it reasonable to assume that the visual image of Moore's two sculptures was buried somewhere in Ayrton's brain. When it emerged from his own unconscious, it moved in a very different direction from Moore's version. *Maze Head* does have a mask-like face, but the composition of the head itself suggests a rich complexity, not a hollow entity.[42]

From seeing the maze in terms of the intricacies of one's mind, with its tangled web of thought and its discrete, discontinuous ideas in its many chambers, it is a small but logical step to view the maze as the jumble of one's emotions. This is the essential message of *Contained Maze* (Cat. No. 583; April 1966; Plate 21), a striking collage that employs corrugated paper, sand, umber paint, tissue paper over card, and two colors of string to develop its narrative. Like *Maze Player* (Cat. No. 551), *Contained Maze* winds the string "out from the maker's guts and nerves to supplant the navel cord." But this web appears more complex and intricate, for it extends upward to encompass the head, dividing it into various compartments, and outward from both navel and clavicle to create a box-like enclosure within which the tortured emotional struggles occur. Here the focus is shifting imperceptibly but inexorably from the maze maker to the maze inhabitant, a progression which led to a series of figures placed inside a cage, exposing them and their struggles to view in three dimensions.

This new conception of the maze inhabitant began with *Cage Contingency* (Cat. No. 495; 1965; Figure 134), advanced with *Mirror Maze* (Cat. No. 596; 1966; Figure 135), concluded temporarily with *Cage Mirror Maze* (Cat. No. 609; 1967; Figure 136), and finally ended in 1972 with *Web* (Cat. No. 783; Figure 137). *Cage Mirror Maze,* as the title implies, combined elements of both the preceding sculptures. The figures within these cages have been compared to the work of Giacometti: Ayrton may have been influenced by the fact that he had three drawings by Giacometti in his own collection,[43] or simply by his earlier contact with Giacometti (see chapter 1) and by Giacometti's sculpture in general. Since Giacometti influenced Ayrton's move into sculpture, it would not be unlikely that he should also contribute to Ayrton's creative expression at times. Whereas in *Cage Contingency* the walls of the cage are only an illusion for the prisoner within them, since the tubular shapes defining the boundaries merely suggest confinement, in *Mirror Maze* the use of mirrors makes them actually become illusory. The translucent, golden walls that multiply the image of the crouched, maze-making inhabitant of the maze also serve as conduit and anchor for the red thread that should provide the means for escape but appear instead to increase the entanglement and entrapment. By adding red thread to his sculpture, Ayrton was using a technique employed by Henry Moore in a series of Stringed Figures over a period of two or three years (ca. 1937–1939). Moore attributed his use of this idea to mathematical models he saw at the Science Museum in London, but, he said, "It wasn't the scientific study of these models but the ability to look through the strings *as with a bird cage* [italics mine] and to see one form within another which excited me."[44] Since Ayrton's contacts with Moore began around this time, these stringed figures may have been buried in his rich visual memory from which he constantly drew new ideas and approaches. The use of strings would be repeated in a number of later works, also to great effect.

T. G. Rosenthal offered the following analysis of *Mirror Maze,* which he saw as "crucial to Ayrton's theme and to his execution of it" and as "the central work around which the others are grouped, and to which they are related":

> Inside this complex construction a man half kneels, half crouches, his hands entangled in the wires of the maze, wires which fan out through a screen as if from an altar, making of the man an almost hieratic figure, for all his being

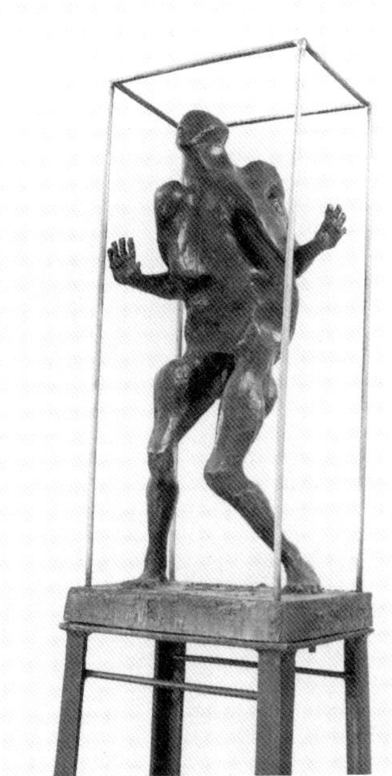

Figure 134. **CAGE CONTINGENCY** (Cat. No. 495; 1965).

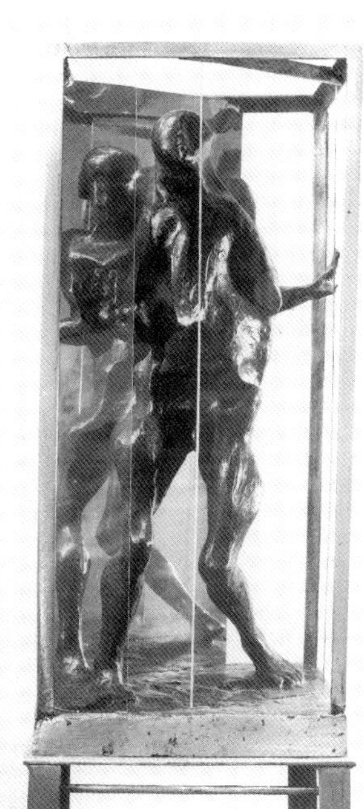

Figure 136. **CAGE MIRROR MAZE** (Cat. No. 609; 1967).

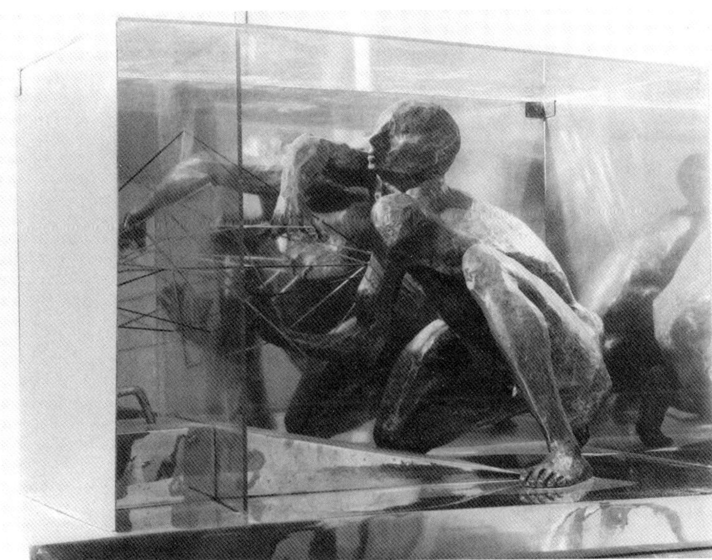

Figure 135. **MIRROR MAZE** (Cat. No. 596; 1966).

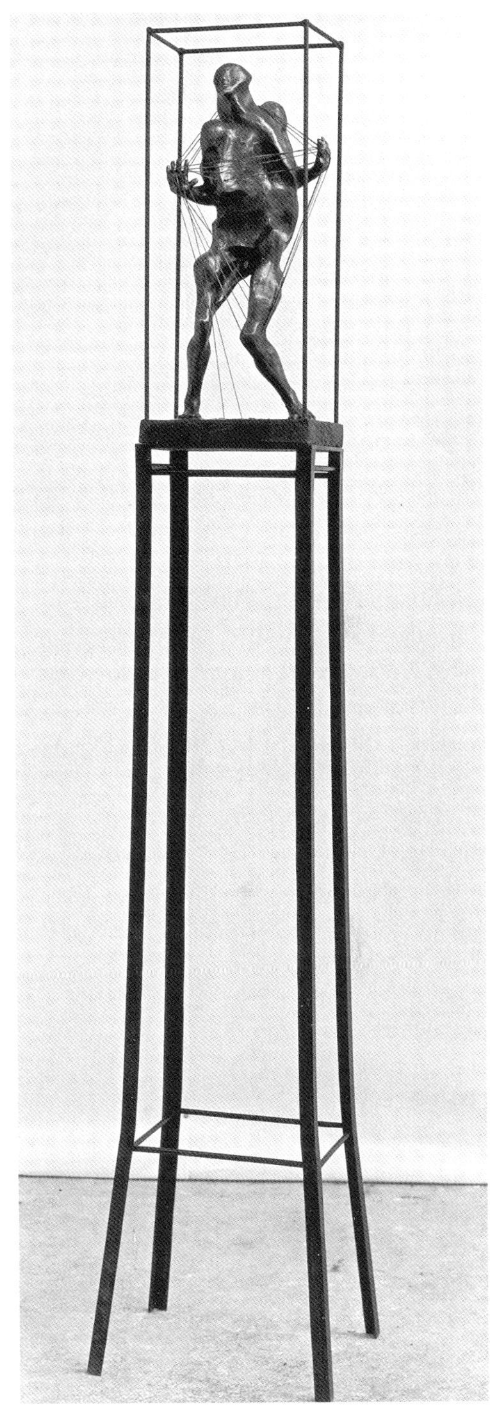

Figure 137. **WEB** (Cat. No. 783; 1972): full view.

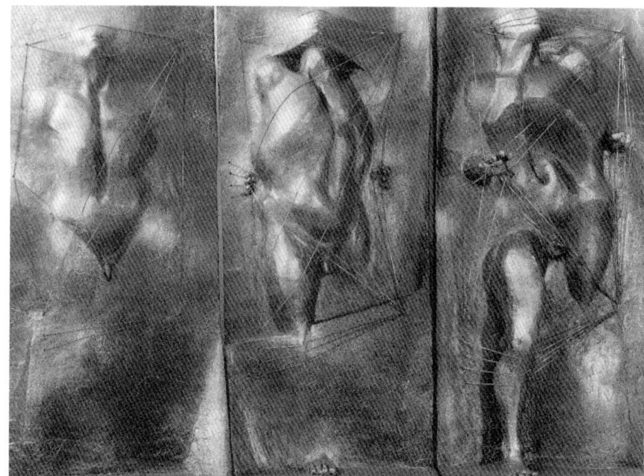

Figure 138. **TRIPTYCH I EMERGING FIGURE** (Cat. No. 597; 1966). J. S. Lewinski, London.

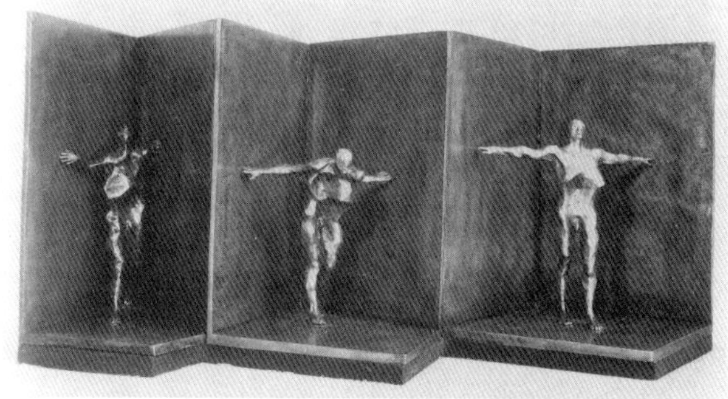

Figure 139. **TRIPTYCH II EMERGING FIGURE** (Cat. No. 616; 1967).

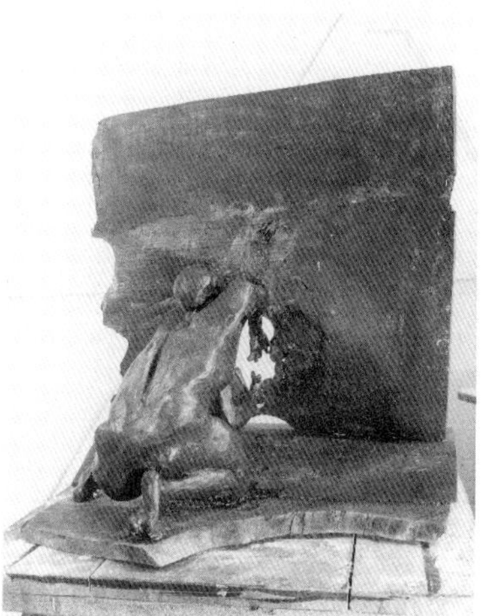

Figure 140. **RE ENTRY** (Cat. No. 614; 1967). J. S. Lewinski, London.

> trapped. Not only is he trapped in the maze corporeally but his image is also trapped by the gleaming, polished metal surfaces—the mirrors—which reflect and cause to ricochet and reverberate the multiple images of this single but universal lost man.
>
> The theoretical, the intellectual, and the moral points are all made in one's visual apprehension of the work. But there is, there must be, more to sculpture than that. Sculpture is, of its very nature, a physical thing, demanding consideration in terms of space and form, and the problem with *Mirror Maze* is that it is boxed in. One cannot, in the usual sense, walk round it, and it ought, therefore, to be, theoretically, inaccessible. Yet such is Ayrton's Daedalic skill that the spatial effects are achieved, by the mirrored surfaces, with a multiplicity of images which one could not achieve by more conventional means; once again Ayrton has demonstrated his rare combination of emotional force and consummate artistic intelligence.[45]

In *Cage Mirror Maze* Ayrton added sheets of perspex, both clear and colored, to heighten the feeling of tension and to multiply the reflections of its twisting, turning, trapped occupant.

At about the same time as the completion of these two mirrored sculptures, or possibly between them, Ayrton discovered yet another way of expressing the fundamental metaphor of the maze. *Triptych I Emerging Figure* (Cat. No. 597; 1966; Figure 138) shows a man, any man, in three stages of emergence through a wall, but not just any wall: he is emerging through the wall of *his* labyrinth. Across the figure in each stage is strung, at various angles and from several points around him, a progressively larger number of cords. As the figure emerges farther from the maze, he moves deeper into the entangling, confining, and all-embracing network of wires. This "harsh, brutal, and at the same time deeply compassionate piece of sculpture" dramatizes the human condition and translates Ayrton's view of his own life into an enduring poetic statement.[46] Ayrton himself later confirmed the validity of this interpretation when he declared unequivocally that his work between 1964 and 1966 had "centred on a series of images called Maze Maker.... [A]ll of them... express in metaphor my view of the human condition and *of my own life*" (1969, 200; italics mine).

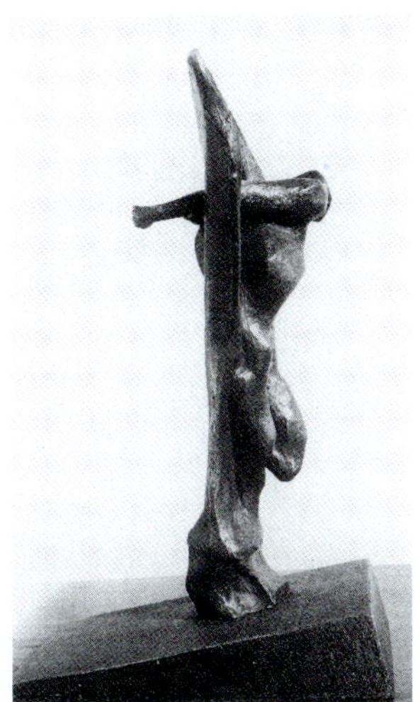

Figure 141. **THROUGH THE BLADE I** (Cat. No. 615; 1967): side view. J. S. Lewinski, London.

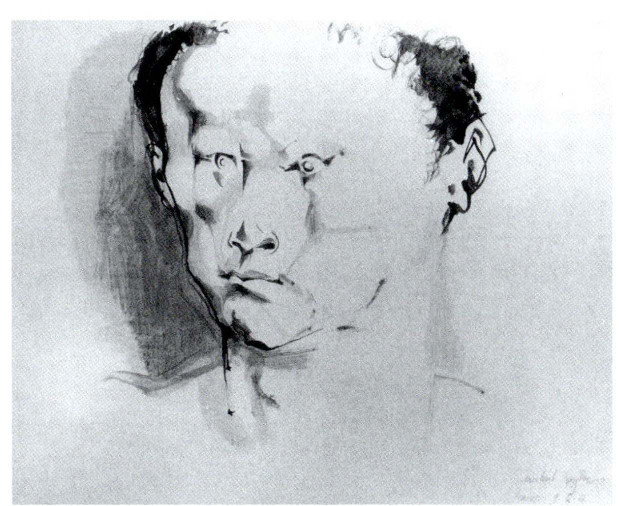

Figure 142. **ICARUS** (Cat. No. 566; 9 February 1966). J. S. Lewinski, London.

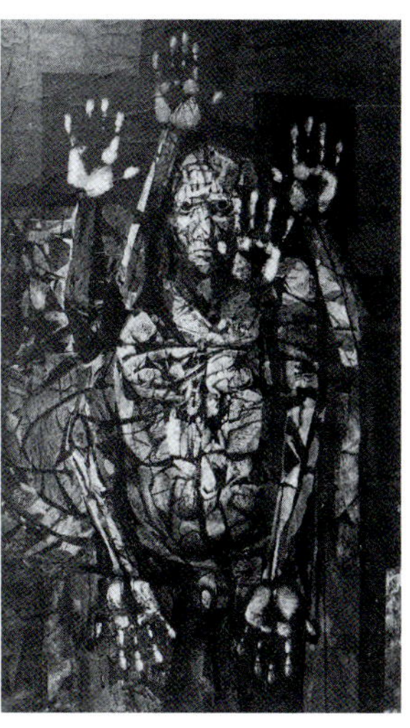

Figure 143. **END MAZE** or **DAEDALUS IN DARKNESS II** (Cat. No. 602; 1967). J. S. Lewinski, London.

In two subsequent variants, one of them in both fiberglass and bronze versions (Cat. Nos. 616, 617 and 618; 1967; see Figure 139), Ayrton replaced the wires with invisible restraints, which are equally effective, both in a literal sense and metaphorically. Similarly, in *Through the Blade I* (Cat. No. 615; 1967; Figure 141), a man passes through the *labrys* symbol, which itself is drawn from the material environment of the *Maze Maker (Large version)* (Cat. No. 544; Plate 19; see above). Although the man is passing through the double axe, he is nevertheless unable to extricate himself from it. This work represents yet another confirmation of the artist's plight: "As for my own maze, Daedalus made me aware of it but now leaves me in it."[47]

While Ayrton was creating all these figures of maze makers, he was also writing about the most famous maker of a maze, Daedalus. When *The Maze Maker* was published in 1967, it became clear how much Ayrton had learned about Daedalus and about himself since the publication five years earlier of *The Testament of Daedalus. The Maze Maker* is at once a tour de force as the "autobiography" of Daedalus and, at the same time, a skillful example of mythmaking. Although this book inevitably invites comparison with the well-known reconstructions of myth and history made by Mary Renault and Robert Graves, to name but two among many others, it is nonetheless distinctive because of the unique experiences Ayrton brought to the writing of it. The vividness of his descriptions is attributable not merely to his adroitness at storytelling, but especially to his long experience in drawing, painting, and sculpture, as well as to his participation in filmmaking, all of which require keen observation and attention to detail. The "autobiography" of the archetypal craftsman is told with great sympathy by an artist who aspired to make as great a mark on the history of art.

Ayrton's profound understanding of both myth and art revealed in *The Maze Maker* elicited extraordinarily high praise from Mary Renault, who wrote to the publisher that she "read it enthralled, solidly for a day": "What an achievement to have fused this powerful, profound and poetic myth-making, with so luminous an interpretation of the artist-craftsman. Each contained in the other and both in the whole. And added to all this, passage after passage of superb descriptive writing, with the heat and glow of molten bronze poured from the crucible."[48] About two months later, on 24 May 1967, Renault wrote directly to Ayrton, who had sent her a copy of *Drawings and Sculpture.* She took great delight in "this book . . . full of new riches, some of them (the Oracle especially) quite breathtaking," but she also expressed the added "fascination

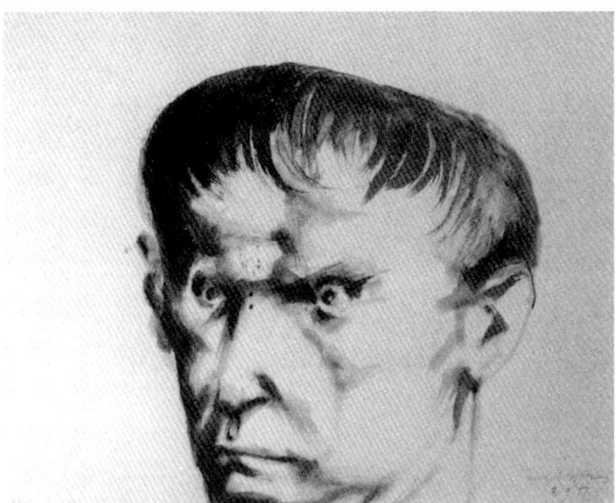

Figure 144. **DAEDALUS, HEAD** (Cat. No. 624; 8 September 1967). J. S. Lewinski, London.

of matching them with their counterparts in the novel," observing that "the way each illuminates the other is profoundly exciting," and further declaring: "There cannot be any artist working today who presents motion, and stress of motion, with such daimonic power."[49]

Clearly evident in this "novel" is Ayrton's own philosophy of life, including his belief that every person is both a maze maker and a maze inhabitant. His attitudes about life and death, about humankind's relation to deity, and his confidence in his own artistic ability, although tempered occasionally by professions of self-doubt, all pervade *The Maze Maker.* In *The Maze Maker,* as in *The Testament of Daedalus,* Ayrton discusses, defines, and dissects the concept of heroism. The duality of Icarus and the frequent ruminations of Daedalus on the question of heroes and heroism in both works illustrate Ayrton's own "obsession with the ambiguities of heroism."[50] As one might expect in a work of this kind, Icarus is much more fully developed than he is in myth. Nor is it hard to imagine that Ayrton's characterization of Icarus, which is carefully designed to illustrate the gulf between the father and son, has been drawn from his own sense of distance from his father as he was growing up.[51] The generational gulf encompasses differences in temperament, skill, understanding, sense of mission and purpose in life, indeed, in everything. When Icarus makes his final run against the sun, the father experiences such emotions as rage and jealousy when he realizes the wastefulness of his son's brand of heroism, and even after the death of his son, he experiences no grief for him, but only self-pity, shame, and anger.

In his development of the relationship between Daedalus and his father and between Icarus and his parents, Ayrton clearly follows Freud. Ten-year-old Daedalus accompanied his father, King Metion of Athens, to Delphi, where they encountered a troop of Dionysus's Maenads. In a cave that night, in his dreams he "saw a sweet and dissolute face, its brow horned like a goat, then like a bull, change smiling before my eyes, into an animal mask and vanish in the dark" (Ayrton 1967, 18). The brow of this great beast—Dionysus in bull form—was "ringed with ivy in which the small black serpents of Crete were twined" and "one snake in the smiling creature's crown had [his] father's face" (Ayrton 1967, 18). The language used to describe Daedalus's perception of Icarus and the gulf between father and son is overtly Freudian (Ayrton 1967, 63–64 and 90–92). Naucrate's maternal pride and the gradual separation between Daedalus and his wife and son (Ayrton 1967, 64 and 78) also reflect Freudian influences.

Presenting Icarus's soaring ascent as a hubristic attempt to commit homosexual rape is but one of Ayrton's many alterations of myth.[52] In this instance, he uses myth-making as a vehicle for preaching to his contemporaries about the significance of myth, as he makes it into an etiological myth and relates this story to the atomic bomb:

> Icarus, first and last a fool, did not become a man although his name became immortal. I do not think he ever discovered who he was. He had pride, such pride that the god himself could scarcely match it and when Icarus flew to rape the sun and throw him down, the god spurned him as you would expect. Yet before you dismiss what I say as folly, mark that Icarus died in orgasm and that Apollo's responding orgasm, long retarded, still took place. Man has taken the god's seed and you now live in terror that with this semen the world itself may yet be cindered. Mark that when you may be tempted to dismiss a myth and bear with me when I try to describe the paradox of Icarus and the enigma of his conquest and defeat. (1967, 134)

Describing Ariadne and Icarus, Daedalus says: "her hatred was so powerful that it came close to love, while

Icarus endured a love so jealous that it came close to hatred and only the destruction of its object could hope to quench it" (Ayrton 1967, 124–25). In this profound revision of the myth, with Icarus dying in orgasm with the sun-god Apollo, Ayrton again is following Freud very closely. Here we have both Eros, the life-affirming instinct, and Thanatos, the destructive instinct—the two basic instincts identified by Freud. Elsewhere he has Daedalus say, "I projected myself from two alter-egos, divine and bestial, and then saw myself mirrored in their shape."[53] It is perhaps worth recalling that Ayrton claimed to have met Freud in Vienna in 1937 (see chapter 1), although Freud's influence on Western culture during Ayrton's life was so strong and so pervasive that Ayrton most likely would have employed Freudian ideas in his novel, even if he had never met him.

Another alteration of the myth involves the relation between Daedalus and Minos. Daedalus was not imprisoned in the labyrinth by Minos, says the narrator (Daedalus/Ayrton), but entered it of his own will and out of fear (1967, 113 and 117). As Daedalus and Icarus made their way into the labyrinth, Daedalus found that the necessary linkages between separately constructed parts of the labyrinth had already been completed, so he knew that Minos had preceded them into the labyrinth, for only Daedalus and Minos knew the "way to the center" (1967, 116f.). And when Daedalus and Icarus arrived at the chamber of the sun (having gone there to avoid the Minotaur, who Daedalus knew would be in the chamber of the moon [1967, 117]), they found a fully furnished room with Minos seated on his throne and Ariadne kneeling at his feet (1967, 118). Ayrton also made Minos privy to all the preflight planning. Daedalus even explained to Minos how it is possible not merely theoretically but actually to fly, by describing to Minos how he will build the wings, stating his underlying assumptions about flight, based on his observation of birds, and articulating the principle that "the dynamics of soaring rather than muscular propulsion must be the key to human flight [and the] air itself must do the work" (1967, 119). But on the last day in the chamber of the sun, Minos told Daedalus: "You have built me my maze. In return I shall put you and your son into my cup and throw you into the air" (1967, 129). Ayrton here hints at the divinity of Minos,

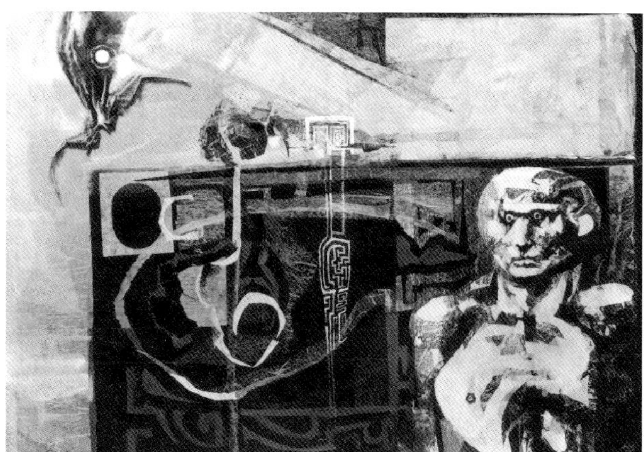

Figure 145. **JACKET DESIGN FOR THE MAZE MAKER** (Cat. No. 594; 1966).

as he does elsewhere in the novel, and suggests that Minos may be "the ultimate arbiter of the flight's success."[54] Other accretions to myth include: 1) the attribution to Daedalus of the discovery of the power of a magnifying glass to ignite a fire (1967, 79); 2) Daedalus is credited with killing Sciron, although Greek myth ascribes that act to Theseus (as the narrative acknowledges, 1967, 243); and 3) the claim that it was not Minos but "Tauros, Minos' general, Pasiphaë's lover" who was boiled to death by the daughters of Cocalus (1967, 310).

The preflight instructions of father to son bear little resemblance to the account in Ovid. They are, moreover, filled with modern technical jargon:

> I babbled warnings to Icarus about stress and the adjustment of the wing camber and gave him other useful information which went unheard. We strapped and buckled each other into our trappings, adjusting wires, tautening gut, looping and binding off the cat's-cradle strings of these fragile wired instruments to which we were about to trust our fragile bodies. . . . I shouted warnings to him about height and distance, about thermal lift and the pressures brought about by the conflict of hot and cold air. . . and we struggled to be ready when the wind reached its full force. (Ayrton 1967, 130)

Ayrton's treatment of Pasiphaë's "false and hollow cow" is much more convincing than any to be found in ancient literature, making it conceivable that such a preposterous

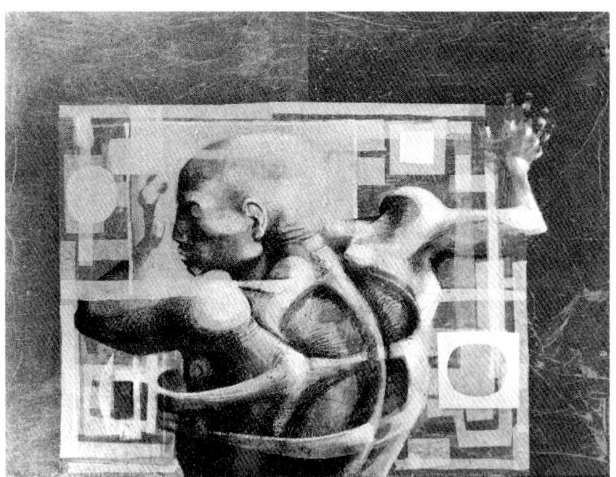

Figure 146. **TRANSLUCENT MAZE** (Cat. No. 545; 1965). J. S. Lewinski, London.

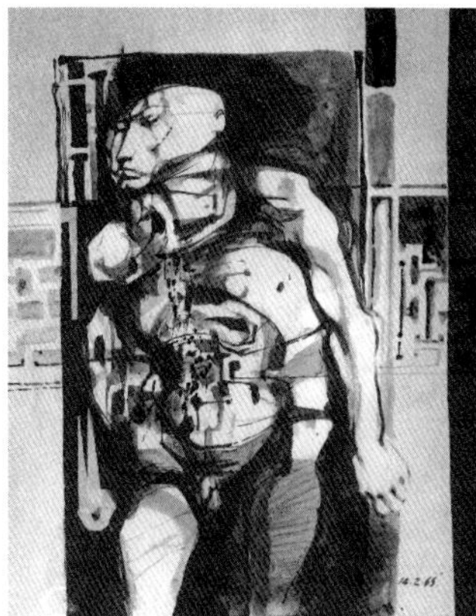

Figure 147. **EMERGING MAZE FIGURE** (Cat. No. 490; 14 February 1965). J. S. Lewinski, London.

union could have occurred. The technical skill of the expert craftsman informs other descriptions as well, such as the temple of Apollo at Cumae with its bronze doors, dedicatory gifts for the gods, and gifts for hosts and friends.

Not only is the characterization of Icarus effectively accomplished, but equally masterful are the portraits of Daedalus, Pallas (e.g., Ayrton 1967, 54), Minos, Ariadne, and Cocalus. The description of Daedalus's romance with Naucrate, the mother of Icarus, and of his gradual withdrawal from her reveals Ayrton's ability to perceive and describe the subtleties and nuances of human emotional responses (1967, 54f., 71f., and 89f.). The living reality of the gods for the ancients is clearly demonstrated throughout the novel, although rationalism and euhemerism are evident at times in Ayrton's mythmaking. Cretan mythology, culture, and history are presented with as much accuracy as could be expected. Knowledge of comparative mythology and various interpretations of myth, ranging from Frazer to the psychoanalysts, is evident. The most obvious ideas about this myth come, however, from Robert Graves, *The Greek Myths.* Etymological explanations (e.g., that Icarus means "dedicated to the Moon goddess Car") and many anthropological explanations can be traced directly to Graves (especially sections 88–96). Although Graves summarily rejects Jungian interpretations of myth (20–21), arguing instead for his "historical and anthropological approach," Ayrton was by no means so quick to reject Jung. Given the strong resemblance between mazes and mandalas, moreover, it is hardly surprising that Ayrton did not dismiss Jung, since this very important symbol became a central focus of Ayrton's life and work. Ayrton's description of the "last eternal maze" built by Daedalus, which he built for Cocalus at Kamikos (Camicus), reflects an awareness of Jungian ideas, as well as expressing Ayrton's own philosophy:

> A maze is a map of ironies, a pattern of paradox and its nature is revealed only to the maze maker and not to its inhabitants. . . . As for myself, I have built labyrinths for others, imprisoned myself in them in the hope of safety and once safe I have instantly begun the struggle to escape from my security. I have even gone into the open labyrinth of the sky to free myself from earth and watched my son die there to free himself from me.
>
> The labyrinth is not merely a dancing floor, nor a complex of passages nor a web of air: it is a field of force. Its architect, as I have learned, embarks upon the construction of a maze, believing that its force lies within his control only to discover that the field is held in equilibrium by opposed forces, at once containing and excluding, and his life's labyrinth has the laugh on him. (1967, 288)

The novel has many exquisitely phrased passages and many quotable sentences and paragraphs (e.g., 92, 111, 116f., 125, 133f., 141, 249, and 288) in this very readable work. Joycean passages (e.g., 198f.) are likewise noteworthy. The novel ineluctably draws the reader along, following the skein of narrative that leads not to a dark and foreboding inner chamber, but to the light of self-realization and understanding.

At the conclusion of the writing of *The Maze Maker* and near the end of the concomitant development of *Maze Maker* sculptures, Ayrton designed the jacket for the British edition of the novel (Cat. No. 594; 1967; Figure 145), creating a montage of his experience of the myth. On the front of the dust jacket, at the top, the title and the author's name are set against a red and yellow landscape which spreads its glow across the top of the spine and over the back, evoking both the sun and Ayrton's Cretan landscapes. Below, *Tense Figure* (Cat. No. 467; September 1964), a principal image of Daedalus (see catalogue), emerges forcefully from a maze configuration. On the spine, the temple concept crowns the maze below, suggesting both *Cumaean Gate* (Cat. No. 365; 1963) and *Maze Below* (Cat. No. 436; 16 July 1964), one of the paintings in the series, *Aspects of Gaia.* On the back of the dust jacket, a reproduction of the wax and bone relief *Icarus Falls I* (Cat. No. 47; see chapter 4), set against the spreading glow of the sun, vies for attention with an inverted *Translucent Maze* (Cat. No. 545; 1965; Figure 146), which retains only a hint of the maze maker who dominated the original collage and charcoal drawing. These images, although undoubtedly chosen especially to represent the multiple aspects of the narrative, nevertheless also summarize Ayrton's own journey, through the Cumaean Gate and into the labyrinth.

The artist's journey and his condition—indeed, the odyssey, condition, and destination of any man, or of Everyman—are largely circumscribed in the closing passage of the novel. Implicit in it also are the various *Maze Maker* images in paint and bronze by which Ayrton sought to reflect the human condition:

> I have called myself Maze Maker with a certain irony because although I believe myself pre-eminent in many crafts, I have been, as Minos described me, first and last a maker of labyrinths. I have made them as simple as a dancing-floor for partridges and as complex as the deep tomb for Minos which was also a prison for the Minotaur. I have inhabited labyrinths I did not make, of which one was the sky, Apollo's web, which I penetrated and from which I escaped, but which drew Icarus into its blazing heart to destroy him. Into another I was driven, and that was the earth maze of Gaia where she confined me until I could placate the sky-god. Then there was the fortress maze I built at Kamikos to exclude Tauros, and within that bastion another maze to frustrate those who might come to rob his grave. Nor am I finished, for I shall build one more and that will be my last. It will be in Sardinia and there I shall dig a twisting path back into Gaia so that the sun will no longer persecute me, for he will have no further cause.
>
> All this long burrowing and building, to protect or to imprison, this flight through the sky and tunnelling in the earth, seems to me now to add up to no more than the parts of a single great maze which is my life. This maze for the Maze Maker I made from experience and from circumstance. Its shape identifies me. It has been my goal and my sanctuary, my journey and its destination. In it I have lived continually, ceaselessly enlarging it and turning it to and fro from ambition, hope and fear. Toy, trial and torment, the topology of my labyrinth remains ambiguous. Its materials are at once dense, impenetrable, translucent and illusory. Such a total maze each man makes around himself and each is different from every other, for each contains the length, breadth, height and depth of his own life.
>
> I, Daedalus, maze maker, shall take this that I have written with me to Sardinia and dedicate it at the entrance to the maze which leads to death. Then you, before you follow me down into Gaia, who is the Mother, will know what is to be known of my journey and the fate of my son, Icarus. Before you follow me, look into the sky-maze and acknowledge Apollo who is the god. (1967, 319–20)

At the conclusion of *The Testament of Daedalus,* Ayrton wrote: "I am sure that all things are ordered and I shall presently grasp the design of these things which concern us here. I shall leave all this that I have written down, burying it under the rock" (1962c, 60–61). During the intervening five years he much more clearly grasped the design, as is evident from his tremendous creative outpouring as he moved from oracles, sentinels, and minotaurs to maze makers, and to *The Maze Maker* itself. Through his progressive discovery of the meaning of the myth and, thereby, of the meaning of life, as he understood it, he also peeled back several layers of understanding for all who would read his words and his images. But the journey was not yet ended. The chambers of the nautilus still hid answers, and the maze maker still inhabited the maze of his own making.

The Genesis of a Maze

6

The Maze Maker is much more than a retelling of the life story of the mythical Daedalus. Its penetration into the myth reveals Ayrton's profound learning and his sense of myth, but it goes beyond the known tradition of the myth to become itself a tour de force of mythmaking. The author also employs these living myths of the past to comment on the present, personalizing the universal expression of myth for his own time. His prescience about this myth's modern-day implications is at once remarkable and chilling.[1]

Just as Ayrton wrote *The Testament of Daedalus* to free himself from the myth, his writing of *The Maze Maker* half a decade later was another such attempt.[2] Yet instead of freeing him, his "novel" drew him still deeper into the myth. Ayrton's sculpture lent plausibility to the flight of Daedalus and Icarus even before he wrote the narrative of *The Maze Maker,* but through the narrative he was able to make it appear even more plausible. In like fashion, he gave credence to Daedalus's many other remarkable feats through his retelling and expansion of the story. It is therefore not surprising that the artist was challenged to prove his literary solution of various technical problems, which had been of no concern to the original mythmakers. Although he was never asked to recreate Pasiphaë's "false and hollow cow," the engineering masterpiece capable of deceiving even Poseidon's bull, he did receive two important commissions as a result of the publication of *The Maze Maker.*

One was to reproduce a golden honeycomb for a New Zealand patron. Whereas Diodorus Siculus in the first century B.C.E. reported that this extraordinary honeycomb was dedicated to Aphrodite at Mt. Eryx in Sicily, Ayrton judged it more appropriate to an earth goddess, presumably because a honeycomb is another metaphor of a maze or labyrinth, but also because he viewed the "labyrinth below the rock of Cumae as the entrails of the Earth and believed, as Daedalus would have done, that the Earth was female. Her name in Greek is Gaia" (Ayrton 1970b, 63). Hence, Ayrton's Daedalus makes the first one for Gaia at Cumae, then later produces a replica of it for Aphrodite.[3] He briefly summarized the process of creating *Golden Honeycomb* (Cat. No. 648; Figure 148) for his client in the catalogue of an exhibition at Stowe in 1970:

> In writing *The Maze Maker* in 1965, I stumbled upon the way in which the "miracle" had been achieved and included a speculative description of the methods Daedalus must have used. As a result I was challenged to prove my contention by producing a golden comb to match the description. This I did, in collaboration with the goldsmith John Donald, and as

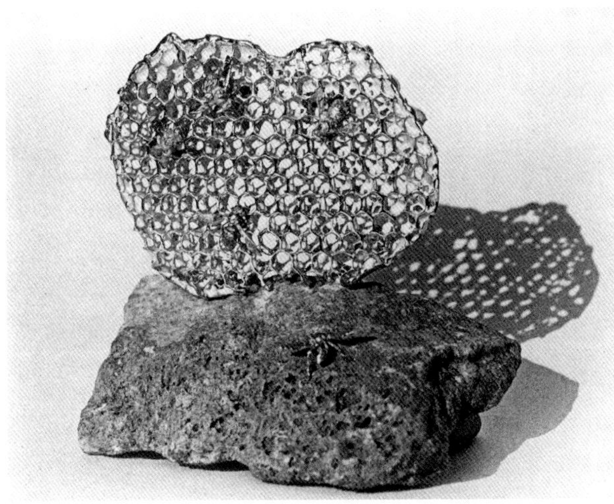

Figure 148. **GOLDEN HONEYCOMB** (Cat. No. 648; 1968).

> a result, 3000 years after the time of Daedalus, another golden honeycomb exists. The "secret" lies in the fact that, in ancient times, certain metals were cast, as they still are cast, by the "lost wax" process *and a honeycomb is the only wax model in nature*. What Daedalus did was to use *a real honeycomb* and not, as with any other artifact or sculpture, make a wax model to be "lost" in casting. He also used real bees which burn out of the mould as readily as wax. We also used real bees. The amazement of those who passed the legend down through the centuries was simply the result of ignorance of the processes of casting on their own part and on the part of the historians who later recorded it. (14)

The mythical Daedalus succeeded on his first attempt, but his modern-day counterpart required sixteen attempts to achieve similar results. Nor was Ayrton able to cast it whole, as Daedalus had done in the novel, but he found it necessary to cast it in sections which were then joined together. Forty bees were "sacrificed" to find seven nearly perfect ones to inhabit the comb, but live bees apparently overlook this offense, as the following description shows: "When the honeycomb was taken to New Zealand by the man who commissioned it, he showed it to Sir Edmund Hillary who, apart from being the conqueror of Everest, is a celebrated apiarist. Sir Edmund placed the golden comb in the grass among his beehives, whereupon his bees adopted it as their own. There is no news as yet of the quality of the honey produced in this Midas-touched environment."[4]

It is reasonable to identify a honeycomb as a labyrinth metaphor, as Ayrton did,[5] because of the complexity of its multiple chambers, but its small size makes it less than suitable for human penetration. The second commission inspired by *The Maze Maker,* however, was not only complex but also very large, and it would readily admit human visitors. Before Ayrton even began to create a miniature honeycomb in gold for his New Zealand patron, he had also received a commission to construct a maze![6] In the novel Minos says to Daedalus: "You will build beneath this palace a place so deep, so tortuous beyond its entry, so convoluted in its winding passages, that no one but you and I will know the way to its centre. You will build a labyrinth. That is the central purpose of your life. Master of many crafts you may be, but finally you will discover that all your life you have been a maze maker. I set you your first maze to make" (Ayrton 1967, 83). Ayrton's commission may not have been so eloquently and prophetically stated, but the challenge was every bit as real. The following account of the genesis of that maze illustrates not only the patron-artist relationship but especially the creative process of the artist himself.

The Maze Maker was published in England in May 1967, but the American edition did not appear until the following fall. The author was in America at that time, en route to California to assume a visiting lectureship at the University of California, Santa Barbara. While visiting friends in New York, he attended a cocktail party where, he said, he "met a singular gentleman who said he'd read it. I said, oh yes, and he said, I want one."[7] The "singular gentleman" was Armand Grover Erpf, a millionaire senior partner in the Wall Street investment firm of Loeb, Rhoades and Company,[8] who added: "if you know something about mazes, when you're out in California, why don't you make a sketch or two and then when you're back here maybe we'll fix it up together?"[9] These instructions are scarcely more precise than Minos's commission to Daedalus cited above, and Ayrton's response appears to have resembled that of Daedalus in similar circumstances, who said: "It was only when I had left him that I realized I had not asked him the purpose of this maze" (Ayrton 1967, 84).

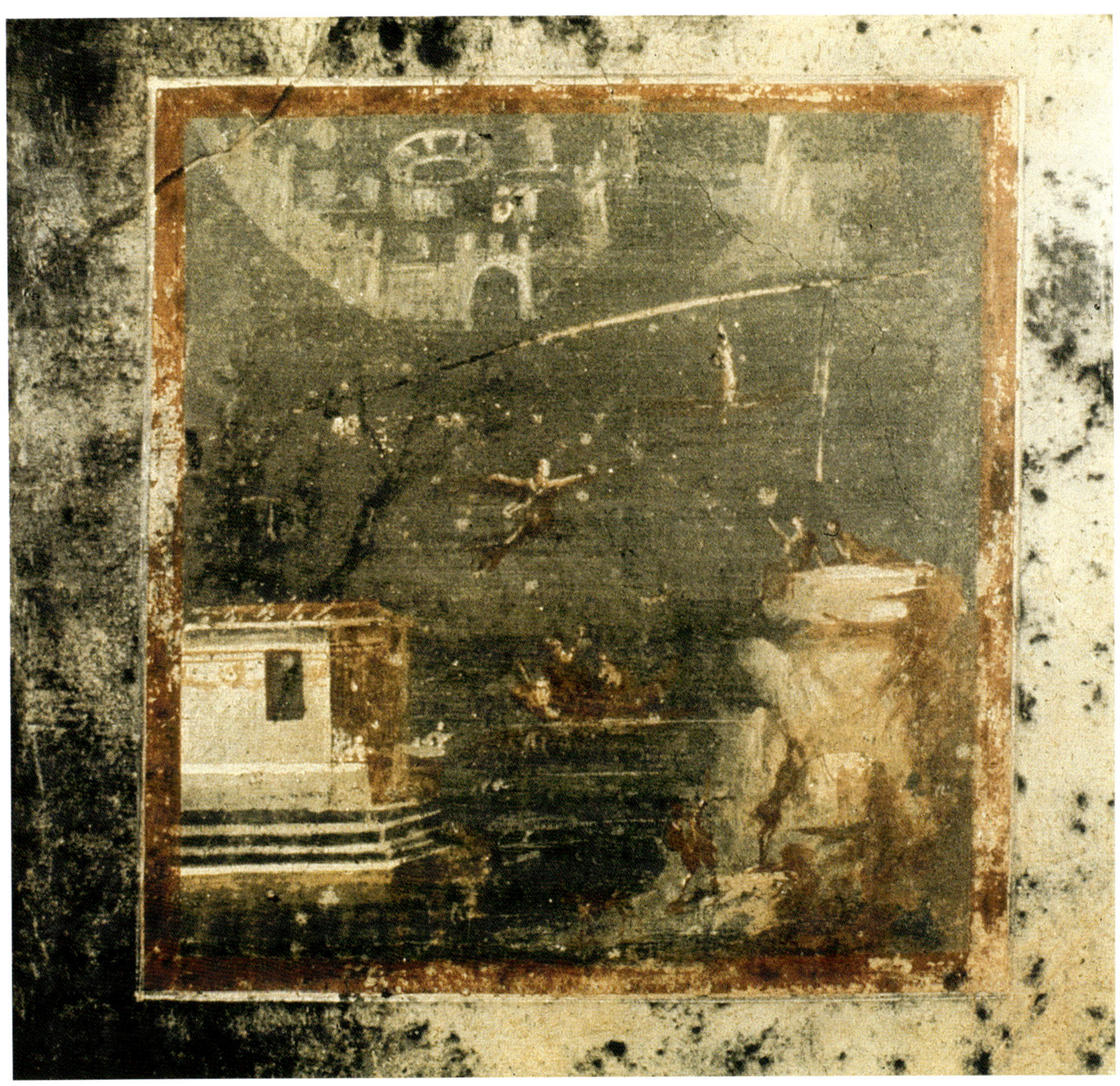

Plate 1. **FALL OF ICARUS** (Pompeii, 1st c. C.E.). British Museum.

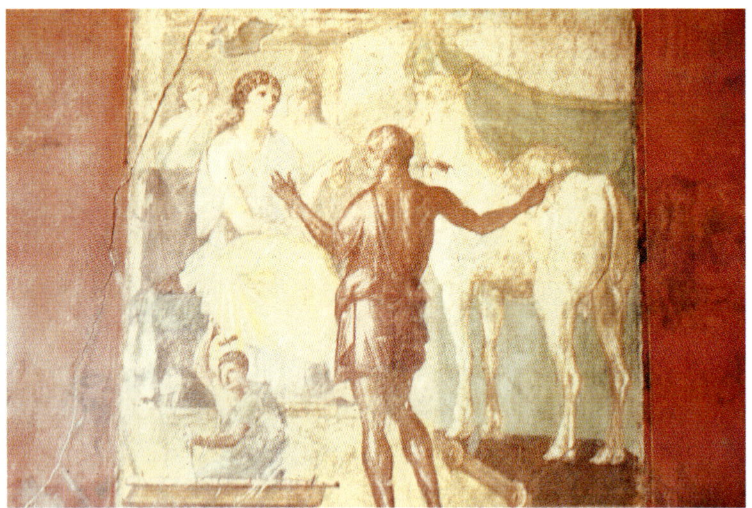

Plate 2. **DAEDALUS AND PASIPHAË** (Pompeii, House of the Vettii, 1st c. C.E.).

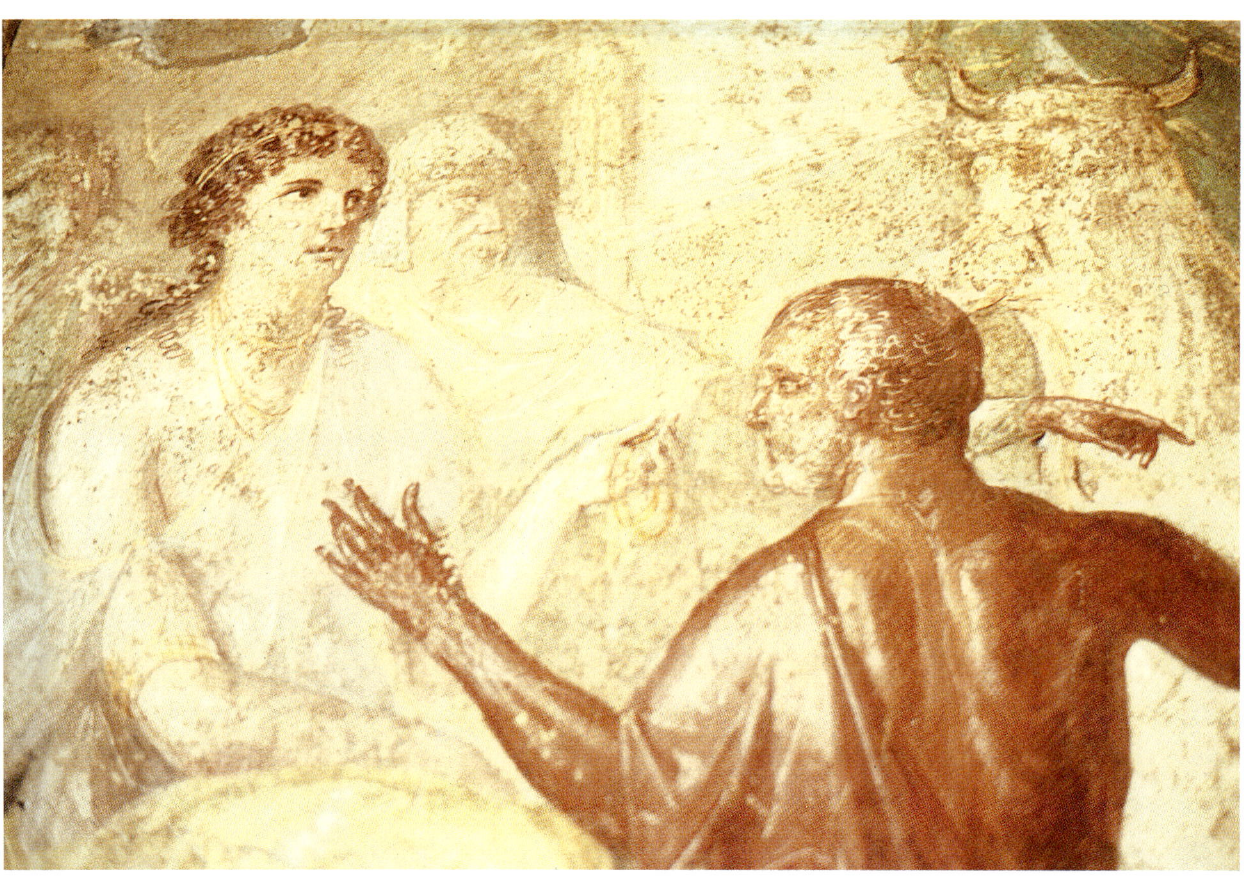

Plate 3. **DAEDALUS AND PASIPHAË** (detail).

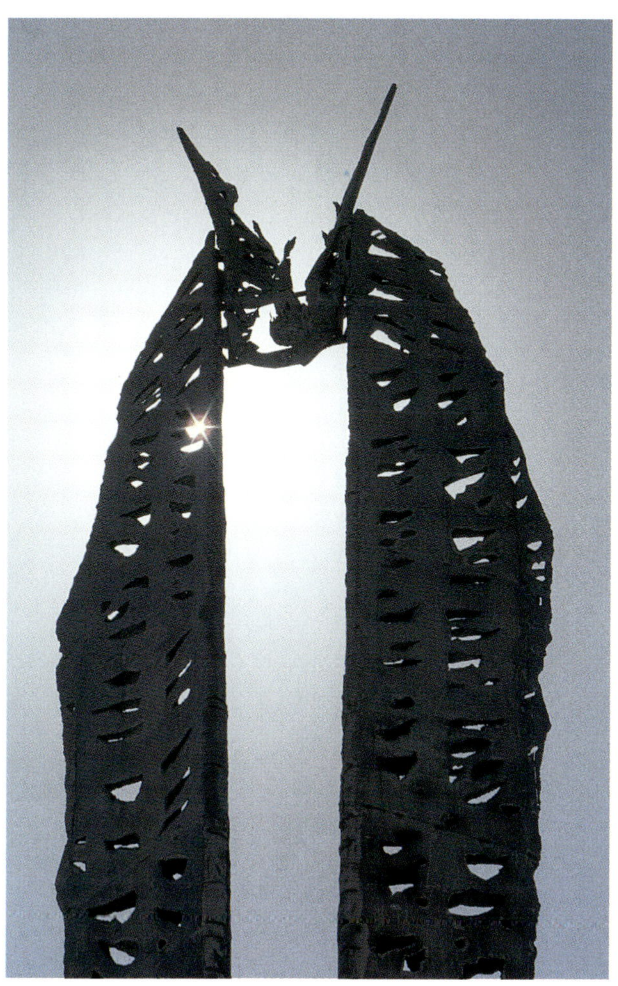

Plate 7. Nicholas Ikaris, **ICARUS MONUMENT ON IKARIA** (1981).

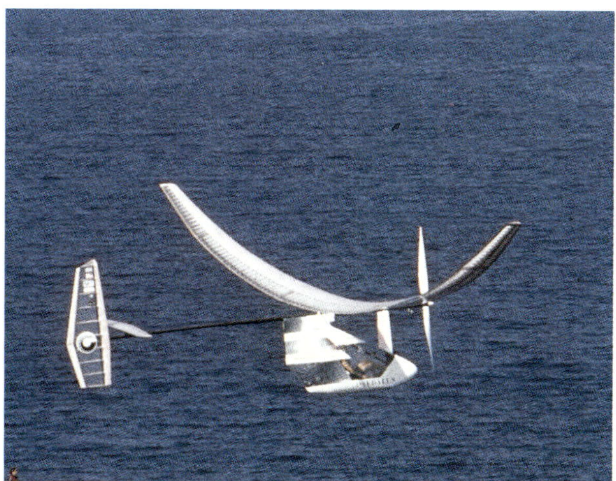

Plate 8. **DAEDALUS AIRCRAFT**, 1988, over the Aegean Sea. Steve Fineberg.

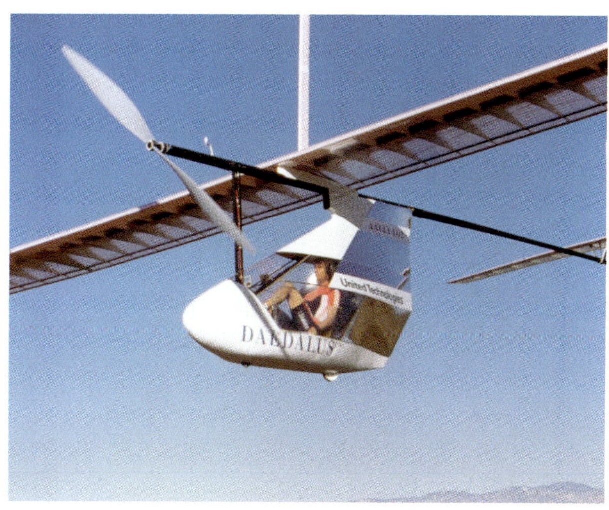

Plate 9. **DAEDALUS AIRCRAFT**, 1988, just after takeoff from airbase on Crete. Steve Fineberg.

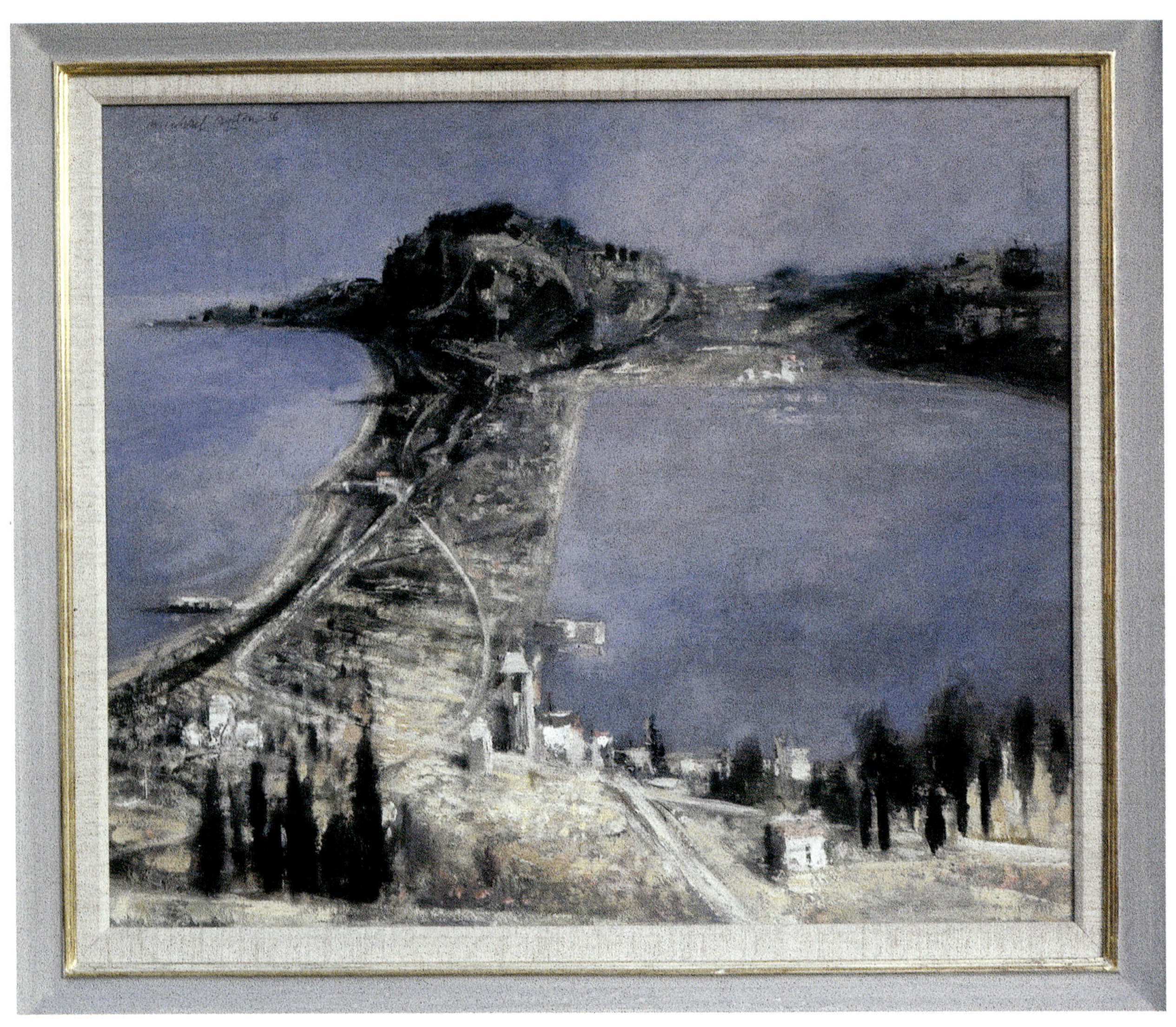

Plate 10. **ACROPOLIS OF CUMAE** (Cat. No. 14; 1956).

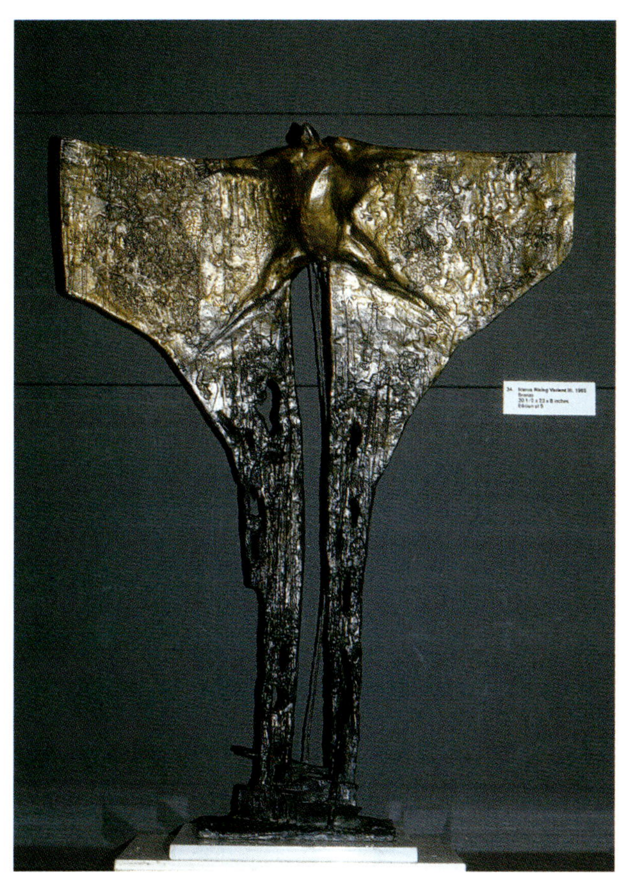

Plate 11. **ICARUS RISING, VAR. III** (Cat. No. 513; 1965).

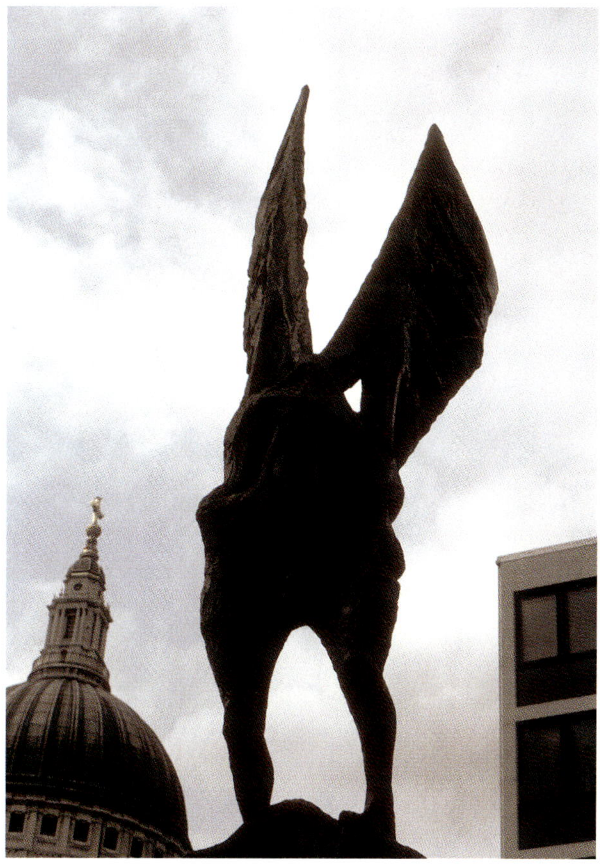

Plate 12. **ICARUS III, VAR. I** (Cat. No. 756; 1972).

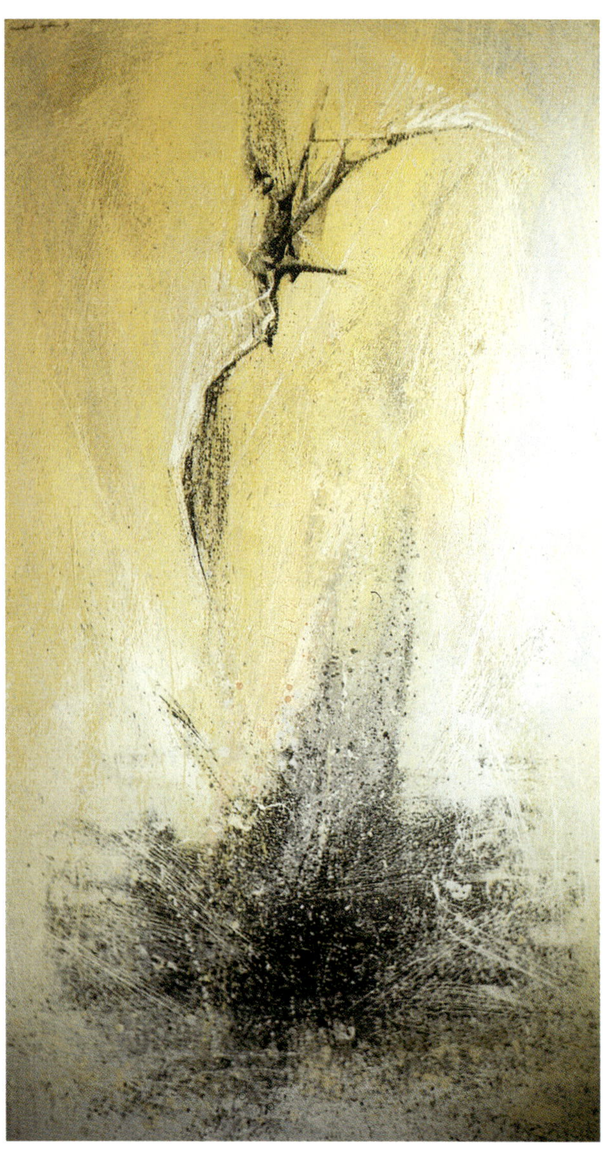

Plate 13. **ICARUS FALLS IV** (Cat. No. 87; 1959).

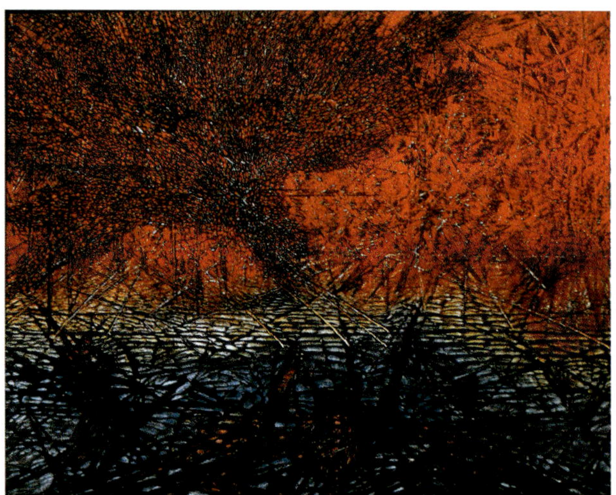

Plate 14. Jimmy Ernst, **ICARUS III** (1963).

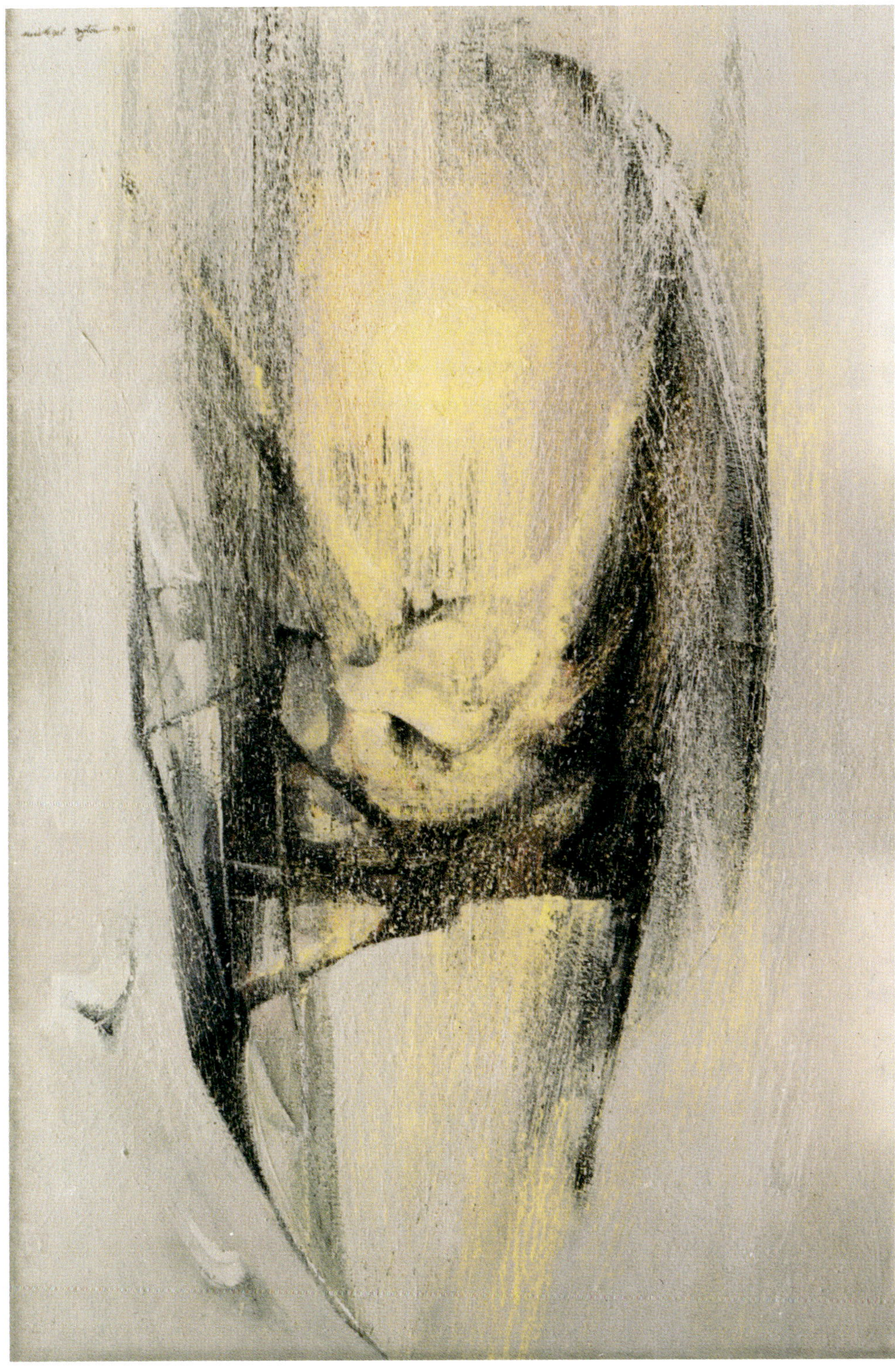

Plate 15. **ICARUS FALLS VI** (Cat. No. 89; 1959–60).

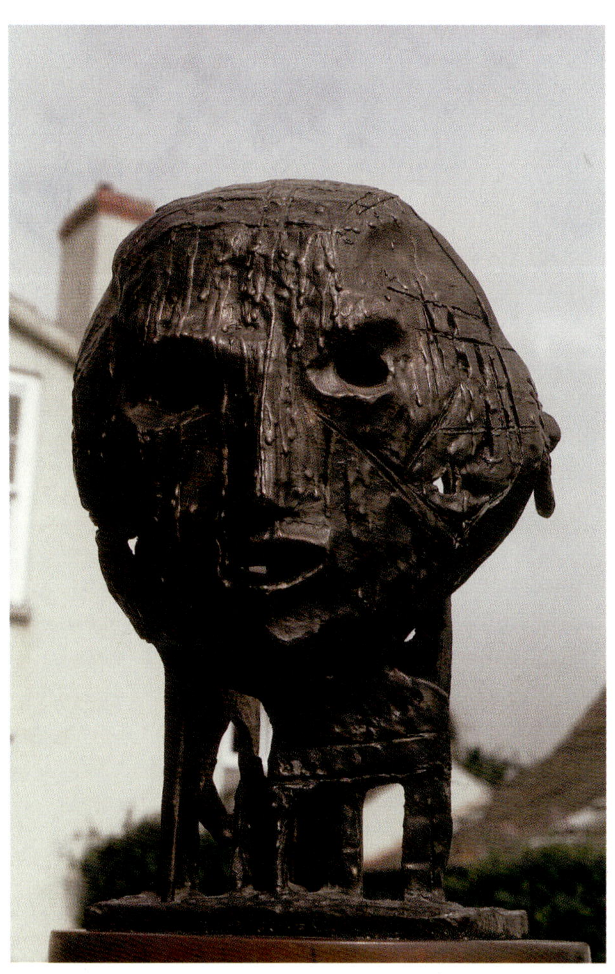

Plate 16. **MAZE HEAD** (Cat. No. 522; 1965).

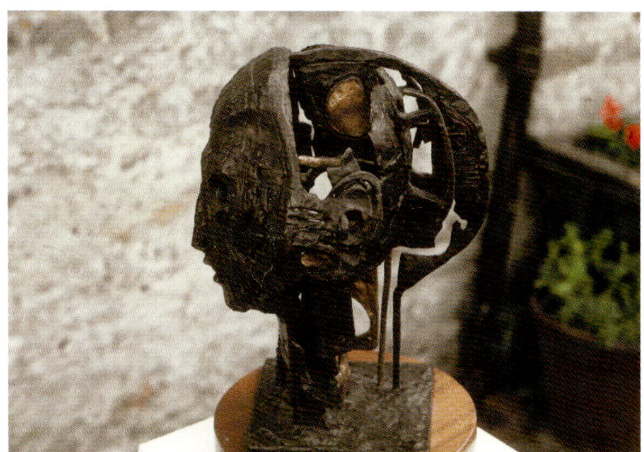

Plate 17. **MAZE HEAD** (Cat. No. 522).

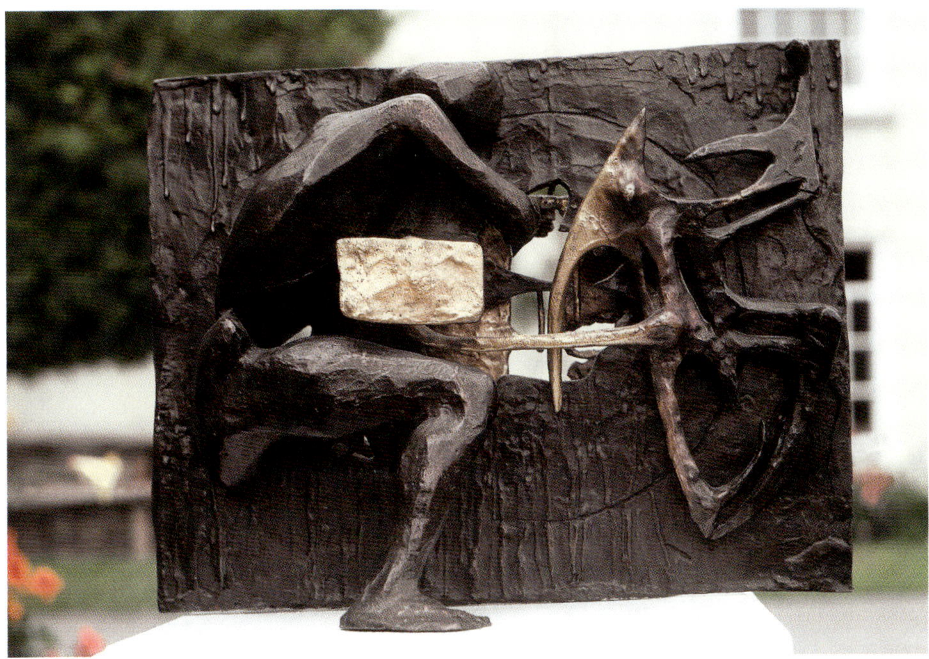

Plate 18. **MAZE MAKER II** (Cat. No. 523; 1965).

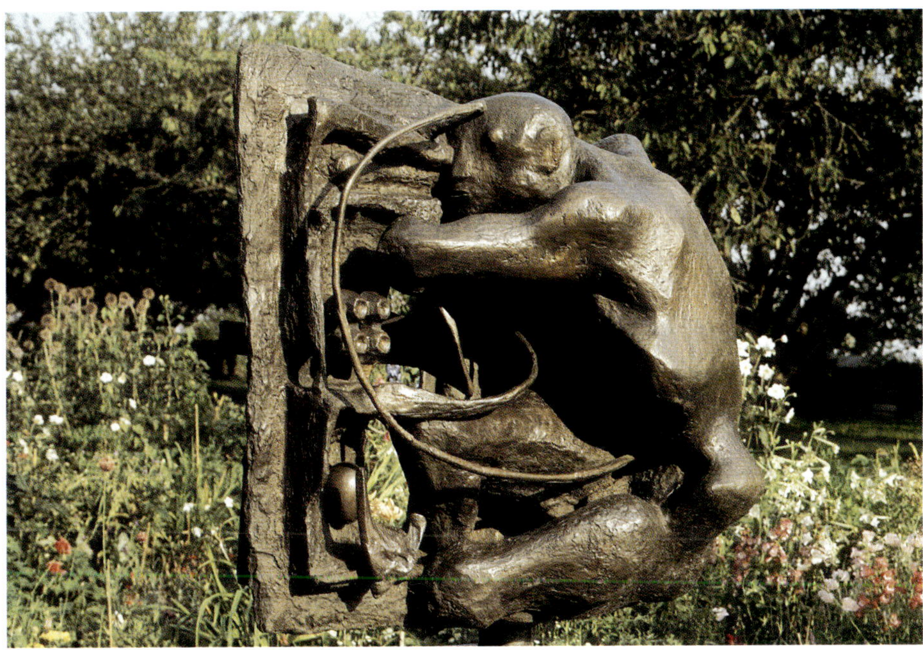

Plate 19. **MAZE MAKER** (Large version) (Cat. No. 544; 1965).

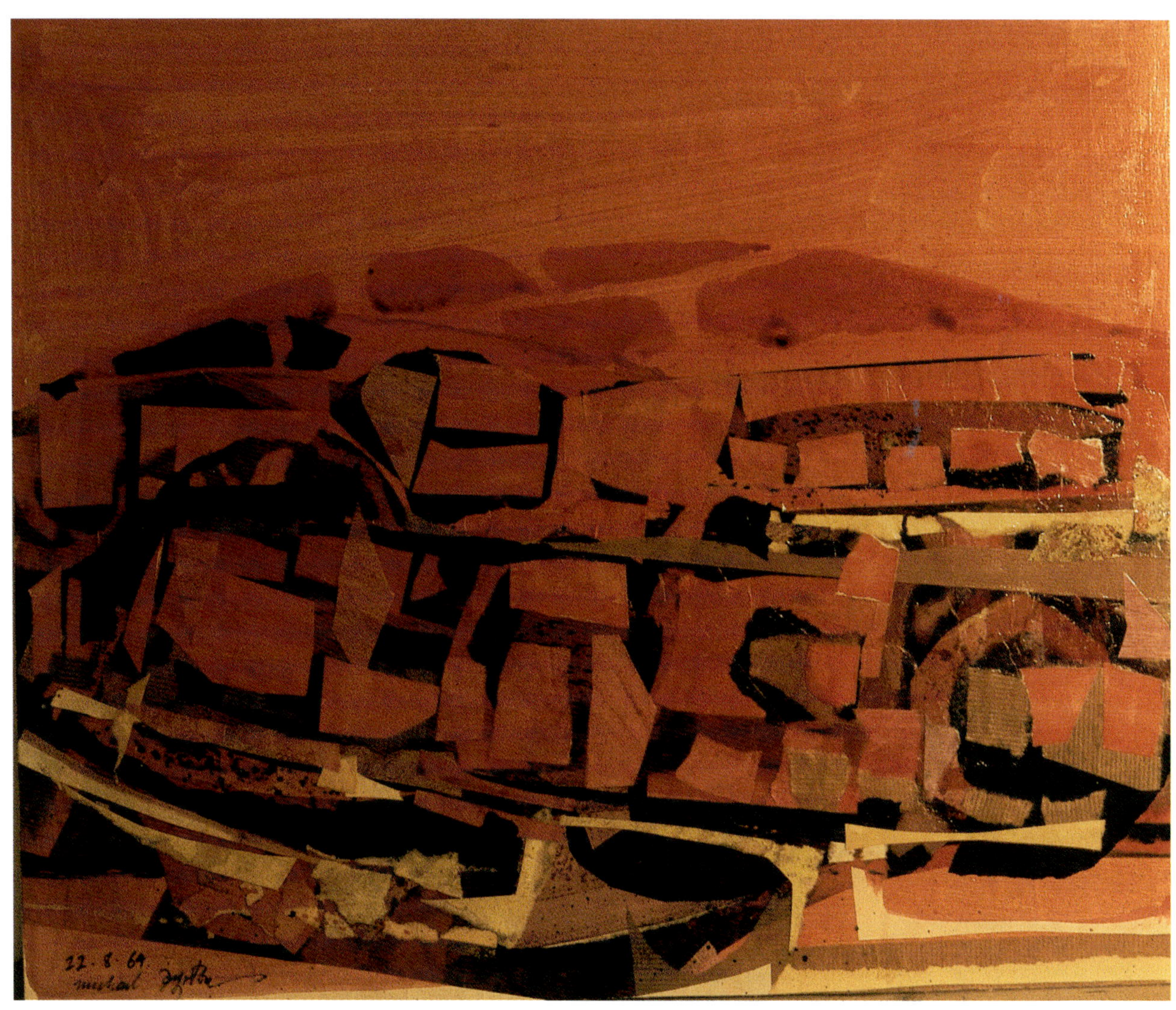

Plate 20. **ASPECTS OF GAIA: COMPRESSED RED** (Cat. No. 452; 22 August 1964).

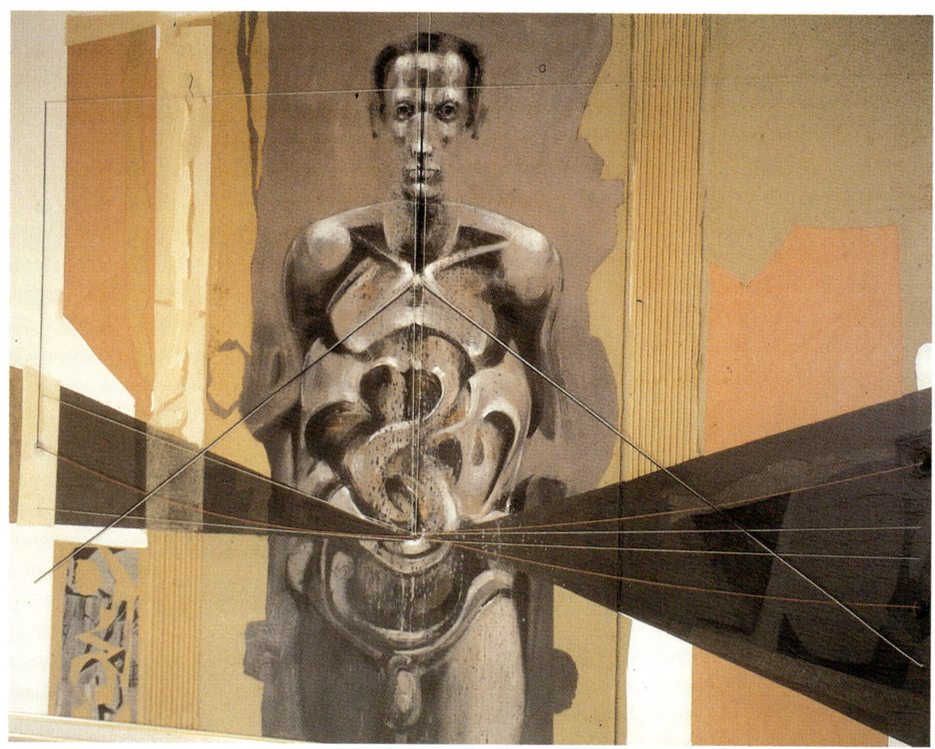

Plate 21. **CONTAINED MAZE** (Cat. No. 583; April 1966).

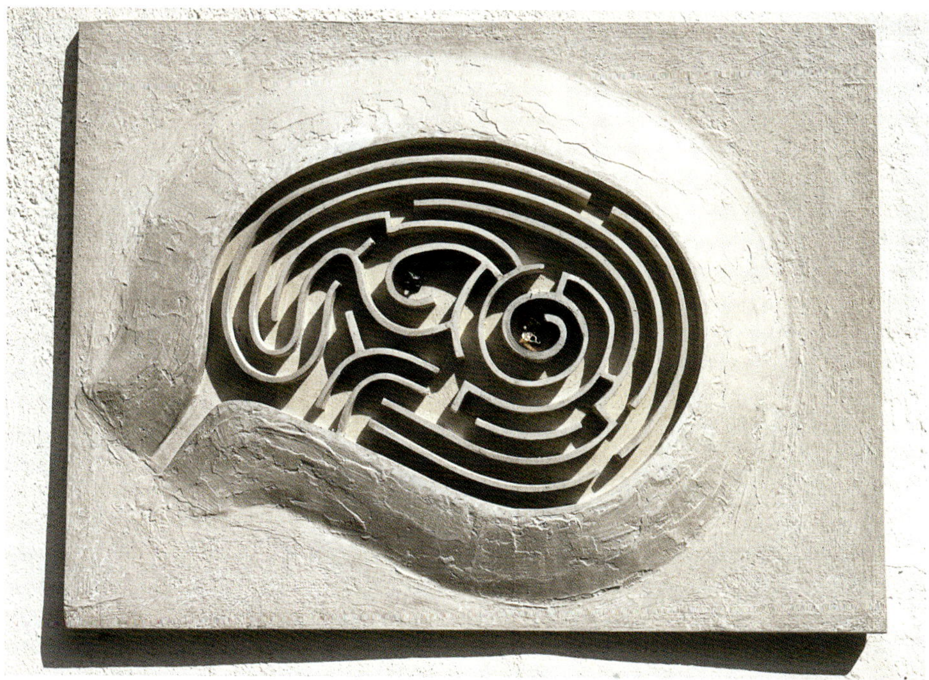

Plate 22. **ARKVILLE MAZE MAQUETTE** (Cat. No. 641; 1968).

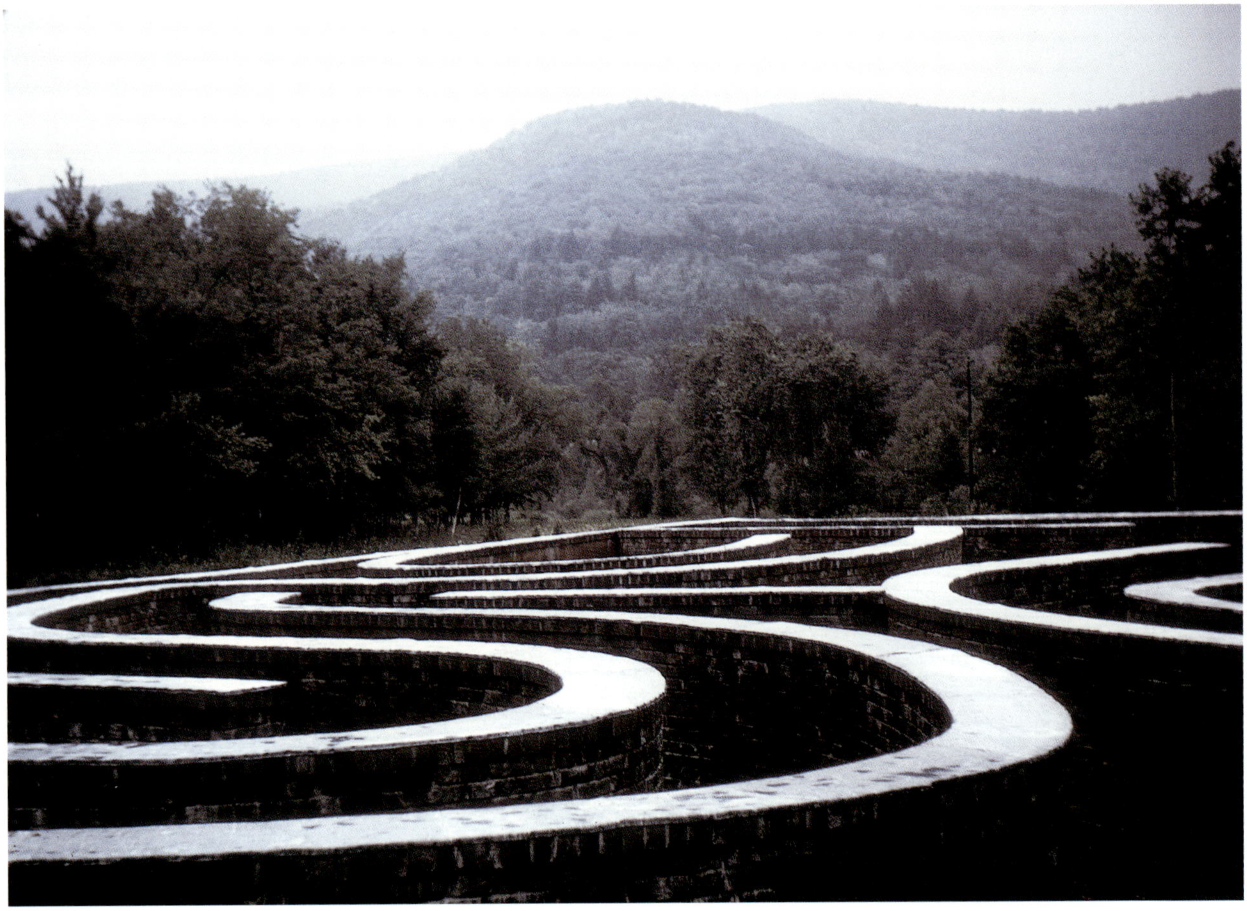

Plate 23. **ARKVILLE MAZE** (Cat. No. 673; 1968–70): overview.

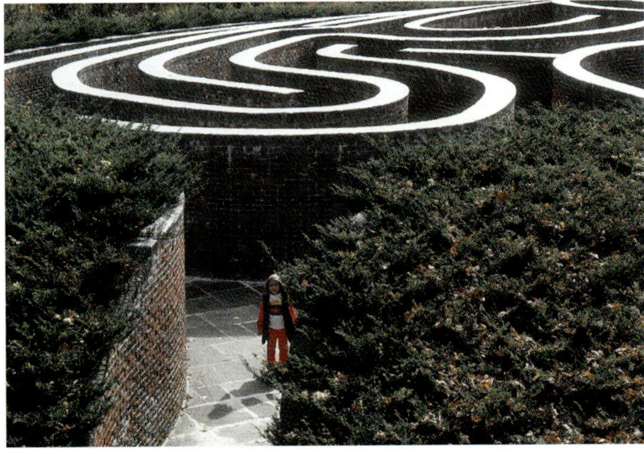

Plate 24. **ARKVILLE MAZE** (Cat. No. 673): Sarah exits maze.

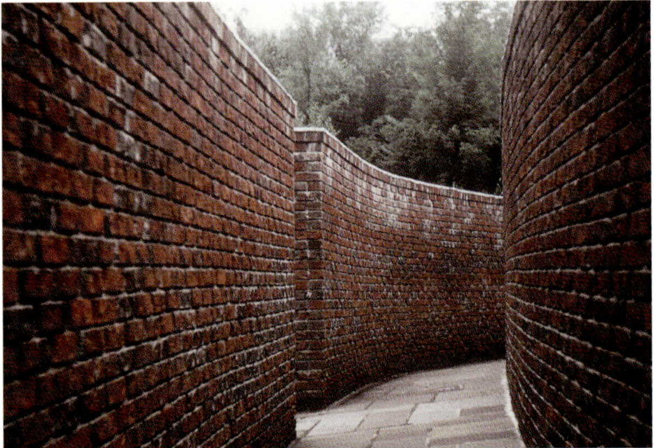

Plate 25. **ARKVILLE MAZE** (Cat. No. 673): corridor view.

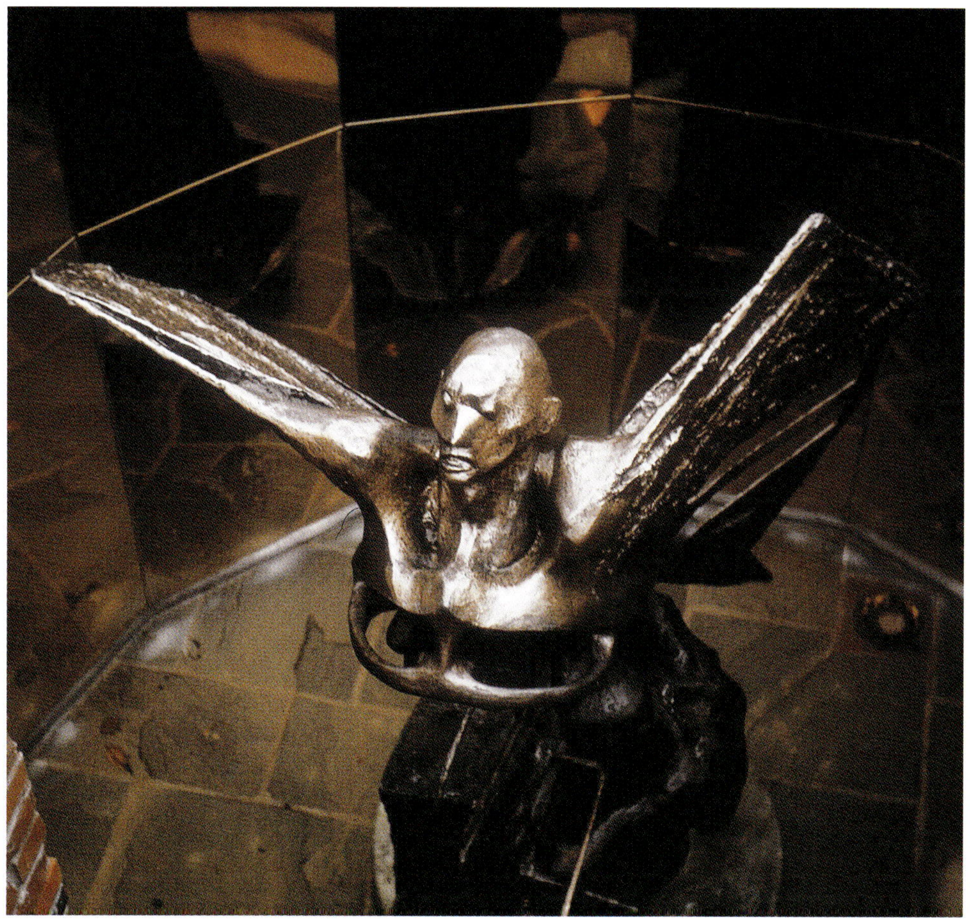

Plate 26. **DAEDALUS/ICARUS MATRIX** (Cat. No. 640; 1968).

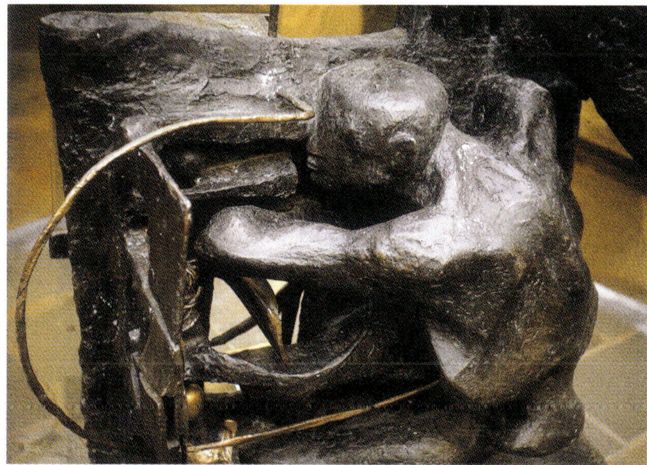

Plate 27. **DAEDALUS/ICARUS MATRIX** (Cat. No. 640): Daedalus from the side.

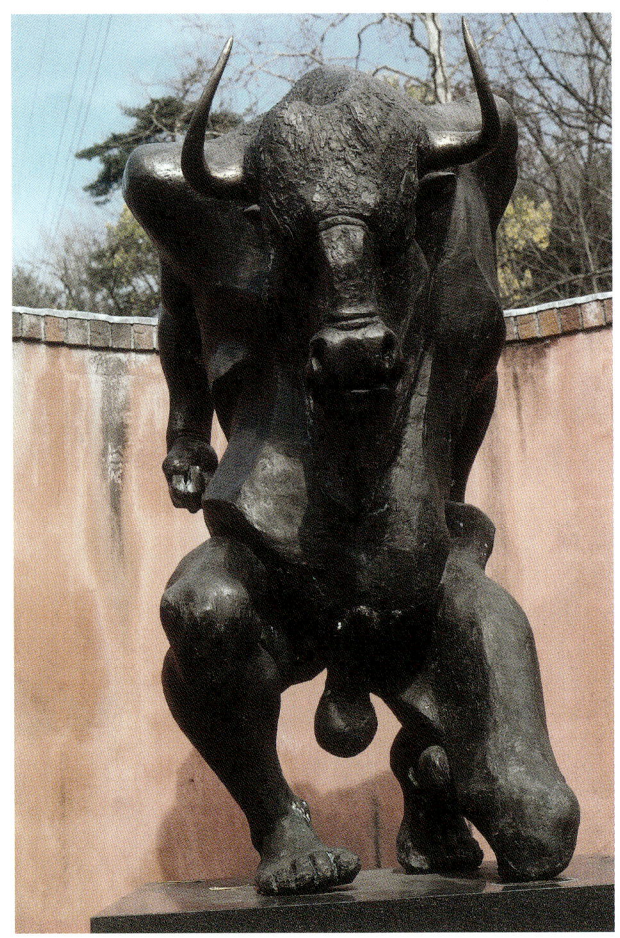

Plate 28. **ARKVILLE MINOTAUR** (Cat. No. 663; 1968–69).

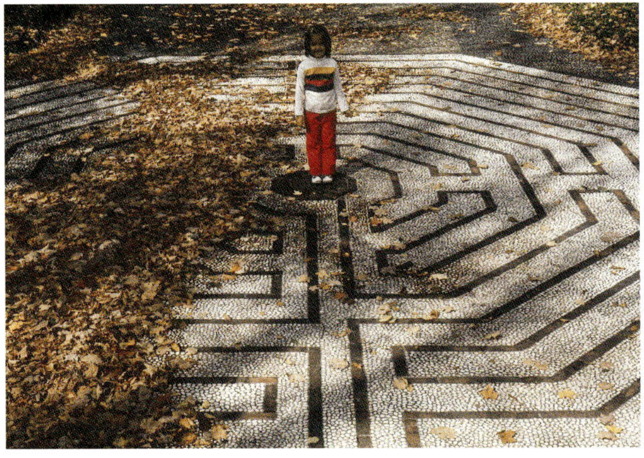

Plate 29. **JERUSALEM MAZE AT ARKVILLE** (Cat. No. 718; 1970).

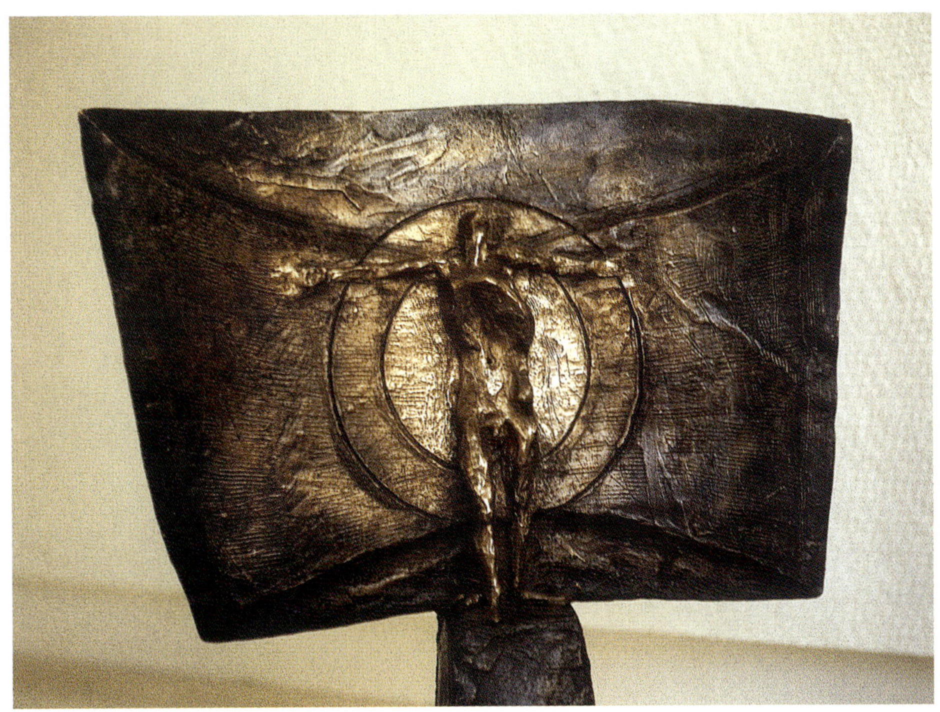

Plate 30. **END MAZE I** (Cat. No. 688; 1970).

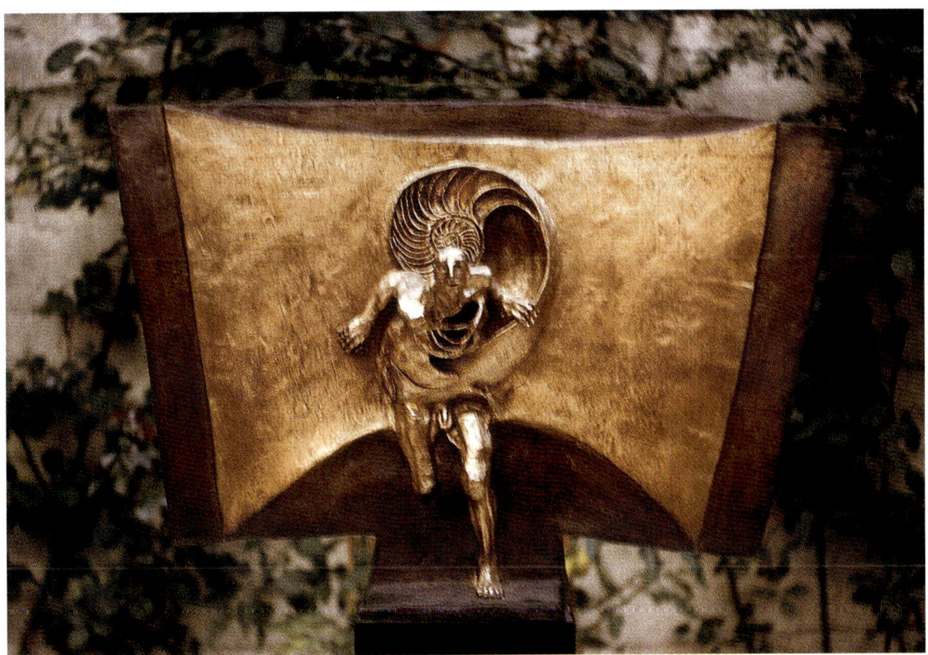

Plate 31. **END MAZE III** (Cat. No. 690; 1970).

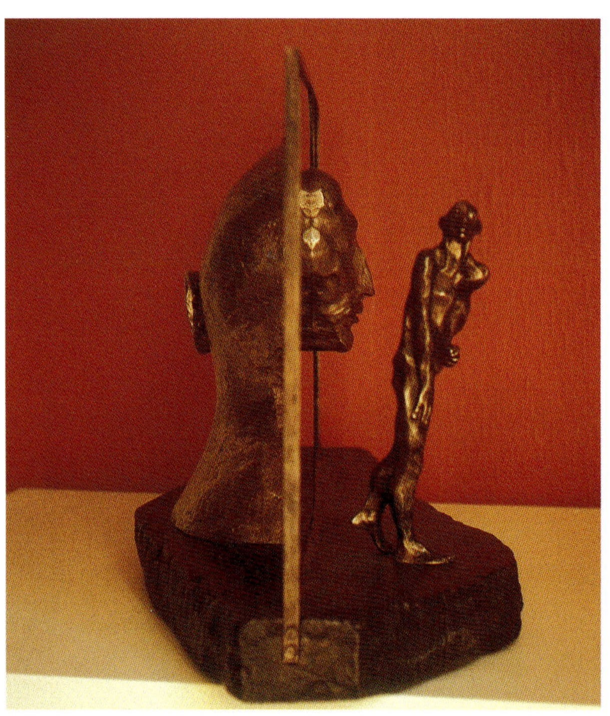

Plate 32. **REFLEX I** (Cat. No. 658; 1969): viewed along perspex.

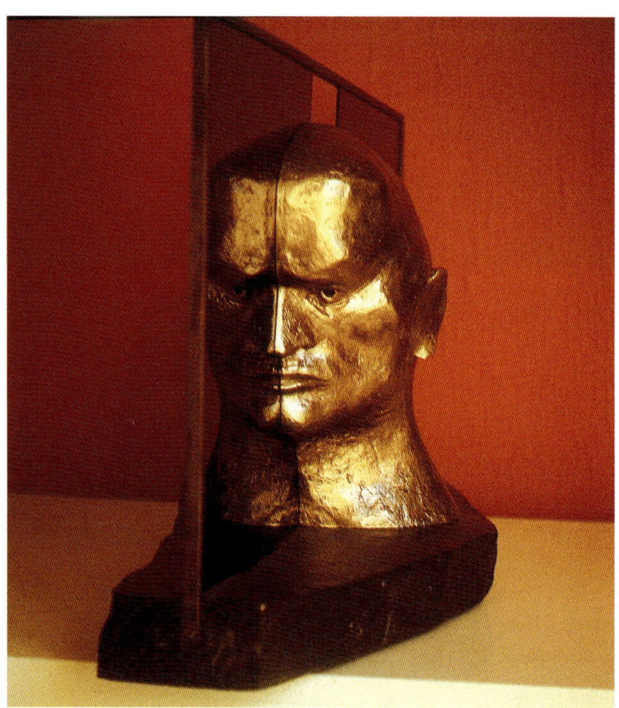

Plate 33. **REFLEX I** (Cat. No. 658): head reflected.

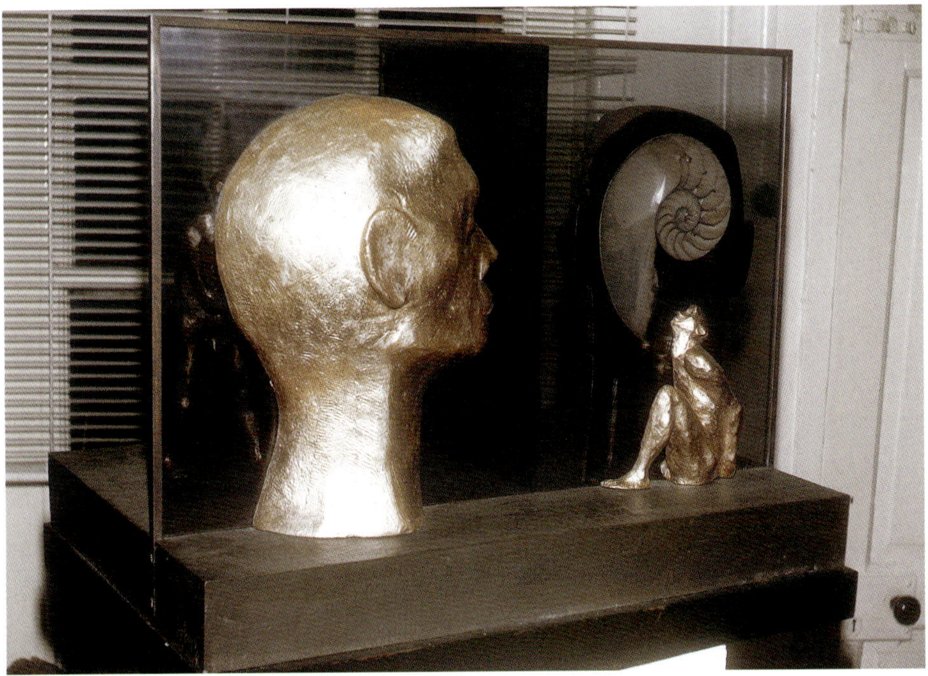

Plate 34. **DISCOVERY OF NAUTILUS** (Cat. No. 667; 1969): half head from rear, seated figure looking up into nautilus.

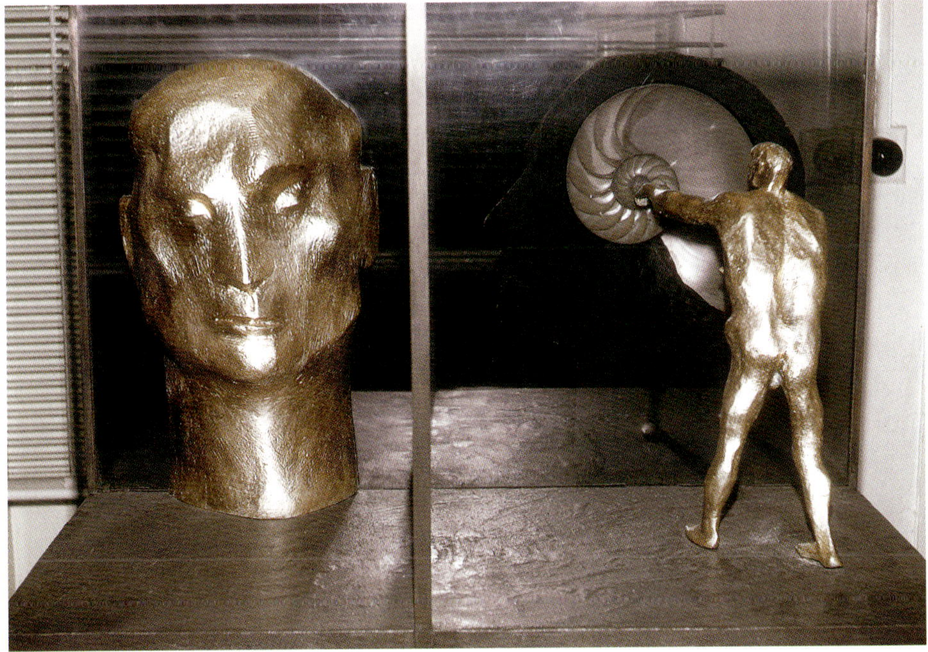

Plate 35. **DISCOVERY OF NAUTILUS** (Cat. No. 667): penetrating the nautilus.

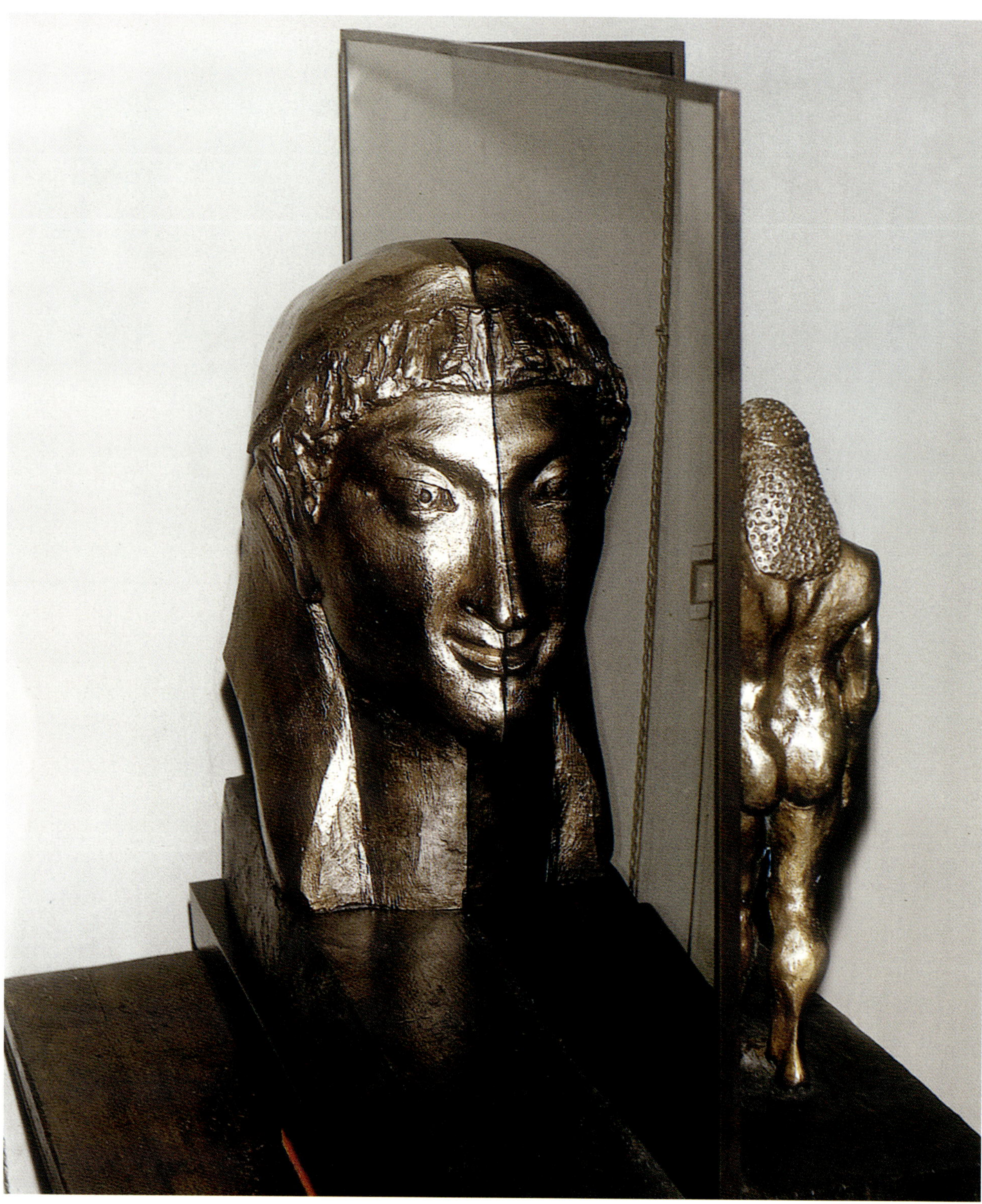

Plate 36. **KOUROS** (Cat. No. 659; 1969): head reflected.

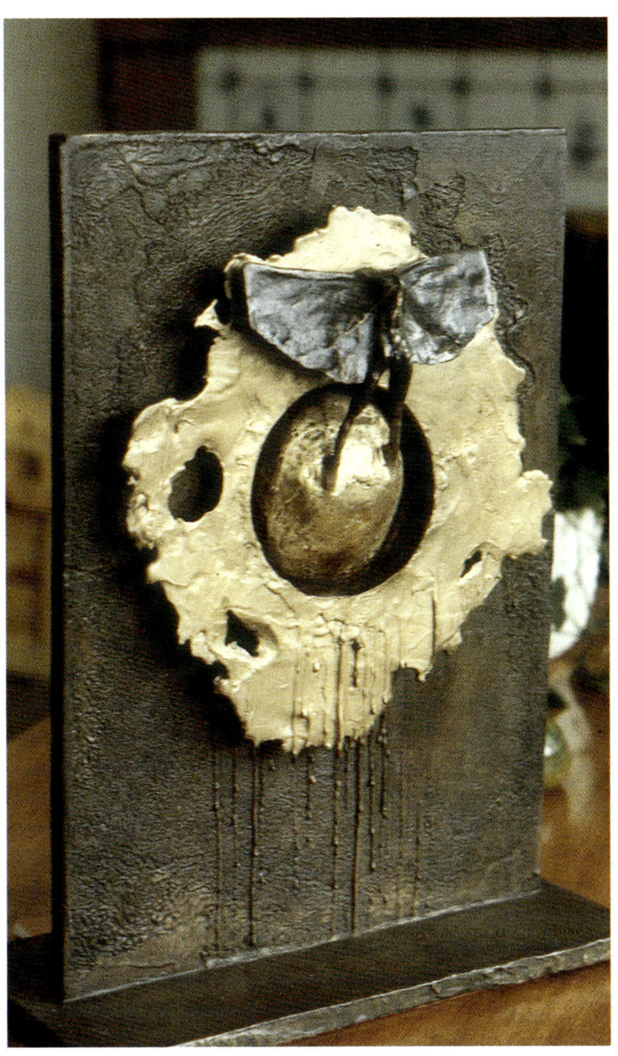

Plate 37. **SUN MAZE** (Cat. No. 721; 1970): Icarus rising.

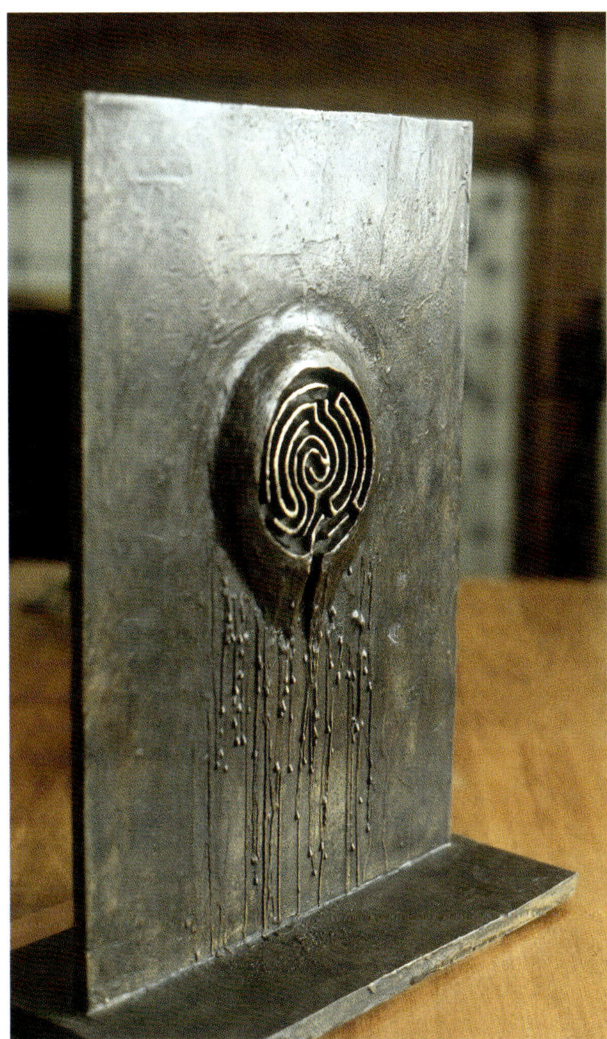

Plate 38. **SUN MAZE** (Cat. No. 721; reverse): maze.

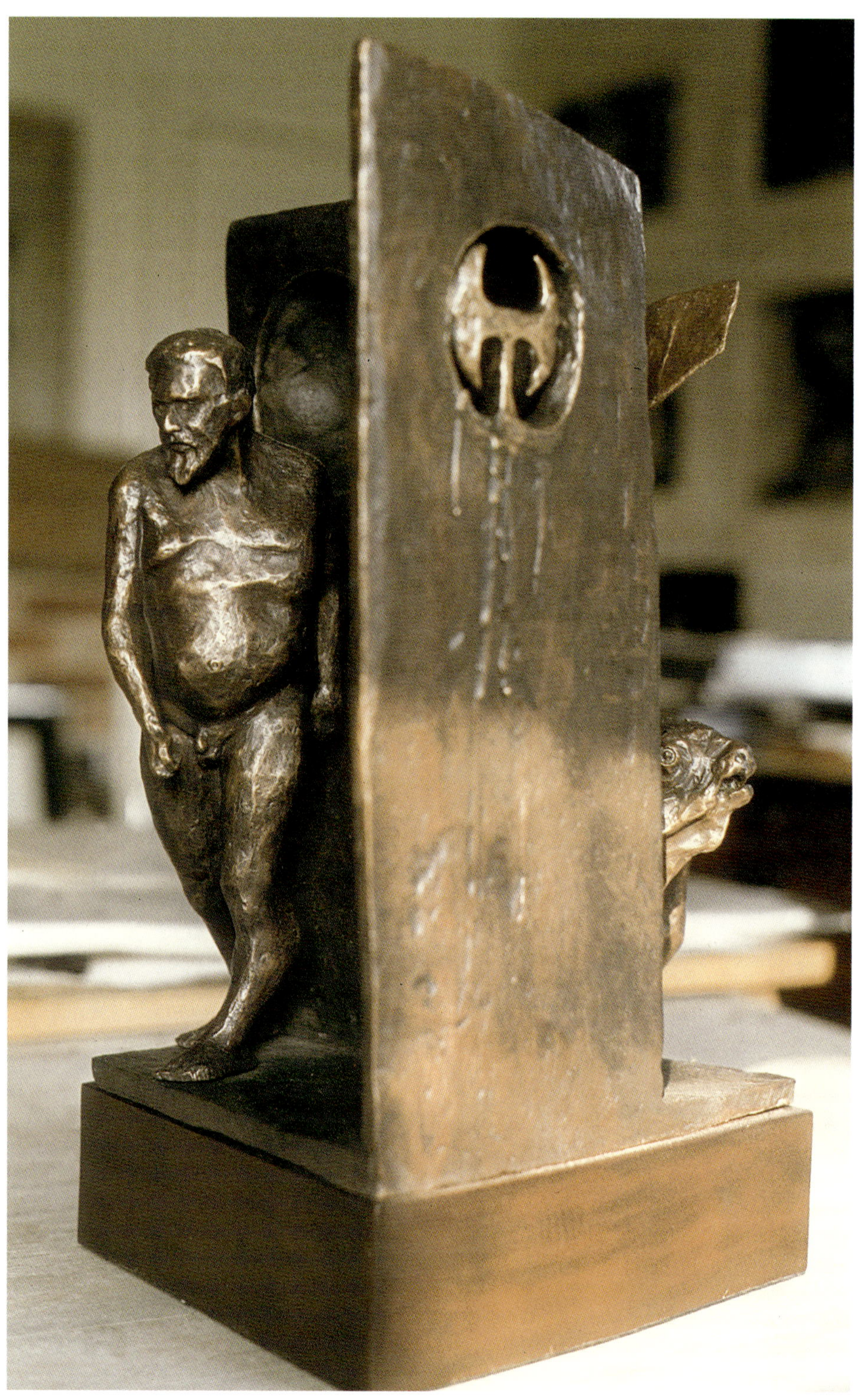

Plate 39. **POINT OF DEPARTURE** (Cat. No. 704; 1970): Daedalus and double axe.

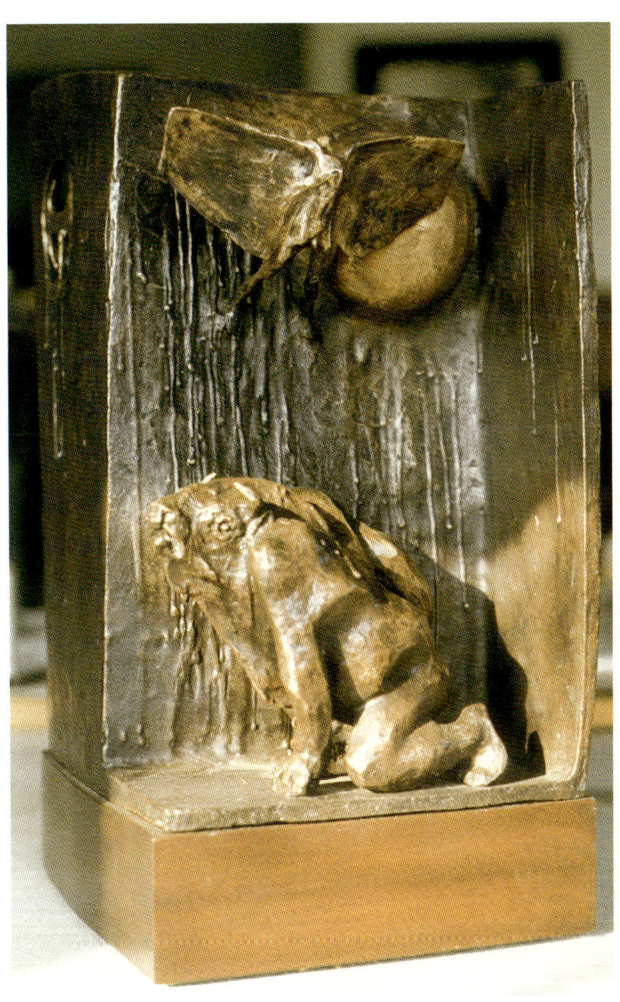

Plate 40. **POINT OF DEPARTURE** (Cat. No. 704): Minotaur and Icarus, rising.

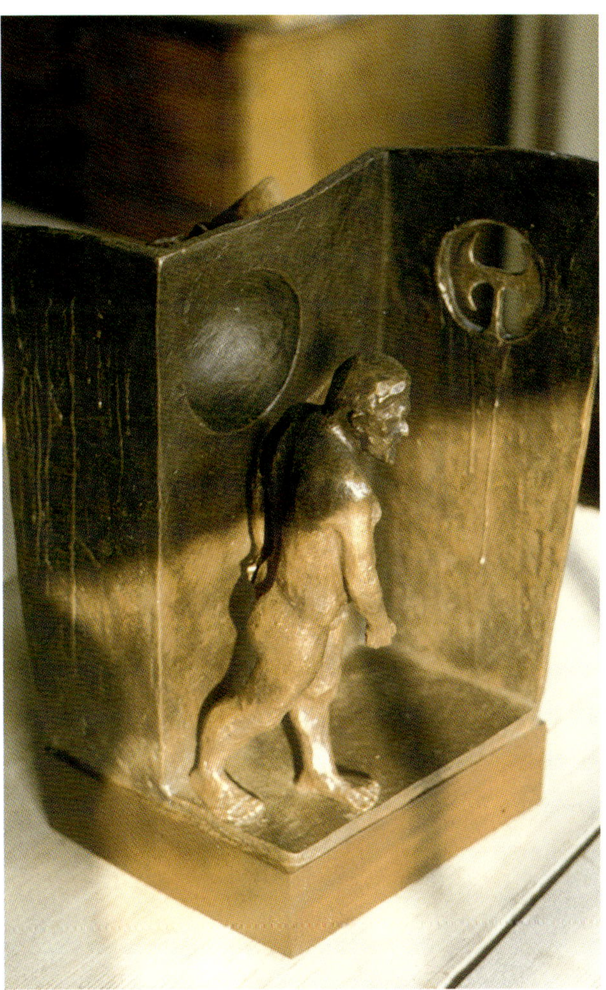

Plate 41. **POINT OF DEPARTURE** (Cat. No. 704): Daedalus, alone.

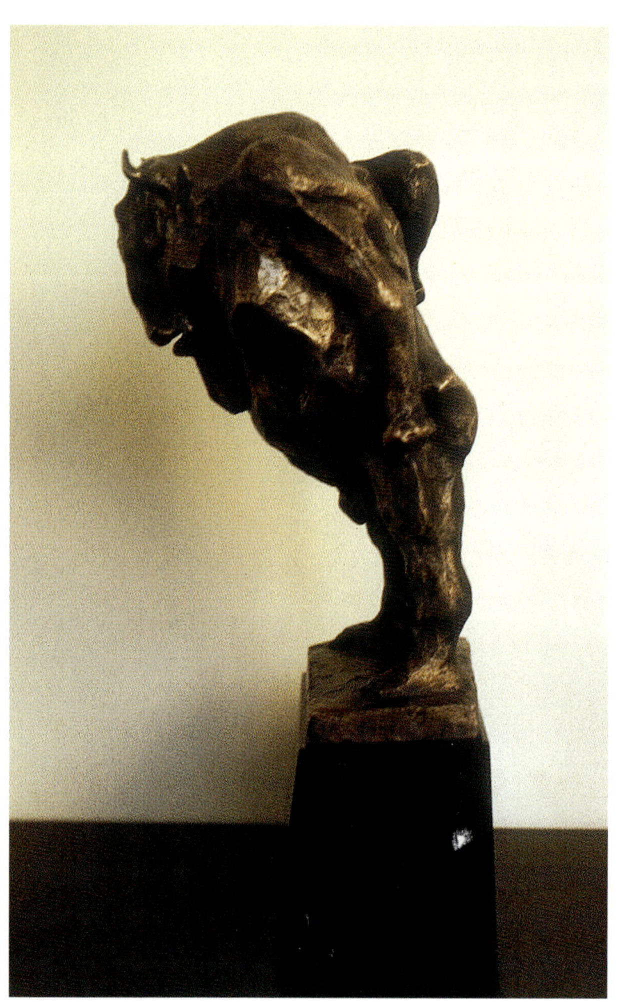

Plate 42. **MINOTAUR RISEN** (Cat. No. 723; 1971).

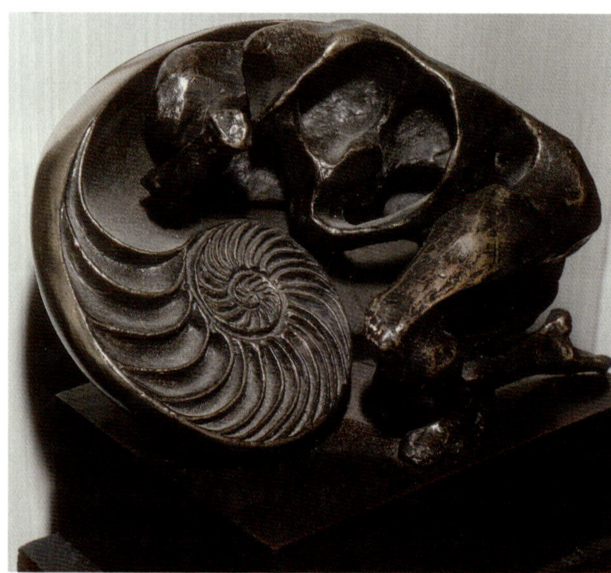

Plate 43. **CARAPACE** (Cat. No. 762; 1972).

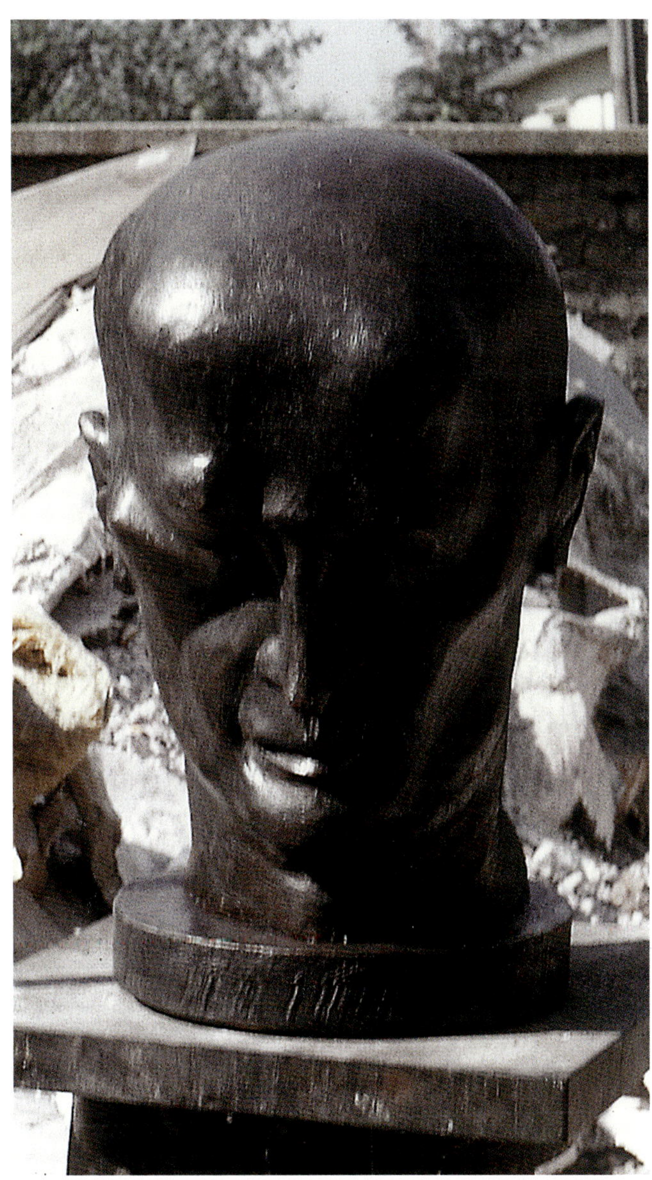

Plate 44. **CONTAINED HEADS**
(Cat. No. 707; 1970): in foundry yard.

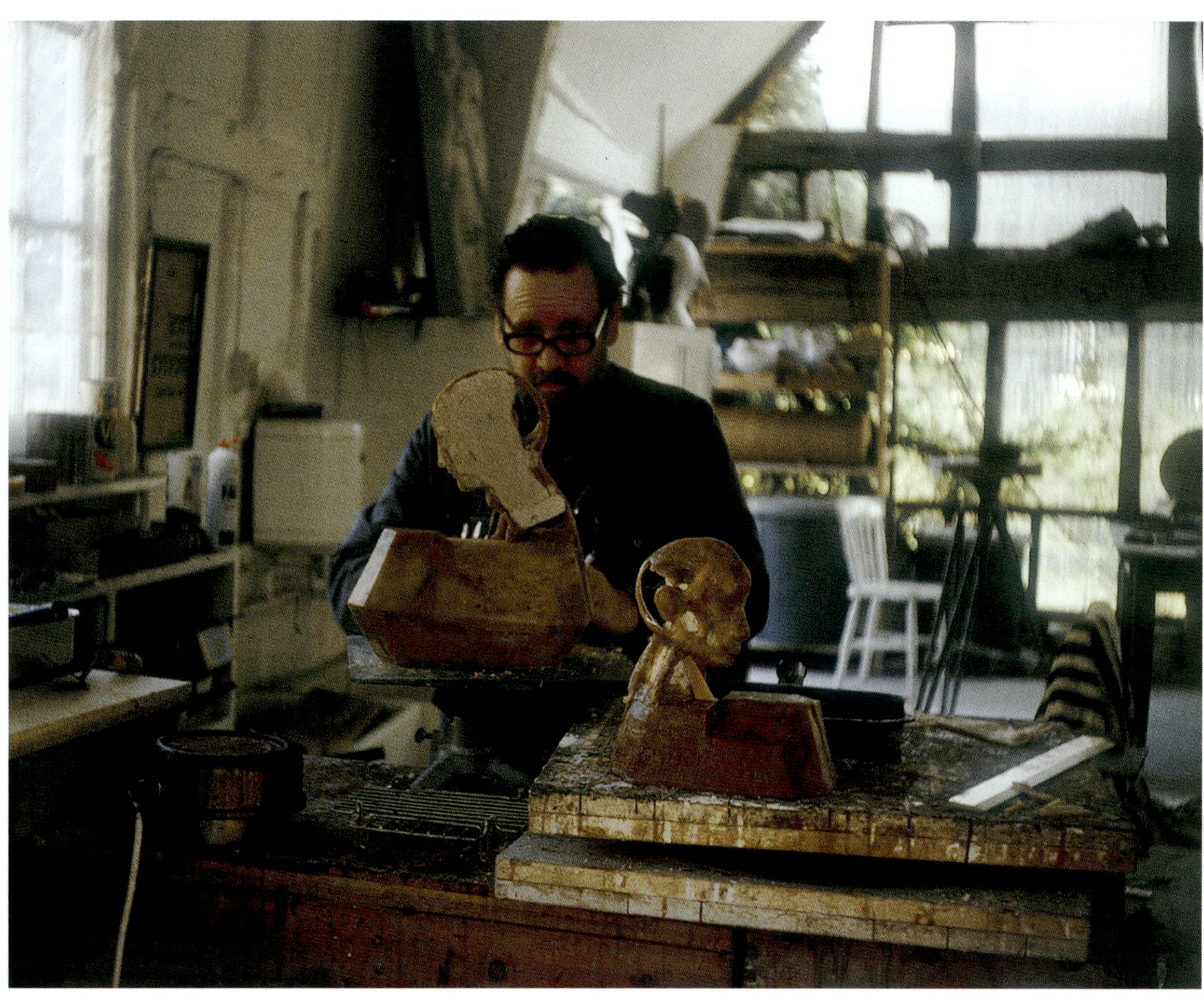

Plate 45. Ayrton at work in his studio on **REFLECTIVE HEAD II** (Cat. No. 743, 1971), the final maquette for the Kresge commission.

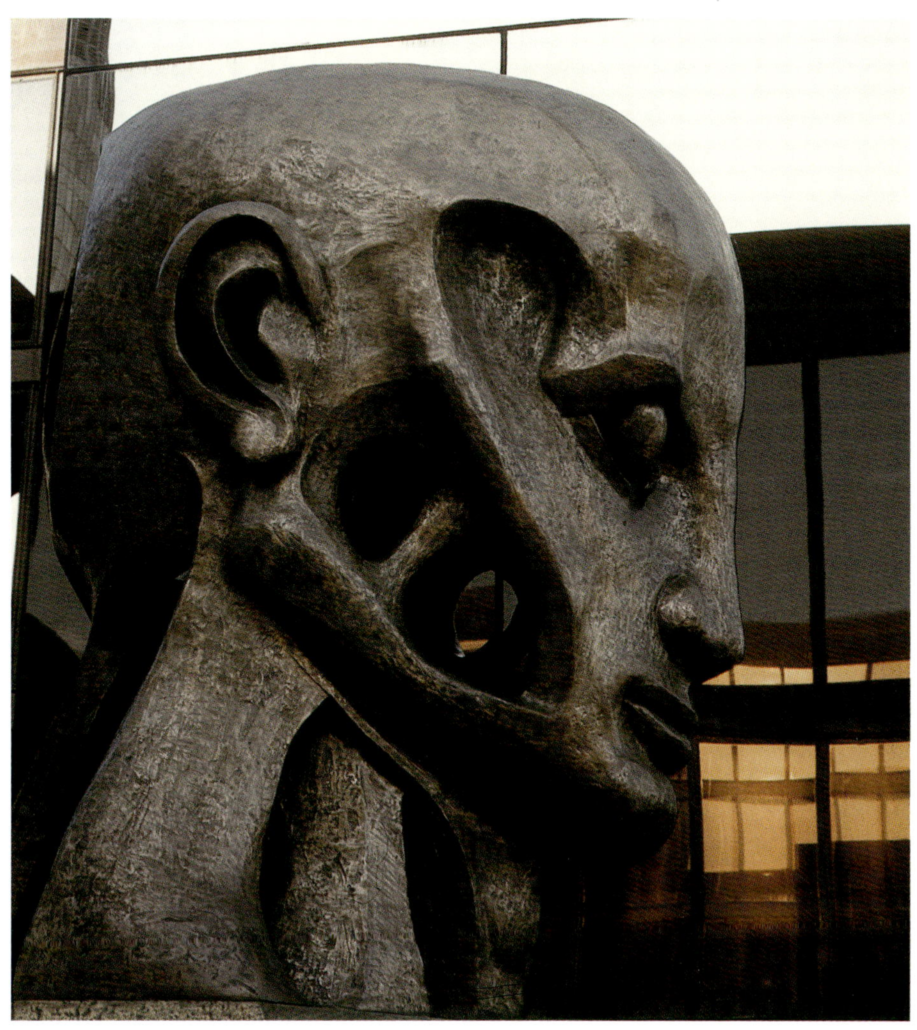

Plate 46. **CORPORATE HEAD** or **REFLECTIVE HEAD** (Cat. No. 772; 1972): side view.

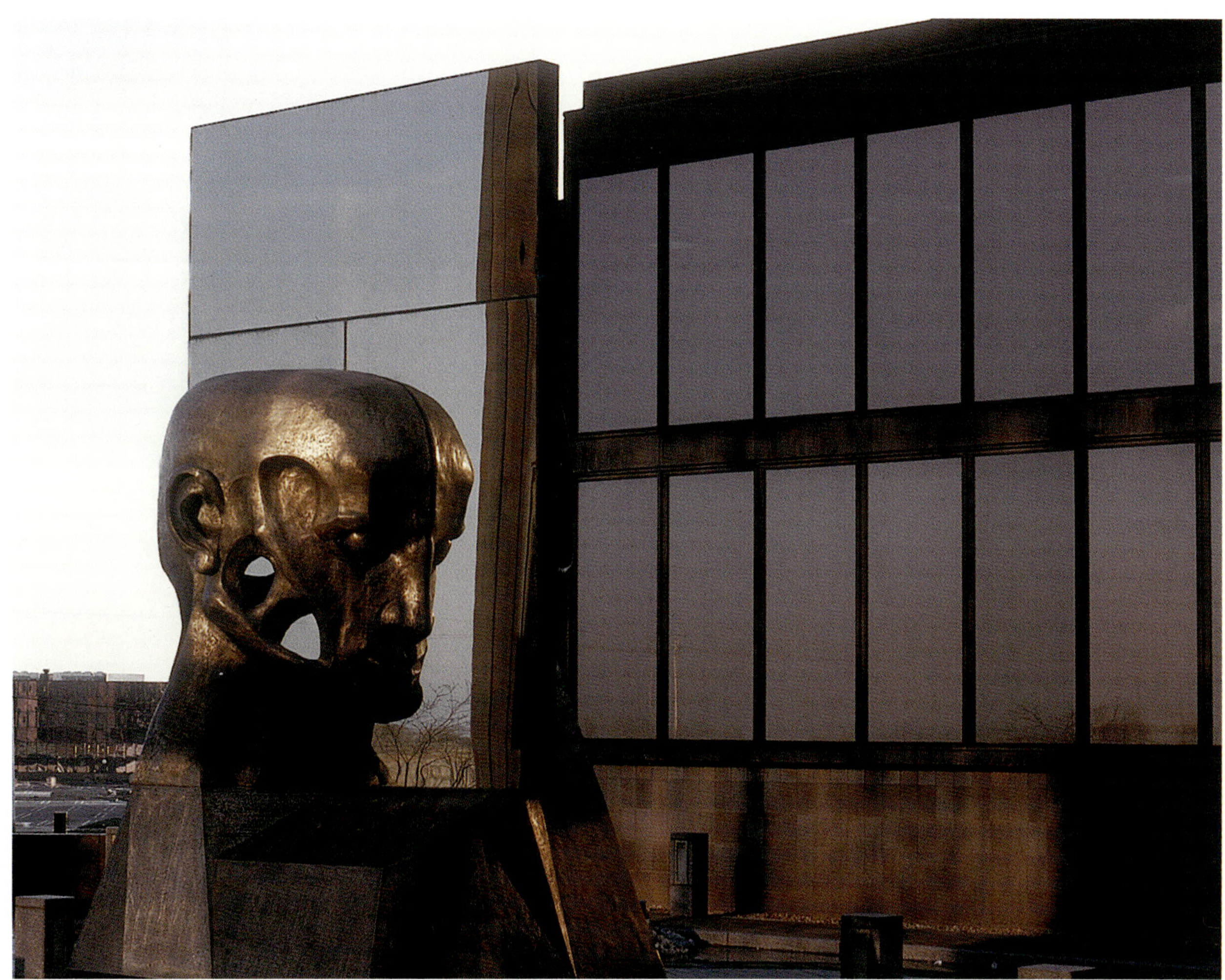

Plate 47. **CORPORATE HEAD** or **REFLECTIVE HEAD** (Cat. No. 772): head reflected.

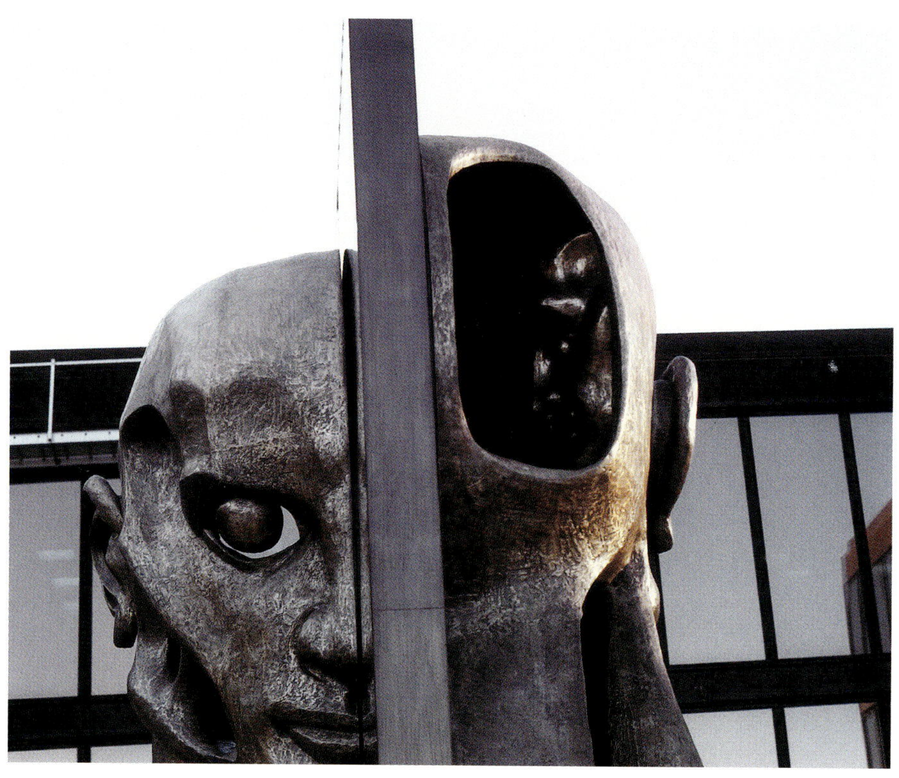

Plate 48. **CORPORATE HEAD** or **REFLECTIVE HEAD** (Cat. No. 772): split heads.

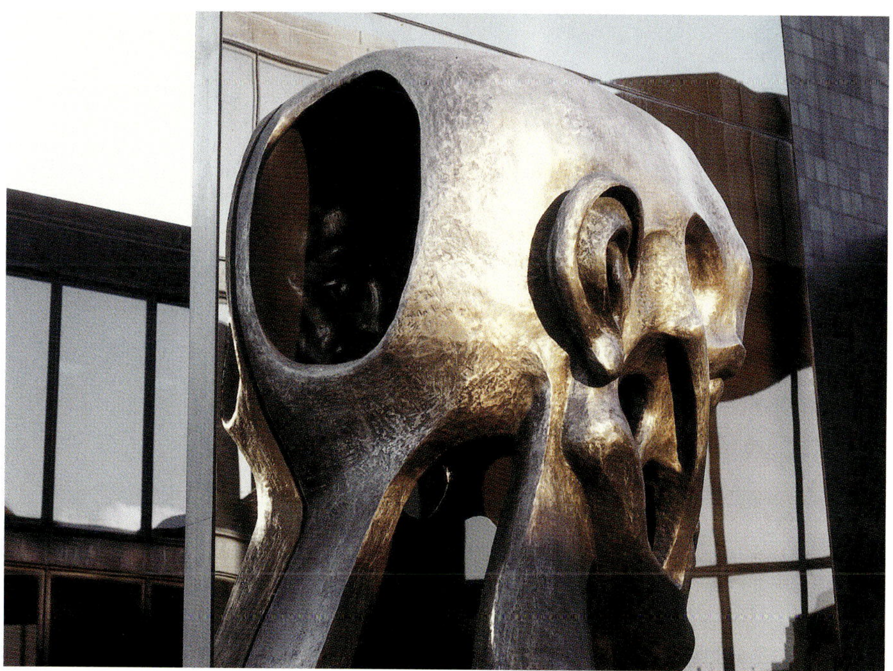

Plate 49. **CORPORATE HEAD** or **REFLECTIVE HEAD** (Cat. No. 772): interior head reflected.

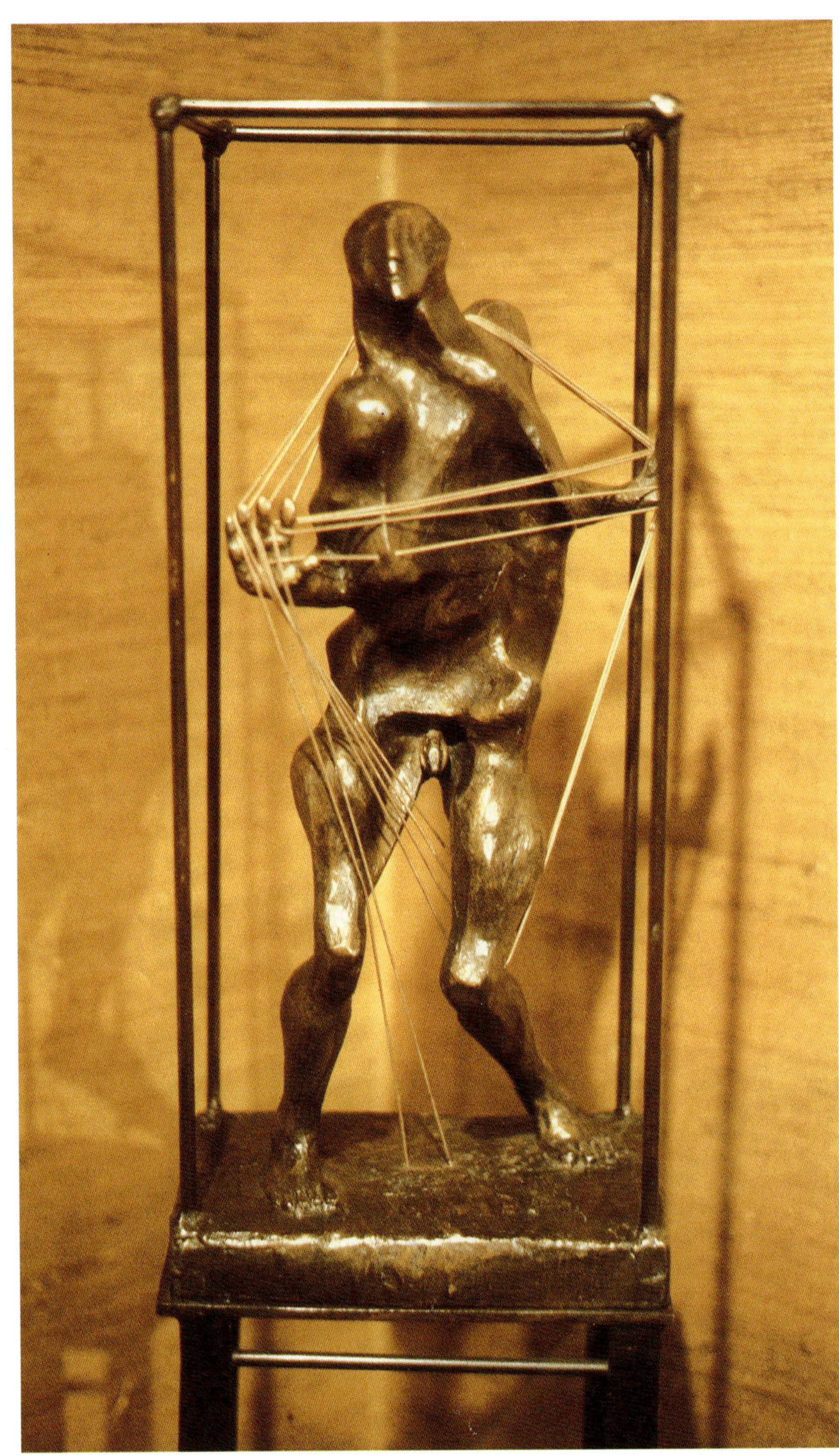

Plate 50. **WEB** (Cat. No. 783; 1972).

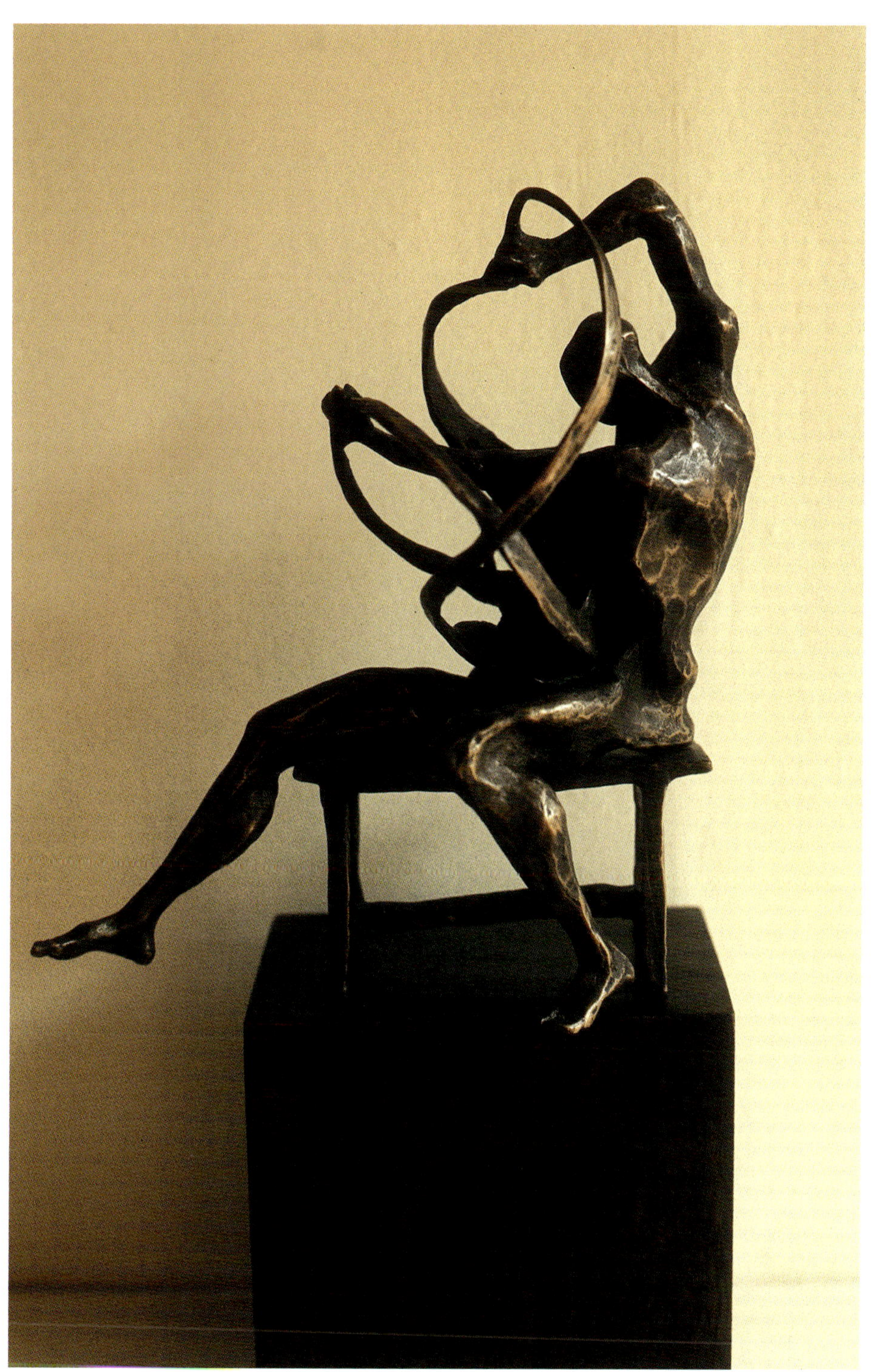

Plate 51. **LAOCOÖN MAZE FIGURE II** (Cat. No. 761; 1972).

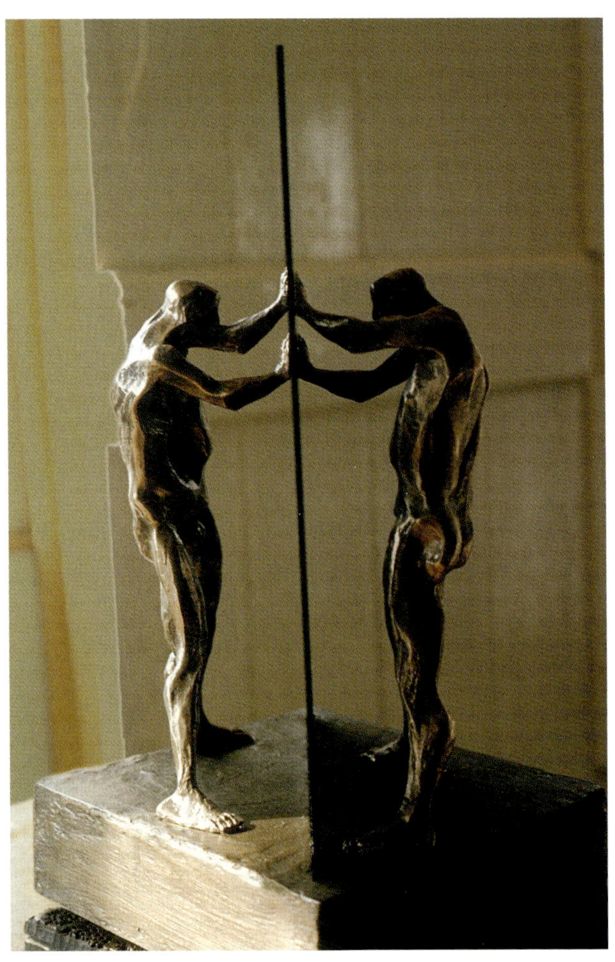

Plate 52. **MIRROR TWINS** (Cat. No. 790; 1973).

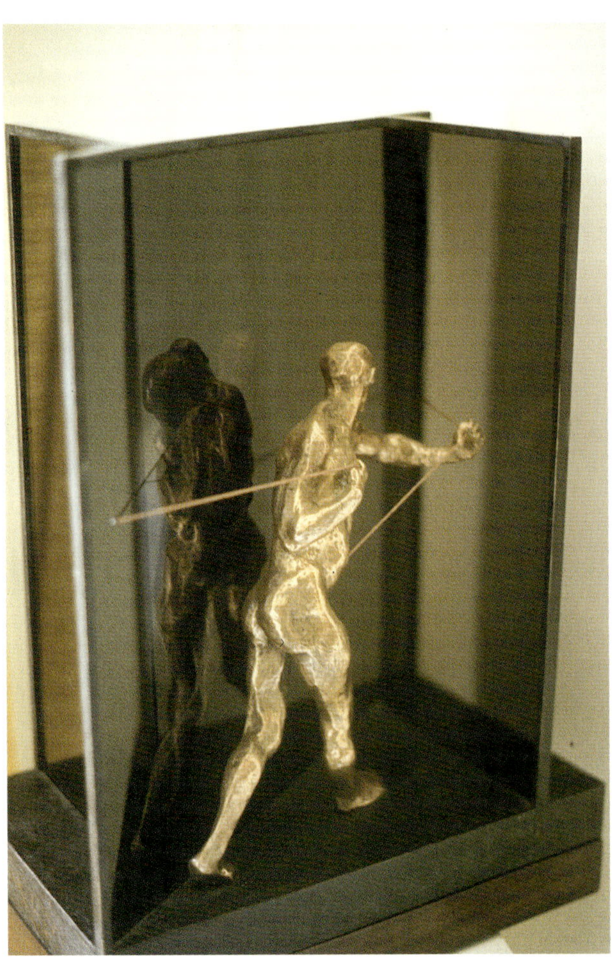

Plate 53. **CORD** (Cat. No. 792; 28 June 1973).

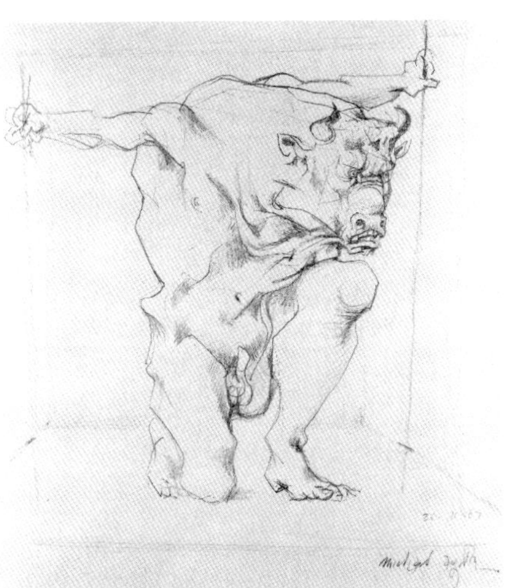

Figure 149. **STUDY FOR ARKVILLE MINOTAUR** (Cat. No. 629; 25 November 1967).

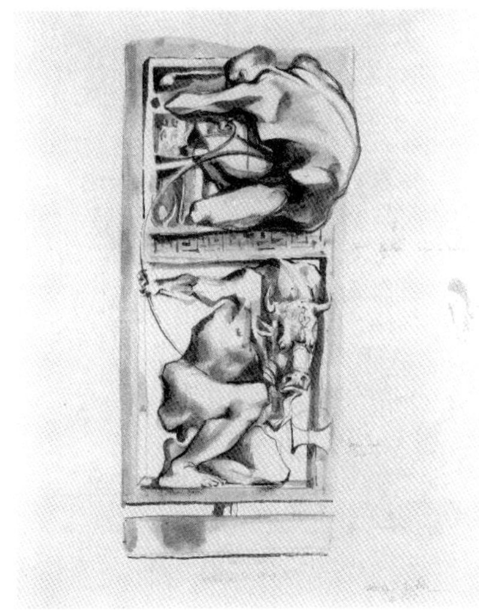

Figure 150. **STUDY FOR ARKVILLE MAZE MAKER/ MINOTAUR MATRIX** (Cat. No. 631; 2 January 1968).

The proposed maze was for Erpf's estate of some five hundred acres in the Catskill Mountains in New York, approximately a three-hour's drive from New York City. The artist saw the setting as "a cup between two mountains" that was "curiously an amazingly Greek landscape, like northern Greece, like the Epirus."[10] The estate already had "a distinguished collection of sculptures scattered about the lawns," but Erpf had his reasons for wanting to add a maze:

> Well, I think it was partly a matter of coincidence, because I happened to have these five huge granite urns on my place. So the thought occurred that there ought to be some sort of a plaza at one end and perhaps another one at the other end, so that this little quasi-formal area could be a spot for meditation and for poetic insights. And I happened to be reading a report and at the end of the report there was a graphic presentation of some sort of a maze so I tore this out and said, "Here, this is what I want, a maze. Put a maze here. It's mysterious, it's mathematical, it has a certain amount of magic to it."[11]

But the motives of Ayrton's client actually go deeper than the above statement might imply, as he himself revealed in these words recorded after the event:

> The whole idea is [that] after two centuries of an age of enlightenment, of the rise of science, the arrogance of reason, perhaps it might be an idea . . . to show some sense to symbolism, to ritual, to reverence and pave the way for a new morality where the presumption of reason and the arrogance of enlightenment and of science might be more appropriately, religiously or artistically blended with the mystery and the myth of man from the very beginning 'till eternity.[12]

The challenge to design a maze so imprecisely described in the original instructions, with only a suggestion that its size range from two to three hundred feet across and that there be sculpture in the center, did not daunt Ayrton, who summarized his activities and his patron's response in these words:

> So I went away and I worked it out and I thought what I would put in the middle and how it would be planned out and I wrote to him and nothing happened. Then I was in California, it was about four months later and I got a telephone call and it went like this. "Hullo, this is Armand Erpf." "Hullo, Mr. Erpf." "Go ahead." He rang off. And that was it, I mean there was no more talk, there was nothing. That was it, just go ahead. So I went ahead.[13]

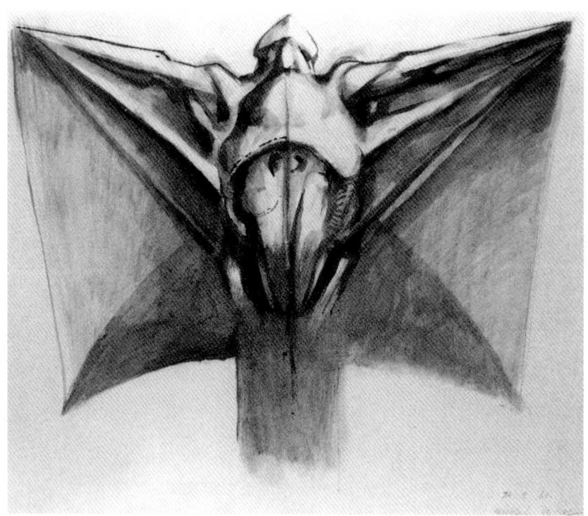

Figure 151. **STUDY FOR ARKVILLE MATRIX: ICARUS RISING I** (Cat. No. 634; 24 February 1968).

The artist's account compresses the story with suitably dramatic effect, but the evolution of the *Arkville Maze* (Cat. No. 673, 1968–1970) and its sculptural inhabitants stretched over a much longer span. Rooted in the past of his own sculpture and his narrative of Daedalus's life, Ayrton's commissioned maze underwent even further transformation after his original plans were accepted. Just as Rudolf Arnheim and others used preliminary sketches by Picasso of *Guernica* to gain insight into his creative process (see chapter 3), so we can gain a deeper understanding of the creative process by tracing Ayrton's progress while he was completing this monumental commission. Moreover, because the commission resulted from the publication of *The Maze Maker,* we will see that myth continues to play a major role in the creative process.

Perhaps the most striking revision in his conception of the maze was the development of the idea that the maze should have not one but two central chambers. In his early comments on the maze and in early sketches, he clearly conceived of it with only a single chamber at the center. Given that the labyrinth described in *The Maze Maker* has two central chambers—one the chamber of the sun, the other of the moon—it is somewhat surprising that he began this project with the conception of a single chamber. Nonetheless, it is clear that he did so. In December 1967, for example, Ayrton wrote to a friend: "I have landed a sculpture commission to make a great stone maze in the Catskills with Daedalus and the Minotaur in bronze at the centre."[14] In the same letter, written from California during his lectureship, he also remarked that he himself had done no sculpture except in his head during this time, but would resume sculpting upon his return home in February 1968.

The catalogue of drawings reveals that studies for bronze minotaurs were gradually taking shape in his mind, that he was returning to a theme he had explored in some depth between 1962 and 1965 (see chapter 5). The first study for the Arkville sculptures, *Study for Arkville Minotaur* (Cat. No. 629; 25 November 1967; Figure 149), continued the process of discovery: here the rising Minotaur is framed by a lightly sketched box. By the next sketch, Study for *Arkville Maze Maker/Minotaur Matrix* (Cat. No. 631; 2 January 1968; Figure 150), the sense of confinement of the Minotaur becomes even more explicit. Ayrton gave a new dimension to the Minotaur's enclosure by linking him umbilically to the maze-making Daedalus, who is in the upper story of the conceptual sculpture. This umbilical attachment graphically states both his plight and his condition. Not only is he a monstrosity trapped in the maze, he also is inextricably linked to Daedalus. In the Greek myth, of course, Daedalus created the contrivance that enabled Pasiphaë to be impregnated by the bull and he devised the labyrinth in which the bull-man was to be hidden from the public. Perhaps Ayrton's choice of the umbilicus to tie the Minotaur to Daedalus was intended to symbolize Daedalus's responsibility for both the birth and the imprisonment of the Minotaur, but it also hints at the link between intellect and passion, between rationality and bestiality contained in each of us. One of Ayrton's later sculptures, *Personal Janus* (Cat. No. 706; see chapter 7), reinforces this theme very dramatically. The design of the maze itself undoubtedly was also influenced by the concept of birth behind this development in his conceptualization of the sculpture that would inhabit the center of The *Arkville Maze* (see below).

This drawing illustrates an early stage in the genesis of the maze and its sculpture, for it is clearly intended as a single piece to be set in a single chamber. But scarcely a month later, soon after Ayrton's return home, the Minotaur appears in a sketch (Cat. No. 633) not only risen but also detached from Daedalus, and in a subsequent drawing Icarus appears, rising, with double-axe wings (Cat. No. 634; see Figure 151; cf. Cat. Nos. 635–637). The artist himself remarked that these "drawings for the Arkville sculptures . . . show how the concept of the *Matrix* changed from one into two separate sculptures. . . . [I]n a sense, they were crucial to the evolution of these sculptures and to the Maze itself."[15] Although one cannot precisely date the crystallization of the artist's ideas about the Maze sculptures, one can place it within the span of a month or so, simply from the dates of these drawings. The decision to divide the central chamber must have been reached by the end of February, for an interview with Ayrton published in the *New Yorker* in early March quotes him as saying: "My maze will have stone walls six and a half feet high, so nobody can see from one passageway to the next, and the correct passage will lead into two secret inner chambers, one of which will contain a sculptured figure of the Minotaur, the other a figure of Daedalus. The maze will probably be oval, and will be about a hundred feet across."[16] This interview presumably took place immediately after Ayrton's meeting with his patron, at which time he must have presented Mr. Erpf with explanatory notes on his plans for the *Arkville Maze*, in which he argued: "[T]he Minotaur must needs occupy a separate chamber from that of Daedalus and Icarus, who, in turn, must be combined into a single image. The aspiration of the Minotaur to achieve humanity is held by the binding force of the animal in him. To convey this he must be seen in solitude, for his prison is also his sanctuary."[17]

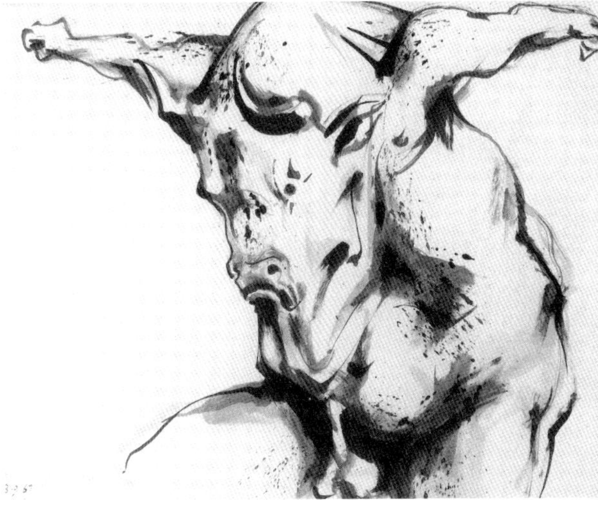

Figure 152. **MINOTAUR RISING I**
(Cat. No. 626; 8 September 1967). J. S. Lewinski, London.

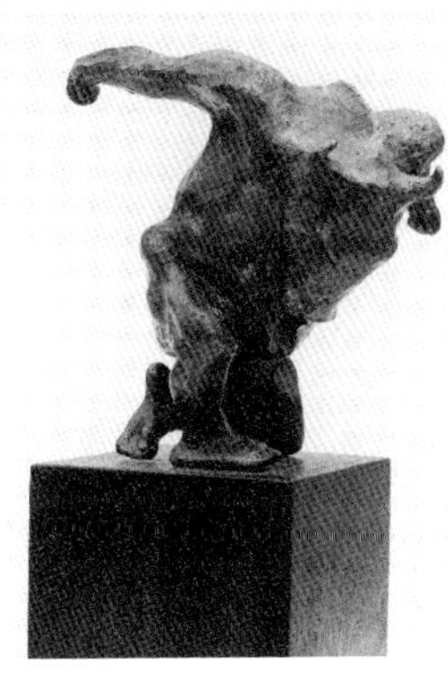

Figure 153.
MINOTAUR RISING I
(Cat. No. 613; 1967).
J. S. Lewinski, London.

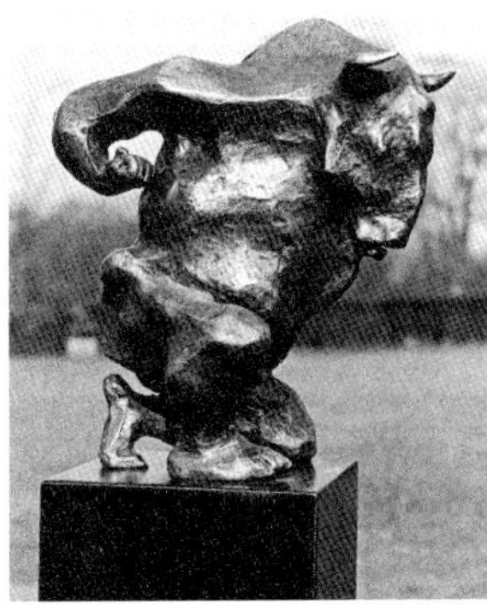

Figure 154.
MINOTAUR RISING III
(Cat. No. 644; 1968): side view.

Once Daedalus and the Minotaur were separated and placed in two distinct chambers, further modifications in conception could—and did—take place. The Minotaur, freed, could express a sense of autonomy because his cage had been enlarged, although he remained a prisoner within the larger maze. The three bronze maquettes, *Minotaur Rising I, II* and *III* (Cat. Nos. 613, 643 and 644), illustrate this point (see Figures 153 and 154). The first one resembles the first drawing (Cat. No. 629; see Figure 149), in which his extended arms enable his hands to grasp the bars of his cage, but the absence of the confining bars causes the outstretched arms of the sculpture to lend a sense of

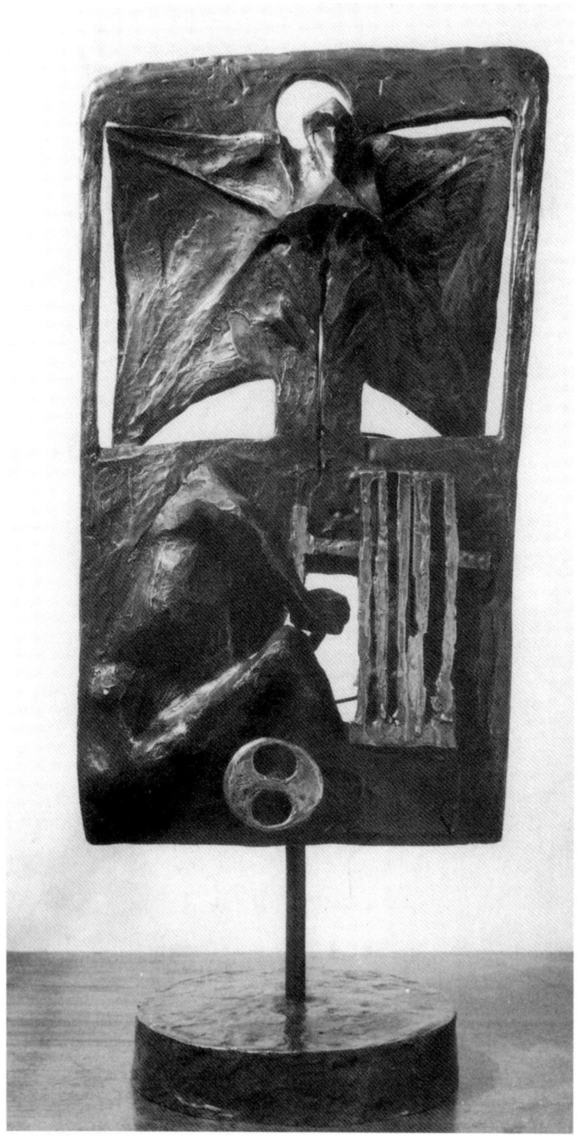

Figure 155. **DAEDALUS/ICARUS MATRIX I** (Cat. No. 638; 1968): front view. J. S. Lewinski, London.

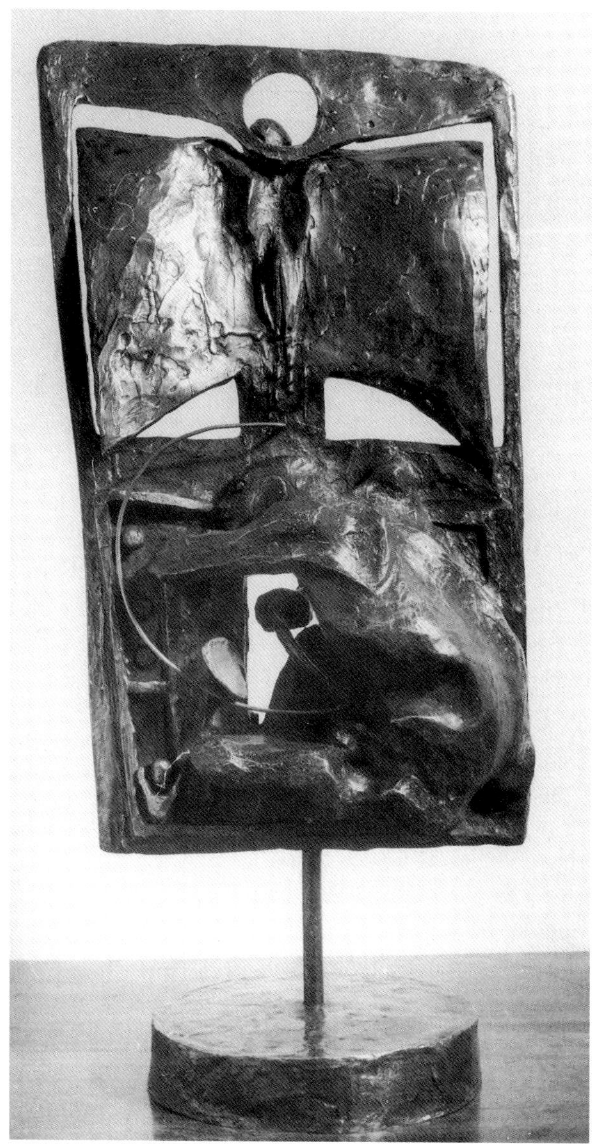

Figure 156. **DAEDALUS/ICARUS MATRIX I** (Cat. No. 638): back view. J. S. Lewinski, London.

imbalance—and suggest an attempt to stabilize himself —as he struggles to his feet, seeking to express his humanity (see also chapter 4). In the second and third ones the arms are brought closer to his side, thus investing him with both a coiled inner tension more expressive of his hybrid condition and a more threatening appearance appropriate to his bestial characteristics. The third maquette (Cat. No. 644; Figure 154), a minor modification of the second (Cat. No. 643), which became the model for the final sculpture (Cat. No. 663), conveys this internal tension and external hostility with particular effectiveness.

By the same token, the detachment of Daedalus from the Minotaur enabled Ayrton to extend the image of the maze maker. Whereas the *New Yorker* interview quoted above mentions only Daedalus as the inhabitant of the second chamber, Ayrton's notes for his patron, as well as his drawings (Cat. Nos. 634–637) and maquettes (Cat. Nos. 638 and 639; Figures 155–157) for the second sculpture, clearly reveal that he did not conceive of him as alone. Appropriately, Daedalus is joined by Icarus, already rising, while the archetypal craftsman himself is still preoccupied with making his maze.

Although the symbolism of the *Study for the Arkville Maze Maker/Minotaur Matrix* (Cat. No. 631; Figure 150) was both appropriate and effective (since the mythical Daedalus worked above ground to design the presumably underground prison for the Minotaur), the transfer of Daedalus into the lower frame of this new *Matrix* produces results that are at once more dramatic and symbolically richer. In his notes for his patron Ayrton wrote: "Daedalus and Icarus are bound by a further dimension of aspiration, one aspect of which is shown in the making of the maze, the other in the desire to fly upwards to escape from it. This image too must be seen as separate from the earth-bound Minotaur" (appendix B).

The evolution of the *Daedalus/Icarus Matrix* created new technical challenges, but their resolution also wrought subtle but important changes in the symbolism as well as the form of the sculpture. The first maquette (Cat. No. 638; Figures 155 and 156) appears almost two-dimensional, whereas the second (Cat. No. 639; Figure 157), the one selected for the final bronze, is unquestionably three-dimensional. In the first one, Daedalus is a virtual replica

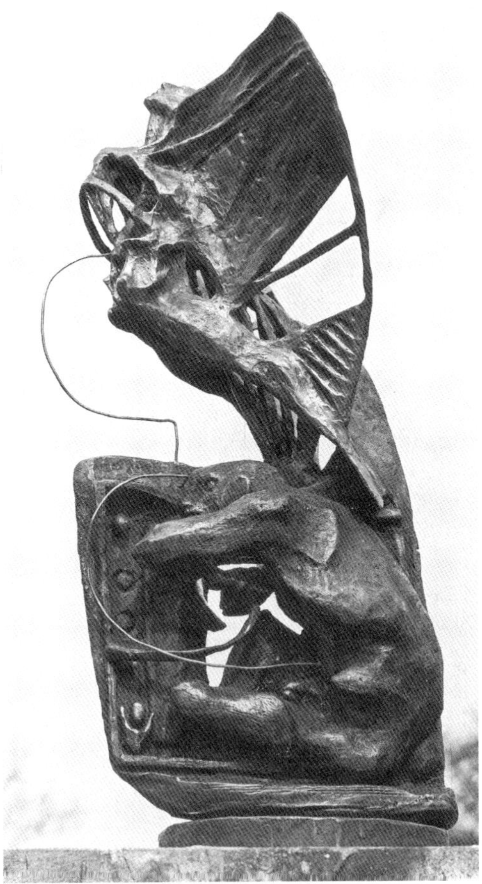

Figure 157. **DAEDALUS/ICARUS MATRIX II** (Cat. No. 639; 1968).

of the earlier bronze *Maze Maker (large version)* (Cat. No. 544; Plate 19; see chapter 5), with the egg-carton section elongated and reduced to two compartments, although the umbilical cord is attached not to the framework of material events that surrounds the maze maker but to the tail (or base) of the Icarus figure in the upper frame. The *labrys* or double-axe imagery of *Icarus Rising* (Cat. No. 206) is carried even further here, leaving no question of the artist's vision of how Icarus would have appeared against the sun (see chapter 4).[18] In the second maquette (Cat. No. 639) Icarus appears bird-like, with his wings extended, and the gap between his lower torso and the maze maker more nearly creates the illusion of flight. But there is a further, more subtle change: the umbilical cord no longer

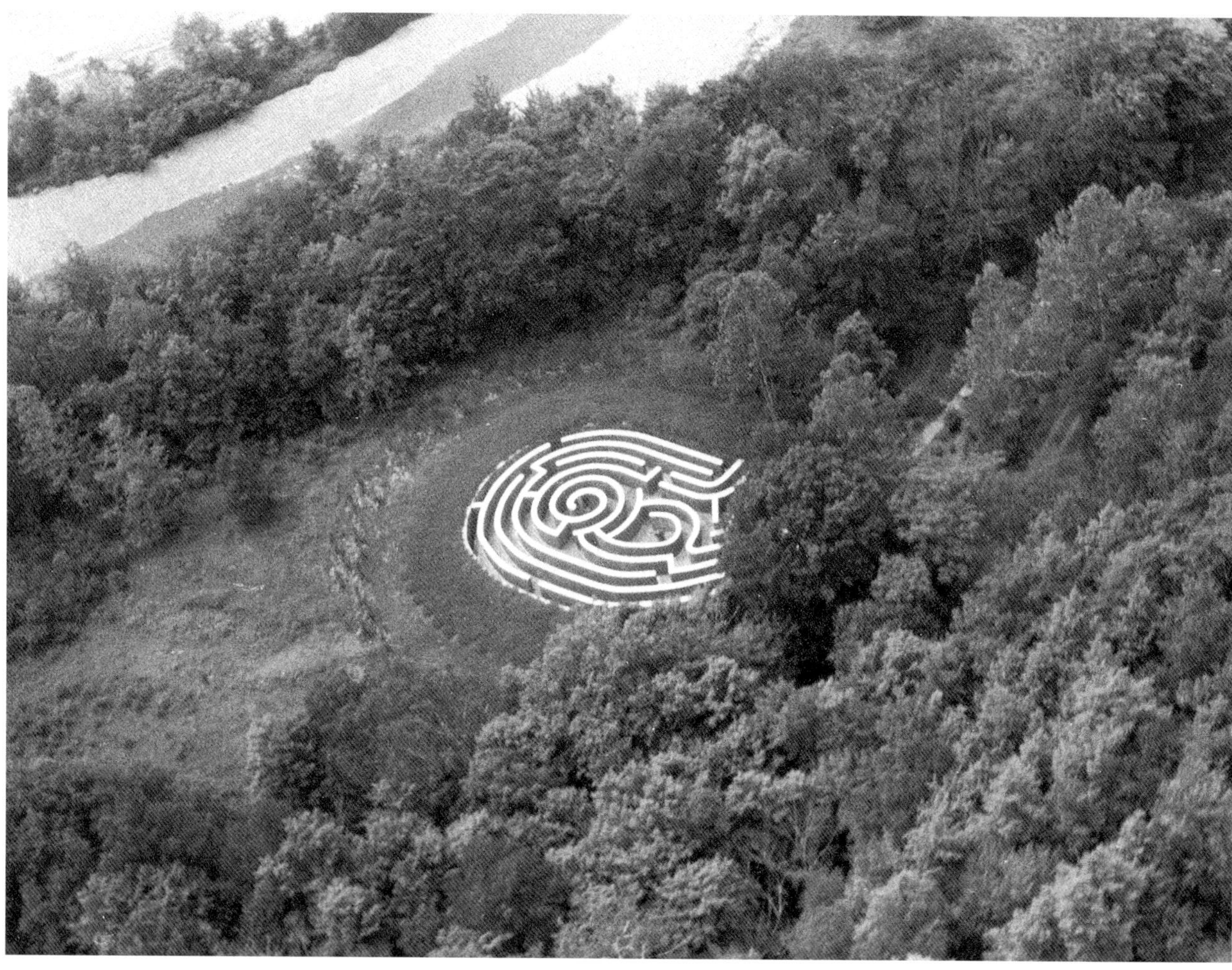

Figure 158. **ARKVILLE MAZE** (Cat. No. 673; 1968–70): aerial view.

links him directly to his father but passes through the maze maker's framework, revealing the paradox of their relationship.

The considerable additional weight of Icarus in the second version required not only a reinforcement of the struts that linked him to the base but also an enlargement of the maze maker portion to sustain him. As a result, *Daedalus/Icarus Matrix* (Cat. No. 640; Figure 160, Plate 27) became at once larger and more complex. The maze maker's enlarged workshop therefore contains more tools than *Maze Maker (large version)* (Cat. No. 544; Plate 19), and the trap he is making for himself has consequently become more complex. The working tools, such as the punch, chisels, T square, and tongs, are all included in the workshop. Since the tongs in the myth [as told in *The Maze Maker*] were made from lobster claws, an actual lobster claw was cast in bronze. The claw also serves as a metaphor of the compass, which Talos allegedly invented. The egg carton that recurs here is intended as a metaphor for the maze. It represents the idea about the maze as separate chambers, it serves as a working model for interlocking cells which can be traversed, and it doubles for the honeycomb, said Ayrton, who also noted that his metaphors tended to double up because he worked on the ancient principle that everything represents itself and something else.[19] There also is an egg in the sculpture, as in the earlier version (Cat. No. 544), which was inspired by a painting of Piero della Francesca in Milan, frequently identified merely as *The Madonna of the Egg.* The egg naturally suggests creation and birth, just as it did in one of the wax and bone reliefs, *The Birth of Phanes.*[20]

Meanwhile, the design of the maze itself was also taking shape for Ayrton. He had already studied the history of mazes while writing *The Maze Maker* and incorporated his understanding of that history into the narrative. In unpublished notes for his patron (printed below as appendix B) he speculated on the significance of the maze as background for his design:

> In antiquity the Maze was endowed with a number of different but connected symbolic functions arising from the elision, over several thousand years, of one legend with another. I have tried to explain some of these in *The Maze Maker*, but it seems to me that one or two significant factors which lie outside the book, yet are relevant to the shape and form I have designed for the Arkville project, might explain the speculations and intentions behind the models and maquettes I have made.
>
> The obvious functions of the maze, to arrest the intruder by confusing him, to protect the centre from intrusion and to contain no less than to exclude, could be and were signified by ideograms of great simplicity at an early date: the Greek *meander* and *key* patterns are maze derivations. As such symbols of protection they were painted on walls at the entrances to houses and found their way into woven textiles, were incised on funerary urns and were heraldically displayed on coins of Knossos from the 5th to the 1st centuries B.C. Although in Roman times the archaic significance of these rituals had much decayed, they remained protective in the form of mosaic floor patterns and even entered children's games, where indeed they have remained to this day—*in pavimentis puerorumve ludicris campestribus,* as Pliny put it, or hopscotch as we might call it.[21] After the fall of Rome, floor mazes passed into Christian iconography and reasserted their ancient power on the floor of the naves of Chartres and other cathedrals.

Following an excursus on the dancing floor for Ariadne mentioned by Homer in *Iliad* 18 (see chapter 2), which was designed for an intricate dance "imitating the mating ceremony of either the crane (the most familiar version) or the partridge,"[22] Ayrton notes that "Eustathius of Thessalonika, writing in about 1100 A.D. relates that Theseus learned Ariadne's dance from Daedalus and danced it *to represent his passage through the labyrinth to kill the Minotaur.*" From this elision of rituals Ayrton drew two conclusions: "firstly that the only escape from the maze would be either to fly out of it, as would cranes or partridges, or to retrace one's steps, which raises the second point: the red thread of Ariadne which was unwound to lead Theseus to the centre of the maze and rewound as it guided his passage back into the outer world. The significance of this red thread surely represents death and rebirth."[23]

Ayrton concludes his explanation for his patron of his choice of the design for the *Arkville Maze* as follows:

> At this point we return to Ariadne's red thread, an umbilical symbol clearly to be identified with the process of birth and in adult life (i.e., in legend) of rebirth and salvation. It is from this metaphor that the Christian significance and therefore the survival of the maze, as a living symbol into our own time, must in some degree derive.
>
> In consequence of these speculations, the pattern and shape of the design I have evolved for the Arkville Maze is organic rather than heraldic in form, unlike most European designed mazes during the last two thousand years. I have derived the overall shape from the models designed for the Etruscan *haruspex* and suggested, in the pattern of paths which contain within their coils the traditional seven turns or "decision points," an entrail rather than a rigidly formal or heraldic pattern.[24]

The *Arkville Maze Maquette* (Cat. No. 641; Plate 22) reveals a rather atypical maze pattern. The classical labyrinth design,[25] which is the archetype for mazes found around the world, usually is either circular or rectangular, with seven rings of path and one central chamber. This type of labyrinth is unicursal, and the points where the path changes direction are always found on the axis between the entrance and the center. The pattern for the *Arkville Maze,* however, is neither circular nor rectangular, but oval; there are, moreover, *two* central chambers, and there is no central axis between the entrance and these chambers. The *Arkville Maze,* furthermore, is multicursal, with seven decision points, where error may compound error, and the path changes direction in seemingly random fashion, causing one repeatedly to retrace one's steps. Ayrton found it necessary to employ two central chambers in order to preserve an equilibrium between the force of the Minotaur and that of Daedalus and Icarus. The explanation offered at the conclusion of his notes for his patron also clarifies an aspect of the decision points in the maze and its larger significance:

> A symbol of the opposition of those forces which preserve equilibrium may, I suspect, be one of the meanings of the sacred Minoan double axe called *labrys,* from which the word labyrinth may derive. This axe, images of which survive in numerous materials, from Minoan times, is also thought to represent the cycle of the waxing and waning of the moon.

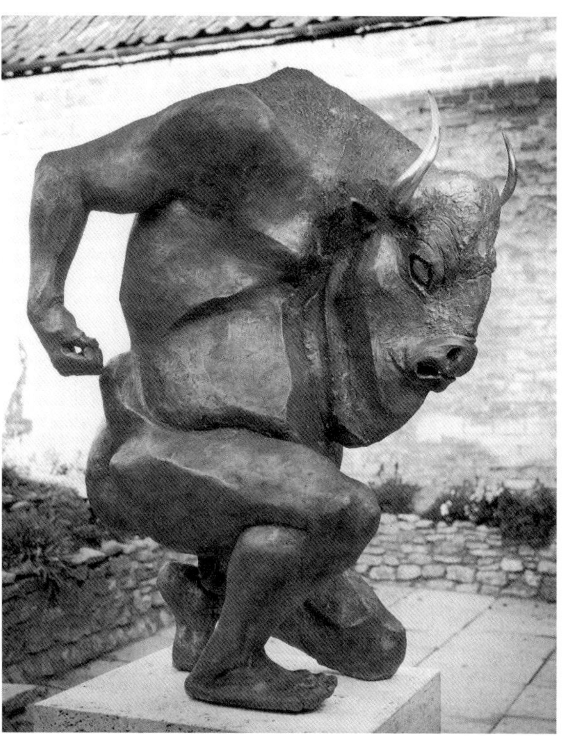

Figure 159. **ARKVILLE MINOTAUR**
(Cat. No. 663; 1968–69): side view, at Bruton Gallery, Somerset.

> At the seventh "decision point" in the Arkville Maze, the traveller will be at the haft of the axe, as it were. The two chambers or coils which lie on either hand will each contain one of two opposed forces, one in the form of the Minotaur and one in the form of Daedalus and his son. Thus "the constrictions separating death and life" will not be forgotten.
>
> The metaphor of the maze is a pregnant one. The complexity and richness of its meanings must be contained and represented as far as possible in the Arkville Maze, for we are, after all, attempting more than *ludicris campestribus.* We are attempting to create an image in which life unwound becomes death and death unwound becomes life.

Various critics have looked for the source of the design for the *Arkville Maze.* One compared the "continuous smooth flowing series of curves which presumably are all the much more easy to get lost in" to the chambered nautilus that recurs as a maze symbol in *The Maze Maker.*[26]

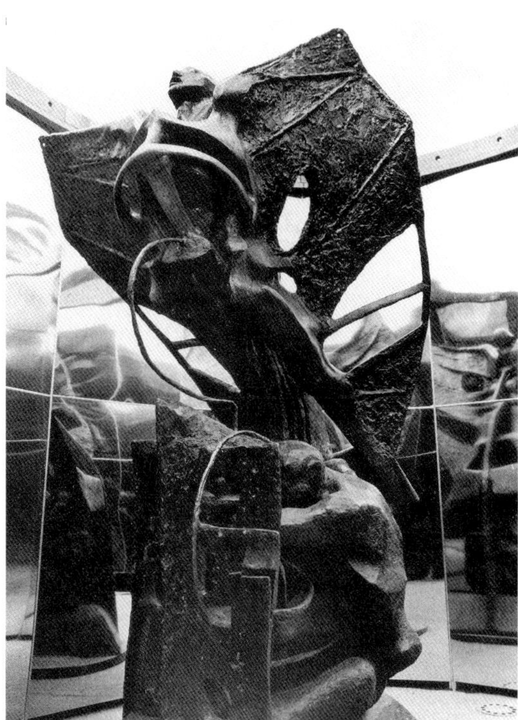

Figure 160. **DAEDALUS/ICARUS MATRIX** (Cat. No. 640; 1968): matrix, with focus on Maze Maker.

Aside from relating his design to the Etruscan haruspex, as noted above, Ayrton acknowledged its connection with that of a nautilus shell cut in half, which, he said, "is one of the most perfect geometrical forms in nature and therefore gives me a special and very exact kind of pleasure."[27] One reason for this pleasure is that he saw the natural organic concretion that produces the geometrical perfection of the nautilus shell as "an extraordinary symbol of what in fact all of us build around ourselves. Because we all live in our own mazes which we make for ourselves." These self-made mazes are "a concretion of experiences, hope, life itself."[28]

Although Ayrton did not mention the womb as a model for his maze pattern, the fetal configuration is unmistakable.[29] His comments about Ariadne's red thread as an umbilical symbol identified with the process of birth offer undeniable evidence that the womb was linked, at least in his subconscious, with the maze design he presented to his patron in maquette form. It is equally easy to discern a cervical inspiration for the entrance to this womb-maze. In Ayrton's description of Mt. Eryx on Sicily, upon which the sanctuary of Aphrodite ("the Mother") stood, Ayrton uses sexual imagery: "the sanctuary is cut into the rock and at the clitoris of this entrance to the earth . . . each man who brings a gift [to the goddess] . . . is received between the thighs of a priestess, to make his gift of seed" (1967, 298). Moreover, the umbilical cord of the *Daedalus/Icarus Matrix,* although derived from the earlier bronze *Maze Maker (large version)* (Cat. No. 544; Plate 19; see chapter 5), offers further reinforcement to the womb symbol. Considering the extensive sexual imagery in *The Maze Maker* and the emphasis on the womb of Gaia in Part Two (147–254) of the novel, it would hardly be surprising to discover a continuation of the concept here. Rather, it is a logical and entirely natural development.

One also must not overlook psychoanalytic explanations for the design of the *Arkville Maze.* From ancient times, caves have served not only as entrances into the earth but also as cult places, for worship of the Great Mother and for mystery religions (and, in later times, by Christians). In the archetype of the Great Mother, "who from the remotest times has been the Earth Mother presiding over caves and mountains,"[30] the earth is conceived of as a womb. Beyond the sexual implications of the uterine shape of the *Arkville Maze* lies a deeper archetypal symbolism transcending the personal: "Being contained in something maternal that is greater than oneself, and emerging from it regenerated, are genuine psychic emotions felt by everyone who enters a world transcending his ego consciousness and is transformed by this experience of mystery. But toward that which surrounds and contains him he feels childishly small, and this feeling awakens echoes of his own infancy, when he groped his way about the mother."[31]

When the maquettes were translated into reality to form the *Arkville Maze* (Cat. No. 673; Figure 158, Plate 23), the result was the largest brick and stone maze in the world, which the artist believed to be "of much the same dimensions as the tomb-labyrinth of Lars Porsena."[32] Over 200,000 bricks were required to construct the eighteen-inch thick, eight- to ten-foot-high walls, which comprise a coil of approximately 1,680 linear feet, wound up within a space no more than 120 by 200 feet across.[33] The deeper one goes into the maze and the nearer one comes to the center, the higher the walls, for the path descends gradually deeper into the earth as one approaches the center. Although the walls at the entrance start at shoulder height and soon are slightly above one's head, they are ten feet high at the very center. Dr. Justine Hopkins, describing her own experience of the maze, says that this gradual deepening "adds considerably . . . to the general disorientation of the journey, and, of course, fits precisely with everything mazes were to Michael"[34] (Plates 24 and 25).

As one enters the maze and begins to follow the involuted passageways, one can very quickly begin to identify with the sacrificial troop of Athenian youth. When, moreover, one finds the path blocked by a solid brick crosswall, one naturally begins to wonder which new trap awaits as one retraces one's steps to another of the crucial decision points. Nonetheless, one ventures forward, awaiting the next point of decision, the next challenge, the next surprise.

Suddenly, as the path opens into a central chamber, one is confronted with a crouched *Minotaur* (Cat. No. 663; Figure 159, Plate 28) who glares threateningly. To my mind come these words from a fragment of Euripides' lost *Eurystheus* (372 N.): "Nay, old man; fear them not; all Daedalus's statues seem to move and to see; so clever was that man." Or these words of Socrates, who talks of Daedalus's statues in Plato's *Meno* 97 D: "If they are not tied fast, they slip away like runaway slaves, but if they are tied, they stay in their place." This lifelike Minotaur has evolved a long way from the earlier grotesque beast (*Minotaur I;* Cat. No. 282). His lower torso and arms are human, but "he begins as bull at the loins and he bears a hump of sinews upon his shoulders which carries the great horned skull and the cattle brute mask of his head."[35] His hybrid shape and the weight of his crest and skull contribute to a certain sense of imbalance, but they also make him a more imposing figure. The reddish stucco walls surrounding him create a special mood, as they call to mind both the palace at Knossos and the bull fights in Spain and Mexico where "the Minotaur is killed every Sunday," says Ayrton, "and as Picasso knows, he does not die."[36]

The other chamber is separated from this one by a single wall and not, as in *The Maze Maker* (1967, 117), "by a maze within the maze." But to gain access, it is necessary to resume one's wanderings in the curving passages, risking frustration, fear, and failure. If, however, success crowns one's decisions, the deceptively similar path will open into a startlingly different chamber. The highly polished bronze walls in the "chamber of the sun" multiply his rays, and the walls are alive with reflected images.[37] Whoever penetrates this chamber becomes a part of the narrative on the wall, merged in reflection with the sculpture that graces the center of the chamber.

The sculpture, of course, is the *Daedalus/Icarus Matrix* (Cat. No. 640; Plate 26). A golden Icarus appears to launch himself upward, escaping the confinement of the maze. From below, he appears already airborne, and his disproportionate chest is expanded, bellows-like, as he hubristically inhales the upper atmosphere on his way to challenge Apollo. The pride conveyed in the earlier bronze *Icarus Rising* (Cat. No. 206; see chapter 4) reverberates through this gilt bronze, but a closer inspection of this evocative sculpture reveals Icarus's umbilical connection to his maze-making father: the artisan, trapped in his own labyrinth, impedes the escape of his hubristic son.

For an artist who has described one page of Virgil's *Aeneid* as the source for a decade of inspiration (see chapter 4), it is only natural to draw further insights from Virgil's most famous medieval interpreter. One should not be surprised, therefore, to learn that Ayrton drew from Dante's *Purgatory,* Canto X, his idea for the mirrored chamber to house *Daedalus/Icarus Matrix:* Dante's description of relief sculpture inspired Ayrton's conception that people who journey through the maze should read it as both mirror image and sculpture.[38] The final paragraphs of *The Maze Maker* (qtd. at the end of chapter 5) offer a key to understanding the idea that the walls of the maze are alive and carry a message: "part of the ambiguous topology of the end of *The Maze Maker* is that you read past and present in the walls as Dante describes them; you do not read them as written words, but as visual imagery (the relief sculpture in Dante is read as an illusion and as a mirror)."[39]

Drawing upon myth and literature for his conception of the maze he designed for Erpf's estate at Arkville, Ayrton went through a process of "visual thinking" at both the conscious and unconscious levels, which was revealed in his drawings and sculptural maquettes. The choices he made—as he discarded the idea of a single chamber at the center, as he separated Daedalus from the Minotaur but then linked him umbilically to Icarus, as he selected reddish stucco for the walls of the Minotaur's chamber and bronze mirrors for the chamber of Daedalus and Icarus, and as he enlarged the maze maker component of *Daedalus/Icarus Matrix* (Cat. No. 640)—all offer profound insights into the creative process. Evident in this process is a constant interplay with the myth he had recounted, modified, and enlarged in *The Maze Maker.* It is a richly complex process, a process even deeper and more complex than is evident in any account of it, for no one can know fully what is (or was) in the mind of another. A well-informed reader will likely extend the analysis further and find new and deeper insights, using the raw materials I have provided, as I have sought to understand and explain Ayrton and his process of making the invisible visible.

In the *Arkville Maze* Ayrton further extended a very ancient and terrible image and enriched a durable and mysterious human symbol. This image of human consciousness extends back some five thousand years into the remote past of human history.[40] Beside his aesthetically pleasing artistic achievement with this sculptural maze, Ayrton has added to the long history of mazes a statement on its meaning to humankind. Through this maze, as well as in his writings and by his other sculptures, he suggests that the maze is both external and internal. It is brick and stone, bronze and glass, but it is also flesh and blood, an organic model of the human body. Abstract, ethereal, and insubstantial, it is likewise real, concrete, and tangible. It is intellectual, spiritual, and emotional. It is simultaneously universal and intensely personal. It is the sum total of human experience and, concurrently, a single, individual, very secret event. Hidden in it are our fears and our hopes, our passions and the rationality that can order and control them. We enter it to escape, we leave it to seek refuge and safety. And yet we depart it only to enter another labyrinth. We are at once the maker and the prisoner of our own maze. Daedalus, Icarus, the Minotaur—all are separate figures in myth and in Ayrton's work, yet all merge into one, for each is a different facet of human experience, each an aspect of the human condition, of the individual personality. At Arkville the metaphor has become reality and reality a metaphor.

Beyond the Maze?

7

The *Arkville Maze* is in a very real sense a portrait of the artist as a mature thinker. Ayrton, in his search for Daedalus and thus also for his own identity as a sculptor, discovered with him that making labyrinths was his calling. He also perceived that, as he says in *The Maze Maker:*

> Each man's life is a labyrinth at the center of which lies his death, and even after death it may be that he passes through a final maze before it is all ended for him. Within the great maze of a man's life are many smaller ones, each seemingly complete in itself, and in passing through each one he dies in part, for in each he leaves behind him a part of his life and it lies dead behind him. It is a paradox of the labyrinth that its center appears to be the way to freedom. (1967, 12)

Ayrton's patron who commissioned the maze at Arkville enjoyed its completion and experienced its mystery for less than two years; in February 1971 Mr. Erpf was buried just outside the maze. About a month later, Ayrton wrote in a letter: "I wish that he had elected to be buried at the centre of the Maze, instead of just outside it. The Maze would have made such an appropriate tomb for him, in addition to being a monument to his remarkable imagination as a patron."[1]

Ayrton meanwhile had moved on to new images that were a further outgrowth of the myth and his discoveries at Arkville. In 1969 Ayrton completed symbolic paintings of Cumae (Cat. No. 656) and Arkville (*Maze,* Cat. No. 661) and a relief *Maze Table* (Cat. No. 672). Painted after the artist had had a long acquaintance with Daedalus, this *Cumae* is much deeper and much more symbolic than his first painting of Cumae (Cat. No. 13): it presents Cumae from a totally different perspective. Whereas the earlier painting records the scene literally, this symbolic version presents more nearly a bird's-eye view, as if Ayrton were Daedalus descending upon this site. The symbolic representation of the Arkville Maze in *Maze* (Cat. No. 661) is echoed in *Maze Table* (Cat. No. 672). Here the Arkville Maze is set in an imaginary, symbolic landscape that summarizes in both form and content the richness of the myth for Ayrton. In it are included the sun, the honeycomb (created from a snake's skin, giving it double significance), wax, and a fish bone, which recalls not only the Icarus relief but also the fish-bone saw of Talos. The uterine form of the maze is even more distinct here than in the *Arkville Maze Maquette* (Cat. No. 641; Plate 22); it is also easy to see in this relief a symbolic representation of impregnation.

Extending further the concepts inherent in the earlier *Emerging Figure* series of triptychs (Cat. Nos. 597, 616, 617, and 618; see chapter 5), in 1969 Ayrton cast two bronzes, *Penetrator I* and *II* (Cat. Nos. 660 and 664; Figures 162 and 163): a twisting, struggling

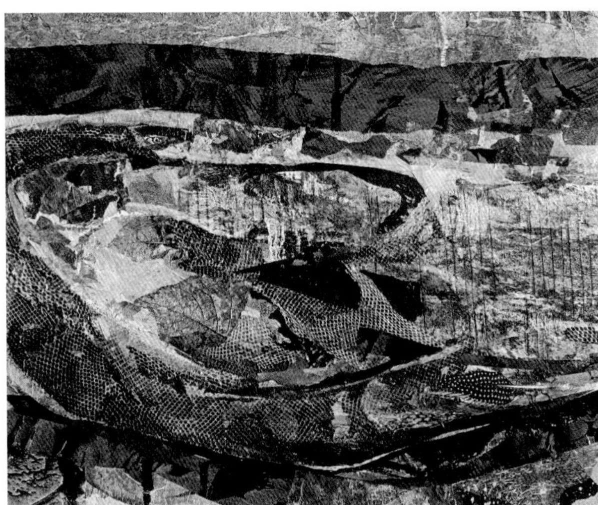

Figure 161. **THE LANDSCAPE OF THE PYTHONESS** (Cat. No. 671; September 1969).

figure is seen breaking through a wall, with only his hands and arms actually penetrating its resistant surface. The hands appear to reach out in a vain effort to grasp either the freedom or the security that lies on the other side, beyond his reach. The sense of struggle present in the Maze Maker series (see chapter 5) continues in these bronzes, but the wall of the maze has replaced the other circumstances and experiences with which the maze maker had struggled. Having made his maze, he now seeks to penetrate it, to attain its center, which, paradoxically, "appears to be the way to freedom."

The struggling figure in the *Penetrators* closely resembles the contorted form of *Laocoön Maze Figure, Version I* (Cat. No. 642; Figure 164), completed the preceding year, when the artist was engrossed in designing the *Arkville Maze* (Cat. No. 673) and its sculptural inhabitants. Virgil's dramatic picture of Laocoön in the Second Book of the *Aeneid* (2.40–56, 199–227) may have inspired Ayrton's bronze, but he may equally well have come to his conception by way of the Vatican Laocoön group found in 1506 C.E. near the Baths of Titus. This marble sculptural group, which had a profound influence upon Michelangelo and which "is probably the most widely discussed work of sculpture which we possess from antiquity,"[2] was certainly well known to Ayrton. Whatever his source, Ayrton chose in this sculpture to focus only upon Laocoön, and he further enriches both the myth and its artistic tradition by interpreting it within the context of the labyrinth.

In Virgil's superb retelling of the story of the fall of Troy, Laocoön serves as a powerful motif. Aeneas tells Dido that the priest of Neptune, as he came racing down the hill,

> Cried in alarm: "Are you crazy, wretched people?
> Do you think they have gone, the foe?
>   Do you think that any
> Gifts of the Greeks lack treachery? Ulysses,—
> What was his reputation? Let me tell you,
> Either the Greeks are hiding in this monster,
> Or it's some trick of war, a spy, or engine,
> To come down on the city. Tricky business
> Is hiding in it. Do not trust it, Trojans,
> Do not believe this horse. Whatever it may be,
> I fear the Greeks, even when bringing presents."
> (Aeneid 2.42–49, trans. R. Humphries [New York: Charles Scribner's Sons, 1951])

Laocoön's forceful challenge to the public response to the wooden horse, heightened by hurling his spear into its side, was interrupted by the arrival of Trojan shepherds with a Greek hostage, Sinon, who had purportedly been abandoned by the Greeks as they sailed away from Troy. The Trojans were beguiled by Sinon's perjury into believing that the wooden horse was an offering to Minerva. Immediately, and with dramatic force, the woeful tale of Laocoön resumes. While Laocoön, Neptune's priest, was slaying a bull at the altar, a "pair of serpents with monstrous coils" came over the sea from Tenedos and onto land, where they headed

> Straight toward Laocoön, and first each serpent
> Seized in its coils his two young sons, and fastened
> The fangs in those poor bodies. And the priest
> Struggled to help them, weapons in his hand.
> They seized him, bound him with their mighty coils,
> Twice round his waist, twice round his neck,
>   they squeezed
> With scaly pressure, and still towered above him.
> Straining his hands to tear the knot apart,
> His chaplets stained with blood and the black poison,

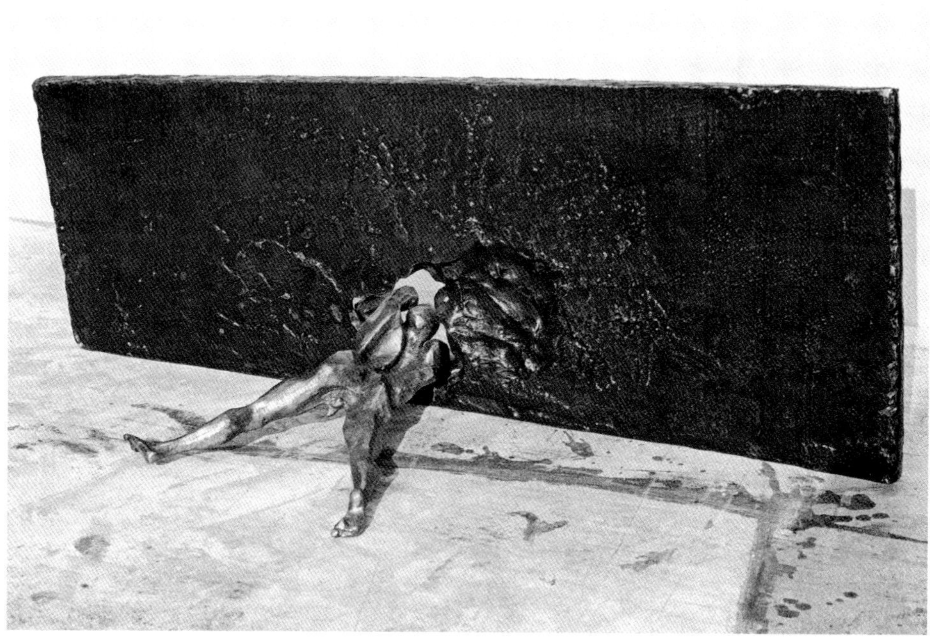

Figure 162. **PENETRATOR I** (Cat. No. 660; 1969): figure from behind.

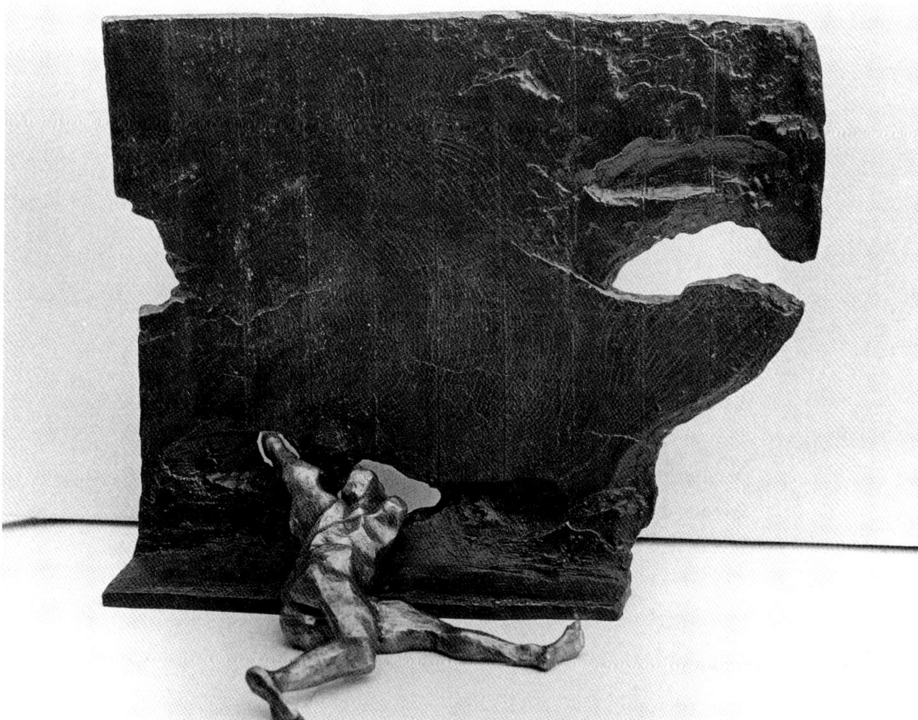

Figure 163. **PENETRATOR II** (Cat. No. 664; 1969): figure from behind.

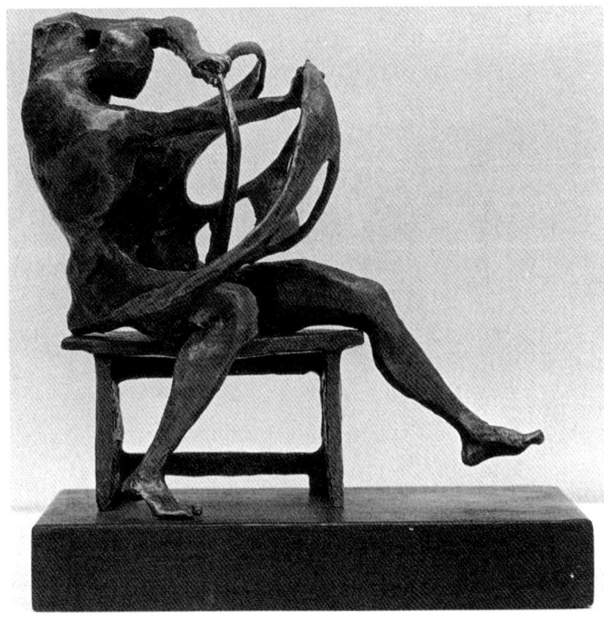

Figure 164. **LAOCOÖN MAZE FIGURE** (Version I) (Cat. No. 642; 1968).

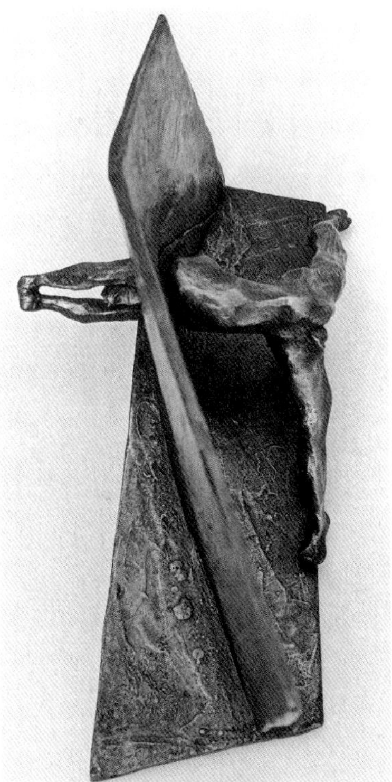

Figure 165. **PENETRATOR III** (Cat. No. 665; 1969): top view.

> He uttered horrible cries, not even human,
> More like the bellowing of a bull, when, wounded,
> It flees the altar.
> (Aeneid 2.212–24, trans. Humphries)

Despite one famous art historian's description of the ancient Laocoön group as "the most tarnished by familiarity,"[3] Ayrton's reinterpretation of the Laocoön story once again demonstrates the seemingly inexhaustible potential of myth.[4] In Ayrton's sculpture, and perhaps even more clearly in his drawings for the Laocoön sculptures (including *Laocoön Maze Figure II* [Cat. No. 761, 1972; Plate 51]), the snakes are not presented as external forces but rather seem to be drawn from within the figure itself. The struggle therefore is with the demons or dragons within oneself rather than with a serpent that attacks from without. Laocoön is enmeshed in a maze of his own making, not ensnared by a serpent sent by one of the gods.

Conceptually related to the *Penetrators* is the series of *Extricators* (*I* and *II*, Cat. Nos. 719 and 720) that were cast the following year. Whereas the *Penetrators* show a male figure thrusting his way through a wall—which in *Penetrator III* (Cat. No. 665; Figure 165) has become convex from the thrust not only of the figure's arms but also of his upper torso through the wall—the *Extricators* reverse the process. In *Extricator I* (Cat. No. 719; Figures 166–168) the wall is still nearly rectangular, and it bulges inward under the strain of the figure's vehement tugging, as he braces his feet to increase his leverage against a barely tractable surface. But in *Extricator II* (Cat. No. 720; Figure 169) the wall becomes more symbolic, assuming an S-shape that resembles a snake's coils, a bent scythe blade, or the convolutions of the *Arkville Maze.* Of these sculptures the artist himself said: "The sculptures called *Penetrators* and *Extricators* I discovered to be essentially optimistic in that the notion of escape is illusory. The metaphor of the labyrinth is too embracing; to escape from it is to return, wishing to return. My imagery has remained mazed because it cannot be otherwise, being both microcosm and macrocosm and independent of scale."[5] The failure of all these figures either to penetrate or escape from the walls is a symbol not merely of Ayrton's own inability to free himself from the myth and the maze, but especially

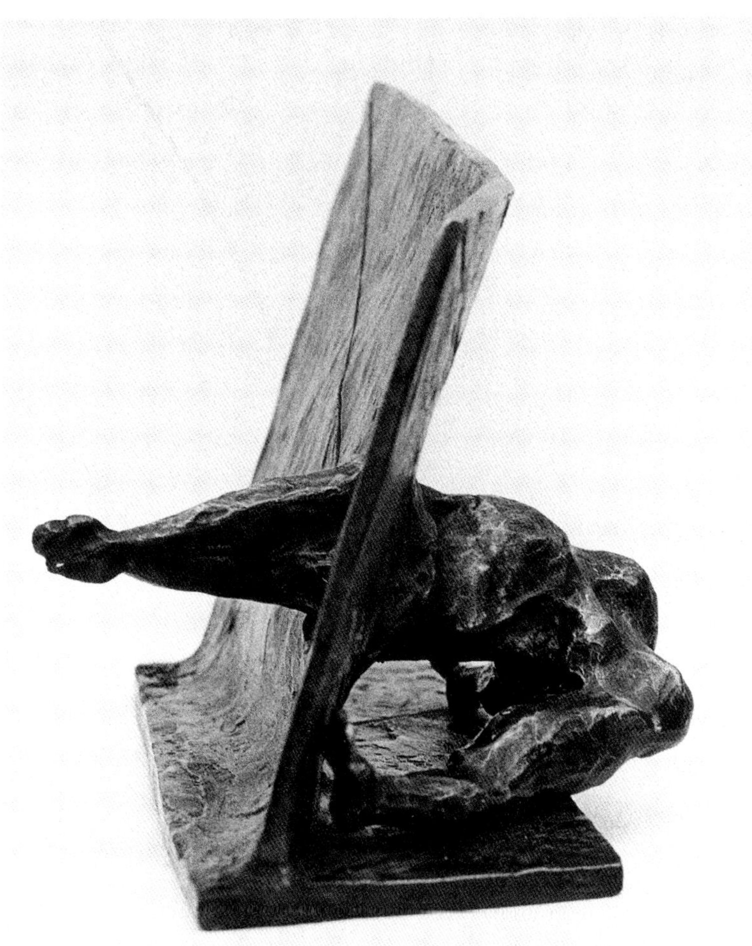

Figure 166. **EXTRICATOR I** (Cat. No. 719; 1970): side view.

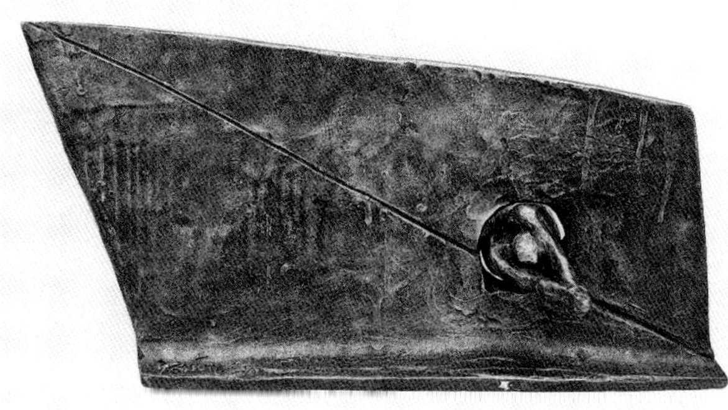

Figure 167. **EXTRICATOR I** (Cat. No. 719): frontal view.

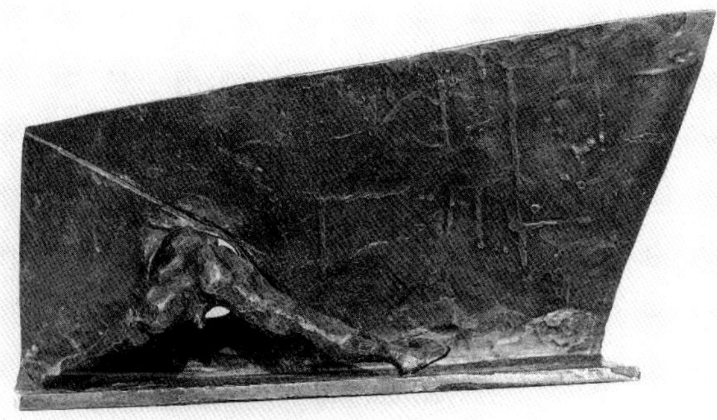

Figure 168. **EXTRICATOR I** (Cat. No. 719): back view.

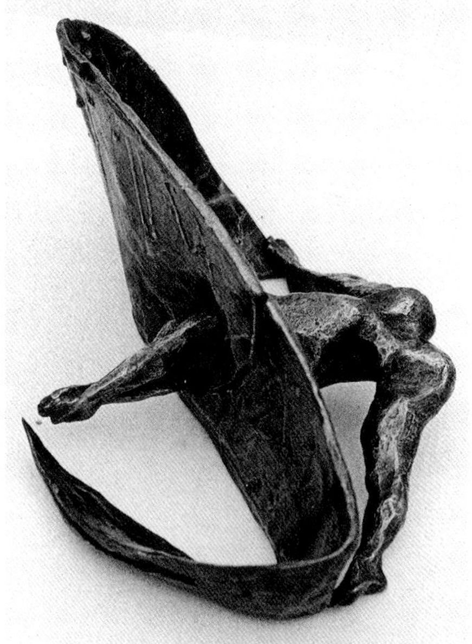

Figure 169. **EXTRICATOR II** (Cat. No. 720; 1970).

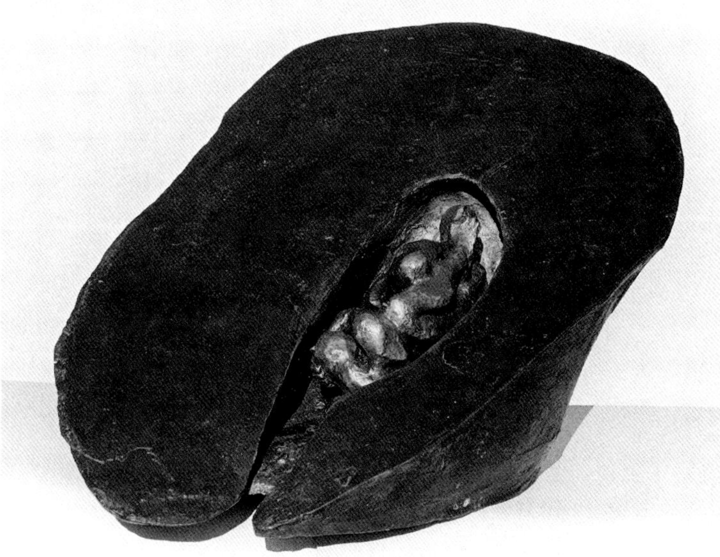

Figure 170. **DEEP IN** (Cat. No. 657; 1969).

for the human condition. Or, as one critic asserts: "Ayrton concluded that man cannot escape and neither could he; that the half of his nature that is physical and of the flesh does not really will itself to psychic liberation but clings to the protection and safety that the maze/fortress accords it."[6]

Similarly, *Deep In* (Cat. No. 657; Figure 170) has imbedded in it a human figure in fetal position (which exists independently as *Return*, Cat. No. 674), reinforcing the idea expressed by both Ayrton and his critic. *Deep In* appears to be a cross-section of the uterus, but one with walls so thick that the possibility of release is almost inconceivable. It would be consistent with Ayrton's other sculpture, but especially of the *Arkville Maze*, and his published remarks to view this piece as a symbol of man's final return to the womb of the earth. In Nikos Kazantzakis's *The Odyssey: A Modern Sequel* (Trans. Kimon Friar [New York: Simon and Schuster, 1958]), Odysseus, in his passionate quest for freedom, discovers that the ultimate freedom is death. So also Ayrton's archetypal figures repeatedly make this discovery for him, although always from a new, yet linked, perspective.

In 1969 Ayrton made another discovery that shaped the direction of most of his subsequent work. Professor Richard Gregory, a neuropsychologist, gave him a piece of neutral density perspex. Gregory's interest in illusion and human perception kept him abreast of technological developments that might further his research.[7] The nature of this slightly tinted plastic is such that it combines translucency with a degree of opaqueness and, as a result, it both creates reflections and permits one to see through it. Since Ayrton had already used bronze and copper mirrors in *Mirror Maze* (Cat. No. 596; 1966) and in the chamber of the sun at Arkville (see Cat. Nos. 640 and 673; also chapter 6), he was quick to recognize the potential of this perspex for further extending the metaphor of the maze. The result was a series of sculptures known as *The Translucent Maze Sequence.* Ayrton's description of this series accompanied its first exhibition to the public in December 1970: "These images are deliberately ambiguous in that they depend upon solid forms related to one another by illusion. Each group turns on its own axis to reveal human beings completed or duplicated to merge in reflection. They seek to represent man exploring the labyrinth of his own mind, aware but uncertain of his identity. They are beyond the maze because they no longer map the journey but rather reveal the condition."[8] Regarding ambiguity it is worth noting the following observations of R. E. Kantor: "At the heart of the mature precept lies the essential notion that ambiguity of meaning need not convey confusion, but rather multiplicity: a single symbol can carry rich manifolds of relationships."[9]

This series of sculptures in the *Translucent Maze Sequence* is intimately, perhaps even integrally, related to *Fabrications* (1972), for both are concerned with a whole series of enigmas. How close the relationship is can be seen especially in "Enigma" (Ayrton 1973, 113–19; discussed below) and "The Autobiography of Lameich Trojan" (207–17).[10] The name "Lameich" is obviously a rearrangement of the letters in the name "Michael," whereas the letters of "Trojan" can be reassembled as "Ayrton," provided that one equates "j" with "y" (which is a logical thing for one who knows some Latin, as Ayrton clearly did).[11] In "Autobiography," Lameich Trojan discovers in Ayrton's workshop an apparatus in which an open copy of his book was suspended on a turntable between two translucent sheets of neutral perspex. By means of this apparatus, he "was able to see not only what [he] had written but what [he] would come to write" (214). By Ayrton's careful placement of a light source, moreover, says Lameich Trojan, "a number of apparent phenomena coincidentally existed." He continues:

> I saw in the smoky depths of the translucent mirrors, so cunningly arranged, my own appearance curiously engaged, combined and duplicated with that of Ayrton, whose image appeared of course reversed at some points in the rotations while I appeared reversed at others. I also observed, and I was illuminated by the fact, just how difficult my autobiography appeared to be to read when focused upon with the clarity required for it to emerge, vanish, re-emerge and complete itself. (214)

The first work in the *Translucent Maze Sequence* is entitled *Reflex I* (Cat. No. 658; 1969; Figures 171 and 172; Plates 32 and 33). Viewed along the perspex, either horizontally or perpendicularly, the sculpture appears reasonably simple and obvious; there is one half of a split head, the profile of another, smaller head, and a twisted figure that seems to be walking out of the image. But as one turns the group on its axis and permits the interplay of light on the translucent surfaces, exciting things begin to happen. The profile face, Janus-like, duplicates itself in the mirror, simultaneously looking back into the past and forward into the uncertain future. Turned farther, the head assumes a mask-like quality reminiscent of the so-called mask of Agamemnon found at Mycenae, although one must visualize the Mycenaean mask as bent to conform to the shape of the head.[12] The viewer also finds his own reflection in the mirror, discovers his own features muted and ambiguous. Like a great work of literature, the sculptures in this series hold a mirror up to our lives and reveal dimensions unknown to us before. The ambiguity of these works intentionally reflects and reveals the ambiguities of human existence, the ambiguities of each individual viewer's life.

The impact of Jorge Luis Borges, the Argentine author of numerous short stories based on the labyrinth motif, is also apparent in these sculptures.[13] Whereas Borges experiments in his stories with such ideas as endless recurrence, the circular repetition of history, the dream within a dream, and the hallucinatory nature of the world, Ayrton not only gives visual form to these ideas, he also casts such a spell over the viewer as to draw him or her imperceptibly but relentlessly deeper and deeper into the labyrinth, blending illusion and reality as one's mind so often does.

With a further turning of this work, the half head completes itself in the mirror and, for a moment, gives the illusion of wholeness. The pattern, and the experience, can be endlessly repeated, although the discovery of subtle nuances of meaning and the evocation of differing emotional responses to the sculpture may result from further study, or from the change of one's line of vision, or by the alteration of lighting. The classical imagery of this and other Ayrton sculptures contributes to a certain sense of timelessness, but the use of contemporary materials to create the intriguing reflections focuses attention on the present moment. Time therefore becomes fluid, as in *The Maze Maker*, simultaneously linear, circular and punctiliar.

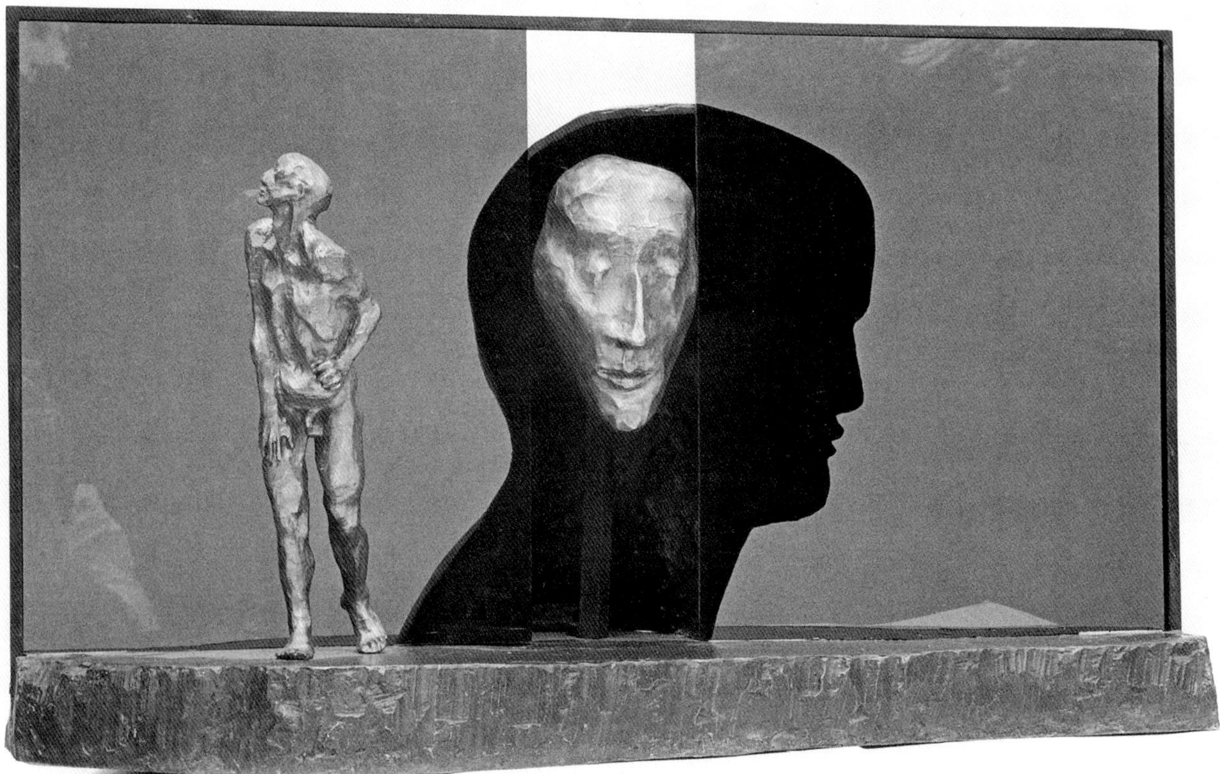

Figure 171. **REFLEX I** (Cat. No. 658; 1969): Janus head.

Borges begins one of his stories, "Tlön, Uqbar, Orbis Tertius," with "I owe the discovery of Uqbar to the conjunction of a mirror and an encyclopedia."[14] It is reasonable to argue that this statement inspired Ayrton's description of an apparatus that conjoined a book and mirrors, particularly since Borges is specifically named in the concluding paragraph of "The Autobiography of Lameich Trojan" (1973, 217), where he seems to acknowledge the extent of his indebtedness to Borges: "Only when this astonishing formula had revealed itself did I descry, deep in the mysterious darkness of both mirrors, joined by their opposition a labyrinth of barely penetrable interfaces, at once translucent and reflective—only then did I descry, without surprise, but with nothing less than reverence, an infinite number of immutable, multiple, blind, but smiling simulacra of the face of Jose [*sic*] Luis Borges."

There are other ways in which Ayrton was influenced by Borges's imaginary region of Tlön, where the metaphysicians "judge that metaphysics is a branch of fantastic literature. . . . One of the schools of Tlön goes so far as to negate time: it reasons that the present is indefinite, that the future has no reality other than as a present hope, that the past has no reality other than as a present memory."[15] Borges also declares: "Things become duplicated in Tlön; they also tend to become effaced and lose their details when they are forgotten."[16]

In the reflector sculptures, Ayrton created an imaginary, illusory world through the conjunction of a mirror and solid bronze forms. In this world, as in Tlön, time is in a sense negated and the duplicated images, when lost and forgotten, grow indistinct. And just as Borges's Tlön is "a labyrinth devised by men, a labyrinth destined to be deciphered by men,"[17] so also Ayrton's illusory world "beyond the maze" is a decipherable labyrinth.

The clues lie not in a single work but are to be found in his many other works and in his writings. The development, therefore, of *The Translucent Maze Sequence*

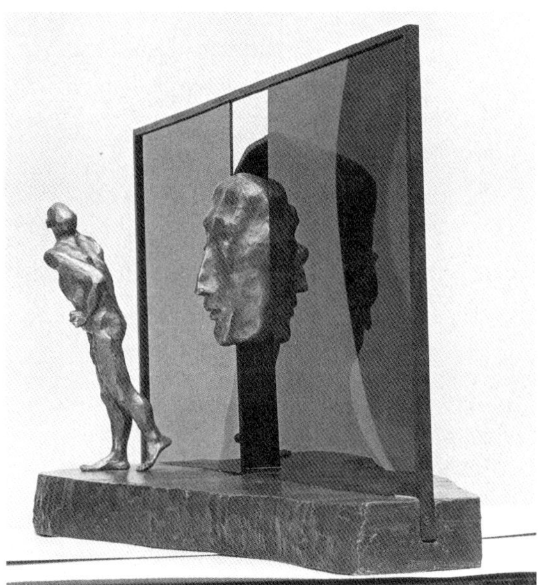

Figure 172. **REFLEX I** (Cat. No. 658): mask head.

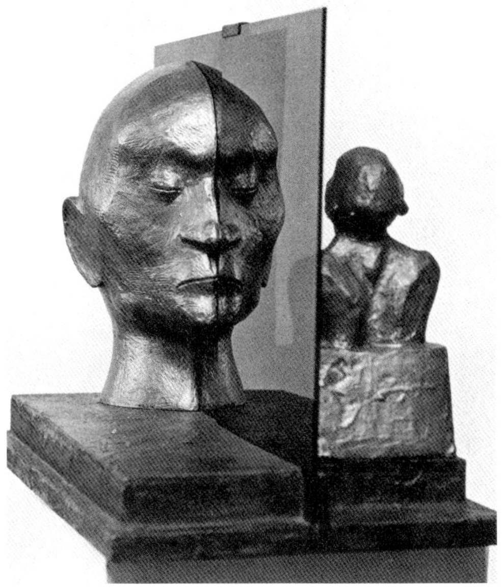

Figure 173. **REFLEX II** (Cat. No. 668; 1969): head reflected.

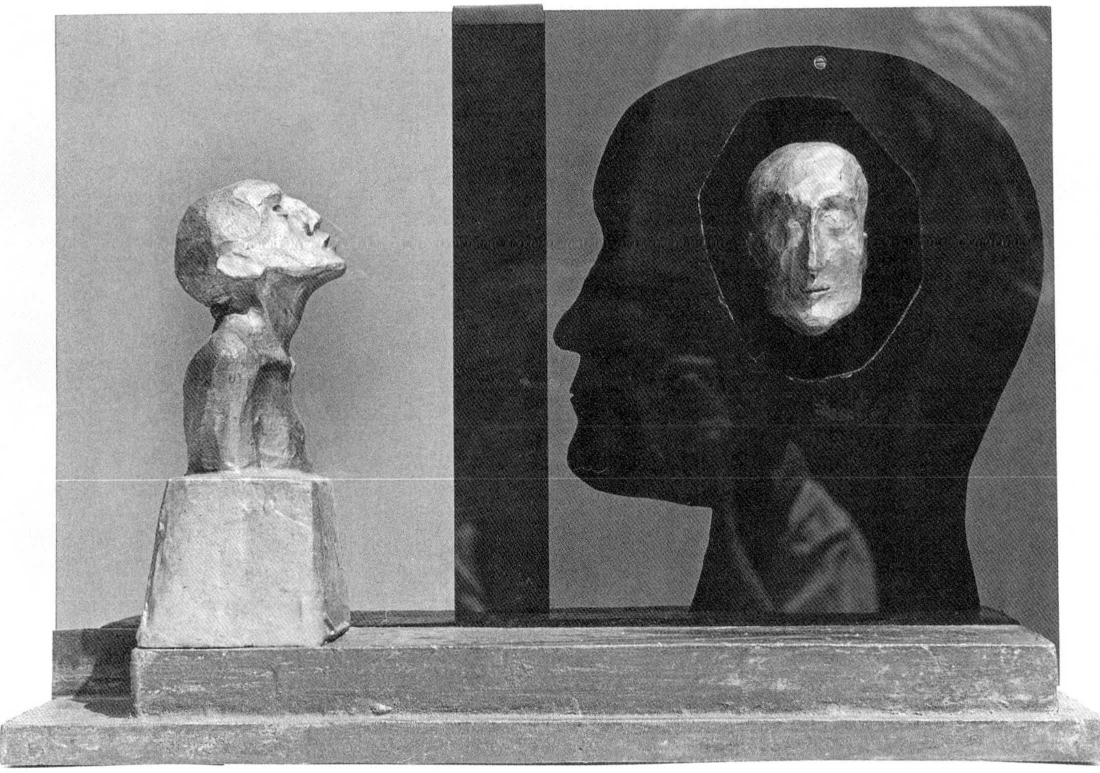

Figure 174. **REFLEX II** (Cat. No. 668): side view, with mask head.

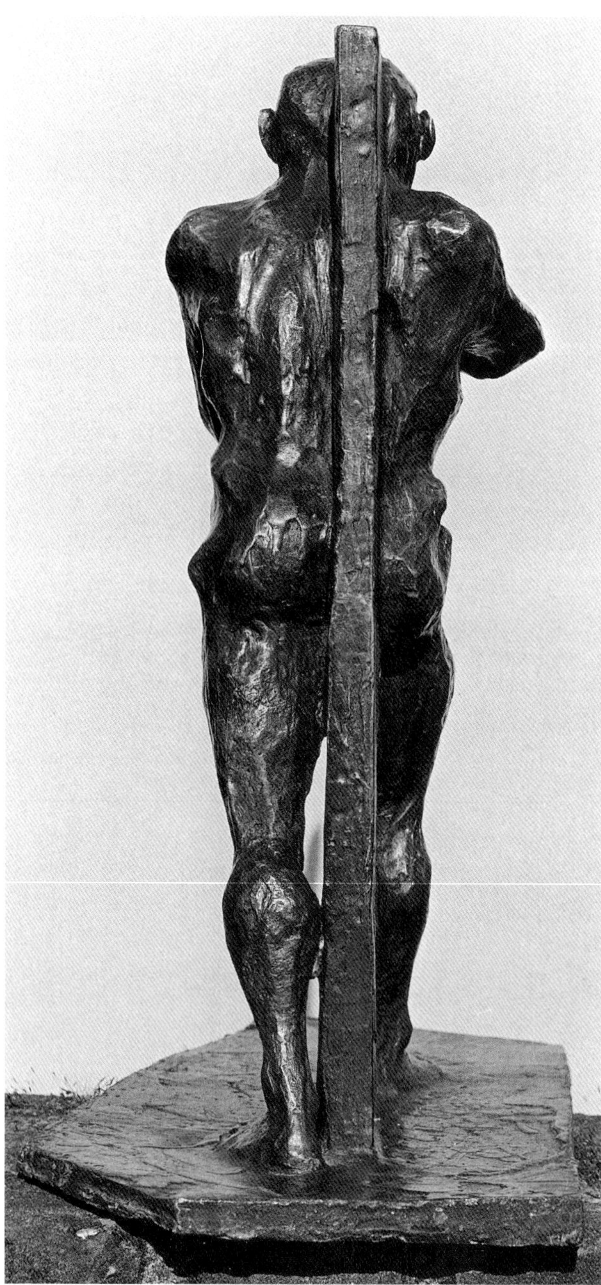

Figure 175. **SPLIT FIGURE** (Cat. No. 675; 1969): back view.

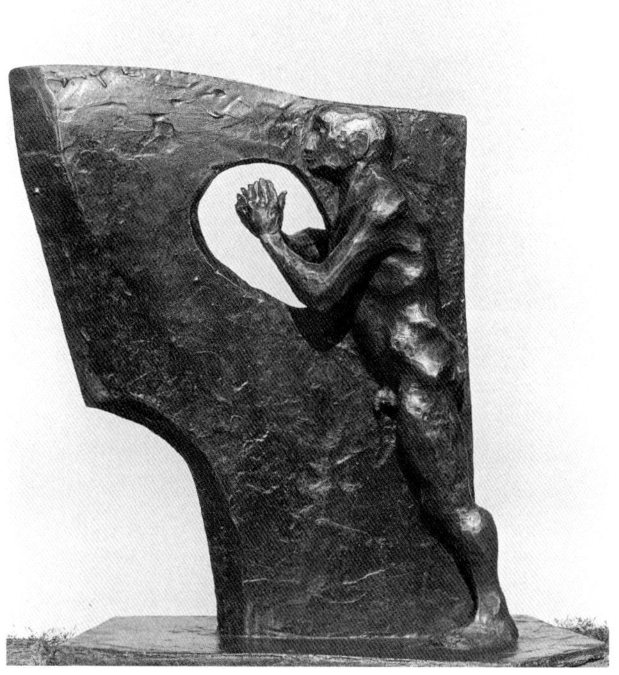

Figure 176. **SPLIT FIGURE** (Cat. No. 675): side view.

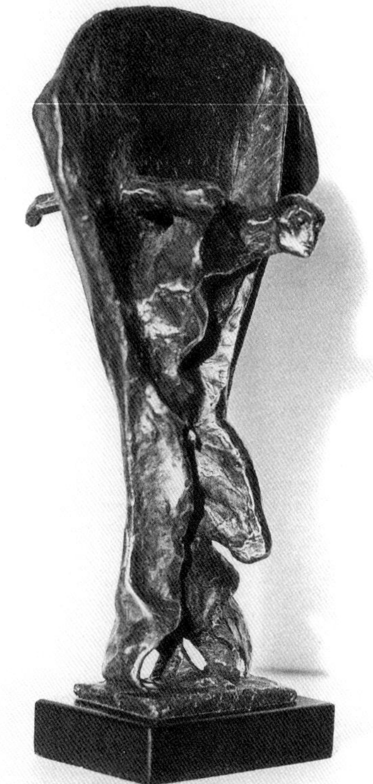

Figure 177. **THROUGH THE BLADE II** (Cat. No. 677; 1969).

must be viewed in the context of Ayrton's total creative expression, as well as in terms of the progression of ideas and the parallels between works in the series itself.

In a public lecture, "Journey Through a Labyrinth," delivered in Detroit in October 1972, Ayrton summarized some of his views on the metaphor of the labyrinth and its significance for his art. These excerpts cast further illumination on his work[18]:

> But aside from the legendary, and literary, and dramatic, elements of the Daedalic myth, the Maze as a concept, *as a model of the human condition*, goes even farther beyond and perhaps deeper into our deep, combined memory than the protagonists in a single ancient legend—even if that legend is one I personally seem to have lived in for many years and which I find central to my own life as an area of operation and of speculation.
>
> Consider then the maze—the labyrinth—as a thing —an object—a diagram. One of its ancient functions was . . . to imprison or hide away a secret. . . . It was also contrived to protect. . . . At one level it is a toy, or a convention, or even a game. . . . But the Maze is more than that—more profound and even older in its importance as a metaphor. *It is an image, a contrivance whereby mankind can identify himself, and come to terms with his environment.* (1–2)

In the reflector sculptures, Ayrton continued his effort to penetrate the meaning of the maze. As he created the reflective images, he not only saw his own reflection in the mirror, he also was searching for new ways of entering the maze or new ways of escaping it. The metaphor became more personal for him at the same time that it continued to elude his grasp.

His use of natural elements, such as the nautilus, in these sculptures gains new meaning when set in the context of the following excerpt from the same lecture:

> *But at the same time, surely mankind sees the earth as an extension, a model of himself.* It is at once his source—his mother element—and it will become his physical destination—which is death—or at least physical death—no matter what afterlife may procede with the soul. Man therefore not only inhabits his environment, but symbiotically *it inhabits him* and he has known this metaphorical double-act instinctively since prehistory, whatever worship or praise he has laid upon the altars of his innumerable deities. This then, I propose is the primary purpose of the Maze. This is its *meaning.* (3)

One theme, which Ayrton stressed in this lecture is that it is important to be able to personify, for "what we can personify we can bring into some proportion and in some measure govern" (16). Without personification, he argued, we not only lose "power over circumstance, over the elements and over ourselves," but we even lose ourselves and our ability to create: "In our corporate arrogance, as a generation raised to assume that scientific progress is the one valid chart of the demonstrable penetration of reality, we may have lost certain vitally important absurdities. We have surely, for a start, lost *our ability to personify.* And in doing so we have accidentally discarded a great if irrational strength—the strength of *poesis*" (11).

Enlightened by these quotations, one can begin to understand more clearly Ayrton's own "irrational strength . . . of *poesis.*" The act of creating has often been attributed by artists and writers to a special inspiration or to a personal *daimon,* from Hesiod around 700 B.C.E. right up to the present time. In and through the act of creating the *Arkville Maze* and his numerous labyrinthine drawings, paintings, and sculpture, Ayrton was exercising the irrational strength gained from personifying reality. He was also mapping his own personal journey through life. As he remarked in the Detroit lecture:

> Now as to the function of the Maze itself and its possible relevance *as a model of the human condition* quasi-eternally and therefore at this moment, there remains another important aspect of the metaphor and one which bridged the psychological leap from paganism into Christianity. This is the image of the maze as the map of the journey through life, into death and hence into resurrection. . . .
>
> [T]he Christian or unicursal Maze differs profoundly from the more ruthless view of chance and necessity which was general before the birth of Christ. It leaves nothing to chance. The Christian Maze . . . *without risk of error . . .* leads . . . to redemption. (13–14)

It is significant that Ayrton did not initially design a unicursal maze for Arkville but a multicursal and curvilinear

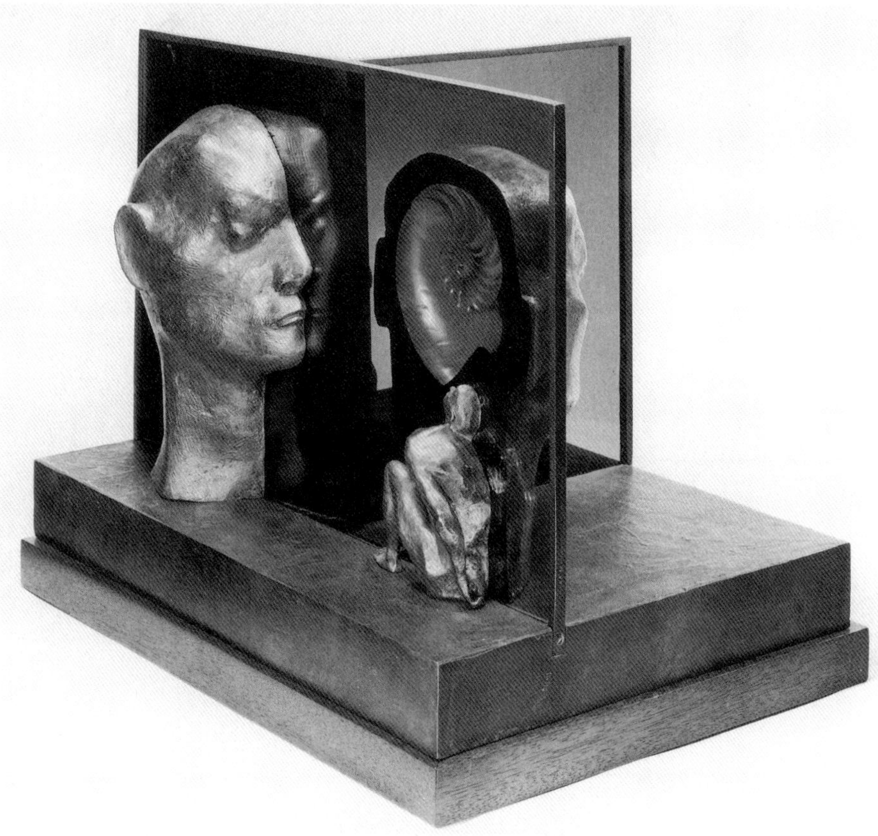

Figure 178. **DISCOVERY OF NAUTILUS** (Cat. No. 667; 1969): head reflected and seated figure, from back. John Webb, FRPS/Brompton Studios.

one, with multiple decision points and two central chambers, neither of which offered redemption. It was only at the urging of his patron, Armand Erpf, that he designed a second maze, a Christian floor maze, *The Jerusalem Maze at Arkville* (Cat. No. 718; 1970; see below).

Noting that "for most of human history and prehistory we have devised formulae to give us power," using personification to bring things "into some proportion" so that we can "in some measure govern," in his Detroit lecture Ayrton offered this conclusion, which further clarifies the images he created: "that is why I inhabit a labyrinth with which I identify and whose inhabitants I identify as meaning many things at once in symbol—in metaphor —in person" (16–17).

The device of the bronze half head employed in *Reflex I* to create a full head by reflection in a mirror is repeated not only in *Reflex II* (Cat. No. 668; Figures 173 and 174) but also in many other sculptures of this type. The bisection of the human body by an axe blade in *Split Figure* (Cat. No. 675; 1969; Figures 175 and 176) may have started the process of physically dissecting human beings, but the spiritual and intellectual dissection of humankind in Ayrton's work had by this time long been evident. In these reflector sculptures, however, the use of a hollow-cast half head serves a clearly functional purpose: it enables the artist to hide another form or object within the vacant space behind the dense perspex. Then, as the sculpture rotates, this hidden figure is suddenly brought into the light, and the inner recesses of the mind are laid bare as deftly as a surgeon exposes the physical interior of the human head.

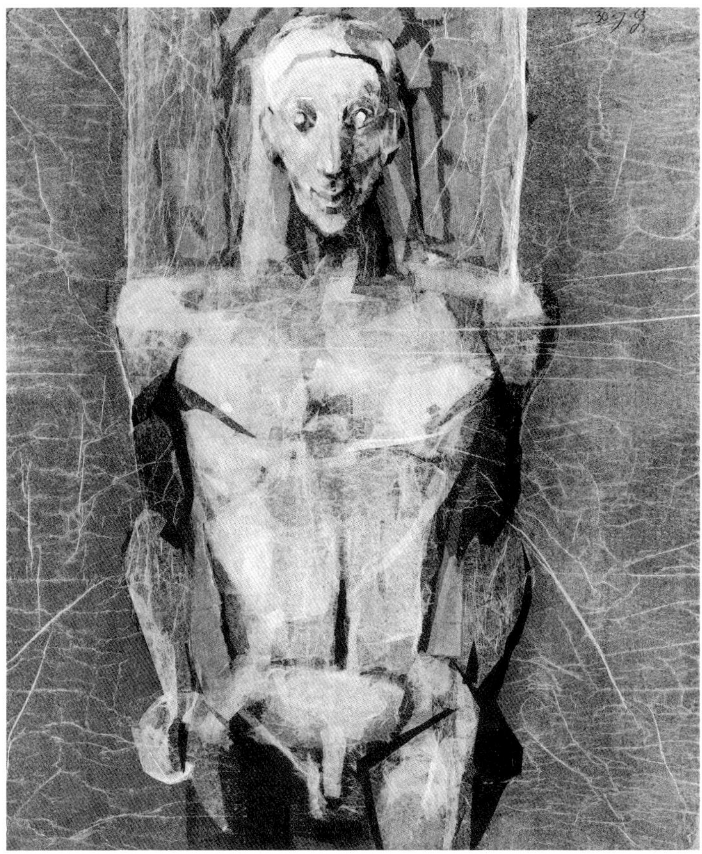

Figure 179 **KOUROS** (Cat. No. 349; 30 July 1963). Stearn & Sons Ltd., Cambridge.

Ayrton began fully to exploit this feature in *Discovery of Nautilus* (Cat. No. 667; Figure 178, Plates 34 and 35) and *Kouros* (Cat. No. 659; Figures 180 and 181, Plate 36). In the former we find a small bronze seated figure at the outer point of a bisected nautilus, which is set in the back of the head on the other side of the perspex. The reverse depicts an erect figure penetrating the inner chamber of the nautilus, again imbedded in a head beyond the perspex interface. The addition of a second piece of perspex, set perpendicular to the longer one, further multiplies the reflections and increases the complexity of the work. The presence of the nautilus shell within both heads is at once significant and obvious, since it "recurs in Ayrton's art as a symbol of the maze, the convolutions of the brain and the ideal, perfect form."[19] In *The Maze Maker,* moreover, Ayrton's Daedalus declares (136):

> yet I knew that in the nautilus of night there were many further nights, each in proportion smaller than the last and each a measured room; I also knew how they narrowed imperceptibly towards the last, toward the curled center of the shell forever shut against the morning. I knew and feared the trap and end of night, where the shell could never be broken, and I felt it closing on me so that I should come to crouch curled like a foetus in the night to come, in a cold beyond the warming breath of god.

The sky for Ayrton also represents a maze in which Daedalus observed "hawks flying, until gradually [he] found a pattern, a key to the labyrinth of the sky" (1967, 103; cf. 132–36 and 319–20). The bronze *Falcon Watcher* (Cat. No. 763; cf. Cat. No. 108) evokes Daedalus engaged in this activity, in anticipation of flying himself, as does

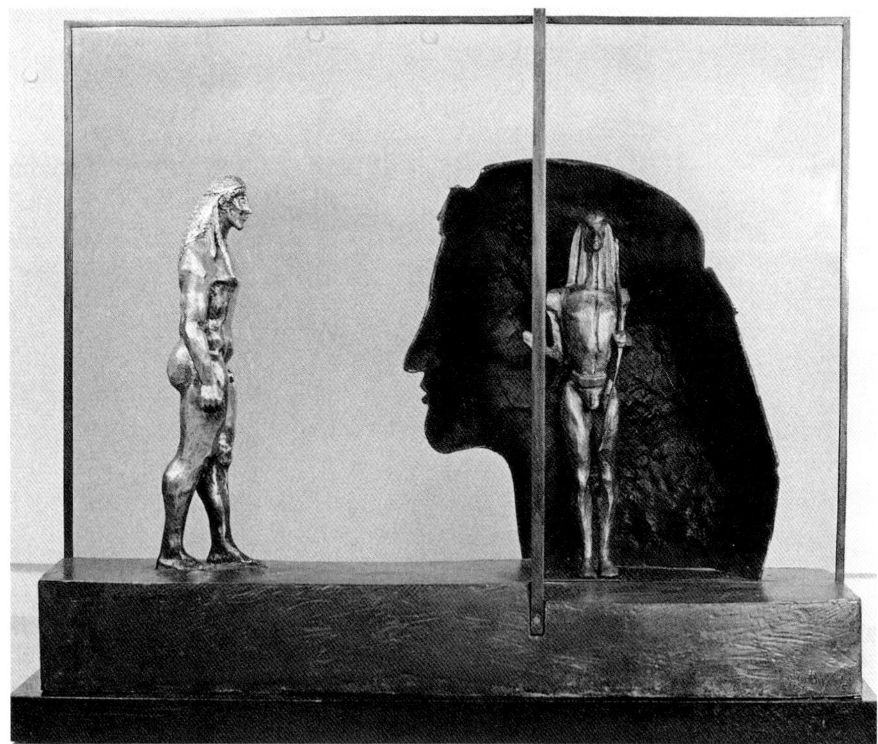

Figure 180. **KOUROS** (Cat. No. 659; 1969): head reflected.

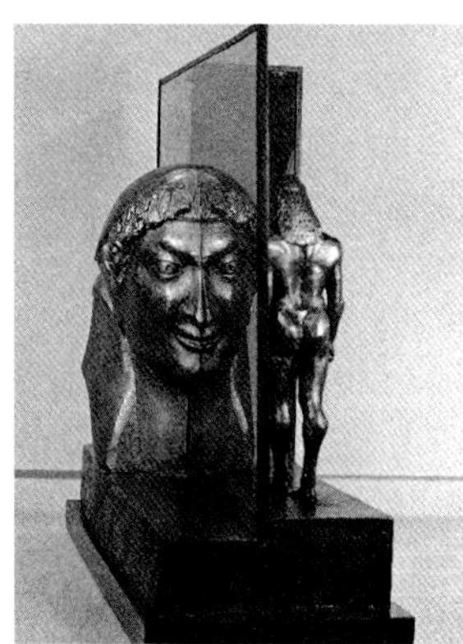

Figure 181. **KOUROS** (Cat. No. 659): large head, side view, but with Mantiklos in sharp focus.

the seated figure in *Discovery of Nautilus.* Since, however, the seated figure stares upward in a mixture of wonderment and uncertainty, perhaps he also symbolizes the sense of awe felt by early humans as they looked up into the maze of the sky. The erect figure penetrating the center of the nautilus would then be a suitable representation of the stance of man in classical Greece, boldly and proudly answering profound questions about the origin and nature of the universe. Such a view would be consistent with Ayrton's professed admiration for classical Greece, but one must be wary of single or simple answers to the creations of Ayrton's complex mind. The erect figure may well also represent Daedalus—and thus Ayrton—threading the nautilus and, thereby, revealing to us its mysteries. To my mind comes a fragment of Oliver Wendell Holmes's "The Chambered Nautilus":

> And every chambered cell,
> Where its dim dreaming life was wont to dwell,
> As the frail tenant shaped his growing shell,
> Before thee lies revealed.[20]

It is also worth noting that "Borges' much-noticed labyrinth, his symbol for the universe, is not the objective universe but the human mind,"[21] for Ayrton here gives visual reality to this concept, which Borges repeatedly pursued in his stories.

The classical context for *Kouros* (Cat. No. 659; Figures 180 and 181, Plate 36) is unmistakable. The large half head on the one side of the longer sheet of perspex clearly derives from a marble kouros found in Volomandra and dated in the middle of the sixth century B.C.E., [22] although Ayrton did not have photographs of it before him as he worked on this reproduction.[23] The resultant slight modifications are most noticeable in the shape of the nose and mouth. The mouth in particular bears a marked resemblance to that of the bronze kouros found at Peiraeus in 1959 (Richter 159 bis, figs. 478–80).[24]

The smaller, erect kouros on the other side of the perspex was originally a separate, unique bronze (Cat. No. 414). Cast solid in 1964, it was adapted from the marble kouros from Anavysos in the National Museum,

Athens (Richter 136, figs. 395–98 and 400–1). Ayrton had long had in his studio a photograph of the Anavysos kouros, which is sometimes referred to as the Croesus kouros and dates from "around 535 B.C."[25] Since the idea of originality as a goal was no more than a Romantic absurdity to Ayrton, he saw it as a mark of humility to borrow from and copy the great masters. Also, since he wanted a classical bronze kouros but knew that he would not be able to have an original one, he decided in 1964 to recreate the Croesus kouros, but in bronze rather than marble, employing as nearly as possible the tools and techniques used in ancient Greece for bronze casting.[26]

Hidden behind the longer perspex, inside the hollow half head and just to the right of the perpendicular sheet of perspex, is yet another kouros. Its inspiration was the Boston kouros, a "bronze statuette . . . inscribed with a dedication to Apollo by Mantiklos," which has been dated in the "first half of the seventh century B.C."[27] Ayrton, however, restored a bow to the left hand of this wasp-waisted kouros, whom he identified as "clearly an Apollo figure."[28] By placing these three kouroi together in a modern plastic context, Ayrton not only gave a virtuoso performance of imitating more than a century's development of Greek sculpture, he especially illustrated his belief that the past is reflected in the present. This enigmatic evocation of the past of Greek sculpture, with the three replicas in illusory relation to each other and the present moment, further contributes to our understanding of Ayrton's view of time.

The narrator of one of Borges's stories, "The Garden of the Forking Paths," says: "I thought of a labyrinth of labyrinths, of one sinuous spreading labyrinth that would encompass the past and the future and in some way involve the stars. Absorbed in these illusory images, I forgot my destiny of one pursued. I felt myself to be, for an unknown period of time, an abstract perceiver of the world."[29]

In a sense, all the reflector sculptures thus far discussed are such a labyrinth, absorbing the viewer in their illusory images. But in another sense, *Dioskouroi* (Cat. No. 701; 1970; Figures 182 and 183) most nearly expresses the concept imagined by Borges, for as figures of myth the Dioskouroi "encompass the past and the future" and, as constellations, they of course also "involve the stars." In Greek myth the Dioskouroi are pictured as inseparable twins, although Castor, like Clytemnestra, was the child of Tyndareus and Leda, while Pollux (also called Polydeuces), like Helen, was the offspring of Zeus and Leda. Since only one of the sons of Leda was fated to die, her son by Zeus was predictably chosen for immortality, but Pollux declined the honor unless he could share it with his brother, so Zeus set them both among the stars as Gemini, or Twins.[30]

The interrelationship between word and image involved in this reflector series and *Fabrications* has already been noted, but it merits further elaboration at this point, since "Enigma" (Ayrton 1973, 113–19) primarily concerns the concept of the *Dioskouroi* sculpture and a closely related one, *Mirror Twins* (Cat. No. 790; 1973; Figure 184). Close study of these two sculptures reveals not only Ayrton's ingenuity but especially how myth invades the creative process, which in turn perpetuates and extends the power of myth. In "Enigma" Ayrton explores "a mystery mirrored in the flesh by mirror twins."[31] Mirror twins are identical twins but with one fundamental distinction: their features, and sometimes their organs, mirror each other. Studies of twins, moreover, have revealed that mirror twins lack the customary fascination of infants between the ages of six and nine months with their own image in a mirror (114). In the sculptural *Mirror Twins* (Plate 52), Ayrton placed mirrored bronze statuettes on either side of a sheet of translucent perspex in an attempt visually to recreate the myth of the contest of two sets of twins, the Dioskouroi, Castor and Polydeuces (Pollux), and the twin sons of Poseidon, Idas and Lynceus. As this sculpture revolves on its turntable, Idas and Lynceus appear, vanish, and reappear in the reflective perspex, whereas the Dioskouroi, being bronze, remain constant.

Commenting on these two reflector sculptures involving twins, *Dioskouroi* (1970) and *Mirror Twins* (1973), Peter Cannon-Brookes calls attention to the three images the eye receives from the placement of a bronze figure on either side of the neutral density perspex: "that of the polished bronze figure on the side closest to the observer, the virtual image of that figure obtained by reflection and the transmitted image of the second bronze figure seen through the sheet."[32] Cannon-Brookes shows

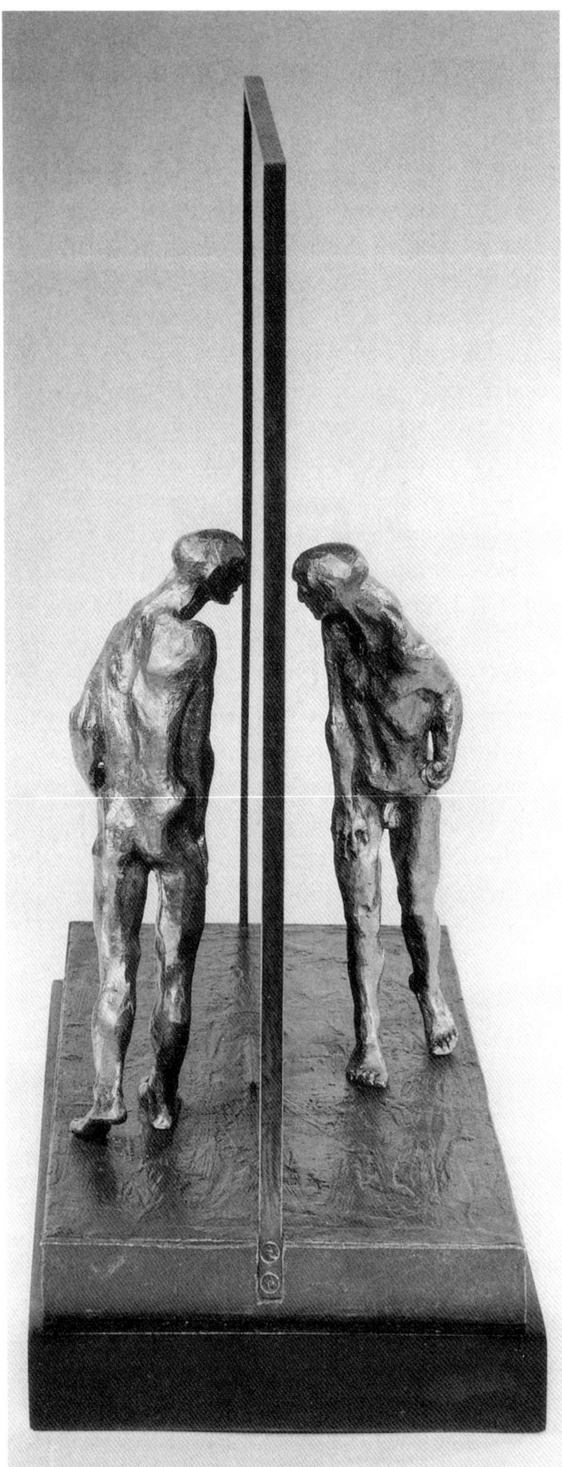

Figure 182. **DIOSKOUROI** (Cat. No. 701; 1970): along perspex. John Webb, FRPS/Brompton Studios.

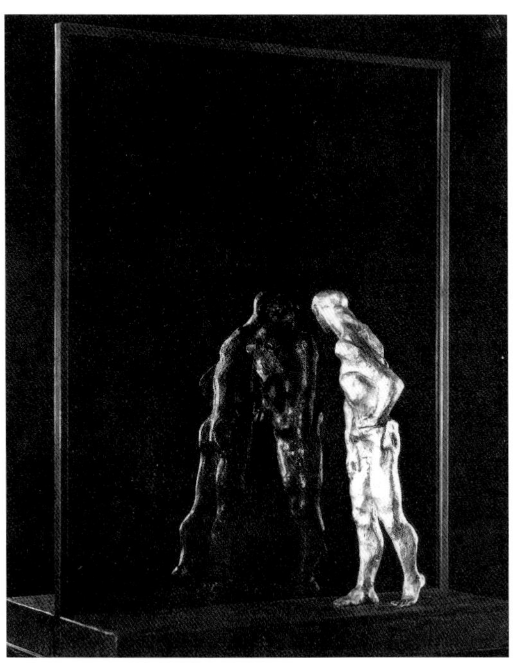

Figure 183. **DIOSKOUROI** (Cat. No. 701): reflected. Henry Morgan, Somerset.

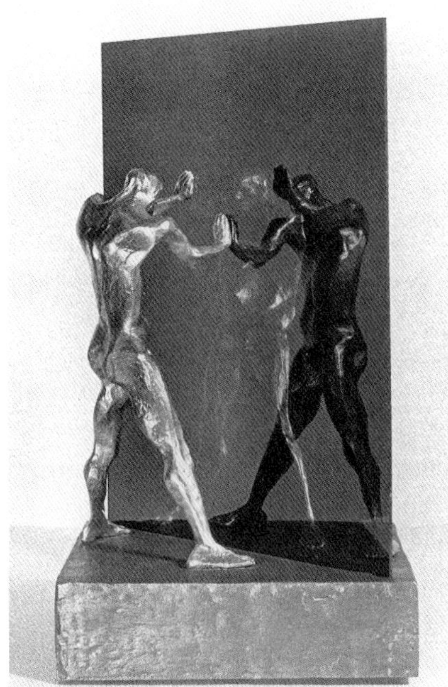

Figure 184. **MIRROR TWINS** (Cat. No. 790; 1973): reflected.

that this unusual creation by Ayrton goes beyond technological novelty to significant achievement: "The use of neutral density perspex ensures that the virtual image and the transmitted image are of the same intensity and when the reflector is turned on its vertical axis a complex changing interplay between three images is obtained. What could be merely an interesting scientific toy is, in the hands of Michael Ayrton, the means by which he challenged the generally accepted limits of reality."[33]

The opening paragraph of "Enigma" sets the stage: "TO PENETRATE the mirror, as Alice did when she went through the looking glass and as Orphée did when Cocteau took him by the hand of Death . . . is an act of exploration. It is also a mystery mirrored in the flesh by mirror twins" (114). After retranslating St. Paul's famous assertion, "Now we see through a glass darkly" (I Corinthians 13:12), to read "Now we see in an enigma by means of a mirror" (114), Ayrton proceeded to solve the enigma by words and images revolving around the myth of the Dioskouroi. Recalling the myth of their less famous twin cousins, Idas and Lynceus, whose story and fate were intertwined with those of the Dioskouroi, Ayrton revealed that, through his discovery of the neutral density perspex, "the twin sons of Poseidon could be seen to merge with the Dioskouroi as a memory of the relationship of mortality mirrored in divinity. And so I made images in bronze of the Dioskouroi and set them face to face on either side of the mirror and this mirror I contained in a bronze frame consistent with their symbol. . . . In this sculpture, which I also made to revolve, Castor and Polydeuces reflect one another and . . . Idas and Lynceus show themselves as inextricably confused with one another, vanishing and reappearing, whereas the Dioskouroi remain constant" (118–19). Through Ayrton's ingenuity, his *Dioskouroi* pass through the dividing mirror, when the light is right, to form an illusory union, as their images merge in reflection to resurrect the ghosts of their cousins. Momentarily, this reflected image seems every bit as real as the heavenly constellation, but this illusion is easily broken by an alteration of light or the line of vision. Enigmatically and ambiguously, Ayrton conjoins past and present, myth and reality.

Although the Dioskouroi may seem far removed from the myth of Daedalus, very little of Ayrton's work throughout this period was not related in his mind to Daedalus, even if only tangentially or subconsciously. Moreover, in speaking of "mortality mirrored in divinity," Ayrton reminds us of the dual nature of humankind, which suggests other symbolic parallels. For example, in his Minotaur sculptures, the duality involves humanity and bestiality rather than divinity. One must also allow the fertile mind of a creative artist to pursue whatever direction the creative daimon might lead, whether or not it leads to the Daedalus myth and the maze concept. Since, moreover, Ayrton himself chose to include *Dioskouroi* and *Mirror Twins* in *The Translucent Maze Sequence,* there is no reason to argue that they are unrelated to the maze.

Ayrton's interest in mirrors and reflected images in the early 1970s brought to a central position ideas that were present in his thought at least as early as 1966, when he created *Mirror Maze* (Cat. No. 596; chapter 5), and it is implied in his description of the maze built by Daedalus for the Minotaur: "his eyes, reading the walls of his prison, registered again their double image" (1967, 198). Even before he developed the idea further with the use of polished bronze panels in one of the central chambers at Arkville, the chamber housing the *Daedalus/Icarus Matrix,* he wrote of the significance that he attached to the mirrored images in a letter written in December 1967. In reply to a friend's detailed, serious comments on *The Maze Maker,* Ayrton wrote:

> The Maze is both hard and soft; certainly it is the prison of the personality and formed by each individual in his own terms, but it is not only that. It is formed . . . of *circumstances and experiences.* These impinge from without and are extra-personal. They are hard. Hence the image of the mirror-polished or curved walls which occupy part of each maze. Your [*sic*] disregard, for some reason, the important factor of the mirror image, the perpetual double and multiplication of the double theme—the imprisoning prisoner, the invented inventor, ant and man, microcosm and macrocosm. These images perhaps relate to Eliot's "time conquered by time" and my way of interpreting it.

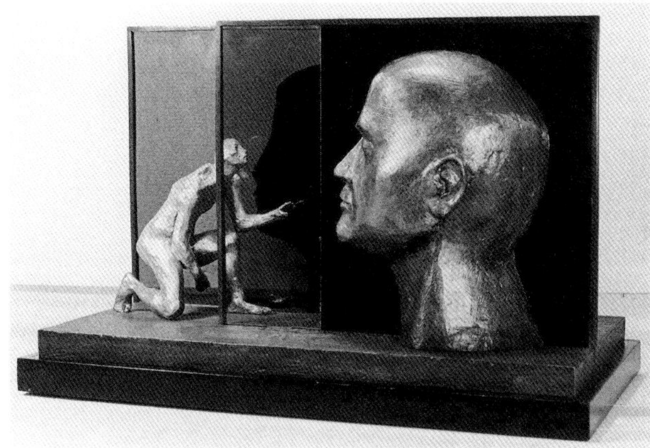

Figure 185. **ENCOUNTER** (Cat. No. 682; 1970): side view, male.

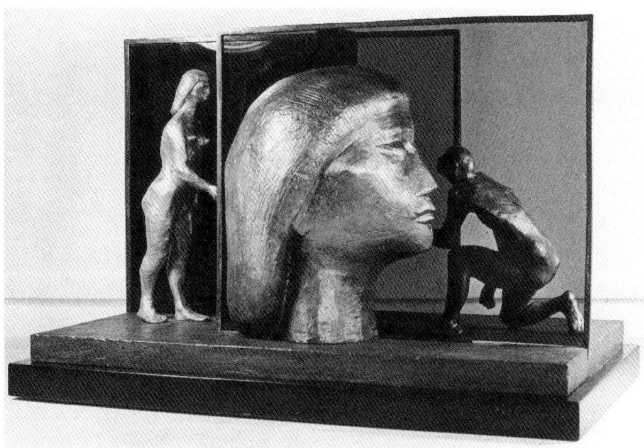

Figure 187. **ENCOUNTER** (Cat. No. 682): side view, female.

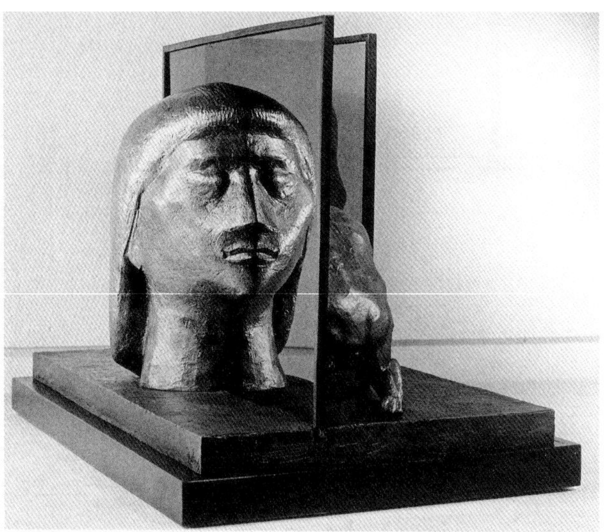

Figure 186. **ENCOUNTER** (Cat. No. 682): female head reflected.

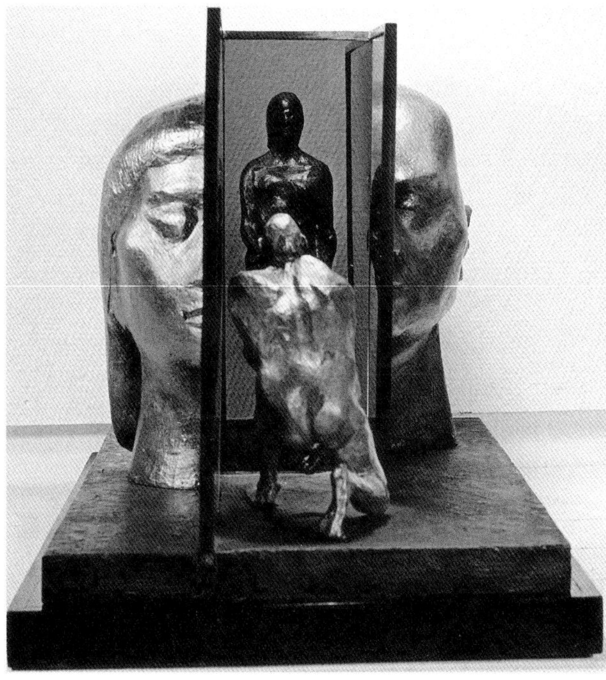

Figure 188. **ENCOUNTER** (Cat. No. 682): frontal view of heads and female figure.

Although these words were written in a letter dated 16 December 1967, i.e., before Ayrton's discovery of either the neutral density perspex or Borges's stories, they clearly are appropriate to the reflector sculptures, since these sculptures give visual reality to the artist's ideas. In the same letter, commenting on Daedalus's [i.e., Ayrton's] view (in *The Maze Maker*) of time as a helix, he remarked: "If time is a helix, then significant events are eternally coexistent at different levels and many of them will mirror each other in the polished surfaces of the helix. Memory is kept at the centre. . . . I recognise that this is a sculptural or visual and not a verbal conception and that my use of words may have failed here."

In his reflector sculptures, Ayrton successfully extended the ideas for which he found words inadequate. Likewise, in *Contained Heads* (Cat. No. 707; 1970; Figures 196, 199, 200, and 203, Plate 44) he expressed similar ideas, without the use of the translucent perspex, although he again employed the principle of rotation upon a fixed base. As one turns the head on its base, one discovers an opening in the back of the head and another head within. Further rotation reveals new faces, new images. The multiple interior heads, which in 1972 gained independence from their cephalic case as *Tricephalic* (Cat. No. 758; Figure 202), evoke an early Celtic representation, in stone, of a tricephalic deity, which was found in the British Isles around 1956 and later acquired by the British Museum.[34] Although one might be tempted to interpret this sculpture as an expression of the complexities of Ayrton's own mind or to find its inspiration in Borges's "The Circular Ruins" (in which the dreamer discovers that he himself is the dreamed one),[35] Ayrton himself declared in a letter that "it came directly from *The Celtic Deity* and from my own feeling that everyone's personal maze is in his own brain (I have just finished a new sculpture even more directly about this) and that we all have within our heads, to put it very simply, several personalities, intelligences, or what you will."[36] It is an interesting coincidence that Leonard Baskin also produced a tricephalic image, *D., H., and J. Hopfer, about 1530,* a print dating from 1964. Perhaps he also had seen the endpiece of *Antiquity* that inspired Ayrton's image.

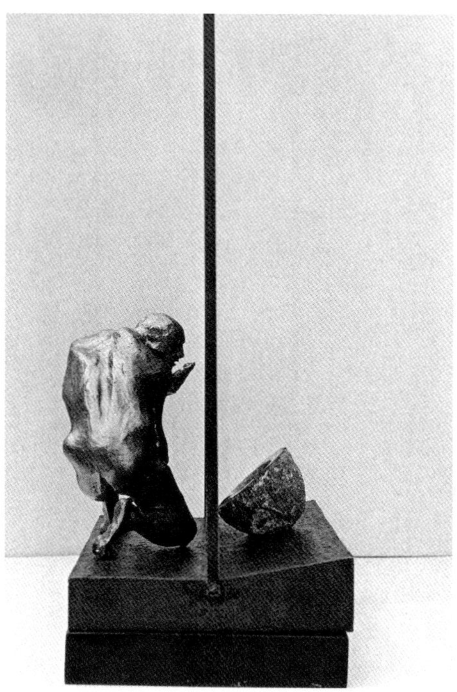

Figure 189. **GEODE** (Cat. No. 703; 1970): along perspex.

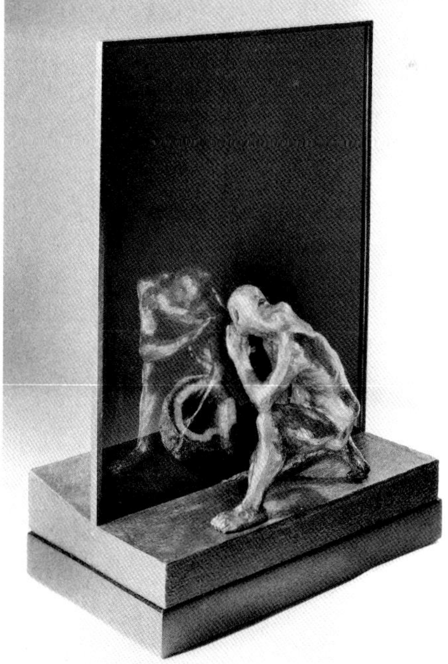

Figure 190. **GEODE** (Cat. No. 703): figure reflected. John Webb, FRPS/Brompton Studios.

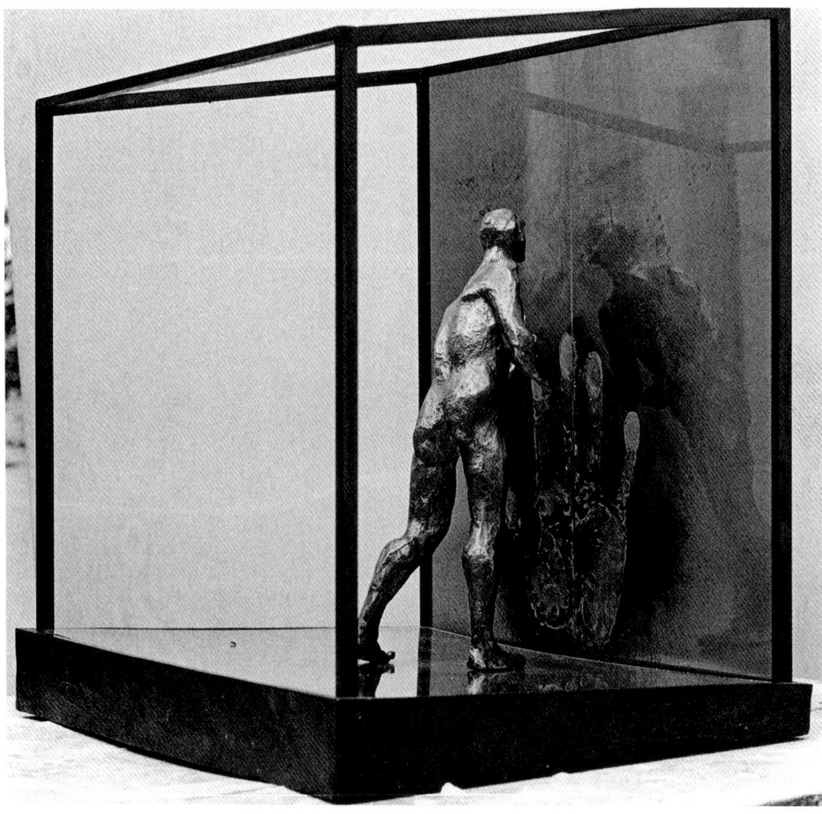

Figure 191. **QUEST** (Cat. No. 716; 1970).

Contained Heads was anticipated earlier in the year by *Captive* (Cat. No. 700; Figure 205), in which a single smaller head appears to float suspended in the hollow casement of a larger head. The interior head, moreover, resembles the small inset heads of *Reflex I* and *II* (Cat. Nos. 658 and 668; above). When considered in the light of the artist's foregoing statement and in relation to a contemporaneous bronze, *Personal Janus* (Cat. No. 706; Figure 206), perhaps *Captive* also can be seen as another expression of Ayrton's own captivity in the maze and in the myth.

Personal Janus portrays a Janus figure at the top of a small, nearly square, column that strongly resembles a classical herm. The symbolic significance of *Personal Janus* is obvious, for the Janus figure combines the artist's own head and the head of the Minotaur. It is clear, however, from one of Ayrton's sketch books, that he did not begin with this conception; it apparently evolved naturally from an earlier idea. Its evolution illustrates anew the powerful role of myth in the creative process. The sketch book, dated around 1968,[37] contains several sketches of a double figure, entitled either "Double Figure" or "Double Key Figure." In sketches of the former, one sees the Minotaur on the right and an unidentifiable human head on the left, each totally a part of the other, revealing once again Ayrton's view of the Minotaur as another aspect of the human personality. The sketch of the latter, "Double Key Figure," is less fully developed, but the intertwining of bestial and human characteristics appears, in intention, to be more intricate. The human figure in "Double Key Figure" is none other than the oracle.[38] By combining these two powerful images into a Janus-headed figure, holding the numinous potency of the oracle in tension with the hybrid bestiality of the Minotaur, Ayrton created a new image that reverberates with intensity, ambiguity, and evocative force. From Ayrton's own identification with Daedalus and, to only a

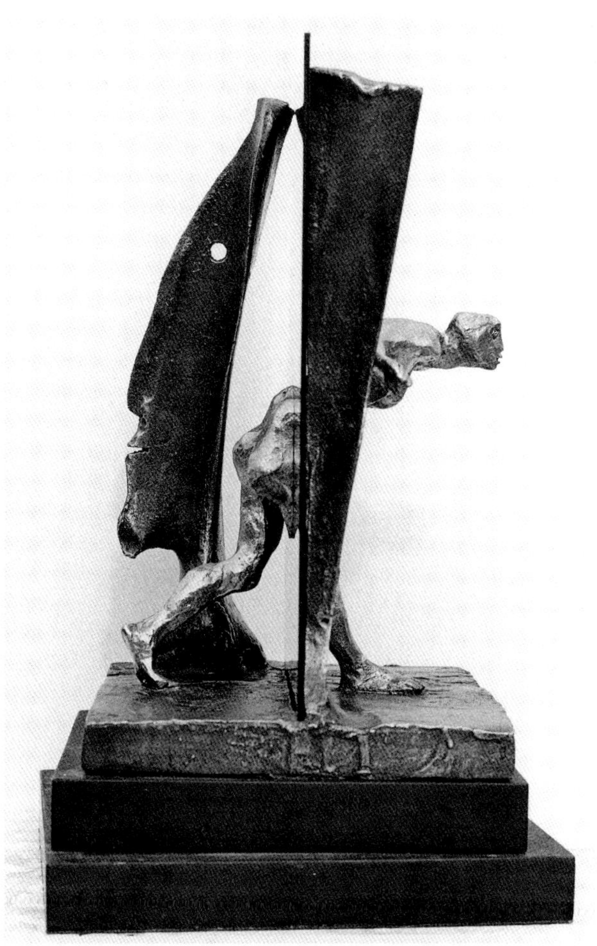

Figure 192. **ENTRANCE** (Cat. No. 717; 1970): side view.

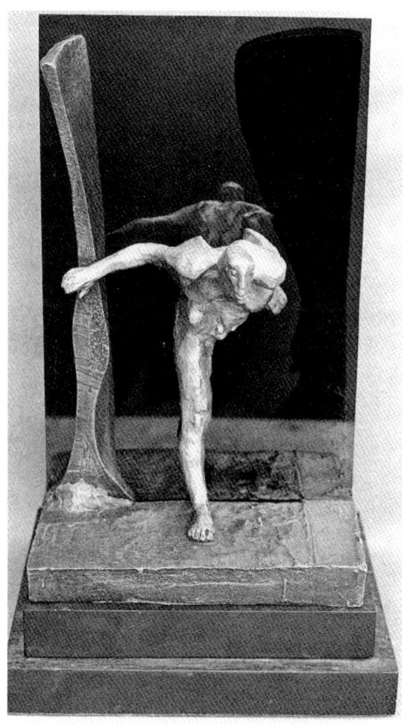

Figure 193. **ENTRANCE** (Cat. No. 717): frontal view of figure.

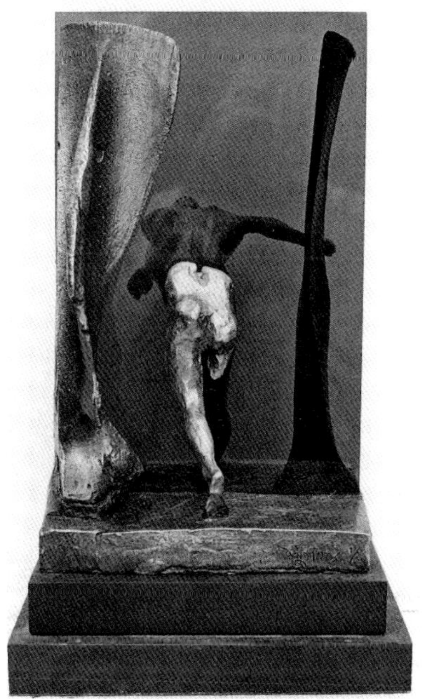

Figure 194. **ENTRANCE** (Cat. No. 717): back view.

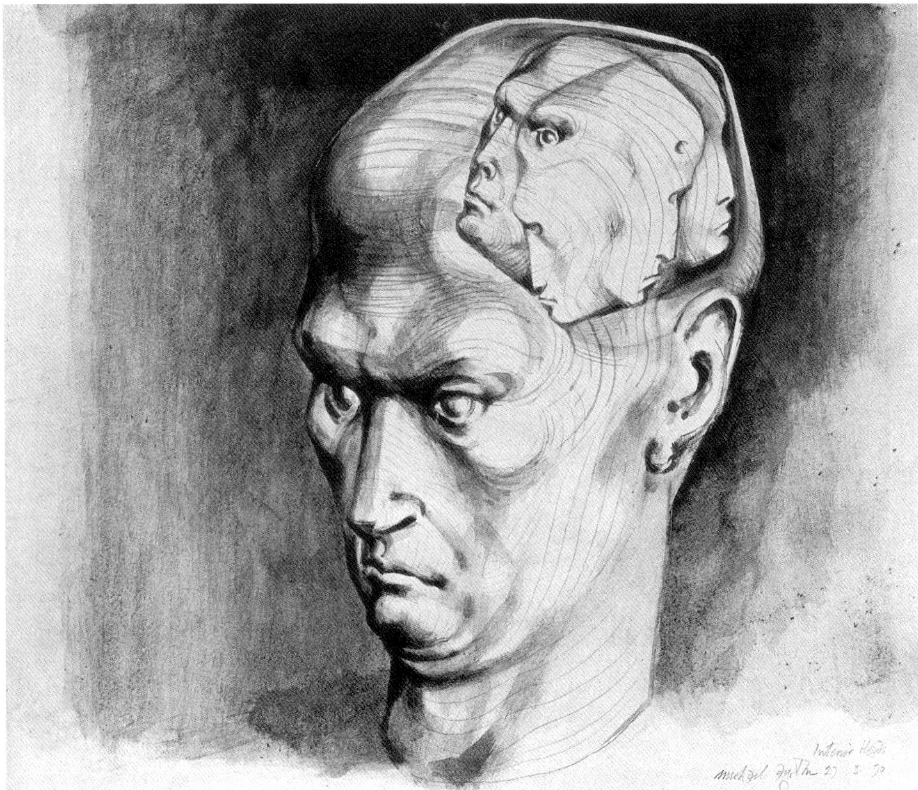

Figure 195. **STUDY FOR CONTAINED HEADS III** (Cat. No. 699; 27 March 1970).

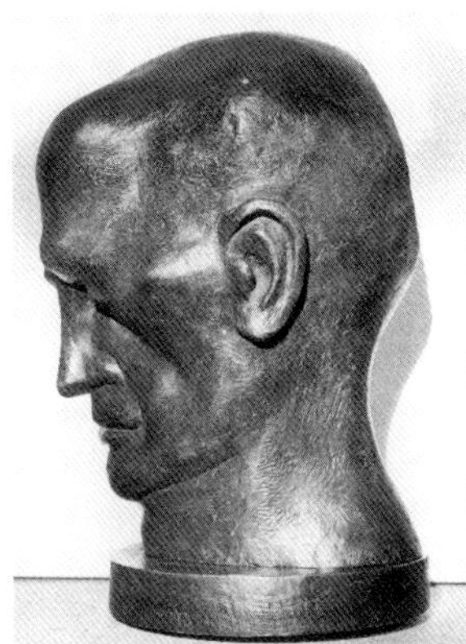

Figure 196.
CONTAINED HEADS
(Cat. No. 707; 1970): side view.

slightly lower degree, with the Minotaur, out of these sketches evolved this 1970 self-portrait in bronze, *Personal Janus,* in which he paired himself with the Minotaur.

Leonard Baskin created a similar Janus figure, *Sacrifice of Isaac,* as a woodcut in 1960. The face of Isaac is paired with the face of Abraham, combining the father and son into a single entity, with age facing in one direction and youth the other way. Since Ayrton created a new dimension of the myth with the rumor that Daedalus had fathered the Minotaur with Pasiphaë (1967, 114–15), *Personal Janus* could also express this new version of the myth. It is more likely, however, that the Minotaur face merely embodies the "brute part of man" (1967, 127).

Virtually contemporaneous with *Captive* and *Personal Janus* is another key sculpture that is both a personal statement and a kaleidoscopic chronicle of Ayrton's involvement with the myth of Daedalus. *Point of Departure* (Cat. No. 704; Figure 208, Plates 39–41), said Ayrton, refers to the beginning of Daedalus's flight and is related to a collage of the same title (Cat. No. 470; Figure 207), which evolved through three stages, from 1962 to 1966.[39] In the bronze *Point of Departure,* a wall separates a crouching Minotaur[40] from an erect male figure who has his back turned to the wall. The male figure in this narrative sculpture obviously represents Daedalus, but it is highly significant that this bronze figure is a nude self-portrait of the artist himself; i.e., he is none other than Michael Ayrton identifying with and representing Daedalus. The fact that he is nude may indicate full self-disclosure, that the identification is complete. Another striking feature about this work is that a golden Icarus (who resembles *Icarus Ascendant,* Cat. Nos. 137 and 321; see chapter 4) is launching himself from the chamber in which the Minotaur, alarmed, crouches. Next to Icarus the wall bulges spherically, while behind him the wall takes on the appearance of melting, dripping wax. In the other chamber, all alone, is Daedalus-Ayrton. Responsible for the existence of both Icarus and the Minotaur—and, to

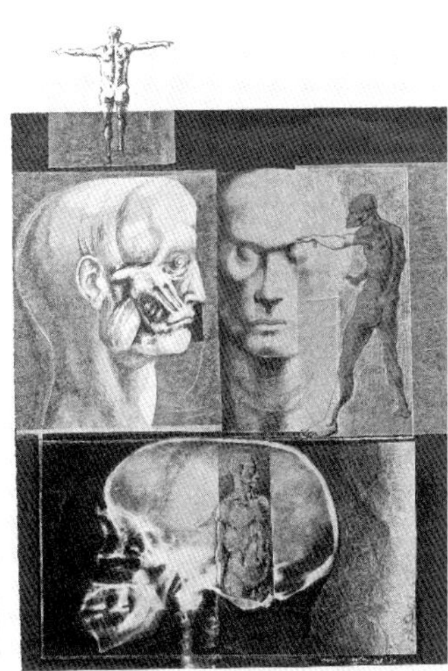

Figure 197. **JOURNEY THROUGH THE HEAD** (Cat. No. 715; October 1970).

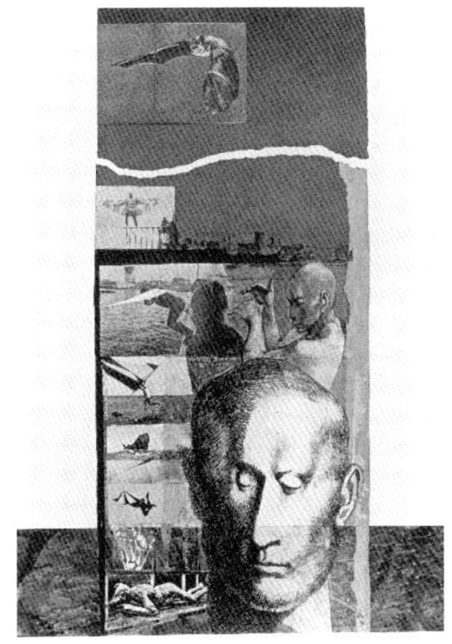

Figure 198. **L'OISEAU CHANT AVEC SES DOIGTS** (Cat. No. 751; March 1972).

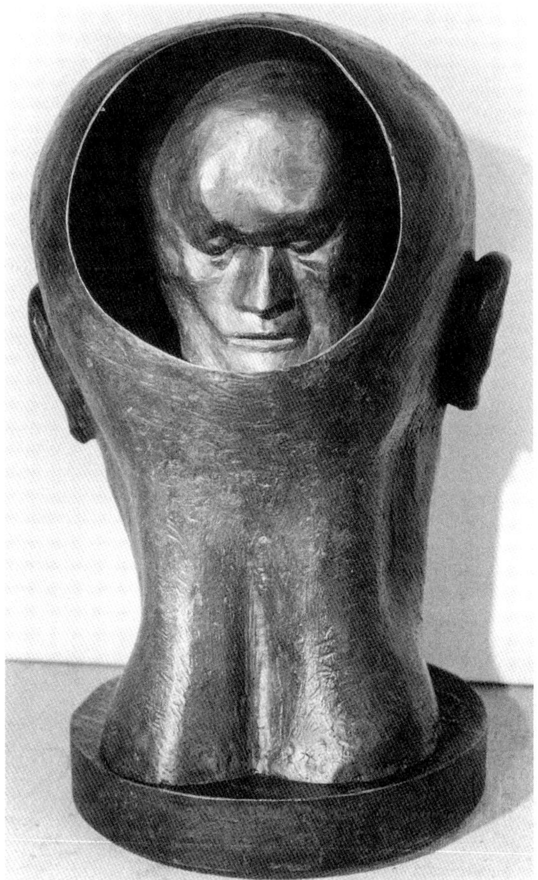

Figure 199. **CONTAINED HEADS** (Cat. No. 707; 1970): back view, downcast head.

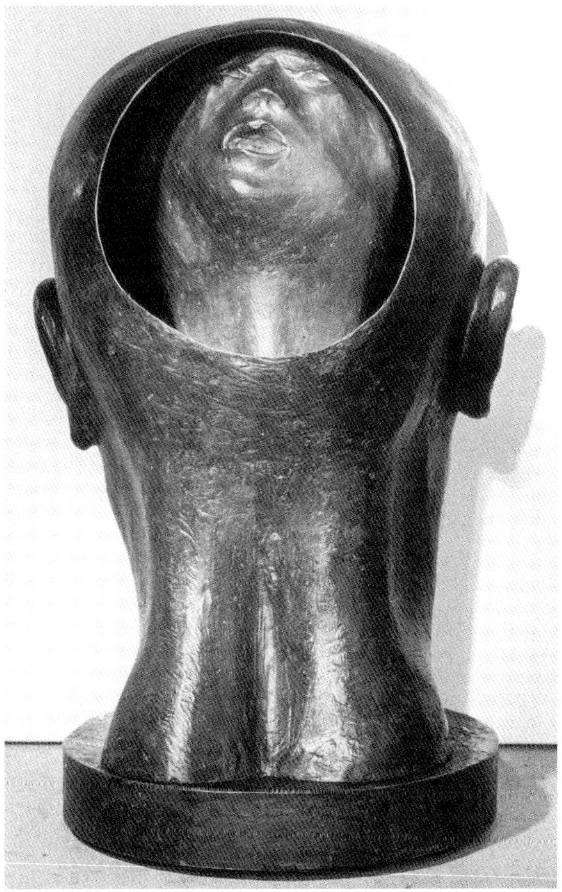

Figure 200. **CONTAINED HEADS** (Cat. No. 707): back view, upcast head.

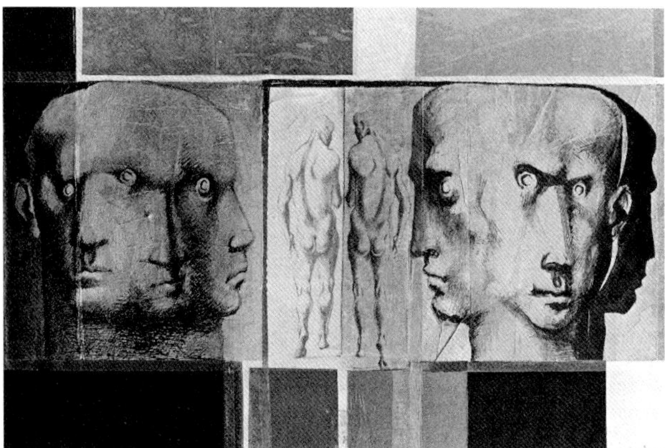

Figure 201. **TRICEPHALIC** (Cat. No. 750; March 1972).

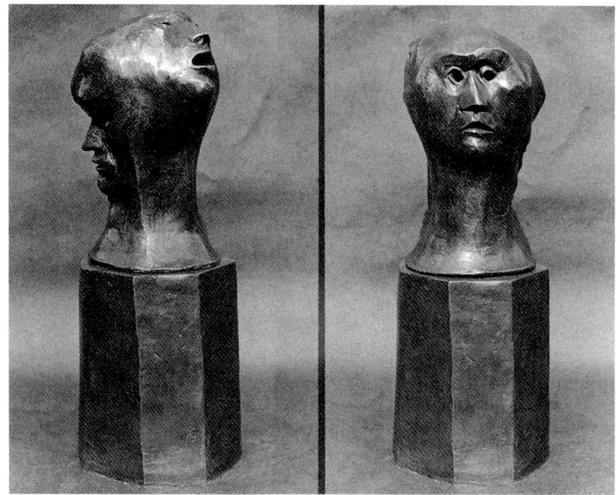

Figure 202. **TRICEPHALIC** (Cat. No. 758; 1972): two views on one plate.

a considerable degree, for their fate—he is cut off from them, brooding in isolation on what he has wrought. And in another wall of his chamber, there is a circular opening dominated by a double axe, the *labrys,* the potent Minoan symbol found during the excavations of Crete—where it appears not only as actual bronze axe heads of varying sizes but also carved into the walls of the palace of Minos at Knossos and painted on walls and such other places as the exterior of the famous sarcophagus from Hagia Triadha.[41] Clearly, *Point of Departure* expresses Ayrton's condition fully as much as it narrates the mythical event of the departure from Crete. The ambiguity of this work is heightened by its contemporaneity with *Captive* and *Personal Janus,* as well as with *Sun Maze* (Cat. No. 721; 1970; Plates 37 and 38).

At about this same time Ayrton was at work on a further commission for the Catskill estate of Armand Erpf. He had been asked to design a second maze for the area at the opposite end of the corridor of urns leading into the *Arkville Maze* (Cat. No. 673; see chapter 6). This maze, however, was to be a floor maze in the manner of the penitential Christian mazes imbedded in the floors of many European cathedrals, including cathedrals at Amiens and Chartres. Mr. Erpf, whom the artist described as "a very pious Catholic," wanted to illustrate the continuity of the maze pattern into Christianity,[42] but although he may have had religious motives for commissioning this second maze, Erpf also revealed thereby his seriousness about the significance of the maze concept. There can therefore be no doubt that his first commission went beyond mere ostentation or eccentricity, that the maze expressed his inner, deeply felt views about the nature and meaning of human experience.

Ayrton's sketches for *The Jerusalem Maze at Arkville* (Cat. No. 718; Plate 29) are dated October 1969, although the floor maze itself was not completed until the following year, less than a year before Erpf's death. This maze is a twenty-six-foot octagon set within a rectangular piazza. Based on the Christian maze in Amiens Cathedral (see catalogue), this octagonal design is fairly typical of medieval mazes and is related to the polygonal pulpits such as Giovanni Pisano designed:

> The square of the earth may be geometrically if imperfectly related to the circle as the symbol representing heaven (self-enclosed and without angles, since God has neither beginning nor end) by "squaring the circle," an insoluble geometrical problem which had obsessed mathematicians for many centuries. The nearest practical resolution of this problem is the polygon which, although it can only be an approximation, creates a union of both symbols (Ayrton 1970c, 28).

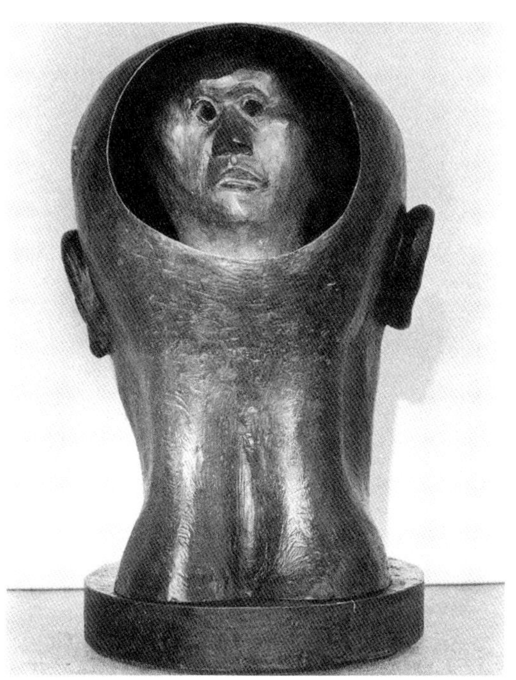

Figure 203. **CONTAINED HEADS** (Cat. No. 707; 1970): back view, direct face.

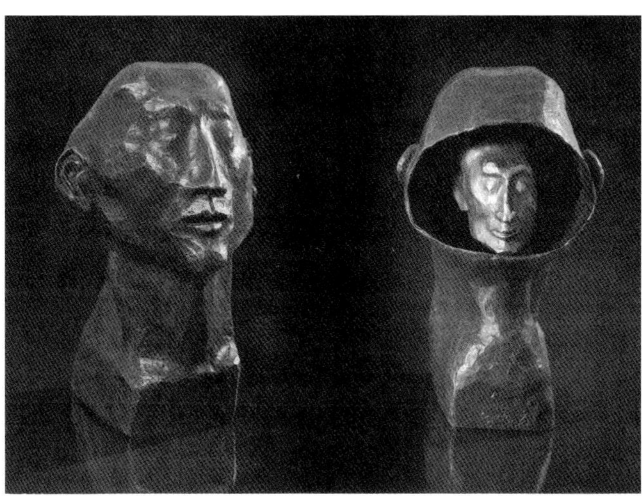

Figure 205. **CAPTIVE** (Cat. No. 700; 1970): front and back views on one plate. Henry Morgan, Somerset.

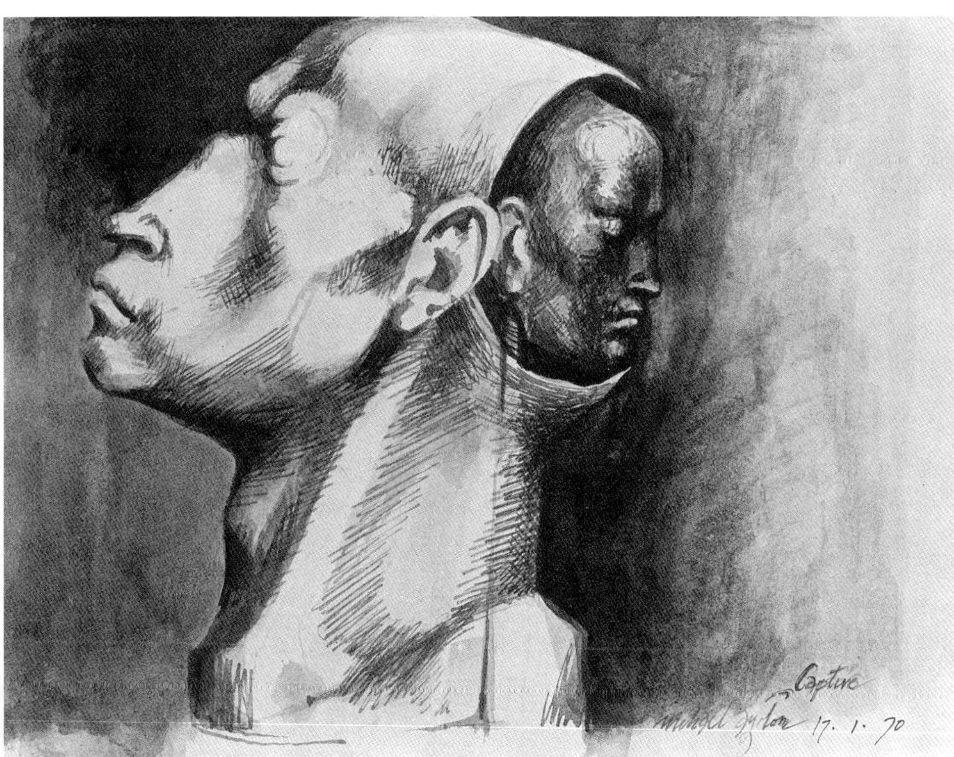

Figure 204. **CAPTIVE** (Cat. No. 680; 17 January 1970).

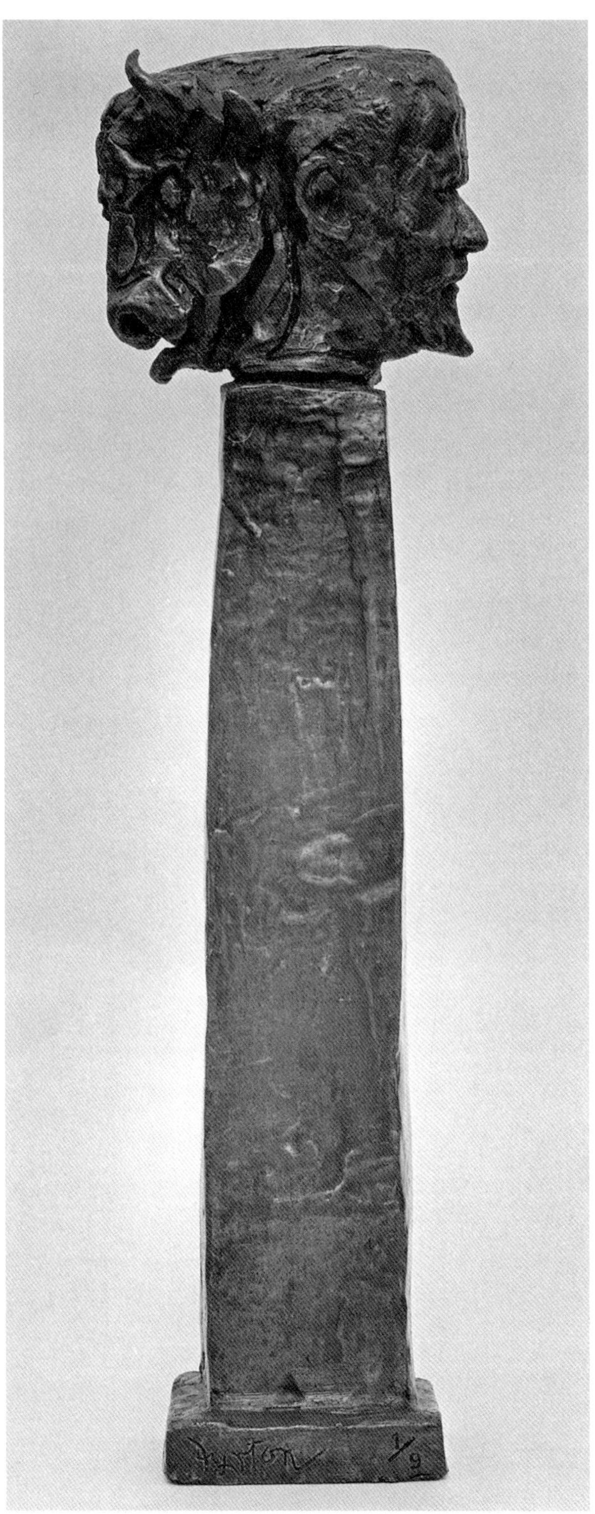

Figure 206. **PERSONAL JANUS** (Cat. No. 706; 1970).

Thus the artist once again succeeded in satisfying his patron's demands while drawing upon and expressing his own ideas and experiences. One may suspect, moreover, that his choice of red brick to delineate the unicursal maze pattern on the floor was rooted in the myth of Ariadne's red thread, although he was well aware of the fact that a Christian would naturally see a different symbolism in the color (i.e., the blood of Christ). There is, of course, also an obvious link with the reddish bricks employed in the walls of the *Arkville Maze* (Cat. No. 673), but it would do Ayrton an injustice to think that this obvious reason for the choice of bricks would be the sole explanation.

At the far end of the piazza, beyond the floor maze and in front of a stand of trees, there was to have been a final sculpture. The sketches for *The Jerusalem Maze at Arkville* (Cat. No. 718) reveal that this sculpture was intended to be 8 x 10 feet and set upon a four-foot-high plinth. *End Maze I, II* and *III* (Cat. Nos. 688–690; see Figure 210) were maquettes for this bronze, which represented for Ayrton his concluding expression on the ideas explored earlier in *Triptych I, II* and *III* (*Emerging Figure*) (Cat. Nos. 597 and 616–618; see chapter 5) and *Penetrator I, II* and *III* (Cat. Nos. 660, 664, 665; see above).[43] As in the earlier bronzes, a figure passes through the wall, but without effort or restraint, for in this last stage in the progression through the maze the individual (homo sapiens) passes out of the maze and into the final maze of death: *End Maze* represents the problem of the maze essentially solved and, therefore, it is by implication posthumous.[44]

Sketches for the emerging figure in *End Maze* also contain a number of revealing observations by Ayrton. On 8 October 1969 he wrote on his first sketch: "Icarus + Minotaur emerged = D. = Homo sap.; Vitruvian circle; Wingform as maze matrix; horns fallen." The following day, on the second sketch, he noted: "Relate Icarus to Daedalus as one. The Minotaur, horns fallen to the ground at his feet, emerges fully human: as part of the Maze Maker [that has] come out from the maze. Contain all in one figure. Head of figure to be heads of father and son combined. Keep a trace of Minotaur in torso." Several sketches later, on 19 October 1969, he added these notations: "Circular maze deeply engraved *behind* figure. Head at center. Double axe form—arcs through navel and penis."

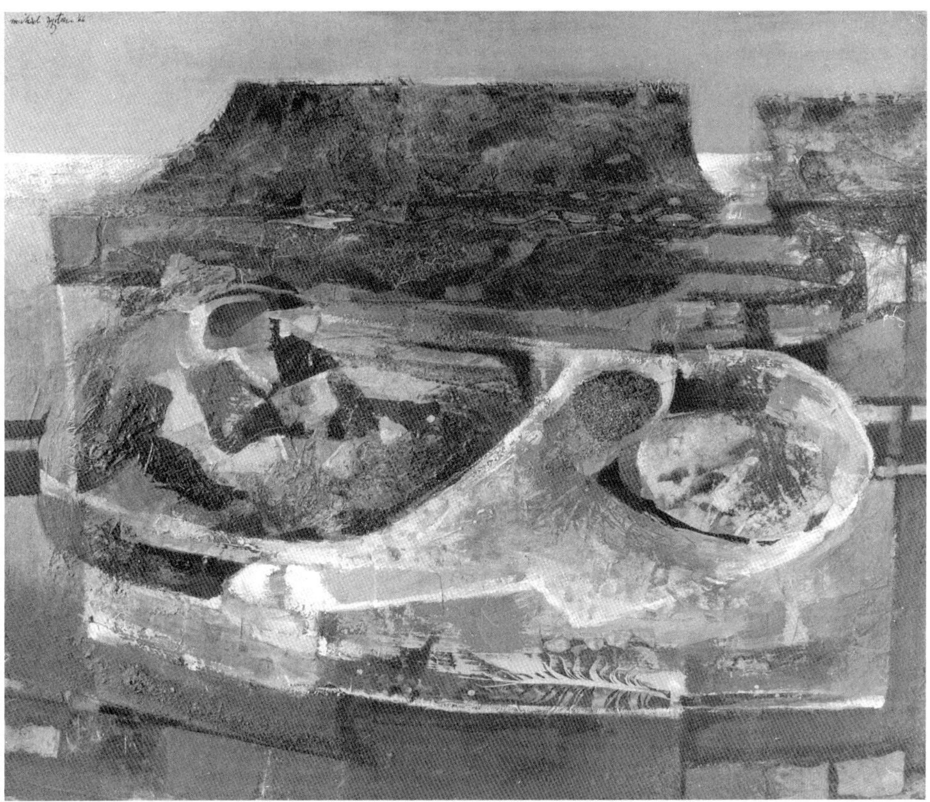

Figure 207. **POINT OF DEPARTURE** (Cat. No. 470; 1962–66); final state, 1966. J. S. Lewinski, London.

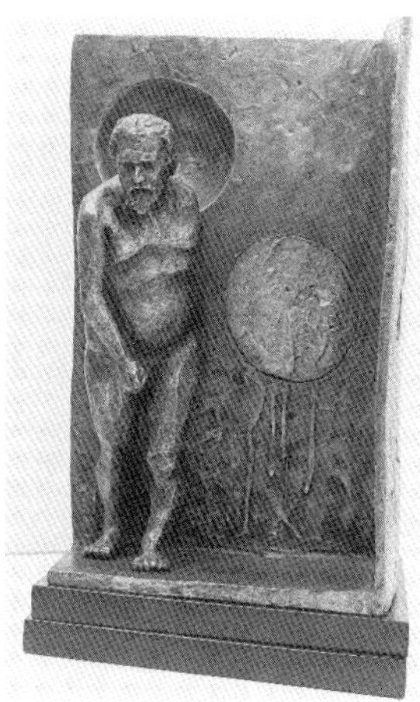

Figure 208. **POINT OF DEPARTURE** (Cat. No. 704; 1970): Daedalus.

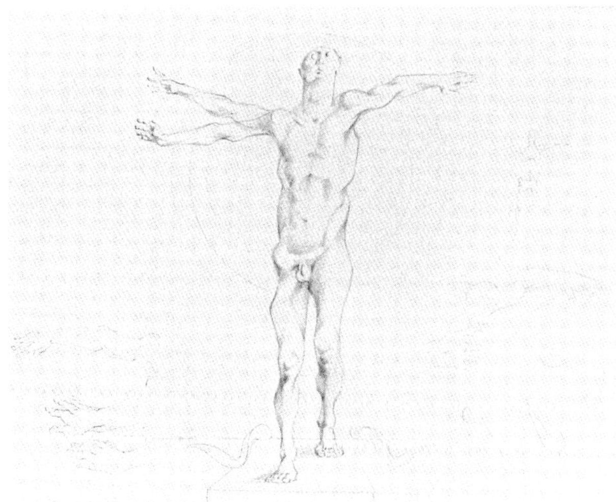

Figure 209. **STUDY FOR END MAZE I** (Cat. No. 676; 10 November 1969).

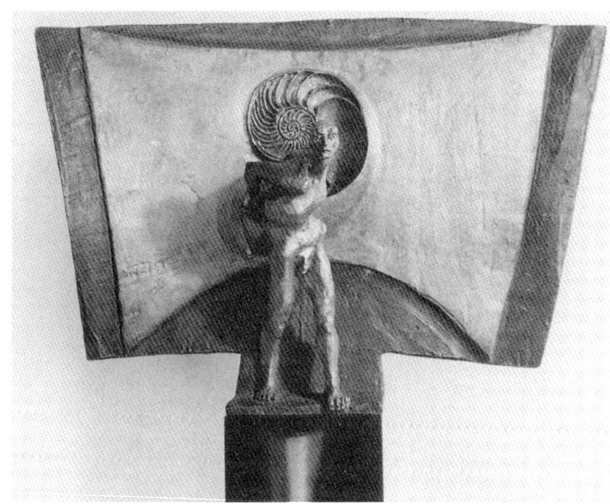

Figure 210. **END MAZE II** (Cat. No. 689; 1970). J. S. Lewinski, London.

The maquettes thus are richly illuminated by the artist's notations on his preliminary sketches. *End Maze I* (Cat. No. 688; Plate 30) portrays an erect figure, with arms outstretched, against two concentric circles incised in a bronze sheet that clearly suggests the Minoan double-axe motif. At his feet, at first unnoticed by the casual observer, lies a pair of horns. The figure must represent the Minotaur emerging from the maze as human, freed from his animal bondage, as well as signifying Daedalus, Icarus, and Everyman. *End Maze II* and *III* (Cat. Nos. 689 and 690; Figure 210, Plate 31), however, show no trace of horns, revealing that the emerging figure is definitely human. The nautilus has replaced the incised circles and the emergent figure, like Ayrton, still appears caught in the coils of the maze, although the artist clearly intended that we should view this as the effortless entrance into death. Mr. Erpf himself passed through the wall into the final maze of death before he had a chance to choose among the maquettes, so the final sculpture never materialized at Arkville. Leaving it behind him, like an unfinished symphony, Ayrton turned his attention once again to the Minotaur.

Minotaur Risen (Cat. Nos. 722 and 723; Figures 214 and 215, Plate 42) was only one of many studies arising out of Ayrton's fixation on this figure of myth who once had also been Picasso's concern. An important development in his treatment of the Minotaur was a set of etchings (Cat. Nos. 726–735; 1971; Figures 216–226). Just as many of Picasso's etchings were a response to the acknowledged master of etching, Rembrandt (see chapter 3), so Ayrton's etchings of *The Minotaur* were a response and a challenge to Picasso. Whereas Picasso depicted the Minotaur in many different settings, but with the Minotaur always a mature creature, Ayrton chose to demonstrate his own prowess by chronicling the entire life cycle of the Minotaur. This series of ten etchings is the only known representation of the entire history of the Minotaur. Never before had anyone attempted to portray, in art or literature, the life of the Minotaur from embryo to adulthood. This unique achievement received favorable critical acclaim: "Surely among the most powerful graphic representations he has ever done, the series portrays the man-beast from birth to tortured maturity. In the course of it he discovers by stages his elements of humanity and brutishness and is

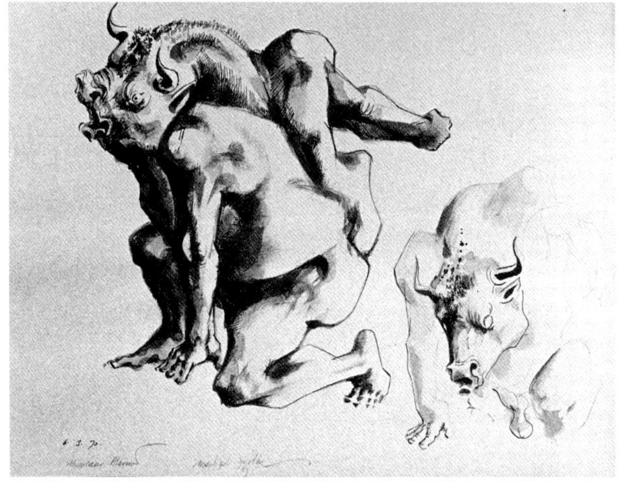

Figure 211. **MINOTAUR ALARMED [II]**
(Cat. No. 692; 6 March 1970).

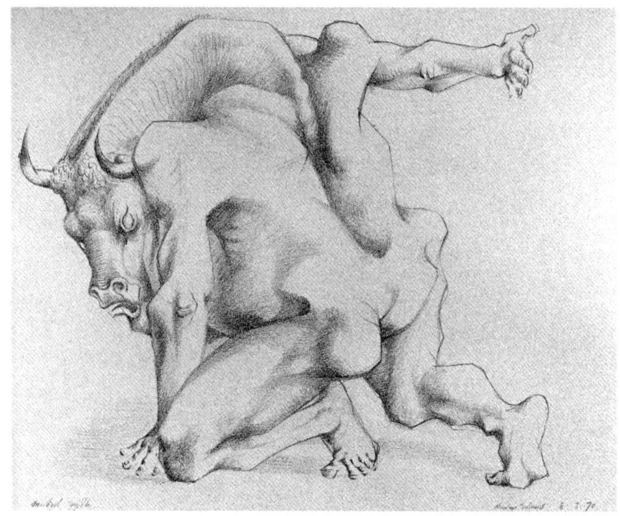

Figure 212. **MINOTAUR DISTRAUGHT**
(Cat. No. 693; 8 March 1970).

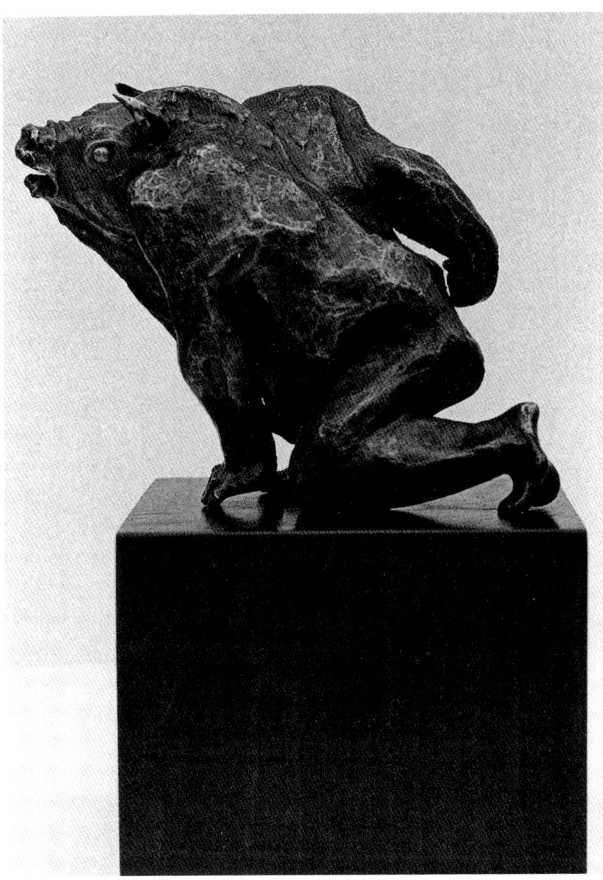

Figure 213. **MINOTAUR ALARMED** (Cat. No. 705; 1970).

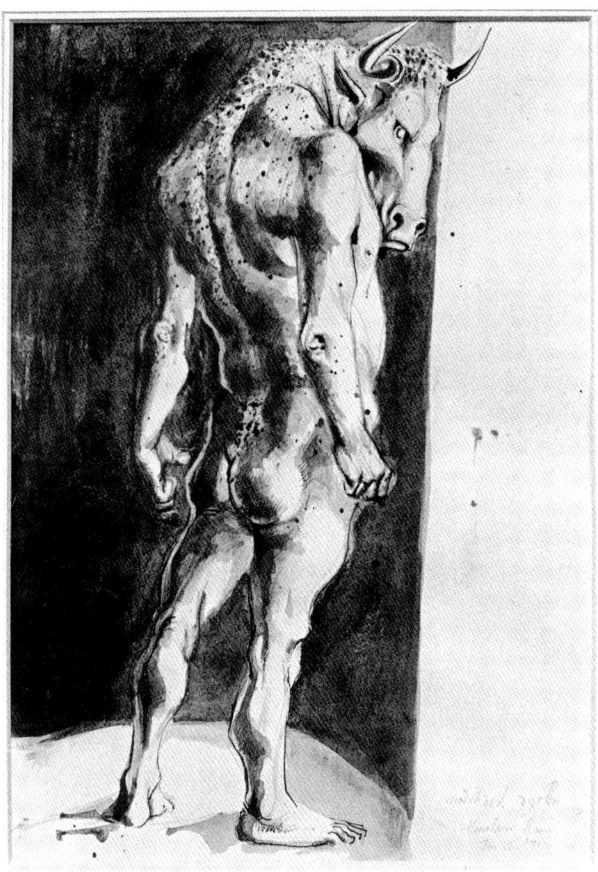

Figure 214. **MINOTAUR RISEN** (Cat. No. 722; 2 January 1971).

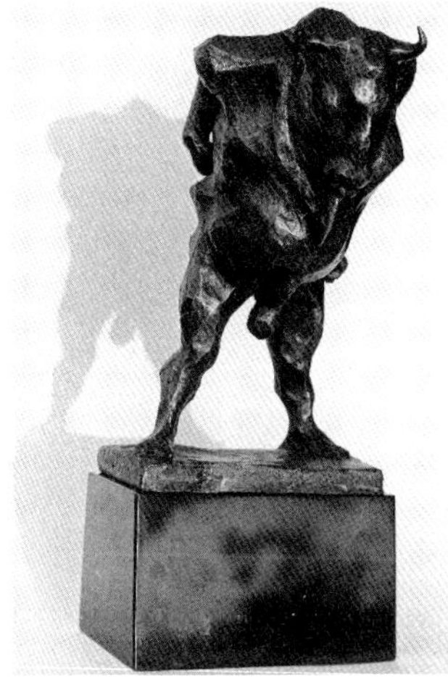

Figure 215. **MINOTAUR RISEN** (Cat. No. 723; 1971): frontal view.

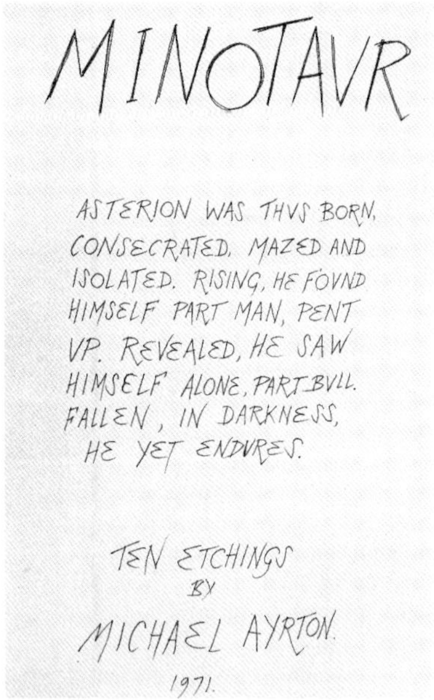

Figure 216.
MINOTAUR ETCHINGS
(Cat. Nos. 726–735; 1971): cover.

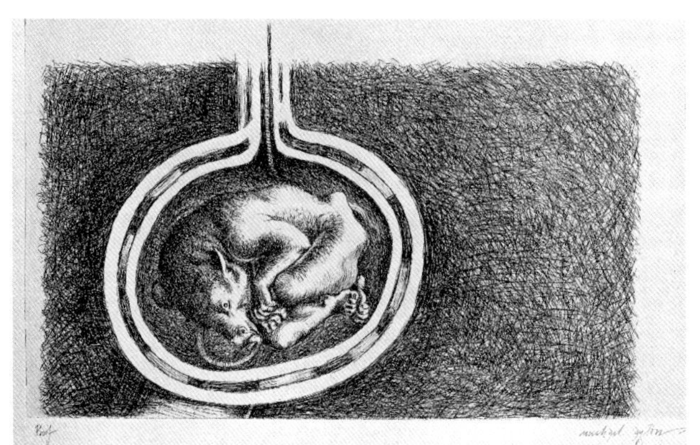

Figure 217. **AS EMBRYO** (Cat. No. 726).

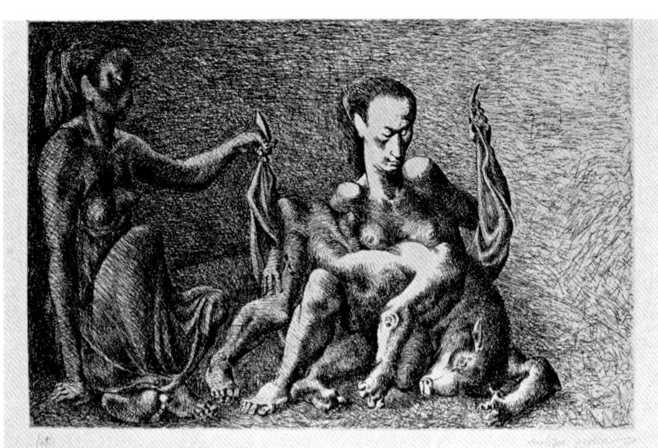

Figure 218. **CONSECRATED** (Cat. No. 727).

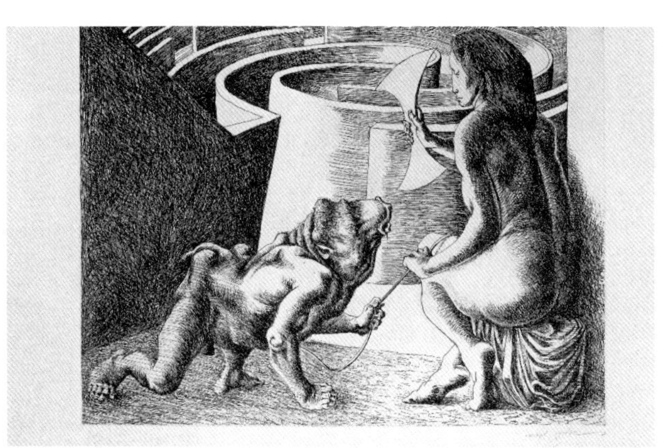

Figure 219. **AS CALF** (Cat. No. 728).

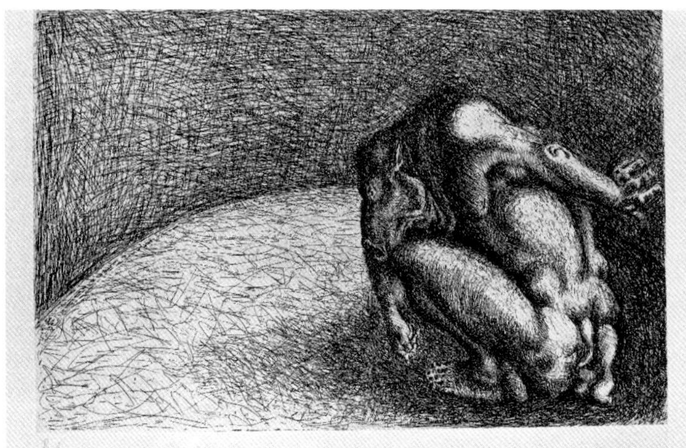

Figure 220. **AS YEARLING** (Cat. No. 729).

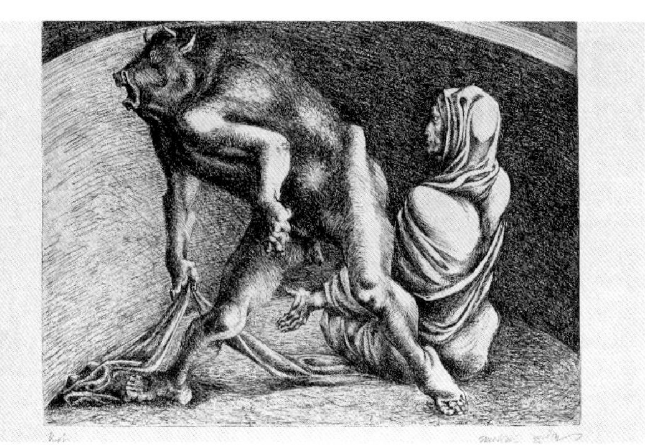

Figure 221. **RISING** (Cat. No. 730).

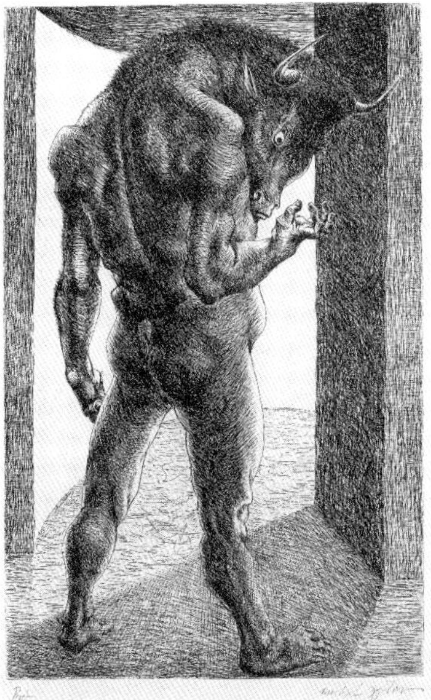

Figure 222. **RISEN** (Cat. No. 731).

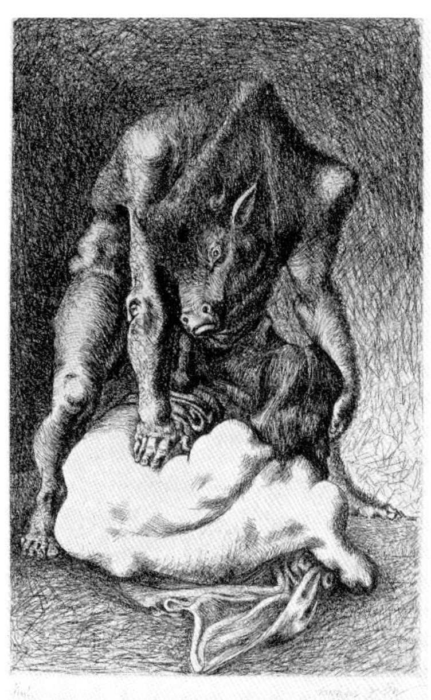

Figure 223. **FULL GROWN** (Cat. No. 732).

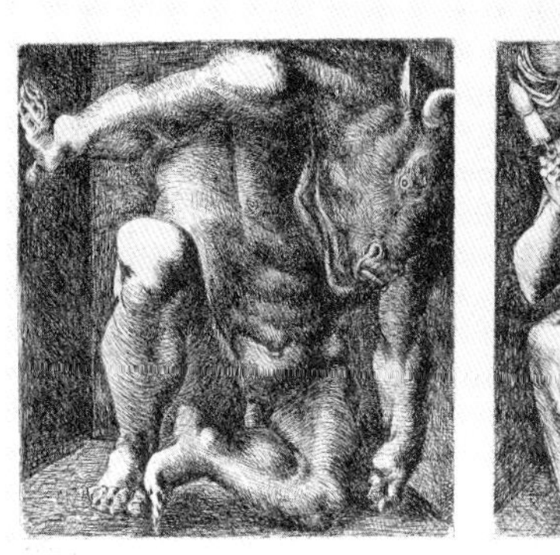

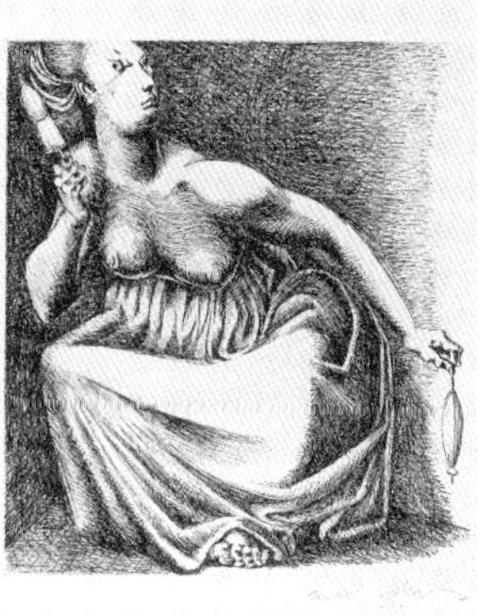

Figure 224. **PENT** (Cat. No. 733).

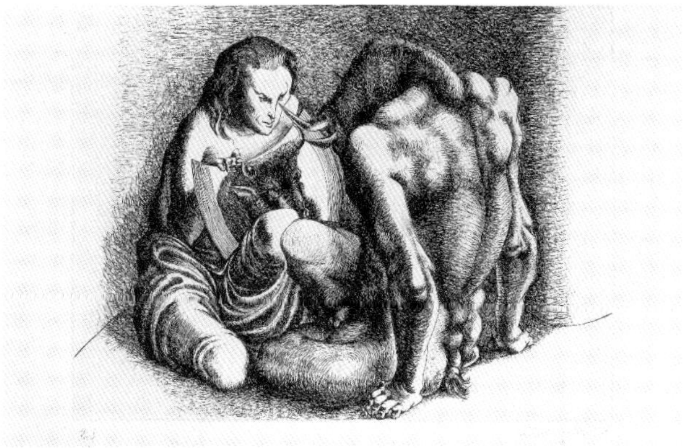

Figure 225. **REVEALED** (Cat. No. 734).

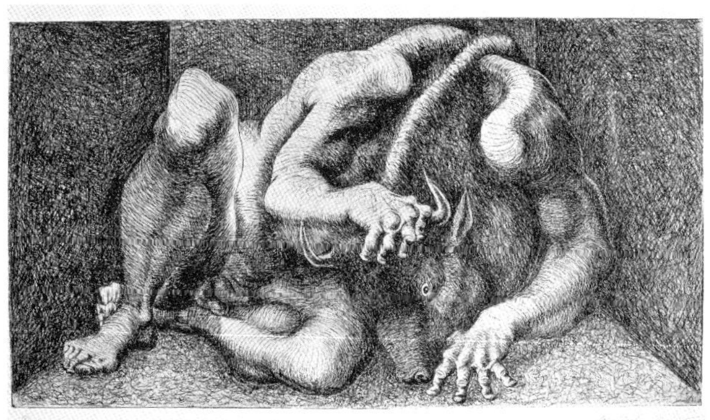

Figure 226. **ALONE** (Cat. No. 735).

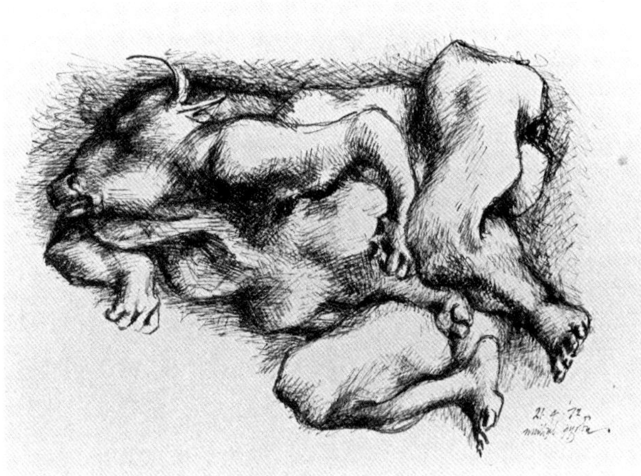

Figure 227. **MINOTAUR ASLEEP II** (Cat. No. 753; 21 April 1972).

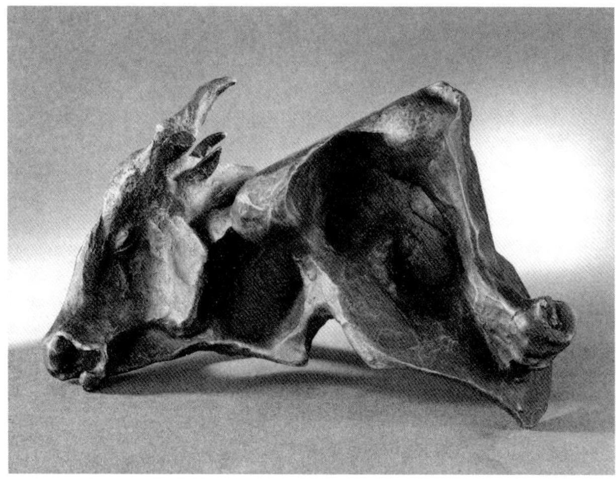

Figure 228. **MINOTAUR SLEEPING** (Cat. No. 757; 1972). Henry Morgan, Somerset.

left in the end to live terrifyingly alone, prisoner not merely of the maze but of his own horrified apperception of himself. The metaphor is clear: Here is Everyman."[45]

The artist's description of this series is likewise revealing: "Asterion was thus born, consecrated, mazed and isolated. Rising, he found himself part man, pent up. Revealed, he saw himself alone, part bull. Fallen, in darkness, he yet endures."[46] The fallen Minotaur was a common theme in Greek art, particularly during the sixth and fifth centuries B.C.E. when Theseus was developing into a national hero,[47] but Ayrton's deepened perception of who, or what, the Minotaur was compelled him to extend the myth, to expand it, to enrich it. Rejecting the heroic values typified by Theseus, Ayrton ignored him in his art just as he dismissed him in his antiheroic *The Maze Maker* (1967, 244). He also ridiculed him in *The Midas Consequence,* by giving Capisco's pet baboon the name Theseus (1974b, 86–87).[48]

This series of etchings is the visual equivalent to *The Maze Maker,* for Ayrton is presenting an autobiography (or "transposed autobiography" as he called *The Maze Maker*) once again, revealing the depth of his self-identification with the Minotaur, just as in the novel he reveals how closely he came to identify with Daedalus. Was he thereby also challenging Picasso's claim to the Minotaur as his alter ego? If so, he gave his alter ego a less explicit sexuality than Picasso did. Ayrton's identification was not limited to seeing the bestial nature within himself; it was also strongly associated with his own physical limitations, as Dr. Justine Hopkins so clearly sees:

> Michael's identification with the Minotaur was as strong, although different, as with Daedalus—not only in terms of the struggle with the beast within, but also in a physical context; when he wrote in "The Landscape of the Minotaur" "I cannot fully raise my loaded head. I cannot raise my head," he spoke all too accurately of his own difficulties under the continuing ravages of the ankylosing spondalitis which stiffened his spine and drastically limited his movement. And it was the Minotaur who continued to recur in his work: even after he had moved Daedalus from the particular to the universal Maze Maker, he still found himself, time and again, compelled to make "one more bloody Minotaur."[49]

Himself a prisoner in the maze as well as its maker, Ayrton saw himself in his fellow prisoner and his fellow prisoner in himself. Although in Borges's story Asterion

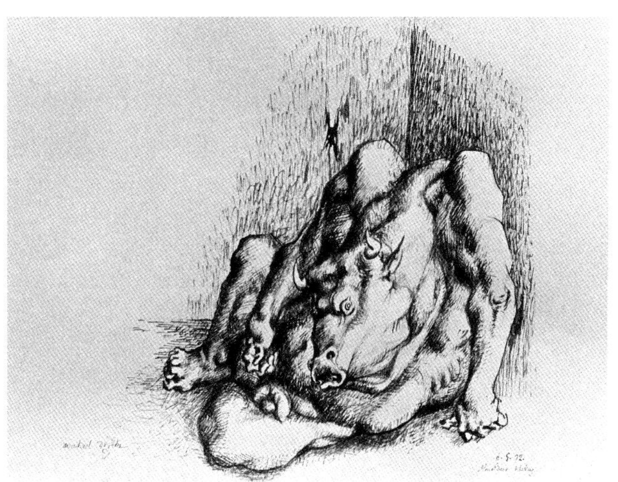

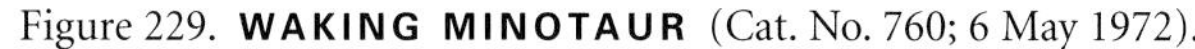

Figure 229. **WAKING MINOTAUR** (Cat. No. 760; 6 May 1972).

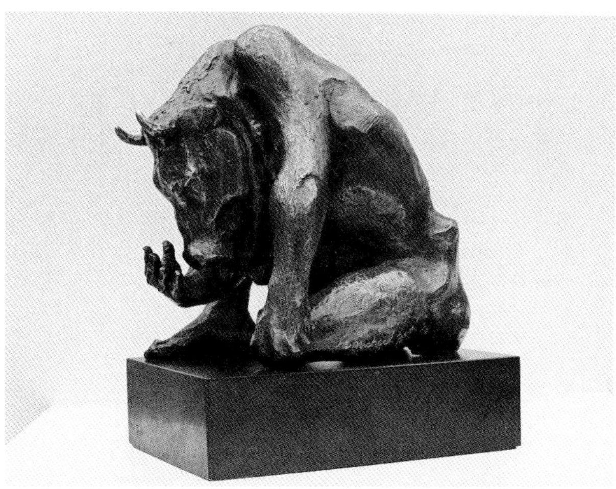

Figure 230. **MINOTAUR WAKING** (Cat. No. 765; 1972).

views Theseus as his redeemer and finds his redemption in death—to which he yields with barely a struggle[50]—Ayrton's Asterion will not die: "Fallen, in darkness, he yet endures."

In 1971 Ayrton turned for a time from the Minotaur to complete a major commissioned work (see *Corporate Head/Reflective Head,* below), but in 1972 the Minotaur came back: first, asleep (Cat. No. 757; Figure 228; cf. Cat. No. 759), then, waking (Cat. No. 765; Figure 230). In these later sculptures of the Minotaur, Ayrton gave new life to his own words: "He was the colour of weathered bronze and . . . I saw him as beautiful in his majestic absurdity. I saw him indomitable and ridiculous in all the grandeur and all the fragility of useless physical strength. Icarus, in his foolishness, had once believed himself half-brother to the Minotaur and believed me the father of both. In that moment I felt I could have been"(1967, 197). The gentleness and sensitivity expressed in these bronzes reveal the depth of Ayrton's bond with his enduring mythical offspring.

The 1971 commission to design an outdoor sculpture that would stand at the focal point of the new international headquarters of the S. S. Kresge Company (later renamed the Kmart Corporation) gave Ayrton the opportunity to extend his use of mirrors and bronze heads. Nearly twenty-two feet high, *Corporate Head/Reflective Head* (Cat. No. 772; Figures 236–239, Plates 46–49) was unveiled in September 1972 in the entrance court of a gigantic, labyrinthine building. It is set at the center of a series of concentric octagons formed by rows of bricks laid in concrete. The outermost octagon opens up, unwinding and extending itself down the two legs of the entrance drive, showing the visitor his way into the labyrinth. The octagonal pattern appropriately recurs in all the service towers that link the thirteen modules that comprised the original building; the building was designed to accommodate additional modules as the need arose.[51]

Progressing up the path to the building entrance, the visitor is unavoidably drawn toward the sculpture that graces the courtyard, for its reflections are not limited to the mirrored surface of the sculpture; the reflective glass of the window-walls of the building itself picks up and multiplies its answering reflections. As one circles the imposing sculpture, one not only sees the half heads completed in the mirrored surface but also discovers interior heads, which in turn are duplicated, full face, in the mirror, inside the head: "When viewed from the rear, each head is seen to be cavitated by carved recesses in

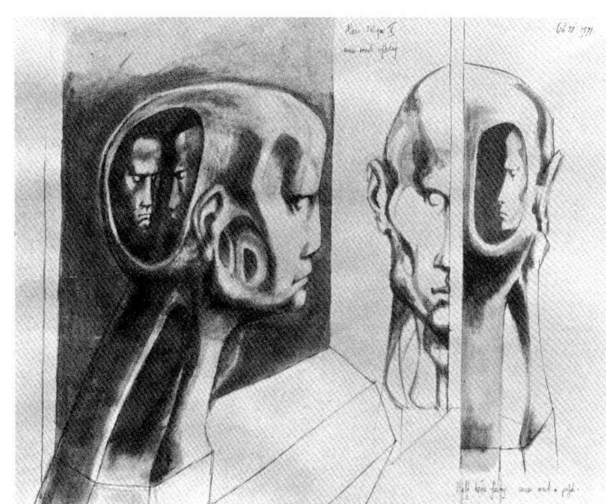

Figure 231. **KRESGE SCULPTURE: MAIN OBLIQUE II** (Cat. No. 740; 28 October 1971).

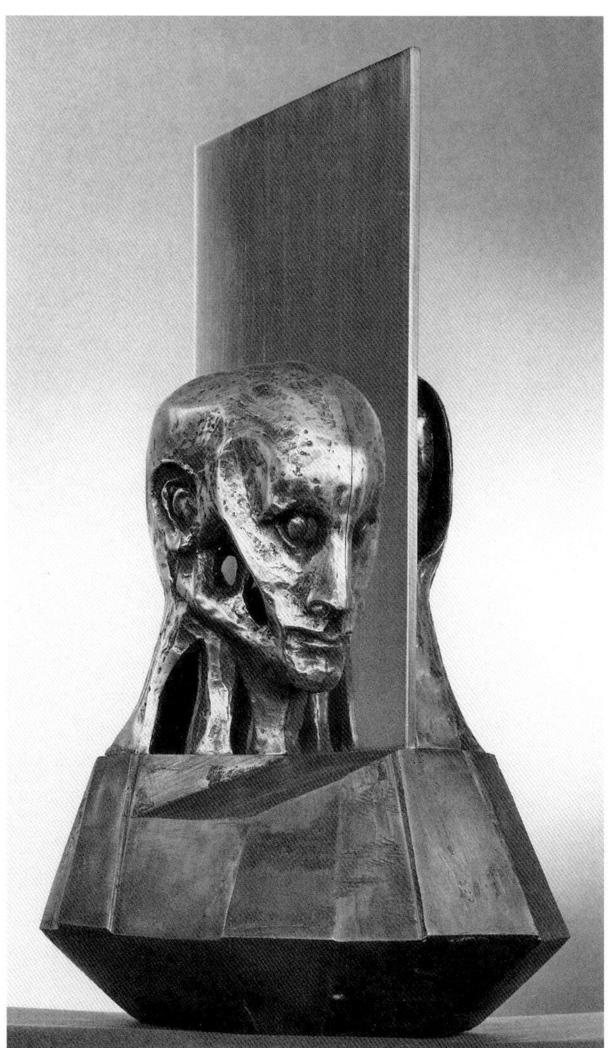

Figure 232. **REFLECTIVE HEAD II** (Cat. No. 743; 1971): head reflected. Henry Morgan, Somerset.

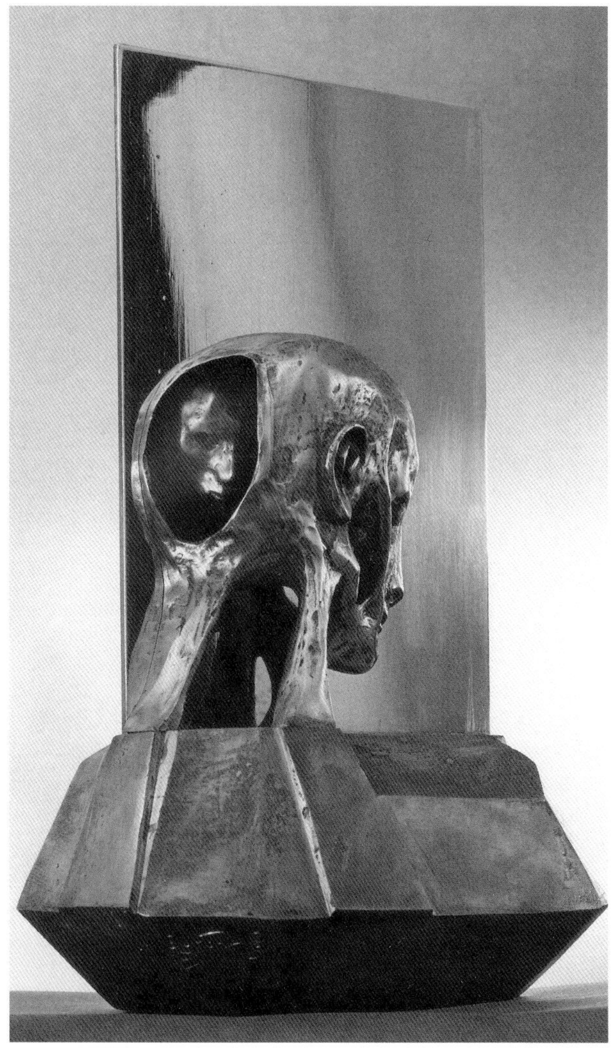

Figure 233. **REFLECTIVE HEAD II** (Cat. No. 743): side view. Henry Morgan, Somerset.

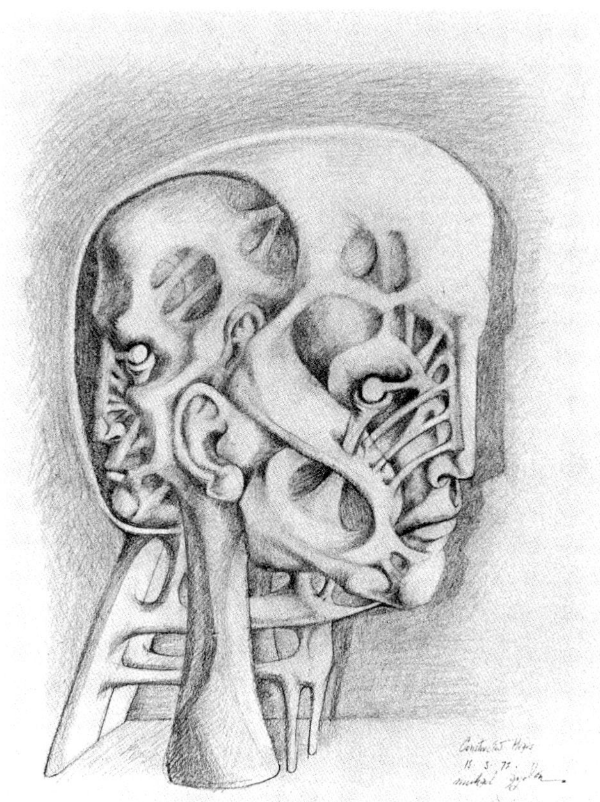

Figure 234. **CONSTRUCTED HEADS** (Cat. No. 746; 15 March 1972).

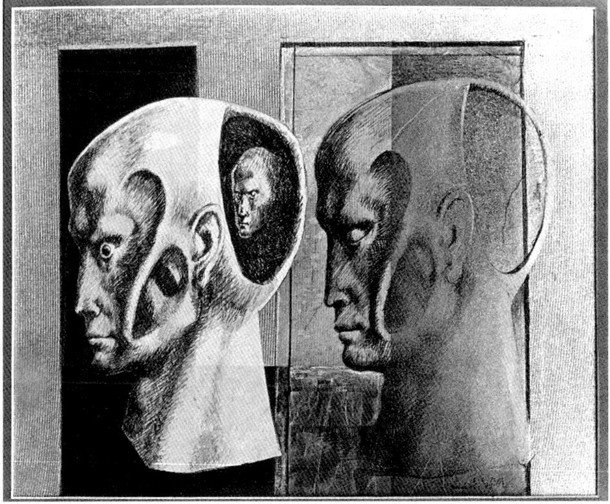

Figure 235. **REFLECTIVE HEADS** (Cat. No. 747; 18 March 1972).

which are set partly abstract head forms. These are the brain's occupants who have installed themselves, uninvited but not to be expelled, in the mind and psyche."[52] And once inside the building, the visitor and the more than 2,000 employees of this international corporation are never far from a view of *Corporate Head/Reflective Head,* for the nature of the building is such that the sculpture and its court are visible from many different levels and many different angles, to intrigue as well as please the viewer.

Ayrton's description of this work for the catalogue of the Maze and Minotaur touring exhibition (appendix A), written in 1972, places it clearly in the context of his earlier works. Although his statement repeats some of the earlier discussions, it is essential to reproduce it here to convey the full sense of his conception of it:

> The labyrinth is at once ambiguous in its form and in its nature. To Daedalus its walls were dense and impenetrable, translucent and illusory. It may also be as implacable as stone or as impalpable as smoke. As a metaphor it developed for me as MIRROR MAZE [Cat. No. 596] in 1966 . . . and as the faceted walls of the innermost coil of the ARKVILLE MAZE [Cat. No. 673] in 1968. These walls throw back the reflection of the bronze DAEDALUS AND ICARUS MATRIX [Cat. No. 640] distorted. In 1969 a small piece of neutral perspex, a substance at once dense and translucent yet with the power to reflect, extended my means to give physical expression to metaphorical form as to the idea of what lies within or beyond the mirror. The idea itself is not new, except in sculpture. Lewis Carroll took Alice through the looking-glass and Jean Cocteau conceived, on film, the means to take Orpheus through the mirror and into the nether world. In ancient legend it was sometimes believed that a man's image, reflected in clear water, was possessed of a separate spirit from his own, while all of us see ourselves in the looking-glass not as we are but in reverse, a maze concept because, although the mirror reflects the image and may even suggest the journey, it gives no clue to its destination. The mystery of the mirror was defined in 10th century China when it was pronounced that at one hundred yards the mirror can see the man, but the man cannot see the mirror and also that the mirror can exist without the image but is incomplete because it is alone, whereas the image cannot exist without the mirror,

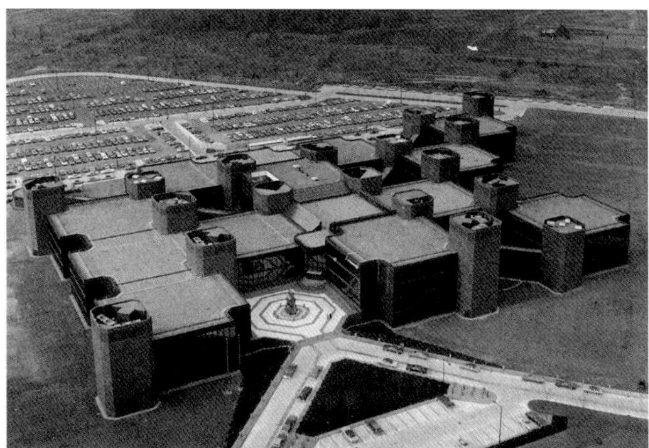

Figure 236. **CORPORATE HEAD** or **REFLECTIVE HEAD** (Cat. No. 772; 1972): aerial view. Balthazar Korab, Troy, Michigan.

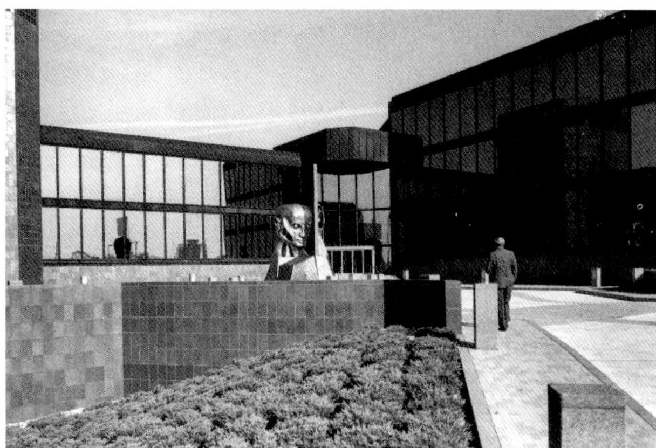

Figure 237. **CORPORATE HEAD** or **REFLECTIVE HEAD** (Cat. No. 772): approaching entrance court. Balthazar Korab, Troy, Michigan.

> but is not itself empty. This riddle can be resolved and perhaps has been, in a sculpture 22 feet high, now in Detroit, and the solution may be imagined in terms of the model for it [Cat. No. 743, REFLECTIVE HEAD II (see Figures 232 and 233)]. . . . On the large scale, each 9 ft. 6 in. head is half illusory, being completed in reflection, and each large head contains a smaller interior head, which is duplicated by the double mirror. Thus the image cannot exist without the mirror which is not itself empty. Each of the fourteen sculptures on this theme, of which five are exhibited here, depends for its effect upon being rotated on its central axis. The exception is the one in Detroit and there the spectator must move round the object, yet it remains an extension of the idea of the maze even if the winding passages exist only in the convolutions of the spectator's brain. (above pl. 39)

A giant corporation such as this one, with all its complexities of corporate structure and multitudinous operations, is no more intricate than this sculpture, which further extends the interplay of mirrors and mazes to penetrate the labyrinthine mind of humankind.

There is considerable irony in the fact that this building and its sculpture are located in a suburb of Detroit named Troy. For the classical scholar or an erudite sculptor this fact recalls the Troy Maze and the Troy games described in connection with the funeral games for Aeneas's father, Anchises, in the Fifth Book of Virgil's *Aeneid.*[53] It is no surprise, then, to find among Ayrton's subsequent work a *Troy Maze* (Cat. No. 777; 1972; Figures 240, 242, 243). On the concave side of a slightly curving bronze wall stands a figure (also separate, as *Invader,* Cat. No. 778; 1972; Figure 241), peering into an opening in the wall that casts back his reflection from a mirror-window of translucent perspex. From the other side one can see the head of the "Invader" peering through the glass. His face and head bear marked resemblance to an earlier bronze, *Advancing Figure* (Cat. No. 605; 1967; Figure 244), as well as to various serpentine figures, such as some of the oracles and a contemporaneous bronze *Serpentine Figure* (Cat. No. 745; Figure 245), although one can also see a certain similarity to *Chimaera II* (Cat. No. 233), which Ayrton drew a decade earlier when he was concerned with the distortions of Icarus in flight. Leading from the base of the irregularly shaped window, on the convex side, a raised line winds in a series of folds to form a maze configuration that recalls a pattern on an Etruscan vase, an oenochoe of the seventh century B.C.E., from Tragliatella [see catalogue Cat. No. 767]. Within the outer wall of this maze pattern is a graffito, "TPVIA" (Truia), in retroscript, as on the Tragliatella oenochoe. The influence of Henry Moore upon Ayrton is evident

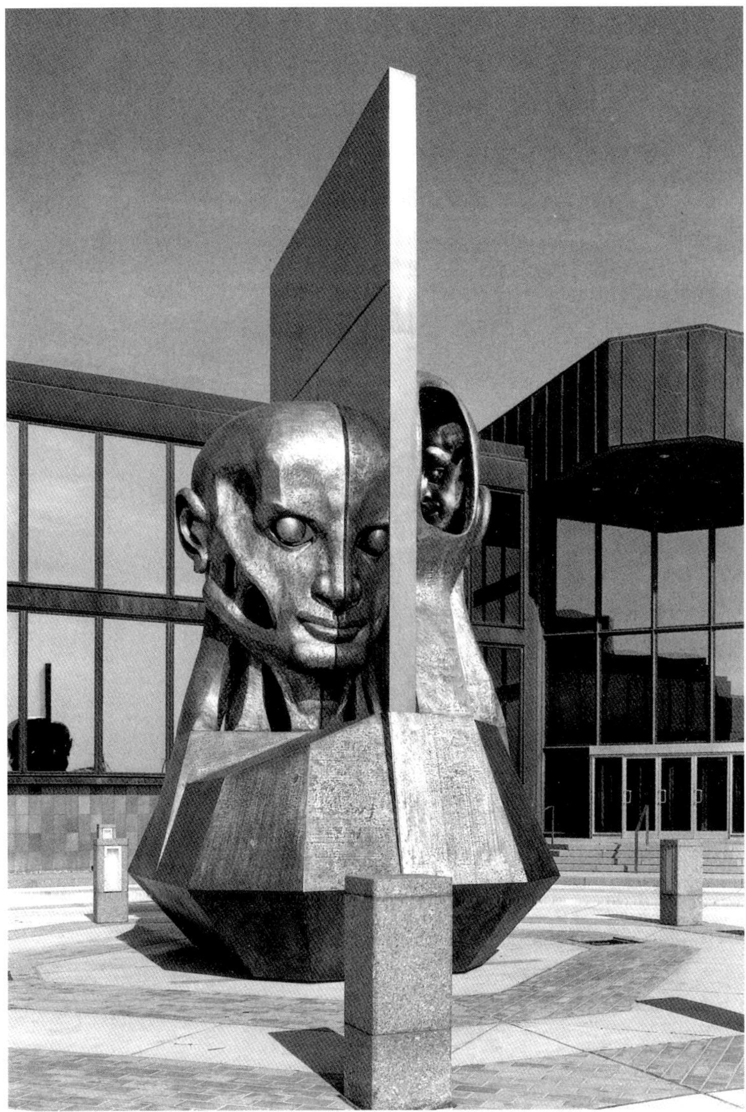

Figure 238. **CORPORATE HEAD** or **REFLECTIVE HEAD** (Cat. No. 772): sculpture, close up. Balthazar Korab, Troy, Michigan.

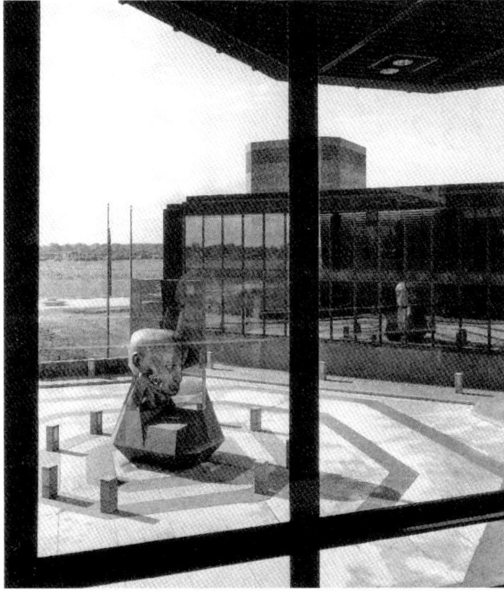

Figure 239. **CORPORATE HEAD** or **REFLECTIVE HEAD** (Cat. No. 772): entrance court, from inside the building. Balthazar Korab, Troy, Michigan.

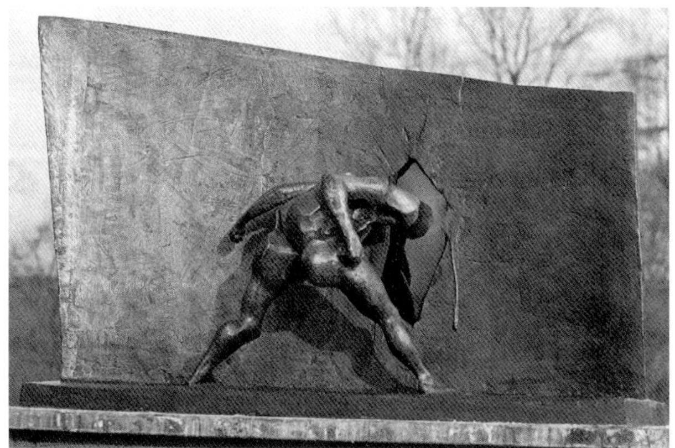

Figure 240. **TROY MAZE** (Cat. No. 777; 1972): back view of **INVADER**.

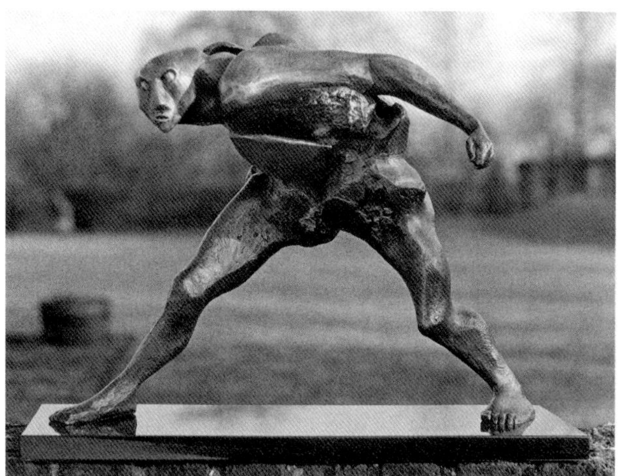

Figure 241. **INVADER** (Cat. No. 778; 1972).

in *Troy Maze,* as one can see by comparing it with Moore's *Girl Seated Against a Square Wall* (1957–1958; Coll. Norton Simon Museum, Pasadena, CA). *Invader* vaguely resembles another of Moore's sculptures, *Maquette for Warrior* (bronze; 1952–1953), and the life-size bronze *Warrior with a Shield* (1953–1954).[54]

In May 1973, while he was visiting fellow of the Institute for the Arts and Humanistic Studies at Pennsylvania State University, Ayrton wrote:

> I find myself lecturing on my "use of" Virgil on Monday and it seems to me that my whole, or almost my whole, work during the last twenty years exists in precis in Book VI, lines 1 to 38 of the *Aeneid*! This apart, the "Troy Game" sculpture ("Troy Maze" however is not equestrian in my version) owes a good deal to Book V but it seems to me that Virgil has been using me rather than I him. One irony I had forgotten is that Deiphobe tells Aeneas to stop gawping at the works of art on the Daedalic doors of the Cumaean Temple and get on with his chores. Could it be that Virgil here instructs me too?[55]

Before writing these words, he had completed several sculptures that further expressed the labyrinth motif and his own predicament. *Carapace* (Cat. No. 762; 1972; Plate 43) reveals a figure, in near fetal position, partially inside a bisected nautilus.[56] *Maze Music* (Cat. No. 780; 1972; Figure 246) is a variation on *Maze Player* (Cat. No. 551; 1965; see chapter 5), and its meaning is clear from Ayrton's statement in the Catalogue of the Maze and Minotaur touring exhibition (appendix A): "Daedalus called the maze his toy, as well as his trial and his trap, and in this aspect I find that it is sometimes strung with the skein of red thread which Ariadne gave to Theseus, so that my hands are perhaps on a stringed instrument which produces a music to me no less haunting for being silent" (above pls. 30 and 36). The same statement could apply, to a degree, to three bronzes cast in 1972: *Figure With a Skein, Version II* (Cat. No. 764), *Red Thread* (Cat. No. 779; Figure 247) and *Web* (Cat. No. 783; Plate 50) are all strung versions of earlier works. Perhaps he intended to symbolize his own entrapment, although in all probability he would not have permitted these works to be limited to personal statements. Like the earlier strong Maze Makers, these

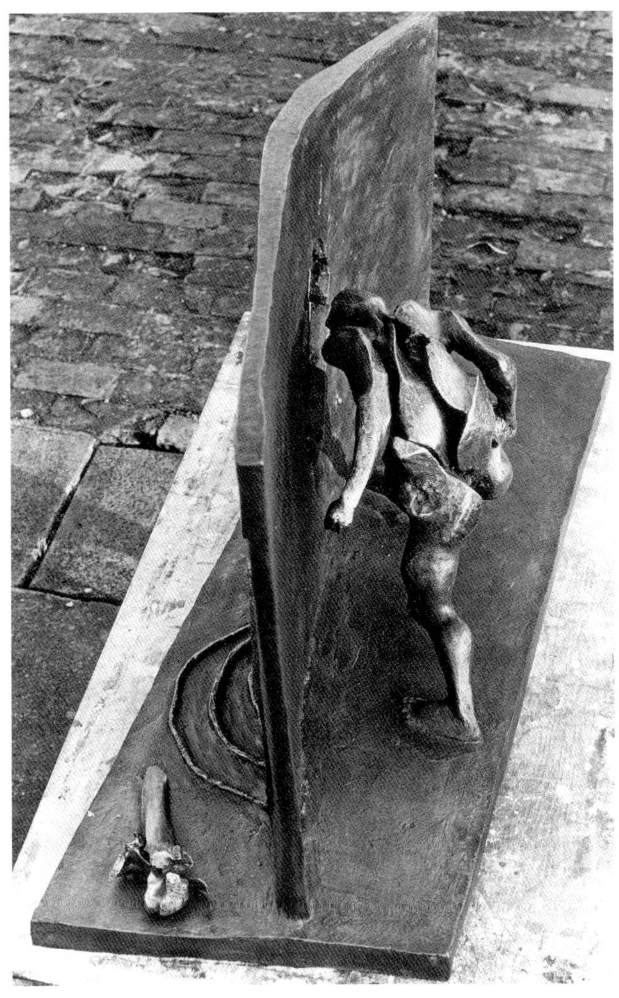

Figure 242. **TROY MAZE** (Cat. No. 777; 1972): back view of **INVADER**, above.

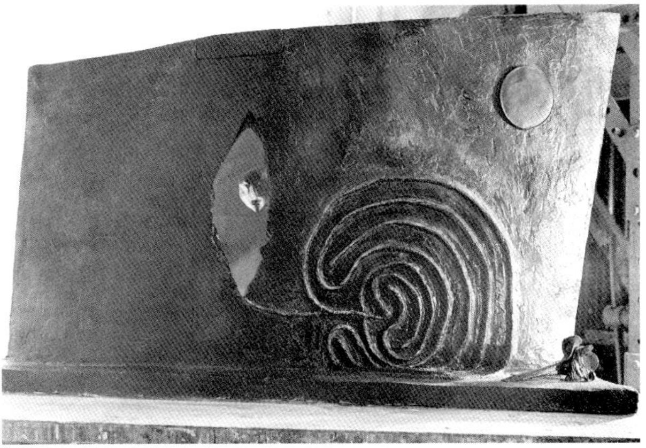

Figure 243. **TROY MAZE** (Cat. No. 777): **INVADER** peering through glass.

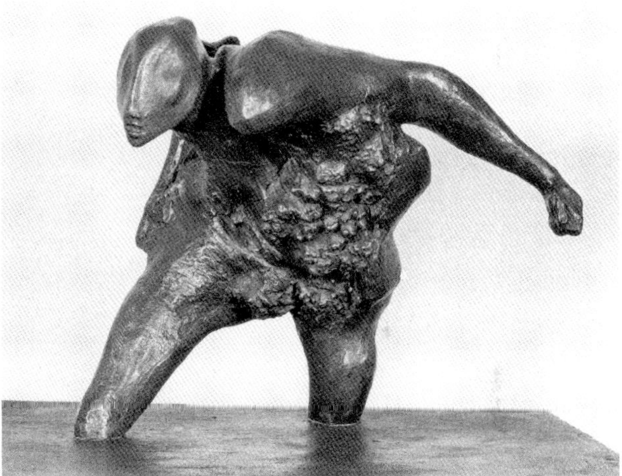

Figure 244. **ADVANCING FIGURE** (Cat. No. 605; 1967): front view.

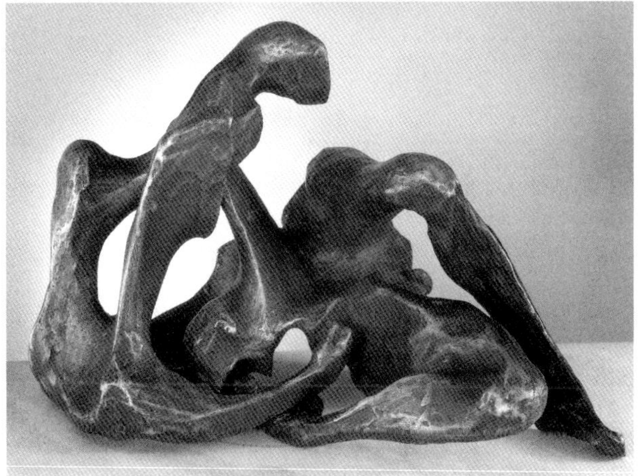

Figure 245. **SERPENTINE FIGURE** (Cat. No. 745; 1972). Henry Morgan, Somerset.

works echo the Stringed Figures created by Henry Moore (1937–1939). Ariadne appears in bronze for the first time in *Red Thread* (Cat. No. 779), which was adapted from a much earlier sculpture, *Minoan Landscape* (Cat. No. 42; 1958): Ariadne inhabits this landscape, and she holds in her hands the umbilical cord that not only passes through the horns of the Minotaur but also ties her to her physical environment.

In *Smoke Mirror Circle* (Cat. No. 776; 1972), figures resembling those in *Dioskouroi* (Cat. No. 701; 1970) and *Mirrored Figure I* (Cat. No. 744; 1972) appear to be caught in a revolving door, their images multiplied by the translucent perspex. In actuality, however, *Smoke Mirror Circle* represents a circling dance movement, calling to mind the dancing floor of Ariadne mentioned in the *Iliad* (see chapter 2).[57] Closely allied in concept is *Cord* (Cat. No. 792; 1973; Figure 249, Plate 53), in which the above-mentioned strung versions are also recalled. A man and a woman lead each other, in illusion if not in fact, through a series of perspex plates by means of a red cord that symbolizes the umbilical cord, as well as the red thread of Ariadne.

Although any of these complex sculptures may seem the ultimate form for the metaphor of entrapment in a maze, a more appropriate final statement may perhaps lie in Ayrton's *Brain Maze* (Cat. No. 782; 1972; Figures 250–252), since he remarked at about this time: "My life circles around making as complete a statement about the idea approached from every possible angle of metaphor of which I am capable,"[58] and since the ideas for all his expressions of the metaphor, after all, are wound out from his brain.[59]

As had so often happened, the potentially final work in relation to the myth proved otherwise. In 1973 Ayrton returned to the enigma of mirror twins he had explored in *Dioskouroi* (Cat. No. 701; 1970), creating a variation on that theme, *Mirror Twins* (Cat. No. 790). Another intriguing late work also depends on illusion to achieve its effect, but it does so without the benefit of mirrors. *Imprint* (Cat. No. 794) is a bronze block that appears solid, save for one concave side. This concavity derives its essential shape from the negative impression of a head such as Ayrton used in *Captive* (Cat. No. 700; 1970) and, earlier, in *Reflex I* and *II* (Cat. Nos. 658 and 668; 1969). When one withdraws a certain distance from this bronze, a curious reversal effect causes the face to appear almost convex.

Ayrton's antepenultimate sculpture is a very personal statement, for it even includes an X-ray of the artist's lower spine and pelvis. *Treadmill* (Cat. No. 795; 1974; Figure 253) expresses the idea of being trapped in one's own limbs, one's own body, as well as expressing the idea of the labyrinth as Ayrton's personal treadmill. The extraordinary distortion of his spine, evident in the X-ray, resulted in exceptional pain for Ayrton, thus limiting his capacity to carry on his creative activities. He summed up in this single work his sense of physical inadequacy and a degree of creative fatigue, evoking his similarly poignant *Daedalus at Cumae* (Cat. No. 204; 1961; see chapter 4), cast over a dozen years earlier as what he had hoped would be his final statement on the myth.

One can be grateful that Ayrton did not conclude his explorations of the Daedalus myth as he had hoped in 1961, for his creations during succeeding years greatly enriched the myth, adding to our understanding not only of myth but also of the creative process itself and of our own times. Ayrton's deadly scalpel unerringly probed the intimate recesses of human thought and emotions in a superb blend of psychology and artistry. His art reveals, as T. S. Eliot once said of Henry James, "a mind so fine that no idea could violate it" (qtd. in *Saturday Review*). Behind his works lies an overwhelming intelligence, which was fortuitously coupled with a dramatist's gift for effect and a draftsman's eye for detail.

Having begun the use of mirrors with *Mirror Maze* in 1966 and expanded their use not long thereafter at Arkville (see chapter 6), Ayrton soon perceived their rich potential for further penetration into the meaning of the Daedalus myth in general and of the maze in particular. As his figures grew seemingly more simple, more primitive, the mirrors transformed them into modern, complex, intriguing images. Like the *Labyrinth* stories of Borges, Ayrton's reflective sculptures offer as much insight into the human mind and humankind's predicaments and paradoxes as we are willing to see. No cursory glance will

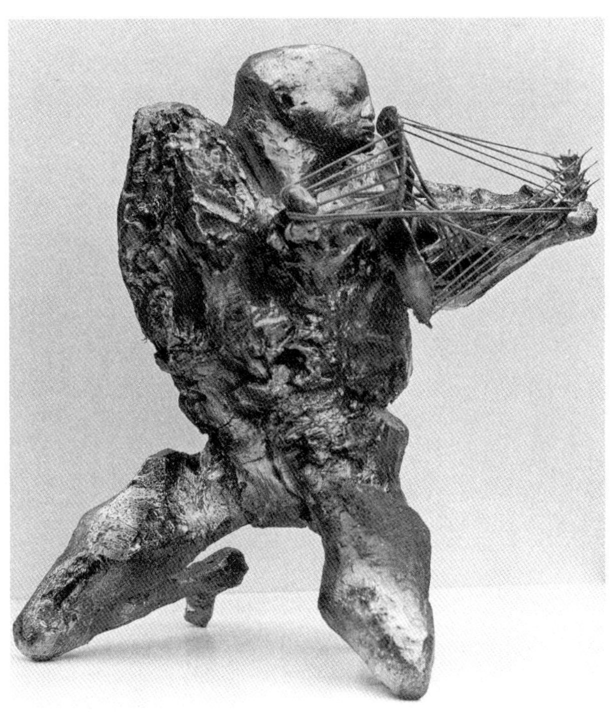

Figure 246. **MAZE MUSIC** (Cat. No. 780; 1972).

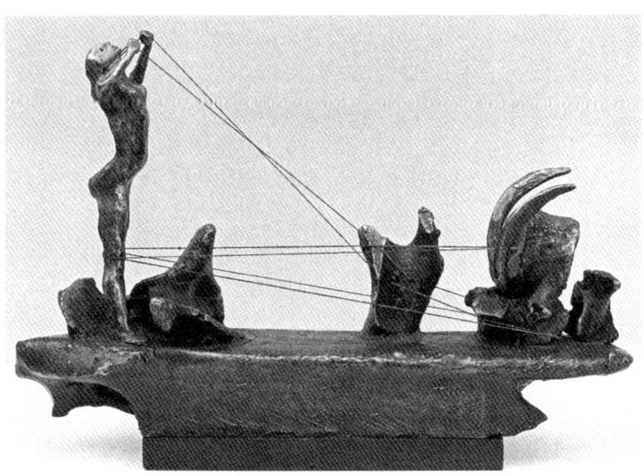

Figure 247. **RED THREAD** (Cat. No. 779; 1972).

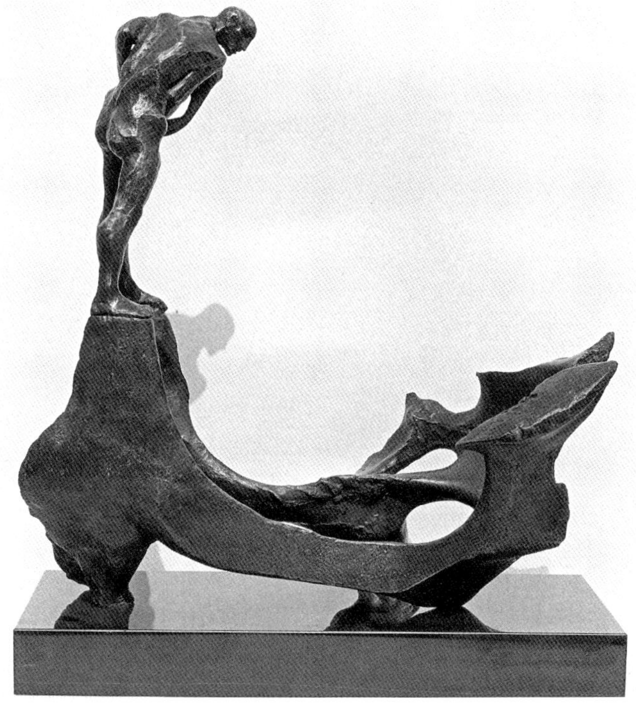

Figure 248. **ORPHEUS SEEKING, VERSION II** (Cat. No. 724; 1971).

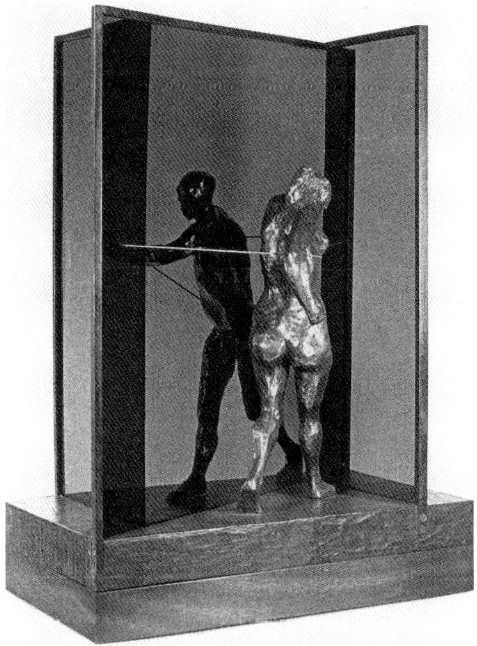

Figure 249. **CORD** (Cat. No. 792; 28 June 1973): female, back.

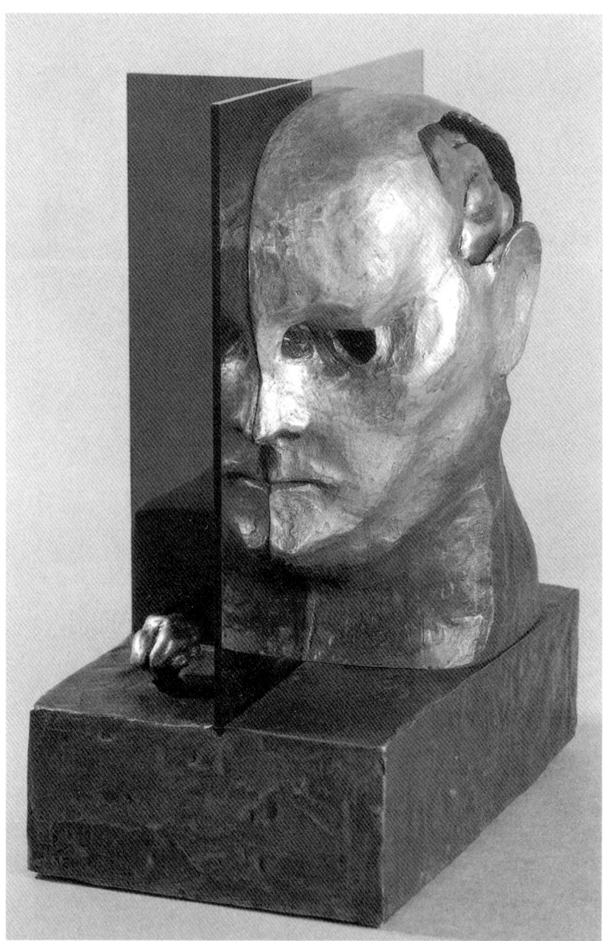

Figure 250. **BRAIN MAZE** (Cat. No. 782; 1972): head reflected. Henry Morgan, Somerset.

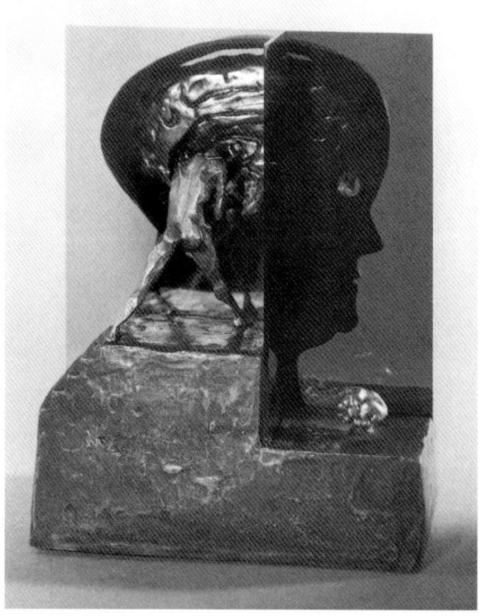

Figure 251. **BRAIN MAZE** (Cat. No. 782): head in profile. Henry Morgan, Somerset.

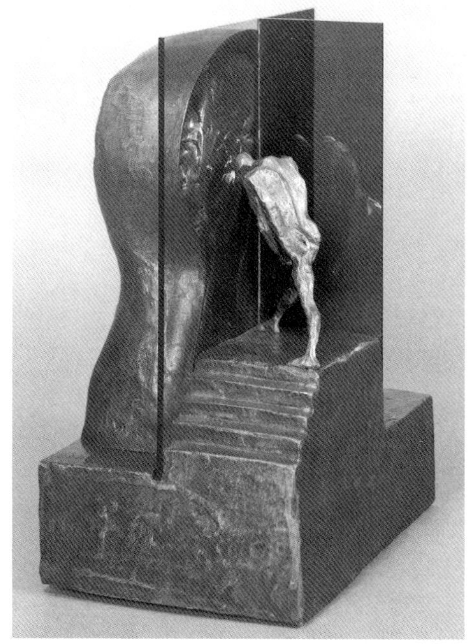

Figure 252. **BRAIN MAZE** (Cat. No. 782): back of head. Henry Morgan, Somerset.

suffice, no superficial sampling will reveal the answers. As one studies Ayrton's bronze and perspex sculptures, slowly turning each on its axis or walking around the Kresge sculpture, new images appear, hinting at the deeper truth hidden beyond them. They offer the paradigm and the paradox of life itself.[60] Truth is discovered to be at once simple and profound, singular and multiple, obvious and elusive, permanent and yet constantly changing. As one is about to penetrate the reality lurking just beyond the mirror, that figure vanishes, only to be replaced by another. A new reflection beckons, and again we totter dangerously, alarmingly on the precipice of infinity. Daedalian Ayrton draws us into the maze as surely as the Minotaur's rumblings drew the hero Theseus into the Cretan labyrinth, but like his archetypal inspiration he holds out to us—through word and image—the red thread of escape.

André Maurois has said of Borges:

> He likes to quote Novalis: "The greatest of sorcerers would be the one who would cast a spell on himself to the degree of taking his own phantasmagoria for autonomous apparitions. Might that not be our case?" Borges answers that indeed it is our case: it is we who have dreamed the universe. We can see in what it consists, the deliberately constructed interplay of the mirrors and mazes of this thought, difficult but always acute and laden with secrets. In all these stories we find roads that fork, corridors that lead nowhere, except to other corridors, and so on as far as the eye can see. For Borges this is an image of human thought, which endlessly makes its way through concatenations of causes and effects without ever exhausting infinity, and marvels over what is perhaps only inhuman chance. And why wander in these labyrinths? Once more, for aesthetic reasons; because this present infinity, these "vertiginous symmetries," have their tragic beauty. The form is more important than the content.[61]

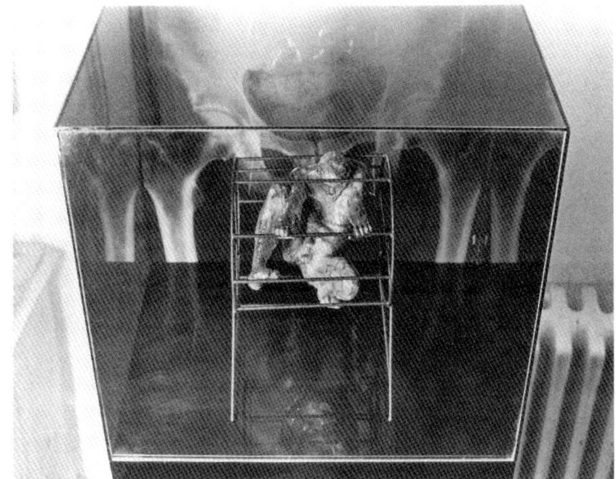

Figure 253. **TREADMILL** (Cat. No. 795; 1974).

Ayrton would of course disagree with Maurois's final sentence, since for Ayrton the content, the narrative, the message, took precedence over form, if he could not bring the two into the desired delicate balance so often achieved in his art. But he clearly would have found a resonance with Maurois's description of the sorcery of Borges, whose creative power he greatly admired. The Borgesian image of human thought, moreover, is consistent with much of Ayrton's own thinking.

To make Maurois's rhetorical question more personal, one might well ask: Why did Ayrton himself continue to wander in these labyrinths? Perhaps for intellectual reasons, since the quest for insight drew him ever deeper into the inner recesses of the human imagination; probably, for psychological reasons, for myth lies deep within the human psyche and in its creative urge; surely, for aesthetic reasons, since "these 'vertiginous symmetries' have their tragic beauty." For Ayrton, moreover, as for Henry James, art was "an act of life." And as James also said, "Art *makes* life, makes interest, makes importance."[62]

Conclusion

Joseph Campbell, one of the foremost mythologists of the twentieth century, describes the symbols of myth as "telling metaphors of the destiny of man, man's hope, man's faith, and man's dark mystery."[1] And C. G. Jung declares, "The primitive mentality does not *invent* myths, it *experiences* them. Myths are original revelations of the preconscious psyche.... Myths ... have a vital meaning."[2] In *Cumaean Gates,* W. F. Jackson Knight explains the development of myth and archetypal patterns as follows: "Myth first arises from some single event of human and personal relations and acts, then becomes in a sense general, as a statement of truth rather than an account of what once happened, and lastly is used as a mental container to hold the facts of some new event. The container can be called an archetypal pattern."[3] The maze or labyrinth is one "archetypal pattern" that particularly interested Knight, who identified the "general principle of the maze" as "exclusion, with conditioned admission."[4] Michael Ayrton, who acknowledged his debt to Jackson Knight on a number of occasions, began his wanderings in myth at Cumae, entering through his own Cumaean Gate. Having discovered on the acropolis at Cumae the numinous presence of the site, he moved on to explore the myth of Daedalus and Icarus in all its ramifications. From his single act of drawing the landscape at Cumae in May 1956, Ayrton entered into a myth that became for him "general, as a statement of truth," and that he "used as a mental container" (ibid.). The "archetypal pattern" that came to dominate his life was the labyrinth, a symbol or metaphor replete with history and rich in its implications for contemporary humanity.

In an age of tremendous invention and extraordinary scientific and technological advances, Ayrton reached back to archetypal figures from Greek myth to give meaning to and make visible psychological realities of our time. He gave expression to the enduring dream of flying and invested the archetype of Daedalus and Icarus with new significance in an age seemingly free from myth and its power. Through his multiple intonations on the labyrinth, moreover, he expressed the unconscious archetype of his age fully as much as Henry Moore did for the archetype of the eternal feminine, the primordial mother. Through multiple intonations on the archetype of the creative artist, expressed in Daedalus as the archetypal craftsman and Icarus as the archetypal overreacher, he gave visual reality to enduring symbols that have captivated artists and writers throughout the centuries.

By tracing Ayrton's progressive involvement with this myth and interpreting its significance for his creative process, I have sought to generalize his experience not only to provide a deeper understanding of the creative act, but especially to gain deeper insight into the human condition. From this study it has become very clear that, even in the latter half of the twentieth century, human beings discover reality through myth, that even a sophisticated mentality "*experiences*" myths, and that even in our own age myths "have a vital meaning" (ibid.)

"Certainly the history of my life and of the works of art which have especially enriched it is precisely that: the depiction or incantation of a handful of metaphors whose splendour rests upon their intonation."

The relatively comprehensive but not exhaustive survey in chapter 3 (and appendix C) of the literary and artistic treatments of the myth of Daedalus and Icarus reveals over and over how versatile and how persistent this myth is. Taken together, Daedalus and Icarus throughout the centuries have provided poets, dramatists, allegorists, and moralists with rich material for contrasting the exuberance of youth with the restraint of maturity; expressing and exploring the natural tension between father and son; revealing the innate human desire to join the birds in the air, either to see the world whole or challenge divine prerogatives; illuminating the contrast between the practical contributions of the artisan and the flights of fancy of the unfettered artist; or illustrating the risks associated with the use and misuse of human invention. Treated separately, Daedalus and Icarus often functioned as vehicles for expressing an artistic or a moral vision, whether as objects to admire and emulate or scorn and repudiate. At times, they became such commonplace symbols that it was sufficient to mention them by name or even merely by allusion. Visual artists throughout the centuries also found in this myth an endless source of inspiration and creativity. Their representations of the myth of the flight and the fall kept the dream of flight alive, even when artists used the myth only paradigmatically, to illustrate the folly of thinking that humans could conquer the air and fly among the birds.

Other aspects of the myth also intrigued and inspired poets and artists, who found a rich resource in the story of the unnatural mating of Pasiphaë with the bull from the sea, the monstrous progeny of this union, and the labyrinthine prison built to hide this hybrid creature from public view. Although I have not followed every passageway in the maze that contains the entire literary and artistic history of each aspect of the myth, it is my hope that I have offered enough of an overview to enable the interested reader to determine where to enter this labyrinth and explore more fully its uncharted passageway. Other scholars, viewing the labyrinth from a different vantage point, will undoubtedly see new patterns emerge, find new meaning in its meanderings. Perhaps they, too, will find that the path into the maze is unicursal but the way out is multiple and oft-times complex and confusing, with many a dead end, many a forking path that leads only to another detour away from the most direct route out, a route that is obvious to the external observer but hidden from the inhabitant or the transient in the maze.

The association of the maze with both the mind and the body, the brain and the intestines, birth and death, imprisonment and freedom, time and eternity, is demonstrated extensively in word and image by Ayrton's creative products during the final two decades of his life. For him the metaphor of the maze, along with the myth of Daedalus and Icarus, was all consuming, the greatest of his obsessions and, to an extent, his final obsession, although he had been moving during the last year of his life into a new passion, with his efforts to bring the poetry of Archilochos to life in word and image. The posthumously published *Archilochos* (1977), in which Ayrton's translations of the poetic fragments and his etchings are set side by side (but he explicitly warns that the etchings are not to be considered as literal illustrations of the translations), contains an introduction by him that hints at his identification with Archilochos as an alter ego: "I found him established, out of time, in the first person singular. And that in my time he is; the first in the first person, self established peremptorily" (1). *The Maze Maker* similarly was cast in the first person singular, as a "transposed autobiography" of Daedalus.

One can perhaps hear Ayrton's own voice in these words expressed by Daedalus in the second paragraph of *The Maze Maker:*

> I never understood the pattern of my life so that I have blundered through it in a maze. I did not know until now that in places the walls of this maze were cunningly polished so that the perils I have endured, my fears and hopes and the joy I have taken in my tasks have time and again been

> reflected in one another. I did not know that those I have loved and hated have been mirrored images of one another. In all my life I never learned from one experience how to encounter its reflected twin. (1967, 11)

At the very least, these words could describe some of the personal experiences revealed in Dr. Justine Hopkins's biography, since they were written during a time of "extreme and traumatic tensions which . . . he had precipitated in his personal life" as a result of marital infidelity and duplicity.[5]

Hopkins has with great perceptivity captured an essential element of the labyrinth in Ayrton's life, the sense of isolation of "all the characters with whom Michael found himself most intimately involved": "The final image of St Anthony is alone. . . . The last image of the Minotaur Suite is *Minotaur Alone,* and the ending of the saga of Daedalus is *Daedalus at Cumae,* alone with empty hands upturned in his lap."[6] To reinforce this idea, she quotes from a letter from Michael to Joan Walsh, with whom he lived for over six years (see chapter 1): "Human beings are eventually alone and they can only get through life by accepting this at the outset," and adds that the final page of the *Archilochos* book contains an image in which "*Archilochos Alone* glares out . . . and his features . . . bear a striking resemblance to Michael's own."[7] In this view of life he echoes Nikos Kazantzakis, whose Odysseus comes to realize, in his search for freedom, that the ultimate freedom is to be all alone, and that this ultimate freedom is found in death.

Less than five years before his death, Ayrton assembled a number of his essays into a collection entitled *Rudiments of Paradise.* He derived this title from an alleged quotation from the Reverend Robert South quoted by Borges: "Aristotle is but a fragment of Adam and Athens but the rudiments of paradise."[8] This collection of essays by Ayrton is valuable not merely for his interpretations of many artists and works of art but especially for what it provides by way of Ayrton's revelation of himself.

In his brief introductory essay, Ayrton also quotes two other statements from Borges's essay, "The Fearful Fear of Pascal": "'Nature is an infinite sphere, whose centre is everywhere and whose circumference is nowhere'; 'It may be,' as Borges concludes, 'that universal history is the history of the different intonation given a handful of metaphors.'"[9] Immediately thereafter Ayrton revealed this significant insight into himself and his work:

> Certainly the history of my life and of the works of art which have especially enriched it is precisely that: the depiction or incantation of a handful of metaphors whose splendour rests upon their intonation. About the fearful sphere which we inhabit, whose centre may be calculated and whose circumference is physically established, there spin metaphors whose centre is everywhere and whose circumference shows itself only through holes in the dark. (1971, 10)

Ayrton's "handful of metaphors" encompasses the labyrinth, its creator and his son, and its occupant. Drawing deeply from the artistic traditions of classical antiquity and their extension through the Middle Ages and the Renaissance, and even into the modern era, Ayrton himself enriched the tradition with his own intonations of these metaphors.

The visual reality Ayrton gave to these metaphors rarely attracted favorable comment, if any comment at all, from the critics. He was too often dismissed as idiosyncratic or as a dilettante who dabbled in too many media to become expert in any of them, or as too cerebral, too old-fashioned in his artistic vision.[10] Nonetheless, his works sold quite well, and he continued to give expression to the bottomless source of inspiration that he found in myth and by observing human nature. To understand him and what motivated him, one must look not only to his creations in the plastic arts but also to his extensive writings.

Rudiments of Paradise contains two sets of three essays, one set focusing on Michelangelo, the other on Picasso, which are crucial to understanding Ayrton and his work. His first essay on Michelangelo, "Prometheus Bound," opens with these sentences:

> Michelangelo's contemporaries thought him the greatest artist who had ever lived and they called him "divine." His reputation as sculptor, architect, painter and draughtsman has not subsequently been surpassed and who is to say that his contemporaries were wrong? Their opinion has not

> dated. He was, and is, the archetype of genius in the visual arts. He is also the archetypal artist and the central paradox around which his life revolved is the basis of the mystique which surrounds the term. *That paradox, put simply, is one of success and failure, the failure of a superhuman achievement in the light of an even more superhuman ambition.* (1971, 121; emphasis mine)

Ayrton saw Michelangelo's "failure" as a "failure at the level of Prometheus, a condition central to the problem of being the archetypal *artist* whose achievement fell short of his ambition" (1971, 145).

This same kind of towering ambition was present in Picasso, as I have shown in chapter 3, but it was also present in Henry Moore. When Moore was eighty years old, poet Donald Hall visited him at Hoglands. Hall first met Moore in 1959, when he was commissioned to do an interview of Moore for *Horizon* magazine, and he interviewed him twice more for other magazines. Through the years, they maintained contact, so Hall "knew [his] man" and could ask him: "Now that you're eighty, you must know the secret of life. What is the secret of life?" Hall continues the story:

> With anyone else the answer would have begun with an ironic laugh, but Henry Moore answered me straight. "The secret of life is to have a task, something you devote your entire life to, something you bring everything to, every minute of the day for your whole life. And the most important thing is—it must be something you cannot possibly do!" Henry Moore's work was the high road of art, and the "something you cannot possibly do" was to be the greatest sculptor who ever lived and know it.[11]

"My own high road," says Hall, "is to make poems better than Dante, Homer, and Virgil, not to mentions folks closer to home like Whitman, Dickinson, Frost, Stevens, and Kinnell."[12]

Michael Ayrton devoted his whole life to "something you cannot possibly do": Both by name and by ambition, I believe, Michael Ayrton strove to emulate Michelangelo, to achieve the Promethean heights attained by this archetypal *artist.* In short, he sought to be and to be recognized as the legitimate successor to Michelangelo, but he did so by pursuing relentlessly the classical archetype of the artist, none other than Daedalus himself. In his pursuit of Daedalus, moreover, Ayrton came to identify himself with the prototypical artisan. Jungian Erich Neumann, in *The Archetypal World of Henry Moore,* declares: "In the creative act the artist identifies himself with the thing created, as though giving out a part of himself, like a mother with her child" (25). Although Neumann describes the creative act as "an extremely concrete expression of . . . the 'matriarchal consciousness'" (ibid., 25), Ayrton's identification with Daedalus should not be construed in these terms but as a projection of himself into the mythical embodiment of the exceptionally gifted artist.

Ayrton's self-identification with his subject, with Daedalus, is not surprising, if one considers this assertion in his first essay on Michelangelo: "The greatness of his painting and sculpture exists paradoxically not in a triumph of 'self-expression' but in the reverse, in a triumph over the self, the greater because as the archetypal *artist,* Michelangelo was in fact the image-maker confronted with *himself.* . . . A man who cannot *become* the thing he seeks to portray by an imaginative transference which requires the rejection of himself, cannot truly portray it" (1971, 128). He seems to me here to be expressing his raison d'être as artist, even as he implies why, "by an imaginative transference," he *became* Daedalus as he sought to portray him.

Ayrton also came to identify himself with the Minotaur and, to a much lesser extent, even with Icarus. Nonetheless, his primary self-identification was with Daedalus, whose achievements he sought to emulate, particularly as he moved from painting to making sculpture. Like Michelangelo, whom he admired passionately and understood deeply, Ayrton moved from word to image, from image to word. To understand both artists, therefore, one must follow them as they move from one medium to another and back again. Even as Ayrton described Michelangelo's struggles, he could also have been describing his own struggle with the metaphor of the Minotaur: "Michelangelo's war within himself, his struggle to survive the Promethean eagle, was, I believe, a struggle to withstand the pressure of his own personality. The twin forces at war, good and evil, God and the devil, the spirit and the flesh, as they may variously be called, may seem to be represented in the artist by a struggle between the impersonal and the personal" (1971, 127).

In "The Translated Image," written in 1960, Ayrton both reveals his profound regard for his artistic predecessors and justifies the act of copying great masters—which he did in his youth (see chapter 1), following a tradition of artistic education dating back to pre-Renaissance times—as a means for penetrating the mind and the art of these masters: "the copyist, acting intuitively, will bring out those aspects of the work he studies which touch him most nearly, but he will also be thinking himself into the mind of the master whose secrets he hopes will be revealed to him, by copying. . . . The copyist is in the act of questioning, examining, accepting and discovering the thought of his predecessor" (1971, 155–56). Ayrton buttresses his argument by citing prominent artists, such as Michelangelo, Rubens, Poussin, Constable, and Seurat, who copied works of earlier artists as part of their own artistic education. In this essay, Ayrton clearly implies that he was not only paying homage to the artists whom he copied, but especially had striven to gain access to the source of their artistic greatness.

Working figuratively in an age dominated by abstraction, Ayrton appeared to be out of step with the times. Ayrton's observations about Leonard Baskin may help to explain his own view of life and his reasons for not accommodating himself to the prevailing fashions in art: "Human beings are his single concern and human life is to him tragic, splendid and paradoxical. . . . Of all Baskin's qualities, the two which impress me most are his wit and his courage. . . . It is courageous for any man of intelligence deliberately to hold that mirror, cracked in a peculiarly idiosyncratic way, to his vision of corruption."[13] From the "idea of sin made corporeal [which] shapes Ayrton's painting in the 1940s"[14] through his depictions of the maze maker to his representations of the Minotaur in the 1970s, there is evident in Ayrton's work a consistent pattern of holding up his idiosyncratically cracked mirror to himself and his fellow human beings, revealing a "vision of corruption" that reflects an artistic pessimism oft-belied by Ayrton's own apparent cheerfulness when engaged in witty and animated conversation with those whom he respected and enjoyed as friends. His use of mirrors, moreover, to extend the concept of the maze, relating bronze sculptures to each other by and through reflective perspex surfaces, adds a special irony to Ayrton's commentary on the work of Baskin and, by extension, upon his own work.

Perhaps it was his great admiration for classical, proto-Renaissance and Renaissance artists that drove him to write so often and so critically about Picasso, for although at age seventeen, in 1938, Ayrton wrote "a panegyric on *Guernica*," he believed passionately that Picasso had plundered the work of his predecessors, had in the process been guilty of "pure artistic vampirism" (Ayrton 1971, 219), had produced nothing but "a vast series of brilliant paraphrases based on the history of art" (ibid. 227), and by his eclecticism had practiced "his extraordinary cannibalism upon the body of the art itself" (ibid. 236). Although some of these intemperate phrases came from his earliest diatribe against Picasso, "The Master of Pastiche," written in 1944 when Ayrton was twenty-three, when he felt the full weight of Picasso's dominance of art and artists, Ayrton never repudiated his criticism of Picasso's method of mining the work of earlier artists. In 1956, however, Ayrton declared, "In any case I am not dispassionate for there is too much to envy and my admiration, no matter what I say, is too great for me to follow the impertinence of an attack at twenty-three with a judgement at thirty-five" (1971, 234).

A partial explanation for his harsh attack on Picasso also may well lie in the Neo-Romantic vision that flourished during war-time England, a vision that Ayrton thoroughly imbued as a young artist. In "Wartime Romances," William Feaver provides a keen insight into this period of British art:

> Today they are fast becoming the Grand Old Men of British Art. Thirty years ago, when they were far from being world famous, Henry Moore and Graham Sutherland were identified, for a while, with a peculiarly insular and now little-known phenomenon of the war-conscious years—English neo-Romanticism. A tendency in art, rather than a full-blown movement, it flourished between the Abdication crisis and the conquest of Everest. Excessive in many respects, occasionally absurd, this art of lyrical over-statement and wishful thinking, developed

> during the Thirties by Sutherland and Piper, was taken up by younger artists Ayrton, Craxton, Minton and Vaughan, to become a significant undercurrent in wartime Britain. Regarding isolation as something splendid, the neo-Romantics took an almost gloating delight in rural retreats and the London of blackout and blitz.[15]

When one recalls that Ayrton was strongly influenced by Pavel Tchelitchev, a Parisian Neo-Romantic from whom he was cut off by the isolation of the war years, it is not at all surprising that he took part in this short-lived movement (or "tendency").

There is, however, more than a personal vision at stake here. The isolation of this period nurtured a cultural nationalism that gave Ayrton the confident belief that British art would prevail over the defunct or discredited art of the continent. The rediscovery of the English land and the Neo-Romantic landscapes were the foundation upon which such a vision was built.[16] In an essay in 1946 Ayrton boldly proclaimed this vision of British art filling a cultural void in European art: "Great Britain is, I believe, the European nation now most likely to undertake the maintenance of that great and general tradition which has been handed down from country to country throughout history."[17] But, and this is a very large *but,* the "obstacle to the realisation of such a fantasy was Picasso's continued authority in the post-war world and his mythical potency. In 1944 Ayrton denounced Picasso at length as 'A Master of Pastiche.' . . . Ayrton's imaginary Picasso was simply one more patriarchal tyrant, on the Fascist model, the sinful father and one more dark monster such as populated Ayrton's paintings."[18]

It took a good deal of courage to challenge the primacy of an artist who cast such a long shadow over twentieth-century art, but Ayrton was never one to shrink from expressing opinions that were either unfashionable or ridiculed the current fashion in art or art criticism. A recent critic offers a less kindly view of Ayrton's antagonism toward Picasso, declaring that it "was perhaps finally explicable as an act of refusal; refusing the belated, secondary and inferior position that Picasso's priority had imposed on all other Modernist painters of the early and mid century. An 'anxiety of influence' beset those *ephebe* British Neo-Romantics who gazed upon the strong maker, Picasso; an anxiety ill-hid by the professions of boredom, mistrust and aggression from such as Sutherland, Minton and Ayrton."[19]

Ayrton's repeated representations of the Minotaur can be explained on several different levels. At one level, Ayrton gave visual expression to a unique figure in Greek mythology, the only one to wear an animal head on a human body (although such representations were common in Egyptian art). At another level, he was expressing his own struggle with that which was bestial within him. At yet another level, he deliberately challenged Picasso's artistic renderings of the Minotaur, revealing the towering ambition that drove him, just as he believed that Michelangelo was driven by a Promethean ambition to excel.

In 1956, at about the time he was being drawn ineluctably into the myth of Daedalus and Icarus, Ayrton declared that he "must obstinately remain, at the moment, among those who cannot see Picasso in the ultimate pantheon" (1971, 234). By challenging Picasso, Ayrton asserted the height of his own ambition, striving to be recognized as the legitimate successor to Michelangelo, just as Picasso sought to establish his primacy in the twentieth century by rivaling Rembrandt's etchings and Rembrandt's reputation. His obstinate refusal to grant Picasso a place "in the ultimate pantheon" of artists may reflect his awareness of the fact that there were many examples of artists, such as Puvis de Chavannes, who were immensely popular in their day but lost favor in succeeding generations. Confident of his own ability and the validity of his artistic vision, Ayrton continued throughout the next two decades to give his own intonation to the metaphors of Daedalus, Icarus, the Minotaur, and the labyrinth, disappointed and frustrated by the lack of recognition he was receiving at the time because of Picasso's dominance of the art world, yet confident that his work would stand the test of time.[20] Now, more than twenty years after his death, there is a renewed interest in his work, particularly in his painting. It is ironic that this interest is directed particularly at his Neo-Romantic works, since he destroyed some of that work because of its unpopularity and tried to modify his style to adapt somewhat to the prevailing abstraction,[21] whereas his inclination and special abilities lay in figurative or representational approaches to painting.

It is too early to declare that Michael Ayrton will assuredly make it into the pantheon of great artists, but there is no denying that some of his sculptures of Daedalus and Icarus, as well as the *Arkville Maze* and his reflector sculptures, achieve an emotive force comparable to that of great artists, from Michelangelo to Moore, Poussin to Picasso, Rembrandt to Rodin. We are indeed fortunate that he left a vast quantity of work in drawing, painting, sculpture, prose, and verse, which enable us to gain insights into his artistry and the creative process itself. For him the myths were not simply amusing stories to tell one's children but an inexhaustible source of inspiration and challenge to his genius. He drew deeply from that source, but he also replenished it by adding his own creative vision to the long history of myth-inspired art. For him, myth and creativity were inextricably intertwined, the metaphor of the labyrinth becoming a powerful vehicle for his creative expression. Image-maker,[22] maze-maker, inhabitant in a maze of his own making, Daedalus-Ayrton found that to escape one maze was to enter another. The metaphor of the labyrinth or maze released his creative energies but held him captive; he remained a penetrator still entrapped in the red thread of escape.

It is perhaps appropriate that Ayrton, in the final days of his life, was at work not only on the Archilochos project, which may have been leading him in a new direction, but also on a series of television programs, *A Question of Mirrors,* which would lead him "back through the mirror of his own past"[23] and enrich the multiple reflections of his entanglement in the meanderings of the labyrinth and the characters of myth with whom he had at various times and in various ways come to identify himself. His death came late on 16 November 1975. The next morning, at 9:00 A.M., he was scheduled to join Karl Sabbagh, the executive producer of the BBC Science and Features Department, for the recording of the first program in this series.

Bold to the end, Michael conceived this fourteen-part series as a challenge not merely to Sir Kenneth Clark's *Civilisation* series, but also to Professor Jacob Bronowski's then-recent *The Ascent of Man* series, which he admired much more than the former. *A Question of Mirrors* developed, in his writing of the scripts, into "a kaleidoscopic review of past preoccupations,"[24] and it led him to combine art and science in ways that extended beyond his earlier combinations of neutral density perspex and bronze sculptures. He pursued his own research and writing with an intensity resembling his obsessive pursuit of Daedalus at an earlier stage in his life. Perhaps he was drawing together the various strands of his heritage—especially from his scientific maternal grandparents and his poet-father—but surely he also was making yet another attempt to articulate his artistic vision to a public that had been largely shaped by a different artistic vision. The series would also have added another, more complex, mirrored self-portrait, of which he had produced many in recent months. His sudden death did not completely cancel the series, but the fourteen programs were reduced to a single hour-long program into which Karl Sabbagh condensed all the scripts Michael had written.[25]

For the headstone of Michael's grave at Hadstock cemetery, Elisabeth selected a bronze version of the maquette for the *Arkville Maze* and a bronze plaque on the obverse, with his name, his identification not as "image-maker" but as "painter and sculptor," and the dates of birth and death. The maze symbol is a most appropriate memorial, for it at once condenses and at the same time expands the complex and confusing passageways of his life and his art. In this replica of the maquette for the large brick-and-stone maze in the Catskill Mountains of New York are expressed the human condition as Michael Ayrton understood it: to the maze maker, it is infinitely complex, confusing, and all-consuming, but to the spectator, qua Daedalus, who is able to look upon it from above, it is simple and obvious. Although it would violate convention and propriety, it would also have been very appropriate to add, at the foot of the grave, a second bronze maquette, *End Maze I,* to give expression to his view of death. The maze maker (Ayrton) passes through the wall between life and death, with the horns of his bestiality shed and lying at his feet: "Each man's life is a labyrinth at the center of which lies his death, and even after death it may be that he passes through a final maze before it is all ended for him. Within the great maze of a man's life are many smaller ones, . . . and . . . in each he leaves behind him a part of his life. . . . It is a paradox of the labyrinth that its center appears to be the way to freedom" (Ayrton 1967, 12).

In the introduction to *Archilochos,* Ayrton declares that he chose to "show Archilochos naked, because he is, to me, the most naked man who ever wrote" (1977, 4). And because Ayrton wrote so much—books, articles, reviews, letters—and created so many images of himself, including nude self-portraits in bronze, he may also have given a self-description in these words. But it is the interweaving of myth and creativity that inspired and has sustained me during this long wandering in the many passageways of Ayrton's life. Myth has shown itself capable of constant renewal, with each age attracted to and enhancing different myths or different aspects of a particular myth. But it is through the interplay of myth in the mind of the creative artist that myth expands and contracts and winds itself around our lives, enriching our understanding of ourselves and our cultural heritage, enlarging our sense of self, entrapping us and yet also giving us freedom.

Rudolf Arnheim's study of the creative process through his analysis of the creation of Picasso's *Guernica* describes the work of the artist as simultaneously growth and execution. Whereas "nature grows" and a "bricklayer executes," a work of art "is grown and executed at the same time."[26] The creation of a work of art depends on the collaboration of the artist's "brain and . . . its tools: the eyes and the hands," and in the act of creating, the artist employs various faculties: seeing and acting; organizing and differentiating; experimenting and selecting; elaborating and modifying. Arnheim's generalization that "the work of art cannot unfold straightforwardly from its seed, like an organism, but must grow in what looks like leaps, forward and backward, from the whole to the part and vice versa,"[27] applies to Ayrton's treatment of the myth of Daedalus. There is no progressive movement from a single cell to a complex organism, but a meandering path with detours and retracing of steps, with increases in subtlety followed by simpler and more direct images, which are, in turn, succeeded by works of greater complexity and deeper symbolism.

Only by viewing Ayrton's entire oeuvre on the myth of Daedalus—in all its richness and complexity—can one see the tremendous power of Ayrton's artistic vision. Just as Arnheim sought to discover the structure and meaning of Picasso's *Guernica* through the analysis and comparison of the many sketches drawn by Picasso, so I have sought to find the structure and meaning of Ayrton's multiple representations of Daedalus, Icarus, the Minotaur, the labyrinth (or maze), and various related mythological figures. Summarizing Picasso's creative efforts, Arnheim declares: "Visual thinking, then, was goal-directed throughout. However, the goal was neither perceptual harmony nor originality. . . . But, as always in the arts, beauty and originality were only means to the end of making the vision visible" (1962, 133). He then asks, "Was this vision given from the beginning? Or did it emerge only gradually?" To these rhetorical questions he replies: "A germinal idea, precise in its general tenor but unsettled in its aspects, acquired its final character by being tested against a variety of possible visual realizations. When, at the end, the artist was willing to rest his case on what his eyes and hands had arrived at, he had become able to see what he meant" (1962, 134). It is safe to say that Ayrton did not take up the myth of Daedalus in 1956 with a clear vision at the beginning but that he explored an enormous "variety of possible visual realizations" of the myth until he understood Daedalus, Icarus, the Minotaur, and the labyrinth, and until he understood their significance for our time and for all time. Through his obsessive engagement for nearly two decades with this rich cycle of Greek myth, Ayrton made his own "vision visible."

His vision was to sustain a tradition in drawing and sculpture that extended back through Rodin, to Michelangelo and Giovanni Pisano, and to ancient Greece. With Leonard Baskin, he rejected the presumption of the past 150 years about art, the presumption "that truth travels on the current of change" (Jaffe, 200). Like Baskin, therefore, he challenged the prevailing trends in modern art, reclaiming the figurative tradition and the myths that had so often fed this tradition. In the process, he invested the myth of Daedalus with contemporary relevance and transformed it, by investing it with psychological overtones and psychoanalytic symbols and significance. Following protean Ayrton through his mature stage as an artist provides many insights into the role of myth in the creative process. His attempts to express his understanding of this particular cycle of myth in bronze, paint, and ink, led to mythmaking in the novel, *The Maze Maker,* which led, in turn, to new visual images and a deeper understanding of the archetypal craftsman and his idealistic, hubristic son. In the end, however, both the mythical Daedalus and his modern successor remain, as one critic said of *Guernica,* "triumphantly mysterious." Deep, very deep, is the well of the past. And deep, very deep, is the well of myth from which this creative artist drew to make his artistic vision visible.

Notes

INTRODUCTION

1. Neumann 2.
2. See, for example, Nyenhuis 1967, and Ward.
3. "Sight Unseen," in Ayrton 1971, 195. Ayrton notes that Berlioz had "expressly stated that painting meant nothing to him" and adds: "When I first encountered this remark in his Memoirs, it came as rather a blow to me personally, for Berlioz is surely of all great composers the painter's composer" (ibid.).
4. Searle 1978, 99–100.
5. Capisco is, of course, also an Italian verb meaning "I understand." The double entendre would have been deliberate, for Ayrton delighted in wordplay and double meanings, as is evident, for example, in his *Fabrications*.
6. Kern. See also Ernst Krause; Matthews; Santarcangeli; Bord 1976; Faris; and Reed Doob.
7. Lewis 1949b; rpt. Michel and Fox. He precedes this prophecy with the assertion that Ayrton's "stamina is unmistakable, since it is of a piece with the air of stability possessed by his work. . . . With Michael Ayrton, unlike the other 'young,' we have emphasis on subject-matter. . . . He may be the bridge by means of which the British 'young' move over into a more literary world again."
8. Raphael 67.
9. Raphael 68: "How the English hate a polymath . . . and how much more they hate a polymorph!"
10. Ayrton 1970e.

CHAPTER 1

1. He offered this explanation to me during one of our many conversations at Bradfields in the early 1970s. Variations on the reasons for changing his name follow in the text and n. 4.
2. Fletcher. Another reviewer says: "We must linger with him and see closely within his thoughts, always straining after the finer mysteries, the less tangible consummations. But when his language does unveil the full substance of his passionate search, we find it hard to think of a modern poet who excels him in the intimate spiritual revelation of human love" (Anon., *Nation and Atheneum,* 28 [19 February 1921], 709).
3. Hopkins 1994, at 23, offers a poignant description of Gerald Gould's declining health and alcoholic life during Michael's teen age years.
4. Raphael. This statement follows the assertion that "Because he was not a scholar, he aped scholarship with scholarly impressiveness: his book on Pisano . . . could be read as furious and not unworthy—evidence of his desire to please the highest examiners." A writer in the *New Yorker* (9 March 1968, 30, col. 1) quotes Michael Ayrton's story that his mother demonstrated her equality with her husband by adding her name to his, with the result that "their son was born Michael Ayrton-Gould; he later lopped off the Gould, as professionally clumsy." Peter Cannon-Brookes 1978a, 7, repeats the story that Ayrton chose his mother's surname because "an artist whose name begins with 'A' will always be close to the top of the list in mixed exhibitions" and adds: "For some years, following the example of Utrillo, he signed his name 'Michael Ayrton.g' in deference to his father's name but dropped the 'g' shortly after 1945."
5. Frye 6.
6. Jaffe 83.
7. Schneider 19.
8. Barbara Bodichon Ayrton was named for Madame Bodichon, one of the founders of Girton College, Cambridge, and a benefactor of Hertha Marks, who went up to Girton in 1876, just seven years after its founding at Hitchin and three years after it had been established just outside Cambridge. Hopkins 1994, 2, dates the birth of Barbara Ayrton in 1892, but Sharp, at 123–26, quotes from correspondence between Madame Bodichon and Hertha Ayrton regarding Barbara prior to the death of Madame Bodichon in June 1891.
9. Hertha Ayrton, quoted in Sharp 192f.
10. Professor Ayrton had another daughter, Edith, by his first wife, his cousin Matilda Chaplin, a pioneering woman doctor whose premature death aborted a promising career. Edith Ayrton married writer Israel Zangwill in 1903; she also had a literary career of her own. For a complete account, see Sharp 111ff. and passim.
11. At the time of his first marriage, Ayrton held a government post in India; subsequently he held a professorship in the new University of Tokyo, prior to assuming the chair at Finsbury; still later, he became professor of applied physics at Central Technical College, South Kensington (Sharp, 114, 129f., and 205). According to another source, however, in 1884 he became "professor of electrical engineering at South Kensington" (*Encyclopedia Britannica,* 1952, 2, 823). That same source reports that "in 1868 [he] went out to Bengal in the service of the Indian Government telegraph department." One of Michael Ayrton's stories in *Fabrications* (97ff.) concerns his interesting and illustrious maternal grandfather, who was credited with having introduced electrical engineering into Japan in the 1860s and was reported to have lectured at the Imperial University of Tokyo with a loaded gun on his desk (notes on a conversation with the artist).

    Hertha Marks was born Phoebe Sarah Marks at Portsea to Levi and Theresa Moss Marks. Levi Marks was a poor watchmaker and jeweler who had fled his native Poland to escape the persecution of Jews by the czarist regimes. The name Hertha was invented for Phoebe at sixteen: Ottilie Blind, younger sister of one of the biographers of George Eliot, invented this unusual name for her, inspired partly "by admiration for Swinburne's poem . . . and partly by a fancy of Ottilie's that . . . Sarah Marks resembled the goddess Erda" (Sharp 27–28). Miss Marks was brought up in London by her aunt, Mrs. Alphonse Hartog, who introduced her to Madame Bodichon, founder of the new women's college in Cambridge, Girton College, where Hertha Marks subsequently enrolled in 1876.
12. Letter from the secretary of the Royal Society, Professor J. Larmor, quoted in Sharp 181. Madame Curie had earlier received the Davy medal from the Royal Society jointly with her husband, but Mrs. Ayrton was the first woman medalist of the Royal Society in her own right (Sharp 181).
13. This account of Ayrton's recollections of his childhood is based on his remarks to me during a personal interview in August 1972. For much greater detail about Ayrton's childhood, see Hopkins 1994, 1–22. Hopkins, at 17–20, clearly implies that his tenure at the Beeches extended for five years, not two, as

reported to me by Ayrton himself. She dates his "bout of osteomyelitis" at age eleven and describes the cure as almost worse than the illness, for the cure went awry and necessitated surgery, which "left the boy with an ugly, depressed scar adhering to the bone [of his leg] beneath, and a slight but definite lameness" (18).

14. Quoted in the *Listener,* 16 April 1970, 512, cols. 1–2. Ayrton, in a letter to the author dated 19 June 1973, states that he would have said "expelled" rather than "fired," so he may have been misquoted in this article. In Hopkins's 1994 account of this episode, the young woman was in fact "the French mistress, a young and pretty girl, whom he eventually seduced in a haystack," and the discovery of their misdeed "led to her instant dismissal and return to France" and a prompt summons to Gould by the headmaster (20).
15. Schneider 170–73.
16. Denvir 1947, 79.
17. For further details on Ayrton's furtive trip to Barcelona and his subsequent stay in Vienna with cousin Millie, see Cannon-Brookes 1978a, 7. See also Ayrton's own account of his cousin Millie in "An Imperfect Copy of Antichrist" (1973, 20–23), upon which Cannon-Brookes's account appears to be based.
18. Ayrton 1962a (rev. ed. 1966), 13. Subsequent references in the text will be drawn from this edition without footnote. The "Biographical Note" in the introduction to the catalogue of the 1949 retrospective exhibition at the Wakefield City Art Gallery states that this lengthy stay in Vienna occurred when he was fourteen and that "during the pre-war years he explored, either alone or in company with parents or friends, a considerable part of Western Europe, returning to England from time to time to study for short periods at innumerable arts schools from which he does not consider he learnt much."
19. Warncke 19.
20. Cannon-Brookes 1978a, 8, follows the official statement in *Drawings and Sculpture,* when he declares that "Ayrton returned to London and exhibited for the first time, at the Zwemmer Gallery." Perhaps Ayrton considered the earlier exhibitions as inconsequential, but still he recorded them in his master record book.
21. Cannon-Brookes 1978b, 117. For another view of Ayrton's place within English neo-Romanticism, see Feaver, esp. 83, col. 2; 84, col. 4; and 85, cols. 3–4. Also see Mellor.
22. Gielgud notes that before the war Ayrton "worked in Paris with Pavel Tchelitchev, on the Jouvet production of Giraudoux's *Ondine*" (115). James Laver, in his introduction to *Paintings by Michael Ayrton,* adds the name of Jack Beddington ("then in Shell Mex") as one of Ayrton's first patrons and assigns the Gielgud commission to 1941 (6). Hopkins 1994, at 41, quotes from a letter dated in January 1941, from Michael to Sir Hugh Walpole, in which he thanks him for having shown to John Gielgud the works by Ayrton in his collection, and, at 54, recounts the terms of the agreement between Gielgud and Ayrton regarding his designs for the production of *Macbeth.*
23. Cannon-Brookes 1978a, 8. Hopkins 1994, at 54, states that "in 1939, inspired by their theatrical experiences in Paris, they had produced at Les Baux a series of designs for a hypothetical production of *Troilus and Cressida;* returning to London they began work on Purcell's *Dido and Aeneas* for Tristram Jellinek, at the Unity Theatre, and made four set and twenty-four costume drawings before the project folded."
24. For further information on Ayrton's relationship with Joan Walsh, see Cannon-Brookes 1978a, 11–35 and passim; also Hopkins 1994, 70ff., 80f., 112f., 128–39, and passim. Hopkins, at 112, notes that in Ayrton's painting *Joan in the Fields,* Joan is depicted wearing on her finger "the heavy ring which Michael had given her in exchange for one of hers, without the ceremony of marriage but with similar connotations." Although or because Michael declined to marry her, Joan had her name legally changed to Joan Ayrton; she used that name until she married George Foa (notes on a conversation with Elisabeth Ayrton, 7 August 1984). A number of works in exhibitions during their relationship attribute ownership to Mrs. Joan Ayrton (by a printer's error, one painting attributed to her collection is listed in *Paintings by Michael Ayrton* [no. 38] as in the collection of "Mrs. John Ayrton"). The Christmas card which Michael Ayrton sent out in 1948 (created by him, using a signed drawing, NATIVITY NO VII, dated 29 October 1948) had the following inscription inside: "From Michael and Joan Ayrton/Christmas 1948. 4 All Souls Place/London W.1." The Christmas cards in 1949 and 1950 are from Michael Ayrton alone.
25. This information is based on *Drawings and Sculpture,* 14, and the biographical note in the catalogue for the 1949 exhibition arranged at the Wakefield City Art Gallery. Denvir 1947, 79, offers a slightly different sequence of events and gives the name of the school as the London County Council Art School at Camberwell. Hopkins 1994, 69, states that he applied for and accepted the job at Camberwell in July 1942 and that it involved teaching "life drawing and design on Fridays."
26. See, for example, Melville 1949; also *Drawings and Sculpture,* 14; Cannon-Brookes 1978a, 10, and 1978b, 116–17; and Mellor.
27. Hopkins 1994, 75. For a full account of his tortured wrestling with his love for Minton, see Hopkins 1994, 72–78.
28. Reprinted in Ayrton 1971, 217–27, as "The Master of Pastiche," this was presented in 1945 as a BBC broadcast, "Picasso as Black Magician," and later published as an article in John Lehmann's *New Writing and Daylight,* (London: Hogarth Press, 1946) vii, 108–17. For a more complete account of the extent of the hostility engendered by the BBC broadcast, see Hopkins 1994, 120ff.
29. "The Enemy as Friend," in Ayrton 1971, 257–67, esp. 262 and 267. See also Rosenthal 1971, 5ff.
30. Searle 1978, 99.
31. Laver 7.
32. Introduction to the catalogue of the exhibition arranged in 1949 by the Wakefield City Art Gallery [7], and a letter to the author dated 19 June 1973. Ayrton's master record book indicates that this one-man show, held in January–February 1946, was the fiftieth occasion on which his work was exhibited and that there were eight other occasions in 1946 when one or more of his drawings and paintings were put on public view.
33. Hopkins 1994, 127ff. In a letter to the author, dated August 31, 1996, Hopkins, commenting on a draft of this manuscript, asserts: "One note I would make is that where you question

my dating (as in the case of MA's sojourn at Felcourt, and his trips to Italy), I have generally made use of dated letters, in view of Michael's (admitted) lack of concern with precision of dates and durations, which often led him to telescope or extend experiences in keeping with their subjective importance." I modified my version to take her comments into account.

34. Denvir 1947, 80, also notes the link of Ayrton's art with that of the Renaissance in northern Europe, calling particular attention to the Isenheim altarpiece: "Anyone who has seen this masterpiece . . . must have been struck by how deeply its spirit has influenced the painting of Michael Ayrton." This powerful work also had a tremendous impact upon an American sculptor, Leonard Baskin, who described his experience during a trip to Colmar in these words: "For months afterwards I could not regard other work, being haunted by the swollen gaunt green with the pustules of disease, lacerated, rutted, bloody body of Christ, hung in the black landscape of despair . . . [and] the weeping and imploring figures of Mary, John, and the Magdalen" (*Baskin: Sculpture, Drawings, Prints* [1970], 5; qtd. in Jaffe at 47.).
35. Jaffe 41.
36. See Jaffe's comments on Valentiner's establishment of the linkage between Tino and Maillol, Lehmbruck, and Barlach (49).
37. D. C. Barrett, in *Contemporary Artists,* 3rd ed., ed. Colin Naylor (Chicago: St. James Press, 1989), 69.
38. Jaffe 9.
39. Jaffe 27.
40. Jaffe 30.
41. Recounted to the author by Mr. Christopher Hull, then director of Fulham Fine Arts, Fulham Road, during an interview on 15 August 1984, shortly before his opening of the Christopher Hull Gallery, 17 Motcomb Street, London. By this time, Elisabeth Ayrton had chosen Mr. Hull to represent the estate in the sale of work by Michael Ayrton.
42. Jaffe 30.
43. Accounts of Ayrton's personal life during this period are based upon conversations with his widow in 1989, as well as upon Hopkins 1994, 140ff. Cannon-Brookes 1978a, 28–35, gives slightly different details and dates, stating that the trio traveled to Italy together in 1948 and that Michael and Elisabeth traveled there alone in 1949. Whatever the dates, the outcome of the trip(s) to Italy is not in dispute.
44. Cannon-Brookes 1978a, 35.
45. Introduction to the 1949 Wakefield catalogue [7]. This exhibition at the Redfern Gallery included nineteen paintings and thirteen drawings from the years 1947–1949, but it was not the first exhibition of Ayrton's Italian paintings: in September–October 1948 the Hanover Gallery, London, mounted an exhibition of twenty small oils under the title "Italian Journey." The catalogue of the exhibition at the Redfern Gallery contained an introduction by Wyndham Lewis (reprinted in the 1949 Wakefield catalogue), in which he asserts, "MICHAEL AYRTON, though the youngest of 'the young,' is one of the most intellectually mature" and "a great classical artist in the making."
46. Lewis 1949b, 988, col. 1. The review was reprinted both in Rosenthal's introduction to the 1971 National Book League Catalogue, and in Michel and Fox, 393. It should be noted that Michel and Fox's notes to 393 (469) neglect to mention Lewis's introduction to the 1949 Redfern and Wakefield catalogues among his writings on Ayrton. Much less enthusiastic than either Wallis or Lewis is Eric Newton ("North & South," *Sunday Times,* 5 June 1949), who remarked that "a draughtsman-turned-painter *adds* colour to form" and stated that he finds color "an intrusion" in Ayrton's paintings, although he also described Ayrton's drawings as "always urgent and often memorable."
47. Hendy 1949b, 34–35.
48. Catalogue of the retrospective exhibition at Whitechapel Art Gallery, September–October 1955, 3 and 27. The revival was newly choreographed by John Cranko and produced by Christopher West.
49. Catalogue of the retrospective exhibition at Whitechapel (1955), 3 and 27. There are internal discrepancies in the catalogue, for the film is erroneously dated 1955, at 27, even though it is stated (at 3) that Ayrton introduced the film at an international seminar at Harvard University in 1954. *Drawings and Sculpture* and subsequent catalogues all ascribe it to 1951. The catalogues also attribute its production to the British Film Institute. Basil Wright produced the film, Adrien de Potier directed it, Sir Laurence Olivier and C. Day Lewis were the narrators, and Alan Rawsthorne wrote the music.
50. Baskin, quoted in Peter Selz, *New Images of Man* (1959), 35; qtd. in Jaffe, at 38–39.
51. For full details of the discovery, acquisition, and renovation of Bradfields, see Hopkins 1994, 172ff. She notes with interest that Bradfields was acquired from an old friend of Michael's father, Sir Francis Meynell, and that Michael visited the home as a child.
52. See Hopkins 1994, 170 ff., for a full discussion of Ayrton's maturation through his life with Elisabeth. She notes that with these changes in his life also came a change in his name. Until then "he had been Micky or Mike to his friends. Now he began to establish himself as Michael and for the rest of his life he resisted all attempts at shortenings" (171).
53. Ayrton 1953d. Ayrton's 1949 "Portrait of Dylan," a 9″ x 6″ wash on grey paper, was reproduced both here (opposite 32) and in the Whitechapel catalogue (catalogue no. 77, pl. X).
54. *Baskin* 19; qtd. in Jaffe (52).
55. Barrett 69.
56. Jaffe 59.
57. Letter from Dr. Justine Hopkins, 31 August 1996.
58. Wright 101.
59. Sigmund Freud, "Symbolism in Dreams," from *The Complete Introductory Lectures on Psychoanalysis* (1966, trans. James Strachey), rpt. in F. Parvin Sharpless, *Symbol and Myth in Modern Literature* (Rochelle Park, NJ: Hayden Book Company, Inc., 1976), 190.
60. Jaffe 37.
61. Irving Sandler, *The Triumph of American Painting* (1970), 62; qtd. in Jaffe (37).
62. Haskell 1978, 98.
63. Rosenthal 1964.
64. Hamet Gallery Exhibition Catalogue Number 24, "Michael Ayrton: A Debt to Hector Berlioz" (November 18–December

20, 1969), inside back cover. The *Times Literary Supplement,* 18 July 1968, 759, reports that Ayrton received the award at a ceremony on that date.

65. Regarding the television special on Berlioz, Ayrton wrote, in a letter to the author dated 19 June 1973: "The idea was Berlioz' invention of *L'idée fixe* (his own obsession) and mine with him. L'idée fixe was translated as 'A Singular Obsession.'"
66. The Daedalus I Gallery formerly bore the unfortunate name "The Generous Critic Art Gallery," but it was renamed upon Ayrton's advice. It did not last long, however, under its new name, for it went out of existence in 1973.
67. Letter to the author, dated 17 July 1973, from E. G. Chandler, F.R.I.B.A., F.R.T.P.I., City Architect and Planning Officer, Corporation of London. The sculpture was presented by the Bernard Sunley Investment Trust.
68. Three scripts (numbers I, VII, and XIII) from this projected series were published in *Labrys,* 3 (October 1978): 36–57. See also Sabbagh's essay in the same issue.
69. Jaffe 38–39.
70. Qtd. in Sabbagh (60).
71. Letter to the author from Dr. Justine Hopkins, dated August 31, 1996.
72. 1978c, 18.
73. Karl Sabbagh produced a one-hour posthumous version of the planned fourteen-hour series. Hopkins 1994 (418), also reports that Ayrton "received a second memorial tribute, for although Exeter University had no mechanism for awarding an honorary doctorate posthumously, the address which would have marked its presentation was given at the Congregation in July 1976."
74. Donald Davie, *In the Stopping Train* (Manchester: Carcanet New Press, 1977), 21–22. Davie earned an international reputation for his translations of Boris Pasternak, as well as for his poetry and books of literary criticism. Among his works of criticism was a review of Ayrton's *The Maze Maker.*

CHAPTER 2

1. Because this book is primarily concerned with the role of this myth in the creative process, I have limited myself to a rather straightforward recounting of the myths, rather than exploring and expatiating on theories of myth. Nonetheless, it is essential that I call attention to a work of major significance, Sarah P. Morris's *DAIDALOS and the Origins of Greek Art.* The scope of her interpretations of myth and art is extraordinary, and many of her conclusions are bold and provocative, but also often based upon compelling arguments and persuasive examples. Her insights into the origins of Greek art and her theories about Athenian appropriation of the myth of Daedalus from Cretan and Near Eastern sources demand serious consideration.
2. In a narrow technical sense Apollodorus should not lead this list, since the extant text derives from an abridgement made in the first or second century C.E., but I have placed him in this position since his original work was written in the second century B.C.E., thus preceding Diodorus's work by about a century, and since Diodorus attached his historical account (drawn from various sources) to a chronological framework dependent on Apollodorus. These sources for the reconstruction of the myth will normally be parenthetically identified in the text of this chapter. Standard abbreviations will be used.
3. On the *Daedalus* of Sophocles, see A. C. Pearson, vol. 1, 110–14, who considers the Talus story to have been an important part of this drama and notes that one scholiast incorrectly referred to it as the *Talus* (113); on the *Camici* see Pearson, vol. 2, 3–8, who tentatively identifies the *Minos* (vol. 2, 69) as an alternate title for this play (4), although there may have been another play by that name; for a discussion of whether there also was a *Theseus,* see Pearson, 1, 184f. On the *Cretans* of Euripides see Cantarella, who impressively assembles testimony, fragments (one is more than fifty lines long, one recently identified papyrus fragment exceeds twenty-five lines, and two are over ten lines in length), and ancient artistic representations presumably related to the drama; and Webster 87–92, who plausibly reconstructs a fair portion of the plot from these sources and presents (299) a brief selection of vase paintings and reliefs that illustrate the play. Webster dates this play early (2–4), possibly as early as 442–441 B.C.E. (32), whereas Cantarella suggests ca. 433 B.C.E. (10f.). This play, which purportedly included a monody by Icarus (Scholiast to Aristophanes *Frogs* 849) and possibly presented him on stage in at least two other scenes (Webster 87), represents the earliest known literary reference to Icarus (see Beazley 1927, 224, and Robert 1920, 364ff.). For the *Theseus* of Euripides see Webster 105–9 and 303, who would date it between the *Cretans* and the known performances of 438 B.C.E. (32), although he can with certainty place it only prior to the *Wasps* of Aristophanes (422 B.C.E.; see 4).

    On the *Daedalus* of Aristophanes, see Edmonds, I, 624–27 (dated 414 B.C.E., 625n.), and on his *Cocalus* see Edmonds 670–75 (dated 387 B.C.E. and produced under the name of Aristophanes' son Araros; see 671). On Plato's *Daedalus* see Edmonds 494–95 (dated either 399 or 387–386 B.C.E., 495n.), who would like to identify Plato's Daedalus with the philosopher Plato and Icarus with Alcibiades. Cantarella (157–58) lists nineteen tragedies and twenty-four comedies on the various aspects of Cretan myth and legend, of which only one (Euripides' *Hippolytus*) is extant. No. 38 in his list is yet another comedy entitled *Daedalus,* by either Eubulus or Philippus, the son of Aristophanes, who produced Eubulus's plays (Scholiast to Plato, *Apology* 19c, cited in Edmonds, II [1959], 16–17, where a single line of this lost play is also to be found). Edmonds, III A (1961), 120–21, includes two fragments of the lost *Theseus* of Diphilus, a poet of the New Comedy (late fourth to early third century B.C.E.), who was the last in a long series of Greek poets to dramatize the myths connected with Crete.

    One should not overlook earlier poetic treatments, such as the dithyrambs of Bacchylides: nos. 17 and 18 (Snell-Maehler; Teubner, 1970) on Theseus and no. 26 on Pasiphaë, which, though fragmentary, is complete enough to reveal that it concerned Daedalus's construction of the cow for the satisfaction of Pasiphaë's lust (for an eloquent and sensitive English translation, see Fagles 66). Earlier literary references to Daedalus (e.g., *Iliad* 18.590ff.) will be treated subsequently.

4. On Pherecydes, who was born around 480 B.C.E., see Felix Jacoby, *Die Fragmente der griechischen Historiker,* I, 58ff. and 97 (F 146). F 146, the Scholiast on Sophocles' *O.C.* 472, not only names the parents of Daedalus but also asserts that the Attic deme Daedalidae derived its name from Daedalus (97). Ancient sources for the life and work of Daedalus are assembled in Overbeck nos. 74–142 (no. 88 = Jacoby *FGrH,* Pherecydes F 146). Plato's *Ion* 533a (Overbeck 86) and D. S. 4.76.1 (Overbeck 87) concur with Pherecydes in naming Metion as his father, although Diodorus adds another generation, inserting Eupalamus between Erechtheus and Metion. Pausanias 7.4.5 (Overbeck 89) places Daedalus in the royal house of Athens, the Metionidae, and elsewhere calls him the son of Palamaon (Paus. 9.3.2 = Overbeck 74). Apollodorus leads the list of eleven sources (Overbeck 75–85) identifying Eupalamus as the father of Daedalus, although not all agree on his mother's name: she is also called Phrasimede (Overbeck 78), Metiadousa (Overbeck 79), and Merope (Overbeck 90). Frontisi offers the following summary: "Among his direct ancestors are Eupalamus, 'skillful hand,' and Palamaon, 'manual,' two names which denote the dexterity and creative skill of the hand. But Daedalus's father is most often said to be Metion, 'the man of *metis,*' and his mother is sometimes Metiadousa, 'she who delights in *metis,*' sometimes Iphinoë, 'she of the vigorous spirit,' and even Phrasimede, 'she who conceives of a plan'"(88).
5. The name Metion for the craftsman's father is, however, not inappropriate, since it is related to the noun *metis,* which means "wisdom, skill, craft" and "counsel, plan, undertaking" (*L.S.J.*). The goddess Metis, or Wisdom, when pregnant with Athena, was swallowed by her mate, Zeus, who subsequently gave birth to Athena from his head (Hes. *Th.* 886–900, 924–26, and fr. 343 [= Chrysippus fr. 908]).

   It should also be noted that Ayrton, in *The Maze Maker,* follows Pherecydes in establishing the lineage of Daedalus.
6. Frontisi 88.
7. Pausanias 1.21.4 and 1.26.4 calls him Calos (Calus), as does the *Souda* (*sub* "temple of Perdix"), whereas Sophocles in the *Camici* (fr. 323, Pearson, 2, 5–6) called him Perdix, i.e., Partridge, and he is followed in this by Ovid (*Met.* 8.236ff.), Hyginus (*Fab.* 39, 244, and 274), and others.
8. Ovid *Met.* 8.244ff. says that the model for Perdix's (Talos's/Talus's) invention of the iron saw was the backbone of a fish. Hyginus *Fab.* 274 and other Latin writers follow Ovid's lead, except Pliny, who does not mention him in his list of inventors, attributing to Daedalus not only carpentry but also many of the tools of the trade, such as the saw, the carpenter's axe, the plumb-line, the auger, glue, and isinglass (*N.H.* 7.198). Pliny also reports that a relative of Daedalus named Euchir was credited by Aristotle with the invention of painting in Greece (*N.H.* 7.205); elsewhere he ascribes the invention of sails to Icarus, the mast and yard to Daedalus, and the anchor to Eupalamus, adding that Minos was the first to engage in a naval battle (*N.H.* 7.209). Cook, 1, 719–30, discusses the myth of Talos, linking him with the sun, the Cretan brazen Talos, and with Zeus himself, suggesting also that the invention of the compass would "naturally [be] attributed to one who, as the Sun, was himself at once circular and discoidal" (725). He also sees in Talos the mythical explanation for the *cire perdue* or "lost-wax" process of bronze casting (723f.).

   Mrs. Judith Binder would date the invention of the compass to the "last quarter of the eleventh century B.C.," since its designs appear on pottery at the Kerameikos which is "datable to 1025–1000 B.C." (notes on a conversation 16 March 1974). I am also indebted to both Mrs. Binder and the late Emeritus Professor Eugene Vanderpool of the American School of Classical Studies at Athens for calling to my attention in 1974 a then-recent discussion of the possible location of the Tomb of Talos (Kalos) on the south slope of the Acropolis (implied by Paus. 1.21.4) in Beschi. See also Judeich.
9. Paus. 7.4.5 says that after Daedalus killed his nephew, he voluntarily went into exile to Minos in Crete, since he knew the customs of his city.
10. Cf. Paus. 8.16.3, where he specifically refers to Homer's comparison (*Il.* 18.590ff.) of the *choros* ("dancing floor" or "dance") wrought by Hephaestus on the shield of Achilles to the *choros* made by Daedalus.
11. Apollod. 3.1.4 says that the Minotaur had a bull's face, but D. S. 4.77.3 declares that the upper portion of the body down to the shoulders was that of a bull. Euripides described him as a "hybrid, monstrous whelp" (F 996) in whom "were mingled the double nature of man and bull" (F 997; Plut. *Thes.* 15.2 quotes both excerpts).
12. Apollod. 3.1.4 describes the labyrinth as a chamber which deceives the way out by means of its tangled windings and this description is assumed to be a quotation from Greek tragedy (Nauck 34). Apollod. 3.15.8 says that it was impossible for anyone upon entering to find his way out (the one entering may in fact specifically refer to the Minotaur in this context, since the report of his imprisonment precedes this statement) because of these same "tangled windings" that blocked the unrecognizable way out.
13. Apollod. 3.15.7 and D. S. 4.60.4–5. Apollodorus offers this story as an alternate version of the myth after recounting the story that Aegeus sent the victorious youth against the bull of Marathon, which killed him, and Paus. 1.27.10 also records the same variant. Although most other sources concur with the story in Diodorus and Apollodorus, there is yet another story in Hyginus *Fab.* 41: he says that Androgeos died in battle during the war waged against the Athenians by his father.
14. Apollod. 3.15.8, D. S. 4.61.1–3, Plut. *Thes.* 15.1, and others. Bacch. *Dith.* 17 (Snell-Mähler) describes a confrontation between Minos and Theseus when on board ship from Athens to Crete with the tribute, and Plato *Phaedo* 58A–B refers to the tribute as if it were a familiar story (as it undoubtedly was). Some sources describe it as an annual tribute (see, for example, Apollod. 3.15.8 and Hyginus *Fab.* 41, as well as Virgil *Aen.* 6.21f.).
15. D. S. 4.61.3–4, but Apollod. *Epit.* 1.7 states that Theseus was included in the third group, a version which is also recorded in Ov. *Met.* 8.171 and Plut. *Thes.* 17. Hellanicus, a fifth century B.C.E. historian whose history included the mythological past,

reported that Minos personally came to Athens to select the Minotaur's victims (cited by Plut. *Thes.* 17.3), among whom was Theseus, but other accounts indicate that they were chosen by lot (Plut. *Thes.* 17.1, Scholiast on Homer, *Il.* 18.590), but Theseus volunteered himself (Apollod. *Epit.* 1.7, Plut. *Thes.* 17.2, Hyginus *Fab.* 41).

16. Apollod. *Epit.* 1.9; see also Hyginus *Fab.* 42 and Plut. *Thes.* 19.1. For an account of the numerous scholia on the subject, see Apollodorus, *The Library* II, 135f., n. 3.
17. Apollod. *Epit.* 1.9. From the scholiasts we learn that Theseus "was to catch the monster by the hair and sacrifice him to Poseidon" (Apollodorus, *The Library* II, 135f., n. 3). Plut. *Thes.* 17.3 cites Hellanicus as his source for the requirement that the Athenians who came as tribute were to carry no weapons, but artistic representations of the myth as early as the seventh century regularly show Theseus slaying the Minotaur with a sword (see Ward 29f., and Illustrations 15, 25–27, 30, 41–42, 111).

    Among the better known representations depicting Theseus slaying the Minotaur with a sword are a stamnos and an amphora of the early fifth century B.C.E., both from Vulci, by the Kleophrades painter and Oinokles, respectively. For a more complete account of these vase paintings, see appendix C.
18. For a full account of the Theseus myth, see Ward.
19. Apollod. *Epit.* 1.12. The twelfth-century Byzantine polymath Johannes Tzetzes in his *Chiliades* 1.498 is the only other writer to name the mother of Icarus (although he calls him Icarius). In *The Maze Maker* (42–44), Ayrton places the union of Daedalus and Naucrate and the birth of Icarus at the home of his cousin Pallas at Sounion, sometime prior to their departure for Crete, significantly expanding the myth at this point. Hyginus *Fab.* 40 merely says that Minos imprisoned Daedalus and that Pasiphaë freed him from his chains, after which he made the wings for their escape.
20. Apollod. *Epit.* 1.12–13 also records the story of the wings, the warnings to Icarus, the flight, the fall of Icarus, and the safe arrival of Daedalus at Camicus in Sicily. D. S. 4.77.7–9 expands the tale somewhat, and his account provides a reasonable outline for Ovid's story, although it is likely that Ovid's sources were Philostephanus of Cyrene and "some Alexandrian poetic source as well" (Hollis 58). Apollod. 2.6.3 records a variant on the burial of Icarus, crediting Heracles with the deed after his discovery of the corpse washed ashore on the island of Doliche, which he renamed Icaria, and Paus. 9.11.5 also credits the burial to Heracles.

    The direction of the flight of Daedalus and Icarus from Crete, as Ovid and others describe it, takes them toward the Aegean island which bears Icarus's name. Recognizing the difficulty of synchronizing this version of the myth with the story of Daedalus at Cumae, Ayrton altered the mythic tradition in *The Maze Maker.* He names none of the islands listed by Ovid, save Delos, over which Icarus appropriately begins his ascent to challenge the Delian god (138f.). Ayrton further "corrects" the myth by having Daedalus declare that he neither saw Icarus fall into the sea nor found his corpse, thus eliminating the problem of the location of Icaria, and Ayrton's Daedalus then "flew on without clear direction" (142), thus resolving the geographical inconsistencies of the myth.
21. Silius Italicus *Punica* 12.89ff. also records the story of the temple at Cumae, with one rather interesting rationalistic twist: the two winged figures merely glided until Icarus's wings melted and he plunged into the sea (92–99); then Daedalus in grief beat his breast, thus unwittingly propelling himself forward (99–101).
22. Although one of the manuscripts (C = Codex Vaticanus) reads "honeycomb" (*kerion*), editors as early as 1888 (Fr. Vogel's Teubner edition) emended the text to read "ram" (*krion*) and this reading prevails in current texts, but the tradition of the golden honeycomb appears to be too well ingrained to be set aside by a mere textual emendation (see, for example, *OCD* 2, 309f., and Cronin). Ayrton, however, like many another mythmaker, cleverly combines these traditions: Daedalus makes both a golden honeycomb and a golden ram (1967, 292 and 298).
23. Apollod. *Epit.* 1.14–15 and Zenobius 4.92. Ovid *Met.* 8.260–62 compresses the story, merely stating that Daedalus arrived in Sicily and that Cocalus took up arms in defense of the suppliant.
24. Paus. 10.17.4 names Aristaeus as the leader of the Sardinian colonists and rejects the possibility that Daedalus could have participated in the colonization, on the grounds that he was a contemporary of Oedipus, whereas Aristaeus was husband to a daughter of Cadmus.
25. Apollod. 2.6.3 records the story of a statue at Pisa made by Daedalus in return for the burial of Icarus. This statue, which closely resembled Heracles, was mistaken at night by him for a living person, so he threw a stone at it and hit it.
26. Skylax 39, 4 Fabr. (qtd. in Jones [6]). *The Encyclopedia of World Art,* 7, 34, locates it at Solossa, in Libya, and describes it as "probably a Carthaginian work." Both sources also list a sculpture of Artemis in Caria (Jones 7), and *EWA* adds a "crater with gigantomachy and Kronos, for Kokalos."
27. Fpl = KN 200. See Ventris and Chadwick 128 and 303–12. Also see Palmer 1963, 235–37. In the fourth century B.C.E. there apparently also was a Daidaleion in Attica, since a marble stele found in the Athenian Agora and recording the transactions of the poletai for 367–366 B.C.E. describes the sale of a confiscated house, "of which the boundaries are on the north the road leading to the Daedaleion and the Daidaleion" (Crosby 18.) I am indebted to Mrs. Judith Binder for calling this item to my attention.
28. Ventris and Chadwick 128.
29. Ibid. 303. Palmer, however, inclines toward the view that "these texts are simply store-room dockets accounting for the disbursement of oil" (235).
30. Ventris and Chadwick 305f.; also Palmer 1963, 236f., who concludes: "In the above texts the sole commodity booked is oil, which, it may be surmised, was intended for ritual anointing."
31. Ventris and Chadwick 308.
32. Fs 32 and Fs 723. Both are recorded in the first three editions of *The Knossos Tablets: B.I.C.S.,* Suppl. 2 (January 1956), 49; Suppl. 7 (1959), 49; Suppl. 15 (1964), 94–95. The fourth edition, ed. John Chadwick et al. (Cambridge: Cambridge Univ. Press, 1971), deletes Fs 723 without explanation.
33. Gg 702 = KN 205. Ventris and Chadwick (310) accept it only tentatively, but Palmer 1963 (238f.) appears to harbor no doubts.

For a discussion of the implications of these discoveries for Mycenaean religion, see Palmer 1965, 130–42.

34. If one accepts the thesis that the Knossos Tablets date not from 1400 B.C.E. but from a period contemporaneous with the Pylos Tablets, i.e., ca. 1200 B.C.E., as do Palmer 106–10 and Blegen (cited by Palmer 106), then there would have been a longer period of time for the deification or semi-deification of the palace builder.
35. This is the conclusion reached by Davaras. I am indebted to Mrs. Judith Binder for calling this work to my attention. In *The Maze Maker,* Ayrton displays an uncanny sense of the evolution of the myth, even though he was unaware of the occurrence of the word "Daedaleion" on the Knossos Tablets (notes on a conversation with the artist, 10 April 1974).
36. Ibid.
37. Pliny *N.H.* 3.102 adds to the sons of Daedalus a King Iapyx, who gave his name to a river in southern Italy, near Brindisi, and to the Iapygian Point (the latter story may derive from Herod. 7.170, where he records the story that off Iapygia there was a shipwreck of the Cretans who had unsuccessfully besieged Camicus for five years in an attempt to avenge the violent death of Minos). Strabo 6.3.2 similarly identifies Iapyx as a son of Daedalus by a Cretan woman, but says that the Iapygians, who perpetuated their leader's name, were Cretans who accompanied Minos to Sicily and were driven off course en route home after his death. Not to be taken seriously is the claim of another alleged descendant of Daedalus: Socrates, whose father Sophroniscus was a sculptor, parried Alcibiades' claim to divine descent with the assertion that he was descended from Zeus through Hephaestus and Daedalus (Plato *Alc.* I, 121A).
38. Callias was one of the wealthiest Athenians during the sixth century. He was victorious in the Olympic Games in 552 B.C.E. See Jones 7.
39. Varro *Res Divinae,* qtd. in Lact. *Inst.* 1.6.8–12. For a full discussion of oracles, see, for example, Parke; Parke and Wormell; and Flacelière.
40. Dion. Hal. 4.62.1–6; Pliny *N.H.* 13.88; Lact. *Inst.* 1.6.10–11; Servius on Virgil *Aen.* 6.72. The Sibylline Books were hidden under the statue of Apollo dedicated on the Palatine Hill in Rome in 28 B.C.E. (Norden 143). These enigmatic writings were used for political purposes, so it is not surprising that when Christianity became the official religion of Rome, they were "Christianized." Hathorn explains the consequence of this development: "This led to the Sibyls' elevation in medieval and Renaissance thought to a venerable position conterbalancing that of the Hebrew prophets. Hence on the ceiling of the Sistine Chapel Michelangelo painted the Libyan, Cumaean, Delphic, Erythraean, and Persian Sibyls as pagan companions to Ezekiel, Jonah, Jeremiah, Joel, Isaiah, Zachariah [*sic*], and Daniel" (183). He also notes that Dante, recalling Virgil's "description [in *Aeneid* VI] of the Sibyl writing her secrets on scattered leaves," evokes her story in his final vision of the Trinity: "In its depths I saw that all which is scattered throughout the universe is here encompassed, bound by love into one volume" (*Paradiso,* Canto XXXIII 61–66 and 85–87).
41. Hesiod *Works and Days* 140ff. describes the bronze race of mortals as the third of his five Ages of Man.
42. For a detailed discussion of Talus, see Roscher vol. 5, 22–37; for a shorter account, see *Apollodorus,* I, 118f., n. 1.
43. Simonides, as qtd. in the Scholiast on Plato *Resp.* 337a, Eustathius on Homer *Od.* 20.302 (1893.5ff.); and the *Souda* (*sub* "Sardonic laughter").
44. Frontisi 88. The analysis that follows is a condensation of several of Frontisi's key points found at 88–90.
45. Frontisi 89.

CHAPTER 3

1. This book on Michael Ayrton grew out of my initial research into the artistic renderings of the myth of Daedalus and Icarus, but my own entanglement with the life and work of Ayrton has kept me from that task. I hope eventually to return to that project, although I have colleagues at other institutions who are also working on some aspects of this myth and its expression in art and/or literature.
2. Nyenhuis 1986. The present summary of the iconography of Daedalus and Icarus in classical antiquity is based largely on the commentary which I wrote to accompany this catalogue. Used by permission of the editors of *LIMC.*

   Any study of the iconography of Daedalus must take into account Sarah P. Morris's, *Daidalos and the Origins of Greek Art.*
3. Brommer 1971–1976, 59–64, 522, and 528. For a partial listing of works on Daedalus and Icarus in classical antiquity, with selected bibliographical references, see Rudd 247–49; his list is limited to those representations for which he was able to find illustrations in publications. The list, which also includes works of later eras (249–53), accompanies two essays on Daedalus and Icarus (21–53).
4. Simon offers persuasive arguments in favor of identifying several additional figures as Daidalos, including many in Brian Cook's "Aristaios I" in *LIMC.* I am indebted to a former student, Professor Larry Alderink of Concordia College, Moorhead, MN, for bringing this very significant article to my attention.
5. Simon 407.
6. Simon 412 and fig. 24.5.
7. Simon 409–10 and figs. 24.3–24.4.
8. Beazley 1927. Also see Beazley 1963, Beazley 1956, and Beazley 1971. For an assemblage of all the fragments of this black-figure vase by the Acropolis Painter 601, see Morris, pl. 9. On the date of *The Cretans* of Euripides, see chapter 2, n. 3.
9. There are two late exceptions, a Roman ringstone of the end of the first century B.C.E. and an Imperial bronze statuette (*LIMC* nos. 17 and 18).
10. Hanfmann. See also Morris, pls. 8a and 8b. Simon notes that TAITLE is a later syncopation of TAITALE, the spelling on the *bucchero olpe* from Cerveteri (407).
11. Walters 1926, no. 663 and pl. 11. This same gem is no. 862 in Richter 1968; she dates this gem very early—in the first half of the fifth century B.C.E.—and she rejects the identification of the inscription with Daedalus, perhaps overlooking the bulla studied by Hanfmann and by Eva Fiesel, "The Inscription on the Etruscan Bulla," *AJA,* 39 (1935): 195–97. Hanfmann also notes the parallelism between the bulla and the gems (191f.).

12. The earliest epigraphical evidence for Daedalus comes from Sicily, on a bronze krater of the first half of the sixth century B.C.E., inscribed "Daidalos gave me as a gift of [guest-]friendship to Kokalos" (Dunbabin).
13. Beazley 1927, 226–30. He declares that the making or fitting of wings "is a favorite device on Italic and Roman gems from the third century before Christ to the second after, perhaps, as Furtwängler conjectures, because of the connection between Daedalus and Campania which is immortalized in the sixth book of the Aeneid" (230).

    Furtwängler 1900 lists four gems depicting Daedalus and Icarus together (28.27, 37.12, 42.1, 63.32), one of Icarus alone (25.2), and one of Daedalus and Icarus with Pasiphaë and Artemis (58.9). Walters 1926 lists a dozen: six of Daedalus, four of Icarus and two of both (nos. 663, 727, 728, 1863, 3130, 4041; 3132–35; 1864 and 3131; pls. 11, 12, 24, and 31). See also Richter (above, n. 11), Part II, *Engraved Gems of the Romans* (London: Phaidon, 1971), nos. 330–31 (Daedalus is attaching wings to Icarus) and 332 (Daedalus making wings). See also *LIMC* nos. 1–11, 12, 12a–d, 13, 17, 25–30, 33, and 53 for a description of gems depicting Daedalus and/or Icarus.
14. Walters 1899, lvi and 237 (nos. 1451 and 1452). No. 1451, which is 3-5/8 inches high, depicts Icarus with large wings "attached to his arms, which are extended diagonally, the 1. upwards, the r. downwards; on his feet are smaller wings." No. 1452, which is 4-1/2 inches high, has large wings "attached to his arms by straps on the wrist and upper arm, spread nearly at a right angle to the body."
15. It is also depicted on a bronze relief disc from Lausanne, dated ca. 100–150 C.E. (*LIMC* no. 44).
16. Von Blanckenhagen 114-38.
17. Von Blanckenhagen. See also Dawson 1944 and 1950. Dawson 1944, 140–42, provides a reasonably complete summary of Daedalus and Icarus in Greek and Roman art.

    Only Actaeon, Polyphemus and Galatea, and the Liberation of Andromeda occur more frequently than the theme of Daedalus and Icarus. These four themes account for about fifty-five (ca. two-thirds) of the approximately eighty paintings on Roman walls.
18. Schefold 1962, 83ff.
19. This theme also occurs on a Roman sarcophagus (*LIMC* 24).
20. Pollak compiles a list of bas-reliefs, sarcophagi, urns, and wall paintings on the Daedalus-Pasiphaë theme. For a more recent and more complete summary of artistic representations of this theme, see Cantarella (chapter 2, n. 3), 37–51 and pls. I–X. Also see Karl Scherling, *RE* 18 (1949), cols. 2069–82, who lists twenty-six artistic representations of Pasiphaë (cols. 2077–82). For my brief summary of this subject I am, in part, indebted to Richard Evans for the results of his researches on the Pasiphaë theme presented in my seminar at the American School of Classical Studies at Athens in early 1974. See also Robert 1890.

    According to Dawson 1944, 141, the fallen Icarus appears on only one sarcophagus (third century C.E.). Helbig 1899 lists two reliefs of Daedalus and Icarus from the Villa Albani (nos. 826 and 851) and one relief of Daedalus and Pasiphaë from the Palazzo Spada (no. 990 = Friedrich Matz and F. von Duhn, *Antike Bildwerke in Rom,* III [Leipzig: von Breitkopf and Hartel, 1882], no. 3567). On the Roman wall paintings also see Helbig 1868), nos. 1205–08 (Daedalus and Pasiphaë) and 1209–1210 (Daedalus and Icarus); Robert 1877; and Mau. Also see Hinks and Reinach. Schefold 1957 includes more than a dozen Pompeian paintings on Daedalus-Icarus-Pasiphaë themes.
21. Walters 1983, nos. B148, 174, 175, 205, 246, 247, 308, 313, 403, 593, 596, 600.47, and 642. C. H. Smith, nos. E37, 48, 84, 304, 441, and 5094. A. H. Smith, no. 2198 and fig. 32. Walters 1903, nos. A 107–13 (Subject: Theseus slaying the Minotaur; nos. A 107–19 are "Fragments of Colossal Statues, with painted patterns, representing the ornamentation of drapery or of a cuirass").
22. See, for example, Roscher, vol. 2.2, 3004–11. Ward includes over 200 illustrations of the Theseus theme, from antiquity to the present, but with a primary emphasis on ancient works. On the frequency of the theme in Roman wall paintings, see for example Reinach, 213–14; Maiuri 81; Helbig 1868, nos. 1211–47; and Schefold 1957. For a possible addition to the list, see the discussion of a gold ring from the Athenian Agora in Immerwahr. Attention should also be called to a seal ring in the collection of the Detroit Institute of Arts (28.121: *Seal Ring: Theseus Slaying the Minotaur*); this Greek seal ring of Ionian gold and bronze dates from the late sixth to early fifth century; on the face, which is only 4.2 cm (1-5/16 in.) in length, one sees Theseus avoiding the horns of the Minotaur as he plunges his dagger into its skull.
23. Doob 40 and pls. 1–3. See also Fisher and Gerster 11–56 and passim.
24. Doob declares: "What is most significant . . . is that, except for one fresco at Knossos . . . and a wall labyrinth . . . at Poitiers, all classical and medieval mazes share a remarkable characteristic: *they are unicursal, with no forked paths or internal choices to be seen*" (40).
25. Otis 284f.
26. Doob 227–28. For the full discussion, see 227–53.
27. Doob 40f.
28. Doob 254.
29. Doob 254f.
30. Doob 255.
31. Doob 257f.
32. Doob 265.
33. Doob 269.
34. Turner 23.
35. Ibid.
36. Doob 272, 281, and 273, respectively.
37. Doob 277.
38. Daedalus is named in *Inferno* 17.111 and 29.112–17 and in *Paradiso* 8.126, Icarus in *Inferno* 17.106–11 (where he is paired with Phaëthon, who also fell from heaven after having soared too high, because he could not control Apollo's horses when he borrowed his chariot).
39. Qtd. in Rudd at 31. Turner declares that Dante was "the first to link the myths of Icarus and Phaethon, [who had been] treated quite differently by classical poets" (24).
40. Doob 302–3.

41. Some critics date his birth as early as ca. 1266 (e.g., *Gardner's Art through the Ages,* 7th ed., rev. by Horst de la Croix and Richard G. Tansey [New York: Harcourt Brace Jovanovich, 1980], 466).
42. Hartt declares that Giotto "in an astonishingly short time revolutionized the art of Florence, of Tuscany, and in fact of most of Italy and eventually of the entire Western world" (64). Hartt credits Giotto with introducing an approach to painting that laid the foundation for empiricism in both art and science. Even his contemporaries recognized the importance of his contributions: Boccaccio declared that Giotto had brought "back to light [the art of painting] that for many centuries had been buried under the errors of some who painted more to delight the eyes of the ignorant than to please the intellect of the wise" (*Decameron* VI, 5), and Dante records his encounter in Purgatory (*Divine Comedy* XI, 94–96) with a painter who compared his own loss of public esteem to that experienced by Cimabue:

    Cimabue believed that he held the field
    In painting, and now Giotto has the cry,
    So that the fame of the former is obscure.

    A revolutionary figure in the history of painting, Giotto displaced the Byzantine style of painting and restored the naturalism of classical antiquity. So great was Giotto's fame as a painter that he was entrusted, near the end of his life, with the task of overseeing the construction of the Campanile, even though he lacked experience in architecture or engineering. The campanile was begun just three years before Giotto's death. After his death, it was continued by Andrea Pisano, who worked on the second and third stories. The remaining stories of the planned seven-story Campanile were completed in the 1350s by the architect Francesco Talenti (Hartt 135, who notes that Talenti completed the Campanile "according to radically different designs," adapting his designs "to the entirely different taste of the late Trecento.").
43. Rudd credits Andrea Pisano with the artistic vision responsible for the choice of Daedalus for a bas-relief on the Campanile: "By including him Andrea revealed himself as a harbinger of the Renaissance in his thinking as well as in his style" (34). He goes on to suggest that Andrea may have envisioned himself as imitating Daedalus at Cumae (recalling Virgil's description in *Aeneid* 6) when he fashioned the bronze temple doors on the Baptistery in 1336.
44. Rudd acknowledges that Andrea used Giotto's designs: "But what is really breath-taking in this parade of culture-heroes is the presence of Daedalus" (34).
45. Doob 40f.
46. Quotations are from Robinson. He points out (783, note on line 919) that Daedalus and Icarus are mentioned in the *Roman de la Rose* 5226–27 but asserts that Chaucer "certainly knew Ovid's version of the familiar story" and thus no specific source for this "brief reference" can be clearly identified.
47. In *The House of Fame* 712, Chaucer calls Ovid's *Metamorphoses* Geoffrey's "oune bok," and he used Ovid's *Heroides* as a model for his *Legend of Good Women.* His knowledge of Ovid therefore clearly extended far beyond this reference to Daedalus and Icarus.
48. Doob 309.
49. Doob 308 and 310–11.
50. Doob 311–12.
51. Doob 313.
52. Doob 319ff.
53. Doob 337–39.
54. Clark 1961, 27.
55. Morford.
56. Auden 1940.
57. Auden 1960, 14, qtd. in John G. Blair, *The Poetic Art of W. H. Auden* (Princeton: Princeton Univ. Press, 1965), 90.
58. Bluestone.
59. Bluestone.
60. Madden.
61. W. C. Williams; copyright William Carlos Williams. The poem first appeared in the *Hudson Review* 13, No. 1 (Spring 1960): 11–12, under the title "Brueghel: 1."
62. Wallace Stevens in *William Carlos Williams: A Collection of Critical Essays,* ed. J. Hillis Miller (Englewood Cliffs, NJ: {Prentice-Hall, 1966), 65.
63. Rudd 40–41. The translation of the poem comes from Rudd 40.
64. Turner 26, 50ff., and 58ff.
65. For Richard Garnett's translation of the opening eight lines of this sonnet, see Rudd 40.
66. Turner 59.
67. For an extensive account of these developments, see Turner, esp. 27–46.
68. Turner 79.
69. Ibid.
70. Turner 84
71. Levin 1952, 17. To illustrate his point, he quotes a line from "The Passionate Shepherd to His Love": "Come liue with me, and be my loue. "
72. Levin 24.
73. Levin 26. He expands the idea further with these comments: "In the stricter categories of theology, his Epicureanism might have been *libido sentiendi,* the appetite for sensation; his Machiavellianism might have been *libido dominandi,* the will to power; and his Atheism *libido sciendi,* the zeal for knowledge. Singly and in combination he dramatized these ideas . . . pushing them to limits beyond which no writer had gone, and toward which we shall follow him with mixed feelings of exhilaration and temerity."
74. Harris and Platzner 993.
75. Levin 158f. See also Murray; and Ogilvie, who applies the concept to a study of the artist Marc Chagall and the murderer Perry Smith (cf. the novel, *In Cold Blood*).
76. Levin 159.
77. Ibid.
78. Levin 161.
79. Martin 28–30.
80. Cust 1900, 46 and 241.
81. Ayrton 1971, 26: "all painting is in some sort a self-portrait." Baskin (qtd. in Jaffe 10): "I fully believe that all my figures are me."

82. That sketch is now in the Musée Ancien, Musées Royaux des Beaux-Arts, Brussels. A similar sketch, enlarged on the left side, belongs to the Johnson Collection on permanent loan to the Philadelphia Museum of Art. The decorations of the hunting lodge were painted by many collaborators: "all are now in the Prado, Madrid, except for one: 'Jupiter and Semele,' which was destroyed in the sack of the Torre de la Parada, 1710" (Beaux-Arts catalogue, Brussels, 1953, 113).
83. The canvas (6'4-7/8" x 5'10-7/8") bears the signature "goui f." on a rock at the left.
84. Fred Licht, *Canova* (New York: Abbeville Press, 1983), states that Canova was lionized in his lifetime "by patrons as diverse as the upstart Napoleon and the diehard Hapsburgs, by popes and subversive liberals, by English bankers and American senators" (17).
85. Licht states that Canova was brought up by his grandfather, a stone mason, and was apprenticed at age eleven to the "atelier of Giuseppe Bernardi (Il Torretti), whose stock in trade was large sets of garden sculptures" (18).
86. Licht describes this sculpture as "his first truly original work . . . which brought him decisive recognition in the Venetian art world" (19). It also afforded him the financial means to take the obligatory artist's pilgrimage to Rome, where he quickly came under the tutelage of Girolamo Zulian, ambassador from Venice to the Vatican. Later Canova would also achieve prominence as a highly skillful diplomat, particularly at the Congress of Paris in 1815.
87. Licht 20. See also 157.
88. Licht 157.
89. Ibid.
90. Giulio Carlo Argan, *Antonio Canova* (9 [cited in Licht at 159 and n. 32]), reads this statue as "an allegory of Canova's ideal of sculpture."
91. Licht 159, paraphrasing Argan.
92. Licht 159.
93. Simon Tidworth, "From the Renaissance to Romanticism," in Ward, ed., suggests that the "image of the dead Minotaur goes back to a Pompeian fresco" (226). He also considers the composition of Canova's *Theseus and the Minotaur* to be indebted to one of Gavin Hamilton's paintings.
94. Licht 159. It is worth noting that Licht challenges the conventional view that Canova's inspiration for the *Theseus and the Minotaur* was probably the classical *Ares Ludovisi,* suggesting instead that his antecedent was very likely Alfonso Lombardi's *Seated Hercules* (ca. 1525), since Canova's notebooks documenting his journey from Venice to Rome record that he had stopped in Bologna, where "he was particularly struck by the talent of a sixteenth-century sculptor he had never heard of before" (160).

    Although it is outside the scope of this discussion, one should perhaps note that Canova later in life portrayed yet another episode in the labors of Theseus, his slaying of a centaur at the wedding of Perithous and Hippadameia. In that case, Canova elected to portray the moment of struggle, showing a vehement Theseus ready to strike with his club while also attempting to strangle the semi-recumbent centaur. Both by its composition and by its intensity, *Theseus and the Centaur* (1804–1819) evokes the memory of the Laocoön sculpture, without directly imitating it, thereby revealing yet again how neoclassical sculpture relates to its classical antecedents. Tidworth asserts that, in this second sculpture on the labors of Theseus, "Theseus the hero is here decidedly reborn, appropriately enough in the age of Napoleon and of the beginnings of nationalism" (226).
95. Shroder 59. A dramatically different view is expressed in a more recent book on French Romanticism: Frank Paul Bowman, *French Romanticism: Intertextual and Interdisciplinary Readings* (Baltimore: Johns Hopkins Univ. Press, 1990), calls attention to the comparison of Jesus and Socrates beginning with Jean-Jacques Rousseau and declares that the Romantics gave "new figural meaning to the topos—not only is Socrates a figure of Jesus, but the two are figures of the modern poet, or of the political leftist" (11).
96. Although one scholar argues that "the first wave of romanticism began to swell in about 1760" and another uses the term *Romanticism* for French thought between 1789 and 1848, other scholars have restricted it to a period covering the quarter century extending from 1820 to 1845. Peyre, at viii, roots romanticism in 1760; see also chapter 2 ("French Romanticism and Romanticism in Other Countries", 26–41), and chapter 3 ("The Word 'Romantic' and the Chronology of Controversies over Romanticism in France," 42–53). Bowman, at xii, uses it broadly for French thought, rather than to refer to a group of writers within this period. Shroder identifies the period "from 1820 to 1843, or at most to 1848" as the one in which Romantic ideas and ideals existed "in their purest form" (vii).

    As with most artistic developments, it is better not to try to employ procrustean methods for dating Romanticism. The difficulty of the task of dating a movement arises, in part, from retrospection into an earlier period and perceiving elements sympathetic to the new movement. Henri Bergson has rightly remarked that "the romantic aspect of classicism only emerged as the retroactive effect of romanticism, once the latter had appeared" (qtd. in Peyre, at 4).
97. Shroder 58. He concedes, however, that the Renaissance also could appropriately be identified with Icarus, for "Leonardo dreamed of a flying machine; Ariosto multiplied in his epic images and instances of actual flights; Marlowe . . . is . . . the prototype of the Icarian artist" (58). Rudd questions the validity of Shroder's thesis: "One doubts whether an adequate essay on French Romanticism could be written around the theme of Icarus. (M. Z. Shroder's study interprets the myth very broadly.) But it is certainly true that images of flight recur at numerous points in the movement" (48).
98. Peyre 44.
99. For an extended discussion of Romantic pessimism and *mal du siècle,* see Peyre 71–87, and Shroder passim.
100. Shroder 93.
101. Shroder 97.
102. Shroder 148–49.
103. Shroder 59.
104. Gautier, *Histoire du romantisme* (153 [qtd. in Shroder at 55]).

105. Hugo, "Préface de l'édition définitive" (dated 23 February 23, 1880), in *Odes et ballades* (1 [qtd. in Shroder at 61]).
106. Shroder 66.
107. Shroder 185f.
108. Shroder 186.
109. For a more extensive discussion of the contrast between these two Icarian ages, see Shroder, esp. 217ff.
110. Bowman (above, n. 95), 201.
111. Ibid.
112. This painting was bought by the Chantrey Bequest and presented to the Tate Gallery in the same year. The painting won a gold medal at the 1900 Paris International Exhibit.
113. Dr. Justine Hopkins, commenting on this manuscript in a letter to the author dated 31 August 1996, provided the information about Draper.
114. Ibid.
115. Gombrich, at 422, says that dissatisfaction with the solutions of Impressionism on the part of Cezanne, Van Gogh, and Gauguin led to three distinct movements in the art of the twentieth century—Cubism, Expressionism, and Primitivism, respectively.
116. *My Life in Sculpture,* by Jacques Lipchitz, with H. Harvard Arnason (London: Thames and Hudson, 1972), 136.
117. Lipchitz 139.
118. Lipchitz 140 and 151.
119. Lipchitz 144 and 159.
120. Campbell 1970, 170–71.
121. See Brann 619–20. For a reproduction of the sketch, see Arnheim 1986, 141, fig. 14.
122. Myers 492.
123. Sigmund Freud, *An Outline of Psycho-Analysis* (1940), trans. James Strachey (London: Hogarth Press, 1949), 1–4.
124. Ibid. 5.
125. Jung 1964, 27.
126. Ibid. 21.
127. Ibid. 29.
128. Ibid. 32 and 38. For a much more complete account, see C. G. Jung, 1956.
129. Joseph L. Henderson, "Ancient myth and modern man," in Jung 1964, 104–57; quotation at 121.
130. Ibid. 121–22.
131. Henderson 125.
132. Ibid.
133. Ibid.
134. M.-L. von Frantz, "The process of individuation," in Jung 1964, 171.
135. Arnheim 1962, 2.
136. Ibid. 3–4.
137. See Arnheim, ibid. 4ff., for a more complete treatment of this topic.
138. Consider, for example, this list of poems compiled by Helen H. Law and published in 1955 by the American Classical League Service Bureau (Bulletin XXVII; page numbers have been added, wherever possible): A. K. Sabin, *The Death of Icarus* (1906); A. J. Burr, "Icarus," in *Roadside Fire* (1912); G. Litchfield, "Icarus," in *Collected Poems* (1913); E. Casson, "Icarus," in *Masques and Poems* (1915); W. Drummond, "Icarus," in *Poems* (1916); S. V. Benet, "Winged Man," in *Heavens and Earth* (1920); O. R. Thompson, "Quaesitor Aeternus," in *Literary Digest* 64, January 3, 1920, x; C. Hamilton, "Icarus," *Literary Digest* 84, March 14, 1925, 38; V. McCormick, "Daedalus," *New Republic* 46 (1926): 272; G. O'Neil, "Young Icarus," in *The White Rooster* (1927); R. Montgomery, "Daedalus," in *Many Devices* (1929); M. Moore, "Icarus: France 1917," *Sewanee Review* 37 (1929): 37; J. R. Anderson, "Icarus," in *Transvaluations* (1932), 9; J. Auslander, "Elegy for Icarus: The Winged Horseman," in *No Traveller Returns* (1935); E. Marlatt, "Icarus," in *Cathedral* (1937); S. Rodman, "Icarus Lost," in *The Airmen* (1941), 13; and M. Carlson, "A Masque for Icarus," *Poetry* 83 (1953): 6.
139. Levin 1941, 45–46, attaches even further importance to this choice of name for the hero: "As the hero of a pedagogical novel, Stephen is significantly baptized. Saint Stephen Protomartyr was patron of the green on which University College was located, and therefore of the magazine with which Joyce had had his earliest literary misadventures."
140. Ellmann 1959, 153f.
141. Ellmann; also Redford. For the embryonic Daedalian imagery of Epiphanies 30 and 31, see Scholes and Kain 40f.
142. For a fuller discussion of "baby tuckoo" and other facets of the bird imagery, see Kelleher; Levin 1941, 61; Ryf passim (also for a discussion of other uses of imagery); Tindall 82f.; and Redford 22.
143. Kaye calls attention to the cow imagery in *Portrait* and identifies these epithets of Stephen with it ("Bous" is simply the transliteration of the Greek word for bull or cow): "Stephen himself is marked as a sacrifice—as St. Stephen, the first Christian martyr, and as 'Bous Stephanoumenos! Bous Stephaneforos!'—i.e., the sacrificial cow bearing the Divine Power and also bearing the crown of martyrdom." The epithet "Bous Stephanoumenos" is repeated at least twice in *Ulysses* (207 and 408; "bullockbefriending bard" [references are to the Random House 1946 edition]). Ryf also comments on the cow imagery in general (85–87). Pasiphaë's wooden cow, whereby she mated with the white bull from the sea, thus adds another dimension to our understanding of the Daedalian imagery in *Portrait.*
144. See Ryf 19 and 24. For further identifications of Stephen with Icarus, see 26, 81, and 159; Levin 1941, 61f.; and Kenner 131f.
145. Ryf 77–79.
146. Quotations are from the Random House edition of 1946. It is interesting to note Joyce's identification here of the lapwing with Icarus. Perhaps it results from a misreading of Ovid *Met.* 8.236ff., which recounts the transformation of Daedalus's nephew Perdix into a lapwing (usually translated as partridge, but occasionally also as lapwing—see Scholes and Kain 269). Rudd, at 50–51, however, suggests a possible conflation of Daedalion, who was transformed into a hawk (*Met.* 11.344f.), with Daedalus. For further examples of Stephen's Icarian identification, see *Ulysses* 554, 555, 557, and 603f.
147. Faris 10. See esp. her discussion in chapter 2 ("Labyrinth of Words: James Joyce's *Ulysses,*" 15–40).
148. Warncke 27. See also 19 and 26.

149. Warncke 140.
150. George Frederick Watts (qtd. in Gibson at 78).
151. Illustrated in Rubin 270.
152. See *Pablo Picasso: A Retrospective,* pp. 253, 270, and 276–343 passim.
153. Cowling and Mundy 223.
154. Ibid.
155. Cowling and Mundy 210.
156. Read 1959, 160. For a psychoanalytical interpretation of Picasso, and particularly of the *Minotauromachy* and *Guernica,* see Schneider chapter 9 ("Three Modern Painters," 152–87, but esp. 164–79).
157. Read 1968, 161. For a full discussion of this painting, see, for example, Arnheim 1962; Proweller; and Darr.
158. Warncke 157.
159. Herbert Read, "The Dynamics of Art," in *Aesthetics Today,* ed. M. Philipson (Cleveland, 1961), 339; qtd. in Harries 120.
160. Ibid. 341; qtd. Harries 120f.
161. Arnheim 1962, 9–10. See also his "Pleas for Visual Thinking," in Arnheim 1986, 135–52.
162. Carla Gottlieb, "The Meaning of the Bull and Horse in Guernica," *Art Journal* XXIV, No. 2 (Winter 1964–1965): 106–12.
163. Darr 338.
164. Ibid.
165. Darr 341.
166. Darr 342–43.
167. Darr 345.
168. Darr 346.
169. Pablo Picasso, qtd. in Read 1959, at 162.
170. *Lettres françaises,* 24 March 1945, written for Simone Tery; qtd. in Read 1959, 160.
171. Picasso, qtd. in Chipp 44.
172. Gide 76. This work was first published, in French, in New York in 1946 and in 1947 in Paris.
173. Gide 81.
174. Gide 82. For a fuller discussion of Gide's book, see Herbert, esp. 179–84. See also O'Brien 201–6 and passim.
175. See Harries 85–87.
176. André Maurois, preface to Borges's *Labyrinths,* 9.
177. For an illustration, see *Leonard Baskin* (Washington DC: Smithsonian, 1970), 47.
178. Ibid. 68 (illustration).
179. See Jaffe 170 for a brief discussion and 172–73 (fig. 117 a, b) for two views of this bronze.
180. Jaffe 165–70 and figs. 114 and 115.
181. Ibid. 165.
182. Jaffe 168. Baskin also made a relief of *Prometheus Bound* in 1970 (fig. 116).
183. Ibid. 170. See 216 for the details on the *Minotaur* and *Theseus* bronzes.
184. I have by no means exhausted the lengthy list of treatments of this myth by twentieth-century artists and writers. I should note, moreover, that I have excluded music completely from this survey. Nonetheless, it would be appropriate to note that rock music contributes a number of songs to the twentieth century's treatments of the myth. In the 1970s, in particular, rock musicians turned to mythology and religion for themes they enlarged with their music.

    Icarus appears to have had a special appeal, as is evident from the following list of titles, which is only a sample of the many treatments: "Icarus Ascending," by Steve Hackett (this song is to be found in his album *Please Don't Go*); "Flight of Icarus," by the heavy-metal group Iron Maiden (this is also the title of the album); "Icarus," by Paul Winter (the album bears the same title); and "Icarus, Borne on the Wings of Steel," by Kansas (this song can be found in any of the following albums by Kansas: *Kansas, Masque,* and *Two for the Show*). This list comes directly from Morford and Lenardon 532 (the identification of the names of the albums, however, is my own). I am indebted to my former colleagues for bringing these songs to my attention through this vehicle.
185. Malinowski, qtd. in Jung and Kerényi, 5.
186. Schorer 355.
187. MacLeish, qtd. in Hopper, 113f.
188. Vickery ix.
189. Paz 211.

CHAPTER 4

1. Letter from the artist to the author, 19 June 1973. Also see Ayrton 1969, 176–79. Subsequent references to this essay will be parenthetically included in the text. It should be noted that although Ayrton here (177) dates his first visit to Italy in 1947, in *Drawings and Sculpture* (14) he assigns it to 1946 (see chapter 1).
2. Notes on a conversation with the artist, 9 April 1974. Also see Ayrton 1969.
3. Herring 106.
4. Hopkins 1994, 42.
5. Ibid.
6. Ibid.
7. Ibid.
8. In the frontispiece to *Testament* Ayrton quotes this passage from Plato, *The Greater Hippias:* "Our sculptors say that if Daedalus were born today and created such works as those that made him famous, he would be laughed at."
9. Quotations are from the Holt, Rinehart, and Winston edition of 1967, unless otherwise noted (e.g., when Ayrton uses slightly different wording in the Longmans, Green edition).
10. 1970b, 57. Hereafter, this article will be cited in the text.
11. In Ayrton 1978c, 10–11. An uncut, uncorrected transcript of a recording on 16 October 1966 for transmission on 17 January 1967 as part of a BBC program entitled "A Silence Filled With Greek" (BBC reference no. DA 495 D) was re-edited by Elisabeth Ayrton after Michael's death and published in a special issue of *Labrys,* 3 (October 1978): 9–20. The program was written by Ayrton and produced by Douglas Cleverdon. Hereafter, references will be included in the text.
12. Dr. Justine Hopkins, letter commenting on a draft of this manuscript, dated 31 August 1996.
13. In the nineteenth century, British artist William Blake gave visual reality to the "common dream of flying" in his drawing, "O, How I Dreamt of Things Impossible." For an illustration of this drawing, see Jung 1964, 54.

14. This drawing was retouched on 16 May 1956. See Cat. No. 5, note.
15. Note to the author, September 1972.
16. Notes on a conversation with the artist, 12 September 1971.
17. Also see Ayrton 1962c, 64.
18. Jimmy Ernst, son of Max Ernst, was born in 1920 and died in 1984. For further information on Jimmy Ernst, see the brief treatment of his painting in appendix C. A brief biographical sketch is included in *Who's Who in American Art,* 16th ed. (New York: R. R. Bowker, 1983), 268.
19. See, for example, Bernini's *Apollo Pursuing Daphne* (1622–1623), an exquisite marble sculpture in the Borghese Gallery in Rome. The Renaissance tendency to moralize myth is evident in the inscription on the base of this sculpture: "Any lover who follows the pleasures of ephemeral appearance, fills his hands with leaves or plucks bitter berries" (qtd. in Mayerson 130). For another treatment of this myth in a different medium, see Poussin's painting, *Apollo and Daphne* (ca. 1664).
20. Ayrton 1962b, 11.
21. See also Hopkins 1994 for a much more complete treatment of this subject.
22. Herring 106, who credits George Steiner, however, with the observation that "in all Ayrton's portraits of his friends, the artist can be seen subtly but lucidly reflected in their images."
23. Green.
24. Just as Michael and Elisabeth had "sparked each other off" on Crete (Ayrton 1978c, 12).
25. Ayrton 1962b, 11.
26. Notes on a conversation with the artist, 27 August 1972.
27. Robertson 1961, 36.
28. Roberts.
29. Ted Hughes, in Alan Fern and Judith O'Sullivan, eds., *The Complete Prints of Leonard Baskin* (Boston: Little, Brown, 1984), 21.
30. Wallis. In *Drawings and Sculpture* (16), Ayrton acknowledges his debt to Rodin, which is especially evident in this piece.
31. Bertram.

CHAPTER 5

1. Dr. Anthony Storr, typescript entitled "The Relevance of Myth," 6. This typescript is one of a series of drafts prepared for a program on BBC television. Since these drafts in the Ayrton archives are not dated or numbered, it is uncertain whether any part of this statement was actually included in the program.
2. "The Cumean Gate," a typescript in the Ayrton archives, 1. This piece seems to have been written in 1964, since Ayrton opens with the assertion, "Eight years ago I went to southern Italy and there discovered Greece."
3. Hopkins, letter to the author, dated 31 August 1996.
4. It is conceivable that Ayrton may have been influenced in this synthesis by the anthropologist A. B. Cook, who had similarly fused the two separate figures into one (see chapter 2). For further information on Talos, also see chapter 2.
5. Wraight, in an article in which he reviews an exhibition of Michael Ayrton's work at Matthiesen Gallery, London.
6. Ibid.
7. Wallis.
8. Notes on a conversation with the artist, 27 August 1972.
9. Whittet.
10. Rosenthal 1964.
11. The *Fat Man* studies are also related to Ayrton's conception of Cephalon in *Maze Maker,* 202 (notes on a conversation with the artist, 26 August 1972).
12. These comments are based on a conversation with the artist on 26 August 1972. On that occasion, Ayrton stated to me that this drawing was a very important one for him.

    Commenting on an earlier draft of this manuscript, Charles A. Huttar raised the question of whether the breaking up of the oracle's head under the stress of receiving the message of the god was not another kind of god-related orgasm. My own discussion of subsequent treatments of the oracle emphasizes the increasingly sexual nature of Ayrton's depiction of the union between Apollo and his oracle, but Huttar's suggestion has helped me to see this work's probable adumbration of those later treatments.
13. In Hedgecoe and Moore, Moore observes (157) that his obsession with reclining figures has been "discussed and explained in great detail in a book called *The Archetypal World of Henry Moore* by Erich Neumann, the favorite disciple of Jung. I began reading it but gave up half-way through the first chapter as I decided I did not want to be psycho-analysed, nor understand what makes me tick." See Neumann, 175, fig. 91, for an illustration of *Mother and Child.*
14. Davie (646) suggests that this passage should call to mind "a series of small bronzes," perhaps thinking of the five plates (157–61) assembled on a single page in *Drawings and Sculpture* (=Cat. Nos. 314, 315, 330, 334, 380 in the catalogue below), and he further remarks that "these sentences 'program' a bronze sculpture he has yet to execute," but surely Ayrton had this single bronze in mind when he composed this passage.
15. Ayrton makes the Cumaean Sibyl "a relative both of her Delphic counterpart, the Pythian oracle, and of Queen Pasiphaë: the female factor in myth is no less powerful than it is in life" (1970b, 59 = *Rudiments* [1971], 297). Pasiphaë is, of course, the daughter of Helius (and sister to both Circe and Aeëtes), so one can perhaps understand how Ayrton might have made the leap of imagination to relate Apollo's oracles to the daughter of the sun.
16. Jackson Knight 1967, 266. Knight's *Cumaean Gates,* originally published in 1936 by Basil Blackwell, comprises Part II (135–287) of this work. Ayrton acknowledged his indebtedness to Jackson Knight's *Cumaean Gates* in "Path," 182.
17. Although one might suspect that a similar concept underlies *Landscape with Wild Oats* (Cat. No. 401; 1963–1964), the artist described this collage as merely a typical "landscape in late autumn when the landscape tends to be dry, burnt up"; most of his Greek landscapes imply late summer, for he favored this kind of landscape (notes on a conversation with the artist, 28 August 1972). Titles such as *Summer's Last Will* (Cat. No. 534; 1965–1969) and *Dry Landscape* (Cat. No. 542; 1965) further illustrate the point.

18. Although the drawing of *Seasons of Demeter II. Summer* preceded that of *Seasons of Demeter I. Spring* by a week, Ayrton modified the titles after he decided to make them into a series, which he completed with two drawings on the same day in May 1965.
19. Undoubtedly Ayrton had this series in mind, as well as his Demeter bronzes, when he wrote this passage in *Maze Maker:* "'for the moment Demeter commands me, in all her harvest.' And I took Cameira and kissed her breasts and sowed her and was harvested: and she, 'the sharer,' shared herself with me. As I say, when I was not afraid, I was happy during those months. Through the winter she became thin as Demeter does" (104). Ayrton produced a charcoal drawing of *Cameira* (Cat. No. 332; 21 March 1963).
20. Notes on a conversation with the artist, 26 August 1972.
21. Notes on a conversation with the artist, 26 August 1972.
22. Rosenthal 1966, 271.
23. Notes on a conversation with the artist, 28 August 1972.
24. Notes on a conversation with the artist, 26 August 1972.
25. Notes by the artist, dated August 1955, in the catalogue of the retrospective exhibition at the Whitechapel Art Gallery in September–October 1955, 8. Reprinted in the catalogue of the exhibition at the R. S. Johnson-International Gallery in December 1972, 43.
26. "Landscape of the Minotaur" (1964), 48. Hereafter referred to in the text simply as "Ayrton 1964."
27. Notes on a conversation with the artist, 28 August 1972.
28. Notes on conversations with the artist in August 1972.
29. The idea of the underground connections was suggested by the artist in a conversation on 28 August 1972, although the elaboration and interpretation are mine.
30. Notes on a conversation with the artist, 27 August 1972.
31. Rykwert 1968.
32. Causey 26.
33. Ibid.
34. Ayrton 1966. Rpt. in *Studio International,* 171, No. 878 (June 1966): 273.
35. Tuve 135. I am indebted to Professor Charles A. Huttar for calling to my attention the possible connections between Herbert's poetry and Ayrton's *Maze Player.*
36. Tuve 144.
37. Dr. Justine Hopkins, letter to the author dated August 31, 1996, commenting on a draft of this manuscript.
38. Baker, 207 (from *The Temple: Sacred Poems and Private Ejaculations (1633.)*
39. Tuve 145–46.
40. Stanford [2].
41. Ayrton 1966.
42. For a discussion of Moore's sculptures, see Neumann 146ff.
43. Causey.
44. Hedgecoe and Moore 105.
45. Rosenthal 1966, 272.
46. Rosenthal 1966, 272.
47. Ayrton 1966.
48. Mary Renault, letter to John Guest Esq., Longmans Green, dated 19.3.67.
49. Mary Renault, letter to Michael Ayrton, dated 24.5.67.
50. Dr. Justine Hopkins, in a letter dated 31 August 1996, commenting on a draft of this manuscript, reminded me of the importance of this issue to Ayrton and encouraged me to make the point more explicit. I therefore am again indebted to her for her insights and her advice.
51. For a full account of his relationship with his parents, but especially with his father, see Hopkins 1994.
52. Myths are sometimes corrected (e.g., 113, 141f., and 241f.). Ayrton's version of the legend of the madness of Heracles, which contradicts the accounts of both Euripides and Apollodorus, is not well handled. Dr. Justine Hopkins, however, in a letter dated 31 August 1996, disagrees with my assessment: "Even the account of Heracles . . . is actually a reinforcement of Daedalus' perception of heroes and heroism."
53. First edition (Longmans), 175. In the Holt, Rinehart and Winston edition of the same year, 202, "two other selves" replaces "two alter-egos."
54. Dr. Justine Hopkins, commenting on a draft of this manuscript in a letter dated 31 August 1996. She stresses the importance to Ayrton of leaving "a generous margin for divine intervention, and both Minos and Tros represent that leeway." I am grateful to her for helping me to clarify my own interpretation of *Maze Maker* and of Ayrton's view of the relation between Minos and Daedalus.

CHAPTER 6

1. For further comment on *Maze Maker,* see chapter 5. Also, see the reviews by Davie, Finley, Hughes, and myself (1968) cited in the bibliography.
2. Ayrton 1970b, 59.
3. Ayrton 1967, Part Two, esp. 171 and 180–84, and Part Three, esp. 282f., 292, and 296–98. See also Ayrton 1970e, where he describes both the process and his reasoning. See chapter 2, for the record of the event in myth.
4. Ibid. 46.
5. Consider, for example, Ayrton's description of his discovery of the underground maze at Cumae: he entered into "the labyrinth of passages that honeycomb the great rock" (1970b, 57).
6. Ayrton, ibid., places both commissions within *the same week* —an amazing coincidence appropriate to the mythmaker himself, for elsewhere the dates do not coincide quite as closely: whereas in "Daedalus and I" Ayrton places his commission to create the golden honeycomb in January, 1968 (64), the earliest study for the *Arkville Minotaur* (Cat. No. 629) is dated 25 November 1967 and the artist reports his commission to design the maze in a letter to Donald Davie on 16 December 1967. In another account of the commission to create the *Arkville Maze,* as recorded in a draft script for a potential BBC film prepared in August 1969, Ayrton stated that at a cocktail party in New York while he was en route to teach in California, he was invited to "make a sketch or two" for the prospective patron's approval: since in 1967 the fall quarter at the University of California, Santa Barbara, began in early October, the gap between the two commissions may have been several months, although he elsewhere reports that he received the approval to go ahead with

the commission by telephone. Even if Mr. Erpf did not officially grant the commission for the *Arkville Maze* until December 1967, the gap still would have been several weeks, if the commission for the golden honeycomb did not come until January 1968.

7. Michael Ayrton, as quoted in a draft script and cutting order prepared in August 1969 for a possible BBC film, then tentatively entitled "Ayrton's Maze," 2. The ensuing account is based largely on this draft script, which is used, after editing, by permission of Michael Ayrton, granted in 1972.
8. During the expansionist era of the 1980s, this firm went through a series of mergers. In May 1990, the Associated Press reported the reorganization of Shearson Lehman Hutton Inc., "the nation's second-largest securities firm." The history of some of the mergers of Loeb, Rhoades and Company is contained in this summary: "Shearson, formerly known as Shearson-American Express, acquired the venerable Lehman Brothers, Kuhn Loeb Inc. in 1984. The merged Shearson Lehman purchased E. F. Hutton & Co. in 1988" (*Grand Rapids Press,* May 20, 1990, F5).
9. Draft script for the BBC (see note 7), 2.
10. Ibid. 4.
11. Ibid. 3, but punctuation has been added to make the text more readable, since the draft script is merely an unedited typescript of a recorded interview.
12. Ibid. 5–6.
13. Ibid. 3. It seems, however, that Ayrton's recollection of the duration of the elapsed time is inaccurate, or at least imprecise, since his letter to Donald Davie on 16 December 1967 (above, n. 6) must have been written less than three months after the original meeting of the artist and his prospective patron.
14. Letter to Donald Davie, dated 16 December 1967.
15. Letter from the artist to the author, dated 30 November 1972.
16. "The Talk of the Town: *Artificer,*" *New Yorker,* 9 March 1968, 30.
17. "Some Notes on the Form of the Arkville Maze, Prepared by Michael Ayrton for Armand G. Erpf, March 1968" (appendix B below).
18. The *labrys* symbol also appears below the bent right leg of the Maze Maker on the reverse, with the tips of the blades extended to form a circle, within which are formed two circular apertures. For Ayrton the double-axe symbol represented not only the Minoan *labrys* but also the waxing and waning of the moon (notes on a conversation with the artist, 28 August 1972). Given the associations between Icarus (and Naucrate) and the moon in *Maze Maker* (54–58 and 74f.), Ayrton's choice of this symbol is not at all surprising.
19. Notes on a conversation with the artist, 28 August 1972. These notes, however, have been further expanded through a study of the artist's sketch books for this project, which bear no precise dates, although one can approximate the dates for most items. The sketch book also lists a blade bone that "passes through [the] window in [the] shield," a bone and socket element, a horned element, a coil of twine, and a bar in the window. In "Some Notes on the Form of the Arkville Maze" (appendix B), Ayrton quotes Joseph Rykwert (*The Idea of a Town* [Hilversum: Lectura Architectonica, 1961]): "In antiquity the notion that everything means both itself and something else was so general and ingrained that it was taken for granted."
20. Not included in my catalogue, since they concern another, unrelated myth.
21. The quotation from Pliny (*N.H.* 36.85) may very well refer to the Troy Game performed in the Campus Martius (cf. Virgil *Aen.* 5), rather than to a game like hopscotch, as Ayrton suggests here.
22. For an elaboration on this point, see his essay, "The Making of a Maze," in Ayrton 1971, esp. 297ff.
23. "Some Notes on the Form of the Arkville Maze" (appendix B).
24. In a draft script for "Ayrton's Maze" (above, n. 7), 9, Ayrton declares that he drew his inspiration for the "organic curve" of his maze design from "the idea that the intestines are the origin of the maze."
25. For illustrations not only of the classical unicursal labyrinth, but also of the Roman and medieval Christian unicursal labyrinths, see Fisher and Gerster, 60ff. and passim.
26. Robert Hughes in the draft script for "Ayrton's Maze" (above, n. 7), 7.
27. Ayrton, draft script for "Ayrton's Maze" (above, n. 7), 9.
28. Ibid.
29. Fisher and Gerster say: "On a symbolic level, the Cretan labyrinth with its golden thread portrays the cycle of life, by representing the womb and the umbilical cord. The male seed enters and explores the dark and secret passages, until he successfully penetrates and transforms the inner half-completed life-form; the umbilical cord is vital to his safe exit from the womb. For Theseus, the crane dance was part of his ritual initiation into adulthood, before he went out into the world to accomplish his life's work, and gain his kingdom" (18). Similarly, when describing the labyrinth found in "the creation myth of the Tohono O'otam (formerly known as Papago) and Pima tribes of Southern Arizona," which is frequently depicted in basketwork, Fisher and Gerster declare: "At one level, the labyrinth symbolizes the female womb, only penetrable if one is pure and perfect. The male figure outside, representing the human seed, can penetrate the womb, fertilize the ovum, produce new life, which then emerges as a new birth or a reincarnated existence. Entry into the labyrinth gives new life to Iitoi, thus achieving reincarnation and eternal life" (19–20).
30. Neumann 74.
31. Neumann 75.
32. Michael Ayrton, in a letter to the author, dated 24 June 1968. Also see Ayrton 1970b, 59, and Matthews 37–39.
33. Ayrton 1970b, 65.
34. Dr. Justine Hopkins, in a letter to the author dated 31 August 1996.
35. Ayrton 1967, 194. His ensuing description of the Minotaur's appearance and behavior also merits reading, for it is both rich in drama and deep in its understanding of the man-beast condition. The reason for the skill of the narrative and empathetic portrayal of the Minotaur may lie in these words of the artist: "in another chamber, kept separate, is the mazed prisoner, the tragic and brutal creature of the Minotaur with whom I equally identify myself" (draft script, cited in n. 7), 4.
36. Ayrton 1970b, 59.
37. In *Maze Maker* there are also two central chambers: "the Minotaur. . . would be in the chamber of the moon. . . . In the chamber of the sun we should be safe" (117). For the significance

that he attaches to these two chambers, see his notes for his patron (appendix B).

38. Notes on a conversation with the artist, 16 August 1972. He derived further ideas about the walls from the inscription of laws on walls in Gortyna, Crete, and from the narrative expressions inset in the walls of pulpits carved by Giovanni Pisano. In *Giovanni Pisano,* Ayrton describes what Dante saw: "As Dante goes upwards through Purgatory he comes upon a curving terrace above a precipice, and gazing upon this circling bank he sees . . . that it is carved in relief in pure white marble with such skill that not only Polyclitus but Nature herself were put to shame. He stands rejoicing in these carved images of humilities, finding them precious for their craftsman's sake, and he recognizes that he is contemplating a *visible speech* new to him because no such sculptures exist in the ordinary world, but that they were made by one who never beheld a new thing" (163f.).
39. Notes on a conversation with the artist, 16 August 1972.
40. See Ayrton 1970b, 59, and Ayrton 1971, 297ff., for his history of mazes and labyrinths. See also the books on labyrinths cited in the bibliography, such as Doob, Matthews, Bord, and Fisher and Gerster.

CHAPTER 7

1. Michael Ayrton, in a letter to the author, dated 12 March 1971. The *Detroit Free Press,* February 4, 1971, carried this notice: "Armand G. Erpf, 73, a millionaire Wall St. broker; died at his desk in the investment firm of Loeb, Rhoades & Co., New York, where he was a senior partner" (12C, col. 1).
2. Bieber 11. This slender volume offers a valuable summary of the history of the Laocoön group since its rediscovery in 1506 C.E., and its presentation of photographs of Filippo Magi's careful reconstruction of the group further enhances its usefulness. See also *P. Vergili Maronis,* AENEIDOS *Liber Secundus,* with commentary by R. G. Austin (Oxford: Clarendon Press, 1964), 44f. and 94ff. (bibliography on the literary tradition of the Laocoön myth and on its representation in art, 97f.).
3. Clark 1956, 228.
4. Also see Cat. No. 761 and Plate 51 for a later version of this work.
5. Michael Ayrton, Catalogue of the Maze and Minotaur touring exhibition (see appendix A), dated 1972, above plates for catalogue nos. 30 and 36.
6. Friendly 52.
7. Gregory, Professor of Neuropsychology and Director of the Brain and Perception Laboratory at the University of Bristol, was also the source of the mirror perspex used in *Mirror Maze* (Cat. No. 596; see chapter 5).
8. Michael Ayrton, Catalogue of an exhibition at Sears Vincent Price Gallery, Chicago, December 1970.
9. Kantor 237. As he concludes the article, Kantor declares: "The clear implication . . . is that opulence of perception when it includes the ability to tolerate the ambiguities and contradictions of the culture goes together with psychological health. This is in fact the mark both of emotional maturity and the most superior vision" (239).
10. Cf. also *Mirror Query,* Cat. No. 748, and *Fabrication,* Cat. No. 788.
11. See Ayrton 1973, where he declares: "only then did I recognize in Lameich Trojan, Michael Ayrton conjoined and indivisibly interlocked" (217).
12. For an account of the discovery of this and other golden burial masks at Mycenae, see H. Schliemann, *Mycenae: A Narrative of Researches and Discoveries at Mycenae and Tiryns* (London: John Murray, 1878), passim, but esp. 289 and 311f., and pl. 474. For the definitive publication of the Shaft Graves, see Karo 121 (no. 624) and pl. LII, for this mask; other masks are shown on pls. XLVII to LI. These graves from Grave Circle A are also discussed by Mylonas 103–27.
13. Borges. Quotations and references in the notes will be from the Penguin edition (1970). Borges was for Ayrton not a direct influence upon these sculptures but rather a part of the climate in which they arose. Ayrton first discovered Borges's stories in late 1968 (notes on a conversation with the artist, 16 August 1972).
14. Borges 27.
15. Borges 34.
16. Borges 39.
17. Borges 42.
18. Ayrton, "Journey Through a Labyrinth," corrected typescript of a public lecture delivered at Wayne State University, Detroit, 2 October 1972. This lecture succeeded by a few days the unveiling of *Corporate Head/Reflective Head* (Cat. No. 772), which is discussed later on in this chapter. Qtd. by permission of Michael Ayrton, granted in 1972.
19. Robertshaw. See also the discussion of the nautilus in relation to the maze in chapter 6.
20. Whicher 293.
21. Wheelock 67. I am indebted to one of my former graduate students, Richard Muegge, for calling this analysis of Borges's work to my attention; he did so prior to my discovery of Ayrton's acquaintance with the Argentine writer's labyrinthine world.
22. The Volomandra kouros is No. 1906 in the National Museum, Athens, and No. 63 in Richter 80–81 and figs. 208–16; hereafter referred to in the text as Richter, followed by her number and the number of the illustration.
23. Notes on a conversation with the artist, 16 August 1972.
24. I am indebted to Mrs. Judith Binder for calling this resemblance to my attention following my lecture at the American School of Classical Studies at Athens in March 1974.
25. Notes on a conversation with the artist, 16 August 1972. The date is based on Richter 115f.
26. Notes on conversations with the artist, 16 August 1972 and 7 April 1974. See also his "Unwearying Bronze" (1965b).
27. Richter 26 and figs. 9–11 (a detail of fig. 9 is included in the epilogue).
28. Notes on a conversation with the artist, 16 August 1972. A sketch book, dated 1968–1969 on the cover, contains two sketches of this interior kouros. The ancient technique of solid casting of bronze applies even more precisely to this bronze (notes on a conversation with the artist, 7 April 1974).
29. Borges 48.
30. An entire issue of PARABOLA: *The Magazine of Myth and Tradition* (Vol. XIX, No. 2 [May 1994]) is devoted to the subject of twins. One article, "Gemini and the Path of Paradox,"

by Kate Duff (12–17), is particularly relevant to this myth, but a number of other articles are at least tendentially relevant.

31. Ayrton 1973, 114. Ayrton argues that the enigma of penetrating the mirror would be more readily understood if it were not for "a poetic mistranslation" of I Corinthians 13:12 ("Now we see through a glass darkly"), which "in the Vulgate . . . reads: *Videmus nunc per speculum in aenigmate* which, literally translated, means: 'Now we see in an engima by means of a mirror'" (114).
32. Cannon-Brookes 1978a, 118.
33. Ibid.
34. Jackson. Ayrton, in a conversation in August 1972, informed me that his inspiration for this sculpture came, in part, from the back piece of *Antiquity.*
35. Professor Donald A. Yates, coeditor of the collection of Borges's stories (see bibliography) and professor of Spanish at Michigan State University, suggested the Borgesian inspiration following my lecture at Michigan State University on 28 November 1972. After seeing Ayrton's reflector sculptures illustrated during the lecture, Professor Yates expressed the opinion that if Borges himself were to see these works, he would judge them infinitely superior to his own attempts to give reality to his ideas. It is worth noting, moreover, that Yates had studied the work of Borges since 1954, had known the author personally since 1962, and had accompanied the then-blind writer as his escort on a lecture tour of the United States not long before he made this observation.
36. Michael Ayrton, letter to the author, dated 21 December 1972. The "new sculpture" is *Brain Maze* (Cat. No. 782; Figures 250–52).
37. Notes on a conversation with the artist, 7 April 1974.
38. Dr. Justine Hopkins, in a letter to the author dated August 31, 1996, commenting on a draft of this manuscript, unequivocally makes this identification.
39. Notes on a conversation with the artist, 18 August 1972. See also the note in the catalogue, Cat. No. 470.
40. This bronze also exists as a separate sculpture, *Minotaur Alarmed,* Cat. No. 705.
41. The Archaeological Museum at Heraklion is replete with examples of the *labrys,* but one can also find many examples of the symbol engraved upon the walls of the palace at Knossos.
42. Notes on a conversation with the artist, 7 April 1974.
43. Ibid.
44. Ibid.
45. Friendly 51.
46. Michael Ayrton, cover of a brochure announcing the publication of the etchings (London: Icarus Press, 1971). Incorporated into this concise description are titles of several of the etchings (see Cat. Nos. 726–35).
47. For a very important discussion of Theseus as a national hero, see Connor.
48. *Midas Consequence* (1974) was Ayrton's final novel. By naming Capisco's baboon "Theseus," Ayrton revealed the extent of his disdain for the hero glorified by the Peisistratids in the sixth century and honored especially by the Athenians of the Golden Age of Greece. For further illustration of the ridicule, see also 105–10, 128, and 132. For an extensive treatment of the development of the heroic status of Theseus, see Ward.
49. Dr. Justine Hopkins, letter dated 31 August 1996.
50. Borges, "The House of Asterion," in *Labyrinths,* 170–72. See also the analysis of this story by Wheelock 147–49.
51. For a more detailed account of the building, see Patton and Patton 6–7. For a description of the building and its materials, but particularly of the mirrored glass, see the anonymous trade magazine article, "In Troy, Michigan." The octagonal shape used in the building and its courtyard of course recalls the shape of *The Jerusalem Maze at Arkville* (Cat. No. 718), although its use here was merely coincidental, but Ayrton's involvement with the myth is filled with such coincidences.
52. Friendly 47.
53. For discussions of the Troy Maze and the Troy games, see, for example, Matthews 1978a (see catalogue, Cat. No. 767); Jackson Knight 1967, 202–14; Cruttwell 83–97; R. D. Williams 145ff. (Williams provides a concise but useful further bibliography, 146f.); Camps (100f.) relates it to historical events. Cruttwell remarks: "the connecting link in Virgil's mind between Crete and Troy and Italy is that Italian 'game of Troy' (*Troiae lusus*)" (86). Perhaps Ayrton intended to recall similar connections in his sculptures which were created after he received the commission for the Kresge headquarters. His knowledge of the work of Jackson Knight and others would undoubtedly have provided both the intellectual and the emotive basis for these creations.
54. Neumann, figs. 93–95.
55. Letter to the author, dated 10 May 1973.
56. In a sketch book dated 1968–1969 I found a drawing for "Coil" (which never materialized) that clearly anticipates *Carapace.* When I pointed out this sketch to Ayrton on 30 August 1972, he evinced great surprise at the discovery, admitting he had completely forgotten the earlier conception when he created *Carapace.*
57. Notes on a conversation with the artist, 10 April 1974.
58. Notes on a conversation with the artist, 28 August 1972.
59. There is a surprising parallel, in conception but not in execution, to *Brain Maze* in a work by American artist Seymour Lipton, whose *Fountainhead* was created for Remington Rand, the manufacturer of the UNIVAC computer. The following comments from Elsen would, for the most part, also apply to Ayrton's *Brain Maze:*

> *Fountainhead* is an imaginative and scientifically inspired equivalent of the human brain, itself the first computer and source of the electronic UNIVAC. The sculptor's medical training, received before 1928, and which included brain dissection, provided the source but not the daring for the image, about which Lipton said: "*The convolutions of the human brain are the inner mirror of the human soul as much as the face is its outer mirror. This sculpture is a study of what goes on, what spatially happens inside the head of a man. If what is seen in a face is emotion, sad, happy or thoughtful, here in the brain is the inside of this mystery. The enigma of the soul still remains.*" (116)

Ayrton's *Brain Maze* may also be his tribute to intelligence, a quality he valued highly, as he makes very clear in his essay on Leonard Baskin's sculpture, as well as in his portrait of Daedalus (see chapter 4). He could equally well be speaking of himself in this mordant comment on Baskin: "Baskin is a learned man, which further sets him apart from the public image of a modern artist" (Ayrton 1962–1963, 54).

60. Concerning Ayrton's *Penetrators* and *Extricators,* as well as his reflector sculptures, Friendly observes:

> In Ayrton's view, the best man can hope for is a continual voyage of exploration and discovery of himself and a continuing struggle in the process. Hence his present work, exemplified in the massive piece at the Kresge building: a brooding search in which man's image both appears through a glass darkly and is also reflected by it, sometimes and from some angles completed, at other times left fractured, and at all times occupied by beings or forces that have intruded from the outside.
>
> Ayrton's drawings, etchings and sculpture are to me inordinately powerful but profoundly pessimistic; there is irony but not humor. This is the more remarkable since he himself is a witty and genial man, of sunny manner and outgoing disposition, maintained despite chronic poor health. (52)

61. André Maurois, in a foreword to Borges, *Labyrinths,* 12f.
62. Letter to H. G. Wells, 10 July 1915 (Leon Edel, ed., *Henry James Letters*, vol. IV, 770).

CONCLUSION

1. Campbell 1956, 260; qtd. in Leeming 270.
2. C. G. Jung, *Psychology of the Child Archetype,* in Jung and Kerényi 73.
3. W. F. J. Knight 1936, 215.
4. Ibid. A second principle which he enunciates to explain the appearance of the name Troy (Truia) "in distant parts of Europe" in conjunction with "Homer's city, the Italian military ride, and indeed mazes and maze dances," is "the rule that in the development of legends facts attract to themselves as mythological accretions those myths which are in form similar to themselves."
5. Hopkins 1994, 304ff.
6. Hopkins 1994, 406.
7. Ibid.
8. Qtd. in Ayrton 1971, 7 and 9. Borges's essay, "The Fearful Sphere of Pascal," is contained in *Labyrinths* (224–27), where Anthony Kerrigan translates the quotation slightly differently than Ayrton remembered it: "An Aristotle was but the fragment of an Adam, and Athens the rudiments of Paradise" (227).
9. Ayrton 1971, 10, but again the quotation is imprecise, for Borges used the plural of intonation (227).
10. Sir Anthony Hopkins, commenting on Welsh writer Gwyn Thomas during a television program from BBC Wales (broadcast following Masterpiece Theatre as "Select Exits" on 3 October 1993, on Channel 35/52 in Grand Rapids, MI), suggested that Thomas may have been cast aside by critics as a writer because he became a television personality. Ayrton's critics, likewise, were well enough aware that Ayrton had been a member of the BBC "Brains Trust" and that he refused to restrict himself to painting, writing, or sculpture, but chose to pursue all three, and more: doing television shows, scripting and collaborating on movies, writing novels as well as art criticism, doing whatever his fertile imagination and insatiable creativity drove him to do.
11. Hall 1993, 53–54.
12. Hall 1993, 54–55.
13. Quoted in Friendly 53–54.
14. Mellor 67.
15. Feaver 74.
16. Mellor 67.
17. Ayrton 1946c, 148.
18. Mellor 68.
19. Mellor 69.
20. Hopkins repeatedly comments on his disappointment and speaks of his belief in the enduring quality of his work, although there were often moments of self-doubt.
21. Elisabeth Ayrton, in a telephone conversation on 21 December 1989, commenting on an earlier draft of chapter 3, declared: "He painted landscapes more abstract than he would have if he had felt that he could avoid it—there was such an emphasis on abstraction that he felt that he had to try it" (notes on that conversation). Dr. Justine Hopkins, however, in a letter dated 31 August 1996, in which she comments on a draft of the complete manuscript, asserts:

> in all his working life he never consciously modified or adapted his work for or to anyone or anything. The increasing abstraction of his Greek landscapes, and the abstract qualities of some of his bronzes are not concessions against the grain to any fashions or fluctuations of the art market, but rather represent his growing sense of the universality of his imagery—the plastic equivalent of his belief that *myth moves in the human mind so that the mind is gradually, imperceptibly, changed as the landscape is modified by erosion and flood and sun and wind.* . . . Abstraction for its own sake, far less for the sake of ephemeral popularity, he found entirely unsympathetic, and altogether rejected—his uncompromising attitude well expressed by his defiant justification of his own mythopoeic activity, which I am sure you know.

Although I agree with Hopkins's essential point and respect her vast knowledge of Michael's life shown in her biography, I cannot ignore the statement by Elisabeth, who obviously knew Michael longer and more intimately than Justine did.

22. In the epilogue to her biography of Ayrton, Hopkins quotes from Ayrton's notes for a television program, "The Painter as Sculptor," broadcast on *Monitor,* BBC1, 21 June 1959: "If it were not that it would increase an already apparent distrust in the variety of my activities I should like to describe myself simply as an *image-maker.* I should like to be so described in my passport. . . . The purpose of an image when made is, to me, ultimately that of a votive."
23. Hopkins 1994, 405.
24. Ibid.
25. Hopkins 1994, 418.
26. Arnheim 1962, 130.
27. Arnheim 1962, 131.

Catalogue

Although this catalogue represents the bulk of Ayrton's work from 1956 to 1975, it is not a catalogue of his entire output during this period. No portraits are included, for example, nor is the Berlioz series, nor individual works that have no relevance to Ayrton's exploration of the Daedalus myth. What *is* presented here is a catalogue as complete as possible for all works related in any way to the thematic focus of this book. Ayrton was a prolific artist during his prime, often completing two drawings a day, for example, during several months on Crete, so it is inevitable that, despite strenuous efforts, some works may not have been located. Ayrton was consulted on a daily basis during my extended visits to Bradfields from 1971 to 1974, and I was given full access to his photographic and other records of his work. Michael and Elisabeth reviewed a first draft of this catalogue in 1974–1975 and found it both comprehensive and accurate. After Michael's death, Elisabeth and her daughter Prue helped me acquire information about later exhibitions and publications. I have also benefited from the assistance of Prue's daughter, Dr. Justine Hopkins, in recent years.

EXPLANATION OF SYMBOLS USED IN THE ENTRIES

The following symbols are used immediately after the number of a catalogue entry or following a citation in a publication to indicate that information about the work listed in that place differs in certain respects from the information provided in this catalogue:

*	the dimensions given in the exhibition catalogue or other publication differ somewhat from those given in this catalogue;
(date)	the date given in the exhibition catalogue or publication differs from that given in this catalogue;
(T)	the title differs (often only slightly) from that given in this catalogue;
(R)	reproduced in the catalogue or publication (the plate or page number normally immediately follows "R").

In addition, the Master Record Book—a bound and lined book in which Ayrton kept a record of virtually every work and every exhibition, from his earliest work until 1969, at which time his record keeping took on a different form—is abbreviated as MRB. The numbering for exhibitions in the MRB is employed in the list of exhibitions in appendix A.

ORGANIZATION OF THE CATALOGUE AND RELATED INFORMATION

Arrangement: The arrangement is chronological, although within a given year there may be an occasional work out of sequence because it was not always possible to establish precise dates, especially for some of the paintings and sculpture. It is important to note, however, that Ayrton kept exceptionally accurate records of his work, so there was less guesswork in dealing with his oeuvre than often is required for works of art.

Measurements: Except where noted, measurements are in inches, height preceding width; for sculpture, width precedes depth.

Dates: Artist's dates on drawings usually give day, month and year, in sequence. Paintings are more likely to have only the year or just the month and year recorded.

Illustrations: Works illustrated are noted parenthetically immediately after the title.

Collections: Names of collectors are indictated only if the name has appeared in print. The location of a work is provided wherever possible.

Exhibition(s): For more detailed information on exhibitions, see appendix A.

Editions: Sculpture editions are limited. Some are unique; others are limited to three casts; still others may include up to twelve. Only casts in public collections are listed, although the number in private collections is noted, if known.

Foundries: From 1953 to 1972 Ayrton's bronzes were cast almost exclusively by the Art Bronze Foundry, Fulham, London, first under the direction of Mr. Charles Gaskin, later under his son, Michael Gaskin. After 1972, the majority of the works were cast by Meridian Bronze Company, Peckham, London, but Morris Singer Foundry, Basingstoke, cast the large *Corporate Head* (Cat. No. 772) and a few smaller bronzes.

1. **ICARUS**
Pen and gouache. 1940.
COLLECTION The MRB lists E. Currie as the collector.
EXHIBITION Leicester Galleries 1940.
BIBLIOGRAPHY Hopkins 1994, 42.

2. **BONE WARRIOR**
Bronze. 1954. 25 x 8-1/2 x 6. Edition of 2.
COLLECTION Private collection, Philadelphia, PA.

3. **TALOS ARMED HEAD I** (Figure 58)
Bronze. 1954–56. 20-1/2 x 13 x 6. Edition of 6.
COLLECTION The artist's estate.
EXHIBITIONS James Goodman Gallery 1965, no. 2*; Mazelow Gallery 1966, no. 7*; Sears Vincent Price Gallery 1967, no. 24* (R).
BIBLIOGRAPHY Ayrton 1962a, pl. 50. Hopkins 1994, 198, 274f.

4. **SCEPTIC**
Bronze. 1956. 15 x 7 x 5. Edition of 9.
COLLECTION Private collection, Chicago.
EXHIBITIONS James Goodman Gallery 1965, no. 3 (T); Mazelow Gallery 1966, no. 10 (T); Bruton Gallery 1981, no. 70 (T; R).

5. **CUMAEAN SIBYL**
Pen and sepia wash, retouched with white on left foot. 3 April and 16 May 1956. 20 x 14.
INSCRIPTIONS Signed in pencil and dated: *3.4.56* and *16.5.56.* Annotated *Cumae* in sepia ink.
COLLECTION The artist's estate.

This drawing was a study for the left-hand figure in the large painting, *Cumaean Sybil* (Cat. No. 17; 1957): "This figure of a woman was drawn before the conception of the painting and simply represents a Cumaean peasant woman. Her identification with the Sibyl was post hoc" (notes by the artist to the author, September 1972). There is no consistency in the spelling of Sibyl, since Ayrton used Sybil and Sibyl almost interchangeably.

6. **CUMAEAN SIBYL (II)**
Oil sketch on board. 1956. 8-3/4 x 11-1/4.
INSCRIPTIONS Signed top left. Below, left of signature: *56.* On back of board: *lst oil sketch for Cumaean Sibyl in Merriam Collection, Phila.*
COLLECTION Private collection, Holland, MI.

In a letter to the author (*30th November, 1972*), Ayrton wrote that this "little oil sketch . . . was the first study in colour for the big Cumaean Sibyl painting in the Merriam Collection in Philadelphia" (see preceding entry). The exact sequence of the drawings and sketches between the first (Cat. No. 5) and fifth (Cat. No. 9) drawings is uncertain, and one drawing is still unaccounted for.

7. **GOAT I. CUMA**
Sepia and black ink wash. 7 May 1956. 20 x 11-1/2?.
INSCRIPTIONS Signed top right. Below signature: *7.5.56.*
COLLECTION The artist's estate.
EXHIBITIONS Manchester 1957; Folio Society 1957; Brasenose, Oxford 1957; Bensons (exhibition of contemporary British artists held by this advertising agency) 1959.

This drawing is closely related to the large painting, *Cumaean Sybil* (Cat. No. 17; 1957), and to the print, *Acropolis at Cumae* (Cat. No. 16).

8. **CUMAEAN SIBYL (IV)**
Sepia and black ink wash. 7 May 1956. 17-1/2 x 11-1/2.
INSCRIPTIONS Dated *7.5.1956.*
COLLECTION The artist's estate.

This drawing of the Sibyl's head follows the first *Cumaean Sibyl* (Cat. No. 5) and precedes by one day the next entry (Cat. No. 9), which is titled *Cumaean Sybil V.* The existence and location of one of the two intervening drawings are uncertain, as is the number of the present drawing in the sequence of these drawings.

9. **CUMAEAN SYBIL V** (Figure 18)
Sepia wash. 8 May 1956. 17 x 11.
INSCRIPTIONS Signed bottom right. Below signature: *8.5.56.* Below date: *Cumaean Sybil V.*
COLLECTION Private collection, Buckinghamshire.
EXHIBITIONS Folio Society 1957; Brasenose, Oxford 1957.

10. **CUMA** (Figure 17)
Pen and wash. 11 May 1956. 16 x 20.
INSCRIPTIONS Signed bottom right. Below signature: *Cuma. 11.5.56.*
COLLECTION Estate of Hollis S. Baker, U.S.A.
EXHIBITION Hope College 1978, no. 16 (Collection "Hollis M. Baker"; R).
BIBLIOGRAPHY Selvaggi 42 (R, cover); Robertson 1961, 34–44 (R, 42); Cannon-Brookes 1978a, no. 118 (T; R, 67).

This is the first drawing of the acropolis of Cumae.

11. **CUMAE**
Brush drawing. 11 May 1956. 4-3/4 x 6.
INSCRIPTIONS Signed bottom left, in pencil. Bottom right: *11.5.1956.* Below date: *Cumae.*
COLLECTION The artist's estate.
EXHIBITION National Book League 1971, no. 65.
BIBLIOGRAPHY Ayrton 1962c, 61 (line illustration).

12. **[ACROPOLIS OF] CUMAE II**
Pen and wash. 12 May 1956. 14-3/4 x 22.
INSCRIPTIONS Signed lower right.
Below signature: *Cumae.* Below annotation: *12.5.56.*
COLLECTION The artist's estate.
EXHIBITIONS Bruton 1971, no. 40* (T; R); National Book League 1971, no. 62* (T; R, pl. nineteen, no. 30*); Maze and Minotaur Tour 1973, no. 70* (T).
BIBLIOGRAPHY Ayrton 1970b, 57–58 (R, 58); = Ayrton 1971, 293–94 (R, pl. 66); Cannon-Brookes 1978a, no. 117 (T; R, 67).

13. **ACROPOLIS OF CUMAE I**
Oil on board. 1956. 20 x 23-3/4.
INSCRIPTIONS Signed at top. After signature: *56.*
COLLECTION Private collection, London.
EXHIBITIONS Leicester Galleries 1957;
Hamet Gallery November 1969, no. 26*.
BIBLIOGRAPHY *Good Housekeeping,* 144 (April 1957): 91 (R: color).

The sequence of Cat. Nos. 13 and 14 is uncertain, since the photograph in Ayrton's photographic record book is identical to the next painting. Either the photograph was misfiled or the order of these two works should be reversed, but there is no clear way to resolve the discrepancy.

14. **ACROPOLIS OF CUMAE II** (Plate 10)
Oil. 1956. 20 x 23-1/2.
INSCRIPTIONS Signed top left. After signature: *56.*
COLLECTION Private collection, Holland, MI.
EXHIBITIONS Redfern Gallery 1959, no. 18; Stone Gallery 1959; King Street Gallery 1960; Reading Museum Art Gallery 1969, no. 54* (T); Hope College 1978, no. 17 (Collection "Leona M. Nyenhuis, Holland, MI").

15. **ACROPOLIS AT CUMA III**
Oil. 1956. approx. 12 x 18.
COLLECTION Trinity College, Cambridge.
EXHIBITIONS Redfern Gallery 1959, no. 19 (T); Stone Gallery November 1959; King Street Gallery 1960.

16. **ACROPOLIS AT CUMAE**
Print. 1957. 20 x 24.
Edition of 50 color (4 colors, predominantly green and blue), 10 black and white (artist's proofs): Published by St. George's Gallery, London (done in Edinburgh by Harley Brothers Press).
COLLECTION Unknown.
EXHIBITION Gainsborough's House 1962, no. 3 (artist's proof).

17. **'CUMEAN SYBIL'** (Figure 19)
Oil. 1957. 54 x 60.
INSCRIPTIONS Signed bottom left, in white. After signature: *57.*
COLLECTION Private collection, Philadelphia.
BIBLIOGRAPHY Hopkins 1994, 225 and facing 210 (R).

18. **FALCONER I**
Oil. 1957. 25 x 28.
COLLECTION Private collection, Philadelphia.
EXHIBITIONS Galerie Creuse, Paris, 1957; Redfern Gallery 1959, no. 10; Bruton Gallery 1981, no. 102* (R, 39).
BIBLIOGRAPHY Hopkins 1994, bet. 306 and 307 (R).

19. **FALCONER II**
Oil. 1957. 30 x 20.
COLLECTION Unknown.
EXHIBITIONS Galerie Creuse, Paris, 1957; Redfern Gallery 1959, no. 11; Stone Gallery 1959.

20. **DELPHI. TOWARDS ITEA**
Sepia wash. 1957. 14 x 20.
INSCRIPTIONS Signed bottom right.
Above signature: *From Delphi Towards Itea.*
COLLECTION Private collection, U.S.A.
EXHIBITION St. George's 1959.
BIBLIOGRAPHY Cannon-Brookes 1978a, no. 120* (R, 68).

In the MRB, this is listed in the year 1958 and entitled "Delphi, towards the sea," which is equally descriptive.

21. **DELPHI. TOWARDS AMFISSA**
Gouache. 1957. 14 x 20.
INSCRIPTIONS Signed bottom right. After signature: *57.*
Above signature: *From Delphi Towards Amfissa.*
COLLECTION Private collection.
EXHIBITION St. George's 1958.

This drawing was a study for a lithograph of a harvest, *Harvest below Amfissa* (not catalogued), included in the "Greek Suite" 1958 (see note to Cat. No. 41).

22. **CRETAN LANDSCAPE. MAY 1957: ROAD TO PHAISTOS**
Oil on board. May 1957. 20 x 23-3/4.
INSCRIPTIONS Signed bottom right.
Above signature: *5) KPHTH* [= Crete].
COLLECTION Private collection; sold from Redfern Gallery.
EXHIBITION Redfern Gallery 1959, no. 12 (T).

23. **THE PLAIN OF MESARA**
Oil on board. 1957. 20 x 23-1/2.
COLLECTION Stathatos Collection, Athens.

The MRB lists this as "Cretan Landscape (Megara) I."

24. **THE PLAIN OF MESARA**
Oil on board. 1957. 14 x 17.
COLLECTION Sold at auction at Bonham's.
EXHIBITIONS Redfern Gallery 1959, no. 14 (T); Stone Gallery 1959; King Street Gallery 1960.

The MRB entitles this "Cretan Landscape II."

25. **FALCONER III**
Oil on board. August 1957. 39 x 17.
INSCRIPTIONS Signed bottom left. After signature: *57.*
COLLECTION Unknown.
EXHIBITIONS Redfern Gallery 1959 (not catalogued); Stone Gallery 1959; King Street Gallery 1960; Reading Museum Art Gallery 1969, no. 56* (T: "I"); Bruton Gallery 1981, no. 103* (R, 39, detail); Beaux Arts Gallery 1993.

26. **FALCON LANDSCAPE I** or **KESTREL LANDSCAPE**
Oil on board. 1957 (repainted 1958). 20 x 30.
INSCRIPTIONS Signed bottom left. After signature: *57.*
COLLECTION Private collection; sold from Redfern Gallery.
EXHIBITIONS Redfern Gallery 1959, no. 6 (T); Redfern Gallery 1963.
BIBLIOGRAPHY Hopkins 1994, 238, writing about the year 1957, may refer to this painting, although she uses the title, "*Landscape in a Kestrel's Eye*" for it, whereas that title is applied to a painting in 1962 (Cat. No. 277).

27. **FALCON LANDSCAPE II**
Oil on board. July–August 1957 (repainted 1958). 21 x 34.
INSCRIPTIONS Signed lower right, on top of pillar. Below signature, on two lines: *July 57 / August.*
COLLECTION Private collection, Philadelphia.

28. **HERA**
Bronze. 1957. 17 x 4-1/2 x 4. Edition of 2.
COLLECTIONS Private collections, Sussex and London.
EXHIBITION Bruton Gallery and Tour 1981, no. 38 (1967; "Edition of 9;" R, 23).

Also incorporated into *Figure and Image*, Cat. No. 29.

29. **FIGURE AND IMAGE**
Bronze. 1957. 23 x 11-1/2 x 9. Unique.
COLLECTION Private collection, Chicago.
EXHIBITIONS Leicester Galleries 1959, no. 7 (R, 7); Main Street Gallery 1960, no. 16.
BIBLIOGRAPHY Ayrton 1962a, pl. 58.

30. **FIGURE IN LANDSCAPE**
Bronze. 1957. 13 x 25 x 9-1/2. Edition of 9.
COLLECTION Private collection, Chicago.
EXHIBITIONS Leicester Galleries 1959, no. 3; James Goodman Gallery 1965, no. 4* (R); Mazelow Gallery 1966, no. 29*; Daedalus I Art Gallery 1972, no. 9.
BIBLIOGRAPHY Ayrton 1962a, pl. 56.

31. **ORPHEUS**
Bronze. 1957. 9-1/2 x 14 x 4. Edition of 6.
COLLECTIONS Private collections, Yorkshire and Ontario.
EXHIBITIONS Leicester Galleries 1959, no. 6; Main Street Gallery 1960, no. 2 (dated 1958; T); Mazelow Gallery 1966, no. 28 (R); Austin/Desmond Fine Art 1990, no. 35 (R, 19).
BIBLIOGRAPHY Ayrton 1962a, pl. 53 (Collection "Mrs. Fay Pomerance, Sheffield"); Hopkins 1994, 243f.

32. **TALOS ARMED HEAD II**
Bronze. 1957. 24 x 14 x 8. Edition of 6.
COLLECTIONS Private collections, London and the Netherlands
EXHIBITIONS James Goodman Gallery 1965, no. 5; Mazelow Gallery 1966, no. 6 (R); Sears Vincent Price Gallery 1967, no. 23 (R); Bruton Gallery and Tour 1981, no. 83 (R, 44).
BIBLIOGRAPHY Ayrton 1962d, [739] (1956; T; R); Ayrton 1962a, pl. 52 (Collection "Nigel Balchin, Esq, Northiam, Sussex"); Ayrton 1969, pl. XIII (T).

33. **WATCHING FIGURE**
Bronze. 1957. 9 x 14 x 6-1/2. Edition of 9.
COLLECTIONS Private collections, Scotland, New York, Toronto, and Somerset.
EXHIBITIONS Leicester Galleries 1959, no. 2; Main Street Gallery 1960, no. 10 (dated *1959*); Gainsborough's House 1962, no. 20; Mazelow Gallery 1966, no. 18 (R).
BIBLIOGRAPHY Ayrton 1962a, pl. 55 (Collection "Eric Linklater, Esq, Nigg, Rosshire, Scotland"); Hopkins 1994, 244.

34. **DELOS, OCTOBER MORNING. I**
Oil on board. November 1957. 20 x 30.
INSCRIPTIONS Signed top left. After signature: *57.*
COLLECTION Private collection, London.
EXHIBITIONS Redfern Gallery 1958, no. 212 (T); Bensons 1959.
BIBLIOGRAPHY [British] *Vogue* 114, 6 (June 1958): 99 ("Delos [from the collection of Sidney Gilliatt]"; R)

35. **ORPHEUS SEEKING**, Version I
Bronze. 1957. 21 x 27 x 10. Unique.
COLLECTION Unknown.
EXHIBITIONS Leicester Galleries 1959, no. 9 (R, 9); Hamet Gallery 1970, no. 8* (dated 1958; R).
BIBLIOGRAPHY Hopkins 1994, 243f.

For *Version II*, see Cat. No. 724.

36. **SACRED PLACE**
Oil and ripolin on board. January 1958. 14-1/2 x 17-3/4.
COLLECTION Private collection, Essex.
BIBLIOGRAPHY Hopkins 1994, 246.

Ayrton's records on the date of this painting are inconsistent: his photographic record dates it in January 1957, but his MRB lists it second in 1958. The later date therefore seems more plausible.

37. **HAWK & HARVEST**
Oil on board. 1958. 40 x 30.
INSCRIPTION Signed upper right.
COLLECTION Estate of Hollis S. Baker, Grand Rapids, MI.

Ayrton's records disagree; the photographic record dates it in 1957, but the MRB lists it fifth in 1958.

38. **DELOS, MORNING. II** (Figure 37)
Oil on board. 1958. 20 x 48.
COLLECTION Private collection; sold from Redfern Gallery.
EXHIBITION Redfern Gallery 1959, no. 1 (T: "II" omitted).

39. **CRETAN EVENING**
Oil on canvas. 1958. 17 x 20.
COLLECTION Private collection, London.
EXHIBITIONS Redfern Gallery 1959, no. 13; Stone Gallery 1959; King Street Gallery 1960; ?Austin Desmond & Phipps 1992–1993.

The title in the MRB is "Harvest evening, Poros."

40. **DOG AT PHAISTOS**
Pen and India ink wash. 1958. 14 x 20.
INSCRIPTIONS Signed bottom right. Before signature: *Phaistos.*
COLLECTION The artist's estate.
EXHIBITIONS St. George's 1958; Folio Society 1960; King Street 1960; Gainsborough's House 1962, no. 23; Hilton Gallery 1964, no. 30 (dated 1959); National Gallery of Canada 1965, no. 3*.
BIBLIOGRAPHY Cannon-Brookes 1978a, no. 121* (R, 69).

41. **EAGLE LANDSCAPE**
Print. 1958. 17 x 26. Edition of 50.
COLLECTION Unknown.
EXHIBITIONS Whitechapel 1959, no. 5; Gainsborough's House 1962, no. 9 (artist's proof); Austin Desmond & Phipps 1992; Beaux Arts Gallery, 1993.
BIBLIOGRAPHY Hopkins 1994, 254.

This print was included in a series of six lithographs, the "Greek Suite." *Eagle Landscape* is the only "Greek Suite" print included in this catalogue of Ayrton's Daedalian images because Ayrton considered it relevant to the myth: "This one is relevant, since it actually is a view of Delphi, from above" (notes on a conversation with the artist, 27 August 1972).

42. **MINOAN LANDSCAPE**
Bronze. 1958. 6 x 12 x 3. Edition of 6.
COLLECTION The artist's estate.
EXHIBITIONS Matthiesen Gallery 1961, no. 38* (dated 1959); James Goodman Gallery 1965, no. 6 (cast 1/6); Mazelow Gallery, Toronto, May–June 1966, no. 11; Sears Vincent Price Gallery 1967, no. 26.
BIBLIOGRAPHY Ayrton 1962a, pl. 54.

43. **KOUROS IV**
Pencil. 2 June 1958. 14 x 10.
INSCRIPTIONS Dated right center: *2.6.58.* Above date: *Kouros IV.*
COLLECTION The artist's estate.
EXHIBITION Austin Desmond & Phipps 1992.

This drawing was used, more than a decade later, in the development of the bronze and perspex *Kouros* (Cat. No. 659; notes on a conversation with the artist, 10 April 1974).

44. **ICARUS SUSPENDED**
Brush drawing. 1958. 15 x 17-1/2.
COLLECTION Unknown.
EXHIBITION ?National Gallery of Canada, no. 8* (1961).
BIBLIOGRAPHY Ayrton 1962c, pl. 12.

45. **SACRED PLACE**
Wax and bone relief. 1958. 30 x 20.
COLLECTION The artist's estate.
EXHIBITION Leicester Galleries 1959, no. 16.

46. **ICARUS DROWNS** (Figure 22)
Wax and bone relief. 1958. 30 x 20.
COLLECTION Private collection, Milan.
EXHIBITION Leicester Galleries 1959, no. 18.

47. **ICARUS FALLS I** (Figure 21)
Wax and bone relief. 1958–1959. 60 x 48 x 4.
COLLECTION Estate of Gavin Maxwell.
EXHIBITION Leicester Galleries 1959, no. 17.
BIBLIOGRAPHY Robertson 1961 (R, [40]); Grant, pl. 87 (dated 1958; "Collection of Gavin Maxwell"); Ayrton 1962a, pl. 69* (dated 1959; T: "I" omitted); Nyenhuis 1967, 233 (dated 1959; R, 236); Ayrton 1969, 184 and pl. XII; Hopkins 1994, 248, 261, and facing 307 (R).

48. **CONTINGENCY I**
Oil wash, ink, and broken glass. 1959. 13 x 17.
COLLECTION Unknown.
EXHIBITIONS Leicester Galleries 1959, no. 26; Folio Society 1960; King Street Gallery 1960.
BIBLIOGRAPHY Hopkins 1994, 252 and 255.

Quest (Cat. No. 716: bronze and perspex, 1970) employs the technique of hand prints on glass similar to this one.

49. **CONTINGENCY II**
Oil wash, ink and broken glass. 1959. 13 x 17.
COLLECTION Private collection, Yorkshire.
EXHIBITION Leicester Galleries 1959, no. 32.
BIBLIOGRAPHY Hopkins 1994, 252 and 255.

50. **ICARUS I** (Figure 27)
Bronze. 1959. 19 x 20 x 8. Edition of 6.
COLLECTIONS Private collections, Bloomfield Hills, MI, Cornwall, Birmingham, London, and U.S.A.
EXHIBITIONS Main Street Gallery 1960, no. 11 (dated 1960); Matthiesen Gallery, October 1961, no. 36; National Book League 1971, no. 67* (Collection: "Estate of Iain Thompson"; R, pl. 20, no. 31).
BIBLIOGRAPHY Ayrton 1962b, 14; Spencer, [18] (R); Ayrton, 1962a, pl. 91 (Collection "Mrs. H. Turner, Bloomfield, Michigan"); Hopkins 1994, 255.

51. **ICARUS II** (Figure 28)
Bronze. 1959. 15 x 14 x 6-1/2. Edition of 9.
COLLECTIONS Private collections, Greenwich, CT, Louisville, KY, London, and Somerset.
EXHIBITIONS Main Street Gallery 1960, no. 12 (dated 1960); Matthiesen Gallery 1961, no. 37; James Goodman Gallery 1965, no. 7; Mazelow Gallery 1966, no. 3 (R); Sears Vincent Price Gallery 1967, 21* (R); University of Essex, March 1968, no. 2; Hamet Gallery 1969, no. 6; National Book League 1971, no. 68* (Collection "Mr. and Mrs. Lewis Simmons"); Maze and Minotaur Tour 1973, no. 18; Bruton Gallery 1981, no. 39; Austin/Desmond Fine Art 1990, no. 38 (R, 24); Austin Desmond & Phipps 1992; Beaux Arts Gallery 1993.
BIBLIOGRAPHY Robertson 1961, [38]* (R); Ayrton 1962d, [746] (dated 1960; T: "Icarus III;" R); Ayrton 1962a, pl. 94 (Collection "Mrs. B. Gimbel, Greenwich, Connecticut"); Friendly 50 (R); Hopkins 1994, 255.

52. **ICARUS FALLS** (Figure 25)
Oil wash on board. 1959. 17 x 11.
INSCRIPTIONS Signed top left. After signature: *59.*
COLLECTION Private collection, U.K.
EXHIBITION Leicester Galleries 1959, no. 25 (T).

53. **ICARUS FALLS II**
Collage and ink. 1959. 17 x 11.
INSCRIPTIONS Signed top left. Below signature: *59.*
COLLECTION Private collection, Hampshire.
EXHIBITIONS Leicester Galleries 1959, no. 28 (T); Maze and Minotaur Tour 1973, no. 60* (1957; T).

This is the first collage on the subject of Daedalus and Icarus.

54. **EAGLE LANDSCAPE**
Oil on board. 1959. 19 x 30.
INSCRIPTIONS Signed bottom right. Below signature: *59.*
COLLECTION Private collection, Essex.
EXHIBITIONS Redfern Gallery 1959, no. 7; Stone Gallery 1959; King Street Gallery 1960.
BIBLIOGRAPHY Hopkins 1994, 246; at 238 she also seems to refer to this painting, but she places it in the context of comments about the year 1957. Her comments about the work are valid, even if the date appears to be in error.

55. **ICARUS FALLS I**
Oil, sand and wax on board. 1959. 40 x 20.
INSCRIPTIONS Signed bottom left. Below signature: *59.*
COLLECTION The artist's estate.
EXHIBITION Christopher Hull Gallery 1987.

Sepia and lemon colors predominate in this painting.

56. **ICARUS FALLS II**
Oil and encaustic on board. 1959. 40 x 20.
INSCRIPTIONS Signed top left. After signature: *59.*
COLLECTION The artist's estate.
EXHIBITION Christopher Hull Gallery 1987.

57. **ICARUS FALLS III** (a)
Oil on board. 1959. 48 x 60.
INSCRIPTIONS Signed bottom right. Below signature: *59.*
COLLECTION Private collection, Chicago.
EXHIBITION Ringling Museum of Art 1972–1973, no. 4 (T: "Icarus I").

Black and white are the essential colors in this painting (notes on a conversation with the artist, 27 August 1972). The MRB lists two "Icarus Falls III" and attributes the first of them to the collection of Mrs. Jack N. Pritzker of Chicago. Ayrton's photographic record, however, lists this one as "Icarus Falls II," whereas Mrs. Pritzker exhibited it as "Icarus I." There is no fully satisfactory way to resolve the discrepancies in numbering, since there is an obvious duplication. I have attempted to clarify matters by adding the letters (a) and (b) to Ayrton's titles.

58. **ACROPOLIS I**
Oil on board. 1959. 30 x 40.
INSCRIPTIONS Signed top left. After signature: *59.*
COLLECTION Private collection, London.

59. **ICARUS FALLS III** (b)
Oil on board. 1959. 72 x 40.
INSCRIPTIONS Signed bottom left. After signature: *59.*
COLLECTION The artist's estate.
EXHIBITIONS Society of Mural Painters Tour 1961; ?Reading Museum Art Gallery 1969, no. 59 ("Icarus Falls I 1959 oil 70 x 35 the artist").
BIBLIOGRAPHY Cannon-Brookes 1978a, no. 134 (R, 77).

Silver grey, lemon, white, and black are the dominant colors in this painting.

60. **ICARUS FALLS—STUDY FOR V**
Oil on board. 1959. 40 x 20.
COLLECTION Unknown.
EXHIBITION Lidchi Art Gallery 1965, no. 9 (T).

The colors of the rainbow, in warm tones, were used in this oil study for *Icarus Falls V* (Cat. No. 88).

61. **WHITE ROCKY LANDSCAPE**
Oil on board. 1959. 30 x 40.
INSCRIPTIONS Signed top left. After signature: *59.*
COLLECTION Unknown.
EXHIBITIONS Sorsbie Gallery 1963, no. 6 (dated 1959–62; R); Sears Vincent Price Gallery 1969, no. 1.

62. **SEAPASSAGE I**
Oil on board. 1959. 30 x 40.
INSCRIPTIONS Signed top left. After signature: *59.*
COLLECTION Purchased by the artist in 1969 from the collection of the Sorsbie Gallery.
EXHIBITION Sorsbie Gallery 1963, no. 7 (T).

63. **STANDING FIGURE**
Monochrome oil on board. 1959. 40 x 20.
INSCRIPTIONS Signed bottom right. Below and right of signature: *59.*
COLLECTION Private collection; sold by the Campaign for Nuclear Disarmament, to whom Ayrton had donated it.

64. **NEAP TIDE**
Oil on board. 1959. 30 x 40.
COLLECTION Private collection, Cape Cod, MA.

Ayrton's MRB lists this painting in 1960, with the title "Estuary or Flood Tide," and attributes it to the collection of "Ben Sonenberg Jun.," but I have followed his photographic record.

65. **ISLAND & GULL**
Oil. 1959. 20 x 40.
INSCRIPTIONS Signed top left. After signature: *59.*
COLLECTION Unknown.

66. **NIGHT THOUGHT I**
Oil and collage on board. 2 August 1959. 13 x 20.
INSCRIPTIONS Signed bottom left. Below signature: *2.8.59.*
COLLECTION National Gallery of New South Wales.
EXHIBITION Austin/Desmond Fine Art 1990, no. 14 (R, 21, in color).
BIBLIOGRAPHY Hopkins 1994, 252.

Ayrton's photographic record book provides a different provenance (with a question mark), but I have followed his MRB.

67. **PREDICAMENT I**
Collage and oil on board. 8 November 1959. 30 x 20.
INSCRIPTIONS Signed bottom left. Below signature: *8.11.59.*
COLLECTION Private collection, London.
EXHIBITIONS Folio Society 1960; King Street Gallery 1960; Main Street Gallery 1960; Matthiesen Gallery 1962.
BIBLIOGRAPHY Ayrton 1962a, pl. 84; Hopkins 1994, 252 and 255.

68. **PREDICAMENT II**
Collage, pen, and oil on paper. 10 November 1959. 18 x 24-1/2.
INSCRIPTIONS Signed bottom left. After signature: *10.11.59.*
COLLECTION Private collection, London.
EXHIBITIONS Folio Society 1960; Main Street Gallery 1960; Reading Museum Art Gallery 1969, no. 92.
BIBLIOGRAPHY Ayrton 1962a, pl. 86; Hopkins 1994, 252 and 255.

69. **PREDICAMENT III**
Pen, collage, and oil on paper. 1959. 11 x 17.
INSCRIPTIONS Signed top left. After signature: *59.*
COLLECTION Unknown.
EXHIBITIONS Folio Society 1960; King Street Gallery 1960; Main Street Gallery 1960.
BIBLIOGRAPHY Hopkins 1994, 252 and 255.

70. **ICARUS FALLS**
Collage and charcoal on paper. November 1959. 30 x 22.
INSCRIPTIONS Signed bottom left, ink over pencil, with a consequent blurring, particularly of surname. After signature, in pencil: *59.* Below signature, in ink: *November 1959.*
COLLECTION Private collection, Chicago.
EXHIBITIONS Folio Society 1960; King Street Gallery 1960; Main Street Gallery 1960.

71. **ICARUS FALLS (STUDY)** (Figure 26)
Pen, sepia wash, and tissue paper collage. 28 November 1959. 30 x 22?
INSCRIPTIONS Signed bottom right. Below signature: *28.11.59.*
COLLECTION The artist's estate.

The identity of this collage was tentatively confirmed by the artist in a letter from Mrs. Elisabeth Ayrton to the author dated 27th October 1973. In the MRB this work follows the preceding one.

72. **ICARUS FALLS (STUDY)**
Pen and tissue paper collage on black paper. November 1959? 30 x 22?
COLLECTION Unknown.

In the MRB there are three *Icarus Falls* studies listed sequentially among works dating from late 1959 and early 1960. This one is the third in the sequence (see note to preceding entry).

73. **ICARUS WITH RAISED ARMS**
Oil on board. 1959. 50 x 30.
INSCRIPTIONS Signed top left. After signature: *'59.*
COLLECTION Private collection, Sheffield.
EXHIBITION Sorsbie Gallery 1963, no. 1.

The MRB lists this painting second in 1960, contrary to the date on the painting. This painting closely resembles the bronze *Icarus III* (Cat. No. 136), although the hand print technique (like the hand print in *Contingency I* [Cat. No. 48]) anticipates several other works, including *Quest* (Cat. No. 716).

74. **DAEDALUS III** (Figure 51)
Pen and wash. 30 November 1959. 11 x 17.
INSCRIPTIONS Signed bottom right.
Below signature: *Daidalos. III.* After annotation: *30.11.59.*
COLLECTION Unknown.
EXHIBITIONS Folio Society 1960; King Street Gallery 1960; Mazelow Gallery 1966, no. 15.
BIBLIOGRAPHY Ayrton 1962d (R) [745*].

Ayrton's photographic record book indicates that this drawing was exhibited at the Hilton Gallery in 1964, but this is apparently erroneous, since the title and dimensions correspond far more closely to *Daedalus Winged* (Cat. No. 76).

75. **DAEDALUS HEAD** (Figure 55)
Bronze. 1959–1960. 12-1/2 x 8 x 10-1/2. Edition of 6.
COLLECTION Private collection, London.
EXHIBITIONS Matthiesen Gallery 1961, no. 40 (R); James Goodman Gallery 1965, no. 8*; Mazelow Gallery 1966, no. 1* (R); Sears Vincent Price Gallery 1967, no. 20* (R); Bruton Gallery 1981, no. 21; Austin Desmond & Phipps 1992; Beaux Arts Gallery 1993 (dated 1959).
BIBLIOGRAPHY Ayrton 1962a, pl. 89; Ayrton 1970b, 61 (R).

76. **DAEDALUS WINGED**
Pen and sepia wash. 1 December 1959. 14 x 20.
INSCRIPTIONS Signed at bottom, right of center.
Below signature: *1.12.1959.*
COLLECTION Private collection, London.
EXHIBITIONS Folio Society 1960; King Street Gallery 1960; Main Street Gallery 1960; Matthiesen Gallery 1962; Hilton Gallery 1964 (see note to Cat. No. 74), no. 43*.
BIBLIOGRAPHY Ayrton 1962c, pl. 1.

Ayrton's photographic record book originally entitled this work "Icarus-Daedalus Winged," because he was unsure of who it was, but he revised the title after he became convinced that it was Daedalus (conversation with the artist, 26 August 1972).

77. **DAEDALUS WINGED** (Figure 52)
Bronze. 1959–1960. 16 x 17 x 14. Edition of 6.
COLLECTIONS Art Gallery, Southport (cast 2); private collections, Northampton, MA, London, and the Netherlands.
EXHIBITIONS Matthiesen Gallery 1961, no. 39; Grosvenor Gallery, London, February–March 1965, no. 39* (R); Reading Museum Art Gallery 1969, no. 21 (dated 1962; Collection "Atkinson Art Gallery, Southport"); National Book League, London 1971, no. 69 (dated 1959; Collection "The Art Gallery, Southport"); Maze and Minotaur Tour 1973, no. 13.
BIBLIOGRAPHY Robertson 1961, 37* (T: "Daedalus I;" R); Ayrton 1962d, [735] (dated 1960; R); Ayrton 1962a, pl. 93 (Collection "Mr. Leonard Baskin, Northampton, Massachusetts"); Ayrton 1970b, 61 (T: "Daedalus I;" R).

78. **SHORE I**
Oil sketch on board. 24 December 1959. 23-3/4 x 19-1/2.
INSCRIPTIONS Signed bottom right. After signature: *24.12.59.*
COLLECTION Private collection.
EXHIBITION Folio Society 1960.

Ayrton's photographic record book contains this note: "Identical version in collage & oil, same size, exists." Immediately following this entry in MRB is a collage and oil entitled "Shore II," which is crossed out and retitled "Rock Pool" (see Cat. No. 79).

79. **ROCK POOL**
Collage and oil. 1959. 23-3/4 x 19-1/2.
COLLECTION Honourable Mrs. Frost.
EXHIBITION Matthiesen Gallery 1961, no. 22*.

In the MRB this painting was originally entitled "Shore II," but that title was lined out, "Rock Pool" was entered above it, and the remaining "Shore" sketches were renumbered.

80. **SHORE II**
Oil sketch on board. 1959. 14 x 20.
INSCRIPTIONS Signed bottom right. Below signature: *59.*
COLLECTION Private collection, London.
EXHIBITION Folio Society 1960.

81. **SHORE III**
Oil sketch on board. 1959. 19-1/2 x 25-3/4.
INSCRIPTIONS Signed bottom right. After signature: *59.*
COLLECTION Private collection.
EXHIBITIONS Folio Society 1960; King Street Gallery 1960.

82. **HEAD AT HIGH VELOCITY**
Pen. 1959. 8 x 10.
COLLECTION Private collection.
BIBLIOGRAPHY Ayrton 1962c, pl. 8.

83. **MEDITATIVE HEAD (DAEDALUS)** (Figure 54)
Pen and wash. 1959. 14 x 20.
INSCRIPTIONS Signed bottom right. After signature: *59.*
COLLECTION Private collection, Cambridge.
EXHIBITIONS Folio Society 1960; King Street Gallery 1960.
BIBLIOGRAPHY Ayrton 1962a, pl. 87 (T); Ayrton 1970b, 61 (R; T).

84. **ACROPOLIS II**
Oil on board. 1959–1960. 30 x 40.
INSCRIPTIONS Signed top left. After signature: *59–60.*
COLLECTION Private collection.

85. **SHORE I**
Oil and sand on board. 1959–1960. 30 x 50.
INSCRIPTIONS Signed bottom left. After signature: *59–60.*
COLLECTION Estate of Lord and Lady Snow, London.
EXHIBITION Reading Museum Art Gallery 1969, no. 60 (T; Collection "Lady Snow"; R, pl. 16).
BIBLIOGRAPHY Cannon-Brookes 1978a, 75 (no. 132: T; R, 76).

86. **LARGE CYCLADIC I** (Figure 74)
Oil and sand on board. 1959–1960. 30 x 50.
INSCRIPTIONS Signed bottom left. After signature: *59–60.*
COLLECTION The artist's estate.
EXHIBITIONS Matthiesen Gallery 1961, no. 12 (1959; T); Austin/Desmond Fine Art 1990, no. 16 (1959; R, 8).
BIBLIOGRAPHY Cannon-Brookes 1978a, 75 (no. 135, R, 78).

This was one of Ayrton's talismanic figures; he would never let it out of his house. He also considered it his best painting in response to Greece in 1959–1960 (notes on a conversation with the artist, 27 August 1972). At the middle of this painting, as in other Cycladic paintings (Cat. Nos. 91–94), there is a configuration that evokes memory of Cycladic marble images of the third and second millenia B.C.E. Ayrton tended to associate these figures with Icarus (notes on a conversation with the artist, September 1971).

87. **ICARUS FALLS IV** (Plate 13)
Oil on board. 1959. 72 x 40.
COLLECTION Unknown.
EXHIBITIONS Sorsbie Gallery 1963, no. 3 (1960; T); Lidchi Art Gallery 1965, no. 7 (T); Grosvenor Gallery 1967.

The primary colors are gold, white, black, and pale ochre, with some red accents. The exact sequence of these *Icarus Falls* paintings is uncertain and, therefore, frequently confused in exhibition listings. On the basis of Ayrton's MRB I have reversed *Icarus Falls IV* and *V*.

88. **ICARUS FALLS V**
Oil on board. 1960. 72 x 48.
COLLECTION Unknown.
EXHIBITIONS Matthiesen Gallery 1961, no. 4* (1959–1960; T); Sorsbie Gallery 1963, no. 5 (1960–1961; T); Lidchi Art Gallery 1965, no. 8 (T); Stowe School 1970, no. 1 (T: "II").

The dominant colors are silver grey, black, white, and lemon. See previous note (Cat. No. 87) regarding sequence.

89. **ICARUS FALLS VI** (Plate 15)
Oil on board. 1959–1960 (reworked in 1960). 72 x 48.
INSCRIPTIONS Signed top left. After signature: *59–60.*
COLLECTION Unknown.
EXHIBITIONS Sorsbie Gallery 1963, no. 4 (1961; T); ?Lidchi Art Gallery 1965, no. 10 (T: "Icarus Sunstruck"); Austin/Desmond Fine Art 1990, no. 19 (T: "Icarus Sunstruck;" R, back cover, in color).

The predominant colors are gold and red, expressing the full blaze of the sun (notes on a conversation with the artist, 27 August 1972).

90. **MORNING SHORE**
Collage and oil on board. 1960 (reworked 1962). 19-3/4 x 23-3/4.
INSCRIPTIONS Signed top left. After signature: *60.*
COLLECTION Private collection; sold from Matthiesen Gallery.
EXHIBITION Matthiesen Gallery 1961, no. 31*.

It appears virtually certain that this painting was originally entitled "Shore III" in the MRB (see note to Cat. No. 79).

91. **LARGE CYCLADIC II**
Oil on board. 1960. 30 x 40.
INSCRIPTIONS Signed top left. After signature: *60.*
COLLECTION The artist's estate.
EXHIBITION Austin/Desmond Fine Art 1990, no. 17 (R, 4).

See note on Cat. No. 86.

92. **CYCLADIC I**
Oil on canvas. 1960. 15 x 18?
INSCRIPTIONS Signed bottom right. After signature: *60.*
COLLECTION Unknown.

See note on Cat. No. 86.

93. **SMALL CYCLADIC**
Oil on canvas. 1960. 15 x 18.
INSCRIPTIONS Signed top left. After signature: *1960.*
COLLECTION Private collection, South Africa.
EXHIBITIONS Lidchi Art Gallery 1965, no. 30; Bruton Gallery 1981, no. 122*.

See note on Cat. No. 86.

94. **CYCLADIC II**
Oil on canvas. 1959–1960. 15 x 18?
INSCRIPTIONS Signed at bottom left and dated below signature: *59–60.*
COLLECTION Unknown.

See note on Cat. No. 86.

95. **MEDITATIVE HEAD II (DAEDALOS)**
Pen and black ink. 1960. 14 x 20.
INSCRIPTIONS Signed bottom right. After signature: *60.*
COLLECTION Artist's estate (ex private collection, New York).
EXHIBITIONS Main Street Gallery 1960; Hilton Gallery 1964, no. 44* (T); Maze and Minotaur Tour 1973, no. 57 (T).
BIBLIOGRAPHY Ayrton 1962c, 9 (R); *Sunday Times,* 1962 (R, acc. to Ayrton's photographic record book); Graham 1972, 23 (R).

96. **ICARUS RISING**
Monochrome oil on board. 1960. 19-1/2 x 23-1/2.
INSCRIPTIONS Signed bottom left. After signature: *60.*
COLLECTION Private collection, Birmingham.
EXHIBITION Main Street Gallery 1960.
BIBLIOGRAPHY Ayrton 1962c pl. 4; Ayrton 1962d, (R) [736*].

97. **SPECULATIVE HEAD**
Pen and wash. 1960. 17 x 11.
INSCRIPTIONS Signed bottom right. After signature: *60.*
COLLECTION Unknown.
EXHIBITION Main Street Gallery 1960.

98. **DAEDALUS**
Pencil. 1960. 14 x 20.
COLLECTION Private collection, Northampton, MA.
BIBLIOGRAPHY Ayrton 1962d, [740] (R).

99. **NIGHT THOUGHT II**
Oil and collage on board. 1960. 14-1/2 x 21.
INSCRIPTIONS Signed top left. After signature: *60.*
COLLECTION Private collection, Oxfordshire.
EXHIBITIONS Matthiesen Gallery 1962; Reading Museum Art Gallery 1969, no. 94; National Book League 1971, no. 66.
BIBLIOGRAPHY Ayrton 1962a, pl. 85; Hopkins 1994, 252.

100. **NIGHT THOUGHT III**
Oil and collage on board. 1960. 14-1/2 x 21.
COLLECTION Private collection, NY.
EXHIBITION Reid Gallery 1961.
BIBLIOGRAPHY Hopkins 1994, 252.

101. **THE FEATHER** (Figure 23)
Oil, ink, and collage. 1960. 14 x 20.
INSCRIPTIONS Signed at bottom, left of center. After signature: *60.*
COLLECTION Private collection.
EXHIBITION Reid Gallery 1961.

Ayrton said he always felt that the woman in this drawing was Pasiphaë, although he had no logical reason for this identification (notes on a conversation with the artist, 11 September 1971).

102. **ICARUS HEAD**
Oil on board. 21 February 1960. 14 x 11.
INSCRIPTIONS Signed bottom left. After signature: *21.2.60.*
COLLECTION Private collection.
EXHIBITION Austin/Desmond Fine Art 1990, no. 18 (R, 22, in color).

103. **SEA PASSAGE II**
Oil on canvas. 1960. 20 x 24?
INSCRIPTIONS Signed top left. After signature: *60.*
COLLECTION Private collection, London.

The 3rd last entry for 1960 in the MRB is entitled "Sea passage between islands—night." The dimensions are derived from that entry.

104. **HILL AND BLACK ROCKS**
Oil on board. 1960. 20 x 24.
INSCRIPTIONS Signed bottom left. After signature: *59/60.*
COLLECTION Private collection, London; sold at auction by Bonham's ("on behalf of The Appeal for Amnesty for Spanish Political Prisoners and Exiles") on 12 October 1961 (no. 20*; "Presented by the artist").

105. **CLIFFS AND STORMY SKY**
Oil on board. 1960. 27 x 32?
INSCRIPTIONS Signed bottom left. After signature: *60.*
COLLECTION Private collection, London.

106. **DARK SHORE**
Oil and sand. 1960. 30 x 40.
INSCRIPTIONS Signed bottom left. After signature: *60.*
COLLECTION Private collection, NY.
EXHIBITION Matthiesen Gallery 1961, no. 11.

This painting carries implications of the flight of Daedalus and Icarus from Crete, as do the shore pictures generally (notes on a conversation with the artist, 27 August 1972).

107. **DAEDALUS WINGMAKER** (Figure 56)
Bronze. 1960. 18 x 22 x 15. Edition of 6.
COLLECTIONS Private collections, New York, London, Detroit, and Paris.
EXHIBITIONS Matthiesen Gallery 1961, no. 41; Reading Museum Art Gallery 1969, no. 13; National Book League 1971, no. 75 (R, pl. 22, no. 34); Maze and Minotaur Tour 1973, no. 14; Bruton Gallery 1981, no. 23 (R, 13).
BIBLIOGRAPHY Robertson 1961, 35 (R); Grant, pl. 88; Ayrton 1962b, 13 (R); Ayrton 1962a, pl. 88 (Collection "Mrs. Morton Rosenfeld, New York"); Nyenhuis 1967, 234 (R, 224); Ayrton 1969, pl. VII (Collection "M. Maurice Druon, Paris"); Ayrton 1970b, 61 (R).

108. **FIGURES WATCHING A BIRD IN FLIGHT (DRAWING FOR SCULPTURE.)**
Pen. 21 March 1960. Dimensions not recorded.
INSCRIPTIONS Signed near the bottom, right of center, below the feet of the middle figure. After signature: *21.3.1960.*
COLLECTION Private collection, South Africa.
EXHIBITION Lidchi Art Gallery 1965, no. 42.

109. **ICARUS TAKING FLIGHT**
Pen. 23 March 1960. 20 x 14?.
INSCRIPTIONS Signed bottom right (blurred). Below signature: *23.3.1960.*
COLLECTION Private collection, London.
EXHIBITIONS Reading Museum Art Gallery 1969, no. 95* (T); National Book League 1971, no. 73* (T).
BIBLIOGRAPHY Ayrton 1962c, pl. 3* (T); Petit (R, 684); Cannon-Brookes 1978a, no. 144* (R, 83).

The flawed signature and the date provide the basis for positive verification. This drawing was a study for the large bronze of Icarus (presumably *Icarus Rising* [Cat. No. 206]), according to Ayrton's note in his photographic record book.

110. **ICARUS ASCENDANT**
Pen. 1960. 8-1/4 x 6.
COLLECTION Unknown.
BIBLIOGRAPHY Ayrton 1962c, 40 (R).

111. **STUDY FOR ICARUS TRANSFORMED I**
Pencil. 1960. 12 x 18.
COLLECTION Private collection, NY.

112. **ICARUS TRANSFORMED (ICARUS HELD)**
Pen. 29 March 1960. 20 x 15.
INSCRIPTIONS Signed bottom right. Below signature: *29.3.60.*
COLLECTION Private collection, London.
BIBLIOGRAPHY Ayrton 1962c, pl. 7* (T).

The identity of the reproduction in *Testament* was verified by the signature and date. Ayrton attributed the discrepancy in dimensions to framing. He expressed a slight preference for the title used in *Testament* (*"Icarus Held"*), since there are several other drawings of "Icarus Transformed" (notes on a conversation with the artist, 11 September 1971).

113. **SEA I**
Oil and sand on board. 1960. 14 x 16?
COLLECTION Mrs. Jack N. Pritzker, Chicago (sold from Matthiesen Gallery, London, November 1960, according to a letter from the collector to the artist, dated 25 September 1972).

114. **CLIFF FACE**
Oil and sand on board. 1960. 9 x 14.
COLLECTION Private collection, Oregon.
EXHIBITION Matthiesen Gallery 1962.

115. **CLIFF AT NIGHT**
Oil and stucco on board. 1960. 13-1/2 x 17-1/2.
INSCRIPTIONS Signed top left, in white. After signature: *60.*
COLLECTION Unknown.

116. **ICARUS HEAD AT G. I**
Oil on board. 1960. 13 x 17.
INSCRIPTIONS Signed bottom left. After signature: *60.*
COLLECTION Private collection, London.

The 19th entry for 1960 in the MRB reads: "Modified head—I Icarus 15 x 16 : oil on board."

117. **ICARUS HEAD AT G. II**
Oil on board. 1960. 13 x 17?
COLLECTION Private collection, London.

118. **BLACK ROCKS**
Sand and oil on board. 1960. 18 x 24?
COLLECTION This painting was in the collection of the late Gavin Maxwell, but it was destroyed by fire.

Ayrton placed the fire in 1966, but Cannon-Brookes 1978a (at 73) places the fire at Sandaig in 1967. I have not resolved the discrepancy.

119. **NARROW SHORE**
Stucco, sand, and oil. 1960. 8 x 30.
INSCRIPTIONS Signed top left. After signature: *60.*
COLLECTION Formerly in the collection of Mrs. Hess, now in a private collection, London?

This painting was the 28th entry for 1960 in the MRB as "Shore VI."

120. **ROCK AND FLIGHT OF GULLS**
Oil on board. 1960. 16 x 18?
INSCRIPTION Signed at bottom right.
COLLECTION Private collection, Surrey.
EXHIBITION Reading Museum Art Gallery 1969, no. 61 (T; Collection "Mrs. D. Deuchar").

121. **WHITE ROCKS**
Oil and stucco. 1960. 30 x 40.
COLLECTION Private collection, London.
EXHIBITION Matthiesen Gallery 1961, no. 9.

122. **SPRING TIDE**
Oil on board. May 1960. 30 x 40.
INSCRIPTIONS Signed bottom left. After signature: *V. 60.*
COLLECTION Private collection, Essex.
EXHIBITION Felstead School 1960.

123. **MINOS MASKED** (Figure 100)
Wash drawing. 21 June 1960. Dimensions not recorded.
INSCRIPTION Dated lower left, near the neck: *21.6.1960.*
COLLECTION Private collection; donated by the artist to Oxfam and sold from Bear Lane Gallery.

There is a line drawing in *Testament of Daedalus*, 32, with the same title but dated 1962 (Cat. No. 256). Ayrton took that pen drawing from this one, but he did not know who owned it (notes on a conversation with the artist, 11 September 1971).

124. **ICARUS IN FLIGHT (RELIEF I)** (Figure 38)
Painted stucco. 1960. 16 x 20-1/2.
INSCRIPTIONS Signed bottom left. After signature: *60.*
COLLECTION Arts Council of Great Britain.
EXHIBITIONS Matthiesen Gallery 1961, no. 1 (R, cover); National Book League 1971, no. 71 (R, pl. 21, no. 33).
BIBLIOGRAPHY Robertson 1961, 39* (T; R); Spencer, [18] (R); Ayrton 1962d, [750] (T; R); Ayrton 1962a, pl. 102; Ayrton 1969, (R, pl. X); Cannon-Brookes 1978a, 79 (no. 139, R, 80).

The 2nd entry in the MRB on the 2nd page for 1960 reads: "Icarus modified [painted stucco relief] 13″ x 17″ Arts Council."

125. **ICARUS DROWNED** (Figure 50)
Stucco relief. June–July 1960. 16 x 36.
INSCRIPTIONS Signed top left. Below signature: *June–July 1960.*
COLLECTION National Gallery of New South Wales, Sydney.
EXHIBITION Matthiesen Gallery 1961, no. 5*.
BIBLIOGRAPHY Robertson 1961, 44 (R); Spencer, [19] (R); Ayrton 1962a, pl. 115*; Cannon-Brookes 1978a, 73 (no. 130, R, 75).

126. **ICARUS AT THE CLIMAX** (Figure 39)
Oil and stucco on board. 1960. 42 x 72.
COLLECTION Unknown.
EXHIBITION Matthiesen Gallery 1961, no. 2.
BIBLIOGRAPHY Robertson 1961, 44 (R); Ayrton 1962b, [12] (R, in color); Ayrton 1962a, pl. 104 (detail); Hopkins 1994, 273f.

127. **ICARUS HEAD III** (Figure 40)
Oil on board. 12–15 July 1960. 13 x 17.
INSCRIPTIONS Signed bottom right. Below signature: *12–15/7/60.*
COLLECTION Unknown.

The colors are grey and silver.

128. **ICARUS HEAD AT G**
Painted stucco relief. 1960. 13 x 17.
COLLECTION The artist's estate.
EXHIBITION National Book League 1971, no. 70*.

The 7th entry in MRB on the 2nd page for 1960 reads: "Modified Head IV Stucco relief painted 13 x 17."

129. **SEA II**
Collage and oil. 1960. 20 x 24.
INSCRIPTIONS Signed bottom left. Below signature: *60.*
COLLECTION Formerly in the collection of Charles Williams, now in private collection.
EXHIBITION Matthiesen Gallery 1961, no. 14 ("II" is absent).

130. **BLACK LANDSCAPE**
Collage. 1960. 25 x 30.
INSCRIPTIONS Signed top left, in white. After signature: *60.*
COLLECTION Joslyn Art Museum, Omaha, NE.
EXHIBITION Matthiesen Gallery 1961, no. 10 (R).

131. **ICARUS IN FLIGHT, 1960**
Mixed media with collage. 1960. 16 x 18.
INSCRIPTIONS Signed bottom right. Below signature: *60.*
COLLECTION The artist's estate.
EXHIBITION Christopher Hull Gallery 1987.

132. **PROMONTORY**
Collage on canvas. 1960. 25 x 30.
INSCRIPTIONS Signed top left, in white on black. After signature: *60.*
COLLECTION Private collection.

133. **HOT LANDSCAPE**
Collage on board. 1960. 14 x 17.
INSCRIPTIONS Signed top left. After signature: *60.*
COLLECTION Private collection, Dublin.
EXHIBITION Matthiesen Gallery 1961, no. 21.

134. **DUSTY LANDSCAPE**
Oil and collage on canvas. 1960. 30 x 40.
INSCRIPTIONS Signed bottom left. After signature: *60.*
COLLECTION Private collection, Flint, MI.
EXHIBITION Matthiesen Gallery 1961, no. 17.

Colors are dusty gold and white (notes on a conversation with the artist, 27 August 1972).

135. **THE CITY IN SAND**
Oil and stucco on board. 1960. 40 x 60.
COLLECTION Sir Malin Sorsbie, Nairobi.
EXHIBITION Matthiesen Gallery 1961, no. 13.
BIBLIOGRAPHY Robertson 1961, [43] (T; R); Ayrton 1962b, [12] (R, in color, but with top trimmed off).

136. **ICARUS III** (Figure 29)
Bronze. 1960. 67 x 19 x 24. Edition of 3.
COLLECTIONS Private collections, New York and Chicago.
EXHIBITIONS Matthiesen Gallery 1961, no. 42; James Goodman Gallery 1965, no. 9 ("Collection of Mr. and Mrs. Alexander Racolin, New York, New York"); Seventeenth King's Lynn Festival 1967, no. 2; Reading Museum Art Gallery 1969, no. 15 (R, pl. 5); Bruton Gallery 1971, no. 6; R. S. Johnson-International Gallery 1972, no. 1 (dated 1960–62; R, cover); Bruton Gallery 1981, no. 40.
BIBLIOGRAPHY Robertson 1961, 41* (dated 1960–1961; T: "Icarus IV"); Ayrton 1962b, 14 (R); Spencer, [17] (R); Ayrton 1962a, pl. 98; Read 1964c, 215 (R, pl. 243).

For *Variant I*, see Cat. No. 756.

137. **ICARUS ASCENDANT**
Gilt bronze plastron. 1960. 3-1/2 x 14 x 2. Edition of 4.
COLLECTIONS The artist's estate and private collection, Oxford.
BIBLIOGRAPHY Hopkins 1994, 367f.

For version II, see Cat. No. 321. One cast was buried at Hadstock with Ayrton's grandson, Marlin Jonathan ("Marjon") Hopkins (born 30 April 1962), who died in December 1971 after being struck by an automobile.

138. **ICARUS SUSPENDED**
Collage and charcoal. 7–16 September 1960. 34-1/2 x 44.
INSCRIPTIONS Signed top left. Below signature: *7–16/9/60.*
COLLECTION Private collection, Detroit.
EXHIBITION Matthiesen Gallery 1961, no. 33 (1961; R).
BIBLIOGRAPHY Ayrton 1962b, [13] (R); Ayrton 1962a, pl. 106 (1961).

The 6th last entry for 1960 in MRB reads: "Icarus in suspension collage & charcoal on canv Martin Scholnik."

139. **ICARUS TORSO** (Figure 41)
Charcoal. 20 September 1960. 20 x 30.
INSCRIPTIONS Signed lower right. Before signature: *20.9.1960.*
COLLECTION Private collection, NY.
EXHIBITION Matthiesen Gallery 1961, no. 32 (1961).
BIBLIOGRAPHY Ayrton 1962a, pl. 101 (T; 1961; its identity is verifiable from the date on the plate itself; Ayrton verified and corrected the error on 11 September 1971).

Ayrton himself considered this version his best rendition of this idea (notes on a conversation with the artist, 11 September 1971).

140. **ICARUS PINWHEEL**
Charcoal. 3 October 1960. 20 x 30.
INSCRIPTIONS Signed top left. Before signature: *3.10.60.*
COLLECTION Royal Air Force Museum, London.
EXHIBITIONS Matthiesen Gallery 1961, no. 35 (1961); Sheffields 1964; Hilton Gallery 1964, no. 47 (1961); National Gallery of Canada Tour 1965–1967, no. 3 (R); Esther Bear Gallery 1968; National Book League 1971, no. 72 (R, pl. 21, no. 32); Maze and Minotaur Tour 1973, no. 62* (R).
BIBLIOGRAPHY Ayrton 1962d (R) [749]; Cannon-Brookes 1978a, no. 141* (R, 82).

Ayrton's photographic record book indicates that this drawing was also exhibited in Chicago ("Sta B & Chicago"), but it is not listed in any of the catalogues issued by the Sears Vincent Price Gallery.

141. **ICARUS AT THE CLIMAX**
Monotype. 1960. 22 x 14-1/2.
COLLECTION The artist's estate.
EXHIBITION Maze and Minotaur Tour 1973, no. 61.

142. **ICARUS AT THE CLIMAX**
Black ink, sepia, and red ink wash. October 1960. 13 x 17.
INSCRIPTION Signed.
COLLECTION Royal Air Force Museum, London.

143. **ICARUS AT THE CLIMAX (IX)**
Black ink wash. 8 October 1960. 20 x 14.
INSCRIPTIONS Signed bottom left, in pencil. Below signature: *Icarus at climax IX.* After annotation: *8.10.1960.*
COLLECTION The artist's estate.
EXHIBITION ?Beaux Arts Gallery 1993.

The artist noted that this was "the eleventh drawing for the large painting of the same title in the Sorsbie Collection, Nairobi [Cat. No. 215, which is actually entitled Icarus in Contact], but also closely related to the final large (sunburst) Icarus Falls painting [Cat. No. 89] in the artist's possession" (notes to the author, September 1972). Thus there appears to be a slight discrepancy in the numbering of this drawing.

144. **THE PALACE AT MALLIA**
Black ink wash. 1960. 17 x 22.
COLLECTION Private collection, Hampshire.
EXHIBITION Maze and Minotaur Tour 1973, no. 74.

145. **CITY I (GOURNIA)**
Black ink wash. 18 October 1960. 15 x 22.
INSCRIPTIONS Signed bottom right, in pen. Annotated in pencil and dated in pen at bottom left: *City.I 18.10.60.(Gournia).*
COLLECTION The artist's estate.
EXHIBITION Maze and Minotaur Tour 1973, no. 71 (R).

This drawing depicts "the ruins of Gournia, looking towards the sea" (notes from the artist to the author, September 1972).

146. **ZACROS (EXCAVATION IV)**
Black ink wash. 20 October 1960. 14 x 20.
INSCRIPTIONS Signed bottom left. After signature, in pen: *20.10.60.* In pencil, below and extending to right of date: *Excavation IV. Zacros.*
COLLECTION The artist's estate.
EXHIBITION Maze and Minotaur Tour 1973, no. 72* (T; R).

The artist observed that "this drawing was made at the very outset of Marinatos' excavation. Dig is not in evidence" (notes to the author, September 1972).

147. **TOWARDS ZACROS**
Ink wash—black and deep red. 20 October 1960. 14 x 20.
INSCRIPTIONS Signed bottom left. After signature: *20.10.60.* Title in pencil on the same line.
COLLECTION The artist's estate.

The artist commented that "the dark red containing a strong admixture of black is only present in the foreground and middle ground rocks" (notes to the author, September 1972).

148. **CYCLADIC LANDSCAPE**
Ink and wash. 24 October 1960. 14 x 20.
INSCRIPTIONS Signed bottom left. After signature: *24.10/60.*
COLLECTION The artist's estate.
EXHIBITION Christopher Hull Gallery 1987.

149. **ENTRANCE I**
Black ink wash. 14 November 1960. 14 x 20.
INSCRIPTIONS Signed bottom left, in ink. Below signature, in pencil: *Entrance I. 14.11.1960.*
COLLECTION Unknown.

The artist remarked that "this is a view of the entrance to the Cave of Eileithyia at Amnisos" (notes to the author, September 1972).

150. **THE CLOUD**
Black ink wash. 14 November 1960. 11 x 17.
INSCRIPTIONS Signed bottom left, in ink. Below signature, in pencil: *Cloud I 14.11.60.*
COLLECTION Merriam Collection, Philadelphia.
EXHIBITION Gainsborough's House 1962, no. 24.
BIBLIOGRAPHY Ayrton 1962a, pl. 67.

151. **BROKEN SEAWALL**
Black ink wash. 1960. 24 x 30.
INSCRIPTIONS Signed bottom right. After signature: *60.* Before signature: *Broken Seawall.*
COLLECTION Private collection, London.

152. **ICARUS FALLEN** (Figure 43)
Bronze. 1960. 11 x 16 x 12. Edition of 6.
COLLECTIONS Private collections, London and Detroit.
EXHIBITIONS Matthiesen Gallery 1961, no. 48; James Goodman Gallery 1965, no. 10* (dated 1960–61; T; Collection "Dr. and Mrs. Charles Upton Lowe, Buffalo, New York"); Reading Museum Art Gallery 1969, no. 114 (Collection "Mrs. E. Raffles"); National Book League 1971, no. 74 (Collection "Sir Duncan Oppenheim").
BIBLIOGRAPHY Robertson 1961, 42* (T: "Icarus III;" R); Ayrton 1962b, 14 (R); Ayrton 1962a, pl. 113 (Collection "Mrs. Nathan Shaye, Detroit").

153. **ICARUS FALLS**
Pen. 1960. 22 x 14.
COLLECTION Unknown.
BIBLIOGRAPHY Ayrton 1962c, pl. 14.

154. **STILL SEA**
Oil on canvas. 1960. 30 x 50.
INSCRIPTIONS Signed top left. After signature: *60.*
COLLECTION Sir Robert and Lady Mayer, London.
EXHIBITIONS Matthiesen Gallery 1961, no. 7; Reading Museum Art Gallery 1969, no. 62 (Collection "Sir Robert Mayer").

There is an Icarus underneath this painting, which employs the pentimento technique, and his outline is still slightly discernible, giving a curious flavor to this picture: "It could almost be called 'Where Icarus Was'" (notes on a conversation with the artist, 27 August 1972).

155. **ERODED ROCKS**
Oil, sand, and stucco on board. 1960. 20 x 30.
INSCRIPTIONS Signed top left. After signature: *60.*
COLLECTION Private collection, London.

156. **NIGHT** [formerly **VILLAGE AT NIGHT**]
Collage. 1960 (repainted 1961, as NIGHT). 18 x 24.
INSCRIPTIONS Signed top left, in black. After signature: *61* (the first version was signed and dated, in white: *60*).
COLLECTION Private collection, London.
EXHIBITION Matthiesen Gallery 1961 (not catalogued).
BIBLIOGRAPHY Spencer, [19] (R).

157. **LANDSCAPE IN A HIGH WIND**
Oil. 1960. 20 x 30.
INSCRIPTIONS Signed top left. After signature: *60.*
COLLECTION Viscountess Hampden, Hampshire.
EXHIBITION Reading Museum Art Gallery 1969, no. 64 ("Golden Landscape 1960–1 18 x 24 Viscountess Hampden").

This painting explores the implications of the takeoff of Daedalus and Icarus in a high wind (notes on a conversation with the artist, 27 August 1972).

158. **ICARUS IMPRINT** (Figure 44)
Oil and sand on black board. 1960. 30 x 50 x 3.
COLLECTION Private collection, Chicago.
EXHIBITION Sears Vincent Price Gallery 1967, no. 9 (1962).

The MRB dates this work in 1961, whereas the photographic record book places it in 1960.

159–178.
CYCLADIC LANDSCAPES
Oil on board. 1960–1961. All 9 x 13.

These twenty landscape paintings were exhibited at Bear Lane Gallery in 1962, with the heading "Cycladic Landscapes—1961," although some were actually painted in 1960, as the inscriptions show. Since these works are grouped together, the following entries have been abbreviated to a considerable degree.

Three of these paintings were exhibited at Ringling Museum of Art in 1972–1973 as part of the collection of Mrs. Jack N. Pritzker. They were entitled simply *Greek Landscape I* (signed and dated "Dec. 60"), *II* ("60"), and *III* ("61"). All are on board and all are 8 1/2 x 12 1/2 inches. They were numbered 5, 6, and 7 in the catalogue.

159. **ISLAND**
INSCRIPTIONS Signed top left. After signature: *60.*
COLLECTION Private collection.
EXHIBITION Bear Lane Gallery, no. 15.

160. **BREAKWATER**
INSCRIPTIONS Signed bottom right. After signature: *60.*
COLLECTION Private collection, Cornwall.
EXHIBITION Bear Lane Gallery, no. 7.
BIBLIOGRAPHY Hopkins 1994, 272.

161. **CITADEL I**
INSCRIPTIONS Signed top left. After signature: *60.*
COLLECTION Private collection; sold from Bear Lane Gallery.
EXHIBITION Bear Lane Gallery, no. 2.

162. **CITADEL II**
INSCRIPTIONS Signed top right. After signature: *60.*
COLLECTION Private collection; sold from Bear Lane Gallery.
EXHIBITION Bear Lane Gallery, no. 3.

163. **EXCAVATION I**
INSCRIPTIONS Signed bottom right. After signature: *60.*
COLLECTION Private collection; sold from Matthiesen Gallery.
EXHIBITION Bear Lane Gallery, no. 4.

164. **EXCAVATION II**
INSCRIPTIONS Signed top left. After signature: *60.*
COLLECTION Private collection, London; sold from Matthiesen Gallery.
EXHIBITION Bear Lane Gallery, no. 5.

165. **CYCLADIC SHORE I**
INSCRIPTIONS Signed top left. After signature: *60.*
COLLECTION Private collection; sold from Bear Lane Gallery.
EXHIBITION Bear Lane Gallery, no. 11.

166. **HARVEST [II]**
COLLECTION Ind Coope.
EXHIBITION Bear Lane Gallery, no. 17.

According to Ayrton's photographic record book, this is the only harvest landscape in this series, but the MRB lists this one as "Harvest II," ascribing "Harvest I" to a collection in Chicago.

167. **SEA WRACK**
INSCRIPTIONS Signed bottom right. After signature: *Nov 60.*
COLLECTION Private collection; sold from Matthiesen Gallery.
EXHIBITION Bear Lane Gallery, no. 6
BIBLIOGRAPHY Hopkins 1994, 272.

168. **STILL SEA**
INSCRIPTIONS Signed top left. After signature: *Nov–Dec 60.*
COLLECTION Private collection; sold from Bear Lane Gallery.
EXHIBITION Bear Lane Gallery, no. 14.

169. **RED LANDSCAPE**
INSCRIPTIONS Signed bottom right. After signature: *Dec 60.*
COLLECTION Private collection; sold from Bear Lane Gallery.
EXHIBITION Bear Lane Gallery, no. 20.

170. **CYCLADIC SHORE II**
INSCRIPTIONS Signed bottom right. After signature: *Dec 60.*
COLLECTION Private collection; sold from Bear Lane Gallery.
EXHIBITION Bear Lane Gallery, no. 12.

171. **HILLSIDE-WEST CRETE**
INSCRIPTIONS Signed top left. After signature: *Dec 60.*
COLLECTION Private collection, London.
EXHIBITION Bear Lane Gallery, no. 13.

172. **ACROPOLIS**
INSCRIPTIONS Signed bottom right. After signature: *60.*
COLLECTION Private collection.
EXHIBITION Bear Lane Gallery, no. 8.

173. **CLIFF FACE**
INSCRIPTIONS Signed top left. After signature: *Dec 60.*
COLLECTION Poole College, Poole, Dorset.
EXHIBITION Bear Lane Gallery, no. 10.

174. **ROAD TO THE SHORE—MATALA**
INSCRIPTIONS Signed top left. After signature: *61.*
COLLECTION Private collection, London.
EXHIBITION Bear Lane Gallery, no. 1.

175. **THE GREAT ROCK**
INSCRIPTIONS Signed bottom right. After signature: *61.*
COLLECTION Private collection; sold from Bear Lane Gallery.
EXHIBITION Bear Lane Gallery, no. 9.

176. **HOT LANDSCAPE**
INSCRIPTIONS Signed top left. After signature: *61.*
COLLECTION Private collection, London.
EXHIBITION Bear Lane Gallery, no. 19 ("Collage and oil").

177. **FOUR POOLS**
INSCRIPTIONS Signed top left. After signature: *61.*
COLLECTION Private collection.
EXHIBITION Bear Lane Gallery, no. 16 ("Collage and oil").

Ayrton's photographic record book describes this painting as "collage & sand."

178. **INLET**
INSCRIPTIONS Signed top left. After signature: *61.*
COLLECTION Private collection.
EXHIBITION Bear Lane Gallery, no. 18 ("Collage and oil").

179. **SEA PASSAGE AT NIGHT**
Oil. January 1961. 20 x 24.
INSCRIPTIONS Signed top left, in white on black. After signature: *Jan 61.*
COLLECTION Private collection.
EXHIBITION Matthiesen Gallery 1961, no. 16 (T).

The MRB title is: "Sea passage between islands—night."

180. **STONY PLACE**
Oil on board. 1961. 18 x 24.
INSCRIPTIONS Signed top left. After signature: *61.*
COLLECTION Private collection, Birmingham, MI.
EXHIBITION Matthiesen Gallery 1961, no. 20.

181. **MINOAN LANDSCAPE** (Figure 114)
Oil. 1961 (reworked March 1961). 25 x 30.
INSCRIPTIONS Signed bottom left. After signature: *March 61.*
COLLECTION Private collection, Detroit.
EXHIBITION Matthiesen Gallery 1961, no. 27 (R).
BIBLIOGRAPHY Ayrton 1962b, 11 (R, in color).

This painting carries implications of both the city and the maze (notes on a conversation with the artist, 27 August 1972).

182. **PLAIN BEYOND THEBES**
Black ink wash. 10 April 1961. 11-1/2 x 15-1/2.
INSCRIPTION In pencil: *Plain Beyond Thebes. 10.4.61.*
COLLECTION The artist's estate.
EXHIBITION Austin Desmond & Phipps 1992.

This wash drawing came "from the same sketchbook as the Delos drawings. Made on the way to Delphi where continual rain blotted out the sun throughout. No drawing made there as M. A. [was] stricken with nearly lethal jaundice" (notes to the author, September 1972).

183. **AMNISSOS**
Brush drawing. 16 April 1961. 3 x 4-1/2.
INSCRIPTION At bottom right: *16.4.61.*
COLLECTION The artist's estate.
BIBLIOGRAPHY Ayrton 1962c, 20 (line illustration).

184. **DELOS (I)**
Black ink wash. 28 April 1961. 11-1/2 x 15-1/2.
INSCRIPTION At bottom right: *Delos. 28.4.61.*
COLLECTION The artist's estate.
EXHIBITION ?Austin Desmond & Phipps 1992.

The artist described the setting as follows: "View from the porch of the rest house towards the sacred way. One of four drawings of Delos made in late April and early May 1961 on the island. All are closely related to *The Testament of Daedalus* and originate the poem 'See the earth sparkles, glittering gives ground' [Ayrton 1962c, 43]" (notes to the author, September 1972).

185. **DELOS (II)**
Black ink wash. 29 April 1961. 11-1/2 x 15-1/2.
INSCRIPTION Bottom left, in pencil: *Kynthos from the Palaestra. Delos. 29.4.61.*
COLLECTION The artist's estate.

186. **POINT OF DEPARTURE**
Brush drawing. 30 April 1961. 6-1/4 x 7-1/4.
INSCRIPTION Bottom right: *30.4.61.*
COLLECTION The artist's estate.
EXHIBITION National Book League 1971, no. 65 (1960; T).
BIBLIOGRAPHY Ayrton 1962c, 24 (line illustration).

187. **FROM APTERA. W. CRETE**
Black ink wash. 30 April 1961. 11 x 15.
INSCRIPTIONS Signed bottom right. Below signature: *From Aptera. W. Crete 30.4.61.*
COLLECTION Unknown.
EXHIBITIONS Gainsborough's House Society 1962, no. 25 (1960; T); Galeries Jason Teff 1965.

188. **DELOS**
Brush drawing. 1 May 1961. 6-1/3 x 11.
INSCRIPTIONS Signed bottom right, in pencil. Above signature: *1.5.61.* Above date: *Delos, 5:30 A.M.*
COLLECTION The artist's estate.
EXHIBITION National Book League 1971, no. 65 (1960).
BIBLIOGRAPHY Ayrton 1962c, 42 (line illustration).

189. **DELOS (III)**
Black ink wash. 1 May 1961. 11-1/2 x 15-1/2.
INSCRIPTION In pencil, bottom left, on four lines: *Delos From Kynthos high view of the port. 1.5.61.*
COLLECTION The artist's estate.
EXHIBITION Austin Desmond & Phipps 1992 (T).

190. **DELOS (IV)**
Black ink wash. 2 May 1961. 11-1/2 x 15-1/2.
INSCRIPTION In pencil, bottom right: *Delos.2.5.61.*
COLLECTION Unknown.

The artist noted that this drawing [like Cat. No. 184, Delos (I)] represents "another view from the rest-home towards the port" (notes to the author, September 1972).

191. **CRETAN LANDSCAPE**
Brush drawing. 12 May 1961. 3-1/2 x 5.
INSCRIPTIONS Signed top center, in pencil. Top left: *Snow, stubble, gray, gold 6:30 P.M.* Top right: *12.5.61. Ida from Phaistos.*
COLLECTION The artist's estate.
EXHIBITION National Book League 1971, no. 65 (1960; T).
BIBLIOGRAPHY Ayrton 1962c, 63 (line illustration).

192. **MINOAN LANDSCAPE II** or **CORN RHYTON**
Oil and sand on canvas. May 1961. 25 x 30.
INSCRIPTIONS Signed top left. After signature: *May '61.* Reworked version: signed top left; after signature: *61.*
COLLECTION Private collection, London.
EXHIBITIONS Matthiesen Gallery 1961, no. 28 (T: "Corn Rhyton"); Bruton Gallery and Tour 1981, no. 97 (T; R, 41).
BIBLIOGRAPHY Cannon-Brookes 1978a, 78 (R; Collection "Bruton Gallery, Bruton").

193. **APTERA, SUDDEN STORM**
Oil. May 1961. 30 x 50.
INSCRIPTIONS Signed bottom left. Before signature: *May 1961.*

This painting was destroyed by the artist, although he retained a photographic record of it.

194. **CYCLADIC SHORE (DUSK)**
Oil. 1960 (repainted and cut down, 1961). 16 x 24.
COLLECTION Private collection, London.

195. **DAEDALUS WINGED** (Figure 53)
Charcoal. 2 June 1961. 20 x 30.
INSCRIPTIONS Signed bottom right. Above signature: *2.6.1961.*
COLLECTION Private collection, Sheffield.
EXHIBITION Matthiesen Gallery 1962.
BIBLIOGRAPHY Ayrton 1962a, pl. 90; Ayrton 1970b, 61 (R).

196. **SCREAM**
Pen. 1961. 10 x 8.
COLLECTION The artist's estate.
BIBLIOGRAPHY Ayrton 1962c, pl. 9.

197. **ICARUS AT THE CLIMAX**
Pen. 1961. 10 x 8.
COLLECTION The artist's estate.
BIBLIOGRAPHY Ayrton 1962c, pl. 11.

198. **ICARUS TRANSFORMED**
Pen. 1961. 9-1/2 x 11-1/2.
COLLECTION The artist's estate.
EXHIBITION Hamet Gallery 1969, no. 27*.
BIBLIOGRAPHY Ayrton 1962c, pl. 10.

199. **ICARUS TRANSFORMED** (Figure 47)
Charcoal and collage on board. 4–7 June 1961. 30 x 40.
INSCRIPTIONS Signed bottom left. After signature: *4–7/6/1961.*
COLLECTION Private collection, NY.
EXHIBITION Matthiesen Gallery 1961, no. 34.
BIBLIOGRAPHY Ayrton 1962a, pl. 97; Ayrton 1962b, 12 (R, color).

This is a rather important drawing, since it relates closely to the *Icarus Transformed* sequence of bronzes (notes on a conversation with the artist, 26 August 1972).

200. **ICARUS MULTIPLE**
Charcoal and collage. 24 June 1961. 20-1/2 x 15.
INSCRIPTION Bottom right: *24.6.61.*
COLLECTION Private collection.
BIBLIOGRAPHY Ayrton 1962a, pl. 108.

201. **STUDY FOR ICARUS RISING** (Figure 32)
Pencil. 4 July 1961. 12 x 18.
INSCRIPTION Bottom right: *4.7.1961.*
COLLECTION Private collection, Santa Barbara, CA.
EXHIBITION Sears Vincent Price Gallery 1967, no. 2 (T).

202. **STUDY FOR DAEDALUS AT CUMAE**
Pencil. 7 July 1961. 12 x 18.
INSCRIPTION Bottom right, near center: *7.7.1961.*
COLLECTION Unknown.

203. **DAEDALUS AT CUMAE**
India ink. 1961. 15 x 11.
COLLECTION Merriam Collection, Philadelphia.
EXHIBITION Philadelphia Museum of Art 1963, 7 (T; attributed to G. Michael Ayrton).
BIBLIOGRAPHY Ayrton 1962c, pl. 16.

204. **DAEDALUS AT CUMAE** (Figure 57)
Bronze. 1961. 21 x 11 x 7-1/2. Edition of 6.
COLLECTIONS Private collections, New York and unknown.
EXHIBITIONS Matthiesen Gallery 1961, no. 47; James Goodman Gallery 1965, no. 14 (R); Mazelow Gallery 1966, no. 2 (R); Reading Museum Art Gallery 1969, no. 17 (Collection "Dr. Catherine Storr"); Bruton Gallery and Tour 1981, no. 20 (R, cover and 15, detail).
BIBLIOGRAPHY Spencer, [18] (R); Ayrton 1962a, pl. 116 (Collection "Dr. Anthony Storr, London"); Ayrton 1970b, 61 (R); Hopkins 1994, facing 307 (R).

205. **ICARUS, PIERCED RELIEF** (Figure 45)
Bronze. 1961. 15 x 15 x 3. Edition of 9.
COLLECTIONS Royal Airforce Museum, London (cast 3); private collections, London and Buffalo, NY.
EXHIBITIONS Matthiesen Gallery 1961, no. 48; James Goodman Gallery 1965, no. 11 (R); Christopher Hull Gallery 1987; Austin Desmond & Phipps 1992.
BIBLIOGRAPHY Ayrton 1962a, pl. 105 (Collection "G. F. Pollock, Esq. London").

206. **ICARUS RISING** (Figure 33)
Bronze. 1961. 23 x 30-1/2 x 8. Edition of 3.
COLLECTIONS Private collections, London.
EXHIBITIONS Matthiesen Gallery 1961, no. 43; Hamet Gallery 1969, no. 8.
BIBLIOGRAPHY Ayrton 1962a, pl. 100 (Collection "Sir Frederick Hooper, Tenterden, Kent"); Nyenhuis 1967, 233 (R, 232).

For *Variants I, II,* and *III*, see Cat. Nos. 413, 512, and 513, respectively.

207. **ROCK AT DUSK**
Oil, sand, and collage. 1961. 13 x 21.
INSCRIPTIONS Signed top left. After signature: *61.*
COLLECTIONS Formerly in the Hess collection; now Exeter College Junior Commons Room.
EXHIBITIONS Matthiesen Gallery 1961; Reading Museum Art Gallery 1969, no. 65 (Collection "Exeter College J.C.R.").

208. **BLACK SHORE**
Oil and collage on board. 1961. 34 x 54.
INSCRIPTIONS Signed top left. After signature: *61.*
COLLECTION Private collection, London.
EXHIBITIONS John Moores 1961–1962; Matthiesen Gallery ("House Show"), March 1962; Arts Council Tour 1965–1966.

209. **SEA AND SHINGLE**
Collage. 1961. 30 x 50.
INSCRIPTIONS Signed top right. After signature: *61.*
COLLECTION Formerly in the collection of Sir David Eccles, now in private collection.
EXHIBITION Matthiesen Gallery 1961, no. 18*.

210. **WHITE MOUNTAIN—CRETE**
Oil on canvas. 1961. 20 x 24.

Destroyed by the artist, but a photographic record of it was retained.

211. **LANDSCAPE AT DUSK**
Oil on canvas. 1961. 20 x 24.
COLLECTION Private collection, Los Angeles.
EXHIBITION Matthiesen Gallery 1961, no. 15; October 1962? (Ayrton's photographic record book lists an exhibition at Matthiesen in October 1962, but adds "not hung").

212. **BLEACHED LANDSCAPE**
Oil and sand. 1960–1962. 25 x 30.
INSCRIPTIONS Signed top left. After signature: *July 61.*
COLLECTION Harold Patton and Associates.
EXHIBITIONS Sorsbie Gallery 1963, no. 8 (1959–1962); Hilton Gallery 1964, no. 1 (1962); Lidchi Art Gallery 1965, no. 14 ("Bleached Landscape—Narobi [*sic*]"; "oil and sand on canvas"); Sears Vincent Price Gallery 1969, no. 4 (1963; "Bleached Landscape, Crete"; "oil on canvas").

Ayrton considered this painting to be a type of "proto-maze picture" that anticipated his later explorations of the maze (notes on a conversation with the artist, 27 August 1972).

213. **ELEGIAC LANDSCAPE**
Oil on canvas. July 1961. 20 x 30.
INSCRIPTIONS Signed bottom right. After signature: *July 61.*
COLLECTION Private collection.
EXHIBITIONS Matthiesen Gallery 1961, no. 26; October 1962? ("not hung": see note to Cat. No. 211).

214. **HEADLAND**
Oil and sand on canvas. 1961. 25 x 30.
INSCRIPTIONS Signed bottom right. After signature: *61.*
COLLECTIONS Formerly in the collection of Felix Salmon; now in private collection (London?).
EXHIBITION Matthiesen Gallery 1961, no. 19 ("collage and oil on board").

215. **ICARUS IN CONTACT** (Figure 46)
Oil on canvas. 1961. 60 x 40.
INSCRIPTIONS Signed bottom left. After signature: (virtually illegible date on photograph).
COLLECTION Sir Malin Sorsbie, Nairobi.
EXHIBITIONS Matthiesen Gallery 1961, no. 3; Sorsbie Gallery 1963, no. 2.
BIBLIOGRAPHY Ayrton 1962b, [13] ("Icarus Falls"; R, in color); Read 1964a (R, pl. 30); Hopkins 1994, 273f.

This painting, which has an unusual dark green sky, represented for Ayrton his most complete version of the kind of orgasm he believed Icarus experienced—the explosion of the sun. In the artist's mind this work was related to the bronze *Icarus Transformed I* (Cat. No. 216), which is in the Tate Gallery (notes on a conversation with the artist, 27 August 1972).

216. **ICARUS TRANSFORMED I** (Figure 48)
Bronze. 1961. 8 x 23 x 12. Edition of 6.
COLLECTIONS Tate Gallery, London; private collections, New York City, Buffalo, NY, Los Angeles, Chicago, and London.
EXHIBITIONS Matthiesen Gallery 1961, no. 44 (R); James Goodman Gallery 1965, no. 12; Sears Vincent Price Gallery 1967, no. 1; National Book League 1971, no. 76; Maze and Minotaur Tour 1973, no. 19 (R).
BIBLIOGRAPHY Robertson 1961, [43] (R); Ayrton 1962a, pl. 107.

217. **ICARUS TRANSFORMED II**
Bronze. 1961. 8 x 6-1/2 x 4. Edition of 2.
COLLECTIONS Private collections, New York and London.
EXHIBITIONS Matthiesen Gallery 1961, no. 45; ?University of Essex 1968, no. 3 (title and date correspond, but dimensions are those of *Icarus Transformed III*).
BIBLIOGRAPHY Ayrton 1962a, pl. 96 (Collection "Mr. Benjamin Sonnenberg, Jr., New York").

218. **ICARUS TRANSFORMED III** (Figure 49)
Bronze. 1961. 5-1/2 x 18 x 5. Edition of 6.
COLLECTIONS Royal Air Force Museum, London (cast 6, formerly private collection in Houston, TX); private collections, Milwaukee, WI, Los Angeles, Houston, TX, and Yorkshire.
EXHIBITIONS Matthiesen Gallery 1961, no. 46; James Goodman Gallery 1965, no. 13; Mazelow Gallery 1966, no. 5; Sears Vincent Price Gallery 1967, no. 22; ?University of Essex, March 1968, no. 3 (see note to Cat. No. 217); Hamet Gallery 1969, no. 7; National Book League 1971, no. 77* (Collection "Mrs. Fay Pomerance [Yorkshire]"); Magdalene Street Gallery 1972, no. 2; Maze and Minotaur Tour 1973, no. 20.
BIBLIOGRAPHY Ayrton 1962a, pl. 112 (Collection "Dr. and Mrs. Abraham Melamed, Milwaukee").

219. **NIGHTSHOAL**
Collage and oil on canvas. 1961. 30 x 50.
INSCRIPTIONS Signed bottom left. Before signature: (photographic record appears to record month and year, 1961, but inscription could not be fully verified).
COLLECTION Private collection.
EXHIBITION Matthiesen Gallery 1962, no. 1

220. **NEAPTIDE II**
Collage and oil on canvas. 1961. 25 x 30.
INSCRIPTIONS Signed top left. After signature: *61.*
COLLECTION Private collection.
EXHIBITION Matthiesen Gallery 1962, no. 2.

221. **SEA III**
Collage on card. 1961–1962 (reworked in 1962). 18 x 24.
INSCRIPTIONS Signed lower left. Below and right of signature: *62.*
COLLECTION Lady Balogh, London.
EXHIBITION Matthiesen Gallery 1961, not catalogued.

222. **MINOAN LANDSCAPE II**
Collage, oil and sand on canvas. 1961. 30 x 40.
INSCRIPTIONS Signed bottom left, in white. After signature: *61.*
COLLECTION Estate of Mrs. Stead-Ellis.

223. **ICARUS HEAD**
Wash. 23 October 1961. 11 x 15.
INSCRIPTION Bottom right: *23.10.61.*
COLLECTION Private collection, London.
BIBLIOGRAPHY Ayrton 1962c, pl. 2*.

224. **ICARUS TORSO II**
Charcoal. 1961. 23 x 18-3/4.
INSCRIPTION Signed bottom left.
COLLECTION The artist's estate.
BIBLIOGRAPHY Ayrton 1962a, pl. 95.

225. **FIGURE UNDER STRESS**
Charcoal. 14 November 1961. 23-1/4 x 17-1/2.
INSCRIPTIONS Signed top left. Below signature: *14.11.61.*
COLLECTION Private collection, London.
EXHIBITIONS Matthiesen Gallery 1962; Reading Museum Art Gallery 1969, no. 96 (R, pl. 22); National Book League 1971, no. 78*.
BIBLIOGRAPHY Ayrton 1962a, pl. 118*; Cannon-Brookes 1978a, 84 (no. 145*; R).

226. **ICARUS DROWNED**
Sepia and black ink wash. 1961. 14 x 20.
INSCRIPTIONS Signed bottom left. Bottom right: *For Sidney [Nolan] from Michael 12.12.61.*
COLLECTION Private collection, London.
BIBLIOGRAPHY Ayrton 1962a, pl. 114.

227. **SENTINEL II**
Pen and black ink. 24 December 1961. 18 x 12.
INSCRIPTIONS Bottom right: *24.12.1961.* Bottom left: *Sentinel* (Below title: *II*).
COLLECTION Canberra Grammar School, Australia.
BIBLIOGRAPHY Ayrton 1962a, pl. 119 (1962; T).

This drawing was based on a chicken bone and served as a study for the bronze *Bone Sentinel* (Cat. No. 245) Ayrton sculpted in 1962 (notes on a conversation with the artist, 11 September 1971).

228. **SENTINEL III**
Pencil. 24 December 1961. 18 x 12.
INSCRIPTIONS Bottom left: *24.12.61.* Left of and above date: *Sentinel.* Below title: *III.*
COLLECTION Unknown.
EXHIBITION National Gallery of Canada Tour 1965–1967, no. 10* (T).

229. **HEAD**
Black ink wash. 24 December 1961. 11 x 15.
INSCRIPTION Bottom left: *24.12.61.*
COLLECTION Private collection, Bradford.
EXHIBITION Matthiesen Gallery 1962.
BIBLIOGRAPHY Ayrton 1962a, pl. 117*.

This figure for Ayrton was actually a representation of Icarus (notes on a conversation with the artist, 26 August 1972).

230. **CHIMAERA I**
Pencil. 29 December 1961. 12 x 18.
INSCRIPTION Bottom right: *Chimera I. 29.12.61.*
COLLECTION Unknown.

231. **HEAD AT G** (Figure 42)
Black ink wash. 31 December 1961. 12 x 18.
INSCRIPTIONS Signed bottom right. Before signature: *Head at G.* Above annotation: *31.12.61.*
COLLECTION The artist's estate.
EXHIBITIONS Esther Bear Gallery 1968; Maze and Minotaur Tour, 1973, no. 63*.
BIBLIOGRAPHY Ayrton 1962a, pl. 103 (T).

When the artist completed this drawing, he actually had Icarus in mind (notes on a conversation with the artist, 11 September 1971).

232. **SOMBRE LANDSCAPE**
Oil, sand, and collage on canvas. 1961–1962. 30 x 40.
INSCRIPTIONS Signed top left. After signature: *61–62.*
COLLECTION Private collection, London.
EXHIBITION Matthiesen Gallery 1962, no. 3 (1961; R).

233. **CHIMAERA II**
Pen and ink. 1 January 1962. 12 x 18.
INSCRIPTIONS Signed bottom right. Above signature: *Chimaera II. 1.1.1962.*
COLLECTION R. S. Johnson-International Gallery, Chicago.
EXHIBITION R. S. Johnson-International Gallery 1972, no. 44 (R, 55).
BIBLIOGRAPHY Hadfield, 69 (R).

This drawing grew out of the artist's preoccupation with stresses and distortions that concerned him in connection with Icarus (notes on a conversation with the artist, 11 September 1971).

234. **ICARUS DISINTEGRATED**
Monotype. 1962. 21-1/2 x 14-1/2.
COLLECTION Unknown.
EXHIBITION National Gallery of Canada Tour 1965–1967, no. 4* (1960).
BIBLIOGRAPHY Ayrton 1962c, pl. 13.

235. **ICARUS DROWNED**
Monotype. 1962. 20 x 14.
COLLECTION Unknown.
BIBLIOGRAPHY Ayrton 1962c, pl. 15.

236. **NIGHT SEA**
Monotype. 1962. 19 x 14.
COLLECTION Unknown.
EXHIBITION National Gallery of Canada Tour 1965–1967, no. 5* (1960).
BIBLIOGRAPHY Ayrton 1962c, pl. 5.

237. **NIGHT LANDSCAPE 62: CRETE**
Collage and oil. February 1962. 20 x 24.
INSCRIPTIONS Signed top left. After signature: *Feb. 62.*
COLLECTION Private collection, London.

238. **RUFFLED SEA**
Collage and oil. 1962. 25 x 30.
INSCRIPTIONS Signed top left. After signature: *62.*
COLLECTION Private collection, Los Angeles.

239. **ROUGH SEA AT NIGHT**
Collage and oil. February 1962. 19-1/2 x 20-1/4.
INSCRIPTIONS Signed lower right. Below signature: *Feb. 62.*
COLLECTION Sir Malin Sorsbie, Nairobi.

240. **SITE**
Oil on canvas. 1961–1962. 20 x 30.
INSCRIPTIONS Signed bottom left. After signature: *61–62.*
COLLECTION Private collection, Los Angeles.

This is the first site picture, and therefore it is a rather important painting: "If it's related to anywhere, it's related to Phaistos" (notes on a conversation with the artist, 27 August 1972).

241. **LANDSCAPE WITH THRESHING FLOOR**
Oil, collage, and sand on canvas. 1961–1962. 30 x 50.
INSCRIPTIONS Signed bottom right, in from margin. After signature: *62.*
COLLECTION Private collection, Los Angeles.

This painting is abstractly related to Mallia (notes on a conversation with the artist, 27 August 1972).

242. **ORACLE I**
Pen and wash. 3 February 1962. 12 x 18.
INSCRIPTIONS Bottom right: *3.2.1962.* Before date: *Oracle.* Below title: *I.*
COLLECTION Unknown.

243. **SENTINEL IV**
Black ink wash. 10 February 1962. 18 x 12.
INSCRIPTIONS Bottom right: *10.2.1962.* Above date: *Sentinel.*
COLLECTION Unknown.
EXHIBITION James Goodman Gallery 1965, no. 3 (T).
BIBLIOGRAPHY Ayrton 1962a, pl. 120 (March 10, 1962, although the correct date is visible in the plate itself; T).

244. **STUDY FOR SENTINEL (TALOS)**
Pen and black ink. 12 February 1962. 22 x 15.
INSCRIPTIONS Signed bottom right, in pencil. Above signature, in ink: *12.2.1962.*
COLLECTION The artist's estate.
EXHIBITIONS Hilton Gallery 1964, no. 40 (T); National Gallery of Canada Tour 1965–1967, no. 11 (1960; T); Hamet Gallery 1969, no. 34* (1963; T); Magdalene Street Gallery 1972, no. 17 (T; R).
BIBLIOGRAPHY Ayrton 1962a, pl. 124 (12 March 1962, although the correct date is visible in the plate itself); Ayrton 1962c, 18 (T; R).

245. **BONE SENTINEL** (Figure 62)
Bronze. 1962. 36 x 11 x 7. Edition of 6.
COLLECTIONS Private collections, Hertfordshire and New York.
EXHIBITIONS Grosvenor Gallery 1964, no. 20; James Goodman Gallery 1965, no. 15; National Book League 1971, no. 87 (Collection "E. Sommer").
BIBLIOGRAPHY Ayrton 1962a, pl. 121.

246. **ORACLE II**
Pen and black ink. 12 February 1962. 15-1/2 x 22.
INSCRIPTIONS Bottom right: *12.2.1962.* Above date: *Oracle II.*
COLLECTION The artist's estate.
BIBLIOGRAPHY Ayrton 1962a, pl. 131* (detail; T).

247. **ORACLE III** (Figure 68)
Pen and black ink. 22 February 1962. 15-1/2 x 22.
INSCRIPTIONS Signed bottom right. Below signature: *22.2.1962.* Below date: *Oracle III.*
COLLECTION Private collection, Yorkshire.
EXHIBITIONS Matthiesen Gallery 1962; Reading Museum Art Gallery 1969, no. 97* (T); National Book League 1971, no. 83* (T).
BIBLIOGRAPHY Ayrton 1962a, pl. 129* (T).

248. **FAT MAN I**
Pen and black ink. 27 February 1962. 22 x 15.
INSCRIPTION Top right: *27.2.62.*
COLLECTION The artist's estate.
EXHIBITIONS Grosvenor Gallery 1964, no. 67 (T); Mazelow Gallery 1966, no. 17 (T; R, together with Cat. No. 249 as one entry); Daedalus I Gallery 1972, no. 25 (T).
BIBLIOGRAPHY Ayrton 1962a, pl. 134 (T); Hopkins 1994, 275.

249. **THE FAT MAN, HALF LENGTH**
Pen and black ink. 27 February 1962. 14 x 10.
INSCRIPTION Bottom right: *27.2.62.*
COLLECTION Unknown.
EXHIBITIONS Grosvenor Gallery 1964, no. 68*; Mazelow Gallery 1966, no. 17 (T; R, together with Cat. No. 248 as one entry).
BIBLIOGRAPHY Ayrton 1962a, pl. 135 (T); Hopkins 1994, 275.

250. **FAT SENTINEL** (Figure 67)
Bronze. 1962. 18 x 5-1/2 x 5. Edition of 9.
COLLECTIONS The artist's estate; private collections, London and Chicago.
EXHIBITIONS Grosvenor Gallery 1964, no. 21 (R); James Goodman Gallery 1965, no. 16; Mazelow Gallery 1966, no. 8; Reading Museum Art Gallery 1969, no. 20 ("Estorick Collection"); Magdalene Street Gallery 1972, no. 3*; R. S. Johnson-International Gallery 1972, no. 2 (R, 9); Austin/Desmond Fine Art 1990, no. 39; Austin Desmond & Phipps 1992.
BIBLIOGRAPHY Ayrton 1962a, pl. 126; Hopkins 1994, 275.

251. **SENTINEL FETISH**
Bronze. 1962. 20 x 7 x 3. Unique.
COLLECTION Private collection, the Netherlands.
EXHIBITIONS Grosvenor Gallery 1964, no. 24 (dated 1963; R); Grosvenor Gallery 1965, no. 40 (dated 1963).

252. **SLENDER SENTINEL** (Figure 63)
Bronze. 1962. 24 x 5-1/4 x 5-3/4. Edition of 6.
COLLECTIONS Private collections, New Zealand, London, New York, and Chicago.
EXHIBITIONS Grosvenor Gallery 1964, no. 25 (dated 1963); Grosvenor Gallery 1965, no. 38 (dated 1963); University of Essex 1968, no. 4; R. S. Johnson-International Gallery 1972, no. 3 (R, 10); Bruton Gallery 1981, no. 75.
BIBLIOGRAPHY Ayrton 1962a, pl. 122.

253. **SMALL SENTINEL**
Bronze. 1962. 13 x 5-1/2 x 5. Edition of 6.
COLLECTION Private collection, Paris.
EXHIBITIONS Grosvenor Gallery 1964, no. 23 (R); James Goodman Gallery 1965, no. 17 (T); Mazelow Gallery 1966, no. 9; Sears Vincent Price Gallery 1967, no. 25; Bruton Gallery 1971, no. 7 (R); Bruton Gallery 1981, no. 76 ("edition of 9"); Austin/Desmond Fine Art 1990, no. 40 ("edition of 9"); Austin Desmond & Phipps 1992.
BIBLIOGRAPHY Ayrton 1962a, pl. 125.

254. **ICARUS RISING II** (Figure 34)
Polyester resin. 1962. 34 x 68 x 16. Unique.
COLLECTION Private collection, London.
BIBLIOGRAPHY Ayrton 1962a, pl. 110 (Collection "Bernard Sunley, Esq., London").

255. **NAUTILUS I**
Pen. 1962. 4-1/4 x 5.
COLLECTION The artist's estate.
EXHIBITION National Book League 1971, no. 65 (1960).
BIBLIOGRAPHY Ayrton 1962c, 29 (line illustration).

256. **MINOS MASKED**
Pen. 1962. 4-1/2 x 5.
COLLECTION Private collection.
BIBLIOGRAPHY Ayrton 1962c, 32 (line illustration).

This pen drawing was taken from a 1960 wash drawing of the same title (Cat. No. 123), which is quite similar (notes on a conversation with the artist, 11 September 1971).

257. **NAUTILUS II**
Pen. 1962. 3-1/2 x 6-1/2.
COLLECTION The artist's estate.
EXHIBITION National Book League 1971, no. 65 (1960).
BIBLIOGRAPHY Ayrton 1962c, 37 (line illustration).

258. **JACKET OF THE TESTAMENT OF DAEDALUS** (Figure 35)
Pen and ink. 1962. 13 x 7-3/4.
COLLECTION Private collection, Chicago.
EXHIBITION National Book League 1971, pl. 23, no. 35.

259. **ORACLE**
Black ink wash. 23 April 1962. 14 x 10.
INSCRIPTIONS Bottom right: *23.4.62.* Below date: *Oracle.*
COLLECTION Private collection, New York.
EXHIBITION James Goodman Gallery 1965, no. 4 (T).
BIBLIOGRAPHY Ayrton 1962a, pl. 132 (T)

260. **SLUMPED ORACLE**
Black ink wash. 23 April 1962. 14 x 10.
INSCRIPTIONS Signed in pencil bottom right and dated below signature. Below date: *Slumped Oracle.*
COLLECTION The artist's estate.
EXHIBITION Hamet Gallery 1969, no. 28*.

261. **THE ACROPOLIS OF RHAMNUS**
Black ink wash. 12 May 1962. 15 x 22.
INSCRIPTION Bottom right: *12.5.62.*
COLLECTION Private collection, Athens.
EXHIBITION Hilton Gallery 1964, no. 34.

This wash drawing depicts the Temple of Nemesis on Rhamnus, which was one of several places very important to the artist, who first visited it with his friend, George Savidis (notes on a conversation with the artist, 11 September 1971).

262. **FRAGMENT OF AUGUST**
Collage and oil on canvas. 1962. 25 x 30.
INSCRIPTIONS Signed bottom left. After signature: *62.* Before signature: *Fragment of August.*
COLLECTION The artist's estate.
EXHIBITIONS Hilton Gallery 1964, no. 5; Lidchi Art Gallery 1965, no. 13; Austin Desmond & Phipps 1992–1993.

263. **GRAVEL PIT**
Oil on canvas. 1962. 20 x 24.
INSCRIPTIONS Signed bottom right. After signature: *62.*
COLLECTION Private collection, Colchester.

264. **STANDING STONES**
Collage and sand on paper. 1962. 19 x 14.
INSCRIPTIONS Signed top left, in white. After signature: *62.*
COLLECTION Private collection, Los Angeles.

265. **CLOUD, SEA AND ROCKS AT NIGHT**
Collage on paper. 1962. 19 x 14.
INSCRIPTIONS Signed bottom left, in white. After signature: *62.*
COLLECTION Private collection, Los Angeles.

The MRB's 7th entry on the 2nd page for 1962 reads: "Sea & white rocks at night."

266. **DARK RED LANDSCAPE**
Oil on canvas. 1962. 25 x 30.
INSCRIPTIONS Signed bottom right. After signature: *62.*

Destroyed by the artist, but a photographic record was retained.

267. **AUTUMN LANDSCAPE**
Oil and sand on canvas. 1962. 20 x 24.

Destroyed by the artist, but a photographic record was retained.

268. **OCHRE LANDSCAPE, ANATOLIA**
Collage and oil on board. 1962. 30 x 40.
INSCRIPTIONS Signed top left. After signature: *62.*
COLLECTION Private collection, London.
EXHIBITION Matthiesen Gallery 1962.

269. **THE KESTREL'S PLACE**
Collage on canvas. 1962. 30 x 40.
INSCRIPTIONS Signed bottom left. After signature: *62.*
COLLECTION From the estate of the late James Fisher, transmitted to his son.
EXHIBITION Grosvenor Gallery 1964, no. 28 (R).

270. **SENTINEL** (Figure 60)
Oil on canvas. 1962. 50 x 25.
INSCRIPTIONS Signed top right. Below signature: *62.*
COLLECTION Unknown.
EXHIBITION Sorsbie Gallery 1963, no. 10.

The red and gold colors of this painting create a hot, brazen effect. It is the only painting of a sentinel and also "the only instance where the sculpture clearly crossed the board—there are not painted Minotaur pictures, for example" (notes on a conversation with the artist, 27 August 1972). There is, however, a collage of *Talos* (Cat. No. 358), which originally was recorded as "Sentinel" (MRB).

271. **CROW'S FEATHER LANDSCAPE**
Collage and acrylic. 1962 (repainted 1964). 20 x 24.
COLLECTION Private collection, South Africa.
EXHIBITIONS Grosvenor Gallery 1963; Hilton Gallery 1964, no. 6 (1962); Lidchi Art Gallery 1965, no. 18.

There is an actual feather in the collage (notes on a conversation with the artist, 26 August 1972).

272. **DARK CLIFF. IEREPATRA**
Pen and sepia ink. 12 July 1962. 13 x 18.
INSCRIPTIONS Signed bottom left. Before signature: *Dark cliff. Ierepetra. S. Crete.* Above annotation: *12.7.'62.*
COLLECTION The artist's estate.
EXHIBITIONS ?Gainsborough's House 1962, no. 27 (T: "Ierepatra, East Crete;" dated 1960); Lidchi Art Gallery 1965, no. 46 (T: "Ierepatra, East Crete"); National Gallery of Canada Tour 1965–1967, no. 9* (dated 1961; T: "Ierepatra, East Crete").

273. **ORACLE**
Wash. 12 July 1962. 15 x 22.
INSCRIPTION Bottom right: *July 12 '62.*
COLLECTION Unknown.
EXHIBITIONS National Gallery of Canada Tour 1965–1967, no. 13; ?Hamet Gallery 1969, no. 33 (T).
BIBLIOGRAPHY Ayrton 1962a, pl. 128 (T).

274. **ORACLE**
Pencil and wash. 16 July 1962. 15 x 22.
INSCRIPTIONS Signed at top, left of center. Top left: *July 16 '62.* Above date: *Oracle.*
COLLECTION Private collection.
EXHIBITION Matthiesen Gallery 1962.
BIBLIOGRAPHY Ayrton 1962a, pl. 130 (18 July 1962, although the correct date is visible in the plate itself; T).

275. **NIGHT LANDSCAPE [IN] BLUE, GREEN AND BLACK**
Collage and oil on canvas. 1962. 20 x 24.
INSCRIPTIONS Signed lower left, in from margin. After signature: *62.*
COLLECTIONS Formerly in the Grosvenor collection; presently in private collection, London.
EXHIBITIONS Matthiesen Gallery 1962; Grosvenor Gallery 1964, no. 36 ("Night Landscape").

276. **LANDSCAPE WITH A FEATHER**
Collage on plywood. 1962. 18 x 24.
INSCRIPTIONS Signed top left. After signature: *62.*
COLLECTION Private collection, South Africa.

277. **LANDSCAPE IN THE KESTREL'S EYE** (Figure 36)
Collage, pastel, gouache, and sand on board. 1962. 30 x 40.
INSCRIPTIONS Signed top left. After signature: *62.*
COLLECTION The artist's estate.
EXHIBITIONS Matthiesen Gallery 1962; Grosvenor Gallery, London 1964, no. 29; Stowe School 1970, no. 4; National Book League 1971, no. 90 (R, pl. 25, no. 38); Austin Desmond & Phipps 1992–1993; Beaux Arts Gallery 1993.

Dusty earth colors—gold and bronze—are basic in this painting. This work was a crucial one for Ayrton in his exploration of the flight of Daedalus and Icarus (notes on a conversation with the artist, 26 August 1972).

278. **THE PLAIN OF MESARA**
Collage and oil on board. 1962. 34 x 66.
COLLECTION The artist's estate.
EXHIBITIONS Grosvenor Gallery 1964, no. 26; Reading Museum Art Gallery 1969, no. 67; Stowe School 1970, no. 3 ("The Plain of Messara [*sic*]").

This work was a key Cretan picture for Ayrton (notes on a conversation with the artist, 28 August 1972). Several titles or descriptions are given this work in the MRB (2nd page of entries for 1962, entry no. 20): "The Messara (Large Harvest)" and "Brazen Landscape" (written above the other two). This is the first of several works grouped together in the MRB under August 1962.

279. **ORACLE I (AUGUST 10)** (Figure 59)
Charcoal and collage on beaverboard. 10 August 1962. 50 x 30.
INSCRIPTIONS Signed top right. Below signature: *August 62.*
COLLECTION Private collection, London.
EXHIBITION Grosvenor Gallery 1963.
BIBLIOGRAPHY Ayrton 1962a, pl. 165 ("Study for Oracle [large version]").

280. **ORACLE WITH BAY LEAVES (FLOWERING LAUREL)**
Collage on card. 1962–1964. 27 x 30.
INSCRIPTIONS Signed top right. Below signature: *11th August 62–12 Dec: '64.*
COLLECTION Unknown.
EXHIBITION Lidchi Art Gallery 1965, no. 11 ("Oracle-Figure with flowering laurel").

The original title for this work in the MRB, 2nd page for 1962, was "Oracle August 11 Figure with flowering laurel." Dimensions there are given as 36 x 26. There is a notation above the line indicating that it was reworked in December 1963 and another notation that this work was destroyed (a line was also drawn through the entry), but it appears still to exist.

281. **ORACLE III (AUGUST 12 '62)** (Figure 69)
Collage on beaver board. 12 August 1962. 40 x 30.
INSCRIPTIONS Signed top right, in white. Below signature: *August 12 '62.*
COLLECTION Eric Estorick, London.
EXHIBITION Grosvenor Gallery 1963 (R).

There is a distortion of the head reminiscent of other drawings and paintings of heads under stress. This figure has a blind-eyed, oracular appearance (notes on a conversation with the artist, 1 August 1972).

282. **MINOTAUR I** (Figure 98)
Bronze. 1962. 52 x 33 x 22. Edition of 3.
COLLECTION The artist's estate.
EXHIBITIONS Grosvenor Gallery 1964, no. 1 (R); Seventeenth King's Lynn Festival 1967, no. 6 (R, detail); Reading Museum Art Gallery 1969, no. 22; Maze and Minotaur Tour 1973, no. 1.
BIBLIOGRAPHY Ayrton 1962a, pl. 137.

283. **SEATED MINOTAUR**, Version I (Small Minotaur) (Figure 97)
Bronze. 1962. 11-1/2 x 8 x 5. Edition of 9.
COLLECTIONS Private collections, London, Cambridge, Paris, Essex, Kent, and Whitley.
EXHIBITIONS Grosvenor Gallery 1964, no. 3 (dated 1963; T); Austin/Desmond Fine Art 1990, no. 47* (dated 1963; R, 22, color).

284. **TALOS. MAQUETTE** (Figure 64)
Bronze. 1962. 9-3/4 x 4 x 3-1/2. Edition of 9.
COLLECTIONS Private collections, Indianapolis, IN, Holland, MI, and London.
EXHIBITIONS Grosvenor Gallery 1964, no. 22* (R); James Goodman Gallery 1965, no. 18 (T); Mazelow Gallery 1966, no. 13; Sears Vincent Price Gallery 1967, no. 28 (R); Hamet Gallery 1969, no. 19; R. S. Johnson-International Gallery 1972, no. 4; Hope College 1978, no. 57 (Collection "Mr. and Mrs. Peter Jolivette, Holland, MI"); Austin Desmond & Phipps 1992 (dated 1963); Beaux Arts Gallery 1993 (dated 1963).

285. **LANDSCAPE IN EARTH AND SMOKE**
Collage, sand, sawdust, and oil. 1962. 30 x 50.
INSCRIPTIONS Signed bottom right. After signature: *62.*
COLLECTION Unknown.
EXHIBITION Grosvenor Gallery 1964, no. 33 ("Landscape in Smoke").

286. **AMPHORA (STILL LIFE IN PARODY)**
Collage on canvas. 1962. 40 x 30.
INSCRIPTIONS Signed top right, in white. After signature: *62.*
COLLECTION Formerly in the Grosvenor Gallery collection; sold from Sotheby's in 1969.
EXHIBITION Bruton Gallery and Tour 1981, no. 93* (R, 30).

The MRB titles this work "Spectral Amphora."

287. **MAN O'WAR**
Oil and encaustic on canvas. 1962. 18 x 22.
INSCRIPTIONS Signed bottom left. After signature: *62.*
COLLECTION Private collection, London.
EXHIBITIONS Bear Lane Gallery 1962; Grosvenor Gallery 1964, no. 34; Lidchi Art Gallery 1965, no. 50.

288. **THE MOON'S ECLIPSE**
Collage and smoke on wood. 1962. 24-3/4 x 31-1/4.
INSCRIPTIONS Signed top left, in white. After signature: *62.*
COLLECTION Private collection, London; sold from Matthiesen Gallery.
EXHIBITION Matthiesen Gallery 1962.

Pasiphaë and her relation to the moon provided the stimulus for this painting (notes on a conversation with the artist, 27 August 1972).

289. **PINEWOOD BEYOND A FIELD**
Oil and smoke on plywood. 10 September 1962. 15 x 17.
INSCRIPTIONS Signed bottom left. Below signature, in heavier pen: *10.9.62.*
COLLECTION Private collection, South Africa.

290. **BLUE VINE LANDSCAPE**
Encaustic, oil, and collage. 1962. 20 x 30.
INSCRIPTIONS Signed top left, in white. After signature: *'62.*
COLLECTION The artist's estate.
EXHIBITION Austin/Desmond Fine Art 1990, no. 20 (R, 30).

291. **LANDSCAPE IN SMOKE**
Collage, wood veneer, and smoke on plywood. 13 September 1962. 20 x 24.
INSCRIPTIONS Signed bottom left. After signature: *13.9.1962.*
COLLECTION Unknown.
EXHIBITIONS Grosvenor Gallery 1963; Hilton Gallery 1964, no. 4; Lidchi Art Gallery 1965, no. 6.

292. **STUBBLE BURNING**
Collage on plywood. September 1962. 20 x 24.
INSCRIPTIONS Signed. After signature: *Sept 62.*
COLLECTION Private collection, Essex.
EXHIBITION Matthiesen Gallery 1962.

293. **HILLSIDE IN DROUGHT**
Collage and smoke on board. 1962. 24-1/2 x 31-1/4.
INSCRIPTIONS Signed top left. Below signature: *19.9.62.*
COLLECTIONS Formerly in the Grosvenor collection; presently in private collection, London.
EXHIBITION Grosvenor Gallery 1964, no. 30*.

The original title for this painting was "Rocky Hillside—Sunset" (MRB, 2nd entry on 3rd page for 1962). The colors are red, brown, and smoke. This Cretan landscape is one of the first of Ayrton's burnt pictures, which he created by using an acetylene torch (notes on a conversation with the artist, 27 August 1972).

294. **WHITE WIND**
Collage and oil on wood. September 1962. 20 x 24.
INSCRIPTIONS Signed top left. After signature: *Sept. 62.*
COLLECTION Private collection, London.
EXHIBITION Grosvenor Gallery 1964, no. 38.

295. **WINTER DEMETER** (Figure 86)
Smoke and collage on board. 30 September 1962. 53 x 20.
INSCRIPTIONS Signed top right. Below signature: *30.9.62.*
COLLECTIONS Formerly Mrs. Walton; sold at auction at Sotheby's, in 1973; Bruton Gallery, Somerset.
EXHIBITION Grosvenor Gallery 1964, no. 31.

This collage is closely related to the bronze *Winter Demeter* (Cat. No. 623). "The Demeter and Kore pictures connect more closely to the seasons—the turning year—than all the others" (conversation with the artist, 28 August 1972). The original title was "Shrouded Oracle" (MRB, 4th entry on 3rd page for 1962).

296. **ORACLE I** (Figure 71)
Bronze. 1962. 17 x 8-1/2 x 13. Edition of 6.
COLLECTIONS Private collections, London, Essex, Rosshire, Paris, New York, and Liverpool.
EXHIBITIONS Grosvenor Gallery 1964, no. 9* (T; R); Seventeenth King's Lynn Festival 1967, no. 23 (T; R); University of Essex 1968, no. 5; Hamet Gallery 1969, no. 9*; Reading Museum Art Gallery 1969, no. 19* (Collection "Andrew Carnwath Esq."); National Book League 1971, no. 84.
BIBLIOGRAPHY Ayrton 1962a, pl. 127; Ayrton 1969, pl. XV (Collection "Abe Gottlieb, New York").

297. **BEYOND THE BEACH**
Oil and encaustic on canvas. 1962. 25 x 30.
COLLECTION Private collection (MRB: "given to Anti-Apartheid").
EXHIBITION Sorsbie Gallery 1963, no. 9 ("Behind the Beach").

298. **CORN AND VINE**
Oil. 1962 (repainted February 1963). 25 x 30.
INSCRIPTIONS Signed (version II) top left. After signature: *'62/63.*
COLLECTION Unknown.
EXHIBITIONS Matthiesen Gallery 1962; Hilton Gallery 1964, no. 2 (1963); Lidchi Art Gallery 1965, no. 15; Sears Vincent Price Gallery 1969, no. 6 (R); Stowe School 1970, no. 5 (1965).

299. **ROCKY WHITE**
Collage on card. 7 October 1962. 18 x 24?
INSCRIPTIONS Signed bottom left. After signature: *7.10.62.*
COLLECTION Private collection, London.
EXHIBITION Matthiesen Gallery 1962.

300. **INLET**
Collage and oil on canvas. October 1962. 25 x 30.
INSCRIPTIONS Signed top left. After signature: *Oct 62.*

Destroyed by the artist, but a photographic record was retained.

301. **WHERE THE VILLAGE STOOD**
Collage on wood. November 1962. 20 x 24.
INSCRIPTIONS Signed top left. After signature: "*'62 Nov:.*"
COLLECTION Grosvenor collection, London.
EXHIBITION Grosvenor Gallery 1964, no. 37.

302. **OWL LIGHT**
Oil on canvas. November 1962. 18 x 22.
INSCRIPTIONS Signed bottom right. After signature: *Nov '62.*
COLLECTION Private collection, London.
EXHIBITIONS ?Bear Lane Gallery 1963; Grosvenor Gallery 1964, no. 35.

303. **FOUR TREES**
Oil on board. 1962. 20 x 24.
INSCRIPTIONS Signed top left. After signature: *'62.*
COLLECTION Unknown.
EXHIBITION Sorsbie Gallery 1963, no. 11.

304. **BROKEN BEACH**
Collage on wood. 1962. 10-1/4 x 13-3/8.
INSCRIPTIONS Signed top left. After signature: *'62.*
COLLECTION Private collection, London.
EXHIBITION Matthiesen Gallery 1966.

305. **SILVER HILL THAW**
Oil and encaustic on canvas. 1962. 30 x 50.
COLLECTION Private collection, Milan.
EXHIBITION Grosvenor Gallery 1964, no. 27 (R).

This painting is essentially a winter landscape in England, around Essex (notes on a conversation with the artist, 28 August 1972)

306. **ORACLE**
Pen. 25 November 1962. 10 x 9.
INSCRIPTIONS Signed in pencil bottom left. After signature: *25.11.62.*
COLLECTION The artist's estate.

307. **STUDY FOR TRIPOD ORACLE**
Black ink wash. 25 November 1962. 14 x 10.
INSCRIPTIONS Signed bottom left, in pencil. Below signature, in ink: *25.11.62.*
COLLECTION The artist's estate.
EXHIBITION Mazelow Gallery 1966, no. 5.

308. **TRIPOD ORACLE**
Pen and black ink wash. 25 November 1962. 16 x 10.
INSCRIPTIONS Signed bottom left. Below signature: *25.11.62.*
COLLECTION The artist's estate.
EXHIBITIONS Bruton Gallery 1981, no. 173 (R, 49); National Museum of Wales, Penarth, and Pelter Sands Gallery 1981.
BIBLIOGRAPHY Cannon-Brookes 1978a, no. 179* (R, 101).

309. **MANTIC FIGURE II**
Pen and black ink. 25 November 1962. 10 x 9.
INSCRIPTIONS Signed bottom left. After signature: *25.11.62.*
COLLECTION The artist's estate.
BIBLIOGRAPHY Cannon-Brookes 1978a, no. 181 (R, 102).

310. **LABYRINTH** (Figure 113)
Oil on canvas. December 1962. 25 x 30.
INSCRIPTIONS Signed bottom left. After signature: *Dec '62.*
COLLECTION Unknown.
EXHIBITIONS Grosvenor Gallery 1964, no. 41 (1963; R); Lidchi Art Gallery 1965, no. 16; Sears Vincent Price Gallery, no. 3; Stowe School 1970, no. 9 (1963); Austin Desmond & Phipps 1992–1993.

This painting represents the first total labyrinth picture, although the labyrinth was variously suggested in earlier paintings. Ayrton attempted to convey a general sense of the maze underground. One enters it and exits from it in three dimensions; hence the maze is not precisely diagrammed in this painting, as it would have been if it were conceived of as being viewed from above (notes on a conversation with the artist, 28 August 1972).

311. **MANTIC HEAD**
Oil on canvas. 1962–1964. 12 x 16.
INSCRIPTIONS Signed bottom left. Below signature on two lines: *20.12.62; /15.5.64.*
COLLECTION Private collection, Santa Barbara, CA.

The MRB titles it "Oracle, head."

312. **NIGHT LABRYS**
Collage on board. December 1962. 17 x 24.
INSCRIPTIONS Signed top left. After signature: *Dec '62.*
COLLECTION Sir Roger and Lady Ormrod, London.
EXHIBITIONS Grosvenor Gallery 1964, no. 43 (1963; R); Reading Museum Art Gallery 1969, no. 70 (1963; Collection "Lady Ormrod"); National Book League 1971, no. 89 (1963; Collection "Lady Ormrod").

The imagery of the double axe in this collage is understandably very significant, in view of its importance in Minoan art and religion. The colors in this painting are predominantly blue, a very deep blue (notes on a conversation with the artist, 26 August 1972).

313. **RED MAZE**
Sand, collage, and oil on board. 1962. 25 x 30.
INSCRIPTIONS Signed bottom left. After signature: *62.*

Destroyed by the artist, but a photographic record was retained.

314. **SEATED TRIPOD FIGURE**
Bronze. 1962–1963. 14 x 7-1/2 x 5. Edition of 6.
COLLECTIONS Private collections, New York, Esher, UK, Buffalo, NY, Paris, and Southfield, MI.
EXHIBITIONS Grosvenor Gallery 1964, no. 10 (R); James Goodman Gallery 1965, no. 19 (dated 1962); Seventeenth King's Lynn Festival 1967, no. 24; University of Essex 1968, no. 8; Hamet Gallery 1969, no. 14.
BIBLIOGRAPHY Ayrton 1962a, pl. 160 (Collection "Mr. and Mrs. Alexander Racolin, New York").

315. **TRIPOD ORACLE** (Figure 75)
Bronze. 1962–1963. 17 x 3 x 5. Edition of 9.
COLLECTION Private collection, Paris.
EXHIBITIONS Grosvenor Gallery 1964, no. 11 (R); Sears Vincent Price Gallery 1967, no. 2 (dated 1963); Bruton Gallery 1981, no. 87; Christopher Hull Gallery 1987; Austin Desmond & Phipps 1992 (dated 1962).
BIBLIOGRAPHY Ayrton 1962a, pl. 161 (Collection "M. Maurice Druon, Paris").

316. **LABRYS** (Figure 115)
Collage on board. 1963. 25 x 30.
COLLECTION Private collection, Cornwall.
EXHIBITION Grosvenor Gallery 1964, no. 32 (1962).

In contrast to the deep blue colors of *Night Labrys* (no. 312), this collage consists of warm earth colors. It is the maze in the double axe (notes on a conversation with the artist, August 1972).

317. **THE SITE OF THE CITY**
Collage on wood. 1963–1964. 20 x 24.
INSCRIPTIONS Signed bottom left, in from margin. After signature, on two lines: *23.1.63 /14.4.64.*
COLLECTION Unknown.
EXHIBITIONS Hilton Gallery 1964, no. 7 (1964); Lidchi Art Gallery 1965, no. 19.

318. **JOURNEY**
Collage on board. 1963. 24 x 31.
INSCRIPTIONS Signed bottom left. After signature: *'63.*
COLLECTIONS Formerly in Grosvenor collection; presently in the collection of Sir Roger and Lady Ormrod, London.
EXHIBITIONS Grosvenor Gallery 1964, no. 39 (R); Reading Museum Art Gallery 1969, no. 69 (Collection "Lady Ormrod").

The 2nd entry for 1963 in MRB entitles this work "Journey between Rocks." This collage is the first in a series of journey pictures; a dark grape color predominates. Made from a paint rag, the collage creates "an arbitrarily variegated picture of the rock" (notes on a conversation with the artist, 28 August 1972).

319. **FIGURE WITH A SKEIN**, Version I
Bronze. 1963. 35 x 8 x 12. Edition of 4.
COLLECTIONS Private collections, London, Evanston, IL, and Paris.
EXHIBITIONS Grosvenor Gallery 1964, no. 18 (R); Tate Gallery 1965, no. 9; James Goodman Gallery 1965, no. 25; Mazelow Gallery 1966, no. 30; Sears Vincent Price Gallery 1967, no. 34 (R).
BIBLIOGRAPHY Ayrton 1962a, pl. 162 (T; Collection "Dr. and Mrs. Murray Thomson, London"); Hopkins 1994, 293 and 298.

For version II, see Cat. No. 764.

320. **STRUNG LANDSCAPE**
Collage on board with string. 1963. 30 x 40.
INSCRIPTIONS Signed top left. After signature: *'63.*
COLLECTION Private collection, Cornwall.
EXHIBITION Grosvenor Gallery 1964, no. 40.

321. **ICARUS ASCENDANT**, Version II (Figure 31)
Gilt bronze plastron. 1963. 5-1/2 x 14 x 2. Edition of 9.
COLLECTIONS Private collections, Cambridge, Chicago, London, and Detroit.
EXHIBITIONS Sears Vincent Price Gallery 1970, no. 22* (dated 1969; "gilt bronze and perspex"); R. S. Johnson-International Gallery 1972, no. 5 (R, 11).

For version I, see Cat. No. 137.

322. **SEAPASSAGE. DELOS**
Collage on canvas. 9 February 1963. 16 x 18.
INSCRIPTIONS Signed bottom left, in white on light back ground. Below signature: *9.2.63.*
COLLECTION Unknown.
EXHIBITION Austin/Desmond Fine Art 1990, no. 22* (R, 31, in color).

323. **TATTERED ORACLE**
Collage on board. 25 February 1963. 20 x 24.
INSCRIPTIONS Signed top right. Above signature: *25.2.1963.*
COLLECTION Private collection, Los Angeles.
EXHIBITION Grosvenor Gallery 1963.

324. **SUDDEN STORM**
Collage on canvas. 3 March 1963. 20-1/2 x 24.
INSCRIPTIONS Signed at bottom left, in white, and dated after signature: *3.3.63.*
COLLECTION Private collection, London.
EXHIBITIONS Sheffield University 1964; Grosvenor Gallery 1964, no. 42; Austin/Desmond Fine Art 1990, no. 21 (R, 29, in color).

This collage vaguely represents a port and was probably based on Navarino, just south of Pylos, where one can still see Turkish galleys lying on the bottom of the sea, relics of battles during the Napoleonic era (notes on a conversation with the artist, 28 August 1972).

325. **ORACLE SEATED I**
Black ink wash. 4 March 1963. 20 x 16.
INSCRIPTIONS Signed bottom left. Below signature: *4.3.1963.*
COLLECTION Private collection, London.

326. **SEATED ORACLE AS KORE**
Black ink wash. 4 March 1963. 20 x 16.
INSCRIPTIONS Signed bottom right. Above signature: *4.3.63.* Top right: *Seated Oracle as Kore.*
COLLECTION Private collection, South Africa.
EXHIBITIONS Grosvenor Gallery 1964, no. 73 (T); Hilton Gallery 1964, no. 50; Lidchi Art Gallery 1965.

327. **ORACLE, ASTRIDE** (Figure 72)
Black ink wash. 4 March 1963. 20 x 16.
INSCRIPTION Bottom, right of center: *4.3.'63.*
COLLECTION Private collection, London.
EXHIBITION Grosvenor Gallery 1964, no. 74.

328. **ORACLE WITH BAY LEAVES II** (Figure 83)
Black ink wash. 8 March 1963. 26-3/4 x 18-3/4.
INSCRIPTIONS Signed bottom right. Above signature: *8.3.1963.* Below signature: *Oracle with Bay Leaves II.*
COLLECTION Private collection, London.
EXHIBITIONS Grosvenor Gallery 1964, no. 76 (T); Reading Museum Art Gallery 1969, no. 100 (T); National Book League 1971, no. 85 (T).
BIBLIOGRAPHY Ayrton 1962a, pl. 164 (T).

329. **STUDY FOR DEMETER PREGNANT**
Pen and black ink wash. 9 March 1963. 25-1/2 x 18-1/2.
INSCRIPTION Dated lower right: *9.3.63.*
COLLECTION The artist's estate.
EXHIBITION Christopher Hull Gallery 1987.

330. **KER**
Bronze. 1963. 15 x 5 x 4-1/2. Edition of 6.
COLLECTION Private collection, Paris.
EXHIBITIONS Grosvenor Gallery 1964, no. 13 (R); Mazelow Gallery 1966, no. 15* (dated 1962); Sears Vincent Price Gallery 1967, no. 30* (R); Austin/Desmond Fine Art 1990, no. 41* ("edition of 9"); Beaux Arts Gallery 1993 ("edition of 9").
BIBLIOGRAPHY Ayrton 1962a, pl. 159 (Collection "M. Maurice Druon, Paris").

331. **THE ORACLE AS KORE**
Charcoal. 20 March 1963. 20-1/2 x 15-1/2.
INSCRIPTIONS Signed bottom right. After signature: *20.3.63.*
COLLECTION Private collection, London.
EXHIBITION Grosvenor Gallery 1964, no. 72.

332. **CAMEIRA**
Charcoal. 21 March 1963. 24 x 18.
INSCRIPTIONS Signed top right. Above signature: *21.3.63.*
COLLECTION R. S. Johnson-International Gallery, Chicago.
EXHIBITIONS Bruton Gallery 1971, no. 42* (R); National Book League 1971, no. 94 (Cameira is parenthetically identified as "mistress to Daedalus"; R, pl. 26, no. 39); R. S. Johnson-International Gallery 1972, no. 45 (R, 45).

333. **RED LABYRINTH**
Oil on canvas. 1963–1964 (repainted January 1964). 20 x 24.
INSCRIPTIONS Signed top right. Below signature: *63/64.*
COLLECTION Unknown.
EXHIBITIONS Hilton Gallery 1964, no. 8; Lidchi Art Gallery 1965, no. 20 ("Red Maze").

334. **MANTIC FIGURE** (Figure 78)
Bronze. 1963. 15 x 5 x 4-3/4. Edition of 6.
COLLECTIONS Private collections, London, Dublin, and Paris.
EXHIBITIONS Grosvenor Gallery 1964, no. 12 (R); James Goodman Gallery 1965, no. 20; Mazelow Gallery 1966, no. 12*; Sears Vincent Price Gallery 1967, no. 27*; Reading Museum Art Gallery 1969, no. 23 (Collection "Mr. and Mrs. John Metcalf"); Bruton Gallery 1971, no. 8; R. S. Johnson-International Gallery 1972, no. 6 ("Edition of 9"; R, 12).
BIBLIOGRAPHY Ayrton 1962a, pl. 157 (Collection "Dr. C. S. Lewsen, London").

335. **THERA I**
Black ink wash. 27 May 1963. 16 x 20.
INSCRIPTION Bottom right: *Thera I. 27.5.'63.*
COLLECTION Private collection, Zurich.
EXHIBITIONS Hilton Gallery 1964, no. 36 (T); Lad Lane Gallery 1985, no. 29.

336. **MELOS**
Pencil and black ink wash. 27 May 1963. 16 x 20.
INSCRIPTION Bottom right: *Melos 27.5.63.*
COLLECTION The artist's estate.

This is a drawing of the port and the acropolis on Melos (notes from the artist to the author, September 1972).

337. **KORE, HEAD**
Sepia and black ink wash. 22 June 1963. 20 x 24-1/2.
INSCRIPTIONS Signed bottom right. Above and left of signature, on Kore's left shoulder: *22.6.63.*
COLLECTION Private collection, Yorkshire.
EXHIBITION Seventeenth King's Lynn Festival 1967, no. 8*.

338. **THE ORACLE AS KEY FIGURE** (Figure 73)
Black, sepia and red wash. 22 June 1963. 17 x 23-1/2.
INSCRIPTIONS Signed bottom right. Above signature: *22.6.63.*
COLLECTION Private collection, New York.
EXHIBITION Grosvenor Gallery 1964, no. 75.

339. **SEATED MINOTAUR** (Figure 99)
Pen and sepia wash. 24 June 1963. 19 x 25.
INSCRIPTION Lower right: *24.6.1963.*
COLLECTION Private collection, London.
EXHIBITION Grosvenor Gallery 1964 (not catalogued).

This first Minotaur drawing should be viewed in relation to *Minos Masked* (Cat. No. 256), which first appeared as a line illustration in *Testament of Daedalus* (notes on a conversation with the artist, 26 August 1972).

340. **MINOTAUR IN JEOPARDY**
Sepia wash. 24 June 1963. 24 x 17.
INSCRIPTIONS Signed bottom right. Below signature: *24.6.1963.*
COLLECTION Private collection, London.
EXHIBITION Grosvenor Gallery 1964, no. 59.

341. **MINOTAUR ENRAGED**
Pen and sepia. 25 June 1963. 28 x 20.
INSCRIPTIONS Signed lower right, near left hip. Above signature, in heavier pen: *25.6.63.*
COLLECTION Unknown.
EXHIBITIONS ?Hilton Gallery 1964, no. 39* (1964); Lidchi Art Gallery 1965, no. 39.
BIBLIOGRAPHY M. and E. Ayrton 1984, 52 (R).

342. **RESTLESS MINOTAUR**
Pen and sepia ink. 27 June 1963. 20 x 16.
INSCRIPTIONS Signed upper right. Below signature, in heavier pen: *27.6.63.*
COLLECTION Private collection, London.
EXHIBITION Grosvenor Gallery 1964, no. 60.
BIBLIOGRAPHY Ayrton 1962a, pl. 149 (T).

343. **CROUCHED MINOTAUR**
Pencil and wash. 30 June 1963. 16 x 20.
INSCRIPTIONS Signed at bottom, right of center, between his feet. Below signature: *30.6.63.*
COLLECTION Private collection, London.
EXHIBITION Grosvenor Gallery 1964, no. 61.

344. **LOWING MINOTAUR**
Pen and sepia wash. 1963. 15-1/2 x 11.
INSCRIPTION Signed bottom right.
COLLECTIONS Sold from Hamet Gallery, 1969; sold at auction at Sotheby's, 1972, and purchased by Bruton Gallery, Somerset.
EXHIBITIONS Hamet Gallery 1969, no. 29*; Maze and Minotaur Tour 1973, no. 52.

345. **DRUNKEN MINOTAUR**, 1963
Ink and wash. 9 July 1963. 20 x 16.
INSCRIPTION Dated lower right: *9.7.63.*
COLLECTION The artist's estate.
EXHIBITION Christopher Hull Gallery 1987.

346. **CROUCHED MINOTAUR** (Figure 107)
Bronze. 1963. 26 x 34 x 21. Edition of 6.
COLLECTION The artist's estate.
EXHIBITIONS Grosvenor Gallery 1964, no. 2; Seventeenth King's Lynn Festival 1967, no. 3 (R); Bruton Gallery 1971, no. 10; Maze and Minotaur Tour 1973, no. 4 (R).
BIBLIOGRAPHY Ayrton 1962a, pl. 148 (Collection "The artist and the Grosvenor Gallery, London"); Ayrton 1969, pl. XVII.

347. **MINOTAUR ALARMED** (Figure 102)
Black ink wash. 23 July 1963. 20 x 16.
INSCRIPTIONS Signed bottom right. Below signature: *Minotaur Alarmed.* Below title: *23.7.63.*
COLLECTION Private collection, Cambridge.
BIBLIOGRAPHY Ayrton 1970d, 10 (R); Cannon-Brookes 1978a, no. 168 (R, 95).

348. **ORACLE, TATTERED HEAD**
Collage on canvas. 27 July 1963. 16 x 12.
INSCRIPTIONS Signed top left, in black pen. Above signature, in pencil (?): *27.7.63.*
COLLECTION Private collection, London.

349. **KOUROS** (Figure 179)
Collage on board. 30 July 1963. 30 x 25.
INSCRIPTIONS Signed top right. Below signature: *30.7.63.*
COLLECTION Private collection, London.
EXHIBITIONS Grosvenor Gallery 1964, no. 44 (R); Reading Museum Art Gallery 1969, no. 68 (Collection "Mrs. C. Hemans"; R, pl. 17).

350. **THERA**
Collage on canvas. 1962–1963. 30 x 40.
COLLECTION Private collection, South Africa; sold by Grosvenor Gallery, London, through the Lidchi Art Gallery, Johannesburg.
EXHIBITIONS Grosvenor Gallery 1964, no. 49 (1963); Lidchi Art Gallery 1965, no. 5.

The title in the MRB is "Cliffs & shoal (Thera)."

351. **RESTLESS MINOTAUR** (Figure 106)
Bronze. 1963. 12 x 10 x 9. Edition of 9.
COLLECTIONS Private collections, London, New York, Middlesex, and Buffalo, NY.
EXHIBITIONS Grosvenor Gallery 1964, no. 4 (R); James Goodman Gallery 1965, no. 26; Reading Museum Art Gallery 1969, no. 26; National Book League 1971, no. 80; Maze and Minotaur Tour 1973, no. 3.
BIBLIOGRAPHY Ayrton 1964, pl. facing [48]; Hadfield, [161] (R, with "Minotaur" poem, 160; [Collection "Grosvenor Gallery, London"]); Ayrton 1962a, pl. 147 (Collection "Mr. and Mrs. Carl Foreman, London"); Hopkins 1994, 283.

352. **MINOTAUR REVEALED** (Figure 109)
Bronze. 1963. 25 x 16-1/2 x 20. Edition of 6.
COLLECTIONS Private collections, London, Chicago, New York, Edwardsville, UT, and Buffalo, NY.
EXHIBITIONS Grosvenor Gallery 1964, no. 5 (R); James Goodman Gallery 1965, no. 27 (R); Mazelow Gallery 1966, no. 22; Seventeenth King's Lynn Festival 1967, no. 7; Sears Vincent Price Gallery 1967, no. 33; University of Essex 1968, no. 7; Hamet Gallery 1969, no. 11 (R); Reading Museum Art Gallery 1969, no. 27 (Collection "Mrs. C. Hemans"; pl. 6); Bruton Gallery 1971, no. 9; National Book League 1971, no. 81 (Collection "Dr. C. S. Lewsen"; R, pl. 27, no. 41); R. S. Johnson-International Gallery 1972, no. 8 (R, 14); Maze and Minotaur Tour 1973, no. 5; Museum of Art, Pennsylvania State University 1973, no. 1; Austin/Desmond Fine Art 1990, no. 44.
BIBLIOGRAPHY Ayrton 1962a, pl. 150 (Collection "Dr Michael Hemans, London").

353. **ORACLE, RESPONDING HEAD**
Black and sepia ink wash. 4 August 1963. 16 x 20.
COLLECTION Private collection, London.
EXHIBITION Grosvenor Gallery 1964, no. 77.

354. **ORACLE, RESPONDING HEAD 2.**
Sepia and black ink wash. 4 August 1963. 16 x 20.
INSCRIPTION Bottom left: *4.8.'63.*
COLLECTION ?Private Collection, Buxted.
EXHIBITION Hilton Gallery 1964, no. 37*.
BIBLIOGRAPHY ?Cannon-Brookes 1978a, no. 183* ("I"; R, 102).

355. **PERPLEXED HEAD**
Collage on wood. 9 August 1963. 21 x 20.
INSCRIPTIONS Signed top left, in white. Above signature: *9.8.63.*
COLLECTIONS Formerly in the Grosvenor collection; presently in private collection, Oxford.
EXHIBITIONS Grosvenor Gallery 1964, no. 45; Reading Museum Art Gallery 1969, no. 71 (Collection "Mr. and Mrs. R. D. F. Pring-Mill" [Oxford]).

356. **HEAD ON A YELLOW GROUND**
Collage on wood. 10 August 1963. 21 x 20-1/2.
INSCRIPTIONS Signed top left. Above signature: *10.8.63.*
COLLECTIONS Formerly in the Grosvenor collection; presently Nathan Collection, New Zealand.
EXHIBITION Grosvenor Gallery 1964, no. 46.

The colors in this translucent head are lemon and white (notes on a conversation with the artist, 28 August 1972).

357. **ORACLE. HEAD RAISED PROFILE**
Collage on wood. 12 August 1963. 21 x 20.
INSCRIPTIONS Signed top left, in white. Above signature: *12.8.63.*
COLLECTION Private collection, South Africa.
EXHIBITION Lidchi Art Gallery 1965, no. 12 ("Oracle—Head in Profile").

358. **TALOS** (Figure 61)
Collage on wood. 13 August 1963. 20-3/4 x 12-1/4.
INSCRIPTIONS Signed top right. Before signature: *13.8.63.*
COLLECTIONS Formerly in the Grosvenor collection; presently in private collection, London.
EXHIBITION Grosvenor Gallery 1964, no. 47.

The MRB originally entitled this first Talos collage "Sentinel" (15th entry on the 2nd page for 1963).

359. **ORACLE WITH CROSSED FEET**
Black ink wash. 17 August 1963. 20 x 16.
INSCRIPTIONS Signed bottom right. Below signature: *17.8.63.*
COLLECTION Unknown.
EXHIBITIONS Grosvenor Gallery 1964, no. 78 (T); Hilton Gallery 1964, no. 49; Mazelow Gallery 1966, no. 21 (T); Bruton Gallery 1971, no. 46 (1965); Magdalene Street Gallery 1972, no. 18.

360. **DEMETER PREGNANT**
Ink and wash. 17 August 1963. 19-1/2 x 12-1/2.
INSCRIPTIONS Signed bottom right. Below signature: *17.8.63.*
COLLECTION The artist's estate.
EXHIBITION Christopher Hull Gallery 1987.

361. **PREGNANT ORACLE**
Black ink wash. 19 August 1963. 30 x 20.
INSCRIPTIONS Signed bottom right. Below signature: *19.8.63.*
COLLECTION Private collection, Paris.
EXHIBITION Grosvenor Gallery 1964, no. 79* (R).
BIBLIOGRAPHY Ayrton 1962a, pl. 163*.

362. **MINOTAUR MASK** (Figure 101)
Black ink wash. 19 August 1963. 20 x 16.
INSCRIPTION Bottom right: *19.8.63.*
COLLECTION Private collection, Chicago.
EXHIBITIONS James Goodman Gallery 1965, no. 8*; Mazelow Gallery 1966, no. 19 (T).

This drawing represents one of the earlier instances when the artist used the technique of flicking his brush to produce the hairy, pelt-like quality of this seminal work (notes on a conversation with the artist, 26 August 1972).

363. **MINOTAUR, HEAD ENRAGED**
Black ink wash. 19 August 1963. 20 x 16.
INSCRIPTIONS Signed bottom right. Below signature: *19.8.63.*
COLLECTION Private collection, London.
EXHIBITIONS Grosvenor Gallery 1964, no. 62 (T); Reading Museum Art Gallery 1969, no. 101 (1964; T).
BIBLIOGRAPHY Ayrton 1962a, pl. 144 (19 August 1964, although the correct date is visible in the plate itself).

364. **MINOTAUR PROTESTING**
Collage and wash. 19 August 1963. 22 x 11.
INSCRIPTIONS Signed bottom right. Below signature: *19.8.63.*
COLLECTION Private collection, South Africa.
EXHIBITIONS Hilton Gallery 1964, no. 48* (R); Lidchi Art Gallery 1965, no. 38.
BIBLIOGRAPHY Ayrton 1970d, 7 (1962; R).

365. **CUMAEAN GATE**
Oil on canvas. 1963. 30 x 40.
INSCRIPTIONS Signed top left. After signature: *'63.*
COLLECTION Private collection, South Africa.
EXHIBITIONS Grosvenor Gallery 1964, no. 48 (T); Lidchi Art Gallery 1965, no. 3.

366. **CLOSED HEAD**
Oil on canvas. 1963. 20 x 24.
COLLECTION Formerly in the Grosvenor collection; presently estate of Kingsley Martin.
EXHIBITION Grosvenor Gallery 1964, no. 50.

This painting was part of the series of Oracle figures (notes on a conversation with the artist, 26 August 1972).

367. **STUDY FOR TALOS**
Black ink and red wash. 9 September 1963. 22 x 18.
INSCRIPTIONS Signed bottom right. Below signature: *9.9.'63.*
COLLECTION Unknown.
BIBLIOGRAPHY Cannon-Brookes 1978a, no. 184 (R, 103).

This drawing and the next one relate most directly to the large bronze *Talos* (Cat. No. 381).

368. **TALOS, FULL LENGTH**
Black ink wash. 10 September 1963. 20 x 16.
INSCRIPTION At bottom, left of center: *10.9.'63.*
COLLECTION Unknown.
EXHIBITION Grosvenor Gallery 1964, no. 81.

369. **STUDY FOR PYTHIA**
Black ink wash. 20 September 1963. 16 x 18.
INSCRIPTIONS Signed bottom right, in pencil. Below signature, in ink: *20.9.'63.*
COLLECTION The artist's estate.
EXHIBITIONS James Goodman Gallery 1965, no. 7* (T: "Study for Mantic Figure"); Mazelow Gallery 1966, no. 6.

370. **ORACLE. STUDY FOR PYTHIA**
Black ink wash. 20 September 1963. 10 x 14.
INSCRIPTIONS Signed top right, in pencil. Below signature, in ink: *20.9.63.* After date, in pencil: *Oracle.*
COLLECTION The artist's estate.

371. **KORE**
Oil on canvas. September 1963 (cut down in 1965). 30 x 25.
INSCRIPTIONS Signed bottom right. Below signature: *September '63.*
COLLECTION Unknown.
EXHIBITION Hilton Gallery 1964, no. 3.

372. **HEAD IN DOUBT**
Wash. 5 October 1963. 13 x 20.
INSCRIPTIONS Signed bottom right. Above signature: *5.10.63.*
COLLECTION Private collection, London.
EXHIBITION Grosvenor Gallery 1964, no. 84.

373. **SCEPTIC HEAD**
Black ink wash. 6 October 1963. 16 x 20.
INSCRIPTION At bottom, right of center: *6.10.63.*
COLLECTION Unknown.
EXHIBITION Grosvenor Gallery 1964, no. 85 (R).

374. **ORACLE, MANTIC HEAD** (Figure 77)
Black ink wash. 6 October 1963. 16 x 20.
INSCRIPTION At bottom, left of center: *6.10.63.*
COLLECTION The artist's estate.
EXHIBITIONS Hilton Gallery 1964, no. 45 (T); National Gallery of Canada Tour 1965–1967, no. 16 (T).
BIBLIOGRAPHY Ayrton 1962a, pl. 155 (T).

375. **HEAD IN GRISAILLE**
Oil on board. 13 October 1963. 15 x 12.
INSCRIPTIONS Signed bottom right, in white. Above signature: *13.10.63.*
COLLECTION Private collection.

376. **FAT MAN, UNDER STRESS**
Wash. 13 October 1963. 17 x 11-1/2.
INSCRIPTIONS Signed bottom left. After signature: *13.10.63.*
COLLECTION Unknown.
EXHIBITION Grosvenor Gallery 1964, no. 69.

377. **TALOS. BACK**
Black ink wash. 13 October 1963. 19 x 11.
INSCRIPTIONS Signed bottom right. Above signature: *13.10.63.*
COLLECTIONS Current provenance unknown; the late A. F. C. Turner was the original collector.
EXHIBITION Grosvenor Gallery 1964, no. 82.

378. **TALOS IN PROFILE**
Black ink wash. 16 October 1963. 19 x 13.
INSCRIPTIONS Signed bottom right. After signature: *'63.*
COLLECTION Unknown.
EXHIBITIONS Grosvenor Gallery 1964, no. 83 (R); James Goodman Gallery 1965, no. 6; Mazelow Gallery 1966, no. 11.

This figure was drawn over a preliminary sketch of a different figure that probably was intended to be a female nude, an oracle figure (notes on a conversation with the artist, 26 August 1972).

379. **PYTHIA** (Figure 76)
Bronze. 1963. 13 x 8 x 8. Edition of 9.
COLLECTIONS Private collections, Yorkshire, London, Paris, and Chicago.
EXHIBITIONS Grosvenor Gallery 1964, no. 17 (R); James Goodman Gallery 1965, no. 22; Mazelow Gallery 1966, no. 14; Sears Vincent Price Gallery 1967, no. 29 (R); Hamet Gallery 1969, no. 13 (R); Reading Museum Gallery 1969, no. 24 (Collection "Terence Doherty, Esq."); National Book League 1971, no. 86 (R, pl. 27, no. 40); R. S. Johnson-International Gallery 1972, no. 7 (R, 13); Bruton Gallery 1981, no. 64 (R, 48); Christopher Hull Gallery 1987.
BIBLIOGRAPHY Ayrton 1962a, pl. 156 (Collection "Mrs. Fay Pomerance, Sheffield").

380. **SIREN**
Bronze. 1963. 9-1/2 x 4 x 2-1/2. Edition of 9.
COLLECTIONS Private collections, Essex, New York, and Paris.
EXHIBITIONS Grosvenor Gallery 1964, no. 14 (R); James Goodman Gallery 1965, no. 21; Sears Vincent Price Gallery 1967, no. 3 (R); Magdalene Street Gallery 1972, no. 4 (R); Bruton Gallery 1981, no. 73; Austin/Desmond Fine Art 1990, no. 45*; Austin Desmond & Phipps 1992.
BIBLIOGRAPHY Ayrton 1962a, pl. 158 (Collection "Mr. and Mrs. Andrew Carnwath, Essex").

381. **TALOS** (Large version) (Figure 65)
Bronze. 1963. 68 x 33 x 25. Edition of 3.
COLLECTION Corporation of Cambridge.
EXHIBITIONS Grosvenor Gallery 1964, no. 19 (R); Reading Museum Art Gallery 1969, no. 25; Austin/Desmond Fine Art 1990, no. 42 (R, 27).
BIBLIOGRAPHY Ayrton 1962a, pl. 153 (Collection "The artist and the Grosvenor Gallery, London"); Hopkins 1994, 411f.

382. **MINOTAUR, HEAD EVOLVING** (Figure 103)
Black ink wash. 27 November 1963. 16 x 20.
INSCRIPTION Bottom right: *27.11.63.*
COLLECTION Private collection, Toronto.
EXHIBITIONS Grosvenor Gallery 1964, no. 63 (R); Stone Gallery 1964.
BIBLIOGRAPHY Ayrton 1962a, pl. 145.

This Minotaur drawing represents the first instance when Ayrton began to view him as capable of evolving into human form (notes on a conversation with the artist, 26 August 1972). The brush-flicking technique of this drawing is reminiscent of that employed in *Minotaur Mask* (Cat. No. 362), but it also adumbrates *Fat Man, Head Under Stress* (Cat. No. 399) in orientation and, to a degree, technique.

383. **MINOTAUR EVOLVING**
Black ink wash. 29 November 1963. 20 x 16.
INSCRIPTION Bottom right: *29.11.'63.*
COLLECTION Unknown.
EXHIBITIONS National Gallery of Canada Tour 1965–1967, no. 17 (T); Maze and Minotaur Tour 1973, no. 51 (T).
BIBLIOGRAPHY Ayrton 1970d, 13 (R; T).

384. **EVOLUTION OF THE MINOTAUR** (Maquette) (Figure 105)
Bronze. 1963. 14-1/2 x 4 x 7. Edition of 6.
COLLECTIONS Private collections, London, Berkshire, and Indianapolis, IN.
EXHIBITIONS Grosvenor Gallery 1964, no. 6; Mazelow Gallery 1966, no. 16*; Sears Vincent Price Gallery 1967, no. 31*; Hamet Gallery 1969, no. 10; Maze and Minotaur Tour 1973, no. 2; Christopher Hull Gallery 1987; Austin/Desmond Fine Art 1990, no. 43* ("edition of 9;" R, 26, color).
BIBLIOGRAPHY Ayrton 1964, pl. facing [49] (T); Ayrton 1962a, pl. 140 (T).

385. **EVOLUTION OF THE MINOTAUR** (Figure 110)
Bronze. 1963–1964. 67 x 29 x 18. Edition of 3.
COLLECTION Lord and Lady Beaumont of Whitley.
EXHIBITIONS Grosvenor Gallery 1964, no. 7; Tate Gallery 1965, no. 8* (R); Bruton Gallery 1981, no. 31 (R, 37, both full and detail); Austin/Desmond Fine Art 1990, no. 45 (dated 1964).
BIBLIOGRAPHY Ayrton 1962a, pl. 142 (Collection "The Rev. and Mrs. Timothy Beaumont, London"); Hopkins 1994, 293.

386. **MAQUETTE FOR LARGE ORACLE I** (Figure 80)
Bronze. 1963. 6 x 2 x 4. Edition of 9.
COLLECTIONS Private collections, London, Oxford, Essex, Israel, New York, Buffalo, NY, and Paris.
EXHIBITIONS Grosvenor Gallery 1964, no. 15 (R); James Goodman Gallery 1965, no. 23; Reading Museum Art Gallery 1969, no. 18* (dated 1962; Collection "Basil Wright, Esq. & Kassim bin Said, Esq.").

387. **MAQUETTE FOR LARGE ORACLE II** (Figure 81)
Bronze. 1963. 6-1/4 x 2 x 4. Edition of 9.
COLLECTIONS Private collections, London, Paris, New York, and Dallas.
EXHIBITIONS Grosvenor Gallery 1964, no. 16* (R); James Goodman Gallery 1965, no. 24*.

388. **MINOTAUR TORMENTED**
Pen and black ink. 22 December 1963. 20 x 16.
INSCRIPTIONS Signed bottom left. Below signature: *22.12.63.*
COLLECTION Private collection, London.
EXHIBITIONS Grosvenor Gallery 1964, no. 64 (R); Reading Museum Art Gallery, 1969, no. 99*.

389. **MINOTAUR IN ANGUISH** (Figure 104)
Black ink wash. 22 December 1963. 20 x 16.
INSCRIPTIONS Signed bottom right. Above signature, in heavier pen: *22.12.63.*
COLLECTION The artist's estate.
EXHIBITIONS Grosvenor Gallery 1964, no. 65; Stone Gallery 1964; National Gallery of Canada Tour, part II [1966–1967]; Daedalus I Gallery 1972, no. 41* (1970).

390. **MINOTAUR EVOLVED**
Charcoal. 24 December 1963. 30 x 20.
INSCRIPTIONS Signed top right. Below signature: *24.12.63.*
COLLECTION Unknown.
EXHIBITION Maze and Minotaur Tour 1973, no. 50* (T).

391. **MINOTAUR ENRAGED**
Charcoal. 24 December 1963. 27 x 17-1/2.
INSCRIPTIONS Signed top right. Below signature: *24.12.63.*
COLLECTION The artist's estate.
EXHIBITIONS Bruton Gallery 1981, no. 160 (R, 37); National Museum of Wales, Penarth, and Pelter Sands Gallery 1981.
BIBLIOGRAPHY Cannon-Brookes 1978a, no. 163* (R, 94).

392. **DENSE LANDSCAPE**
Collage and oil on board. 24–25 December 1963. 31 x 48.
INSCRIPTIONS Signed bottom left. After signature: *24–25/12/63.*
COLLECTION Gruber Collection, New York.
EXHIBITION Grosvenor Gallery 1964, no. 51.

393. **FIGURE IN A DOORWAY**
Collage on board. 25 December 1963. 40 x 30.
INSCRIPTIONS Signed top left. Below signature: *25.12.1963.*
COLLECTION The artist's estate.
EXHIBITIONS Grosvenor Gallery 1964, no. 54; Lidchi Art Gallery 1965, no. 2 (R, cover).

394. **FIGURE WITH LAUREL LEAVES** (Figure 70)
Collage on board. December 1963. 26 x 36.
INSCRIPTIONS Signed at top left, somewhat below margin, and dated after signature: *Dec: 1963.*
COLLECTION Private collection, New York.
EXHIBITION Grosvenor Gallery 1964, no. 52.

395. **KEY FIGURE I**
Oil on canvas. Repainted 1963. 40 x 60.

Destroyed by the artist, but a photographic record was retained.

396. **THE FAT MAN**
Collage on card. 1963. 40 x 30.
COLLECTION Private collection, South Africa.
EXHIBITIONS Grosvenor Gallery 1964, no. 53 (R); Lidchi Art Gallery 1965, no. 1.

397. **ORACLE** (Large version) (Figure 79)
Bronze. 1963–1964. 60 x 36 x 32. Edition of 3.
COLLECTION Sir Leon and Lady Bagrit, London.
EXHIBITIONS Grosvenor Gallery 1964, no. 8; Bruton Gallery 1981, no. 59 (R, 49); Austin/Desmond Fine Art 1990, no. 46 (dated 1963).
BIBLIOGRAPHY Ayrton 1962a, pl. 168 (Collection "Sir Leon and Lady Bagrit, London").

398. **FAT MAN, HEAD**
Black and pink wash. 2 January 1964. 16 x 20.
COLLECTION The artist's estate.
EXHIBITION Grosvenor Gallery 1964, no. 70.

399. **FAT MAN, HEAD UNDER STRESS**
Black ink wash. 3 January 1964. 16 x 20.
INSCRIPTIONS Signed bottom right. Below signature, in heavier pen: *3.1.'64.*
COLLECTION R. S. Johnson-International Gallery, Chicago.
EXHIBITIONS Grosvenor Gallery 1964, no. 71 (R); National Gallery of Canada Tour 1965–1967, no. 18; R. S. Johnson-International Gallery 1972, no. 46 (T).

400. **VILLAGE**
Collage. 1963–1964. 20 x 30.
INSCRIPTIONS Signed top left. After signature: *Jan '64.*
COLLECTION Private collection, London.
EXHIBITION Grosvenor Gallery 1969, no. 45.

401. **LANDSCAPE WITH WILD OATS**
Collage on canvas. 1963–1964. 25 x 30.
INSCRIPTIONS Signed top left, in white. After signature: *63–64.*
COLLECTION Messrs. George Rowney Ltd., London.
EXHIBITION Grosvenor Gallery 1964, no. 55.
BIBLIOGRAPHY Hopkins 1994, 291.

The color of this collage is predominantly black, with mixed dust and rock comprised largely of yellow, orange, grey, and sand colors, and real oats are part of it (notes on a conversation with the artist, 28 August 1972).

402. **DELOS. SACRED PORT**
Oil on canvas. 1963–1964 (repainted September 1964). 25 x 30.
INSCRIPTIONS Signed top left. After signature: *'64.*
COLLECTION Gruber Collection, New York .

403. **SACRED PLACE. DELOS**
Collage on canvas. 1964. 25 x 30.
COLLECTION Estate of Roger Senhouse, Sussex.

404. **THEATRE AT MILETUS**
Oil on canvas. 1964. 12 x 16.
INSCRIPTIONS Signed top left. After signature: *'64.*
COLLECTION Private collection, Milan.

405. **DEIPHOBE (CUMAEAN SYBIL)** (Figure 84)
Black wash. 9 February 1964. 16 x 20.
INSCRIPTIONS Signed bottom left.
Bottom right: *Cumaean Sybil.* Below annotation: *9.2.1964.*
COLLECTION Private collection; sold from Hamet Gallery, London.
EXHIBITIONS Seventeenth King's Lynn Festival 1967, no. 20 (T); University of Essex 1968, no. 24.

This drawing is closely related to the bronze *Pythia* (Cat. No. 379).

406. **DEIPHOBE WAITING**
Pen and ink wash. 1964. 16 x 20.
INSCRIPTIONS Signed bottom left. Top left: *Deiphobe Waiting.*
COLLECTION R. S. Johnson-International Gallery, Chicago.
EXHIBITION R. S. Johnson-International Gallery 1972, no. 47.

Deiphobe is drawn in profile, looking upward. She is seated, but only the upper half of her body is clearly discernible.

407. **STUDY FOR NAUTILUS MAZE FIGURE**
Black ink wash. 15 February 1964. 10 x 14.
COLLECTION Unknown.
EXHIBITIONS Grosvenor Gallery 1966, no. 83; Sears Vincent Price Gallery 1967, no. 6 ("pencil wash").

408. **THE ORACLE AS PYTHIA**
Pen and sepia ink. 16 February 1964. 20 x 25.
INSCRIPTIONS Signed bottom left. Above signature: *16.2.1964.*
COLLECTION Exeter College, Oxford, Junior Commons Room.
EXHIBITION Grosvenor Gallery 1964, no. 80 (R).
BIBLIOGRAPHY Cannon-Brookes 1978a, no. 182 (R, 102).

409. **MINOTAUR EVOLVING II**
Sepia wash. 16 February 1964. 23-1/2 x 18.
INSCRIPTIONS Signed top left, in pencil. Below signature, in sepia: *16.2.64.*
COLLECTIONS Sold from the Mazelow Gallery, Toronto, in 1966. Later purchased by the artist from the collection of Duncan Melvin. The artist's estate.
EXHIBITIONS Grosvenor Gallery 1964, no. 66 (T; R); James Goodman Gallery 1965, no. 9 (1963; T); Mazelow Gallery 1966, no. 18 (R); Maze and Minotaur Tour 1973, no. 53 (T).
BIBLIOGRAPHY Ayrton 1962a, pl. 143 (T).

410. **LANDSCAPE WITH STARS**
Collage on board. 1964. 18 x 22.
INSCRIPTIONS Signed top left, in white. After signature: *'64.*
COLLECTION Private collection, London.
EXHIBITION Grosvenor Gallery 1966.

411. **KEY FIGURE** (Figure 82)
Collage on canvas. February 1964. 40 x 60.
INSCRIPTIONS Signed upper left, in white. After signature: *Feb '64.*
COLLECTION Private collection, Surrey.
EXHIBITIONS Grosvenor Gallery 1964, no. 56 (R); Bruton Gallery and Tour 1981, no. 106 (R, 47).
BIBLIOGRAPHY Hopkins 1994, 281.

412. **ORACLE**
Collage on board. February 1964. 40 x 60 (30 x 40?).
INSCRIPTIONS Signed top left, in white. After signature: *'64.* Below signature and date: *February.*
COLLECTION Unknown.
EXHIBITIONS Grosvenor Gallery 1964, no. 58 (R); Lidchi Art Gallery 1965, no. 4.

Ayrton's records present conflicting dimensions for this work. His photographic record gives the dimensions as 30 x 40 inches, but the MRB records them as 40 x 60 inches. The Grosvenor
catalogue entry corresponds with the MRB.

413. **ICARUS RISING**, Variant I
Bronze. 1964. 60 x 30-1/2 x 8. Unique.
COLLECTION Hobson Partners Ltd.
EXHIBITION Grosvenor Gallery 1965, no. 37 (1961 variant 1963).

For the original version, see Cat. No. 206; see also Cat. Nos. 512 and 513.

414. **KOUROS**
Bronze. 1964. Dimensions unknown. Unique.
COLLECTION The artist's estate.

Adapted for use in Cat. No. 659 (*Kouros:* bronze and perspex; 1969).

415. **CROUCHED MINOTAUR**
Pen and black ink. 5 March 1964. 14 x 10.
INSCRIPTION Lower right, below left knee, right of his right foot: *5.3.64.*
COLLECTION Private collection, Buffalo, NY?
EXHIBITIONS James Goodman Gallery 1965, no. 11* (1963; T); ?Mazelow Gallery 1966, no. 13 ("Minotaur Kneeling").
BIBLIOGRAPHY Ayrton 1964, 52 (R); Ayrton 1970d, 14 (R).

416. **MINOTAUR, CROUCHED EVOLVING**
Pen and black ink. 6 March 1964. 14 x 10.
INSCRIPTION Lower left: *6.3.'64.*
COLLECTION Unknown.
EXHIBITION National Gallery of Canada Tour, part II [1966–1967].

417. **MINOTAUR EVOLVING II** version 2
Pen and black ink. 6 March 1964. 14 x 10.
COLLECTION Private collection.

418. **MINOTAUR, HEAD-PROFILE**
Pen and black ink. March 1964? 7 x 10.
COLLECTION Unknown.
BIBLIOGRAPHY Ayrton 1964, 51 (R).

419. **MINOTAUR, HEAD EVOLVING 2**
Pen and black ink. March 1964? 14 x 10.
COLLECTION Unknown.
BIBLIOGRAPHY Ayrton 1964, 49 (R).

420. **MINOTAUR AT BAY** (Figure 108)
Pen and black ink. March 1964? 14 x 10.
COLLECTION Minotaur Restaurant, London.
BIBLIOGRAPHY Ayrton 1970d, 25 (R).

This half-length portrait of the Minotaur virtually ends at the knees, with a short additional line extending downward from each incomplete lower appendage. Ayrton described this drawing as "one of the few where he is particularly menacing" (conversation with the artist, 27 August 1972).

421–452.
ASPECTS OF GAIA
Gouache, collage, and ink, under acrylic. 1964. 16 x 20 maximum size, with slight variations.

These small landscapes are closely related to the narrative in *Maze Maker*, part two.

Since this group is distinctive and unified, the format of the catalogue here also is deliberately different and somewhat compressed. Unless otherwise noted, these works are in the artist's estate. The MRB lists twenty titles under the heading "Twenty one Aspects of Gaia June–July 1964" and eight under the heading "Gaia Subsequent Aspects." Items missing from that list are duly noted below.

421. **DEEP BLUE, CONTAINED**
18.6.64
INSCRIPTIONS Signed bottom left, in margin. Dated below signature.
COLLECTION Private collection.

422. **DEEP GREEN CONVERGING**
20.6.64.
INSCRIPTIONS Signed bottom right, in white. Dated above signature.
COLLECTION Estate of Joseph Rykwert, London.

423. **EARTH ENTRAIL**
20.6.64
INSCRIPTIONS Signed top right, in white and blue. Dated after signature.
COLLECTION Unknown.

Colors are black, deep and bright blue, violet, and grey.

424. **CUMAEAN SECTION**
22.6.64
INSCRIPTIONS Signed bottom right, in white. Dated below signature.
COLLECTION Leopold de Rothschild, London.
EXHIBITIONS Grosvenor Gallery 1966, no. 48*; Reading Museum Art Gallery 1969, no. 73; National Book League 1971, no. 93 ("Landscapes of Gaia VIII").
BIBLIOGRAPHY Ayrton 1969 (1965; R, pl. IX).

425. **EARTH CORDS**
22.6.64
INSCRIPTIONS Signed at bottom left, in white. Dated at bottom, just to right of center, in black.
COLLECTION Private collection, Johannesburg.
EXHIBITIONS Hilton Gallery 1964, no. 22; Lidchi Art Gallery 1965, no. 28.

426. **DARK IN DEPTH**
23.6.64
INSCRIPTIONS Signed top right, in pale blue. Dated after signature.
COLLECTION Unknown.

Colors include black, pale blue, lavender, and violet.

427. **BLUE DEEP, LIQUID**
25.6.64
INSCRIPTIONS Signed top left, in white. Dated before signature.
COLLECTION Private collection, London.

428. **LUNG DEEP, BLUE DISPERSING**
25.6.64
INSCRIPTIONS Signed bottom right, in white. Dated above signature.
COLLECTION Unknown.
EXHIBITIONS Hilton Gallery 1964, no. 18 (T); Lidchi Art Gallery 1965, no. 49 (T).

429. **INTRUSION ON DARK RED**
12.7.64
INSCRIPTIONS Signed bottom right, in white. Dated bottom left, in white: *11/12.7.64.*
COLLECTION Unknown.
EXHIBITION Lidchi Art Gallery 1965, no. 26 (T).

430. **DEEP GREEN, STATIC**
12.7.64
INSCRIPTIONS Signed top left, in white. Dated before signature.
COLLECTION Private collection, Gloucestershire.
EXHIBITION Hilton Gallery 1964, no. 17.

431. **OMPHALOS I**
13.7.64
INSCRIPTIONS Signed bottom left, in white. Dated above signature.
COLLECTION Private collection, London.

432. **OMPHALOS II**
13.7.64
INSCRIPTIONS Signed top left, in white. Dated above signature.
COLLECTION Private collection, Athens.
EXHIBITION Hilton Gallery 1964, no. 23.

433. **RESTLESS FIELD**
14.7.64
INSCRIPTIONS Signed bottom right. Dated above signature.
COLLECTION Estate of Hollis S. Baker, Grand Rapids, MI.
EXHIBITION Hilton Gallery 1964, no. 15.

434. **PILLAR**
15.7.64
INSCRIPTIONS Signed bottom left, in white. Dated above signature.
COLLECTION Unknown.
EXHIBITIONS Grosvenor Gallery 1966, no. 51; Magdalene Street Gallery 1972, no. 22*; Austin/Desmond Fine Art 1990, no. 26 (R, 31, in color).

Yellow, brown, and grey ink are combined with brown, black, and red tissue paper.

435. **ACROPOLIS AND CLOUD**
16.7.64
INSCRIPTIONS Signed top left, in white. Dated above signature.
COLLECTION Carter Collection, Johannesburg.
EXHIBITION Hilton Gallery 1964, no. 14.

436. **MAZE BELOW**
16.7.64
INSCRIPTIONS Signed bottom left, in white. Dated below signature.
COLLECTION Private collection, Sudbury.

437. **INTRUSION ON BLACKNESS**
16.7.64
INSCRIPTIONS Signed bottom right, in light blue. Dated below signature, in pencil.
COLLECTION Unknown.
EXHIBITIONS Hilton Gallery 1964, no. 19; Lidchi Art Gallery 1965, no. 25.

438. **EARTH PELVIS**
20.7.64
INSCRIPTIONS Signed bottom left, in white. Dated before signature.
COLLECTION Unknown.
EXHIBITIONS Grosvenor Gallery 1966, no. 53*; Magdalene Street Gallery 1972, no. 21*.

In ink and gouache, this landscape comprises reds, browns, black, grey, white, blue, and yellow or cream. This work was inadvertently omitted from the MRB.

439. **BRAZEN PLACE**
21.7.64
INSCRIPTION Signed bottom left, in white. Dated before signature.
COLLECTION Private collection, London.

440. **HARVEST ENTRANCE**
21.7.64
INSCRIPTIONS Signed bottom left. Dated below signature.
COLLECTION Estate of Hollis S. Baker, Grand Rapids, MI.
EXHIBITION Hilton Gallery 1964, no. 20.

441. **MEETING OF PATHS (CORINTHIAN LANDSCAPE)**
21.7.64
INSCRIPTIONS Signed bottom left. Dated above signature.
COLLECTION Private collection, Surrey.
EXHIBITION Grosvenor Gallery 1966, no. 49* (T).

442. **VERTEBRATE COPPER**
21.7.64
INSCRIPTIONS Signed bottom right. Dated below signature.
COLLECTION Unknown.

This work was not included in the MRB. Although the photographic record dates this work *21.8.64*, Ayrton himself identified as *Vertebrate Copper* this work, which was completed a month earlier.

443. **EARTH PECTORAL**
22.7.64
INSCRIPTIONS Signed top left, in pencil.
Dated before signature, in pen.
COLLECTION Unknown.
EXHIBITIONS Arts Council Tour 1965–1966; Magdalene Street Gallery 1972, no. 20*.

Predominant colors are bright yellows, shading into almost olive green, brown, and black, with touches of white.

444. **ERODED SILVER**
2.8.64
INSCRIPTIONS Signed bottom right. Dated below signature.
COLLECTION Carter Collection, Johannesburg.
EXHIBITION Hilton Gallery 1964, no. 16.

445. **ROCK ARMOUR**
3.8.64
INSCRIPTIONS Signed top left, in white. Dated before signature.
COLLECTION Unknown.
EXHIBITIONS Hilton Gallery 1964, no. 13; Lidchi Art Gallery 1965, no. 27.

Colors included in this collage are violet, orange, white, yellow, brown, and black.

446. **EARTH CORTEX**
6.8.64
INSCRIPTIONS Signed bottom right. Dated above signature.
COLLECTION Private collection, London.
EXHIBITIONS Magdalene Street Gallery 1972, no. 19*; Bruton Gallery 1981, no. 98* (T); Austin/Desmond Fine Art 1990, no. 24* (R, 4).

447. **CEPHALON**
7.8.64
INSCRIPTIONS Signed bottom right. Dated above signature.
COLLECTION Carter Collection, Johannesburg.
EXHIBITION Hilton Gallery 1964, no. 21 (T: "Encephalon").

448. **TRILOBITE COIL**
7.8.64
INSCRIPTIONS Signed at bottom right, in white, but partially traced over in black ink. Dated below signature.
COLLECTION Private collection, London.
EXHIBITION Grosvenor Gallery 1966, no. 52*.

449. **TEMPORAL GYRUS (CEPHALON)**
10.8.64
INSCRIPTIONS Signed bottom left. Dated above signature.
COLLECTION Private collection, London.

450. **PROCENCEPHALON (CORTEX)**
10.8.64
INSCRIPTIONS Signed bottom left. Dated after signature.
EXHIBITION Arts Council Tour 1965–1966 (T: "Cortex").

Various shades of grey dominate this painting, with black, white, and traces of pastel green.

451. **MATRIX (CONSTRICTED FLOW)**
21.8.64
INSCRIPTIONS Signed bottom right, in pencil.
Dated after signature, in white.
COLLECTION Unknown.

This work is not included in the MRB, but it is in the photographic record.

452. **COMPRESSED RED (RED HARUSPIC)** (Plate 20)
22.8.64
INSCRIPTIONS Signed bottom left. Dated above signature.
COLLECTION Unknown.
EXHIBITIONS Grosvenor Gallery 1966, no. 50 (T: "Landscape, Compressed Red"); Christopher Hull Gallery 1987 (T: "Red Landscape, Greece"); Austin/Desmond Fine Art 1990, no. 25 (T: "Red Landscape;" R, 31, in color).

Ayrton originally entitled this work "Red Haruspic," since he wished to convey an idea about the liver, but he changed the title to "Compressed Red" when exhibitors failed to comprehend the meaning of the original title (notes on a conversation with the artist, 23 August 1972). This work is not included in the MRB, but it is in the photographic record.

453. **CUMAEAN SYBIL**
Gouache and ink. 23 July 1964. 16 x 20.
INSCRIPTIONS Signed top right. Below signature: *23.7.64.*
COLLECTION Private collection, South Africa.
EXHIBITION Lidchi Art Gallery 1965, no. 24 (T).

454. **SYBIL ON BLUE**
Gouache and ink. 23 July 1964. 16 x 20.
INSCRIPTIONS Signed top right. Below signature, in white ink: *23.7.64.*
COLLECTION Carter Collection, Johannesburg.
EXHIBITION Hilton Gallery 1964, no. 24* (T).

455. **MAZE HEAD I** (Figure 132)
Charcoal and gouache. 1 August 1964. 16 x 20.
INSCRIPTION Signed at bottom, right of center. Below signature: *1.8.1964.*
COLLECTION Private collection, NY?
EXHIBITION James Goodman Gallery 1965, no. 10*.

456. **ANATOMY OF DAEDALUS** (Figure 133)
Drawing. 1 August 1964. Dimensions unknown.
INSCRIPTIONS Signed bottom right. Below signature: *1.8.64.*
COLLECTION Private collection, Cambridge.

457. **MAZE HEAD** (Figure 116)
Oil on canvas. 1964. 20 x 30.
INSCRIPTIONS Signed top left. After signature: *'64.*
COLLECTION Unknown.
EXHIBITIONS Lidchi Art Gallery 1965, no. 17; Sears Vincent Price Gallery 1965, no. 5 (T: "I" added; R); Stowe School 1970, no. 11; Austin/Desmond Fine Art 1990, no. 23 (R, 30, in color).

458. **MINOTAUR MAZE HEAD**
Gouache and charcoal. 10 August 1964. 16 x 20.
INSCRIPTIONS Signed bottom right. Above signature: *10.8.64.*
COLLECTION Unknown.
EXHIBITIONS Hilton Gallery 1964, no. 26 (T); Lidchi Art Gallery 1965, no. 33? (T).
BIBLIOGRAPHY Hopkins 1994, 284 ("*Maze Head [Minotaur]*").

This is the only maze-headed Minotaur created by Ayrton (notes on a conversation with the artist, 27 August 1972).

459. **MAZE HEAD**
Gouache, charcoal, and pastel. 10 August 1964. 16 x 20.
INSCRIPTIONS Signed bottom left. Above signature, in heavier pen: *10.8.64.*
COLLECTION R. S. Johnson-International Gallery, Chicago
EXHIBITION R. S. Johnson-International Gallery 1972, no. 48 (R, 59).
BIBLIOGRAPHY Hopkins 1994, 284 ("*Maze Head [Daedalus]*").

Ayrton apparently overlooked this drawing in his sequential numbering of the *Maze Head* drawings: it should be number II.

460. **MAZE MAKER I** (Figure 118)
Bronze. 1964. 16-3/4 x 9 x 6. Edition of 9.
COLLECTIONS Private collections, London, New York, Athens, Buffalo, NY, Toronto, Auckland, and Suffolk.
EXHIBITIONS Tate Gallery 1965, no. 10* (T: "Maze Maker 1964"); James Goodman Gallery 1965, no. 29*; Mazelow Gallery 1966, no. 19*; Grosvenor Gallery 1966, no. 2.
BIBLIOGRAPHY Ayrton 1962a, pl. 182 (Collection "Mr. and Mrs. K. Danzig, London"); Hopkins 1994, 293.

461. **MAZE HEAD II**
Charcoal and gouache. 15 August 1964. 16 x 20.
INSCRIPTIONS Signed bottom right. After signature: *15.8.'64.*
COLLECTION Private collection, Santa Barbara, CA.
EXHIBITION National Gallery of Canada Tour 1965–1967, no. 20 (R).

462. **MAZE HEAD III**
Gouache. 16 August 1964. 16 x 20.
INSCRIPTIONS Signed top right. Bottom right: *16.8.64.*
COLLECTION Private collection, South Africa.
EXHIBITIONS Hilton Gallery 1964, no. 25 (T); Lidchi Art Gallery 1965, no. 33 (T).

463. **RED MAZE HEAD**
Gouache and ink. 16 August 1964. 16 x 20.
INSCRIPTIONS Signed bottom right. Below signature: *16.8.'64.*
COLLECTION Unknown.

464. **MEMBRANE MAZE HEAD**
Collage. 3 September 1964. 15 x 22.
INSCRIPTIONS Signed bottom left. Below signature: *3.9.64.*
COLLECTION Private collection, South Africa.
EXHIBITION Lidchi Art Gallery 1965, no. 32.

465. **DEEP**
Collage on canvas. 1964. 20 x 24.
COLLECTION Formerly in the collection of Sir Gerald Barry.
EXHIBITION Grosvenor Gallery 1966, no. 46.

The dark blue colors depict the sea at night.

466. **CORE OF BLACK ROCK**
Collage on canvas. September 1964. 20 x 24.
INSCRIPTIONS Signed bottom right. After signature: *Sept. '64.*
EXHIBITION Lidchi Art Gallery 1965, no. 23 (T).

Destroyed by the artist, but a photographic record was retained.

467. **TENSE FIGURE**
Collage on board. September 1964. 30 x 20.
INSCRIPTIONS Signed top left. After signature: *Sept: 64.*
COLLECTION Unknown.
EXHIBITIONS Grosvenor Gallery 1966, no. 59; Seventeenth King's Lynn Festival 1967, no. 6; Reading Museum Art Gallery 1969 (Ayrton's photographic record book lists this exhibition for this work, but the exhibition catalogue does not).

This principal Daedalus image also appears on the jacket of *The Maze Maker* (Cat. No. 594). Ayrton said he also called this work "Daedalus in Darkness," although there is another collage (Cat. No. 601) bearing that same title (notes on a conversation with the artist, August 1972).

468. **DISLOCATED FIGURE**
Black ink wash. 30 September 1964. 16 x 20.
INSCRIPTIONS Signed bottom right. Below signature: *30.9.64.*
COLLECTION Art Institute of Chicago.
EXHIBITIONS Grosvenor Gallery 1966, no. 78; Sears Vincent Price Gallery 1967, no. 5 (T; R); R. S. Johnson-International Gallery 1972, no. 49 (R, 5).
BIBLIOGRAPHY Ayrton 1962a, pl. 202.

469. **CITADEL**
Collage. October 1964. 25 x 30.
INSCRIPTIONS Signed top left, in white. After signature: *Oct: 64.*
COLLECTION Unknown.
EXHIBITIONS Grosvenor Gallery 1966, no. 40; Sears Vincent Price Gallery 1967, no. 6; Stowe School 1970, no. 6.

470. **POINT OF DEPARTURE** (three stages) (Figure 207)
Collage on board. 1962–1966. 20 x 24.
INSCRIPTIONS Signed at top left, all three stages, and dated after signatures: *October '62* (first stage); *'64* (second stage); *'66* (final stage).
COLLECTION Private collection, Essex.
EXHIBITIONS Matthiesen Gallery 1962 (first stage, as "Feather Among Rocks"); Grosvenor Gallery, London 1967, no. 47.
BIBLIOGRAPHY Causey 27 (1964–1966; R); Hopkins 1994, 275.

The three stages of this collage illustrate the working method of the artist as he wrestled with conveying the idea of the point of departure for the flight of Daedalus and Icarus from Crete. Although the first stage was completed in October 1962, Ayrton did not record it in his MRB until late 1964, so I have followed his lead.

471. **MINOTAUR IN JEOPARDY** (Figure 111)
Bronze. 1964. 11-1/2 x 6 x 6-1/2. Edition of 9.
COLLECTIONS Minotaur Restaurant, London; private collections, New York, New Bedford, MA, Paris, Somerset, and Southfield, MI.
EXHIBITIONS James Goodman Gallery 1965, no. 28* (R, back cover); Mazelow Gallery 1966, no. 17; Grosvenor Gallery 1966, no. 1; Seventeenth King's Lynn Festival 1967, no. 20; Sears Vincent Price Gallery 1967, no. 32; University of Essex 1968, no. 6; Hamet Gallery 1969, no. 12; Reading Museum Art Gallery 1969, no. 28 (Collection "T. G. Rosenthal, Esq."); Hamet Gallery 1970, no. 11; Maze and Minotaur Tour 1973, no. 6; Hope College 1978, no. 5 (Collection "Mrs. Richard B. Cole, Southfield, MI"; R); Bruton Gallery 1981, no. 53.
BIBLIOGRAPHY Ayrton 1962a, pl. 146 (Collection "Mr. A. Lublin, New York"); Hopkins 1994, 281f.

472. **COMPRESSED FIGURE: STUDY FOR MIRROR MAZE (BACK)**
Sepia wash. 10 December 1964. 19 x 24-1/2.
INSCRIPTIONS Signed bottom right. Below signature: *10.12.64.*
COLLECTION Private collection, Auckland.
EXHIBITION Grosvenor Gallery 1966, no. 66 (T; R).
BIBLIOGRAPHY Ayrton 1962a, pl. 184*.

473. **SMOKE-MAZE FIGURE**
Collage. 1964. 30 x 50.
INSCRIPTIONS Signed bottom left. After signature: *'64.*
COLLECTION Private collection, Chicago.
EXHIBITIONS Grosvenor Gallery 1966, no. 29; Wycombe Arts Festival 1967; Sears Vincent Price Gallery 1967, no. 8; Museum of Art, Pennsylvania State University 1973, no. 28 ("Collection P. J. H. Bentley").

474. **SMOKE MAZE HEAD**
Collage on wood. 1964. 23-1/2 x 35.
COLLECTION Salford Art Gallery.
EXHIBITION Grosvenor Gallery 1966, no. 36.

475. **LANDSCAPE ON RED WOOD**
Collage. 1964. 23-1/2 x 35.
COLLECTION Private collection, London.
EXHIBITIONS Grosvenor Gallery 1966, no. 34 (R); also 1967.

476. **MOONPHASE**
Collage and marble dust. 1964. 25 x 30.
COLLECTION Private collection, London.
EXHIBITION Grosvenor Gallery 1966, no. 39*.

In the MRB this work bears the title "Sea at Full Moon."

477. **ERODED LANDSCAPE**
Black ink wash. 6 January 1965. 15 x 22.
INSCRIPTIONS Signed bottom right. Bottom left: *Eroded Landscape.* After annotation: *6.1.1965.*
COLLECTION Unknown.

478. **NAXOS MARBLE**
Black ink wash. 10 January 1965. 15 x 22.
INSCRIPTIONS Signed bottom right. Bottom left: *Naxos Marble.* After annotation: *10.1.1965.*
COLLECTION Unknown.

479. **PAROS II**
Black ink wash. 12 January 1965. 15 x 22.
INSCRIPTIONS Signed bottom right, in pencil. Bottom left, in ink ("II" in pencil): *Paros II.* After annotation, in pen: *12.1.65.*
COLLECTION Unknown.

480. **PASIPHAË I** [formerly **KNEELING FIGURE (PROFILE)**] (Figure 24)
Black ink wash. 15 January 1965. 20 x 16.
INSCRIPTION Lower right: *15.1.65.*
COLLECTION Minotaur Restaurant, London.
EXHIBITIONS National Gallery of Canada Tour 1965–1967, no. 23 (T); ?Reading Museum Art Gallery, June–July 1969, no. 104 ("Parsiphaë [*sic*] 1965 Wash 20 x 16 Minotaur Restaurant"; it may refer to Cat. No. 532); ?National Book League 1971, no. 88 ("Pasiphaë 1965 Black ink, wash 20 x 16 in *Minotaur Restaurant*"; it may refer to Cat. No. 532).
BIBLIOGRAPHY Ayrton 1970d, 17 (T; R, 9).

481. **COMPRESSED FIGURE: FRONTAL STUDY FOR MIRROR MAZE**
Black ink wash. 16 January 1965. 19 x 24-1/2.
INSCRIPTIONS Signed bottom right. Below signature: *16.1.65.*
COLLECTION Bruton Gallery, Somerset.
EXHIBITIONS Seventeenth King's Lynn Festival 1967, no. 4* (T); University of Essex, March 1968, no. 28* (T); Bruton Gallery 1971, no. 47 (T); Maze and Minotaur Tour 1973, no. 59 (T; R).

Although this figure is clearly related to the earlier *Compressed Figure* (Cat. No. 472) and to the bronze figure in Mirror Maze (Cat. No. 596), Ayrton indicated it was "in fact a study for the large Maze Maker" (notes on a conversation with the artist, 27 August 1972).

482. **BACK** [formerly **KNEELING FIGURE (BACK)**]
Black ink wash. 17 January 1965. 16 x 20.
INSCRIPTIONS Signed at bottom, right of center. Above signature: *17.1.65.*
COLLECTIONS Sold from the collection of the late R. Turner at Christies in November 1968 and purchased by the artist; sold in 1972 to R. S. Johnson-International Gallery, Chicago.
EXHIBITION R. S. Johnson-International Gallery 1972, no. 52.

483. **WINTER DEMETER**
Black ink wash. 28 January 1965. 20 x 16.
INSCRIPTIONS Signed top right. Above signature, in heavier pen: *28.1.65.*
COLLECTION Unknown.
EXHIBITIONS National Gallery of Canada Tour 1965–1967, no. 24 (T; R); Esther Bear Gallery 1968; ?Sears Vincent Price Gallery 1970 (not catalogued?); Bruton Gallery 1971, no. 48 (1966; T); Magdalene Street Gallery 1972, no. 24 (T); Bruton Gallery 1981, no. 177*; National Museum of Wales, Penarth, and Pelter Sands Gallery 1981.

484. **APPREHENSIVE FIGURE**
Pencil. 29 January 1965. 20 x 16.
INSCRIPTIONS Signed top right. Below signature: *29.1.1965.*
COLLECTION Unknown.
EXHIBITIONS National Gallery of Canada Tour 1965–1967, no. 25; Esther Bear Gallery 1968; ?Sears Vincent Price Gallery 1970 (not catalogued?).

485. **SEASONS OF DEMETER II. SUMMER** (Figure 91)
Pencil. 29 January 1965. 16 x 20.
INSCRIPTIONS Signed bottom right. Above signature: *29.1.1965.*
COLLECTION The artist's estate.
EXHIBITIONS Grosvenor Gallery 1966, no. 74 (T); Sears Vincent Price Gallery 1967, no. 10 (T); Bruton Gallery 1981, no. 166* (T; R, 46); National Museum of Wales, Penarth, and Pelter Sands Gallery 1981.
BIBLIOGRAPHY Cannon-Brookes 1978a, 100 (no. 188; R, 105).

For a clarification of the reason for conflicting titles in the exhibition catalogues, see the note on Cat. No. 510, *Seasons of Demeter III. Autumn.*

486. **SEASONS OF DEMETER I. SPRING** (Figure 90)
Pencil. 4 February 1965. 20 x 16.
INSCRIPTIONS Signed top right. Above signature: *4.2.65.*
COLLECTION Eric Estorick or the Grosvenor Gallery, London.
EXHIBITIONS Grosvenor Gallery 1966, no. 72; Sears Vincent Price Gallery 1967, no. 9 (T).
BIBLIOGRAPHY Cannon-Brookes 1978a, 100 (no. 186; R, 105).

487. **DEMETER SEATED**
Pencil. 11 February 1965. 14 x 10.
INSCRIPTION Bottom right: *11.2.65.*
COLLECTION Eric Estorick or the Grosvenor Gallery, London.
EXHIBITIONS Grosvenor Gallery 1966, no. 84; Sears Vincent Price Gallery 1967, no. 14.

488. **DEMETER, HEAD FULL FACE**
Black ink wash. 11 February 1965. 16 x 20.
INSCRIPTIONS Signed bottom left. Bottom right, in pen: *11.2.65.*
COLLECTION R. S. Johnson-International Gallery, Chicago.
EXHIBITIONS Grosvenor Gallery 1966, no. 71 (T); Seventeenth King's Lynn Festival 1967, no. 7 (T); R. S. Johnson-International Gallery 1972, no. 51 (T); Museum of Art, Pennsylvania State University 1973, no. 31 (T).

489. **TURNING HEAD (CREW CUT)**
Black ink wash. 11 February 1965. 16 x 20.
INSCRIPTIONS Signed bottom right. Below signature, in heavier pen: *11.2.65.* Below date: *Turning Head.*
COLLECTION Unknown.

490. **EMERGING MAZE FIGURE** (Figure 147)
Black ink wash and collage. 14 February 1965. 20 x 16.
INSCRIPTION Bottom right: *14.2.65.*
COLLECTION The artist's estate.
EXHIBITIONS Grosvenor Gallery 1967, no. 70; Seventeenth King's Lynn Festival 1967, no. 5; University of Essex 1968, no. 23*; R. S. Johnson-International Gallery 1972, no. 50 (R, 47); Museum of Art, Pennsylvania State University 1973, no. 30.
BIBLIOGRAPHY Ayrton 1962a, pl. 199; Cannon-Brookes 1978a, 84 (no. 148; R, 86).

491. **STRESS MAZE TORSO**
Charcoal and collage on canvas. February 1965. 24 x 20.
INSCRIPTIONS Signed top left. Below signature: *Feb '65.*
COLLECTION Private collection, London.
EXHIBITIONS Grosvenor Gallery 1966, no. 63 (T); National Book League 1971, no. 97 (1962; T; R, pl. 24, no. 37).

492. **FEMALE HEAD IN PROFILE**
Black ink wash. 26 February 1965. 16 x 20.
INSCRIPTIONS Signed bottom right. Above signature: *26.2.65.*
COLLECTION Unknown.

493. **SERPENTINE FIGURE II**
Pencil. 26 February 1965. 20 x 16.
INSCRIPTIONS Signed top right. Above signature: *26.2.65.* After date: *Serpentine Figure II.*
COLLECTION Unknown.
EXHIBITIONS National Gallery of Canada Tour 1965–1967, no. 26 (T); Esther Bear Gallery 1968.

494. **TURNING TORSO**
Charcoal and collage on canvas. 5 March 1965. 20 x 16.
INSCRIPTIONS Signed top left. Above signature: *5.3.65.*
COLLECTION Unknown.
EXHIBITIONS Grosvenor Gallery 1966, no. 69; Seventeenth King's Lynn Festival 1967, no. 2 (R).

495. **CAGE CONTINGENCY** (Figure 134)
Bronze. 1965. 69-1/2 x 13-1/2 x 10. Unique.
COLLECTION Private collection, Detroit.
EXHIBITIONS Grosvenor Gallery 1966, no. 15 ("Edition of 6"; dated 1965–66); Hamet Gallery 1969, no. 24 (R); Reading Museum Art Gallery 1969, no. 32.
BIBLIOGRAPHY Ayrton 1962a, pl. 200.

496. **DEMETER AND KORE I**
Bronze. 1965. 9-3/4 x 8 x 11. Edition of 9.
COLLECTIONS Sir Robert and Lady Mayer, London; private collections, London, Chicago, and Twin Lakes, WI.
EXHIBITIONS Grosvenor Gallery 1966, no. 18* (T); Sears Vincent Price Gallery 1967, no. 12* (R).
BIBLIOGRAPHY Ayrton 1962a, pl. 175.

497. **DEMETER AND KORE II** (Figure 89)
Bronze. 1965. 5-3/8 x 5-1/4 x 6. Edition of 9.
COLLECTIONS Private collections, Johannesburg, London, New York, Oxford, and Chicago.
EXHIBITIONS Grosvenor Gallery 1966, no. 19* (T); Reading Museum Art Gallery 1969, no. 29* (Collection "Basil Wright, Esq. & Kassim bin Said, Esq.").
BIBLIOGRAPHY Ayrton 1962a, pl. 176* (Collection "Mrs. M. M. Finger, Johannesburg").

498. **KORE, HEAD** (Figure 87)
Bronze. 1965. 15-1/2 x 14 x 12. Edition of 9.
COLLECTIONS Private collections, Chicago and Cambridge.
EXHIBITIONS Grosvenor Gallery 1966, no. 20* (R); Seventeenth King's Lynn Festival 1967, no. 22; Sears Vincent Price Gallery 1967, no. 13*; University of Essex 1968, no. 9; Hamet Gallery 1969, no. 15; Stowe School 1970, no. 22*; R. S. Johnson-International Gallery 1972, no. 9 (R, 15); Christopher Hull Gallery 1987; Austin/Desmond Fine Art 1990, no. 50* (R, 6); Austin Desmond & Phipps 1992.
BIBLIOGRAPHY Causey 27* (R); Ayrton 1962a, pl. 171.

499. **MAZED MINOTAUR** (Figure 112)
Charcoal and collage on board. 4 April 1965. 21 x 28.
INSCRIPTIONS Signed bottom left. After signature: *4.4.65.*
COLLECTION Private collection, Alberta, Canada.
EXHIBITION National Gallery of Canada Tour 1965–1967, no. 28 (R).
BIBLIOGRAPHY Ayrton 1969, pl. XVI (1961).

500. **CROSS LEGGED NUDE**
Dark ink wash. 16 April 1965. 20 x 16.
INSCRIPTIONS Signed bottom right. Above signature: *16.4.1965.*
COLLECTION Private collection, Auckland.
EXHIBITION Grosvenor Gallery 1966, no. 77 (T).

501. **KORE**
Charcoal. 17 April 1965. 30 x 21.
INSCRIPTIONS Signed bottom right. Above signature: *17.4.65.*
COLLECTION Private collection, Chicago.
EXHIBITIONS Grosvenor Gallery 1966, no. 61; Sears Vincent Price Gallery 1967, no. 15.
BIBLIOGRAPHY Ayrton 1962a, pl. 169.

502. **UPRIGHT BLACK MAZE MAKER**
White chalk on black paper. 19 April 1965. 22 x 19.
INSCRIPTIONS Signed bottom right. Above signature: *19.4.'65.*
COLLECTION Private collection, London.
BIBLIOGRAPHY Cannon-Brookes 1978a, 84 (no. 147; T; R, 85).

503. **DAEDALUS, MAZE MAKER** (Figure 117)
Charcoal and white chalk on black paper. 20 April 1965. 24 x 19.
INSCRIPTIONS Signed top right. Above signature: *20.4.65.*
COLLECTION Private collection, Holland, MI.
EXHIBITIONS National Gallery of Canada Tour 1965–1967, no. 29 (R); Esther Bear Gallery 1968; Hope College 1978, no. 19 (Collection "Mr. and Mrs. Jacob E. Nyenhuis, Holland, MI").
BIBLIOGRAPHY Program of the City of Birmingham Orchestra, 18 November 1971 (R, [6]).

Humphrey Searle's *Labyrinth* symphony, written in 1971, was "commissioned by the Feeney Trust for the City of Birmingham Symphony Orchestra, for performance at the 1971 Royal Concert" (program notes, [5]). Searle dedicated this symphony to Michael Ayrton "jointly with the CBSO" (ibid.). Program of the Royal Concert 1971, 23 November 1971, at Royal Festival Hall, London (R, 27).

504. **MAZE MAKER**
White chalk on black paper. 20 April 1965. 19 x 24.
INSCRIPTIONS Signed bottom right. Below signature: *20.4.65.*
COLLECTION Private collection, London.
EXHIBITIONS Grosvenor Gallery 1967, no. 65 (T); National Book League 1971, no. 98.
BIBLIOGRAPHY Ayrton 1962a, pl. 187 (T).

505. **MAZE MAKER** (frontal view)
White chalk on black paper. 21 April 1965. 19 x 24.
INSCRIPTIONS Signed bottom right. Above signature: *21.4.65.*
COLLECTION Unknown.

506. **DIONYSUS AND MINOTAUR II**
Black ink wash. 22 April 1965. 16 x 20.
INSCRIPTIONS Signed bottom right. After signature, in pen: *22.4.65.* Top left: *Dionysus and Minotaur II.*
COLLECTION Private collection.
EXHIBITION National Gallery of Canada Tour 1965–1967, no. 30 (T).

507. **BLACK MAZE HEAD**
White chalk on black paper. 24 April 1965. 16 x 20.
INSCRIPTION Bottom right: *24.4.65.*
COLLECTION Private collection, London.
BIBLIOGRAPHY Cannon-Brookes 1978a, 119f. (no. 225; T; R, 125).

508. **MAZE HEAD VI**
Black ink. 1965. 14 x 10.
INSCRIPTIONS Signed in middle, right of center. After signature: *65.* Below signature: *Maze Head VI.*
COLLECTION The artist's estate.
EXHIBITION Mazelow Gallery 1966, no. 10 (T: "Maze Heads").

509. **DIONYSUS IN BULL FORM AND CROUCHED MINOTAUR**
Black ink wash. 25 April 1965. 16 x 20.
INSCRIPTIONS Signed top right. Bottom right: *25.4.1965.* Below date: *Dionysus and Minotaur IV.*
COLLECTION Minotaur Restaurant, London.
EXHIBITIONS Reading Museum Art Gallery 1969, no. 105 (T; R, pl. 24); National Book League 1971, no. 82 (T).
BIBLIOGRAPHY Ayrton 1970d (R, 21); M. and E. Ayrton 1984, 68 (R).

510. **SEASONS OF DEMETER III. AUTUMN** (Figure 92)
Pencil. 4 May 1965. 16 x 20.
INSCRIPTIONS Signed bottom right. After signature: *4.5.1965.* Top left: *Autumn Demeter.*
COLLECTION The artist's estate.
EXHIBITIONS Grosvenor Gallery 1966, no. 73 (T); Sears Vincent Price Gallery 1967, no. 11 (T); Bruton Gallery 1981, no. 140* (R, 46).
BIBLIOGRAPHY Cannon-Brookes 1978a, 100 (no. 191; R, 106).

Since this reclining Demeter figure is clearly related to the bronze *Summer Demeter* (Cat. No. 622), Ayrton confused the titles and identified this drawing in his master photographic record as *Seasons of Demeter II. Summer* (see Cat. No. 485). He corrected the sequence in his records on 27 August 1972, when I noted the conflict between the annotation on the drawing itself and the identification in the official records. This fact explains the confusion in titles in the exhibition catalogues.

511. **SEASONS OF DEMETER IV. WINTER** (Figure 93)
Pencil. 4 May 1965. 20 x 16.
INSCRIPTIONS Signed top left. Top right: *4.5.1965.* Below date: *Winter Demeter.*
COLLECTION Mr. Eric Estorick or the Grosvenor Gallery, London.
EXHIBITIONS Grosvenor Gallery 1966, no. 75; Sears Vincent Price Gallery 1967, no. 12 (T).
BIBLIOGRAPHY Cannon-Brookes 1978a, 100 (no. 187; R, 105).

512. **ICARUS RISING**, Variant II
Bronze. 1965. 41 x 30 x 7. Unique.
COLLECTION Private collection, New York.
EXHIBITIONS Seventeenth King's Lynn Festival 1967, no. 4; Mazelow Gallery 1966, no. 25; Sears Vincent Price Gallery 1967, no. 19.

Original version is Cat. No. 206; see also Cat. Nos. 413 and 513.

513. **ICARUS RISING**, Variant III (Plate 11)
Bronze. 1965. 40 x 30-1/2 x 8. Edition of 9.
COLLECTIONS Minotaur Restaurant, London; private collections, Chicago and Surrey.
EXHIBITIONS Bruton Gallery 1971, no. 14*; National Book League 1971, no. 79* (dated 1961–6); R. S. Johnson-International Gallery 1972, no. 15 (R, 19); Maze and Minotaur Tour 1973, no. 22 (R); Museum of Art, Pennsylvania State University 1973, no. 6 (dated 1966; "Collection Joseph V. and Brenda F. Smith"); Bruton Gallery and Tour 1981, no. 43*; Christopher Hull Gallery 1987.

Original version is Cat. No. 206; see also Cat. Nos. 413 and 512.

514. **BLADE MAZE FIGURE** (Figure 119)
Bronze. 3 May 1965. 19-3/4 x 5 x 6. Edition of 9.
COLLECTIONS Private collections, Yorkshire, New York, Chicago, and London.
EXHIBITIONS Grosvenor Gallery 1966, no. 9*; Seventeenth King's Lynn Festival 1967, no. 21; Sears Vincent Price Gallery 1967, no. 7* (R); University of Essex 1968, no. 10; Hamet Gallery 1969, no. 17; Magdalene Street Gallery 1972, no. 5 (R); Daedalus I Gallery 1972, no. 10; R. S. Johnson-International Gallery 1972, no. 13; Austin/Desmond Fine Art 1990, no. 49* (R, 7).
BIBLIOGRAPHY Ayrton 1962a, pl. 179.

515. **KNEELING MAZE FIGURE** (Figure 120)
Bronze. 1965. 5-1/2 x 3-3/4 x 8. Edition of 9.
COLLECTIONS Private collections, Buffalo, NY, London, Paris, Somerset, Munster, IN, and Cambridge.
EXHIBITIONS James Goodman Gallery 1965, no. 31* (dated 1964–65); Mazelow Gallery 1966, no. 20*; Grosvenor Gallery 1966, no. 13; Seventeenth King's Lynn Festival 1967, no. 16; Sears Vincent Price Gallery 1969, no. 3*; Bruton Gallery 1971, no. 11.
BIBLIOGRAPHY Ayrton 1962a, pl. 177.

516. **DEMETER AND KORE**
Black ink wash. 1 June 1965. 20 x 16.
INSCRIPTIONS Signed bottom right. After signature: *1.6.65.*
COLLECTION Galeries Jason Teff, Quebec.

517. **DEMETER AND KORE** (Figure 88)
Charcoal on blue paper. 1 June 1965. 22 x 15.
INSCRIPTIONS Signed bottom right. Below signature: *1.6.1965.*
COLLECTION Private collection, London.
EXHIBITIONS Grosvenor Gallery 1966, no. 68*; Reading Museum Art Gallery 1969, no. 103* (R, pl. 23).
BIBLIOGRAPHY Ayrton 1962a, pl. 170.

518. **BARLEY FLIGHT I**
Collage on canvas. July 1965. 20 x 24.
INSCRIPTIONS Signed top left. After signature: *July '65.*
COLLECTION Private collection, London.
EXHIBITIONS Reading Museum Art Gallery 1969, no. 77 (1966; "I" omitted; Collection "Lord Jessel;" R, pl. 18).
BIBLIOGRAPHY Hopkins 1994, 291.

519. **LUSH LANDSCAPE**
Acrylic. 1965. 25 x 30.
INSCRIPTIONS Signed bottom left. After signature: *'65.*
COLLECTION Unknown.
EXHIBITIONS Grosvenor Gallery 1966, no. 43; also 1967; Sears Vincent Price Gallery 1969, no. 2 (1964); Stowe School 1970, no. 10; Austin/Desmond Fine Art 1990, no. 28 (R, 30, in color); Beaux Arts Gallery 1993.

Dominant colors are dark green and very dark blue, with a few highlights in chartreuse.

520. **THE FUTURE BARLEY**
Collage. 1965. 19-1/2 x 15.
INSCRIPTIONS Signed bottom left, in white. After signature: *'65.*
COLLECTION The artist's estate.
EXHIBITIONS Grosvenor Gallery 1966, no. 55; Reading Museum Art Gallery 1969, no. 76* (1966); Stowe School 1970, no. 17.

521. **THE FUTURE WHEAT**
Collage. 1965. 19-1/2 x 15.
INSCRIPTIONS Signed bottom right. After signature: *'65.*
COLLECTION The artist's estate.
EXHIBITIONS Grosvenor Gallery 1966, no. 54; Reading Museum Art Gallery 1969, no. 75; Stowe School 1970, no. 18.

The hand print in this collage symbolizes the hand of Kore bringing the harvest back into existence (notes on a conversation with the artist, 28 August 1972).

522. **MAZE HEAD** (Figure 131, Plates 16 and 17)
Bronze. 1965. 10 x 9 x 11. Edition of 9.
COLLECTIONS Private collections, La Jolla, CA, New Haven, CT, and London.
EXHIBITIONS Grosvenor Gallery 1966, no. 7; Seventeenth King's Lynn Festival 1967, no. 10; Sears Vincent Price Gallery 1967, no. 8; University of Essex 1968, no. 11; Hamet Gallery 1969, no. 23 (R, cover); Stowe School 1970, no. 20; Bruton Gallery 1971, no. 13; National Book League 1971, No. 102; R. S. Johnson-International Gallery 1972, no. 10 (R, 17); Maze and Minotaur Tour 1973, no. 17; Museum of Art, Pennsylvania State University 1973, no. 5; Bruton Gallery 1981, no. 47; Austin/Desmond Fine Art 1990, no. 51* (R, 24).
BIBLIOGRAPHY Causey 27 (R); Blakeston (R); Ayrton 1962a, pl. 194 (Collection "Dr J. Bronowski, La Jolla, California").

523. **MAZE MAKER II** (Plate 18)
Bronze. 1965. 11 x 8-1/2 x 14-1/2. Edition of 9.
COLLECTIONS Private collections, New York, London, Glencoe, IL, Green Bay, WI, Chicago, and Cambridge.
EXHIBITIONS James Goodman Gallery 1965, no. 30* (dated 1964–65); Grosvenor Gallery 1966, no. 3 (dated 1964); Sears Vincent Price Gallery 1967, no. 4 (dated 1964); Hamet Gallery 1969, no. 20; National Book League 1971, no. 104*; R. S. Johnson-International Gallery 1972, no. 14; Maze and Minotaur Tour 1973, no. 16; Museum of Art, Pennsylvania State University 1973, no. 4 ("Collection Mr. and Mrs. Max Becker, Jr."); Christopher Hull Gallery 1987.
BIBLIOGRAPHY Ayrton 1962a, pl. 186 (Collection "Michael Gottlieb, New York").

524. **MAZE MAKER III** (Figure 122)
Bronze. 1965. 10 x 4-1/4 x 8. Edition of 9.
COLLECTIONS Private collections, Stamford, CT, London, Chicago, Houston, TX, and Yorkshire.
EXHIBITIONS Grosvenor Gallery 1966, no. 4* (dated 1964–65); Hamet Gallery 1969, no. 18*; Bruton Gallery 1981, no. 48*.
BIBLIOGRAPHY Ayrton 1962a, pl. 181 (Collection "Mr. and Mrs. Richard Lewis, Stamford, Connecticut").

525. **DEMETER AND KORE**
Charcoal drawing on canvas. 16 July 1965. 30 x 25.
INSCRIPTIONS Dated at top, left of center: *16.7.'65.*
COLLECTION Private collection.
EXHIBITIONS ?Austin Desmond & Phipps 1992; ?Beaux Arts Gallery 1993.
BIBLIOGRAPHY Ayrton 1962a, pl. 174 (1964, although the correct date is visible in the plate itself); Cannon-Brookes 1978a, no. 185 (R, 104).

526. **DEMETER AND KORE (HEADS)**
Charcoal on darkest blue paper. 30 July 1965. 16 x 20.
INSCRIPTIONS Signed bottom right. Below signature: *30.7.65.*
COLLECTION Private collection, Yorkshire.

527. **MAZE TORSO**
Charcoal. 30 July 1965. 30 x 21.
INSCRIPTIONS Signed bottom left. Below signature: *30.7.1965.*
COLLECTION Unknown.
EXHIBITIONS Grosvenor Gallery 1966, no. 60; Seventeenth King's Lynn Festival 1967, no. 3 (1963); University of Essex 1968, no. 22.
BIBLIOGRAPHY Ayrton 1962a, pl. 198.

528. **ARIADNE AND MINOTAUR**
Black ink wash. 1965. 16 x 20.
COLLECTION Minotaur Restaurant, London.
EXHIBITION Reading Museum Art Gallery 1969, no. 106.

529. **TURNING MAZE MAKER**
Charcoal. 1 August 1965. 30 x 21.
INSCRIPTIONS Signed bottom right. Below signature: *1.8.65.*
COLLECTION Unknown.
EXHIBITIONS Redfern Gallery 1966; Reading Museum Art Gallery 1969, no. 107 (T).

530. **BARLEY MATRIX**
Collage. August 1965. 30 x 50.
INSCRIPTIONS Signed bottom left, in white. After signature: *August '65.*
COLLECTION Private collection, London.
EXHIBITION Grosvenor Gallery 1966, no. 30.
BIBLIOGRAPHY Hopkins 1994, 291.

This collage "has only the most peripheral kind of associative relevance [to Daedalus and Icarus]. . . . [I]t is connected as much with the Demeter theme as any" (notes on a conversation with the artist, 26 August 1972).

531. **SUNSTRIKE**
Collage. 1965. 25 x 30.
INSCRIPTION Signed top left, in white. After signature: *'65.*
COLLECTION Private collection; sold from Sears Vincent Price Gallery.
EXHIBITIONS Grosvenor Gallery 1966, no. 41; Sears Vincent Price Gallery 1967, no. 7.

532. **PASIPHAË II**
Black ink wash? 9 August 1965. 20 x 16.
INSCRIPTIONS Signed bottom right. Above signature: *9.8.65.*
COLLECTION Minotaur Restaurant, London.
EXHIBITIONS ?Reading Museum Art Gallery, no. 104 ("Parsiphaë [*sic*] 1965 Wash 20 x 16 Minotaur Restaurant"; also see Cat. No. 480); ?National Book League, December 1971, no. 88 ("Pasiphaë 1965 Black ink, wash 20 x 16 in *Minotaur Restaurant*"; also see Cat. No. 480).
BIBLIOGRAPHY Ayrton 1970d (1965; T; R, 18).

533. **VERTICAL LANDSCAPE**
Collage on red wood. 1965. 35 x 23-1/2.
INSCRIPTIONS Signed top left. After signature: *65.*
COLLECTION Private collection, Cambridge.
EXHIBITIONS Grosvenor Gallery 1966, no. 35* (1964); Reading Museum Art Gallery 1969, no. 72 (1964); Hamet Gallery 1969, no. 28 (1964).

534. **SUMMER'S LAST WILL**
Collage and acrylic on board. 1965–1969. 36 x 48.
INSCRIPTIONS Signed top left. After signature: *'65–69.*
COLLECTION Private collection, London.
EXHIBITION Grosvenor Gallery 1966, no. 28 (1964).

535. **BLACK ROCK STRONG TIDE**
Collage on board. 1965 (repainted 1969). 21 x 27.
INSCRIPTIONS Signed top left. After signature:*'65–69.*
COLLECTION Unknown.
EXHIBITIONS Hamet Gallery 1969, no. 31* (T); Stowe School 1970, no. 8* (T).

536. **NAXOS MARBLE**
Collage. 1965. 30 x 40.
INSCRIPTIONS Signed top left. After signature: *'65.*
COLLECTION Private collection, Essex.
EXHIBITIONS Grosvenor Gallery 1966, no. 32; Reading Museum Art Gallery 1969, no. 74 (Collection "Andrew Carnwath, Esq.").

537. **NIGHT SEA AND SHORE**
Collage. 1965. 30 x 40.
INSCRIPTIONS Signed bottom left, in white. After signature: *'65.*
COLLECTION Private collection, London.
EXHIBITIONS Grosvenor Gallery 1966, no. 31 (1964); Wycombe Arts Festival 1967.

This collage relates directly to the flight of Daedalus and Icarus, illustrating aspects of the flight at night (notes on a conversation with the artist, 26 August 1972).

538. **CORN STELE** (Figure 96)
Collage. 1965. 30 x 25.
INSCRIPTIONS Signed top left. After signature: *'65.*
COLLECTION Private collection, Rockford, IL.
EXHIBITIONS Grosvenor Gallery 1966, no. 37; Wycombe Arts Festival 1967; Sears Vincent Price Gallery 1967, no. 5*.
BIBLIOGRAPHY Rosenthal 1966, 271 (T; R).

Persephone is the primary mythical figure evoked by this collage. It is intended to recall her descent into the underworld and her transformation into a gravestone until spring (notes on a conversation with the artist, 26 August 1972).

539. **CORN FRAGMENT**
Collage. September 1965. 20 x 30.
INSCRIPTIONS Signed top left. After signature: *Sept: '65.*
COLLECTION Unknown.
EXHIBITIONS Grosvenor Gallery 1966, no. 44; Beaux Arts Gallery 1993.

540. **GREEN HEAD OF DEMETER**
Acrylic on canvas. 9 September 1965. 12 x 15.
INSCRIPTIONS Signed top left. After signature: *9.9.'65.*
COLLECTION Unknown.

541. **BLACK MAZE HEAD**
Acrylic on canvas. 27 September 1965. 12 x 16.
INSCRIPTIONS Signed bottom left, in white. Well to right of signature: *27.9.65.*
COLLECTION Unknown.
EXHIBITIONS Grosvenor Gallery December 1966; ?Beaux Arts Gallery 1993 (T: "Daedalus Head").

542. **DRY LANDSCAPE**
Collage. 1965. 20 x 25.
INSCRIPTIONS Signed top left. After signature: *'65.*
COLLECTION Unknown.
EXHIBITION Hamet Gallery 1969, no. 30 (1964).

543. **CIRCUMSTANTIAL HEAD**
Acrylic on canvas. 3 October 1965. 25 x 20.
INSCRIPTIONS Signed bottom left. After signature: *3.10.65.*
COLLECTION Unknown.
EXHIBITIONS Grosvenor Gallery 1966, no. 62; Sears Vincent Price Gallery 1967, no. 2 (T: "Icarus" added).

Despite the identification of this head with Icarus in one of the exhibition catalogues, Ayrton described this figure as "another Daedalus image" (notes on a conversation with the artist, August 1972).

544. **MAZE MAKER** (Large version) (Plate 19, Figure 121)
Bronze. 1965. 34 x 36 x 24. Edition of 3.
COLLECTION The artist's estate.
EXHIBITIONS Grosvenor Gallery 1966, no. 5* ("Edition of 4;" dated 1964; R); Seventeenth King's Lynn Festival 1967, no. 1 (R, cover); University of Essex 1968, no. 1; Reading Museum Art Gallery 1969, no. 31 (R, pl. 8); Maze and Minotaur Tour 1973, no. 15 (R).
BIBLIOGRAPHY Causey 26 (R, 27*, dated 1964); Ayrton 1962a, pl. 188; R[ykwert] 1967, 54 (R); Nyenhuis 1967, 234 (R, 235); Ayrton 1969, 200 and pl. XIX; Friendly, 48 (R).

545. **TRANSLUCENT MAZE** (Figure 146)
Collage and charcoal on brown board. 1965. 30 x 40.
INSCRIPTIONS Signed top right. After signature, in white: *65.*
COLLECTION The artist's estate.
EXHIBITIONS Grosvenor Gallery 1966, no. 58; Seventeenth King's Lynn Festival 1967, no. 1 (R); University of Essex 1968, no. 20; Reading Museum Art Gallery 1969, no. 108; Bruton Gallery 1971, no. 45; National Book League 1971, no. 99*; Magdalene Street Gallery 1972, no. 23 (R, but erroneously numbered 18); Maze and Minotaur Tour 1973, no. 58.
BIBLIOGRAPHY Causey 26–27 (R, 27); Ayrton 1962a, pl. 183; Cannon-Brookes 1978a, 84 (no. 149; R, 86).

546. **MAZE MAKER I**
Acrylic and collage on canvas. 1965. 60 x 40.
COLLECTION Private collection, Narbeth, PA.
EXHIBITIONS Grosvenor Gallery 1966, no. 25 (R); Sears Vincent Price Gallery 1967, no. 1 (R); Museum of Art, Pennsylvania State University 1973, no. 29 ("Collection Dr. and Mrs. Milton T. Brown;" R, cover).
BIBLIOGRAPHY Ayrton 1969, 200 and pl. XVIII.

547. **RAINSTORM ON GREEN HILL**
Acrylic. 1965. 25 x 30.
COLLECTION The artist's estate.

548. **IMPASSE**
Collage. 1965. 24 x 20.
COLLECTION The artist's estate.

549. **CLOSED GOLD HEAD**
Acrylic. 1965. 12 x 16.
COLLECTION Private collection.
EXHIBITION Grosvenor Gallery 1966, no. 56.

550. **SEPTEMBER HEAD**
Acrylic. 1965. 12 x 16.
COLLECTION Unknown.
EXHIBITION Grosvenor Gallery December 1966.

This brilliant gold and orange painting depicts Demeter in September (notes on a conversation with the artist, 28 August 1972).

551. **MAZE PLAYER** (Figure 123)
Bronze. 1965. 15-1/2 x 12 x 15. Edition of 9.
COLLECTIONS Private collections, London, Chicago, Oak Lawn, IL, Hillsboro Beach, FL, and New York.
EXHIBITIONS Grosvenor Gallery 1966, no. 8; Sears Vincent Price Gallery 1967, no. 6 (R); University of Essex 1968, no. 13; Hamet Gallery 1969, no. 22; Stowe School 1970, no. 21; Bruton Gallery 1971, no. 12 (R); National Book League 1971, no. 103 (Collection "Mr. Milo Keynes"; R, pl. 28, no. 42); R. S. Johnson-International Gallery 1972, no. 11 (R, 16); Museum of Art, Pennsylvania State University 1973, no. 3 ("Collection Mr. and Mrs. Leonard Lawrence"; R); Hope College 1978, no. 6.
BIBLIOGRAPHY Ayrton 1962a, pl. 192.

552. **MAZE TORSO** (Figure 124)
Bronze. 1965. 14-1/2 x 5-1/2 x 4-1/2. Edition of 2.
COLLECTIONS Private collections, Chicago and Steubenville, OH. Edition closed: "mould lost by foundry" (Sculpture Record Book).
EXHIBITIONS Grosvenor Gallery 1966, no. 6*; Sears Vincent Price Gallery 1967, no. 5* (R).
BIBLIOGRAPHY Ayrton 1962a, pl. 196 (dated 1955).

553. **NAUTILUS MAZE FIGURE (UPRIGHT)** (Figure 125)
Bronze. 1965. 12-1/2 x 5-1/2 x 4-1/2. Edition of 9.
COLLECTIONS Private collections, Highland Park, IL, and Palo Alto, CA.
EXHIBITIONS Grosvenor Gallery 1966, no. 11; Sears Vincent Price Gallery 1969, no. 14; R. S. Johnson-International Gallery 1972, no. 12 (T); Austin/Desmond Fine Art 1990, no. 52*.
BIBLIOGRAPHY Ayrton 1962a, pl. 197.

This work was erroneously reproduced as "Maze Torso" in the Sears Vincent Price Gallery catalogue of an exhibition in 1967.

554. **NAUTILUS MAZE FIGURE (PRONE)** (Figure 126)
Bronze. 1965. 3 x 10 x 5. Edition of 9.
COLLECTIONS Private collections, Somerset and Chicago.
EXHIBITIONS Grosvenor Gallery 1966, no. 10; Seventeenth King's Lynn Festival 1967, no. 19; Sears Vincent Price Gallery 1967, no. 9 (T); Hamet Gallery 1969, no. 21; Reading Museum Art Gallery 1969, no. 30 (R, pl. 7); Bruton Gallery 1981, no. 58 (R, 21); Austin Desmond & Phipps 1992; Beaux Arts Gallery 1993.
BIBLIOGRAPHY Ayrton 1962a, pl. 193.

555. **STUDY FOR CONTAINED MAZE (MIRROR MAZE)**
Pencil and wash. 20 November 1965. 20 x 16.
INSCRIPTIONS Signed right middle. Above signature: *20.11.'65.* Top left: *Contained Maze.*
COLLECTION The artist's estate.
EXHIBITIONS Sears Vincent Price Gallery 1967, no. 8 (T); Daedalus I Gallery 1972, no. 26 (1963; T); Museum of Art, Pennsylvania State University 1973, no. 26 (1963; T); Christopher Hull Gallery 1987; ?Austin Desmond & Phipps 1992.

This drawing was originally conceived as a study for the bronze *Mirror Maze* (Cat. No. 596), but it also gave rise to the painting *Contained Maze* (Cat. No. 583). Since it presents three different aspects of a kneeling figure, this drawing is in fact closer to the bronze than to the painting, which depicts an erect figure (notes on a conversation with the artist, 26 August 1972).

556. **PUPATE FIGURE**
White chalk on black paper. 22 November 1965. 19 x 24.
INSCRIPTIONS Signed top left. Above signature: *22.11.65.*
COLLECTION Private collection, Gloucestershire.
EXHIBITION Grosvenor Gallery 1966, no. 64.
BIBLIOGRAPHY Rosenthal 1966, 272 (R); Cannon-Brookes 1978a, 107 (no. 192; R).

557. **DEMETER AND KORE**
Black wash. 28 November 1965. 16 x 20.
INSCRIPTIONS Signed bottom left. Above signature: *28.11.65.*
COLLECTION Private collection (London?).
EXHIBITION ?Sears Vincent Price Gallery 1967, no. 7.

This drawing was a study for the two bronzes, *Demeter and Kore*, *I* and *II* (Cat. Nos. 496 and 497).

558. **SMALL STANDING MAZE FIGURE** (Figure 127)
Bronze. 1965. 7-1/4 x 4-1/4 x 2-1/2. Edition of 9.
COLLECTIONS Private collections, London, Luxembourg, Chicago, Surrey, Cambridge, and Sussex.
EXHIBITIONS Grosvenor Gallery 1966, no. 12* (T); Seventeenth King's Lynn Festival 1967, no. 18; Sears Vincent Price Gallery 1967, no. 10* (R); Magdalene Street Gallery 1972, no. 6.
BIBLIOGRAPHY Ayrton 1962a, pl. 178.

559. **MAZE HEAD. DRAWING 4**
Black ink wash. 5 January 1966. 16 x 20.
INSCRIPTIONS Signed bottom right. Above signature: *5.1.66.* Above date: *Maze Head. Drawing 4.*
COLLECTION Private collection, Chicago.
EXHIBITIONS Seventeenth King's Lynn Festival 1967, no. 9 (T); University of Essex 1968, no. 25 (T).

560. **STUDY FOR EMERGING FIGURE III**
Pencil and wash. 21 January 1966. 20 x 16.
INSCRIPTIONS Signed at bottom, left of center. At bottom, right of center: *21.1.66.* Below signature: *Emerging Figure III.*
COLLECTION Private collection, London.
EXHIBITIONS Grosvenor Gallery 1966, no. 79 (24.1.1966; the title, "Study for Emerging Figure," might confuse it with Cat. No. 562, but that is a pencil drawing; also, Ayrton's photographic record book ascribes this drawing to this exhibition); ?University of Essex 1968, no. 27.

561. **SERPENTINE FIGURE**
Black ink wash. 22 January 1966. 20 x 16.
INSCRIPTIONS Signed bottom right. Below signature: *22.1.66.* Below date: *Serpentine Figure IV.*
COLLECTION ?Grosvenor Gallery, London.
EXHIBITIONS Grosvenor Gallery 1966, no. 76; Sears Vincent Price Gallery 1967, no. 13 (R).

562. **STUDY FOR EMERGING FIGURE II**
Pencil. 24 January 1966. 20 x 16.
INSCRIPTIONS Signed top right. Bottom right: *24.1.66.* Above date (two lines): *Emerging Figure II / 36″ x 16″ x 3″ (Depth).*
COLLECTION The artist's estate.
EXHIBITIONS Seventeenth King's Lynn Festival 1967, no. 18 (1965; T); Magdalene Street Gallery 1972, no. 26 (T); Maze and Minotaur Tour 1973, no. 64 (T).
BIBLIOGRAPHY Cannon-Brookes 1978a, 113 (no. 200; T; R, 112).

The dimensions annotated on the drawing are for the second figure in the bronze triptych, *Triptych II. Emerging Figure* (Cat. No. 616).

563. **STUDY FOR EMERGING FIGURE**
Black ink wash. 4 February 1966. 22 x 14.
INSCRIPTIONS Signed bottom right. Above signature: *4.2.66.* Above date: *Emerging Figure I.*
COLLECTION Mr. Eric Estorick or Grosvenor Gallery, London.
EXHIBITIONS Grosvenor Gallery 1966, no. 67*; Sears Vincent Price Gallery 1967, no. 17*; Beaux Arts Gallery 1993.
BIBLIOGRAPHY Ayrton 1962a, pl. 205 (entitled "Study for Emerging Figure, II" [here "II" clearly indicates the sequence of the drawings, not of the figures in the bronze triptych, since this is a study for the first of the three bronze figures]).

564. **STUDY FOR MIRROR MAZE**
Pencil and black ink wash. 6 February 1966. 16 x 20.
INSCRIPTIONS Bottom right: *6.2.66.* Above date: *Mirror Maze. 2.*
COLLECTION Mr. Eric Estorick or Grosvenor Gallery, London.
EXHIBITIONS Grosvenor Gallery 1966, no. 80; Sears Vincent Price Gallery 1967, no. 16.
BIBLIOGRAPHY Ayrton 1962a, pl. 204.

This drawing is actually very closely connected with two paintings, *Contained Maze* (Cat. No. 583) and *Maze Maker I* (Cat. No. 546), as well as with the bronze *Mirror Maze* (Cat. No. 596) (notes on a conversation with the artist, 26 August 1972).

565. **MAZE HEAD**
Black ink wash. 9 February 1966. 16 x 20.
COLLECTION Unknown.
EXHIBITIONS Grosvenor Gallery 1966, no. 81; ?University of Essex 1968, no. 25 ("Study for Maze Head"; see Cat. No. 559).

566. **ICARUS** (Figure 142)
Black wash. 9 February 1966. 16 x 20.
INSCRIPTIONS Signed bottom right. Below signature: *Icarus 9.2.66.*
COLLECTION Private collection, Los Angeles.
EXHIBITION Sears Vincent Price Gallery 1967, no. 1* (T).

567. **THESEUS**
Black ink wash. 9 February 1966. 16 x 20.
INSCRIPTIONS Bottom left: *9.2.66.* Bottom right: *Theseus.*
COLLECTION The artist's estate.
EXHIBITIONS Bruton Gallery and Tour 1981, no. 168* (R, 44); Christopher Hull Gallery 1987.

568. **DISTURBED FIGURE**
Black ink wash. 9 February 1966. 16 x 20.
INSCRIPTIONS Signed top right. Bottom right: *9.2.66.* Below and left of date: *Disturbed Figure.*
COLLECTION Private collection, Oakbrook, IL.
EXHIBITIONS University of Essex 1968, no. 30; Magdalene Street Gallery 1972, no. 27 (T: "Oracle Disturbed"); R. S. Johnson-International Gallery 1972, no. 53.

569. **BARLEY FLIGHT II**
Collage. 1966. 30 x 25.
INSCRIPTIONS Signed top left. After signature: *'66.*
COLLECTION Harold Patton and Associates, Detroit.
EXHIBITIONS Grosvenor Gallery 1966, no. 38 (T: "II" omitted); Wycombe Arts Festival 1967; Sears Vincent Price Gallery 1967, no. 4 (T: "II" omitted).

570. **SUNSHROUD**
Collage. 1966. 25 x 30.
INSCRIPTIONS Signed bottom left, in white. After signature: *'66.*
COLLECTION Private collection, London.
EXHIBITIONS Grosvenor Gallery 1966, no. 42; Reading Museum Art Gallery 1969, no. 79 (Collection "Mrs. C. Hemans").

571. **FEBRUARY HEAD**
Acrylic and collage. 1966. 12 x 16.
INSCRIPTIONS Signed bottom right. After signature: *'66.*
COLLECTION Private collection.
EXHIBITION Grosvenor Gallery 1966, no. 57.

572. **PERSEPHONE WITH BARLEY STALKS** (Figure 85)
Black wash. 6 March 1966. 20 x 16.
INSCRIPTIONS Signed top left. After signature. *6.3.66.*
COLLECTION Private collection, Holland, MI.
EXHIBITIONS Esther Bear Gallery 1968 (R, cover); Hope College 1978, no. 20 (Collection "Mr. and Mrs. Jacob E. Nyenhuis").

Ayrton also used "Kore with Corn Stalks" as the title for this work. In myth and in Ayrton's work, Kore (Maiden) is a frequent substitute for Persephone.

573. **STUDY FOR CONTAINED MAZE**
Pencil. 5 April 1966. 14 x 10.
COLLECTION Unknown.
EXHIBITION Grosvenor Gallery 1966, no. 85.

574. **CROUCHED MINOTAUR** (Variant I)
Brush and black ink. April 1966. 10 x 14.
COLLECTION Unknown.
BIBLIOGRAPHY ?M. and E. Ayrton 1984, 50 (R).

575. **CROUCHED MINOTAUR** (Variant II)
Brush and black ink. April 1966. 10 x 14.
COLLECTION Private collection.

576. **CROUCHED MINOTAUR** (Variant III)
Brush and black ink. April 1966. 10 x 14.
COLLECTION Private collection.

577. **CROUCHED MINOTAUR** (Variant IV)
Brush and black ink. April 1966. 10 x 14.
COLLECTION Private collection.

578. **CROUCHED MINOTAUR** (Variant V)
Brush and black ink. April 1966. 10 x 14.
COLLECTION Private collection.

579. **CROUCHED MINOTAUR** (Variant VI)
Brush and black ink. April 1966. 10 x 14.
COLLECTION Private collection.

580. **CROUCHED MINOTAUR** (Variant VII)
Brush and black ink. April 1966. 10 x 14.
COLLECTION Private collection.

581. **CROUCHED MINOTAUR** (Variant VIII)
Brush and black ink. April 1966. 10 x 14.
COLLECTION Private collection.

582. **FEBRUARY WITH MARCH**
Collage. April 1966. 30 x 40.
INSCRIPTIONS Signed top left. After signature: *April '66.*
COLLECTION Private collection.
EXHIBITION Grosvenor Gallery 1966, no. 33 (T).

583. **CONTAINED MAZE** (Plate 21)
Collage. April 1966. 40 x 60.
INSCRIPTIONS Signed top left. After signature: *April '66.*
COLLECTION The artist's estate.
EXHIBITIONS Grosvenor Gallery 1966, no. 27; Museum of Art, Pennsylvania State University 1973, no. 33.
BIBLIOGRAPHY Cannon-Brookes 1978a, 113 (R).

584. **DEMETER PREGNANT** (Figure 94)
Bronze. 1966. 31 x 13 x 14. Edition of 6.
COLLECTIONS Reading Museum Art Gallery; private collections, Oak Lawn, IL, Chicago, Southfield, MI, London, and Evanston, IL.
EXHIBITIONS Grosvenor Gallery 1966, no. 21*; Seventeenth King's Lynn Festival 1967, no. 8; Sears Vincent Price Gallery 1967, no. 14* (R); Hamet Gallery 1969, no. 16; Reading Museum Art Gallery 1969, no. 33 (R, pl. 9); Museum of Art, Pennsylvania State University 1973, no. 2 ("Collection Mr. and Mrs. Granvil J. Specks 1963").
BIBLIOGRAPHY Causey 26* (R); Rosenthal 1966, 272* (R); Ayrton 1962a, pl. 173; Blakeston cover (R).

585. **MINOTAUR DRUNK**
Pen. 1966. 20 x 16.
COLLECTION Minotaur Restaurant, London.

586. **THE MINOTAUR DRUNK AND DANCING I**
Pen. 26 May 1966. 20 x 16.
INSCRIPTIONS Signed bottom right. Above signature: *26.5.'66.*
COLLECTION Minotaur Restaurant, London.

587. **THE MINOTAUR DRUNK AND DANCING II**
Pen. 26 May 1966. 20 x 16.
INSCRIPTIONS Signed bottom right. Above signature: *26.5.66.*
COLLECTION Minotaur Restaurant, London.
BIBLIOGRAPHY Ayrton 1970d, 22 (R, left half of page; erroneously numbered "I," 9).

588. **THE MINOTAUR DRUNK AND DANCING III**
Pen. 27 May 1966. 20 x 16.
INSCRIPTIONS Signed bottom right. Bottom left: *27.5.66.*
COLLECTION Minotaur Restaurant, London.
BIBLIOGRAPHY Ayrton 1970d, 22 (R, right half of page; erroneously numbered "II," 9).

589. **THE MINOTAUR DRUNK AND DANCING IV**
Pen. 28 May 1966. 20 x 16.
INSCRIPTIONS Signed bottom right. Bottom left: *28.5.66.*
COLLECTION Minotaur Restaurant, London.

590. **ASTERION**
Pen. 28 May 1966. 20 x 16.
INSCRIPTIONS Signed bottom right. Bottom left: *28.5.66.* Top left, above the head: *ASTERION.*
COLLECTION Minotaur Restaurant, London.
BIBLIOGRAPHY Ayrton 1970d (R, frontispiece).

591. **STUDY FOR MINOTAUR IN JEOPARDY**
Black ink wash. 30 May 1966. 20 x 16.
INSCRIPTIONS Signed at left margin, below the middle. Above signature: *30.5.66.*
COLLECTION Private collection, Chicago.
EXHIBITIONS Seventeenth King's Lynn Festival 1967, no. 10; University of Essex 1968, no. 26; Magdalene Street Gallery 1972, no. 25 (T); R. S. Johnson-International Gallery 1972, no. 54 (R, 44).
BIBLIOGRAPHY Ayrton 1970d, 26 (R).

592. **VERGIL AT CUMAE**
Pencil and black ink wash. 1966. 14 x 10.
INSCRIPTIONS Top left: *Caslon Roman?* Bottom left, on two lines: *Caption inside flap:— / Jacket design: 'Vergil at Cumae' by Michael Ayrton.*
COLLECTION Private collection, Holland, MI.
EXHIBITION Hope College 1978, no. 18 (dated 1967; Collection "Jacob E. Nyenhuis")
BIBLIOGRAPHY Hopkins 1994, 303.

Jacket design for W. F. Jackson Knight, *Vergil: Epic and Anthropology* (London: George Allen and Unwin, 1967).

593. **MAZE MAKER II** (Figure 128)
Collage and acrylic on canvas. 1966. 60 x 40.
INSCRIPTIONS Signed top left, in from margin and barely legible. After signature: *'66.*
COLLECTION Unknown.
EXHIBITIONS Grosvenor Gallery 1966, no. 26; Reading Museum Art Gallery 1969, no. 78 (R, pl. 19); Stowe School 1970, no. 2 (R); Bruton Gallery 1981, no. 109 (T; R, 40).
BIBLIOGRAPHY Ayrton 1969, 200 (R, pl. XX).

594. **JACKET DESIGN FOR THE MAZE MAKER** (Figure 145)
Collage and acrylic on card. 1966. 16 x 24.
INSCRIPTIONS Signed bottom left. After signature: *'66.*
COLLECTION The artist's estate.
EXHIBITIONS National Book League 1971, no. 100 (R, pl. 23, no. 36); Museum of Art, Pennsylvania State University 1973, no. 34.

This jacket design was used for the edition published by Longmans, Green, but not for the American edition (Holt, Rinehart & Winston).

595. **WAVE**
Collage. 1966. 20 x 24.
INSCRIPTIONS Signed bottom left. After signature: *'66.*
COLLECTION Private collection.
EXHIBITION Grosvenor Gallery July 1967.

596. **MIRROR MAZE** (Figure 135)
Bronze, copper, and perspex. 1966. 14 x 24 x 18-1/2. Edition of 6.
COLLECTIONS Lord and Lady Beaumont of Whitley; private collections, Chicago, Detroit, and Flushing, NY.
EXHIBITIONS Grosvenor Gallery 1966, no. 16* (R); Seventeenth King's Lynn Festival 1967, no. 9 (R); Sears Vincent Price Gallery 1967, no. 18* (R); Hamet Gallery 1969, no. 25; Reading Museum Art Gallery 1969, no. 34*; National Book League 1971, no. 105 (Collection "Lord and Lady Beaumont"); R. S. Johnson-International Gallery 1972, no. 16 (R, 23); Maze and Minotaur Tour 1973, no. 39 (R).
BIBLIOGRAPHY Rosenthal 1966, 273* (R); Ayrton 1962a, pl. 203; Santarcangeli pl. 96 (T: "The Maze Maker"); Hopkins 1994, 318 and 348.

597. **TRIPTYCH I EMERGING FIGURE** (Figure 138)
Bronze. 1966. 36 x 17-1/4 x 10; 36 x 16 x 11; 36 x 16 x 13 (dimensions for each of three bronzes which, when aligned, constitute a single piece of sculpture, 36 x 49-1/2 x 13). Edition of 3.
COLLECTIONS Private collections, Chicago and unknown.
EXHIBITIONS Grosvenor Gallery 1966, nos. 22, 23, 24* ("Emerging Figure I, Emerging Figure II and Emerging Figure III; Edition of 6"; R); Seventeenth King's Lynn Festival 1967, no. 11 ("Triptych—Emerging Figures I 1966, cast 1/6"); Sears Vincent Price Gallery 1967, no. 15* (T); Hamet Gallery 1969, no. 26* (T; statement that "these three pieces can be sold separately" suggests that the entire group may have been displayed); Reading Museum Art Gallery 1969, no. 35* (T; R, pl. 10).
BIBLIOGRAPHY Rosenthal 1966, 272 (R [II & III], 271); Ayrton 1962a, pl. 206; Hopkins 1994, 313.

598. **TURNING MAZE FIGURE** (Figure 129)
Bronze. 1966. 9-1/2 x 4 x 3. Edition of 9.
COLLECTIONS Sir Robert and Lady Mayer, London; private collections, New York, Yorkshire, London, Spokane, WA, and Chicago.
EXHIBITIONS Grosvenor Gallery 1966, no. 14; Seventeenth King's Lynn Festival 1967, no. 17; Sears Vincent Price Gallery 1969, no. 4.

599. **SLEEPING FIGURES I**
Pencil. 4 November 1966. 16 x 20.
INSCRIPTIONS Signed bottom right. Before signature: *Sleeping Figures I.* Above annotation: *4.11.1966.*
COLLECTION The artist's estate.

600. **SLEEPING FIGURES III**
Pencil. 6 November 1966. 16 x 20.
INSCRIPTIONS Signed bottom right. Above signature: *SLEEPING FIGURES III.* Above annotation: *6.11.66.*
COLLECTION Unknown.
EXHIBITION Daedalus I Gallery 1972, no. 27.

601. **DAEDALUS IN DARKNESS**
Collage. 1967. 20 x 24.
INSCRIPTIONS Signed top left. After signature: *67.*
COLLECTION Private collection, Deerfield, IL.
EXHIBITIONS Sears Vincent Price Gallery 1967, no. 3* (R); National Book League 1971, no. 95* (1963).

602. **END MAZE** or **DAEDALUS IN DARKNESS II** (Figure 143)
Collage. 1967. 50 x 30.
INSCRIPTIONS Signed top left, in white. Dated after signature.
COLLECTION Unknown.
EXHIBITION ?Beaux Arts Gallery 1993 ("Daedalus in Darkness 48 x 30").

603. **EARTH CORE**
Collage. 1967 (repainted 1969). 20 x 30.
INSCRIPTIONS Signed top left. Below signature: *67.*
COLLECTION The artist's estate.
EXHIBITIONS ?Austin/Desmond Fine Art 1990, no. 29 (T: "Maze Core"); ?Beaux Arts Gallery 1993 (T: "Maze Core").

604. **CHILL SEA**
Collage on canvas. 1967. 25 x 30.
COLLECTION Unknown.
EXHIBITIONS Grosvenor Gallery 1967; Sears Vincent Price Gallery 1967, no. 10 (T: "Running Sea"); Stowe School 1970, no. 7 (T); National Book League 1971, no. 64 (1960; T).

605. **ADVANCING FIGURE** (Figure 244)
Bronze. 1967. 12-1/2 x 24 x 8-3/4. Edition of 9.
COLLECTION Private collection, St. Paul, MN.
EXHIBITIONS Sears Vincent Price Gallery 1969, no. 6* ("cast 2/6"; R); R. S. Johnson-International Gallery 1972, no. 17 (R, 21).

606. **BONE MAZE FIGURE** (Figure 130)
Bronze. 1967. 7-1/4 x 7 x 5. Edition of 9.
COLLECTION The artist's estate.
EXHIBITIONS Sears Vincent Price Gallery 1969, no. 21* (T: "Improvisation on a Bone"; R); Daedalus I Gallery 1972, no. 11; Bruton Gallery 1981, no. 8.

This bronze was a maquette for the unique fountain variant, Cat. No. 607.

607. **BONE MAZE FIGURE, FOUNTAIN VARIANT**
Cast aluminum. 1967. 7-1/4 x 7 x 5. Unique.
COLLECTION Lord and Lady Beaumont of Whitley.

608. **BONE MAZE FIGURE** (Miniature)
Bronze. 1967. 2-1/4 x 2 x 3/4. Edition of 12.
COLLECTION Bruton Gallery, Somerset.
EXHIBITION Bruton Gallery 1981, no. 9 (dated 1975; R, 53).

609. **CAGE MIRROR MAZE** (Figure 136)
Bronze, perspex, and copper. 1967. 69-1/2 x 13-1/2 x 10. Edition of 6.
COLLECTIONS Private collections, Chicago, Rockford, IL, and Southfield, MI.
EXHIBITIONS Grosvenor Gallery 1966, no. 17; Sears Vincent Price Gallery 1967, no. 11 (dated 1966; R); Daedalus I Gallery 1972, no. 1; Museum of Art, Pennsylvania State University 1973, no. 7 (T: "Cage Mirror Maze/Contingency"; dated 1967–73; "Collection Mr. Elbert Bagus").
BIBLIOGRAPHY Hopkins 1994, 318.

Despite the fact that a sculpture entitled "Cage—Mirror Maze" with this sculpture's dimensions was listed in the Grosvenor Gallery 1966 catalogue, all Ayrton's sculpture records date it in 1967, so I have done the same. It appears that it should properly follow Cat. No. 596.

610. **FALSE PHOENIX**
Relief collage. May 1967. 9 x ?.
INSCRIPTIONS Signed top left. After signature: *May 1967.*
COLLECTION Private collection, London.

A sea urchin, seawater terra-cotta, fish bones, and bird bones comprise the relief elements in this collage (notes on a conversation with the artist, 26 August 1972).

611. **FLIGHT OF GULLS**
Relief collage with wood and bone on board. 1967. 16 x 20.
INSCRIPTIONS Signed bottom right, in white. After signature: *67.*
COLLECTION Private collection, Milan.

612. **THE BIRD IN BONE**
Relief collage. 1967. 16 x 20.
INSCRIPTIONS Signed bottom right. Bottom left: *May. 1967.*
COLLECTION Unknown.

613. **MINOTAUR RISING I** (Figure 153)
Bronze. 1967. 6 x 6 x 5-1/2. Edition of 9.
COLLECTIONS Lord and Lady Beaumont of Whitley; private collections, Southfield, MI, Chicago, London, Essex, Cambridge, and Bristol.
EXHIBITIONS Sears Vincent Price Gallery 1969, no. 16*; Reading Museum Art Gallery 1969, no. 38* (dated 1968; Collection "Lord and Lady Beaumont of Whitley"); Hamet Gallery 1970, no. 9*; Sears Vincent Price Gallery 1970, no. 2* (dated 1968); Magdalene Street Gallery 1972, no. 11*; Maze and Minotaur Tour 1973, no. 17; Hope College 1978, no. 8 (Collection "Mrs. Richard B. Cole"; R).

This bronze was the first maquette created for the Arkville *Minotaur* (Cat. No. 663).

614. **RE ENTRY** (Figure 140)
Bronze. 1967. 23 x 21 x 17. Edition of 9.
COLLECTIONS Private collections, Evanston, IL, Glenview, IL, and Chicago.
EXHIBITIONS University of Essex 1968, no. 16; Sears Vincent Price Gallery 1969, no. 13 (R); Sears Vincent Price Gallery 1970, no. 10; Daedalus I Gallery 1972, no. 12; R. S. Johnson-International Gallery 1972, no. 24 (dated 1968; R, 25); Bruton Gallery and Tour 1981, no. 65.

615. **THROUGH THE BLADE I** (Figure 141)
Bronze. 1967. 15 x 10 x 5-3/4. Edition of 9.
COLLECTIONS Private collections, Deerfield, IL, Chicago, and Yorkshire.
EXHIBITIONS University of Essex 1968, no. 15; Sears Vincent Price Gallery 1969, no. 5; Sears Vincent Price Gallery 1970, no. 20; Bruton Gallery 1981, no. 85 (T: "II").

616. **TRIPTYCH II EMERGING FIGURE** (Figure 139)
Bronze. 1967. 14-3/4 x 32 x 12. Edition of 6.
COLLECTIONS Private collections, London, Chicago, and Luxembourg.
EXHIBITIONS Grosvenor Gallery 1966, no. 23* (T; R); Seventeenth King's Lynn Festival 1967, no. 12 (T); Sears Vincent Price Gallery 1967, no. 16* (T); Sears Vincent Price Gallery 1969, no. 7 ("cast 3/9"); Sears Vincent Price Gallery 1970, no. 5; Bruton Gallery 1971, no. 19*; Magdalene Street Gallery 1972, no. 8*; R. S. Johnson-International Gallery 1972, no. 19*; Maze and Minotaur Tour 1973, no. 24; Hope College 1978, no. 7; Bruton Gallery 1981, no. 88; Austin/Desmond Fine Art 1990, no. 54 (R, 26).

617. **TRIPTYCH III EMERGING FIGURE**
Fiberglass. 1967. 22 x 50 x 18. Unique.
COLLECTION The artist's estate.
EXHIBITION University of Essex 1968, no. 14.

618. **TRIPTYCH III EMERGING FIGURE**
Bronze. 1967. 37 x 50 x 18. Edition of 3.
COLLECTION Private collection, Chicago.
EXHIBITIONS Grosvenor Gallery 1966, no. 24* (T; "Edition of 6"; R); Sears Vincent Price Gallery 1967, no. 17* (T); Sears Vincent Price Gallery 1969, no. 8 (R); Sears Vincent Price Gallery 1970, no. 6; R. S. Johnson-International Gallery 1972, no. 20 ("Edition of 9"; R, 22).
BIBLIOGRAPHY Ayrton 1962a, pl. 206.

619. **SLEEPING FIGURES**
Bronze. 1967. 2 x 12-1/2 x 9. Edition of 9.
COLLECTION Private collection, Chicago.
EXHIBITIONS Seventeenth King's Lynn Festival 1967, no. 13; Sears Vincent Price Gallery 1969, no. 22*; Hamet Gallery 1969, no. 4; Sears Vincent Price Gallery 1970, no. 9; Bruton Gallery 1971, no. 17; Magdalene Street Gallery 1971, no. 10; Daedalus I Gallery 1972, no. 14.
BIBLIOGRAPHY Hopkins 1994, 318.

620. **CURLED SLEEPING FIGURES**
Bronze. 1967. 4 x 10 x 9-1/2. Edition of 9.
COLLECTIONS Private collections, London and Chicago.
EXHIBITIONS Seventeenth King's Lynn Festival 1967, no. 14; Sears Vincent Price Gallery 1969, no. 23*; Hamet Gallery 1969, no. 5; Sears Vincent Price Gallery 1970, no. 7; Bruton Gallery 1971, no. 18; Daedalus I Gallery 1972, no. 15; Bruton Gallery and Tour 1981, no. 19 (R, 20).
BIBLIOGRAPHY Hopkins 1994, 318.

621. **WAKING FIGURES**
Bronze. 1967. 5 x 15-1/4 x 11-1/4. Edition of 9.
COLLECTIONS Lord and Lady Beaumont of Whitley; private collections, Auckland, Normal, IL, and Chicago.
EXHIBITIONS Seventeenth King's Lynn Festival 1967, no. 15; Sears Vincent Price Gallery 1969, no. 11; Reading Museum Art Gallery 1969, no. 36* (dated 1968; Collection "Lord & Lady Beaumont of Whitley"); Hamet Gallery 1969, no. 6*; Sears Vincent Price Gallery 1970, No. 8; Daedalus I Gallery 1972, no. 13; Austin/Desmond Fine Art 1990, no. 55; Austin Desmond & Phipps 1992; Beaux Arts Gallery 1993.
BIBLIOGRAPHY Hopkins 1994, 318.

622. **SUMMER DEMETER** (Figure 95)
Bronze. 1967. 5-1/2 x 16 x 10. Edition of 9.
COLLECTION Private collection, Lake Bluff, IL.
EXHIBITIONS Sears Vincent Price Gallery 1969, no. 19*; Hamet Gallery 1969, no. 7 (T); Bruton Gallery 1971, no. 16; Magdalene Street Gallery 1972, no. 8; R. S. Johnson-International Gallery 1972, no. 18 (R, 20); Bruton Gallery 1981, no. 81 (R, 46); Christopher Hull Gallery 1987; Austin/Desmond Fine Art 1990, no. 53* (R, 5); Austin Desmond & Phipps 1992; Beaux Arts Gallery 1993.
BIBLIOGRAPHY Hopkins 1994, 318.

623. **WINTER DEMETER**
Bronze. 1967. 11-1/2 x 6 x 7-1/2. Edition of 9.
COLLECTIONS Private collections, Chicago and London.
EXHIBITIONS Sears Vincent Price Gallery 1969, no. 20* (R); Hamet Gallery 1969, no. 8 (T); Bruton Gallery 1971, no. 15; Magdalene Street Gallery 1972, no. 7; Bruton Gallery and Tour 1981, no. 91; Beaux Arts Gallery 1993.
BIBLIOGRAPHY Hopkins 1994, 318.

624. **DAEDALUS, HEAD** (Figure 144)
Black ink wash. 8 September 1967. 16 x 20.
INSCRIPTIONS Signed bottom right. Below signature: *8.9.67.*
COLLECTION The artist's estate.
EXHIBITIONS University of Essex 1968, no. 29; Daedalus I Gallery 1972, no. 29; Museum of Art, Pennsylvania State University 1973, no. 39 (Collection "H. Patton and Associates"); Bruton Gallery 1981, no. 147* (R, 44).

625. **MINOTAUR RISING (STUDY FOR I)**
Black ink wash. 8 September 1967. 14 x 10.
INSCRIPTIONS Signed bottom right. Below signature: *MINOTAUR RISING.* Below annotation: *8.9.67.*
COLLECTION Private collection, London; sold via Michael Tollemache Ltd.
BIBLIOGRAPHY Tollemache 1969, no. 4* (R, 6).

626. **MINOTAUR RISING I** (Figure 152)
Black ink wash. 8 September 1967. 16 x 20.
INSCRIPTIONS Signed bottom left, in pencil. Below signature, in pen: *8.9.67.*
COLLECTION Minotaur Restaurant, London.
BIBLIOGRAPHY Ayrton 1970d, 29 (R); M. and E. Ayrton 1984, 56 (R).

627. **EMERGING FIGURE**
Black ink wash. 16 September 1967. 16 x 22.
INSCRIPTIONS Signed bottom left. Before signature: *16.9.67.*
COLLECTION Private collection, Chicago.
EXHIBITION R. S. Johnson-International Gallery 1972, no. 55 (R, 43).

628. **EMERGING FIGURE**
Pen and black ink wash. 19 September 1967. 16 x 22.
INSCRIPTIONS Signed bottom right. Below signature: *19.9.67.*
COLLECTION The artist's estate.
EXHIBITIONS ?Sears Vincent Price Gallery 1970, no. 48 ("Emerging Figure Black ink wash 12-1/2 x 22 1968"); Daedalus I Gallery 1972, no. 28; Museum of Art, Pennsylvania State University 1973, no. 37 (Collection "H. Patton and Associates").

629. **STUDY FOR ARKVILLE MINOTAUR** (Figure 149)
Pencil. 25 November 1967. 20 x 16.
INSCRIPTIONS Signed bottom right. Above signature: *25.11.67*
COLLECTION Estate of Armand G. Erpf, Arkville, NY.

630. **STUDY FOR DAEDALUS/ICARUS MATRIX**
Pencil and ink wash. 29 December 1967. 16 x 20?
INSCRIPTION Dated *29.12.67.*
COLLECTION Private collection, Chicago.

630a. **STUDY FOR DAEDALUS/ICARUS MATRIX**
Pencil and ink wash. 30 December 1967. 16 x 20?
INSCRIPTIONS Signed top right. Top left, below notation: *30.12.67.* Top left, on three lines: *Matrix—Daedalus with Icarus ascendant / rising from his shoulders. Height 8ft—base / to wingtip.* Lower left, one-third from bottom, on five lines: *Crest rising from / central plate to* [*hold (?)*—illegible on photograph of drawing] */ Icarus trajectory / must have steel / core to take strain.* Bottom left, in and up slightly from corner, on three lines: *Height 30″ to / leading edge / Length 36″.* Bottom center: *Double axe: bright bronze.* Straight above this: *cage.* Slightly to the right of center, up slightly from bottom, on three lines: *Workshop. / Tools & / inventions.*
COLLECTION Drs. Paul and Laura Mesaros, Steubenville, OH.
EXHIBITION Marietta College, Marietta, OH, Grover Hermann Fine Arts Center, February 6–March 4, 1972 ("A Personal Collection" Drs. Paul and Laura Mesaros), no. 46 (T, size).
BIBLIOGRAPHY *Marietta, Ohio, Times,* 29 January 1972, 4 (R).

631. **STUDY FOR ARKVILLE MAZE MAKER/ MINOTAUR MATRIX** (Figure 150)
Pencil and black ink wash. 2 January 1968. 20 x 16.
INSCRIPTIONS Signed bottom right. Below signature: *2.1.68.* Bottom center, on two lines: *Circular base / Turntable on Ball bearings.* Right of center, halfway up from bottom: *laquer double axe.* Right of center, just above middle: *Key Maze. laquer in declivities?*
COLLECTION Estate of Armand G. Erpf, Arkville, NY.

632. **STUDY FOR ARKVILLE MATRIX: MINOTAUR**
Pencil and black ink wash. 11 January 1968. 20 x 16.
INSCRIPTIONS Signed at right margin, one-third of distance from bottom to center. Below signature: *11.1.68.* At right margin, one-third down from top: *Umbeliacus leading up to Maze Maker.*
COLLECTION Estate of Armand G. Erpf, Arkville, NY.

633. **MINOTAUR RISEN: STUDY FOR ARKVILLE MINOTAUR**
Pencil and black ink wash. 19 February 1968. 20 x 16.
INSCRIPTIONS Signed bottom right. Below signature: *19.2.68.*
COLLECTION Estate of Armand G. Erpf, Arkville, NY.

634. **STUDY FOR ARKVILLE MATRIX: ICARUS RISING I** (Figure 151)
Black ink wash. 24 February 1968. 16 x 20.
INSCRIPTIONS Signed bottom right. Above signature: *24.2.68.*
COLLECTION Estate of Armand G. Erpf, Arkville, NY.

635. **STUDY FOR ARKVILLE MATRIX: ICARUS RISING II**
Pencil and black ink wash. 26 February 1968. 16 x 20.
INSCRIPTIONS Signed lower right. Below signature: *Icarus Rising.* Below annotation: *26.2.68.*
COLLECTION Estate of Armand G. Erpf, Arkville, NY.

636. **STUDY FOR ARKVILLE MATRIX: ICARUS RISING III**
Black ink wash. 26 February 1968. 16 x 20.
INSCRIPTIONS Signed bottom right. Above signature: *26.2.68.* Above date: *Icarus Rising—upper back.*
COLLECTION Estate of Armand G. Erpf, Arkville, NY.

637. **STUDY FOR ARKVILLE MATRIX: ICARUS RISING IV**
Pencil. 27 February 1968. 16 x 20.
INSCRIPTIONS At bottom, right of center: *27.2.68.*
COLLECTION Estate of Armand G. Erpf, Arkville, NY.

638. **DAEDALUS/ICARUS MATRIX I** (Figures 155 and 156)
Bronze maquette. 1968. 17-1/4 x 8-3/4 x 4-1/2. Edition of 9.
COLLECTION Estate of Armand G. Erpf, Arkville, NY.
EXHIBITIONS Reading Museum Art Gallery 1969, no. 42* (dated 1969); Maze and Minotaur Tour 1973, no. 25.
BIBLIOGRAPHY Tollemache 1969, no. 1* (R, 3); Ayrton 1970b, [56] (R).

639. **DAEDALUS/ICARUS MATRIX II** (Figure 157)
Bronze maquette. 1968. 18 x 9-1/4 x 10. Edition of 9.
COLLECTIONS Tel Aviv Museum; private collections, Hillsboro Beach, FL, Chicago, Steubenville, OH, Wiltshire, and unknown.
EXHIBITIONS Sears Vincent Price Gallery 1969, no. 15 (R); Reading Museum Art Gallery 1969, no. 43* (dated 1969; R, pl. 11); Sears Vincent Price Gallery 1970, no. 1 ("II" omitted); Bruton Gallery 1971, no. 22; National Book League 1971, no. 107*; Marietta College, Marietta, OH, Grover Hermann Fine Arts Center 1972, no. 26* (T); R. S. Johnson-International Gallery 1972, no. 22; Maze and Minotaur Tour 1973, no. 26 (R); Museum of Art, Pennsylvania State University 1973, no. 8 ("Collection Drs. Paul and Laura Mesaros"); Hope College 1978, no. 9; Bruton Gallery 1981, no. 22; Austin/Desmond Fine Art 1990, no. 56 (T: "II" omitted; R, 23, color).
BIBLIOGRAPHY Ayrton 1971, 293 and pl. 69.

640. **DAEDALUS/ICARUS MATRIX** (Figure 160, Plates 26 and 27)
Bronze. 1968. 93 x 46 x 50. Edition of 9.
COLLECTION Estate of Armand G. Erpf, Arkville, NY.
BIBLIOGRAPHY Ayrton 1970b, [62]* (R); Hopkins 1994, 326, 331, and 348.

This sculpture is housed in one of the two central chambers of the *Arkville Maze* (Cat. No. 673).

641. **ARKVILLE MAZE MAQUETTE** (Plate 22)
Fiberglass, with 2 miniature bronzes. 1968. 27-1/2 x 37 x 2-1/2. Edition of 9.
COLLECTION The artist's estate.
EXHIBITIONS Reading Museum Art Gallery 1969, no. 41*; Sears Vincent Price Gallery 1970, no. 4 (R); Bruton Gallery 1971, no. 23; National Book League 1971, no. 108; Magdalene Street Gallery 1972, no. 16; Maze and Minotaur Tour 1973, no. 27.
BIBLIOGRAPHY Ward 253 (R); Ayrton 1970d (R, cover); Ayrton 1971, 294 and pl. 68 (dated 1968–69).

A bronze version is mounted on the headstone of Michael Ayrton's grave at Hadstock.

642. **LAOCOÖN MAZE FIGURE** (Version I) (Figure 164)
Bronze. 1968. 8 x 10 x 4. Edition of 9.
COLLECTIONS Private collections, Oxford, Lake Forest, IL, Chicago, London, and Somerset.
EXHIBITIONS Sears Vincent Price Gallery 1969, no. 12; Reading Museum Art Gallery 1969, no. 37* (Collection "Basil Wright, Esq. and Kassim bin Said Esq."); Sears Vincent Price Gallery 1970, no. 12; Bruton Gallery 1971, no. 21; National Book League 1971, no. 106*; R. S. Johnson-International Gallery 1972, no. 23.
BIBLIOGRAPHY Tollemache 1969, no. 2 (R, 4).

For Version II, see Cat. No. 761.

643. **MINOTAUR RISING II**
Bronze. 1968. 6 x 5 x 4-1/2. Unique.
COLLECTION Estate of Armand G. Erpf, Arkville, NY; the artist's cast was sold in error to a private collector in New York.
EXHIBITION Reading Museum Art Gallery 1969, no. 39*.

This bronze was the second maquette for the *Arkville Minotaur* (Cat. No. 663).

644. **MINOTAUR RISING III** (Figure 154)
Bronze. 1968. 11-1/2 x 4 x 4. Edition of 9.
COLLECTIONS Minotaur Restaurant, London (8/9); private collections, Cambridge, Chicago, London, New York, Viterbo, Cornwall, and Somerset.
EXHIBITIONS Sears Vincent Price Gallery 1969, no. 17*; Reading Museum Art Gallery, 1969, no. 40*; Sears Vincent Price Gallery 1970, no. 3; Bruton Gallery 1971, no. 20 (R, [10]).
BIBLIOGRAPHY Tollemache 1969, no. 3* (dated 1969; R, 5).

This bronze was the final maquette created for the *Arkville Minotaur* (Cat. No. 663).

645. **KOUROS I**
Black ink wash. 6 August 1968. 16 x 20.
INSCRIPTIONS Signed bottom right. Before signature: *6.8.68.* Before date: *Kouros I.*
COLLECTION The artist's estate.
EXHIBITIONS Sears Vincent Price Gallery 1970, no. 46 ("Kouros II"); Bruton Gallery and Tour 1981, no. 156 (R, 50); Christopher Hull Gallery 1987.

646. **KOUROS II**
Charcoal. 20 July 1968. 20 x 16.
INSCRIPTIONS Signed bottom right, in pencil. Bottom left, in pencil: *20.7.68.* Lower left edge, in another hand: *Kouros II.*
COLLECTION The artist's estate.
EXHIBITION Sears Vincent Price Gallery 1970, no. 45 ("Kouros I").

It appears that the numbering in the 1970 exhibition catalogue was correct, but confusion has been created with the titles written on the drawings. The dating would require reversing these two entries, but the titles dictate the current sequence.

647. **HEAD OF THE MINOTAUR**
Sepia. 10 August 1968. 20 x 16.
INSCRIPTIONS Signed bottom right. Bottom left: *10.8.68.*
COLLECTION Minotaur Restaurant, London.
BIBLIOGRAPHY Ayrton 1970d, 30 (R); M. and E. Ayrton 1984, cover, title page, and 8 (R).

648. **GOLDEN HONEYCOMB** (Figure 148)
Gold. 1968. 4 x 2-1/2 x 4.
COLLECTION George Wooller, Auckland.
EXHIBITIONS Stowe School 1970, no. 23 (dated 1969; "Gold and Marble"); National Book League 1971, no. 110.
BIBLIOGRAPHY Ayrton 1970e, 45 (R); Ayrton 1970b, 64 (R, 65); Ayrton 1971, 294 and pl. 67; Friendly 51 (R, 51; "Little Golden Honeycomb"); Hopkins 1994, 331–33.

649. **MINOTAUR ASLEEP I**
Sepia ink wash. 18 November 1968. 20 x 16.
INSCRIPTIONS Signed lower right. Below signature: *18.11.68.*
COLLECTION Private collection, Sussex.
EXHIBITIONS Sears Vincent Price Gallery 1970, no. 47 (T: "I" omitted); Magdalene Street Gallery 1972, no. 28 (T: "I" omitted); Maze and Minotaur Tour 1973, no. 54* (R).

650. **SLEEPING FIGURES**
Pencil. 1968. 16 x 20.
COLLECTION Unknown.
EXHIBITION Sears Vincent Price Gallery 1970, no. 56.

651. **EMBRACE**
Pencil. 1968. 16 x 20.
COLLECTION Unknown.
EXHIBITION Sears Vincent Price Gallery 1970, no. 57.

652. **RISING MIST**
Acrylic. January 1969. 25 x 30.
INSCRIPTIONS Signed bottom right, well in from margin, in white. After signature: *Jan 69.*
COLLECTION Unknown.
EXHIBITIONS Reading Museum Art Gallery 1969, no. 81 (R, pl. 20); Hamet Gallery November–December 1969, no. 32.

653. **CITY UNDER STORM**
Acrylic. 1969. 25 x 30.
COLLECTION Minotaur Restaurant, London.
EXHIBITIONS Hamet Gallery November–December 1969, no. 33; National Book League 1971, no. 43 (Collection "Joseph Berkmann"; R, pl. 29).

654. **LANDSCAPE AFTER FLOOD**
Acrylic. 1969. 10 x 12.
COLLECTION The artist's estate.

655. **STREAM BED AND DOUBLE AXE**
Acrylic. 1969. 30 x 40.
COLLECTION The artist's estate.

656. **CUMAE**
Acrylic. 1969. 25 x 30.
COLLECTION The artist's estate.
EXHIBITIONS Hamet Gallery November–December 1969, no. 27 (T: "The Acropolis of Cumae II"); Museum of Art, Pennsylvania State University 1973, no. 43 (T).

657. **DEEP IN** (Figure 170)
Bronze. 1969. 12 x 19 x 14 (imbedded figure, *Return:* 5 x 9 x 3-1/2; see Cat. No. 674). Edition of 9.
COLLECTION The artist's estate.
EXHIBITIONS Hamet Gallery 1969, no. 10 (T); Sears Vincent Price Gallery 1970, no. 16; Bruton Gallery 1971, no. 25; Daedalus I Gallery 1972, no. 18; Museum of Art, Pennsylvania State University 1973, no. 15; Bruton Gallery and Tour 1981, no. 24 (R, 16).

658. **REFLEX I** (Figures 171 and 172, Plates 32 and 33)
Bronze and perspex. 1969. 16-1/2 x 26 x 11. Edition of 9.
COLLECTION The artist's estate.
EXHIBITIONS Sears Vincent Price Gallery 1970, no. 23*; Daedalus I Gallery 1972, no. 2*; R. S. Johnson-International Gallery 1972, no. 29* (R, 33); Museum of Art, Pennsylvania State University 1973, no. 13; Hope College 1978, no. 10 (R); Austin/Desmond Fine Art 1990, no. 60; Beaux Arts Gallery 1993.
BIBLIOGRAPHY Friendly 52 (R); Nyenhuis 1978a, 2–3 (R, 11).

659. **KOUROS** (Figures 180 and 181, Plate 36)
Bronze and perspex. 1969. 21-1/4 x 28-1/2 x 9. Edition of 6.
COLLECTION Private collection, Chicago.
EXHIBITIONS Sears Vincent Price Gallery 1970, no. 26 (R); R. S. Johnson-International Gallery 1972, no. 27 ("Edition of 9"; R, 31); Museum of Art, Pennsylvania State University 1973, no. 14 (R); Bruton Gallery and Tour 1981, no. 45 ("Edition of 9;" R, 50); Austin Desmond & Phipps 1992.

660. **PENETRATOR I** (Figure 162)
Bronze. 1969. 8 x 19 x 9-1/2. Edition of 9.
COLLECTION Private collection, Fort Wayne, IN.
EXHIBITIONS Sears Vincent Price Gallery 1969, no. 9*; Hamet Gallery 1969, no. 11*; Sears Vincent Price Gallery 1970, no. 13; Bruton Gallery 1971, no. 24* (R); Daedalus I Gallery 1972, no. 16; Bruton Gallery 1981, no. 61.
BIBLIOGRAPHY Hopkins 1994, 347 and 379.

661. **MAZE**
Collage. May 1969. 20 x 24.
COLLECTION The artist's estate.
EXHIBITION National Book League 1971, no. 91 (1968; T).

662. **GREEN MAZE** (Formerly, **PATH THROUGH FIELDS**)
Collage. 1965–1966 (repainted 1969). 20 x 24.
INSCRIPTIONS Signed top left. After signature: *May 1969.*
COLLECTION The artist's estate.
EXHIBITIONS Hamet Gallery November–December 1969, no. 34 (1968); Stowe School 1970, no. 12; National Book League 1971, no. 101 (R, pl. 30, no. 44); Austin/Desmond Fine Art 1990, no. 30 (R, 30, in color).

663. **ARKVILLE MINOTAUR** (Figure 159, Plate 28)
Bronze. 1968–69. 55 x 42 x 36. Plinth: 36 x 36 x 36. Edition of 3.
COLLECTIONS Arkville Maze (Estate of Armand G. Erpf, Arkville, NY; black marble plinth); Corporation of London, Postman's Park (granite plinth); private collection, Somerset (bronze plinth).
EXHIBITIONS Bruton Gallery 1971, no. 27* (dated 1969–70); Maze and Minotaur Tour 1973, no. 8.
BIBLIOGRAPHY Exhibition catalogue, Sears Vincent Price Gallery 1969 (R); Reading Museum Art Gallery 1969, pl. 12; Ayrton 1970b, [62] (T; R); Ayrton 1971, 296 and pl. 70; Patton 9 (R); Friendly 49 (R); Hopkins 1994, 326, 331, 360, 411, and between 210 and 211 (R, both plaster and bronze).

This sculpture is housed in one of the two central chambers of the *Arkville Maze* (Cat. No. 673).

664. **PENETRATOR II** (Figure 163)
Bronze. 1969. 17-1/2 x 22-1/2 x 14. Edition of 9.
COLLECTIONS Private collections, Chicago and Wilmette, IL.
EXHIBITIONS Sears Vincent Price Gallery 1969, no. 10*; Hamet Gallery 1969, no. 12*; Sears Vincent Price Gallery 1970, no. 14 (R; also detail, R, cover); Daedalus I Gallery 1972, no. 17 (R); R. S. Johnson-International Gallery 1972, no. 28 (R, 27); Maze and Minotaur Tour 1973, no. 28; Museum of Art, Pennsylvania State University 1973, no. 10; Austin/Desmond Fine Art 1990, no. 59*.
BIBLIOGRAPHY Hopkins 1994, 347 and 379.

665. **PENETRATOR III** (Figure 165)
Bronze. 1969. 8-1/2 x 15 x 7-1/4. Edition of 9.
COLLECTION The artist's estate.
EXHIBITIONS Sears Vincent Price Gallery 1970, no. 15* (dated 1970); Magdalene Street Gallery 1972, no. 13; Christopher Hull Gallery 1987.
BIBLIOGRAPHY Hopkins 1994, 379.

666. **HEADS INHABITED**
Black chalk. 5 July 1969. 14 x 10.
INSCRIPTION Bottom right: *5.7.69.*
COLLECTION Unknown.
EXHIBITION Daedalus I Gallery 1972, no. 32.

667. **DISCOVERY OF NAUTILUS** (Figure 178, Plates 34 and 35)
Bronze and perspex. 1969. 15-1/2 x 22-1/4 x 15-1/2. Edition of 9.
COLLECTIONS Private collections, Southfield, MI, and Chicago.
EXHIBITIONS Sears Vincent Price Gallery 1970, no. 25 (R); Bruton Gallery 1971, no. 33 (R); R. S. Johnson-International Gallery 1972, no. 25 (R, 29); Maze and Minotaur Tour 1973, no. 40 (R); Museum of Art, Pennsylvania State University 1973, no. 11; Hope College 1978, no. 11 (Collection "Mrs. Richard B. Cole"); Austin/Desmond Fine Art 1990, no. 58* (R, front cover, color).
BIBLIOGRAPHY Robertshaw 44 (R); Nyenhuis 1978a, 3.

668. **REFLEX II** (Figures 173 and 174)
Bronze and perspex. 1969. 13 x 18-1/2 x 10. Edition of 9.
COLLECTIONS City of Troy, MI, donated in 2000 by Kmart Corporation (formerly, S. S. Kresge Company); private collection, Chicago.
EXHIBITIONS Sears Vincent Price Gallery 1970, no. 24; R. S. Johnson-International Gallery 1972, no. 30 (R, 32); Museum of Art, Pennsylvania State University 1973, no. 12; Austin/Desmond Fine Art 1990, no. 61* (R, 5).

669. **STUDY FOR ENCOUNTER**
Pen and black chalk. 4 August 1969. 10 x 14.
INSCRIPTIONS Signed bottom left. Below signature: *4.8.69.*
COLLECTION Unknown.
EXHIBITIONS Sears Vincent Price Gallery 1970, no. 49; Daedalus I Gallery 1972, no. 30*.

670. **LANDSCAPE WITH CAST SKIN**
Collage on canvas. August 1969. 25 x 30.
INSCRIPTIONS Signed top left. After signature: *Aug '69.*
COLLECTION The artist's estate.
EXHIBITION Hamet Gallery November–December 1969, no. 39.

671. **THE LANDSCAPE OF THE PYTHONESS** (Figure 161)
Collage on canvas. September 1969. 20 x 24.
INSCRIPTIONS Signed top left. After signature: *Sept: 69.*
COLLECTION The artist's estate.
EXHIBITIONS Hamet Gallery November–December 1969, no. 37*; Stowe School 1970, no. 13; National Book League 1971, no. 92; Beaux Arts Gallery 1993.
BIBLIOGRAPHY Hopkins 1994, 287.

672. **MAZE TABLE**
Wax, bone, snake skin, acrylic, and smoke. 1969. 19 x 37 x 25. Unique.
COLLECTION The artist's estate.
EXHIBITION National Book League 1971, no. 109.

This table offers an imaginary setting for the Maze.

673. **ARKVILLE MAZE** (Figure 158, Plates 23, 24, and 25)
Brick and stone, with two central chambers, one of stucco, one with polished bronze mirrors. The former houses the *Arkville Minotaur* (Cat. No. 663), the latter the *Daedalus/Icarus Matrix* (Cat. No. 640). 1968–1970. 8 x 200 x 120 feet (approx.), surrounded by an embankment approximately 30 feet across.
COLLECTION Estate of Armand G. Erpf, Arkville, NY.
BIBLIOGRAPHY Anon. 1969, 48 (R); Anon. 1970, 512 (R); Ayrton 1970b, [62] (R); Ward 251; Friendly 50 (R, 48); Nyenhuis 1978a, 2; Hopkins 1994, 320–27.

674. **RETURN**
Bronze. 1969. 5 x 9 x 3-1/2 (figure in *Deep In:* see Cat. No. 657). Edition of 9.
COLLECTION Private collection, London.
EXHIBITIONS Sears Vincent Price Gallery 1970, no. 17; Magdalene Street Gallery 1972, no. 12.

675. **SPLIT FIGURE** (Figures 175 and 176)
Bronze. 1969. 15-3/4 x 16 x 7-1/2. Edition of 9.
COLLECTION Private collection, Chicago.
EXHIBITIONS Sears Vincent Price Gallery 1970, no. 19; R. S. Johnson-International Gallery 1972, no. 31 (R, 26).
BIBLIOGRAPHY Hopkins 1994, 347f.

676. **STUDY FOR END MAZE I** (Figure 209)
Pencil. 10 November 1969. 16 x 20.
INSCRIPTIONS Signed top right. After signature: *10.11.69.* Below date: *Study for End Maze I.*
COLLECTION The artist's estate.
EXHIBITIONS Sears Vincent Price Gallery 1970, no. 58; Daedalus I Gallery 1972, no. 31*.

The discarded horns at the base of the figure suggest that he represents the Minotaur emerging as man from the maze.

677. **THROUGH THE BLADE II** (Figure 177)
Bronze. 1969. 11 x 6 x 4. Edition of 9.
COLLECTION Private collection, Somerset.
EXHIBITION Sears Vincent Price Gallery 1970, no. 21.

678. **STUDY FOR END MAZE III**, Vers. I
Pen and black ink wash. 1970. 16 x 20.
INSCRIPTIONS Signed bottom left. After signature: *'70.* Right of date: *End Maze III.*
COLLECTION Unknown.
EXHIBITIONS ?Bruton Gallery 1971, no. 52 (T); Maze and Minotaur Tour 1973, no. 67 (T); ?Bruton Gallery and Tour 1981, no. 150* (T); Christopher Hull Gallery 1987; ?Austin Desmond & Phipps 1992.
BIBLIOGRAPHY Cannon-Brookes 1978a, 107 (no. 196; R, 109).

679. **STUDY FOR END MAZE III**, Vers. II
Pen and black ink wash. 1970. 16 x 20.
INSCRIPTIONS Signed bottom right. After signature: *'70.* At bottom, left of center: *End Maze III.*
COLLECTION Unknown.
EXHIBITIONS Sears Vincent Price Gallery 1970, no. 62 (1969; T); Daedalus I Gallery 1972, no. 37; Christopher Hull Gallery 1987.

680. **CAPTIVE** (Figure 204)
Pen and black ink wash. 17 January 1970. 16 x 20.
INSCRIPTIONS Signed bottom right, with partial retracing of surname. After signature: *17.1.1970.* Above signature and date, blurred, due to tracing with pen over pencil: *Captive.*
COLLECTION Unknown.
EXHIBITION Sears Vincent Price Gallery 1970, no. 61* (T).

681. **CAPTIVE II**
Pencil. 17 January 1970. 14 x 10.
INSCRIPTIONS Dated bottom right: *Jan 17 70.* Above and left of date: *Captive II.* Bottom middle: *Spindle.*
COLLECTION Private collection, Holland, MI.

682. **ENCOUNTER** (Figures 185, 186, 187, and 188)
Bronze and perspex. 1970. 14-3/4 x 15-1/2 x 26-1/2. Edition of 6.
COLLECTION The artist's estate.
EXHIBITIONS Sears Vincent Price Gallery 1970, no. 27 (dated 1969); Daedalus I Gallery 1972, no. 3; R. S. Johnson-International Gallery 1972, no. 26 ("Edition of 9"; dated 1969; R, 30).
BIBLIOGRAPHY Friendly 51 (dated 1969; R).

683. **CORTEX**
Pencil. 26 January 1970. 14 x 10.
INSCRIPTIONS Signed top right. Below signature: *26.1.70.* Slightly below and to right of date: *Cortex.*
COLLECTION Unknown.
EXHIBITION Daedalus I Gallery 1972, no. 36.

The metaphor of the brain is expressed in this drawing.

684. **JACKET FOR *THE MAZE MAKER*** (Bantam edition)
Black ink wash. 1970. 7 x 9.
INSCRIPTIONS Title and author's name on spine of book. Back cover: THE AUTHOR OF THIS BOOK, FINDING THE JACKET IMPOSED UPON IT BY THE PUBLISHER UNACCEPTABLE, IN THAT IT REPRESENTS A BALINESE LADY RECLINING ON A STUFFED MOOSE, HAS HERE REPLACED IT WITH A DRAWING OF HIS OWN IN WHICH THE MAZE MAKER HOLDS THE TOTEM OF THE PUBLISHER SYMBOLICALLY. FIFTY COPIES IN THIS FORM, EACH SIGNED BY THE AUTHOR, WILL BE DISTRIBUTED AS GIFTS TO HIS FRIENDS AND OTHERS. THOSE TEMPTED TO SEEK THE LADY AND THE MOOSE WILL SACRIFICE TO THEIR PRESENT CURIOSITY A FUTURE BIBLIOGRAPHICAL RARITY OF WHICH THIS COPY IS NO: [numbered and signed in ink].
COLLECTION Private collection, Holland, MI.
BIBLIOGRAPHY A portion of the front cover was reproduced, with appropriate comment, in the *Observer,* 15 March 1970.

685. **STUDY FOR PENETRATOR**
Charcoal. 1970. 16 x 20.
COLLECTION Private collection, Chicago.
EXHIBITION Sears Vincent Price Gallery 1970, no. 51 (T).

686. **STUDY FOR PENETRATOR II**, Vers. I
Pencil. 7 February 1970. 16 x 20.
INSCRIPTIONS Signed bottom left. Bottom right: *7.2.70.* Below and left of date, on two lines: *Stretched Figure. Study for Penetrator. Large Version.*
COLLECTION Private collection, Cambridge.

687. **STUDY FOR PENETRATOR II**, Vers. II
Pencil. 9 February 1970. 16 x 20.
INSCRIPTIONS Signed bottom right. Below signature: *9.2.70.* Considerably to the left of date: *Penetrator.*
COLLECTION Unknown.
EXHIBITIONS ?Sears Vincent Price Gallery 1970, no. 50* (T); ?Magdalene Street Gallery 1972, no. 30 (T); Maze and Minotaur Tour 1973, no. 65 (T).
BIBLIOGRAPHY Cannon-Brookes 1978a, 113 (T; no. 206; R, 115).

688. **END MAZE I** (Plate 30)
Bronze. 1970. 11-1/2 x 11 x 3-1/4. Edition of 9.
COLLECTION The artist's estate.
EXHIBITIONS Sears Vincent Price Gallery 1970, no. 37*; Daedalus I Gallery 1972, no. 19; Bruton Gallery 1981, no. 27; Austin/Desmond Fine Art 1990, no. 64* (R, 24); Austin Desmond & Phipps 1992; Beaux Arts Gallery 1993.
BIBLIOGRAPHY Hopkins 1994, 351f.

689. **END MAZE II** (Figure 210)
Bronze. 1970. 20-1/2 x 22 x 4-1/2. Edition of 9.
COLLECTION The artist's estate.
EXHIBITIONS Sears Vincent Price Gallery 1970, no. 38; Daedalus I Gallery 1972, no. 20 (R).
BIBLIOGRAPHY Hopkins 1994, 351f.

690. **END MAZE III** (Plate 31)
Bronze. 1970. 20-1/2 x 22 x 4-1/2. Edition of 9.
COLLECTION Exeter University.
EXHIBITIONS Sears Vincent Price Gallery 1970, no. 39 (R); Bruton Gallery 1971, no. 30*; R. S. Johnson-International Gallery 1972, no. 33 (R, 36); Maze and Minotaur Tour 1973, no. 29 (R); Bruton Gallery and Tour 1981, no. 28; Austin Desmond & Phipps 1992.
BIBLIOGRAPHY Hopkins 1994, 351f. and 412.

691. **PENETRATOR III**
Pencil. 3 March 1970. 16 x 20.
INSCRIPTIONS Bottom right: *3.3.70.* Below date: *Penetrator III.*
COLLECTION The artist's estate.
EXHIBITIONS ?Magdalene Street Gallery 1972, no. 30 ("Penetrator": it may have been Cat. No. 687, but since the bronze *Penetrator III* was in the exhibition, it is more likely that this drawing was exhibited); Daedalus I Gallery 1972, no. 39; Museum of Art, Pennsylvania State University 1973, no. 45 (Collection "H. Patton and Associates").

692. **MINOTAUR ALARMED [II]** (Fig. 211)
Pen and black ink wash. 6 March 1970. 16 x 20.
INSCRIPTIONS Signed at bottom, left of center. At bottom left: *Minotaur Alarmed.* Above annotation, in pen: *6.3.70.*
COLLECTION The artist's estate.
EXHIBITIONS Daedalus I Gallery 1972, no. 35; Museum of Art, Pennsylvania State University 1973, no. 44 (Collection "H. Patton and Associates"; R).

693. **MINOTAUR DISTRAUGHT** (Figure 212)
Pencil. 8 March 1970. 16 x 20.
INSCRIPTIONS Signed bottom left. Bottom right: *8.3.70.* Before date: *Minotaur distraught.*
COLLECTION Private collection, Oxfordshire.
EXHIBITIONS Sears Vincent Price Gallery 1970, no. 59; Magdalene Street Gallery 1972, no. 29; Maze and Minotaur Tour 1973, no. 55 (R).

694. **MINOTAUR ENRAGED**
Pen and ink wash. 1970. 16 x 20.
COLLECTION Private collection, Winnetka, IL.
EXHIBITION R. S. Johnson-International Gallery 1972, no. 57.

695. **STUDY FOR DISCOVERY OF NAUTILUS I**
Ink wash drawing. 20 March 1970. 16 x 20.
INSCRIPTIONS Signed bottom right. Below signature: *20.3.70.*
COLLECTION Private collection, Southfield, MI.
EXHIBITIONS Sears Vincent Price Gallery 1970, no. 50 (T: "I" is absent; *Study for Discovery of Nautilus II,* Cat. No. 696, is mistakenly *reproduced*); Hope College 1978, no. 21 (Collection "Mrs. Richard B. Cole").

The figure on the right is derived from a drawing by Leonardo da Vinci (notes on a conversation with the artist, 28 August 1972).

696. **STUDY FOR DISCOVERY OF NAUTILUS II**
Black ink wash. 1970. 16 x 20.
INSCRIPTIONS Signed lower left, ink over pencil, on base of planned sculpture. After signature: *71.*
COLLECTION Private collection, Bath.
EXHIBITIONS Bruton Gallery 1971, no. 51 (T: "II" omitted; R); Maze and Minotaur Tour 1973, no. 66 (T: "II" omitted).
BIBLIOGRAPHY Cannon-Brookes 1978a, 118 (no. 214; T; R, 119).

697. **STUDY FOR 'CONTAINED HEADS' I**
Black ink wash. 24 March 1970. 16 x 20.
INSCRIPTIONS Signed bottom left. After signature: *24.3.70.*
COLLECTION Private collection, Surrey.
EXHIBITIONS Sears Vincent Price Gallery 1970, no. 54 (T: "I" omitted); Bruton Gallery 1971, no. 53.
BIBLIOGRAPHY Cannon-Brookes 1978a, 119 (no. 224; R, 124).

698. **STUDY FOR CONTAINED HEADS II**
Pen and black ink wash. 27 March 1970. 10 x 14.
INSCRIPTIONS Signed bottom right. Below signature, traced over in heavy pen: *27.3.70.* Before date, in pencil: *Contained Heads.*
COLLECTION Unknown.
EXHIBITIONS Sears Vincent Price Gallery 1970, no. 55 (T: "II" omitted); Daedalus I Gallery 1972, no. 33 (T: "II" omitted).

699. **STUDY FOR CONTAINED HEADS III** (Figure 195)
Pencil and black ink wash. 27 March 1970. 16 x 20.
INSCRIPTIONS Signed bottom right. After signature: *27.3.70.* Above date: *Interior Heads.*
COLLECTION Private collection, London.

700. **CAPTIVE** (Figure 205)
Bronze. 1970. 8-1/2 x 5-1/4 x 7. Edition of 9.
COLLECTION The artist's estate.
EXHIBITIONS Sears Vincent Price Gallery 1970, no. 33; Bruton Gallery 1971, no. 28; Daedalus I Gallery 1972, no. 22; Bruton Gallery and Tour 1981, no. 11 (R, 18); Austin/Desmond Fine Art 1990, no. 62* (R, 25).
BIBLIOGRAPHY Hopkins 1994, 364.

701. **DIOSKOUROI** (Figures 182 and 183)
Bronze and perspex. 1970. 19-1/4 x 14-1/2 x 8-1/2. Edition of 9.
COLLECTIONS Private collections, Detroit, London, Toronto, and Beverly Hills, CA.
EXHIBITIONS Sears Vincent Price Gallery 1970, no. 28 (R); Bruton Gallery 1971, no. 34; Daedalus I Gallery 1972, no. 6 (R); R. S. Johnson-International Gallery 1972, no. 32 (R, 35); Bruton Gallery 1981, no. 25.
BIBLIOGRAPHY Robertshaw 44 (R); Ayrton 1973, 115–19 (R, 115 and [17]).

702. **EMERGING HEAD**
Bronze. 1970. 14-1/2 x 9-1/2 x 4-1/2. Edition of 9.
COLLECTION The artist's estate.
EXHIBITIONS Sears Vincent Price Gallery 1971, no. 32*; Bruton Gallery 1981, no. 26 (T; R, 42); Austin/Desmond Fine Art 1990, no. 63* (R, 26).

703. **GEODE** (Figures 189 and 190)
Bronze and perspex. 1970. 19-1/4 x 14-1/2 x 8-1/2. Edition of 9.
COLLECTIONS Ipswich Museum, Suffolk; private collections, Hampshire, Oxfordshire, Chicago, London, and Oxford.
EXHIBITIONS Sears Vincent Price Gallery 1970, no. 29* (R); Bruton Gallery 1971, no. 35 (R, cover); Daedalus I Gallery 1972, no. 4 (R); R. S. Johnson-International Gallery 1972, no. 35 (R, 34); Austin/Desmond Fine Art 1990, no. 66* (R, 36); Austin Desmond & Phipps 1992.
BIBLIOGRAPHY Robertshaw 44 (R).

704. **POINT OF DEPARTURE** (Figure 208, Plates 39, 40, and 41)
Bronze. 1970. 14-3/4 x 8-3/4 x 9-3/4. Edition of 9.
COLLECTIONS Private collections, Chicago and Bristol.
EXHIBITIONS Sears Vincent Price Gallery 1970, no. 35*; Maze and Minotaur Tour 1973, no. 33* (R); Bruton Gallery and Tour 1981, no. 63 (R, 58); Austin/Desmond Fine Art 1990, no. 67*.
BIBLIOGRAPHY Hopkins 1994, 353.

705. **MINOTAUR ALARMED** (Figure 213)
Bronze. 1970. 10 x 6 x 6. Edition of 9.
COLLECTIONS Private collections, Somerset, Chicago, and Wiltshire.
EXHIBITIONS Sears Vincent Price Gallery 1970, no. 41; Magdalene Street Gallery 1972, no. 14*; R. S. Johnson-International Gallery 1972, no. 36 (R, 38); Maze and Minotaur Tour 1973, no. 9 (R); Bruton Gallery 1981, no. 50.

706. **PERSONAL JANUS** (Figure 206)
Bronze. 1970. 14-1/2 x 4 x 3-1/2. Edition of 9.
COLLECTIONS Private collections, Somerset.
EXHIBITIONS Sears Vincent Price Gallery 1970, no. 36*; Maze and Minotaur Tour 1973, no. 31 (R); Bruton Gallery and Tour 1981, no. 62 (R, 58, full and detail); Christopher Hull Gallery 1987.
BIBLIOGRAPHY Friendly 47 (R, 46); Hopkins 1994, 313 and 358.

707. **CONTAINED HEADS** (Figures 196, 199, 200, and 203, Plate 44)
Bronze. 1970. 24 x 16 x 24. Edition of 9.
COLLECTION City of Troy, MI, donated in 2000 by Kmart Corporation (formerly, S. S. Kresge Company).
EXHIBITIONS Sears Vincent Price Gallery 1970, no. 34 (R); Bruton Gallery 1971, no. 29; Daedalus I Gallery 1972, no. 21 (R); Museum of Art, Pennsylvania State University 1973, no. 16; Hope College 1978, no. 12 (R, two views); Bruton Gallery 1981, no. 15* (R, 42–43, 3 details).
BIBLIOGRAPHY Exhibition catalogue, Maze and Minotaur Tour 1973 (R, "Acknowledgments" page); Nyenhuis 1978, 4 (R, 6–7); Hopkins 1994, 364.

The interior heads were given separate existence in 1972 as *Tricephalic* (Cat. No. 758). For a full discussion of these two bronzes, see chapter 7.

708. **A LYRE FOR ARIADNE**
Sepia ink wash. 6 August 1970. 16 x 20.
INSCRIPTIONS Bottom center: *8.6.1970.* Before date: *A Lyre for Ariadne.*
COLLECTION The artist's estate.
EXHIBITION Sears Vincent Price Gallery 1970, no. 53.

709. **TRANSLUCENT HEADS III**
Black ink wash. August 1970. 16 x 20.
INSCRIPTIONS Signed bottom right. After signature: *August 70.* Bottom left: *Translucent Heads III.*
COLLECTION R. S. Johnson-International Gallery.
EXHIBITIONS ?Sears Vincent Price Gallery 1970, no. 60 (T: "III" omitted); R. S. Johnson-International Gallery 1972, no. 56 (R, 28); Museum of Art, Pennsylvania State University 1973, no. 48; Bruton Gallery 1981, no. 170* (T: "III" omitted); National Museum of Wales, Penarth, and Pelter Sands Gallery 1981.

The numbering on this drawing would suggest that it should follow Cat. No. 712, but the date necessitates placing it in this sequence.

710. **HEADS REFLECTED**
Black ink wash. 29 August 1970. 16 x 20.
INSCRIPTIONS Signed bottom left. After signature: *29.8.70.*
COLLECTION The artist's estate.
EXHIBITION Daedalus I Gallery 1972, no. 40.

711. **STUDY FOR CONTAINED HEADS IV**
Black ink wash. 5 September 1970. 14 x 10.
INSCRIPTIONS Signed bottom right. Above signature: *5.9.1970.* Lower left: *Contained Heads II.*
COLLECTION Private collection, Chicago.
EXHIBITIONS R. S. Johnson-International Gallery 1972, no. 58 (T: "IV" omitted; R, 48); Museum of Art, Pennsylvania State University 1973, no. 47 ("Collection Dr. and Mrs. Robert Laff").

712. **TRANSLUCENT HEADS II**
Pen and black ink wash. 9 September 1970. 10 x 14.
INSCRIPTIONS Signed lower left. Below signature: *9.9.70.*
COLLECTION Detroit Institute of Arts.
EXHIBITION Daedalus I Gallery 1972, no. 34 (R).
BIBLIOGRAPHY Cannon-Brookes 1978a, 119 (no. 223; R, 124).

713. **MINOTAUR RISEN I**
Pencil. 10 September 1970. 8 x 5-3/4.
INSCRIPTIONS Signed bottom right. Below signature: *10.9.70.* Bottom left: *Minotaur Risen I.*
COLLECTION Private collection, Holland, MI.

714. **COMPACT ANATOMIES**
Pencil. 12 September 1970. 16 x 20.
INSCRIPTIONS Middle right: *12.9.1970.* Above date: *Compact Anatomies.*
COLLECTION The artist's estate.
EXHIBITIONS Daedalus I Gallery 1972, no. 38; Museum of Art, Pennsylvania State University 1973, no. 46 (T); Bruton Gallery 1981, no. 146* (R, 16); National Museum of Wales, Penarth, and Pelter Sands Gallery 1981; Austin Desmond & Phipps 1992.

715. **JOURNEY THROUGH THE HEAD** (Figure 197)
Collage and black ink, with gold and copper metal paint sprayed on. October 1970. 30 x 22.
INSCRIPTIONS Signed bottom right. After signature, in white: *Oct '70.*
COLLECTION R. S. Johnson-International Gallery, Chicago.
EXHIBITIONS R. S. Johnson-International Gallery 1972, no. 59 (1971; R, 49); Museum of Art, Pennsylvania State University 1973, no. 49 (1971; R); Hope College 1978, no. 22.

716. **QUEST** (Figure 191)
Bronze and perspex. 1970. 15 x 12-1/2 x 15-7/8. Edition of 9.
COLLECTION The artist's estate.
EXHIBITIONS Sears Vincent Price Gallery 1970, no. 30; Maze and Minotaur Tour 1973, no. 41.

717. **ENTRANCE** (Figures 192, 193, and 194)
Bronze and perspex. 1970. 13 x 8-1/4 x 8. Edition of 9.
COLLECTIONS Private collections, Somerset and Northfield, IL.
EXHIBITIONS Sears Vincent Price Gallery 1970, no. 31; Bruton Gallery 1971, no. 36; Daedalus I Gallery 1972, no. 5; R. S. Johnson-International Gallery 1972, no. 34 (R, 37); Bruton Gallery 1981, no. 29.

718. **THE JERUSALEM MAZE AT ARKVILLE** (Plate 29)
Brick and local granite. 1970. 26-foot octagon.
COLLECTION Estate of Armand G. Erpf, Arkville, NY.
BIBLIOGRAPHY Hopkins 1994, 350–53.

The design for this floor maze is based on the labyrinth in the Amiens Cathedral (see Matthews [59], 60, and fig. 48). This information was provided to me by Ayrton himself. Hopkins 1994, however (at 352), asserts that it was based on the Chartres Cathedral. It is conceivable that Ayrton was influenced by the floor maze in both cathedrals.

719. **EXTRICATOR I** (Figures 166, 167, and 168)
Bronze. 1970. 7-1/2 x 16 x 7-3/4. Edition of 9.
COLLECTION The artist's estate.
EXHIBITIONS Sears Vincent Price Gallery 1970, no. 43* (T: "Extricator II"); Maze and Minotaur Tour 1973, no. 32; Austin/Desmond Fine Art 1990, no. 65* (R, 25).
BIBLIOGRAPHY Hopkins 1994, 347.

The titles for EXTRICATOR I and II were inadvertently reversed in Ayrton's master sculpture record but corrected in August 1972. Hence, several exhibition catalogues reverse the titles.

720. **EXTRICATOR II** (Figure 169)
Bronze. 1970. 5-1/2 x 11 x 7-3/4. Edition of 9.
COLLECTION The artist's estate.
EXHIBITIONS Sears Vincent Price Gallery, December 1970, no. 42 (T: "Extricator I": see note to no. 719); Daedalus I Gallery 1972, no. 23 (T: "Extricator I"); Bruton Gallery 1981, no. 32.
BIBLIOGRAPHY Hopkins 1994, 347.

721. **SUN MAZE** (Plates 37 and 38)
Bronze. 1970. 16-1/2 x 12 x 4. Edition of 9.
COLLECTION The artist's estate.
EXHIBITIONS Sears Vincent Price Gallery 1970, no. 40*; R. S. Johnson-International Gallery 1972, no. 37 (R, 39); Maze and Minotaur Tour 1973, no. 30 (R); Museum of Art, Pennsylvania State University 1973, no. 17; Hope College 1978, no. 13; Bruton Gallery 1981, no. 82; Austin/Desmond Fine Art 1990, no. 68* (R, 24).
BIBLIOGRAPHY Hopkins 1994, 352f.

722. **MINOTAUR RISEN** (Figure 214)
Black ink wash. 2 January 1971. 14 x 10.
INSCRIPTIONS Signed bottom right. Below signature: *Minotaur Risen.* Below annotation: *Jan 2 '71.*
COLLECTION Private collection, St. Paul, MN.
EXHIBITION R. S. Johnson-International Gallery 1972, no. 60 (R, 46).

723. **MINOTAUR RISEN** (Figure 215, Plate 42)
Bronze. 1971. 8-3/4 x 5 x 5-1/2. Edition of 9.
COLLECTIONS Private collections, Somerset, Scotland, Surrey, Chicago, and Holland, MI.
EXHIBITIONS Bruton Gallery 1971, no. 31; Magdalene Street Gallery 1972, no. 15; R. S. Johnson-International Gallery 1972, no. 38; Maze and Minotaur Tour 1973, no. 10* (R); Bruton Gallery 1981, no. 54.

724. **ORPHEUS SEEKING**, Version II (Figure 248)
Bronze. 1971 (version I, 1957). 21-1/2 x 20 x 12. Edition of 6.
COLLECTION The artist's estate.
EXHIBITIONS Bruton Gallery 1971, no. 32; Bruton Gallery and Tour 1981, no. 60 ("Edition of 9"); Austin Desmond & Phipps 1992.

For *Version I*, see Cat. No. 35.

725. **STUDIES OF MINOTAUR AS CALF**
Pencil. 20 June 1971. 10 x 14.
INSCRIPTIONS Signed bottom left. Bottom right: *20.6.71.* Above date: *Calf Minotaur.*
COLLECTION Private collection, London.
EXHIBITION Maze and Minotaur Tour 1973, no. 56.

726–735.
MINOTAUR ETCHINGS (Figure 216)
Ten etchings. 1971. 31 x 23 (some reverse).
The edition is limited to 75 sets, all signed and numbered, with some sets reserved for the sale of single etchings. Published by Icarus Press, London.
COLLECTIONS British Museum; Salford Art Gallery, Manchester; DePree Art Gallery, Hope College.
EXHIBITIONS Bruton Gallery 1971, nos. I–X (VII, *Full Grown,* R); National Book League 1971, no. 117* (1970–1971; VI, *Risen,* R, pl. 32, no. 47; IX, *Revealed,* R, pl. 32, no. 48); Magdalene Street Gallery 1972, nos. 31–40; Daedalus I Gallery 1972, nos. I–X (VII, *Full Grown,* R); R. S. Johnson-International Gallery 1972, nos. 67–76 (VIII *Pent,* no. 74, R); Maze and Minotaur Tour 1973, nos. I–X, after no. 74 (R, all; I, *As Embryo,* and X, *Alone,* on back cover); Hope College 1978, nos. 27–37 (VI, *Risen,* no. 33, R); Lad Lane Gallery 1985 (VII, *Full Grown,* R); Christopher Hull Gallery 1987; Austin/Desmond Fine Art 1990, nos. 76–78 (VI, *Risen,* R, 38; VII, *Full Grown,* R, 37; IX, *Revealed,* R, 37); Beaux Arts Gallery 1993.
BIBLIOGRAPHY *Fuse* no. 2, Nov. 1971 ? (R), and no. 4, Nov. 1973 (R, II, *Consecrated,* 23; III, *As Calf,* 32; IV, *As Yearling,* 23; V, *Rising,* cover; IX, *Revealed,* and X, *Alone,* 42); Cannon-Brookes 1978a, 93 (no. 174; R, 98–99); M. and E. Ayrton 1984, 12 (R, *As Embryo*), 16 (R, *Consecrated*), 20 (R, *As Calf*), 24 (R, *As Yearling*), 28 (R, *Rising*), 32 (R, *Risen*), 36 (R, *Full Grown*), 40 (R, *Pent*), 44 (R, *Revealed*), and 48 (R, *Alone*); *Times Literary Supplement* November 30–December 6, 1990 (R, 1292); Hopkins 1994, 358f. and 360f.

726. **AS EMBRYO** (Figure 217)
727. **CONSECRATED** (Figure 218)
728. **AS CALF** (Figure 219)
729. **AS YEARLING** (Figure 220)
730. **RISING** (Figure 221)
731. **RISEN** (Figure 222)
732. **FULL GROWN** (Figure 223)
733. **PENT** (Figure 224)
734. **REVEALED** (Figure 225)
735. **ALONE** (Figure 226)

It is conceivable that *Revealed* (no. 734) was unconsciously inspired by Picasso's *La Fin d'un Monstre* (The End of a Monster), in which a garlanded nude woman, with a spear or arrow in her right hand, holds a mirror in her left hand directly in front of the head of a Minotaur (fig. 109, 141, in Arnheim 1974). The reclining Minotaur, himself pierced by an arrow, looks in the mirror with mouth agape at what he sees. In *Revealed*, the Minotaur likewise looks into a mirror held by a woman, as he discovers his true identity. Ayrton's woman is partially draped, and the mirror is much larger, but the confrontation certainly calls to mind Picasso's earlier drawing.

736. **SELF PORTRAIT**
Pen and black ink. 1 August 1971. 14 x 10.
INSCRIPTION Lower left: *1.8.1971.*
COLLECTION The artist's estate.
EXHIBITIONS National Book League 1971 (R, back cover); Lad Lane Gallery 1985, no. 31.

737. **KRESGE SCULPTURE: FULL PROFILE**
Pencil and black ink wash. 15 September 1971. 20 x 16.
INSCRIPTIONS Lower right, approximately midway between center and margins, at the bottom right of the shaded area representing the mirror: *Sept: 15 '71.* Considerably below date, on two lines: '*Reflective Head*' / *Kresge.* Other annotations on this working drawing include dimensions for the glass sheet (*15′ x 10′*), for the neck (*4′*) and for the base (an inset of *3 ft* and the sloping right side of *10′*). Right margin, below middle, in four lines: *Head 9′ x 6′6″. / Neck 4′. / Inner Mask 3 ft. / Depth 2 ft 9″.* Bottom right, on three lines: *Light to penetrate through neck, back of head, under cheekbone and under eyebrows.* Bottom, left of center, in three lines, with arrow extending upward through statement: *Bright bronze sheet in relief to integrate neck and base. (to top of undercut.).* Bottom left, in five lines: *Bright bronze sheet in relief to integrate spine with base.*
COLLECTION City of Troy, MI, donated in 2000 by Kmart Corporation (formerly, S. S. Kresge Company).

738. **KRESGE SCULPTURE: OUTSIDE AND INSIDE OF HEAD**
Pencil and black ink wash. 10 October 1971. 10 x 14.
INSCRIPTIONS Top right, in two lines: *KRESGE SCULPTURE PROJECT.* Below annotation: *Oct: 10 '71.* Bottom right, in two lines: *Reverse of cast half-head: mask in place. / Whites indicate spaces to admit light through to glass.* Other annotations on this working drawing include the dimensions of the head (*9 ft x 6'6"*), the chin (*Depth 2'6"*), and the height of the interior head (*3 ft.*).
COLLECTION City of Troy, MI, donated in 2000 by Kmart Corporation (formerly, S. S. Kresge Company).

739. **KRESGE SCULPTURE: OBLIQUE I**
Pencil and black ink wash. 27 October 1971. 16 x 20.
INSCRIPTIONS Bottom, right of center: *October 27 '71.* Top left: *KRESGE SCULPTURE;* slightly lower: *Oblique I.* The right half of the drawing is a sketch for the siting of the sculpture and contains numerous annotations which have meaning only in that context.
COLLECTION City of Troy, MI, donated in 2000 by Kmart Corporation (formerly, S. S. Kresge Company).
BIBLIOGRAPHY Cannon-Brookes 1978a, 119 (no. 220; T: "Study for Reflective Head"; R, 122).

740. **KRESGE SCULPTURE: MAIN OBLIQUE II** (Figure 231)
Pencil and black ink wash. 28 October 1971. 16 x 20.
INSCRIPTIONS Top right: *Oct 28 1971.* Top center, in two lines: *Main Oblique II / inner mask reflecting.* Bottom right: *Half heads facing* [:] *inner mask in profile.*
COLLECTION City of Troy, MI, donated in 2000 by Kmart Corporation (formerly, S. S. Kresge Company).
BIBLIOGRAPHY Patton, "Letters to the Editor," *Smithsonian* 1973, 18 (R: excerpt of right half, as "*Reflective Head II*"); Cannon-Brookes 1978a, 119 (no. 221; T: "Study for Reflective Head"; R, 122).

741. **REFLECTIVE HEAD I**
Bronze, or bronze and perspex. 1971. 21 x 14 x 9. Edition of 9.
COLLECTION The artist's estate.
EXHIBITIONS Daedalus I Gallery 1972, no. 7; R. S. Johnson-International Gallery 1972, no. 39.

Maquette for the sculpture commissioned by the S. S. Kresge Company (Cat. No. 772).

742. **LANDSCAPE WITH GULLS**
Black ink wash. 4 November 1971. 16 x 20.
INSCRIPTIONS Signed bottom right. After signature: *Nov 4 '71.*
COLLECTION Bruton Gallery, Somerset.

This recollective drawing, said Ayrton, recalled Crete for him, although it had been a long time since he visited there, and it is related to the many other early landscape drawings. Of this drawing he said: "I always see Talos marching around in that landscape, largely throwing rocks at ships" (notes on a conversation with the artist, 20 August 1972).

743. **REFLECTIVE HEAD II** (Figures 232 and 233, Plate 45)
Bronze. 1971. 16 x 10 x 7. Edition of 9.
COLLECTIONS City of Troy, MI, donated in 2000 by Kmart Corporation (formerly, S. S. Kresge Company); Southampton Art Gallery (5/9); private collections, Chicago, Detroit, Steubenville, OH, and South Africa.
EXHIBITIONS Daedalus I Gallery 1972, no. 8* (R, both covers); R. S. Johnson-International Gallery 1972, no. 40 (R, 41); Maze and Minotaur Tour 1973, no. 42 (R, two views); Museum of Art, Pennsylvania State University 1973, no. 18; Hope College 1978, no. 14 (Collection "Kmart Corporation"; R); Bruton Gallery 1981, no. 67 (T).
BIBLIOGRAPHY Nyenhuis 1978, 3–4 (R, 18).

Maquette chosen for the sculpture commissioned by the S. S. Kresge Company [Kmart Corporation] (Cat. No. 772).

744. **MIRRORED FIGURE I**
Bronze and perspex. 1972. 18 x 8 x 5-1/4. Edition of 9.
COLLECTIONS Private collections, London, Evanston, IL, and New York.
EXHIBITIONS R. S. Johnson-International Gallery 1972, no. 43*; Maze and Minotaur Tour 1973, no. 43 (R, 2 views); Museum of Art, Pennsylvania State University 1973, no. 22 (R).

745. **SERPENTINE FIGURE** (Figure 245)
Bronze. 1972. 4-1/2 x 6-1/2 x 4-1/2. Edition of 9.
COLLECTIONS Private collections, Detroit and London.
EXHIBITIONS Daedalus I Gallery 1972, no. 24 (R); Bruton Gallery 1981, no. 72 ("Edition of 12"); Austin Desmond & Phipps 1992 ("edition of 12").

746. **CONSTRUCTED HEADS** (Figure 234)
Pencil. 15 March 1972. 20 x 16.
INSCRIPTIONS Signed bottom right. Above signature: *15.3.72.* Above date: *Constructed Heads.*
COLLECTION The artist's estate.
EXHIBITION Christopher Hull Gallery 1987.
BIBLIOGRAPHY Cannon-Brookes 1978a, 119f. (no. 227; R, 125)

This drawing is an extension of the Kresge sculpture (notes on a conversation with the artist, 30 August 1972).

747. **REFLECTIVE HEADS** (Figure 235)
Collage and black ink, with gold and copper metal paint sprayed on. 18 March 1972. 18 x 21.
INSCRIPTIONS Signed bottom right, considerably in from margin. Above signature: *18.3.'72.*
COLLECTION R. S. Johnson-International Gallery, Chicago.
EXHIBITION R. S. Johnson-International Gallery 1972, no. 61 (R, 51).

748. **MIRROR QUERY**
Pencil. 19 March 1972. 12 x 19-3/4.
INSCRIPTIONS Signed bottom right. Below signature: *Mirror?* Below annotation: *19.3.1972.* All inscriptions are reversed, as if in a mirror.
COLLECTION Unknown.

749. **TWINS REFLECTED**
Collage and black ink, with gold and copper metal paint sprayed on. 20 March 1972. 18 x 21.
INSCRIPTIONS Signed bottom left, in from margin. After signature: *20.3.1972.* At bottom, slightly to the right of the date: *Twins Reflected.*
COLLECTION Private collection, Beverly Hills, CA.
EXHIBITION R. S. Johnson-International Gallery, no. 64 (R, 7).

750. **TRICEPHALIC** (Figure 201)
Collage and black ink, with gold and copper metal paint sprayed on. March 1972. 20 x 30.
INSCRIPTIONS Signed bottom right. Below signature: *March 72.*
COLLECTION Private collection, Miami, FL.
EXHIBITION R. S. Johnson-International Gallery 1972, no. 62 (R, 52).
BIBLIOGRAPHY Cannon-Brookes 1978a, 120 (no. 229; R, 126).

751. **L'OISEAU CHANT AVEC SES DOIGTS** (Figure 198)
Collage and black ink, with gold and copper metal paint sprayed on. March 1972. 30 x 21.
INSCRIPTIONS Signed bottom right, midway between center and margin. Below signature: *March '72.* At mid-center: *L'OISEAU CHANT AVEC SES DOIGTS.*
COLLECTION R. S. Johnson-International Gallery, Chicago.
EXHIBITIONS R. S. Johnson-International Gallery 1972, no. 63 (R, 50); Museum of Art, Pennsylvania State University 1973, no. 50; Hope College 1978, no. 23.

The title ("The bird sings with its fingers") is a quotation from Cocteau, according to Ayrton ("perhaps from *Orphée*"; notes on a conversation with the artist, August 1972), although the quotation comes from the screen play of *Orphée.* As striking in French as in English, this statement was one of a number of unusual messages Orpheus received (in the film) over an automobile radio. This collage likewise is strangely evocative, since it comprises Icarus drawings and press photographs that capture one's attention.

752. **LAOCOÖN MAZE FIGURE III**
Pencil. 7 April 1972. 14 x 20.
INSCRIPTIONS Signed bottom right. Above signature: *April 7 '72.* Below signature: *Laocoön Maze Figure III.*
COLLECTION Unknown.
EXHIBITION Christopher Hull Gallery 1987.

753. **MINOTAUR ASLEEP II** (Figure 227)
Pen and sepia ink. 21 April 1972. 14 x 20.
INSCRIPTIONS Signed lower right. Above signature: *21.4.'72.*
COLLECTION Unknown.
BIBLIOGRAPHY M. and E. Ayrton 1984, 72 (T; R).

754. **LAOCOÖN MAZE FIGURE**, vers. III
Pen and sepia ink. 23 April 1972. 14 x 18.
INSCRIPTIONS Lower right: *April 23rd '72.* Below date, on two lines, *Laocoön Maze Figure, v.III., Drawing 2.*
COLLECTION R. S. Johnson-International Gallery.
EXHIBITIONS R. S. Johnson-International Gallery 1972, no. 65; Christopher Hull Gallery 1987.

755. **LAOCOÖN MAZE FIGURE III**
Pen and sepia ink. 25 April 1972. 14 x 20.
INSCRIPTIONS Signed bottom right. At bottom center: *25.4.72.* At bottom, just left of center: *Laocoön Maze Figure III.*
COLLECTION The artist's estate.
EXHIBITION Daedalus I Gallery 1972, no. 42 (R).
BIBLIOGRAPHY Cannon-Brookes 1978a, 127 (no. 235; R, 129).

756. **ICARUS III**, Variant I (Figure 30, Plate 12)
Bronze. 1972 (original version, 1960). 67 x 19 x 24. Edition of 3.
COLLECTIONS Corporation of London, Old Change Court (nr. St. Paul's Cathedral); Royal Air Force Museum, London; National Air and Space Museum, Washington, DC.
EXHIBITION Maze and Minotaur Tour 1973, no. 23 (R).
BIBLIOGRAPHY Hopkins 1994, 411 and 413.

For original version, see Cat. No. 136.

757. **MINOTAUR SLEEPING** (Figure 228)
Bronze. 1972. 5-3/4 x 9-3/4 x 6. Edition of 9.
COLLECTIONS Private collections, Yorkshire and London.
EXHIBITIONS R. S. Johnson-International Gallery 1972, no. 42* (R, 42); Maze and Minotaur Tour 1973, no. 11 (T: "Minotaur Asleep"; "edition of 12"; R); Bruton Gallery 1981, no. 51 (T; R, 36); Christopher Hull Gallery 1987; Austin Desmond & Phipps 1992 (T); Beaux Arts Gallery 1993 (T).
BIBLIOGRAPHY Hopkins 1994, 360.

758. **TRICEPHALIC** (Figure 202)
Bronze. 1972. 24-3/4 x 9 x 9.
COLLECTION The artist's estate.
BIBLIOGRAPHY Nyenhuis 1978, 4; Hopkins 1994, 364.

This bronze was first created as the interior of *Contained Heads* (Cat. No. 707; 1970). For a full discussion of these two bronzes, see chapter 7.

759. **MINOTAUR SLEEPING—MINIATURE**
Bronze. 1972. 1-3/4 x 2-3/4 x 2. Edition of 12.
COLLECTIONS Private collections, Somerset, Surrey, Westmorland, Cumbria, and London.

760. **WAKING MINOTAUR** (Figure 229)
Pen and sepia ink. 6 May 1972. 16 x 20.
INSCRIPTIONS Signed bottom left. Bottom right: *6.5.72.* Below date: *Minotaur Waking.*
COLLECTION Private collection, Beverly Hills, CA.
EXHIBITION R. S. Johnson-International Gallery 1972, no. 66.

761. **LAOCOÖN MAZE FIGURE II** (Plate 51)
Bronze. 1972 (version I, 1968). 9-1/2 x 8-3/4 x 3-1/2. Edition of 9.
COLLECTIONS Private collections, London, Somerset, Hampshire, and Sussex.
EXHIBITION Maze and Minotaur Tour 1973, no. 34 (R).

For version I, see Cat. No. 642.

762. **CARAPACE** (Plate 43)
Bronze. 1972. 5-1/2 x 8-1/2 x 6-1/2. Edition of 12.
COLLECTIONS Royal Albert Memorial Museum and Art Gallery, Exeter, Devonshire; private collections, Somerset, London, and Detroit.
EXHIBITIONS Maze and Minotaur Tour 1973, no. 37 (R); Museum of Art, Pennsylvania State University 1973, no. 21; Bruton Gallery and Tour 1981, no. 12* (R, 16).

763. **FALCON WATCHER** (Figure 20)
Bronze. 1956–72. 85 x 26 x 14-3/4. Edition of 3.
COLLECTION The artist's estate.
EXHIBITION Bruton Gallery 1981, no. 33* (R, 39).

Figures Watching a Bird in Flight (Drawing for Sculpture) (Cat. No. 108) has been described by the artist as a drawing for the original version of this sculpture, which existed for a number of years in plaster before being modified in 1972 in preparation for casting (notes on a conversation with the artist, April 1974). That drawing, however, is dated *21.3.1960*, making it difficult to reconcile the conflicting dates of these two works.

764. **FIGURE WITH A SKEIN**, Version II
Bronze. 1972 (version I, 1963). 35 x 7-1/4 x 13. Edition of 9.
COLLECTION The artist's estate.
EXHIBITIONS Maze and Minotaur Tour 1973, no. 35* (R); Museum of Art, Pennsylvania State University 1973, no. 20* (R); Austin Desmond & Phipps 1992.
BIBLIOGRAPHY Hopkins 1994, 369.

For *Version I*, see Cat. No. 319.

765. **MINOTAUR WAKING** (Figure 230)
Bronze. 1972. 11 x 8 x 11-1/4. Edition of 12.
COLLECTIONS Southampton Art Gallery; private collections, Somerset, Cleveland, OH, Sussex, Suffolk, London, Chicago, and Wiltshire.
EXHIBITIONS Maze and Minotaur Tour 1973, no. 12 (R); Bruton Gallery and Tour 1981, no. 55 (R, 36).
BIBLIOGRAPHY Hopkins 1994, 360.

766. **TROY MAZE** (Drawing I)
Pen and dilute ink. 16 August 1972. 10 x 14.
INSCRIPTIONS Signed top left, in pencil. Bottom left, in ink: *16.8.72.* Above date, in pencil: *TROY (1).*
COLLECTION The artist's estate.
EXHIBITION Bruton Gallery 1981, no. 174*.
BIBLIOGRAPHY Cannon-Brookes 1978a, 113 (T; no. 208; R, 116).

This drawing is a full-length study of the figure ("Invader") from behind. See *Troy Maze* (Cat. No. 777) and *Invader* (Cat. No. 778).

767. **TROY MAZE** (Drawing II)
Pen and dilute ink. 17 August 1972. 10 x 14.
INSCRIPTIONS Signed top right, in pencil. Bottom right: *17.8.72.* Above date: *TROY I. TRVIA.* In outer corridor of maze design, in retroscript and in ink: *TRVIA.*
COLLECTION The artist's estate.
EXHIBITION Museum of Art, Pennsylvania State University 1973, no. 51.

This drawing reveals a "maze wall with figuration of the Tragliatella graffiti representing TROY from the wine cup in the Conservatori Museum, Rome (Etruscan 7th c. B.C.). Figure of 'Invader' looking through wall" (notes from the artist to the author, September 1972). Representations of the Etruscan wine-vase can be found in Matthews, 157–58, figs. 133–35. This book was an influential source book on mazes and labyrinths for Ayrton.

768. **BRAIN MAZE** (Drawing I)
Pen and black ink wash. 17 August 1972. 14 x 10.
INSCRIPTIONS Signed at bottom, just left of center. Below signature: *17.8.72.* Left margin, near bottom: *Brain Maze I.*
COLLECTION The artist's estate.
EXHIBITIONS Museum of Art, Pennsylvania State University 1973, no. 53 (T; R); Beaux Arts Gallery 1993.

769. **TROY MAZE** (Drawing III)
Pen and dilute ink. 19 August 1972. 16 x 20.
INSCRIPTIONS Signed top right, in ink. Bottom right, in pencil: *19.8.72.* Above date: *TROY 3.*
COLLECTION The artist's estate.
EXHIBITION Maze and Minotaur Tour 1972, no. 68 (T; R).

This drawing is a "full length study of the figure (also cast separately as 'INVADER' [Cat. No. 778]) from the front—seen against the Troy Wall" (notes from the artist to the author, September 1972).

770. **TROY MAZE** (Drawing IV)
Pen and dilute ink. 19 August 1972. 13-1/2 x 18.
INSCRIPTIONS Signed bottom right, in pencil. Before signature: *19.8.1972.* Above date: *Troy. (4).*
COLLECTION The artist's estate.
EXHIBITION Lad Lane Gallery 1985, no. 39*.

This is a drawing of the "figure seen through the wall" (notes from the artist to the author, September 1972).

771. **BRAIN MAZE** (Drawing III)
Pen and diluted ink. 19 September 1972. 10 x 14.
INSCRIPTIONS At bottom left: *Brain Maze (Drawing III).* After title, in heavy pen: *Double eye.* Bottom right: *19 9 '72.* Below date: *Walnut as brain metaphor beyond perspex.* Left margin, center: *Pierce bridge of note* [*sic:* instead of "*nose*"] *in front of frontal facing eye to let light in through perspex.* Right margin, center: *open up side of skull. To show polished brain.*
COLLECTION The artist's estate.
EXHIBITIONS Museum of Art, Pennsylvania State University 1973, no. 53 (T; R); Beaux Arts Gallery 1993.
BIBLIOGRAPHY Cannon-Brookes 1978a, 118 (no. 216; R, 120).

772. **CORPORATE HEAD** or **REFLECTIVE HEAD** (Figures 236, 237, 238, 239, Plates 46, 47, 48, and 49)
Bronze and glass. 1972. 21′6″ x 13′ x 9′6″. Edition of 3.
COLLECTION City of Troy, MI, donated in 2000 by Kmart Corporation (formerly, S. S. Kresge Company).
BIBLIOGRAPHY Patton 8 (R); Friendly 47 (R, [53], as "Reflective Head II"; dated 1971); anon. 1973, 6–7 (R, cover photograph); Nyenhuis 1978a, 3–4 (R, 13); Hopkins 1994, 364–69 and 372.

The title "Corporate Head" was evolved by the Kresge management. It was not so designated by Ayrton, who preferred the title "Reflective Head," as the maquettes were christened (notes on a conversation with the artist, 28 August 1972). In the anonymous article the sculpture is described as follows: "The symbolic head was split in two, then panels of reflective *Solarcool* Clear *Spandrelite* were inserted between the halves" (7).

773. **MAZE MUSIC** (Drawing I)
Pen, sepia ink, and red chalk. 12 October 1972. 18 x 13.
INSCRIPTIONS Signed bottom right, in pencil. Above signature: *October 12 1972.* Above date: *Maze Music (Drawing I).*
COLLECTION The artist's estate.
EXHIBITION Hope College 1978, no. 24.

774. **STUDY FOR MAZE MUSIC** (Drawing II)
Pen, sepia ink, and red chalk. October 1972. 13 x 18.
INSCRIPTIONS Signed bottom right. After signature: *Oct 30 '72.* After date, on two lines (one above signature line): *Maze Music / Study for bronze.*
COLLECTION Private collection, Devon.
EXHIBITION Maze and Minotaur Tour 1973, no. 69 (R).
BIBLIOGRAPHY Cannon-Brookes 1978a, 127 (no. 230*; R).

775. **SMOKE-MIRROR CIRCLE**
Pencil. 30 October 1972. 12 x 20.
INSCRIPTIONS Signed bottom right. Above signature: *Oct 30 '72.* Above date: *Smoke Mirror O (Drawing II).*
COLLECTION The artist's estate.
EXHIBITION Museum of Art, Pennsylvania State University 1973, no. 52 (T: "Mirror").

776. **SMOKE MIRROR CIRCLE**
Bronze and perspex. 1972. 19-1/4 x 14-1/2 x 8-1/2. Edition of 12.
COLLECTIONS Private collections, Narbeth, PA, London, and Somerset.
EXHIBITIONS Museum of Art, Pennsylvania State University 1973, no. 24* (dated 1973); Bruton Gallery 1981, no. 77; Austin/Desmond Fine Art 1990, no. 70* (R, 36).

777. **TROY MAZE** (Figures 240, 242, and 243)
Bronze. 1972. 29 x 48 x 18. Edition of 9.
COLLECTION The artist's estate.
EXHIBITIONS Maze and Minotaur Tour 1973, no. 38 (R: "photographed in plaster, exhibited in bronze"); Museum of Art, Pennsylvania State University 1973, no. 19 (R); Bruton Gallery 1981, no. 89; Austin/Desmond Fine Art 1990, no. 72 ("ed. 6"; R, 32, color, and 33 [back view]).
BIBLIOGRAPHY Lucie-Smith 1975, 77 (R); Hopkins 1994, 379f., 393, and 411.

778. **INVADER** (Figure 241)
Bronze. 1972. 16-1/2 x 21-1/2 x 8-1/2. Edition of 9.
COLLECTION Private collection, Cambridge.
EXHIBITIONS Austin Desmond & Phipps 1992 ("edition of 12"); Beaux Arts Gallery 1993.
BIBLIOGRAPHY Hopkins 1994, 379.

779. **RED THREAD** (Figure 247)
Bronze. 1972. 7-1/2 x 12-1/2 x 3-1/2. Edition of 12.
COLLECTION The artist's estate.
EXHIBITION Bruton Gallery 1981, no. 68.
BIBLIOGRAPHY Hopkins 1994, 298 and 369.

This work is a strung variation on *Minoan Landscape* (Cat. No. 42).

780. **MAZE MUSIC** (Figure 246)
Bronze. 1972. 18 x 13 x 8-1/2. Edition of 12.
COLLECTION Portsmouth City Museums.
EXHIBITIONS Maze and Minotaur Tour 1973, no. 36 (R); Bruton Gallery 1981, no. 49.
BIBLIOGRAPHY Hopkins 1994, 369.

This is a variation on *Maze Player* (Cat. No. 551).

781. **MAZE MAKER RECONSIDERED**
Pen and sepia ink wash. 27 November 1972. 16 x 20.
INSCRIPTIONS Signed bottom right. Below signature: *'72.* Bottom center: *Maze Maker reconsidered.* After annotation: *Nov: 27 72* (*7* is blurred).
COLLECTION Unknown.

782. **BRAIN MAZE** (Figures 250, 251, and 252)
Bronze and perspex. 1972. 10 x 8-3/4 x 6-1/2. Edition of 12.
COLLECTION Unknown.
EXHIBITIONS Museum of Art, Pennsylvania State University 1973, no. 23 (dated 1973); Austin/Desmond Fine Art 1990, no. 69* (R, 34).

783. **WEB** (Figure 137, Plate 50)
Bronze. 1972. 69-1/2 x 13-1/2 x 10. Edition of 9.
COLLECTION The artist's estate.
EXHIBITIONS Bruton Gallery 1981, no. 90 (dated 1971); Austin/Desmond Fine Art 1990, no. 71*; Austin Desmond & Phipps 1992.
BIBLIOGRAPHY Hopkins 1994, 369.

This sculpture is a final variant on *Cage Contingency* (Cat. No. 495) and is a strung version (letter from the artist to the author, dated 28 April 1973).

784. **TURF MAZE** (Drawing I)
Pencil. January 1973. 16 x 20.
COLLECTION Corporation of London

This is a drawing for the Corporation of London, which acquired the second cast (of three) of the *Arkville Minotaur* (Cat. No. 663). The turf maze and the Minotaur are "sited in Postman's Park, Aldersgate Street in the City of London," next to St. Botolph's Without (letter to the author from E. G. Chandler, F.R.I.B.A., F.R.T.P.I., city architect and planning officer, Corporation of London, dated 17th July, 1973).

785. **TURF MAZE** (Drawing II)
Pencil. 10 January 1973. 16 x 20.
INSCRIPTIONS Signed top left. Above signature: *10.1.'73.*
COLLECTION Corporation of London.

This drawing is a detail of the previous one (Cat. No. 784), focusing on the *Arkville Minotaur* in the center of the turf maze.

786. **BRAIN MAZE IV**
Pen, black ink, and wash. 1973. 14 x 10.
COLLECTION The artist's estate.
EXHIBITIONS Museum of Art, Pennsylvania State University 1973, no. 53 (T; R); Beaux Arts Gallery 1993.
BIBLIOGRAPHY Cannon-Brookes 1978a, 118 (no. 218; R, 121).

787. **STUDY FOR BRAIN MAZE**
Ink wash. 1973. 14 x 10.
INSCRIPTIONS Signed top left. Annotated top right: *Brain Maze*?
COLLECTION The artist's estate.
EXHIBITION Lad Lane Gallery 1985, no. 35 (R).

788. **FABRICATION**
Black chalk, pencil, and collage. 11 March 1973. 22 x 30.
INSCRIPTIONS Signed bottom right, in from margin. Below signature: *FABRICATION.* Below annotation: *11.3.'73.*
COLLECTION The artist's estate.

The proof of the book jacket for *Fabrications* comprises part of this enigmatic self-portrait.

789. **STUDY FOR WEB**
Pen, sepia ink, and red chalk. 21 April 1973. 18 x 13.
INSCRIPTIONS Signed bottom right, in pencil. Below signature: *21.4.73.* Above signature: '*Trap.*'
COLLECTION Private collection, U.S.A.
BIBLIOGRAPHY Cannon-Brookes 1978a, 127 (no. 233*; R, 128).

The original title for *Web* (Cat. No. 783) was "Trap," but the artist renamed it in 1973 (letter from Elisabeth Ayrton, dated 11 November 1973).

790. **MIRROR TWINS** (Figure 184, Plate 52)
Bronze and perspex. 1973. 16 x 9 x 8. Edition of 12.
COLLECTION Private collection, Suffolk.
EXHIBITION Bruton Gallery 1981, no. 57.

791. **MIRRORED FIGURE II**
Bronze and perspex. 1973. 15 x 8 x 5-1/4. Edition of 12.
COLLECTIONS Private collections, Falsterbo, Sweden, and London.
EXHIBITION Bruton Gallery 1981, no. 56 (R, 51, 2 views).

792. **CORD** (Figure 249, Plate 53)
Bronze and perspex. 28 June 1973. 18 x 14-1/2 x 8-3/4. Edition of 12.
COLLECTION The artist's estate.
EXHIBITIONS Bruton Gallery 1981, no. 16*; Christopher Hull Gallery 1987; Austin/Desmond Fine Art 1990, no. 73 (R, 35); Beaux Arts Gallery 1993.

793. **ICARUS FLEDGED**
Bronze. 1973. 8 x 7-1/2 x 4. Edition of 12.
COLLECTION Private collection, Somerset.
EXHIBITION Bruton Gallery 1981, no. 41.

This work is a variation on *Icarus Transformed II* (Cat. No. 217).

794. **IMPRINT**
Bronze. 1973. 12 x 7-1/8 x 5-3/8. Edition of 12.
COLLECTION The artist's estate.

795. **TREADMILL** (Figure 253)
Perspex, x-ray, and bronze. 1974. 56 x 16 x 12. Edition of 12.
COLLECTION The artist's estate.
EXHIBITIONS Bruton Gallery 1981, no. 86* (R, 56); Austin Desmond & Phipps 1992.
BIBLIOGRAPHY Hopkins 1994, 394 and between 402 and 403 (R).

796. **SEA FIGURE**
Black ink and wash over pencil. 12 August 1974. 16 x 20.
INSCRIPTIONS Signed bottom left. After signature: *12.8.74.* Bottom right: *Sea Figure.* Below title: *Extension in part of the skull, with back* [illegible].
COLLECTION Unknown.
EXHIBITION Hope College 1978, no. 25.
BIBLIOGRAPHY Cannon-Brookes 1978a, no. 101 (R, 58).

797. **CAVE I**
Pen and black ink. 1974. 15 x 12.
COLLECTION Unknown.
EXHIBITION Austin Desmond & Phipps 1992.

798. **CAVE**
Black ink wash. 30 September 1974. 11 x 14-1/2.
INSCRIPTIONS Signed bottom right. Below signature: *Cave. 30.9.74.*
COLLECTION Unknown.
EXHIBITION Bruton Gallery and Tour 1981, no. 145 (R, 48).

799. **CAVE**
Pencil. 1974. 12 x 15.
COLLECTION Unknown.
EXHIBITIONS Austin Desmond & Phipps 1992; Beaux Arts Gallery 1993.

800. **IDENTITY CARD**
Collage. 31 October 1974. 21 x 29.
INSCRIPTIONS Signed bottom left. Above signature: *IDENTITY CARD.* After signature: *31.10.74.*
COLLECTION Unknown.
EXHIBITIONS Bruton Gallery 1981, no. 154 (R, 57); National Museum of Wales, Penarth, and Pelter Sands Gallery 1981.
BIBLIOGRAPHY Hopkins 1994, 398f.

801. **SEA FIGURE**
Bronze. 1974. 6 x 5 x 17-1/2. Edition of 12.
COLLECTION The artist's estate.
EXHIBITION Hope College 1978, no. 15.

This bronze is suggestive of the death of Icarus in the Icarian Sea.

802. **MASK II**
Pen and black ink wash. 21 November 1974. 16 x 20.
INSCRIPTIONS Signed at top left and dated and titled below signature: *21.11.74/Mask II.*
COLLECTION The artist's estate.
EXHIBITION Hope College 1978, no. 26.

Ayrton's identification with the Minotaur is strongly suggested here. Although not an outright self-portrait, this work clearly implies that the artist is masking—or unmasking—himself as a man within a beast or, conversely, a man struggling to control the bestial elements within himself.

803. **CAVE**
Bronze and perspex. 1974. 15-1/2 x 18 x 15. Edition of 12.
COLLECTION The artist's estate.
EXHIBITIONS Bruton Gallery and Tour 1981, no. 14 (R, 48); Austin/Desmond Fine Art 1990, no. 74* (R, 33).

804. **IMPACT**
Bronze. 1974. 13 x 9-1/2 x 8-3/4. Edition of 12.
COLLECTION The artist's estate.
EXHIBITION Bruton Gallery and Tour 1981, no. 44 (R, 60).

805. **MINOTAUR ERECT**
Sepia ink wash. 1974. 17-1/2 x 13-5/8.
COLLECTION The artist's estate.
EXHIBITION Lad Lane Gallery 1985, no. 36.

806. **REFLECTION OF FLIGHT**
Bronze. 1975. 11-1/4 x 8-3/4 x 6. Edition of 12.
COLLECTION The artist's estate.
EXHIBITIONS Bruton Gallery 1981, no. 66; Christopher Hull Gallery 1987; Austin Desmond & Phipps 1992* (dated 1974).

807. **MINOTAUR ERECT**
Bronze. 1975. 26 x 7 x 12. Edition of 12.
COLLECTION The artist's estate.
EXHIBITION Bruton Gallery and Tour 1981, no. 52* (R, 36).
BIBLIOGRAPHY Hopkins 1994, 393 and 413.

808. **STUDY FOR SUMMER DEMETER, 1975**
Black ink and wash. 27 September 1975. 16 x 20.
INSCRIPTIONS Below and right of central drawing: *27.9.75.* Above lower right sketch: *take out near this?*
COLLECTION The artist's estate.
EXHIBITION Christopher Hull Gallery 1987.

The central drawing is surrounded by about a 3-inch margin, in which are sketches on the right and below. Colors are brown, reddish, and black tones. The nude sentinel figure, wearing a Greek-style helmet, is seated on a high stool, with hands crossed over membra privata.

809. **MINOTAUR SURPRISED**

Pen, black ink, and black wash. 10 October 1975. 20 x 16.

INSCRIPTIONS Signed lower left. Above signature, in heavy pen: *10.10.'75.*

COLLECTION The artist's estate.

BIBLIOGRAPHY Cannon-Brookes 1978a, no. 167 (R, 95).

810. **STUDY FOR 'WINTER DEMETER,' 1975**

Black ink wash. 20 October 1975. 15-1/2 x 19-1/2.

INSCRIPTIONS Below and right of central drawing: *20.10.'75.* Annotation, on four lines: *sieve resin on for skybite/Double biting time / coarser texture—longer bite / Tap plate?*

COLLECTION The artist's estate.

EXHIBITION Christopher Hull Gallery 1987.

The central drawing is surrounded by about a 3-inch margin, in which there is a sketch (head and torso, from left) on the lower right, along with notations.

811. **MASK III**

Sepia, pen, and wash. 27 October 1975. 19-1/2 x 14.

INSCRIPTIONS Dated lower right. Above date: *Mask III.*

COLLECTION Unknown.

EXHIBITION Bruton Gallery and Tour 1981, no. 159 (R, 59).

BIBLIOGRAPHY Hopkins 1994, 398f.

812. **MASK**

Pencil. 30 October 1975. 14 x 10.

INSCRIPTIONS Dated at middle: *30.10.75.*

COLLECTION The artist's estate.

BIBLIOGRAPHY Hopkins 1994, 398f.

This is a fitting final drawing. It shows Ayrton's head with the mask of the Minotaur removed.

Appendix A:
Principal Exhibitions and Collections

PART I. EXHIBITIONS CITED IN THE CATALOGUE

Note: The numbers at the left correspond to the numbering in Ayrton's Master Record Book (M.R.B.), which ends in 1970 with entry No. 219, although he listed several exhibitions in 1971 and 1972 without numbers. The exhibitions included in the following list (except for my lettered insertions and those with an asterisk) were underlined in the M.R.B. by Ayrton and generally appear in the list of principal exhibitions.

When Ayrton did not number an exhibition, I have recorded it with a lower case a, b, or c following the numbered exhibition preceding it. The exhibitions so designated also usually appear in his list of principal exhibitions found in later catalogues; I have used the catalogue of the "Maze and Minotaur" touring exhibition (1973) as my guide in this matter. From 1970 onward, the numbering is my own sequence, continuing from the last number in the M.R.B., based upon my best knowledge of the sequence of his exhibitions after that time. The statements in quotations at the end of certain entries come directly from the M.R.B.

1942

20. *Leicester Galleries, London* (October). Paintings, drawings, and designs for *Macbeth.* Two-man exhibition with John Minton. "23 works & 8 with J. M."

1943

26. *Redfern Gallery, London* (July): "The Temptation of St. Anthony" and preliminary studies. Paintings and drawings. Solo exhibition. "14 gouaches & drawings."

1945

39. *Redfern Gallery, London* (January). Paintings and drawings. Solo exhibition. "33 pictures."

1946

50. *Roland Browse & Delbanco Gallery, London* (January–February). Drawings. Solo exhibition. "Drawings. (17)."

57. *Arts Council, London, and on tour* (August 1946–January 1947): "Four Young Painters." "6 oils."

1947

59. *Redfern Gallery, London* (March). Paintings and designs for *The Fairy Queen.* Solo exhibition. "25 paintings, also Fairy Queen designs."

1948

73. *Hanover Gallery, London* (September–October): "Italian Journey." Paintings. Solo exhibition. "Italian Studies. 20 small oils."

1949

79. *Redfern Gallery, London* (31 May–25 June). Paintings and drawings. Solo exhibition. Catalogue introduction by Wyndham Lewis. "19 paintings 13 drawings."

81–84. *Wakefield City Art Gallery* (August–September); *Harrogate Art Gallery* (September–October); *Bankfield Museum, Halifax* (October–November); *Ferens Art Gallery, Hull* (November 1949–January 1950). Paintings, drawings, illustrations, and theater designs. Retrospective. 48 paintings, 32 drawings, 143 book illustrations for 8 books, and 36 theater designs for 7 productions. Solo exhibition. Introductory catalogue essays by Wyndham Lewis, Philip Hendy, and Constant Lambert.

1950

92. *Galleria Il Milione, Milan* (April). Paintings and drawings. Solo exhibition.

93. *Galleria dell' Obelisco, Rome* (May). Paintings and drawings. Solo exhibition. Introductory catalogue essay by Leonardo Borgese.

98. *City Art Gallery, Leeds* (November–December): "Fifteen [Six?] Painters." Paintings. "Six paintings & six drawings (six painters)."

1951

102. *Heffer Gallery, Cambridge* (January). Drawings. Solo exhibition. "The Shepherd & 14 drawings."

104. *Galerie Orell Füssli, Zürich* (April–May). Drawings. Solo exhibition. "30 drawings & lithographs."

104a. *New Burlington Galleries, London* (May?): "60 Paintings for 1951."

105. *Redfern Gallery, London* (29 May–23 June). Paintings and drawings. Solo exhibition. "18 oils 17 drawings" [but catalogue lists 19 paintings].

1952

109. *Arts Council Gallery, Edinburgh* (January):" Six [Four?] Painters." Paintings. "6 oils (four painters)."

115. *Galerie Galanis-Hentschel, Paris* (20 May–6 June). Paintings and drawings. Solo exhibition. Catalogue preface by Sir Philip Hendy. "12 oils 6 drawings" [the exhibition catalogue lists only the oils].

119. *Redfern Gallery, London* (October). Drawings. Solo exhibition. "30 drawings 6 lithographs."

1953

122. *Riksforbondet for Bildande Konst, Stockholm* (March et seq.). Paintings. "British Council (Sweden) 5 oils, incl. Mirror Image. Mute. Afternoon."

128. *Redfern Gallery, London* (October). Paintings. Solo exhibition. "18 oils."

130. *Tate Gallery, London, Contemporary Art Society* (November et seq.). Painting. "Children with a tortoise."

131. *Heffer Gallery, Cambridge* (November) Drawings for *Tittivulus.* Solo exhibition.

1954

132. *Foyles Gallery, London* (January–February). Drawings for *Tittivulus,* plus other drawings and lithographs. Solo exhibition.

1955

137. *Whitechapel Art Gallery, London* (September–October). Retrospective 1945–1955. Paintings, sculpture, drawings, illustrations, book jackets, and theater designs. Solo exhibition. 63 paintings, 18 sculptures, 45 drawings, 22 book illustrations for 8 books, 6 book jackets, and 18 theater designs for the *Fairy Queen.* "10-year retrospective. 173 exhibits."

137a. *Gesellschaft für Kulturelle Verbindungen mit dem Ausland, Berlin.* Graphics.

1956

*141. *Tate Gallery, London, Contemporary Art Society Exhibition* (February–March): "The Seasons." Painting. "Summer."

141a. *Ritchie Hendricks Gallery, Dublin.* Paintings.

1957

*145. *S.A.E. Manchester* (February). "Skaters, Goat, Collage."

147. *Leicester Galleries, London.* (March–April). Sculpture and drawings. Solo exhibition. "20 bronzes 20 drawings."

147a. *Grand Rapids Art Gallery, Michigan*: "Paintings and Sculpture from Two Private Collections." This exhibition included more than a dozen works by Ayrton in the private collection of the late Hollis S. Baker (notes from the artist, May 1973).

*149. *British Council Tour, Moscow* (July–August): "Aspects of Contemporary British Art." Painting. "Figures in a Red Room."

151–52.
Folio Society, London (September); *Brasenose College, Oxford* (October–November). Drawings, lithographs and sculpture. Solo exhibition. "15 drawings, 10 lithos, 8 bronzes."

1958

*153. *Whitechapel Art Gallery, London, Guggenheim Award Exhibition* (May). Painting. "Terrace at Night."

*159. *Tate Gallery, London, Contemporary Art Society Exhibition* (June–August): "The Religious Theme." Wax and bone relief. "Landscape of Cain (relief)."

161a [162]. *St. George's Gallery, London* (4–29 November). See No. 165.

1959

162. *Leicester Galleries, London* (5–25 June). Sculpture, drawings, and reliefs. 14 bronzes, 8 wax reliefs (there is a brief essay by Ayrton in the catalogue, describing the process), and 11 drawings. Solo exhibition.

163. *Redfern Gallery, London* (9 June–10 July). Paintings. Solo exhibition [but the catalogue includes not only the 22 paintings by Ayrton, but also 16 works by Vieira da Silva and 25 by Jawlensky].

165. *St. George's Gallery, London* ("April?"). Drawings and prints. Solo exhibition. "Greek Suite Lithos & Drawings." As the dates suggest, this exhibition preceded nos. 162–64. Ayrton's uncertainty about the date of this exhibition can perhaps be resolved by the brief catalogue for an exhibition which corresponds in every detail to this entry, but carries the dates of November 4–29, 1958.

166. *Stone Gallery, Newcastle* (November). Paintings and drawings. 18 paintings, 8 drawings, and 6 studies for sculpture. Solo exhibition. The dates given on the brochure are "September 17th until October 19th, 1959," so there is a disparity between it and Ayrton's M.R.B.

1960

167. *Folio Society, London* (January). Drawings. Solo exhibition.

168. *King Street Gallery, Cambridge* (February). Paintings, reliefs, bronzes, and drawings. Solo exhibition.

*169. *Northampton Art Gallery* (March): "Art Alive." Bronzes, reliefs, and painting. "1 relief, three bronzes, 1 painting."

170. *Main Street Gallery, Chicago* (23 May–20 June). Bronzes and drawings. Solo exhibition. A card of the exhibition announces it as Ayrton's "First One-Man Showing in America" and lists 16 bronzes.

1961

*171. *Brooklyn Museum, New York* (January et seq.): "Contemporary Drawings." Drawings. "2 landscapes."

172. *Victoria and Albert Museum, London: Society of Mural Painting* (January): "Mural Art Today." Painting. "Icarus Falls relief, Icarus Falls II oil, Tour [i.e., included in touring exhibition]."

*173. *Reid Gallery, London* (September). "Contemporary drawings." "3 drawings."

174. *Matthiesen Gallery, London* (6–28 October): "The Icarus Theme." Sculpture, paintings, and drawings. Solo exhibition. "60 works [but the catalogue lists only 49 (31 paintings, 4 drawings, and 14 bronzes)]."

*175. *John Moores, Liverpool* (November 1961–January 1962). Paintings. "Black Shore."

1962

177. *Bear Lane Gallery, Oxford* (3–28 April). Paintings. Solo exhibition [but the catalogue presents it as an exhibition shared with Edmond Kapp]. "Cycladic Landscapes 20 small oils."

181. *Gainsborough's House, Sudbury* (11–30 August). Sculpture, drawings, and lithographs. Solo exhibition. "17 lithos, 3 bronzes 8 drawings [Cretan Landscapes]."

182. *Matthiesen Gallery, London* (December). Sculpture, paintings, and drawings. Solo exhibition. "20 bronzes 20 drawings 10 paintings (retrospective) Dec. publication of sculpture book." This exhibition was somewhat hastily assembled to mark the publication of *Drawings and Sculpture* and therefore was uncatalogued (notes on conversations with the artist in 1971 and 1972).

1963

183. *Sorsbie Gallery—Munitalp Foundation, Nairobi* (March–April). Paintings. Joint exhibition with four other British artists (Lawrence Daws, Jack Smith, Keith Vaughan, and Brett Whiteley). Catalogue introduction by Alex F. Mitchell. "12 paintings." Of the twelve paintings, five were on the theme of Icarus; a brochure, "Ayrton & the theme of Icarus" (excerpted from *Testament of Daedalus*), accompanied the exhibition catalogue.

183a. *Philadelphia Museum of Art* (3 October–17 November): "Philadelphia Collects 20th Century." Sculpture and drawing.

*187. *Grosvenor Gallery, London* (November): "First Image." "Minotaur I bronze, Crow's Feather Landscape, Landscape in Smoke."

1964

*187a. *Sheffield University* (April).

188. *Grosvenor Gallery, London* (29 April–30 May). Sculpture, paintings, collages, and drawings 1962–1964. Solo exhibition. Catalogue introduction by T. G. Rosenthal. "Bronzes, paintings, drawings, collages. 80 works [25 bronzes of Minotaur, Oracle, and Talos Sequences; 22 drawings on these themes; and 33 paintings and collages]."

190. *Hilton Gallery, Athens* (2–21 October). Paintings and drawings. Solo exhibition. Catalogue introduction by Georgios P. Savvides. "50 paintings & drawings."

1965

190a. *Grosvenor Gallery, London* (9 February–11 March): "Fifty Years of Sculpture: Some Aspects 1914–1964." 4 sculptures.

*191. *Tate Gallery, London, Contemporary Art Society Exhibition* (25 February–4 April): "British Sculpture in the Sixties". Sculpture. "Mazemaker, Evolution of the Minotaur. Skein."

192. *Lidchi Gallery, Johannesburg* (April). Paintings and drawings. Solo exhibition. "55 paintings & drawings [but catalogue lists only 50]."

193. *James Goodman Gallery, Buffalo, New York* (15 May–5 June). Sculpture and drawings. Solo exhibition. "30 bronzes. 18 drawings [but the catalogue lists 31 bronzes and 11 drawings]."

195. *National Gallery of Canada* (regional tour, October 1965–July 1967). Drawings. Solo exhibition. "30 drawings (6 replaced June 66). Oct 65–May 67. June 66–July 67."

196. *Galeries Jason Teff, Quebec* (November). Drawings and prints. "10 drawings 10 lithos."

196a. *University of Sussex Art Centre.* See No. 201x.

196b. *Leeds Institute Gallery,* "Form and Image." Sculpture.

*198. *Arts Council of Great Britain,* "East Anglian artists" (December 1965–July 1966). Mixed media. Touring exhibition. "Black Shore, Delos, Earth Pectoral, Cephalon II."

1966

200. *Grosvenor Gallery, London* (7 June–2 July). Sculpture, paintings, collages, and drawings 1964–1966. Solo exhibition. "85 exhibits." Catalogue includes 24 bronzes, 33 paintings and collages, 18 drawings and monochrome collages, and an introductory essay, "Maze Maker 1966," by Ayrton. [Entry should follow No. 201x.]

201. *Mazelow Gallery, Toronto* (18 May–4 June). Sculpture and drawings 1954–1966. Solo exhibition. Catalogue includes 30 bronzes and 22 drawings, essays by Ayrton on sculpture and on Daedalus and Icarus, and an essay on Ayrton's drawings by Jim Salt.

*201x. *University of Sussex Art Centre, "Ayrton, Skelton and Cunliffe."* Sculpture (open air). The M.R.B. has two entries numbered 201, the second of which reads: "Sussex University. Crouched Minotaur. Icarus III. Bronzes. May–July 66." Although later catalogues list such an exhibition in 1965, it appears that this was the only exhibition at the University of Sussex at this time (there was another in 1972: see No. 225).

203a. *Matthiesen Gallery, London* (Christmas).

1967

203b. *Wycombe Arts Festival, Buckinghamshire* (February–March). Paintings and sculpture. Solo exhibition. Unnumbered, underlined entry on facing page in M.R.B.: "11 paintings, 6 bronzes."

204. *Gallery 81, Sudbury* (April). Drawings. Solo exhibition. "22 landscape drawings." [Should follow No. 205.]

205. *Dunfermline Arts Festival, Scotland* (March) and *Scottish Arts Council Tour:* "International Sculpture." Sculpture. "2 large bronzes (Talos & Cage Contingency) + Arts Council Tour."

206. *Seventeenth King's Lynn Festival, Norfolk* (21–29 July). Sculpture, drawings, and reliefs. Solo exhibition. 24 bronzes, 20 drawings, and 3 framed reliefs. [Should follow No. 207.]

207. *St. Catherine's College, Oxford* (June). Collages and drawings. Solo exhibition. [Should follow No. 208.]

208. *Grosvenor Gallery, London* (May). Sculpture, paintings, collages, and drawings. Solo exhibition.

209. *Whitechapel Art Gallery, London,* "The Face of Man" (November–December. Sculpture, reliefs, and drawings. [Should follow No. 210.]

210. *Sears Vincent Price Gallery, Chicago* (October–November). Sculpture, drawings, and paintings 1961–1967. Solo exhibition. 34 bronzes, 17 drawings, and 10 paintings.

1968

211. *Esther Bear Gallery, Santa Barbara, California* (14 January–18 February). Drawings. Solo exhibition.

211a. *University of Essex, Colchester* (10–23 March). Bronzes, reliefs, and drawings. Solo exhibition. 16 bronzes, 2 wax and bone reliefs, and 12 drawings. Introductory catalogue essay by Joseph Rykwert. Unnumbered but underlined entry following No. 211 in M.R.B.

211b. *Davenport Municipal Art Gallery, Iowa,* "Collectors' Finds." Sculpture and drawings.

211c. *Scottish Hellenic Society of Edinburgh.* Paintings.

211d. *Camden Art Centre, London,* "Sculpture in a Civic Setting". Sculpture.

1969

212. *Hamet Gallery, London* (4–29 March). Retrospective 1954–1966. Sculpture and drawings. Solo exhibition. 26 sculptures and 8 drawings. "Sculpture 1956–68."

212a. *Scottish Gallery of Modern Art, Edinburgh,* "British Artists 1939–49." Watercolors and drawings.

213. *Reading Museum Art Gallery* (14 June–5 July). Retrospective 1946–1969. Sculpture, paintings, collages, and drawings. Solo exhibition. 43 sculptures, 38 paintings and collages, 29 drawings, and 23 portrait drawings. Catalogue introduction by Eric J. Stanford. [Should follow No. 214.]

214. *Sears Vincent Price Gallery, Chicago* (April–May). Sculpture, paintings, and reliefs. Solo exhibition. 23 bronzes, 4 reliefs, and 6 paintings.

214a. *Leeds City Library.* Drawings.

215. *Hamet Gallery, London,* "A Debt to Hector Berlioz" (18 November–20 December). Drawings, paintings, and sculpture 1947–1969. Solo exhibition. 12 sculptures, 28 paintings, 21 drawings, and 3 costume designs. Catalogue introduction by George Steiner, notes by the artist.

1970

216. *Stowe School, Buckinghamshire* [seven artists] (30 May–30 June). Paintings and sculpture. 18 paintings and 5 sculptures. Introductory catalogue essays by T. G. Rosenthal and George Steiner (excerpted from introductions to catalogues for exhibitions at Grosvenor Gallery, 1964, and Hamet Gallery, 1969, respectively); notes by the artist.

217. *Sheffield University Fine Art Society* (July). Sculpture. "Cage Contingency." [Should follow No. 218.]

218. *London Arts Gallery, Detroit* (May–June): "Michael Ayrton: an Introduction." Sculpture and drawings.

219. *Sears Vincent Price Gallery, Chicago,* "Beyond the Maze" (5–28 December). Sculpture, reliefs, and drawings. Solo exhibition. Catalogue introduction by George Steiner. 23 drawings and 43 sculptures, including one of fiberglass and bronze and 10 reflector sculptures, of bronze and perspex. [Last numbered entry in M.R.B.]

1971

222. *Bruton Gallery, Bruton, Somerset* (9 October–6 November). Retrospective 1954–1971. Sculpture, drawings, and etchings. Solo exhibition. 36 sculptures, 14 drawings, and 10 Minotaur etchings. Catalogue introduction by George Steiner (reprinted from No. 219).

223. *National Book League, London* (December): "Word and Image I & II." Sculpture, paintings, drawings, etchings, manuscripts, page proofs, books, source materials, photographs, and radio and television scripts. Retrospective. Shared with Wyndham Lewis. Catalogue introduction by T. G. Rosenthal.

1972

224. *Magdalene Street Gallery, Cambridge* (22 February–10 March). Sculpture, drawings, and etchings. Solo exhibition. 16 sculptures, 14 drawings, and 10 Minotaur etchings.

225. *University of Sussex.* Sculpture and etchings. Solo exhibition.

226. *Daedalus I Gallery, Detroit* (28 September–28 October): "The Maze and Beyond." Retrospective 1958–1972. Sculpture, reliefs, drawings, and etchings. Solo exhibition. 24 sculptures, 4 reliefs, 18 drawings, and 10 Minotaur etchings. Catalogue introduction by Jacob E. Nyenhuis and an essay on reflector sculpture by Richard Gregory. When this show was organized, this gallery in the Detroit suburb of Brimingham was named "The Generous Critic Art Gallery," but Ayrton encouraged the owner to give it a more appropriate name, wherefore it was rechristened "Daedalus I Gallery." Although the name change was not made early enough to find its way into the announcement or the catalogue, it was effective by the time the show opened.

227. *R. S. Johnson-International Gallery, Chicago,* "The Maze" (November et seq.). Retrospective 1962–1972. Sculpture, drawings, and etchings. Solo exhibition. 43 sculptures, 23 drawings, and 10 Minotaur etchings. Catalogue introduction by David Piper.

228. *Arts Council of Great Britain* (November 1972 to June 1973). "Painting, Sculpture and Drawing in Britain 1940–49."

228a. *Ringling Museum of Art, Sarasota, Fl* (22 December 1972–21 January 1973). "Contemporary British Art from the Collection of Mrs. Jack N. Pritzker." Sculpture and painting. 2 bronzes and 4 paintings.

1973

229–233.
Portsmouth City Art Gallery (3 February–3 March); *Southampton City Art Gallery* (10 March–7 April); *Holburne Museum, Bath* (14 April–12 May); *Exeter City Art Gallery* (19 May–16 June); *Rye Art Gallery* (23 June–4 August): "Maze and Minotaur." Retrospective 1956–1972. Sculpture, drawings, and etchings. Solo touring exhibition, organized by Bruton gallery. 43 sculptures, 25 drawings and 10 Minotaur etchings.

234. *Pennsylvania State University* (6 May–17 June). Retrospective 1947–1973. Sculpture, paintings, collages, drawings, and books. Solo exhibition. 24 sculptures, 9 paintings and collages, 20 drawings (including portraits), 8 books with corresponding manuscripts and page proofs, and 4 books illustrated by Ayrton.

235. *Haverford College, Haverford, Pennsylvania* (19 October–5 November). Bronzes, reliefs, drawings, and etchings. Solo exhibition. 14 bronzes, 4 wax and bone reliefs, 19 drawings, and 8 framed Minotaur etchings (all except VII and X).

236. *David Barnett Gallery, Milwaukee, WI* (Winter 1973): "Michael Ayrton: The Maze." Retrospective 1962–1972. Sculpture, drawings, and etchings. Solo exhibition. 26 bronzes, 9 drawings, and 10 Minotaur etchings.

1974

237. *Bruton Gallery, Bruton, Somerset* (18 May–15 June). Work of the 1950s. Sculpture, paintings, and drawings. Solo exhibition. 22 sculptures, 16 paintings, and 19 drawings. Catalogue introduction by Basil Wright.

1975

238. *Holland Park, London* (22 May–9 July): "Sculpture in Holland Park 1975." Sculpture. Exhibition of figurative sculpture by 11 artists, organized by the *Illustrated London News* in conjunction with the Greater London Council. 5 bronzes, all reproduced in the catalogue.

239. *R. S. Johnson-International Gallery, Chicago* (Fall 1975). Sculpture and drawings 1972–1975. Solo exhibition. 21 sculptures and 20 drawings. Solo exhibition.

1976

240. *Print Room, Fitzwilliam Museum, Cambridge* (16 October–22 December): "Prints and Small Bronzes by Michael Ayrton (1921–1975)." Bronzes, prints, etchings, aquatints, lithographs, and drawing. Solo exhibition. 6 bronzes; 37 prints, including 16 Archilochus etchings, 5 Minotaur etchings, 8 etchings for Verlaine's *Femmes/Hombres,* 3 aquatints, 4 lithographs; and one drawing. Prefatory note on Archilochus by G. S. Kirk and excerpts from Ayrton's translation of poems by Archilochus.

1977

240–244.
City Museums and Art Gallery, Birmingham (14 January–27 February); *Mappin Art Gallery, Sheffield* (16 April–15 May); *The Manor House Museum, Ilkley (Bradford Art Gallery and Museum)* (26 May–30 June); *The Minories, Colchester* (17 July–14 August); *Museum and Art Gallery, Sunderland* (27 August–3 October): "The Compulsive Image." Sculpture, paintings, drawings, reliefs, and theater designs. Retrospective 1940–1975. Solo exhibition. Catalogue text and commentary prepared by Peter Cannon-Brookes.

245. *Bruton Gallery, Bruton, Somerset* (30 April–18 June). Graphics and related drawings, shown with a group of recent sculpture.

246. *Bruton Gallery, Bruton, Somerset* (2 July–17 September): Summer Exhibition 1977. Nineteenth- and twentieth-century artists. Drawings, graphics, and sculpture.

1978

247. *DeWitt Cultural Center Gallery, Hope College, Holland, MI* (27 February–23 March). Sculpture, drawings, etchings, paintings, and collages. Retrospective 1954–1975. Solo exhibition. 15 bronzes, 3 paintings and collages, 8 drawings, 10 Minotaur etchings, and 16 Archilochus etchings. Catalogue introduction and annotations by Jacob E. Nyenhuis.

248. *Gallery Huntly, Canberra* (15 August–12 September). Sculpture, drawings, and etchings. Solo exhibition, organized by Bruton Gallery, Bruton, Somerset.

1979

249. *Macy Darling Gallery, Washington, D.C.* (22 May–30 June). Sculpture, paintings, drawings, and graphics. Retrospective (1949–1975). Solo exhibition. 43 bronzes, 8 paintings, 26 drawings, 46 etchings.

1981

250–252.
Bruton Gallery, Bruton, Somerset (28 March–2 May); *National Museum of Wales, Turner House, Penarth, Wales* (10 May–14 June); scaled down for Clifton Arts Festival and shown at *Pelter/Sands Gallery, Bristol* (10 July–1 August): "Recurring Themes and Images." Sculpture, paintings, drawings, reliefs, etchings, and theater designs. Solo exhibition, organized by Bruton gallery. 92 bronzes, 47 paintings and collages, 4 watercolors, 6 reliefs, 27 theater designs and book illustrations, 12 portraits, 74 drawings, and 41 etchings. Catalogue introduction by Michael Le Marchant.

253–258.
Five Roses National Festival of the Arts, Grahamstown, South Africa (10–17 July). Subsequently toured South Africa (Grahamstown, Cape Town, Port Elizabeth, Johannesburg) and Zimbabwe until October 1982. Sculpture, paintings, drawings, reliefs, collages, book illustrations, and theater designs. Organized (with annotated catalogue of 114 works) by Peter Cannon-Brookes, as an offshoot of "Recurring Themes and Images."

259. *Imperial War Museum, London* (October 1981–January 1982): "Neo-Romantic Watercolours." Paintings. Ayrton and nine others.

260–262.
Artspace Touring Exhibition, Scotland; Collins Exhibition Hall, Glasgow; City Art Centre, Edinburgh; Artspace Galleries, Aberdeen (October 1981–March 1982). Retrospective 1939–1975. Sponsored by Scottish Arts Council. Sculpture, paintings, drawings, and graphics.

1982

263. *Bath Festival Contemporary Art Fair* (28–31 May). Sculpture, paintings, drawings, and graphics. Group exhibition organized by Bruton Gallery, Bruton, Somerset.

264. *Christopher Hull Gallery, London* (September). Sculpture, paintings, drawings, and graphics. Retrospective 1939–1975.

1983

265. *Hobson Gallery, Cambridge* (12 April–7 May). Sculpture, paintings, drawings, and prints 1954–1975. Solo exhibition. 23 bronzes, 2 paintings, 17 drawings, 7 lithographs, 51 etchings (including Minotaur Suite [10], Verlaine Suite [15], Archilochos Suite [16], and 5 aquatints).

266. *Thos. Agnew & Sons Ltd, London* (25 May–22 July): "The Realist Tradition: British Paintings, Watercolours, Drawings, Sculpture and Prints from 1880 to the Present Day." 175 works by 62 artists. 1 bronze and 1 landscape painting.

267. *Welsh Sculpture Trust* (4 June 1983–2 June 1984): "Sculpture in a Country Park: An outdoor exhibition in the grounds of Margam."

268–269.
Fischer Fine Art Limited, London (13 July–19 August); *National Museum of Wales, Cardiff* (27 August–25 September): "The British Neo-Romantics 1935–1950." 21 artists. 10 paintings and drawings.

270. *Galerie Barbara Eicke, Düsseldorf* (11 November–10 December). Sculpture. 28 bronzes.

1984

271. *R. S. Johnson-International Gallery, Chicago* (February): "Homage to Michael Ayrton 1921–1975." Drawings, paintings, and sculpture. Solo exhibition. 46 bronzes, 25 paintings, drawings, and etchings. Catalogue introduction by R. Stanley Johnson.

272. *Thos. Agnew & Sons Ltd, London* (21 March–19 April). Sculpture, paintings, and drawings. 44 bronzes and 32 (33) paintings and drawings. Solo exhibition. Catalogue introduction by Peter Cannon-Brookes.

273. *Beaux Arts, Bath* (22 March–13 May). Sculpture, paintings, drawings, and etchings. Solo exhibition. 26 bronzes, 11 paintings, 19 drawings, and 10 etchings.

274. *Victoria Art Gallery, Bath* (26 May–30 June): "Michael Ayrton, Mazemaker." Sculpture, paintings, reliefs, etchings, and drawings. Solo exhibition. 65 bronzes, 20 paintings, 8 wax and bone reliefs and plaster reliefs, 13 etchings, and 28 drawings.

275. *Christopher Hull Gallery, London* (3–27 October): "Ayrton's Animals." Sculpture, painting, and drawing. Solo exhibition.

1985

276. *Lad Lane Gallery, Dublin* (9 September–4 October). Sculpture, drawings, and etchings. Solo retrospective exhibition. 26 bronzes, 13 drawings, and 13 etchings.

1986

277. *Christopher Hull Gallery, London* (4–28 June): "Michael Ayrton, The Last Decade." Sculpture, Painting, and Drawing 1965–1975. Solo exhibition.

278. *Redfern Gallery, London* (14 October–26 November): "Design." Exhibition of works by 60 artists. 14 set and costume designs for film, ballet, and theater.

1987

279. *Barbican Art Gallery, London* (21 May–19 July): "A Paradise Lost: The Neo-Romantic Imagination in Britain 1935–55." Exhibition of works by 77 artists. Paintings, drawings, book jackets, and book illustrations.

280. *Christopher Hull Gallery, London* (July). Sculpture, paintings, and drawings. Retrospective 1957–1975. Solo exhibition.

281. *Chapman Gallery, London* (12 October–7 November). Paintings, drawings, and sculpture. Solo exhibition.

282. *Goldmark Gallery, Uppingham, Rutland* (11 December 1987–16 January 1988): "Michael Ayrton at the Goldmark Gallery." Sculpture, paintings, drawings, and graphics. Solo exhibition.

1988

283. *Beaux Arts Gallery, Bath* (April–May). Sculpture, paintings, and drawings.

284. *Albermarle Gallery, London* (15 June–29 July): "Nine Neo-Romantic Artists." 2 gouaches, 1 oil, 1 ink and dark wash. Organized in conjunction with the publication of Malcolm Yorke, *The Spirit of Place: Nine Neo-Romantic Artists and Their Times* (London: Constable, 1988).

1989

285. *Christopher Hull Gallery, London* (15 February–11 March). Paintings, drawings, and sculpture. Retrospective 1939–1964. Solo exhibition.

1990

286. *Austin/Desmond Fine Art, London* (December 1990–January 1991). Sculpture, Paintings, Drawings, Prints. Retrospective 1939–1975. 44 bronzes, 31 paintings and drawings, 6 etchings and aquatints. Catalogue introduction by Adrian Heath; biographical and interpretive essay by Justine Hopkins.

1992

287. *Austin Desmond & Phipps, London* (9 December 1992–14 January 1993). Sculpture, paintings, drawings, and prints. Solo exhibition. 26 bronzes, 8 paintings, 28 drawings, and 8 color lithographs. Catalogue notes by Justine Hopkins.

1993

288. *Beaux Arts Gallery, Bath* (20 September–9 October). Sculpture, paintings, drawings, prints, and etchings. Solo exhibition. 15 bronzes, 14 paintings, 12 drawings, 5 lithographs, 51 etchings (including Minotaur Suite [10], Verlaine Suite [15], Archilochos Suite [16], and 3 aquatints).

PART II. REPRESENTATION IN PUBLIC COLLECTIONS

A. **United Kingdom**

Tate Gallery, London
National Portrait Gallery, London
Victoria and Albert Museum, London
Corporation of London
Arts Council of Great Britain
British Council
British Museum
Art Gallery and Museum, Aberdeen
Museum and Art Gallery, Birmingham
City Art Gallery, Bristol
Fitzwilliam Museum, Cambridge
King's College, Cambridge
Pembroke College, Cambridge
St. Catherine's College, Cambridge
Trinity Hall, Cambridge
Education Authority, Derby
Museum and Art Gallery, Dudley
Exeter Art Gallery
Ferens Gallery, Hull
Museum and Art Gallery, Ipswich
Education Authority, Leicester
University of Liverpool
City Art Gallery, Manchester
Ashmolean, Oxford
Brasenose College, Oxford
Exeter College, Oxford
Museum and Art Gallery, Reading
Museum and Art Gallery, Salford
City Art Gallery, Southampton
Museum and Art Gallery, Southport
Museum and Art Gallery, Stoke-on-Trent, Hanley
Museum and Art Gallery, Swindon
City Art Gallery and Museum, Wakefield
City Art Gallery, York

B. **United States**

Library of the University of Texas, Austin
Museum of Fine Arts, Boston
Fogg Art Museum, Cambridge, Massachusetts (graphics collection)
Art Institute, Chicago
Detroit Institute of Arts
Library of Northwestern University, Evanston, Illinois
Wadsworth Atheneum, Hartford, Connecticut
DePree Art Gallery, Hope College, Holland, Michigan
Dartmouth College, Lebanon, New Hampshire
Museum of Modern Art, New York, New York (graphics collection)
Joslyn Art Museum, Omaha, Nebraska
Museum of Art, Philadelphia
Terre Haute Art Museum, Terre Haute, Indiana

C. **Commonwealth Countries**

National Gallery of Canada, Ottawa
Art Gallery of Ontario, Toronto
National Gallery of New South Wales, Sydney

D. **Other Countries**

La Bibliothèque Nationale, Paris
Munitalp Foundation, Nairobi
Tel Aviv Museum, Tel Aviv

Appendix B:

"Some Notes on the Form of the Arkville Maze"

PREPARED BY MICHAEL AYRTON FOR ARMAND G. ERPF
MARCH 1968

> *In antiquity the notion that everything means both itself and something else was so general and ingrained that it was taken for granted.*
>
> Joseph Rykwert, *The Idea of a Town*, Lectura Architectonica, Hilversum 1961

In antiquity the Maze was endowed with a number of different but connected symbolic functions arising from the elision, over several thousand years, of one legend with another. I have tried to explain some of these in *The Maze Maker,* but it seems to me that one or two significant factors which lie outside the book, yet are relevant to the shape and form I have designed for the Arkville project, might explain the speculations and intentions behind the models and maquettes I have made.

The obvious functions of the maze, to arrest the intruder by confusing him, to protect the centre from intrusion and to contain no less than to exclude, could be and were signified by ideograms of great simplicity at an early date: the Greek *meander* and *key* patterns are maze derivations. As such symbols of protection they were painted on walls at the entrances to houses and found their way into woven textiles, were incised on funerary urns and were heraldically displayed on coins of Knossos from the 5th to the 1st centuries B.C. Although in Roman times the archaic significance of these rituals had much decayed, they remained protective in the form of mosaic floor patterns and even entered children's games, where indeed they have remained to this day—*in pavimentis puerorumve ludicris campestribus,* as Pliny put it, or hop-scotch as we might call it. After the fall of Rome, floor mazes passed into Christian iconography and reasserted their ancient power on the floor of the naves of Chartres and other cathedrals. As linear symbols, mazes have had a long history which runs parallel, in antiquity, with both the history of their architecture and the evolution of their more elaborate forms.

The first textual reference to a maze connected with the Minoan Labyrinth occurs in Book 18 of the Iliad. It concerns a maze pattern with which, among other things, the shield of Achilles was inlaid by the bronze-smith god Hephaistos. This pattern depicted "a dancing floor like the one Daedalus designed in the spacious town of Knossos for Ariadne of the lovely locks." Homer does not refer specifically to a maze, but there are other sources from which it becomes clear that the patterns on the dancing floor of Ariadne laid out in plan the intricate manoeuvres required of the dancers imitating the mating ceremony of either the crane (the most familiar version) or the partridge. This dance involved a complicated advance towards and withdrawal from the centre by the male, in which he displayed his plumage, encircled and was circuitously and gradually drawn towards the female. The ritual function of this dance as practiced by Theseus may originally have been totemic or alternatively, but perhaps less probably, *mimesis* to ensure success in the hunt. Eustathius of Thessalonika, writing in about 1100 A.D. relates that Theseus learned Ariadne's dance from Daedalus and danced it "*to represent his passage through the labyrinth to kill the Minotaur.*" On the island of Delos, this ritual was so long maintained that Eustathius tells us that he knew an old sailor who remembered the steps, which suggests a continuing folk tradition of at least two thousand years.

What we have here is an elision of rituals or a "thing which meant itself and something else"; that is to say, a ritual devised for one purpose which comes to represent another. Two points at once arise: firstly that the only escape from the maze would be either to fly out of it, as would cranes or partridges, or to retrace one's steps, which raises the second point: the red thread of Ariadne which was unwound to lead Theseus to the centre of the maze and rewound as it guided his passage back into the outer world. The significance of this red thread surely represents death and rebirth, but I shall return to the physical symbolism of the maze, after a further reference to the connection between the labyrinth and the dance.

At this point we return to Ariadne's red thread, an umbilical symbol clearly to be identified with the process of birth and in adult life (i.e. in legend) of rebirth and salvation. It is from this metaphor that the Christian significance and therefore the survival of the maze, as a living symbol into our own time, must in some degree derive.

In consequence of these speculations, the pattern and shape of the design I have evolved for the Arkville Maze is organic rather than heraldic in form, unlike most European designed mazes during the last two thousand years. I have derived the overall shape from the models designed for the Etruscan *haruspex* and suggested, in the pattern of paths which contain within their coils the traditional seven turns or "decision points," an entrail rather than a rigidly formal or heraldic pattern.

"That in ancient belief a thing was supposed to remain itself on account of strong binding forces so that if the binding force was relaxed the thing would dissolve into its opposite" (as W. F. Jackson Knight put it in *The Cumaean Gates*) seems to me to signify, among other things, that the Minotaur must needs occupy a separate chamber from that of Daedalus and Icarus, who, in turn, must be combined into a single image. The aspiration of the Minotaur to achieve humanity is held by the binding force of the animal in him. To convey this he must be seen in solitude, for his prison is also his sanctuary. Daedalus and Icarus are bound by a further dimension of aspiration, one aspect of which is shown in the making of the maze, the other in the desire to fly upwards to escape from it. This image too must be seen as separate from the earthbound Minotaur.

A symbol of the opposition of those forces which preserve equilibrium may, I suspect, be one of the meanings of the sacred Minoan double axe called *labrys,* from which the word labyrinth may derive. This axe, images of which survive in numerous materials, from Minoan times, is also thought to represent the cycle of the waxing and waning of the moon.

At the seventh "decision point" in the Arkville Maze, the traveller will be at the haft of the axe, as it were. The two chambers or coils which lie on either hand will each contain one of two opposed forces, one in the form of the Minotaur and one in the form of Daedalus and his son. Thus "the constrictions separating death and life" will not be forgotten.

The metaphor of the maze is a pregnant one. The complexity and richness of its meanings must be contained and represented as far as possible in the Arkville Maze, for we are, after all, attempting more than *ludicris campestribus.* We are attempting to create an image in which life unwound becomes death and death unwound becomes life.

Michael Ayrton
March 1968.

Ed. Note: The quotation from Pliny (*Natural History* 36.85) may very well refer to the Troy Game performed in the Campus Martius (cf. Virgil *Aeneid* 5, chapter 7 and note 53), rather than to a game like hopscotch, as Ayrton suggests here.

Appendix C:

Additional Representations of Daedalus and Icarus in Art and Literature

CLASSICAL ANTIQUITY

A full iconographic history of Daedalus and Icarus in classical antiquity is found in my essay, "Daidalos et Ikaros," published in *Lexicon Iconographicum Mythologiae Classicae* (*LIMC*), III. Nonetheless, that catalogue contains less than half of the more than 120 known representations of the myth in classical antiquity. Included here are a number of works excluded from the main text, as well as additional details for some of the works cited briefly there.

One of the early representations of Daedalus alone bears his name in Etruscan and is closely related to the gold bulla described in chapter 3: a fourth-century cornelian scarab, with the inscription "*Taitle,*" is included in the collection of the British Museum (BM 663 = *LIMC* no. 12). On it we see Daedalus, "a beardless winged figure flying with head thrown back, and legs much bent at the knees; in r. hand adze, and in l. a frame-saw; below, waves indicated by the usual pattern."[1]

Given the popularity of the Theseus legend and the interest in his conquest of the Minotaur, it is not surprising that this feat was frequently portrayed in ancient art. As a result, in the British Museum alone one finds over twenty ancient works of art (mostly vases, but also sculpture and terra-cotta) depicting the Minotaur, usually being slain by Theseus.[2]

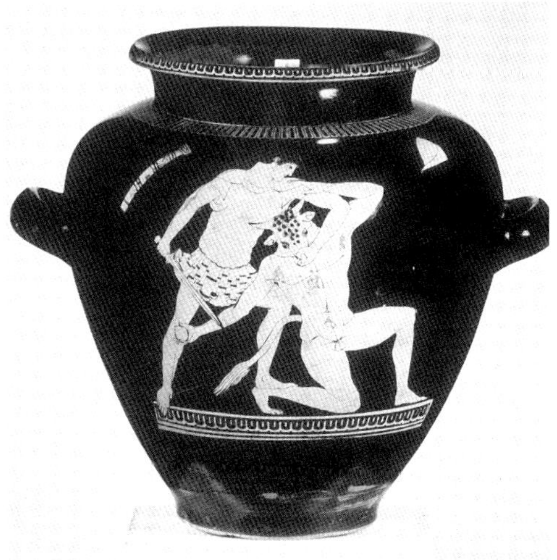

Figure 254. **THESEUS AND THE MINOTAUR**: Stamnos by Kleophrades painter (Vulci, early 5th c. B.C.E.). British Museum.

Three vases from this collection are illustrative of the treatments presented on vases. BM E 441 is a stamnos by the Kleophrades painter, dating from the early fifth century B.C.E. and found at Vulci (see Figure 254). The concise description from the British Museum catalogue tells the story depicted on the stamnos:

> Theseus, a full-grown ephebos with hair on cheek, long hair looped up behind, with the ends falling over a fillet, and short girt chiton, with sword in r. hand, has passed his l. arm around the neck of the Minotaur and grasps its muzzle in his l. hand, pulling its head round *en face*. He steps forward to r. with his l. foot on the r. shin of his opponent. The Minotaur, fleeing to r., has fallen backwards on to his r. knee; with r. he brandishes a stone, with his l. he clutches at the l. shoulder of Theseus; blood flows from wounds in the abdomen, chest and each shoulder. He has a long bull's tail. In the field hang on l. the scabbard, on r. the petasos (archaic form) of Theseus: beside him on the r. [*kalos*].[3]

BM E 304, the Nolan amphora by Oinokles, derives from the same period and site as the stamnos. In this depiction of the slaying of the Minotaur, Theseus grasps the Minotaur by the horn and is about to drive home a second thrust of the sword. A "tottering" Minotaur attempts with his right hand to push Theseus away, but the blood flowing from his wound and his lolling tongue suggest that he lacks the energy to cause any serious injury with the stone that he brandishes in his left hand.[4]

BM E 84 is a red-figure kylix by the Codrus painter, also found at Vulci but of a slightly later date, the middle of the fifth century. The slaying of the Minotaur is portrayed on its interior, as a central scene surrounded by six more of the labors of Theseus. This scene is placed "within a circle of pattern consisting of sets of three maeanders separated by chequer squares": Just as in the amphora, Theseus grasps the horn of the Minotaur, but now he does so not for the actual slaughter, but to drag the dying Minotaur out of a building (implied by a "Doric fluted column with entablature and triglyphs, forming a porch to the main building"), which conceals much of the hybrid creature's body.[5]

FOURTEENTH CENTURY

A friend and contemporary of Chaucer, John Gower, in his *Confessio amantis,* reintroduces the parallel between the amorous lover and Icarus. He uses the Ovidian account of the flight and fall of Icarus to illustrate a moral, that it is a vice for a person of high estate to go too low and for a servant to go too high. Icarus again is used as a symbol of the dangers of a lover's overconfidence.[6]

Other fourteenth-century writers offer allegorical interpretations of Ovid's *Metamorphoses,* such as Giovanni del Virgilio and Pierre Bersuire. The latter, who died in 1362, offers a more sophisticated allegory than the former. In *Ovidius Moralizatus,* Bersuire advises: "Apply it historically against those who devise labyrinths . . . or say in moral terms that Daedalus is a sinner whom Minos, i.e. the devil, shut up in a maze of the concerns and blessings of this world. . . . Set it forth if you wish as an example, applying the story to disobedient and presumptuous sons. . . . Or say that Daedalus the architect is God, who made the structure of the world, his son is any Christian."[7]

SIXTEENTH CENTURY

Among the sixteenth-century artists to treat the theme was Giulio Pippi, known as Giulio Romano (1499–1546), an apprentice to Raphael who completed Raphael's famous *Transfiguration* after Raphael's death in 1520.[8] For the Sala dei Cavalli of the Palazzo Ducale in Mantua he designed a portrayal of the *Fall of Icarus.*[9] This portrait occupies the center of the ceiling. A contorted Icarus appears to reach out toward his father, who flies on. Both figures are nude, with their wings attached by straps crisscrossing their torsos and continuing on down their arms to their wrists. The fate of the rash Icarus is accentuated and reinforced by the misfortune of another impetuous youth, Phaëthon, who is depicted plunging into darkness as Apollo's horses disappear in the opposite direction, into the bright light. This collocation of Icarus and Phaëthon calls to mind the moralizing of Horace and the juxtaposition of these two stories in the wall paintings in Pompeii (see chapter 3).

Brueghel's painting of the fall of Icarus inspired numerous poetic interpretations, but it also was copied in its own time, disseminated by means of engravings and etchings. Although Brueghel himself did engraving, he did not do his own engravings and etchings. One engraving was done by Frans Huys (1522–1562): "Man of War Sailing to the Right, with the Fall of Icarus," is from the set *Vaisseaux de Mer.*[10] The sun, not visible in the painting, is prominent in the engraving, as is Daedalus, who does not appear in Brueghel's landscape.[11] Another engraving after Brueghel was completed by Cornelis Cort (1530–1578).[12]

The last of the sixteenth-century artists to treat the myth was Hans Bol (1534–1593), who has three known representations of the fall of Icarus: a painting at the Musée Mayer Van den Bergh at Anvers; a drawing in the Kunsthalle in Hamburg; and an engraving.[13] They show the farmer, the shepherd, and the fisherman all looking up at Daedalus and Icarus in the sky. In other words, Bol corrects what he must have assumed was a simple error in Brueghel's treatment of the myth, for he makes the attitudes of these peasants fit the description in Ovid. Like Brueghel's other successors, he seems not to have understood Brueghel's intentions, so he followed his style but changed the essence of the presentation of the myth.[14]

In Hurtado de Mendoza's poem, "Pensamiento mío," there is a new dimension to the treatment of the myth of Icarus: Whereas in earlier poets consideration of the risks is followed by anticipation of the glory to be gained by taking the risks, in Mendoza the transition is from glory to defeat, and Icarus plunges into a sea of his own tears. The image of the sea of tears occurs in a number of subsequent treatments by other poets.

Not only Icarus but also Phaëthon and Prometheus are evoked as comparisons for the lover. In one of his sonnets, Mendoza substitutes the image of Phoenix: The lover flies not merely toward but even into the blazing light of his beloved's eyes, where he is consumed by the heat of their fire. In another, the lover expresses the desire "to be burned alive so that his ashes can be offered as a sacrifice on the altar of his beloved's beauty."[15] In yet another sonnet, the overpowering beauty of his beloved's golden hair draws the lover and causes him to fall, like Icarus, to destruction. The lover's ambition, however, outstrips both Icarus's and Phaëthon's, with the result that he expects his memorial to be not merely a river or a sea, but the whole world.

Also among the poets who employed the myth of Icarus in these ways was Cervantes. Like the others, he evokes Icarus with his image of the lover's ambition carried aloft by fragile wings, but unlike the others, he also alludes to the disobedience of Icarus, although he concludes his sonnet with the expectation that immortality will come to the lover through his death.

Luis de Góngora introduced a number of new elements into the treatment of the myth, such as the reduction of Icarus to a "reluctant bridegroom" and his transformation into a female, Violante,[16] and the comparison of the Italian architect Juanelo Turriano, who devised a series of locks for the Tagus River to raise it to the level of Toledo, to Icarus, implying that Juanelo's scheme was similarly ill-fated.[17]

SEVENTEENTH CENTURY

In 1567, Arthur Golding published his translation of Ovid's *Metamorphoses* in England. This translation, which included allegorical comments, was used by Shakespeare and his contemporaries. Golding's comments on the myth of Daedalus and Icarus follow the traditional view that "Daedalus showed how all men love liberty and how necessity brings forth invention, while Icarus illustrated the importance of moderation and obedience."[18] Early in the seventeenth century, however, Francis Bacon (in 1609) articulated a different view, suggesting that Icarus is the more worthy one for having aspired and fallen: "Defects are rightly considered worse than excesses. An excess has an element of magnanimity and of kinship with heaven, like a bird; whereas a defect creeps on the earth like a snake."[19] Popular views of virtue and vice were changing, allowing for the "pride of the questing intellect" to be regarded no longer as a sin and lowliness no longer as a virtue.[20] This shift was already evident in Christopher Marlowe, whose brief life was marked by the Icarian pride of the questing intellect. It also prepared the way for many of the treatments of the myth during the next three centuries.

William Shakespeare (1564–1616)

Shakespeare, like Marlowe, employed the myth of Daedalus and Icarus in his dramas, but used it only paradigmatically and allegorically. He thereby perpetuated the more common view of Icarus that prevailed before Marlowe transformed him into a symbol of the poet's aspirations. In *3 Henry VI,* for example, Icarus is allegorized as rash and presumptuous. Gloucester says to King Henry on the death of his son:

> Why, what a peevish fool was that of Crete
> That taught his son the office of the fowl!
> And yet, for all his wings, the fool was drown'd. (5.6)

King Henry develops the metaphor further, comparing himself to Daedalus, Richard Plantagenet to Minos, Plantagenet's son Edward to the sun, and Gloucester (Plantagenet's son Richard, later Richard III) to the sea:

> I, Daedalus; my poor boy, Icarus;
> Thy father, Minos, that denied our course;
> The sun that sear'd the wings of my sweet boy,
> Thy brother Edward; and thyself, the sea
> Whose envious gulf did swallow up his life.(5.6)

The image of the maze or labyrinth also appears in a number of Shakespeare's other dramas. From his use of this image, it is clear that the concept of the labyrinth had become a commonplace. Two examples will suffice to illustrate the point:

> The quaint mazes in the wanton green
> For lack of threading are undistinguishable.
> (*A Midsummer Night's Dream, 2.1*)

> Thou mayst not wander in that labyrinth;
> There minotaur and ugly treason lurk.
> (*1 Henry VI, 5.3*)

Domenichino (1581–1641)

Domenico Zampieri, a native of Bologna better known as Domenichino, was an assistant to Annibale Carracci (1560–1609). Carracci was the guiding spirit for a group of Bolognese painters who followed him to Rome, soon after his arrival there in 1595. To these painters is attributed the "establishment of classicism in early Baroque art."[21] Carracci was responsible for the decoration of the Galleria Farnese in Rome from 1597 to 1608, with assistance from his brother Agostino (1557–1602) during the first three years of the project.[22] From 1602 to 1604 Domenichino painted a series of small wall panels for the entrance wall of the Galleria Farnese, all on mythological themes.[23] The influence of Carracci is clearly evident in Domenichino's work.

The first panel depicts Daedalus and Icarus, but in a strikingly different interpretation of the myth. The fisherman in the boat and the semi-recumbent shepherd have been startled from their customary tasks, as in Ovid's account, but they have been amazed not merely by the sight of two humans in flight, but specifically and frighteningly by the fall itself. Like Brueghel a half century earlier, Domenichino was responding to the evocative power of the myth but changed it to fit his artistic vision. In his choice of subject, however, Domenichino clearly expresses the baroque spirit.

The baroque spirit or style can perhaps best be described by contrast to the style of Mannerism, which preceded it. Mannerism (ca. 1520–1600) is generally described as implying "an elegant, refined, artificial, and courtly style."[24] Baroque (roughly, seventeenth century, although some scholars extend it from 1600 to 1750), on the other hand, involves a robust naturalism, an emotive power that draws the viewer into the intensity of the feelings depicted in a painting, a "grandeur of conception" or a "bold and imaginative design," and a powerful unity in the midst of "complexity and multiplicity of parts."[25] Whereas a baroque painting or sculpture may express great emotional intensity, a Mannerist work "may appear strangely inexpressive and detached."[26] The definition of baroque, risky as it may be, varies to a considerable degree by reason of the country or the epoch under discussion. The evolution of the baroque may become evident from the small sample of Baroque representations of the myth of Daedalus and Icarus. One can observe the progression from the early baroque of Carracci and Carravaggio, with naturalism as its expression, to the High Baroque realized in the "sensuousness and colourism of Rubens," to the "third or classicistic phase, in which the opulent and emotional qualities of the 'High Baroque' were supplanted by a more rigorous order, clarity and composure," with Andrea Sacchi and Poussin as leading representatives.[27]

Carlo Saraceni Veneziano (ca. 1580–1620)[28]

During the same decade in which Domenichino completed his panels for the Galleria, another group of artists was forming around Caravaggio. Among them was Saraceni, who arrived in Rome between 1602 and 1604. He included three landscapes on the theme of Daedalus and Icarus among a series of nine mythological landscape scenes. Working in a series, Saraceni is functioning in a characteristically baroque manner, for serialization reflects the baroque love for narrative and extension. Caravaggio's innovations in the use of light in landscape painting are evident in Saraceni's landscapes, all of which are on copper (all measure ca. 16″ x 21″).[29]

In the first scene, *The Flight,* Daedalus appears to be launching his son. One observes in this scene a peculiar tangling of limbs and wings, such as one finds at times in Mannerist paintings. In *The Fall,* a new element is added to the story, giving it an undoubtedly contemporary relevance: A noble, mounted on his horse, addresses the fisherman while pointing off into the distance with his left arm; perhaps he is calling the fisherman's attention to the descent of Icarus. On the shore at the lower right are also seen two figures, shepherds among their sheep, gazing intently up into the sky, observing the tragedy. With this scene, in which the coloring is light and rather soft, Saraceni achieves considerable boldness in his landscape vision. In the final scene, *The Burial,* Saraceni uses light very effectively. The corpse of Icarus is starkly accentuated against the dark copse of trees behind the saddened father, who is partially absorbed into the shadow of the trees, even as he is shadowed by his grief. Daedalus stares upward at a bird in the sky, a reminder not only of his son's fatal imitation of birds in flight, but also of birds of prey and of the partridge, Perdix, sister of Daedalus and mother of Talos (see chapter 2).

Sir Anthony Van Dyck (1599–1641), Andrea Sacchi (1599–1661),[30] and Jakob Jordaens (1593–1678)

Sir Anthony van Dyck introduced a new theme into artistic treatments of the myth of Daedalus and Icarus. Van Dyck shifts the focus in his painting to the fastening of the wings, a theme in classical representations (see chapter 3) but a new development in modern times. Once he revivified this emphasis, many of his successors, including Andrea Sacchi and Jakob Jordaens, also turned their attention to depicting this dimension of the myth. Van Dyck became the chief assistant of Rubens, following his earlier training in Antwerp by H. van Balen. Van Dyck's fame came primarily from his portraits of the English nobility, although he also painted a number of large canvases on mythological, allegorical, and religious subjects.

Around the time of the death of Saraceni, or perhaps a bit later, Van Dyck painted his *Daedalus and Icarus.*[31] He very likely chose this mythological story primarily for its potential in terms of portraiture, for Icarus, who dominates the canvas, adopts a pose not unlike figures in other portraits. In fact, in another composition by Van Dyck on this subject, later engraved by John Watts (1778), "Icarus is a self-portrait of the artist, and is posed with his hand on his father's head."[32] There is in this portrait somewhat less of the "subtle flattery and grace of Van Dyck's portraits of Charles I," somewhat more of the fundamental naturalism and "the sense of presence imparted by the greatest portraits of the seventeenth century."[33] Because he was not painting royalty here and because this painting hints at self-portraiture, Van Dyck seems able to express more deeply the soul of his subject.

In the Palazzo Rosso in Genoa is one of two pictures by Andrea Sacchi on the subject of Daedalus binding on Icarus's wings. This large painting (5′7″ x 4′-1/8″) is stylistically similar to the Van Dyck painting. Since Van Dyck spent five years in Italy, including two sojourns in Genoa (1621–1622 and 1626–1627), it is likely that Van Dyck completed his painting in Genoa and that he either directly influenced Sacchi or they had a common source, now lost.

Daedalus fastening the wings on Icarus was also treated twice by the Flemish painter Jakob Jordaens, a native of Antwerp and fellow citizen of Van Dyck. One canvas (62″ x 46-1/2″) has nearly full-length, life-size images of father and son. Daedalus affixes the left wing on Icarus, who occupies the center of the painting and to whom attention is drawn by the red cloth draped over him. Icarus holds the other wing in his right hand as he stares up, almost expressionless, into the sky. His left hand is raised heavenward, but his eyes are turned away from the direction of his pointing index finger.

Giulio Carpioni the Elder (1613–1679) and Johann Karl Loth (1632–1698)

Giulio Carpioni, who worked mainly at Vicenza, was strongly influenced by Poussin's classicism.[34] His distinctive style emerged in the 1640s. In a small gouache (11-1/4″ x 14-3/4″), *The Death of Icarus,* Carpioni chose a subject that had been infrequently treated, since most of his predecessors focused on the flight and fall of Icarus. By focusing his attention on the ultimate end of the fall, rather than on the fall itself, Carpioni expresses a common theme of the baroque, the theme of death. Not only does this treatment set him apart from his predecessors, it also offers him a degree of freedom of expression. His interpretation of the myth includes a bit of mythmaking or artistic license: The corpse of Icarus is attended by numerous Nereids, Neptune or Triton with a trident, and two pudgy cherubs who hover above the scene.

Dedalus Mourning Icarus is a very small pen drawing (3-3/4″ x 5-1/2″) by Johan Karl Loth, a native of Munich and both son and erstwhile student of the artist Johan Ulrich Loth, who studied under Carlo Saraceni. Johan Karl worked in Venice under Pietro Liberi, painted historical pictures, and, for a time, was a portrait artist, painting pictures in Vienna of the emperor and other distinguished individuals. Consistent with baroque subject matter, a number of his works dwell on the theme of death, including *Dead Christ* and the *Death of St. Joseph.*

This pen drawing on grey paper is accented in white.[35] The color of the paper heightens the somber tone of this representation of Daedalus mourning the death of his son. Daedalus is shown hunched over in grief, his wings still intact. He pathetically extends his hand toward the lifeless corpse of his son, whose body is draped indecorously over a boulder. Attention is thus focused on an aspect of the myth generally left unexpressed: Ovid merely tells us that Daedalus

> saw the wings on the waves, and cursed his talents,
> Buried the body in a tomb, and the land
> Was named for Icarus.
> (*Metamorphoses* 8.233–35)

EIGHTEENTH CENTURY

Bernard Picart (1673–1733)

In 1731 Bernard Picart made an engraving, *Icarus Falling,* for a book, *The Temple of the Muses,* which he designed and engraved (see Figure 255). In his "Explication of the Fable," he records the version of the myth told by Pausanias, in which the flight is rationalized as an escape by ship through the use of newly invented sails. The figures in the boat may therefore be intended to recall

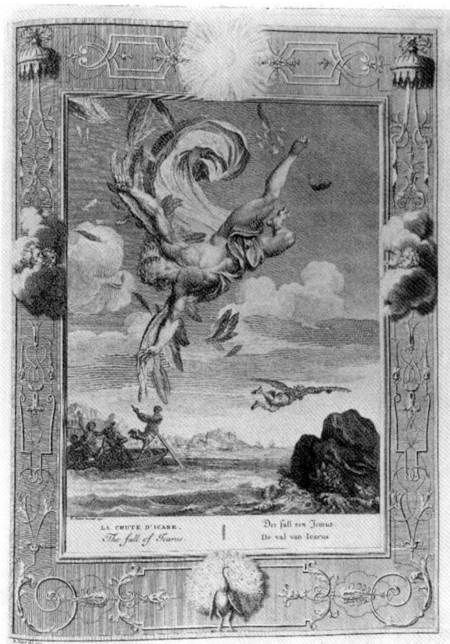

Figure 255. Bernard Picart, **ICARUS FALLING** (1731).

Minos and his comrades who pursued Daedalus, who is flying far ahead of them, gliding along apparently without effort, whereas they strain at the oars. Icarus, says Picart, did not know "how to guide his ship, was shipwracked and drowned."

Charles Paul Landon (1760–1826)

When Charles Paul Landon exhibited his *Daedalus and Icarus* at the Salon of 1799, it was "praised chiefly for its pleasant composition, the 'suavity of its colors,' and 'the fitness of its drawing and handling.' The painting is a nice little cabinet picture [54 x 44 cm.], in which the historical subject, more modest in size than usual . . . , leans more toward anecdotal description than toward the heroization which one would expect."[36]

The influence of his teacher, Jean-Baptiste Regnault (1754–1829), who frequently treated mythological subjects, is evident in this painting. In Regnault's revolutionary painting *Liberty or Death* (1794–1795), one sees at the center the Genius of France, with tri-colored wings, flying above the globe of the earth, flanked by Death on the left and the Republic, with all its symbols, on the right. The youthful figure of the Genius of France and his wings clearly must have been in the forefront of Landon's consciousness when he painted his Icarus.

Although Landon exhibited regularly at the Salon from 1791 to 1812 and won the Grand Prix in 1792, he was "better known as a man of letters than as a painter; during the 1790s, he wrote numerous reviews of works exhibited at the Salons, in which he extolled the superiority of drawing and of idealization."[37] His extensive writings are the primary and often the sole source for current knowledge of paintings exhibited at the Salons during the first quarter of the nineteenth century.

Landon's paintings included such other mythological figures as *Leda* (Salon of 1806) and *Venus* (Salon of 1810). His paintings are characterized by bright, clear colors, such as one sees in *Daedalus and Icarus,* and his subjects are usually pleasant and graceful. It is not surprising that he would therefore present an idealized scene of Daedalus launching Icarus into flight, the moment when optimism dominates. There is in this painting no hint of the risk of failure that lies ahead.

Goethe (1749–1832)

Icarus is twice evoked in Goethe's *Faust.* In *Faust I* (lines 1064ff.) the flight of Icarus is suggested when the hero expresses a longing for taking flight:

> I long to join his quest
> On tireless wings uplifted from the ground.
> Then should I see, in deathless evening-light,
> The world in cradled stillness at my feet. . . .
> Then mountains could not check my god-like flight,
> With wild ravine or savage rocky ways.[38]

The fate of Icarus is poignantly evoked in Goethe's *Faust II* (Act III, lines 1111–16), where Euphorion, the child of Faust and Helen of Troy, attempts to soar Icarus-like up into heaven in pursuit of beauty, but he falls to his death at his parents' feet, while the chorus chants "Icarus! Icarus! / Oh woeful sight!" (lines 1415f.).

It is said that as early as 1775 Goethe had already conceived the idea of employing the medieval legend of Faust's marriage to Helen and that he later considered using the legend "to symbolize the union between classical and romantic poetry. In 1825 Byron's individuality and tragic fate having supplied him with the long-sought motive for his Euphorion, the child of Helena and Faust, the type of modern poetic genius, he applied himself to the completion of the work."[39] Whereas Marlowe used Icarus as the model for his Faust, Goethe transfers the identification to Faust's son, although following Marlowe might have been more appropriate for a poet who himself emulated Icarus in many ways earlier in his career.

NINETEENTH CENTURY

Frederic, Lord Leighton (1830–1896)

In 1869, a year after the completion of several paintings on the theme of Ariadne, Frederic, Lord Leighton painted a portrait of Daedalus and Icarus (4′6″ x 3′5″), which is now in the Lord Faringdon Collection, Buscot Park, Berkshire (see Figure 256). The influence not only of Canova[40] but also of Van Dyck and his early imitators is obvious in this painting, although there are various distinctive touches. In the center of the painting, Daedalus and Icarus stand on a concrete terrace on a promontory overlooking the sea, with a range of mountains in the distance and a coastal city between the figures and the mountains.[41] On the left, behind Daedalus, a statue of Athena Promachos stands atop a lone Doric column. Icarus assumes the pose of a kouros, with his weight on his left leg, forming an s-curve, his face turned to his left, his right arm raised toward the strap on the large wing rising behind him, his left arm at his side, partially enveloped by the garment that billows out behind him. Daedalus, crouching, looks up at or beyond his son as he fastens the strap of the wing. He is half-draped, whereas Icarus is nude except for a narrow band of fabric across his lower torso.

The contrast between father and son is evident in their color, the quality of their flesh, and their hair: Icarus is pale, with the flesh of a kouros and a full head of dark hair; Daedalus, on the other hand, is darkly tanned from exposure to the sun, has lines and furrows of age in his flesh, and is virtually bald. The idealized Icarus seems almost oblivious to the presence of his realistically depicted father.

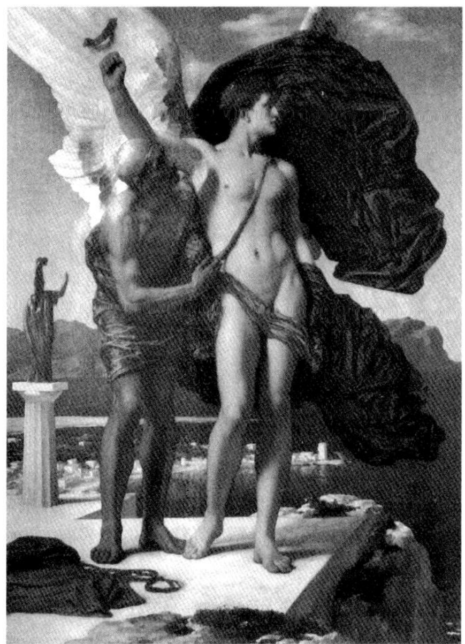

Figure 256. Frederic, Lord Leighton, **DAEDALUS AND ICARUS** (1869).
The Faringdon Collection Trust.
Photograph: Photographic Survey, Courtauld Institute of Art.

The perspective of this painting also warrants special note. Justine Hopkins has called attention to the "visually stunning" impact of the "extreme vertiginous plunge which [Leighton] gives to the perspective, hinting at the flight and the fall to come with the skilful delicacy which was the trademark of [Leighton's] finest pictures, and which his Victorian audience, educated in Classical legend to an extent largely unimaginable today, well knew how to appreciate."[42]

TWENTIETH CENTURY

Algernon Charles Swinburne (1837–1909)

A previously unpublished poem by Swinburne, *Pasiphaë,* was published in 1915 in an edition of no more than twenty by T. J. Wise, but the poem appears to have been largely unknown until it was published again in 1950 by the Golden Cockerel Press, London. Randolph Hughes, who prepared the poem for publication and wrote an introduction to this edition, is harshly critical of Wise's inferior editing of the poem.[43] The manuscript of the poem is in the British Museum, written on foolscap sheets, each bearing a watermark date of 1867, so Hughes reasons that the poem was probably composed either in 1867 or sometime after that date.[44] The poem is untitled in the manuscript, and Hughes suggests the title could just as well be "Pasiphaë and Daedalus," although he accepts the single designation, *Pasiphaë.*[45]

The poem begins with Daedalus addressing the artificial cow he constructed for Pasiphaë, who arrives and is addressed in the opening monologue. In the ensuing dialogue, which sounds rather like a parody of Greek tragedy by A. E. Housman, Pasiphaë discovers the true purpose of this wooden cow:

> O happiest head, O my life's help and stay,
> Be prosperous, and have praise of men and me
> In all time alway; but this one thing more,
> This will I ask thee, and spare not thou to say,
> In what way having put this strange shape on,
> I may fare heifer-wise beneath a bull,
> Being clothed with cow and quite diswomanized.
> (lines 66–72)

Swinburne introduces Pasiphaë's nurse into the dialogue, with a lengthy epilogue to this short poem (137 lines), asking her mistress (lines 111f.): "What god is this that drives thee without sail / Before the wild wind of a wandering will?"

In another poem, *The Masque of Queen Bersabe,* Swinburne gives one stanza to Pasiphaë:

> I am the queen Pasiphaë.
> Not all the pure clean-coloured sea
> Could cleanse or cool my yearning veins;
> Nor any root or herb that grew,
> Flag-leaves that let green water through,
> Nor washing of the dews and rains.
> From shame's pressed core I wrung the sweet
> Fruit's savour that was death to eat,
> Whereof no seed but death remains.[46]

This rather peculiar poem serves as a useful reminder that the offspring of this unnatural union provided the occasion for the construction of the labyrinth, but it also adumbrates the twentieth century in which the Minotaur would function as a potent symbol for Picasso, who overshadowed all his contemporaries, and for Michael Ayrton, who tried to cast off Picasso's shadow.

Bertrand Russell (1872–1970)

Less than a decade after the first installment of Joyce's *Portrait of the Artist as a Young Man* appeared in the *Egoist* in London, the symbol of Daedalus was employed in a very different context elsewhere in England. On 4 February 1923, J. B. S. Haldane read to the Heretics in Cambridge a paper entitled "Daedalus, or Science and the Future," which was published the following year in New York. He predicted a glorious future for the intelligent application of the discoveries of the emerging sciences. Blaming "sentimental interest" in Prometheus for the failure to notice "the far more interesting figure of Daedalus, . . . the first modern man," Haldane offered a rather novel version of the achievements of Daedalus to explain his choice as the symbol for scientific progress in the future (46–47). Daedalus, who invented the art of flying to escape from Minos's "ruthless economies," was the "first to demonstrate that the scientific worker is not concerned with the gods," since he "was neither smitten by a thunderbolt, chained to a rock, nor pursued by the furies," despite the fact that he was responsible for the death of Zeus's son Minos (48). Predicting an especially bright future for the biological sciences, Haldane described the scientific worker of the future as an arbiter of morals and establisher of a new, scientifically acceptable religion, who would "more and more resemble the lonely figure of Daedalus as he becomes conscious of his ghastly mission, and proud of it" (92f.).

Bertrand Russell was quick to respond the following year to Haldane's "Daedalus" with his own *Icarus, or the Future of Science.*[47] Speaking from a skepticism based on "long experience of statesmen and governments," Russell declared: "I am compelled to fear that science will be used to promote the power of dominant groups, rather than to make men happy. Icarus, having been taught to fly by his father Daedalus, was destroyed by his rashness. I fear that the same fate may overtake the populations whom modern men of science have taught to fly" (5–6). Russell distrusted his fellow human beings, since in the past they used the benefits of science primarily for three purposes: "first, to increase the population; then, to raise the standard of comfort; and, finally, to devote more energy to war" (21). It was "one of the comfortable nineteenth-century delusions" to believe that scientific progress is necessarily a "boon to mankind," for the generally corrupt "holders of power" used its fruits merely to increase their power (57). More kindliness was needed instead, but he was pessimistic about the possibility of achieving it (62). His disillusionment pervades the concluding paragraph of his book:

> Science has not given men more self-control, more kindliness, or more power of discounting their passions in deciding upon a course of action. It has given communities more power to indulge their collective passions. . . . Men's collective passions are mainly evil. . . . [S]cience threatens to cause the destruction of our civilization. The only solid hope seems to lie in . . . the gradual formation of an orderly economic and political world-government. But perhaps, in view of the sterility of the Roman Empire, the collapse of our civilization would in the end be preferable to this alternative. (62–64)

The attitude of Russell toward Icarus evokes the negative representations by Spanish poets and writers of the early seventeenth century. For Russell, Icarus represents misguided ambition, arrogance, and misuse of power, all of which lead to dreadful consequences. He therefore projects for an entire society the unique disaster of the brash Icarus. Lord Russell's pessimistic view of humanity led him to believe that people were much more inclined to emulate Icarus than Daedalus and, thereby, turn useful inventions into weapons of destruction or tools of power and self-indulgence.

Lauro De Bosis (1901–1931)

In 1928, at the Olympic contest in Amsterdam, Lauro de Bosis won a prize for his play, *Icaro.*[48] Written in a structure resembling a Greek tragedy, this drama introduces a novel description of the flight of Icarus, which is presented as a solo flight. The messenger speech so familiar in Greek drama is used to describe the fall of Icarus. The concluding lines universalize the myth:

> Wherever in the world a human heart
> burns with desire and love, defying fate,
> always, unseen, will Icarus take its part.

The death of De Bosis a few years later evokes the myth and his prize-winning drama. An ardent opponent of fascism, De Bosis was in self-exile from Mussolini's Italy. To help fight Mussolini's fascist regime, De Bosis purchased an airplane and learned how to fly. On 3 October 1931, two months and six days short of his thirtieth birthday, he flew over Rome, dropping leaflets attacking fascism. It is not known whether he was shot down by Mussolini's troops or crashed into the sea, but he never returned from his ambitious but ill-fated journey.

Henri Matisse (1869–1954)

In September 1947 Henri Matisse published *Jazz,* a collection of twenty often dazzlingly brilliant plates, each set apart by about a half dozen pages of handwritten reflections on a wide variety of topics but scarcely at all related to the plates themselves. These reflections serve, in his own words, a "purely visual" function.[49] One of the plates is his *Icarus* (Plate 5), a black silhouette with a small red heart; this falling Icarus is set against the deep blue background, which is randomly illumined with brilliant yellow star-like forms.

Earlier, Matisse prepared a "scissors-and-paste frontispiece for the *Verve 'De la couleur'* issues, a *Fall of Icarus* dated June 1943, which is clearly an early version of the *Icarus* . . . reproduced in *Jazz.*"[50] Louis Aragon offers special insights based on a confidential conversation with the artist, which revealed deeper implications of this work: "The Fall of Icarus . . . between two bands of deepest blue, contained a central bundle of black rays against which Icarus was set out in white like a corpse, and from Matisse's own confidential comments we gather that the yellow splashes, suns or stars according to mythological interpretation, stood for bursting shells in 1943."[51]

Matisse's Jazz *Icarus* (pl. VIII) is "wryly placed at the end of the 'Airplane' section of the *Jazz* text, which speaks of a return from 'an enchanted world' to 'our modest condition of walking.'"[52] The Jazz *Icarus* has been described as "one of the simplest images in the series . . . [but it] is perhaps the subtlest poetically" because of its relationship to the earlier *Fall of Icarus:* "In the earlier version Matisse has shown Icarus, his heart a red star, shooting down a blue diagonal path between star-studded skies. Here, in the final version, his heart is reduced to a palpitating scarlet dot which scarcely animates his dangling limbs as he falls through deep blue infinity."[53]

Hélène Sardeau (1899–1969)

Hélène Sardeau was born in Belgium and emigrated to America with her family in 1917. She studied for a time "at the Art Students League. Frank Crowninshield saw her early work and aided her immensely."[54] She dealt primarily in small figures and did a number of mural projects; she also received commissions for sculptural reliefs in Brazil and Mexico, and her sculpture *Slave* was chosen for a sculptural group in Fairmont Park, Philadelphia.[55]

In 1951 Sardeau completed a sculpture in plaster of Icarus (75-3/8″ x 75-1/2″ x c. 43″). It was first exhibited in the autumn of 1952 in New York, "at the first artist-juried exhibitions of sculpture . . . which had been organized by Francis Taylor, Director of the Metropolitan Museum in New York."[56] It was cast in bronze and donated in 1961 to the Philadelphia Museum of Art in memory of a Philadelphia doctor.[57]

For many years, her *Icarus* stood near a fountain in front of the museum, but by the mid-1970s it had been moved just inside the main entrance. Sculpted shortly after World War II, this bronze, with its wing-flap arms, bent and broken, evokes images of the warplane crashes of Icarus's modern-day descendants. This sensitive rendition of Icarus presaged some of the interpretations given the myth by Ayrton, beginning five years after this work was created.

William Golding (1911–1993)

Before Golding's fourth novel, *Free Fall,* was published in 1959, he revealed that his new novel would deal with "the patternlessness of life." The novel is a first-person account by Sammy Mountjoy, a well-known painter. Golding invited comparison with Joyce's *Portrait* and other works in that genre with this satirical reference: The heroes in "those books which kept turning up in the twenties . . . [were] bad at games, unhappy and misunderstood at school—tragic, in fact, until they reached eighteen or nineteen and published a stunning book of poems or took to interior decoration" (48). The structure of the novel, moreover, not only invites comparison with his own earlier novels, but also evokes the mythical Daedalus as well as Stephen Dedalus and the labyrinth he created. One scholar has noted that Golding's earlier novels were "mainly concerned with the escape of their protagonists from the maze of the past," but "Sammy's story is an obliquely chronicled account of its narrator's willing—almost obsessive—return to that maze."[58]

In the novel there are explicit references to myth:

> Sammy is linked with Daedalus or Icarus (154–55) and Prometheus (157–58); the rectory itself is like a labyrinth,

> Christian rather than pagan. Unlike Joyce's Stephen, however, who escapes from the labyrinthine streets of Catholic Dublin, Sammy must wait until his imprisonment by Halde to realize that his true labyrinth, like pagan Daedalus's, is self-created, and like his Dantesque inferno, exists within himself.[59]

With Joyce's *Portrait* as a literary context, *Free Fall* further enriches and extends the myth of Daedalus and Icarus in the twentieth century.

Gianfilippo Usellini (1903–1971)

Gianfilippo Usellini was born in Milan, studied at the Brera Fine Arts Academy in Milan, and served as professor of painting at the Brera Art Lyceum, Milan. He has entered works in numerous national and international exhibitions, has had solo exhibitions in Italy and abroad, has been included in group exhibitions in most of the major cities of the world, and has won several prizes for his work, which is included in collections in major Italian cities, Paris, and elsewhere.[60]

In 1961 Usellini won second prize in the Esso Standard Italiana fourth Esso Competition with *The Dream of Icarus.*[61] The theme of the "competition was 'One Hundred Years of Italian Industry' to celebrate the centenary of Italy's political unification."[62] In a blend of realism and Romanticism, Usellini links the flight of Icarus with this century's first experiments with flight.

This whimsical painting depicts Icarus with butterfly wings newly airborne above a garage/hangar. On the ground, the billowing wings of a biplane topped by cherubim with reddish-orange wings contrast with the realistic garage and a tintype photographer, who is photographing a couple standing in front of the biplane. The sentimentality and whimsy of this painting are a far cry from the depth of interpretation given by Brueghel in the sixteenth century or by a number of artists and writers in the twentieth.

Jimmy Ernst (1920–1984)

Jimmy Ernst, the son of Max Ernst, completed several interpretations of Icarus. His abstract-expressionist painting, *Icarus III* (1963, Plate 14), uses color and form to achieve a dramatic statement of the myth of the flight and the fall. The shadow of a giant bird hovers over the bright red, which captures the intensity of the sun's heat, whereas the reddish hue of the mangled mass of rods grouped to form a tangled corpse in the midst of the deep blue sea poignantly expresses the misfortune that befell Icarus.

Nicholas Ikaris[63]

Nicholas Ikaris was born on the Aegean island of Ikaria, the mythical site of the fall of Icarus. A 1950 graduate of the Fine Arts Academy in Athens, Ikaris received a number of important prizes in his homeland and abroad. His public sculptures can be found in Vienna, Dortmund, New York City, New Orleans, and Ikaria. He served for a time as a professor of art at Kingsborough College of the City University of New York.[64] The City Hall of New York City displays his statue, *The Astronaut,* which is dedicated to astronaut John Glenn.[65]

In 1967 it was announced that Ikaris's *The Icarus Monument* (Plate 7) a 115-foot bronze monument, would be unveiled in Greece during the 1969 World Conference of Astronauts,[66] but it was not until 1 August 1981, that the sculpture was erected on the quay of the island of Ikaria, rather than "on the rock off the shore of the island . . . where Icarus . . . fell to his death."[67] This striking sculpture dominates the harbor, with a plummeting Icarus suspended near the top of the V-shaped bronze, catching and reflecting the rays of the sun in constantly changing patterns of light. The two legs of the V that form the struts for the Icarus figure, as well as the Icarus itself, are filled with randomly shaped perforations through which the bright light of the Aegean can flow or be refracted.

In 1967 Ikaris offered insights into his work with these comments:

> I began in Greece; I am an Aristotelian.
>
> As I worked at my art under the strong light of Attica, I was studying in depth another light that comes from the ancient ruins, a light far beyond archaeological interests, far beyond the emotional appeal of historical remains. Behind the first simple impressions, I saw an

> essential reality; the constant decay and change of earthly matter; the vital pulse of a past civilization whose stony symbols are following it back to its natural origin. . . .
>
> I wanted only to swallow the stellar dust, to teach myself the secret technique of incredible nature, the technique by which slowly, in time, through the blending of collisions and the logical balance of powers, without the poetic finger of any god who creates overnight, the earth. . . has brought forth her own shapes. . . .
>
> Whatever comes from nature, even the most abstract, we take without doubt or comment. I want, then, to imitate the impersonality of nature so that my works of art will seem to have made themselves, without any human intervention.[68]

Given the subtitle of one of his sculptures, *The Free Spirit,* his interest in astronauts, his awareness of the "strong light of Attica," and these personal statements, it is hardly surprising that he created the spectacular sculpture that greets all who arrive at the harbor of his native island, which bears in its very name the memory of the free-spirited Icarus.

The Daedalus Project, 1988[69]

On 23 April 1988, the flight of Daedalus became a contemporary reality, when Kanellos Kanellopoulos, a Greek cycling champion, flew under his own power from Crete to Santorini at the controls of a human-powered aircraft that weighed barely seventy pounds yet had the wingspan of a DC-9 (Plates 8 and 9). During all the centuries in which people, spurred on by the myth of Daedalus and Icarus, dreamed of human flight, it was always assumed the flier would supply the power. Nevertheless, the human-powered aircraft came into its own only during the last few decades of the twentieth century, after the remarkable achievements of flight in propeller-driven and, later, jet-propelled airplanes, and of space flight to the moon and beyond. Beginning in 1959, a series of competitions sponsored by British industrialist Henry Kremer provided the impetus for this surge in the development of human-powered flight. The prize that Kremer first offered in 1959 was not claimed until 1977, when Bryan Allen successfully flew the GOSSAMER CONDOR around the required one-mile, figure-of-eight course. Two years later, Allen claimed another, much larger prize, when he accomplished the first human-powered flight across the English Channel, a distance of twenty-two miles, at the controls of the GOSSAMER ALBATROSS. Four years later, Kremer sponsored another competition with the goal of increasing the speed and practicality of human-powered aircraft. The first prize this time was claimed by the team responsible for building MONARCH B, a craft designed and built at M.I.T. by members of a working group. This team decided that the next challenge would be to reenact the flight of Daedalus. The Daedalus Project consisted of a working group of students, professors, engineers, and athletes. After completing a feasibility study in 1985 and 1986, the working group recruited five national-class cyclists, including Kanellos Kanellopoulos, fourteen times the national cycling champion of Greece and a member of the team chosen to compete in the 1988 Summer Olympics.

The working group also chose the flight route after careful deliberation. They selected the route from Crete to Santorini because it was assumed that Daedalus had engaged in island-hopping and because it was a safer route than the one to the mainland, where air currents over the tiny island of Kithera off the southern tip of the Peloponnese were much more dangerous. The distance between Crete and Santorini—seventy-four statute miles—was some five miles farther than to the mainland and more than three times the distance covered by Bryan Allen when he crossed the English Channel. After experimenting in 1987 with a prototype aircraft, the LIGHT EAGLE, the team developed a new, lighter aircraft, DAEDALUS 87. With a wingspan of 112 feet, yet weighing less than seventy pounds, DAEDALUS was constructed of Thornel carbon fiber (embedded in epoxy resin), Kevlar (a high strength organic plastic fiber), Foamular (an extruded polystyrene foam), Mylar (polyester plastic used as the skin of the aircraft), expanded polystyrene foam, and the proverbial steel piano wire. Bicycle pedals and gear box were used to turn the propellor. A second aircraft, DAEDALUS 88, was also constructed as a back-up. This proved to be a wise decision, since DAEDALUS 87 was damaged during a test flight at Edwards Air Force Base in early 1988.

In March 1988 the team left for Crete and set up their operation at an airbase near Knossos. After a series of short test flights, the team prepared for the real thing on 2 April 1988. Because of unfavorable winds, however, the flight was scrubbed, not only on April 2nd, but on a number of subsequent days. These cancellations, however, enabled the team to fly to the island of Ikaria on a Greek Air Force helicopter to attend a special ceremony in their honor. The pilots and project director John Langford were made honorary citizens of Ikaria. The flight occurred on 23 April 1988, when weather conditions finally proved ideal. After pedaling for three hours and fifty-four minutes, pilot Kanellopoulos approached Perissa Beach for a landing, but as he banked the plane slightly, a gust of wind caused the wings to collapse, and the plane plummeted into the Aegean Sea just a few yards off shore. Kanellopoulos emerged unhurt from the craft and waded ashore to an enthusiastic welcome.

Using modern technology and a highly conditioned cyclist, the Daedalus Project Team proved that a human can fly the long distance from Crete to another major island. The completion of this extraordinary flight is not only a triumph for human ingenuity and scientific invention, but also a stunning reminder that the myth of Daedalus still has the power to inspire, challenge, and enrich us, even in a highly scientific, technological age.

NOTES

1. Walters 1926, no. 663 and pl. 11. This same gem is no. 862 in Richter; she dates this gem very early—in the first half of the fifth c. B.C.E.—and rejects the identification of the inscription with Daedalus, perhaps overlooking the bulla studied by Hanfmann and also by Eva Fiesel, "The Inscription on the Etruscan Bulla," AJA, 39 (1935): 195–97. Hanfmann l91f. also notes the parallelism between the bulla and the gems.
2. Walters 1893, nos. B148, 174, 175, 205, 246, 247, 308, 313, 403, 593, 596, 600.47, and 642. C. H. Smith nos. E37, 48, 84, 304, 441, and 5094. A. H. Smith no. 2198 and fig. 32. Walters 1903, nos. A 107–13 (subject: Theseus slaying the Minotaur; nos. A 107–19 are "Fragments of Colossal Statues, with painted patterns, representing the ornamentation of drapery or of a cuirass").
3. C. H. Smith 270.
4. C. H. Smith 220.
5. C. H. Smith 111. Another red-figure kylix from Vulci, signed by the painter Epiktetos (fl. 520–500 B.C.E.), also depicts Theseus, with sword in hand, attacking the Minotaur, who defends himself with a rock, but one of much larger proportions. The Minotaur has sunk to his knees, but he holds the rock in both hands above his head. For an illustration, see Ward 16, ill. 15.
6. For the actual text, see Turner 25.
7. Rudd 37.
8. In 1524 Giulio left Rome for Mantua, where he dominated the duchy in both architecture and painting for the next twenty years. From 1527 to 1534 he constructed and decorated the Palazzo del Te for Federigo Gonzaga, a marquess who became the first duke of Mantua during its construction. The palace has been described as "the most fantastic structure" that "the Mannerist crisis . . . was ever to beget" (Hartt 590). Ceilings and, at times, walls of both major and minor rooms of the ducal palace were covered with scenes drawn largely from classical mythology, including detailed representations of the Gigantomachy and the tale of Cupid and Psyche. The decorations are noted for their bright, sometimes fiery, colors and for their gaudiness.
9. This room was designed by Giulio Romano and executed largely by one of his assistants, Anselmo de Ganis.
10. From the Rosenwald Collection of the National Gallery of Art, which was housed for a time at the Alverthorpe Gallery near Philadelphia.
11. Daedalus does appear in a copy of the painting included in the Van Buuren Collection in Brussels, but not in the original version, which is in the Musées Royaux des Beaux-Arts in Brussels.
12. Cort's career was launched about the middle of the sixteenth century by the engraver-publisher Hieronymus Cock, of Antwerp, who undertook the reproductions of Brueghel. Cort subsequently joined the increasing number of artists from the Netherlands who went to Italy to work. He remained there until his death and established a school of engraving at Rome that influenced Italian engravers for half a century (EWA 12, 142). In his engraving of the Brueghel landscape one finds ingredients of Italian mannerism: "A high viewpoint, a range of craggy mountains and a distant prospect of river and sea coast" (Clark 1961, 27).
13. De Tolnay, I, 29 (the painting in Anvers is reproduced in II, 6).
14. Ibid.
15. Turner 77.
16. In the seventeenth century, Miguel de Barrios, a.k.a. Daniel Leví de Barrios, also portrayed a woman as Icarus (see Turner 135).
17. Turner 94.

18. Rudd 38. Golding's translation, edited by J. F. Nims, was republished in 1965. For further comments, see Rudd, n. 6, 260.
19. Trans. Rudd, 38.
20. Ibid.
21. Martin 1977, 250.
22. Wittkower 63 and 68.
23. The other themes were: a) the disclosure of Callisto's pregnancy; b) Callisto transformed into a bear; and c) Mercury and Apollo. For a discussion of Domenichino's role in the completion of the paintings in the Galleria Farnese, see e.g., Martin 1965, Pope-Hennessy, and Wittkower (esp. 513, n. 21; see also his bibliography, 605).
24. Chilvers and Osborne 310.
25. Martin 1977, 19–22.
26. Martin 1977, 21.
27. Martin 1977, 28–30.
28. The date of birth is deduced from the record of his death, which is preserved in the parish registry of S. Trovaso, which states that at the time of his death he was "about forty years" (Borsook 6 and 83, n. 13). Michael Kitson, *The Complete Paintings of Caravaggio* (New York: Harry N. Abrams, 1967), 15, gives his date of birth as 1578–1579. For a brief treatment and a complete catalogue of Saraceni's oeuvre, see Cavina.
29. Borsook (at 9–10) reports that oil painting on copper was especially popular between 1590 and 1620 among northern European artists, but few Italian artists beside Saraceni adopted this technique.
30. A pupil of Albani and influenced by the Carraccis, Andrea Sacchi was a prominent representative of the classical tradition during the High Baroque period. He was joined in a new movement, formed in the 1630s, by the French painter Nicolas Poussin (1594–1665), who lived in Rome from 1624 to 1640, and two sculptors, Alessandro Algardi of Bologna (1598–1654) and Francesco Duquesnoy of Brussels (1597–1643), who lived in Rome from 1618 until his death. Of this group, Wittkower 261, has said, "What they stand for is not a straight continuation of Bolognese classicism, but a revised version, tinged by the influence of the great masters and, in painting, by a new impact of Venetian colourism which was shared by the leading 'Baroque' artists, Lanfranco, Cortona, and Bernini. Compared with the Early Baroque classicism, the new classicism was first rather boisterous and painterly; it has a physiognomy of its own, and it is this style that by rights may be termed 'High Baroque classicism.'"
31. In 1621, upon the advice of Rubens and after a short stay in England, Van Dyck went to Italy, where he spent the better part of five years in Genoa, with visits to the artistic centers of Rome, Venice and Palermo. Max Rooses, *Fuenfzig Meisterwerke von Anton van Dyck* (Leipzig: Breitkopf, 1900, 70), argues that "this painting appears to date from before his . . . journey to Italy" but other scholars (e.g. Gustav Glueck, *Van Dyck: des Meisters Gemälde in 571 Abbildungen* [London: A. Zwemmer, 1931]) date it anywhere from 1621 to 1630. This portrait (48″ x 33″ in size) is in the collection of the Art Gallery of Ontario, Toronto.

    In the 1630s, Rubens chose to treat the theme of the fall of Icarus, perhaps following the example of his former student. Rubens himself was for a time a pupil of Adam van Noort, as was Jordaens.
32. Cust, 241.
33. Martin 1977, 91, but the judgment about the portrait of Icarus is mine, not Martin's.
34. Wittkower 340, states that Giulio Carpioni "found a way out of the local academic eclecticism [in Venice] through elegant classicizing stylizations." See also 550, n. 70, for bibliographic references, including confirmation of the dates of Carpioni's life (some scholars give his dates as 1611–1674).
35. This drawing is included in the print collection of the Galerie der Bildende Kuenste, Kunstmuseum, Dusseldorf. The drawing is signed on the lower right: "G. Lott." Nonetheless, it was misidentified by a former owner (Krahe) as a drawing by Daniel Seiter.
36. Vilain 523, regarding no. 116, *Daedalus and Icarus.*
37. Vilain 522.
38. Trans. Philip Wayne (Penguin Books); qtd. by Rudd 48.
39. Goethe, *Faust,* trans. Anna Swanwick (New York, n.d.), 417.
40. Dr. Justine Hopkins, commenting on a draft of this manuscript in a letter dated 31 August 1996, notes that Leighton had "trained in Rome, and would certainly have seen Canova's sculpture as a student—he greatly admired the older artist, and there is almost certainly a reminiscence of that work here."
41. Hopkins, ibid., notes that "the landscape behind the pair is based on a series of sketches made while travelling in Greece, and shows the coastline of Rhodes."
42. Hopkins, ibid.
43. Hughes 5ff.
44. Ibid. 7.
45. Ibid. 8.
46. *The Works of Algernon Charles Swinburne: Poems* (Philadelphia: David McKay, n.d.), 92. Other nineteenth-century poems relating to the Cretan myths are these: John Sterling, "Daedalus," in *Poems* (1939), 162–65; Bayard Taylor, "Icarus," in *The Poetical Works of Bayard Taylor* (1851), 88–90; De Tabley, "Daedalus," in *Eclogues and Melodramas* (1864); J. G. Saxe, "Icarus," in *Poetical Works* (1868); H. L. Koopman, "Icarus," in *Orestes* (1888); and F. E. Coates, "Poor Icarus," in *Poems* (1898). For this list, I am in part indebted to Helen H. Law, whose *Bibliography of Greek Myth in English Poetry* was published in 1955.
47. Russell. Quotations are from the third impression of 1925.
48. A translation of the play, with a foreword by Gilbert Murray, was published posthumously in 1933. See Rudd 51f. Rudd also recounts the story of another Italian, Gabriele D'Annunzio, the henchman of Mussolini: his poetic version of the myth diminished it, just as his life as a fascist diminished the human race.

49. Barr 274.
50. Barr.
51. Aragon 35. It is reproduced in color in Aragon, pl. IV, and in Cowart et al., 58, pl. II. For further information, see catalogue no. 14, 100.
52. Aragon 108.
53. Barr 275.
54. Letter to the author from George Biddle, her husband, dated September 27, 1970.
55. Ibid.
56. Ibid.
57. In a letter to me dated September 28, 1970, Dr. Fred B. Rogers, chairman of the department of medicine at Temple University, provided the following information on the individual in whose name the sculpture was donated: "Dr. Edward Weiss (1895–1960), a graduate of the Jefferson Medical College in 1917, came to Temple University School of Medicine from Jefferson in 1932. An internist and Professor of Clinical Medicine at Temple until his sudden death from a heart attack, he was a patron of the arts and, I suspect, a friend of Helene Sardeau (her husband, Mr. Biddle, also a professional artist, being from Philadelphia)."

    In his letter, George Biddle (n. 54) reported that "Henri Marceau, then director of the Museum, had for many years been a friend and constant admirer of Hélène's work. It was he who formally accepted the 'Icarus' for the Museum and was responsible for its installation."
58. Johnson 51.
59. Johnson 61.
60. Letter from Lorenzo Cantini of Esso Standard Italiana to Miss Anne Adams, Managing Director, the *Lamp,* Standard Oil Company (NJ), dated October 2, 1970.
61. At the time of the letter from Mr. Cantini, the painting was the property of Esso Standard Italiana and located in the office of the company's president. The painting was reproduced on the cover of the *Lamp* 44, no. 3 (Fall 1962), a publication of Standard Oil Company (NJ). It was included in an exhibition at the IBM Gallery in New York in fall 1962, along with twenty-four other works brought over from Italy. The paintings in the show were selected from among the eighty-seven entered in the fourth Esso Standard Italiana Competition, which was held in 1961 (catalog of the IBM exhibition).
62. IBM exhibition catalog 1.
63. No date of birth is given for Ikaris because all attempts to find biographical information have proven fruitless; repeated contacts with librarians and other personnel at Kingsborough College have been particularly frustrating. Ikaris apparently returned to Greece after his divorce. His ex-wife, who was said to be a faculty member at Kingsborough College, and his son reportedly still live in the New York area.
64. *Greece* 196.
65. Ibid.
66. Ibid. 197. A photograph of the maquette of the monument, photographed in the Atlantic Ocean, is reproduced with this announcement.
67. Ibid.
68. Ibid. 196.
69. For a somewhat fuller account of this project, see Nyenhuis 1990, 67–72. A much more extensive description of this entire project is to be found in various journals (see Langford 1988 and Dorsey 1990).

Bibliography and List of Works Cited

A. BOOKS AND ARTICLES BY MICHAEL AYRTON

British Drawings. London: Collins, 1946. [1946a]

"Chagall as a Book Illustrator." *Signature: A Quadrimestral of Typography and Graphic Arts,* n.s. 2 (November 1946): 31–36. [1946b]

"The Heritage of British Painting, IV." *Studio* (November 1946): 148. [1946c]

"The Master of Pastiche." In *New Writing and Daylight.* Ed. John Lehmann. London: Hogarth Press, 1946. VII, 108–117. [1946d]

"Entrance to a Wood." *Orpheus: A Symposium of the Arts.* Ed. John Lehmann. London: John Lehmann, 1948. I, 114–16. [1948a]

Hogarth's Drawings. London: Avalon Press, 1948. [1948b]

Introduction to *Chagall* (with notes by the artist). London: Faber and Faber, 1948; 2–5. [1948c]

"Giovanni Pisano." *Royal Society of Arts,* 1953. [1953a]

Introduction and notes to *Degas II.* London: Faber and Faber, 1953. [1953b]

Tittivulus or, The Verbiage Collector. London: Max Reinhardt, 1953. [1953c]

Tribute to Dylan Thomas. "Seventeen Further Memoirs." *ADAM International Review,* XXI, 238 (1953): 32. [1953d]

"The Glutton Eye." [British] *Vogue* 111, no. 10 (October 1955): 140–141, 241.

"The Act of Drawing." *Spectrum,* 1, 2 (Spring–Summer 1957), 3–14. [1957a]

"Homage to Wyndham Lewis: 1884–1957." *Spectrum* 1, 2 (Spring–Summer 1957), 48–52. [1957b]

Golden Sections (essays). London: Methuen, 1957. [1957c]

"Wax and Bone Reliefs." *Painter and Sculptor,* 1, No. 3 (Autumn 1958): 10–12.

"A Painter's Transition to Sculpture." *Impulse* (August 1959): 27–30.

Introduction to *Themes and Variations: 5 Centuries of Master Copies.* London: Thames and Hudson, 1960.

Drawings and Sculpture by Michael Ayrton, with an introduction by C. P. Snow. London: Cory, Adams and McKay, 1962. Rev. ed., 1966. [1962a]

"The Icarus Theme." *Shell Aviation News,* 284 (1962): 11–14. [1962b]

The Testament of Daedalus. London: Methuen, 1962. [1962c] Excerpts printed in *Massachusetts Review,* 3, No. 4 (Summer 1962): 733–52, as "The Testament of Daedalus"; London: Robin Clark Paperback, 1991. [1962d]

"The Sculpture of Leonard Baskin." *Motif,* 10 (Winter 1962–1963): 52–59.

"The Landscape of the Minotaur." *London Magazine,* n.s. 4, 2 (May 1964): 48–54; rpt. in *Labrys,* 3 (October 1978): 30–33.

"On a Self-portrait by Pierre Bonnard." *London Sunday Times,* 23 January 1965; rpt. in *Labrys,* 3 (October 1978): 35. [1965a]

"Unwearying Bronze." *Horizon,* 7, No. 1 (Winter 1965): 16–37; rpt. in Ayrton 1971, 173–92. [1965b]

"Maze Maker 1966." Catalogue introduction. Grosvenor Gallery, London, June–July 1966. Rpt. in *Studio International,* 171, No. 878 (June 1966): 273.

The Maze Maker. London: Longmans, Green 1967; New York: Holt, Rinehart and Winston, 1967; New York: Bantam Books, 1969; Frankfurt: Fischer, 1970; New York: Bard Books/Avon Books, 1975; and London: Solitaire Books, 1982.

"The Path to Daedalus." *Virgil.* Ed. D. R. Dudley. "Studies in Latin Literature and Its Influence." London: Routledge and Kegan Paul, 1969; 176–200.

Berlioz, A Singular Obsession. London: B.B.C. Publications, 1970. [1970a]

"Daedalus and I." *Horizon,* 12, 2 (Spring 1970): 56–65; rpt. as "The Making of a Maze" in Ayrton 1971, 293–305. [1970b]

Giovanni Pisano, Sculptor. Intro. Henry Moore. London: Thames and Hudson, 1970; New York: Weybright and Talley, 1970; Frankfurt: Fischer, 1970; Paris: Braun, 1971. [1970c]

The Minotaur. London: Published privately by Genevieve Restaurants, 1970. [1970d]

"Recreating a Gift for the Gods." *Daily Telegraph Magazine,* 278 (13 February 1970): 45–46. [1970e]

The Rudiments of Paradise: Various Essays on Various Arts. London: Secker and Warburg, 1971; New York: Weybright and Talley, 1971.

Fabrications. London: Secker and Warburg, 1972; New York: Holt, Rinehart and Winston, 1973.

A Meaning to the Maze. The Seventh Jackson Knight Memorial Lecture (Delivered at the University of Exeter 18 May 1973). Abingdon-on-Thames: Abbey Press, 1974. [1974a].

The Midas Consequence. London: Secker and Warburg, 1974; Garden City, NY: Doubleday, 1974. [1974b]

Archilochos. Intro., transl., and illus. Michael Ayrton, with an essay by G. S. Kirk. London: Secker and Warburg, 1977.

"A Question of Mirrors—Three Television Scripts." *Labrys,* 3 (October 1978): 36–57. [1978b]

"A Silence Filled with Greek." *Labrys,* 3 (October 1978): 9–20. (This is a re-edited version of a broadcast originally aired on the BBC Third Programme on Tuesday, 17 January 1967.) [1978c]

"Icarus Poems." *Labrys,* 3 (October 1978): 21–29. [1978d]

Michael and Elisabeth Ayrton. *Minotaur!: Comprising the Minotaur's Nurse: Dealing with the Problem of Asterion by Elisabeth Ayrton, The Minotaur by Michael Ayrton [1970d] and Eighteen Etchings and Drawings by Michael Ayrton.* Frome, Somerset: Bran's Head Books, 1984.

B. UNPUBLISHED WORKS BY MICHAEL AYRTON

"Some Notes on the Form of the Arkville Maze." Prepared by Michael Ayrton for Armand G. Erpf, March 1968.

"Journey Through a Labyrinth." Lecture delivered at Wayne State University, 2 October 1972.

C. FILMS BY MICHAEL AYRTON

In Collaboration with Basil Wright:

The Drawings of Leonardo Da Vinci. London: British Film Institute, 1951.

Greek Sculpture. London: Marsden Films, 1959.

Maze Maker. London: Marsden Films, 1972.

In Collaboration with Charles Collingwood:

The Maze. New York: CBS Television, 1973.

With Ayrton as Commentator, Touring the British Museum:

Prints and Drawings: The Image. London: British Museum.

D. BOOKS ILLUSTRATED BY MICHAEL AYRTON

Acknowledgment: The completeness of this list is in large part due to the comprehensive "An Annotated Checklist of Books Illustrated by Michael Ayrton," by Rigby Graham, included in his "Michael Ayrton—Book Illustrator." Copyright 1972, by William B. Thorsen. Copyrighted material used by permission.

1941 Paul Verlaine. "Fêtes Galantes." 29 illustrations in ink and gouache (unpublished).

1943 David Cleghorn Thompson. *The Hidden Path.* Glasgow: William Maclellan. Frontispiece, pen drawing.

1945 John Webster. *The Duchess of Malfi.* London: Sylvan Press. 11 line drawings, unlimited ed. 10 lithographs and 11 line drawings, limited ed.

Cecil Gray. *Gilles de Rais* (a play). London: Favil Press. 4 line decorations.

Phoebe Pool, ed. *Poems of Death.* London: Adprint, Frederick Muller. 16 four-color lithographs and a cover.

1946 Cecil and Margery Gray. *The Bed, or the Clinophile's Vade Mecum.* London: Nicholson and Watson. 13 illustrations (and end paper spread in color).

John Arlott and Michael Ayrton. *Clausentum.* London: Jonathon Cape. 7 wash drawings.

Thomas Nashe. *Summer's Last Will and Testament.* London: Oxford Univ. Press. 7 pen drawings.

1948 Reinhold Schneider. *Imperial Mission.* New York: Gresham Press. 9 pen drawings.

James Laver, ed. *Paintings by Michael Ayrton.* London: Grey Walls Press. 6 pen and wash drawings and 1 pen drawing.

Oscar Wilde. *The Picture of Dorian Gray.* London: Castle Press. 20 pen drawings and 8 full-page portraits.

Henry Purcell. *The Fairy Queen.* London: John Lehmann. Costumes and sets for the Sadlers Wells production.

Thomas Nashe. *The Unfortunate Traveller, or the Life of Jacke Wilton.* London: John Lehmann. 16 lithographs, including tail piece.

1950 Anon., ed. Dr. E. J. Holmyard. *Ancestors of an Industry.* London: Kynoch Press for I.C.I. 12 black-and-white illustrations, 1st ed. 11 line drawings on a tinted background, 2nd ed.

1951 William Shakespeare. *The Tragedy of Macbeth.* London: Folio Society. 8 four-color lithographs.

Eric Linklater. *Trolleri med gamla ben—A Spell for Old Bones.* Stockholm: P. A. Norstedt and Soners. 16 pen drawings.

1952 Henry Bett. *English Myths and Legends.* London: B. T. Batsford. 10 pen drawings.

Giovanni Battista Basile. Trans. Richard Burton. *Il Pentamerone or The Tale of Tales.* London: William Kimber; reissued by Spring Books. 6 pen drawings.

1953 Michael Ayrton. *Tittivulus or the Verbiage Collector.* London: Max Reinhardt. 60 lithographs.

1954 Louis MacNeice. *The Other Wing.* London: Ariel Poems, Faber and Faber. 1 four-color lithograph and 2 pen drawings.

J. Wentworth Day. *Ghosts and Witches.* London: B. T. Batsford. 20 pen drawings.

1955 Kay Fuller. *Forfeit.* London: James Barrie. 8 scraperboard drawings.

1955–1956

Wyndham Lewis. *The Human Age.* 2 vols. London: Methuen. 9 monotypes and 2 color monotype jackets.

1957 George Foa. *The Blood Rushed to My Pockets.* London: John Calder. 8 line illustrations.

Edgar Allan Poe. *Tales of Mystery and Imagination.* London: Folio Society. 10 monotypes.

1958 George Rylands, ed. *A Distraction of Wits.* Cambridge: Cambridge Univ. Press. 12 two-color line drawings, a title page drawing in one color, and 2 calligraphic borders.

John Keats. *Poems.* London: Peter Nevill. Frontispiece and 32 line decoration headpieces.

1960 Richard Church. *North of Rome.* London: Hutchinson. 7 line drawings.

Gavin Maxwell. *Ring of Bright Water.* London: Longmans. 1 double spread containing 10 drawings.

Lucius Apuleius. *The Golden Ass.* London: Folio Society. 10 two-color lithographs and illustrated cover.

C. S. Lewis. *A Preface to Paradise Lost.* London: Oxford Univ. Press (Oxford Paperbacks). Cover.

Thomas Nashe. *The Unfortunate Traveller, or the Life of Jacke Wilton.* New York: Capricorn Books. 6 line drawings.

1961 Aeschylus. *The Oresteia.* New York: Limited Editions Club and Heritage Club. 11 full-page illustrations.

1962 Michael Ayrton. *Drawings and Sculpture.* London: Cory, Adams and Mackay. 139 illustrations, 1st ed. 209 illustrations, rev. ed. (1966).

Michael Ayrton. *The Testament of Daedalus.* London: Methuen. 27 drawings and monotypes.

1964 William Shakespeare. *The Tragedy of Macbeth.* London: Folio Society. 8 theater designs by Michael Ayrton and John Minton for John Gielgud's 1942 production.

1967 Euripides. *Three Plays: Medea, Hippolytus, the Bacchae.* Trans. Philip Vellacott. New York: Limited Editions Club. 16 ink and wash drawings.

1969 Michael Ayrton. *The Mazemaker.* London: Bantam Books. Cover drawing, ed. of 50, superimposed upon original cover (see Cat. No. 684).

Michael Ayrton. *Berlioz, A Singular Obsession.* London: B.B.C. 33 illustrations and 2 photographs of bronzes.

1970 Michael Ayrton. *The Minotaur.* London: Genevieve Restaurants. 13 pen, wash, and charcoal drawings, and a cover design.

Rigby Graham. *Monotypes.* Wymondham: Brewhouse Press. 3 monotypes.

1971 Michael Ayrton. *The Minotaur.* London: Icarus Press. A set of 10 etchings.

Muriel Spark. *Not to Observe.* London: Observer Books. 1 etching.

Paul Verlaine. *Femmes, Hombres.* London: Douglas Cleverdon. 15 etchings.

1972 Plato. *The Trial and Execution of Socrates.* Trans. Peter George. London: Folio Society. 8 pencil drawings.

The Epic of Gilgamesh. New York: Limited Editions Club.

E. Correspondence between Michael and/or Elisabeth Ayrton and Jacob E. Nyenhuis, 1968–1991; between Jacob E. Nyenhuis and Dr. Justine Hopkins, 1990–1996.

F. Notes by Jacob E. Nyenhuis on Conversations with Michael Ayrton, 1971–1974.

G. CRITICAL WORKS ABOUT MICHAEL AYRTON AND HIS WORK

Note: Works listed by Ayrton in exhibition catalogues but which I could not verify are marked with an asterisk at the end of the item.

Anon. "The Talk of the Town: *Artificer.*" *New Yorker,* 9 March 1968, 30.

———."Aesthetics: Knossos in the Catskills; Largest Maze in the World." *Time* 94 (15 August 1969): 48.

———. "Get Me out of Here." *Listener,* 83, 2142 (16 April 1970): 512.

———. "In Troy, Michigan: Thirteen Modules Form S. S. Kresge Headquarters." *Plans and Specs* (P.P.G. Industries), 4, 2 (Summer 1973): 6–7.

B[askin], L[eonard]. "A Note on Michael Ayrton." *Massachusetts Review,* 3, 4 (Summer 1962): [752].

Bertram, Anthony. "Daedalus and Icarus." *Tablet,* 22 December 1962.

Blakeston, Oswell. "A Profile of Michael Ayrton." *Arts Review,* 18, 11 (June 1966): 270.

Borgese, Leonardo. Catalogue Introduction. Galleria dell' Obelisco, Rome, 1950.

Cannon-Brookes, Peter. "The Wax Reliefs of Michael Ayrton." *Atti del I Congresso Internationale sulla ceroplastica nella scienza e nell'arte* (Florence, 3–7 June 1975). Florence: Leo S. Olschki, 1977, 503–16.

———. *Michael Ayrton: An Illustrated Commentary.* Birmingham: Birmingham Museums and Art Gallery, 1978. [1978a]

———. "Michael Ayrton: Pembrokeshire and Neo-Romanticism." *Labrys,* 3 (October 1978): 115–21. [1978b]

Causey, Andrew. "A Throng of Thoughts and Forms." *Illustrated London News,* 248, 6618 (4 June 1966), 26–27.

Davie, Donald. "Michael Ayrton's *The Maze Maker.*" *Southern Review,* 5 (1969): 640–54; rpt. *Labrys,* 3 (October 1978): 86–95.

Denvir, Bernard. "Michael Ayrton." *Studio,* 133 (January–June, 1947): 78–81.

———. "Four Young English Painters." *Graphis,* Zurich, 1949.* [1949a]

———. "Michael Ayrton." *Arts News and Reviews,* London, 1949.* [1949b]

Feaver, William. "Wartime Romances." *Sunday Times,* 20 May 1973, 74–85.

Finley, M. I. "Daedalus Lives." Review of *The Maze Maker* by Michael Ayrton. *New York Review of Books,* 9, 9 (23 November 1967): 35–36.

Flowers, Charles. "Riding the Wind: When Man Becomes Most Like Bird." *Detroit Free Press Magazine,* 20 October 1974, 6–10.

Friendly, Alfred. "Daedalus Reborn: Michael Ayrton Makes a New Maze." *Smithsonian,* 3, 10 (January 1973): 46–53.

Gaunt, William. Review of *Drawings and Sculpture* by Michael Ayrton. *Connoisseur* 152 (February 1963): 122f.

Gielgud, Sir John. "Before *Macbeth.*" *Theatre Arts,* 26, 2 (February 1942): 113–17.

Graham, Rigby. "Icarus Over England." *American Book Collector,* 18, 5–6 (January–February 1968): 15–25.

———. "Michael Ayrton—Book Illustrator." *American Book Collector,* 22, 7 (May 1972): 11–23. (Also "An Annotated Checklist of Books Illustrated by Michael Ayrton," 18–23).

Grant, Michael. *Myths of the Greeks and Romans.* Cleveland: World Publishing, 1962; esp. 386 and pls. 87–88.

Green, Peter. "Ayrton Airborne." *Yorkshire Post,* 4 October 1962.

Gregory, Richard. "The Reflector Sculpture of Michael Ayrton." Exhibition Catalogue, Daedalus I Gallery, Detroit, September 1972.

Hadfield, John. *A Chamber of Horrors: An Anthology of the Macabre in Words and Pictures.* London: Studio Vista, 1965; Boston: Little, Brown, 1965.

Haskell, Arnold. *Ballet, 1932–45.* London: British Council, 1946.*

———. "Michael Ayrton Remembered." *Labrys,* 3 (October 1978): 98–99.

Hendy, Sir Philip. Catalogue Introduction. Wakefield City Art Gallery, August 1949. [1949a]

———. "New Sculpture and Painting." *Britain Today* 161 (September 1949): 33–35. [1949b]

———. Catalogue Introduction. Galerie Galanis-Hentschel, Paris, May 1952.

Herring, Nigel. "Michael Ayrton's Book Illustrations: An Open Letter." *Labrys,* 3 (October 1978): 105–10.

Hopkins, Justine. Catalogue Introduction. Austin/Desmond Fine Art, London, December 1990.

———. *Michael Ayrton: A Biography.* London: Andre Deutsch, 1994.

Hughes, Robert. "Ayrton's Daedalus." Review of *The Maze Maker* by Michael Ayrton. *Studio International,* 174, 891 (July–August 1967): 68.

Knight, G. Wilson. *Neglected Powers: Essays on Nineteenth and Twentieth Century Literature.* New York: Barnes and Noble, 1971; see 69–75, 82, and 336.

Labrys, 3 (October 1978). Issue devoted to Michael Ayrton.

Lambert, Constant. Catalogue Introduction. Redfern Gallery, London, January 1945.

———. "The Face of Ischia: Three Paintings by Michael Ayrton." *Lilliput,* November 1948, 44–49.

———. "Michael Ayrton as Theatre Designer." Wakefield City Art Gallery, August 1949.

Lask, Thomas. "Old Artificer." Review of *The Maze Maker* by Michael Ayrton. *New York Times,* 117 (4 November 1967): 31.

Laver, James. Introduction to *Paintings by Michael Ayrton.* London: Grey Walls Press, 1947; 5–13.

Le Marchant, Michael. "The Sculpture of Michael Ayrton." *Labrys,* 3 (October 1978): 111–13.

Lewis, Wyndham. Catalogue Introduction. Redfern Gallery, London, May 1949; rpt. Wakefield City Art Gallery, August 1949. [1949a]

———. "Round the Galleries: Michael Ayrton (9 June 1949)." *Listener,* 9 June 1949; rpt. Michel and Fox 393. [1949b]

———. "A Note on Michael Ayrton's 'Passion of the Vine.'" *Nine,* 2, 3 (August 1950): 184–85 (plus four plates).

———. *The Demon of Progress in the Arts.* London: Methuen, 1954; Chicago: Henry Regnery, 1955.

———. "A Note on Michael Ayrton." *Spectrum,* 1, 2 (Spring–Summer 1957): [15]–[18]; rpt. in Ayrton 1957b, 13–16.

Lucie-Smith, Edward. "The Numinous in Modern Art." *Times* (London), 26 May 1964.

———. "The Future of Sculpture." *Illustrated London News* 263, 6923 (June 1975), 75–77.

MacGregor, Martha. Review of *The Maze Maker* by Michael Ayrton. *New York Post,* 14 October 1967.

Matthews, John, ed. *Labrys 3: Michael Ayrton.* October 1978. [1978a]

———. "Oracle (For Michael Ayrton)." *Labrys,* 3 (October 1978), 97. [1978b]

Mellor, David. "Michael Ayrton: The Grotesque Body." In *A Paradise Lost: The Neo-Romantic Imagination in Britain 1935–55.* Ed. David Mellor. London: Barbican Art Gallery, 1987. 67–71.

Melville, Robert. "Michael Ayrton's 'Temptation of St. Anthony.'" Redfern Gallery, London, 1943.

———. "A Panorama of Modern Art." *World Review,* n.s. 1–5 (March 1949): 40–45; rpt. Nendeln/Liechtenstein: Kraus Reprint, 1970.

Michel, Walter, and C. J. Fox, eds. *Wyndham Lewis on Art: Collected Writings 1913–1956.* New York: Funk and Wagnalls, 1969.

Middleton, Michael. "Four English Romantics." *Orpheus: A Symposium of the Arts.* Ed. John Lehman. London: John Lehman, 1948; I, 107–13.

Nyenhuis, Jacob. Review of *The Maze Maker* by Michael Ayrton. *Classical Journal,* 64, 3 (December 1968): 134–36.

———. Catalogue Introduction. Daedalus I Gallery, Detroit, September 1972.

———. *Michael Ayrton: An Exhibition of Sculpture, Drawings, Etchings, and Paintings: 1954–1975.* Introduction and annotated catalogue. Holland, MI: Hope College, February 1978. [1978a]

———. "Michael Ayrton's World: Mazes and Minotaurs." *Labrys,* 3 (October 1978): 72–85. [1978b]

Oettli, Simone. "The Maze Maker." *Kenyon Review,* 5, 1 (Winter 1983): 67–84.

Orlando, Ruggiero. "Prunella Clough e Michael Ayrton." *Letteratura e Arte Contemporanea.* 2, 11 (1951): 57–62.

Patton, Harold. "English Sculptor Designs 'Corporate Head' for World Retailer." *Impresario: Magazine of the Arts and Leisure,* 11, 5 (September–October 1972): 8–9.

Patton, Harold, and Eleanor Patton. "The Birth of a Building." *Impresario: Magazine of the Arts and Leisure,* 11, 5 (September–October 1972): 6–7.

Petit, Edmond. "Le Problème Icare." *Forces Aériennes Françaises,* 16, 187 (December 1962): 673–85.

Piper, David. Catalogue Introduction. Magdalene Street Gallery, Cambridge, February 1972.

———. Catalogue Introduction. Maze and Minotaur Tour, February 1973.

Pryce-Jones, Alan. Review of *The Maze Maker* by Michael Ayrton. *New York Times Book Review,* 72 (5 November 1967): 56.

Raphael, Frederic. "On the Recent Death of an Artist." *Labrys,* 3 (October 1978): 65–71.

Roberts, Keith. Review of *Drawings and Sculpture* by Michael Ayrton. *Burlington Magazine* 105 (January 1963): 40–43.

Robertshaw, Ursula. "Ayrton through the Labyrinth." *Illustrated London News,* 260, 6822 (January 1972): 44.

Robertson, Bryan. Catalogue Introduction. Whitechapel Gallery, London, September 1955.

———. "Ayrton and The Theme of Icarus." *Motif,* 7 (Summer 1961): 34–44.

Rosenthal, T. G. Catalogue Introduction. Grosvenor Gallery, London, April 1964.

———. "The Recent Work of Michael Ayrton: London Commentary." *Studio International,* 171, 878 (June 1966): 271–72.

———. "Ayrton's Work in Retrospect." *Times* (London), 24 June 1969.

———. Catalogue Introduction. "Word and Image I and II, Wyndham Lewis and Michael Ayrton." London: National Book League, December 1971.

Rouve, Pierre. "Michael Ayrton." *Arts Review,* 16, 8 (2–16 May 1964): 4.

R[ykwert], J[oseph]. "Le Sculture di Michael Ayrton a Londra." *Domus,* 451 (June 1967): 54.

———. Introduction to the Catalogue of an Exhibition at the University of Essex, March 1968.

———. "Postscript." *Labrys,* 3 (October 1978): 126.

Sabbagh, Karl. "Michael Ayrton's Mirror Scripts." *Labrys,* 3 (October 1978): 60–64.

Salt, Jim. "Michael Ayrton's Drawings." Catalogue Introduction. Fine Arts Gallery, University of Alberta, Canada, and the National Gallery of Canada Tour, June 1965.

Savvides, Georgios P. Catalogue Introduction. Hilton Gallery, Athens, October 1964.

Schulze, Franz. Review of *The Rudiments of Paradise* by Michael Ayrton. *Saturday Review,* 12 June 1971, 31.

Searle, Humphrey. "Programme Notes (Part 2): *Labyrinth.*" Royal Concert, Tuesday, 23 November 1971 (City of Birmingham Symphony Orchestra), 27.

———. "Michael Ayrton Remembered." *Labrys,* 3 (October 1978): 99–100

Selvaggi, Giuseppe. "I Disegni di Michael Ayrton." *Prospettive Meridionali,* 6, 9 (September 1960): 42.

Sharp, Evelyn. *Hertha Ayrton, 1854–1923: A Memoir.* London: Edward Arnold, 1926.

Snow, C. P. Introduction to *Michael Ayrton, Drawings and Sculpture.* London: Cory, Adams and McKay, 1962; rev. ed., 1966.

Spencer, Charles S. "O Michael Ayrton kai o Ikaros." *Zygos,* 7, 78–79 (May–June 1962): 16–19.

Stanford, Eric. Introduction to the Catalogue of an Exhibition at the Reading Museum Art Gallery, June–July 1969.

Steiner, George. Catalogue Introduction. "Michael Ayrton: A Debt to Hector Berlioz." Catalogue Number 24, Hamet Gallery, London, November 1969.

———. Catalogue Introduction. Sears Vincent Price Gallery, Chicago, December 1970; rpt. Bruton Gallery, Bruton, Somerset, October 1971.

[Thompson, Cynthia.] "Michael Ayrton." *Time,* 58, 2 (9 July 1951): 66.

Tollemache Ltd., Michael. *Catalogue of New Acquisitions, 1969.* London: Tollemache, 1969.

Tucker, Peter. "The Book Illustrations of Michael Ayrton." *Private Library,* 3rd ser., 9, 1 (Spring 1986): 3–52.

Updike, John. Review of *Fabrications* by Michael Ayrton. *New Yorker,* 5 May 1973, 147–49.

Wallis, Nevile. "The Artist's Mind." *Spectator,* 21 December 1962.

Ward, Anne G., ed. *The Quest for Theseus.* London: Pall Mall Press, 1970; 247, 250–51.

Warner, Rex. Introduction to *The Testament of Daedalus* by Michael Ayrton. London: Methuen, 1962.

Whittet, G. S. Review of *Drawings and Sculpture* by Michael Ayrton. *Studio,* 165, February 1963: 86f.

Winkler, Elisabeth. "Loving Mothers: Penelope Leach, the Child Development Expert, and Her Mother Elisabeth Ayrton, the Writer, Talk to Elisabeth Winkler." *London Sunday Times Magazine,* 22 April 1990, 13–16.

Wraight, Robert. "Dishing the Critics." *Tatler,* 15 December 1962.

Wright, Basil. "Michael Ayrton Remembered." *Labrys,* 3 (October 1978): 100–103.

Yorke, Malcolm. *The Spirit of Place: Nine Neo-Romantic Artists and Their Times.* New York: St. Martin's Press, 1988; see 196–224 and 337–53.

H. GENERAL WORKS CITED IN THE NOTES OR WHICH OFFER A BASIS FOR FURTHER STUDY ON THE SUBJECT OF MYTH AND CREATIVITY AND ON THE MYTH OF DAEDALUS

Andrews, John Williams. *Prelude to "Icaros."* New York: Farrar and Rinehart, 1936.

Apollodorus. *The Library.* Trans. J. G. Frazer. 2 vols., incl. *Epitome.* London: W. Heinemann (Loeb Classical Library), 1921.

———. *The Library of Greek Mythology.* Trans., with notes and indices, Keith Aldrich. Lawrence, KS: Coronado Press, 1975.

Aragon, Louis. *Henri Matisse, Roman.* Vol. II. Paris: Gallimard, 1971.

Arnheim, Rudolf. *Picasso's Guernica: The Genesis of a Painting.* Berkeley: Univ. of California Press, 1962, 1973.

———. *Toward a Psychology of Art: Collected Essays.* Berkeley: Univ. of California Press, 1967.

———. *Art and Visual Perception: A Psychology of the Creative Eye. The New Version.* Berkeley: Univ. of California Press, 1974.

———. *New Essays on the Psychology of Art.* Berkeley: Univ. of California Press, 1986.

Artress, Lauren. *Walking a Sacred Path: Rediscovering the Labyrinth as a Spiritual Tool.* New York: Riverhead, 1995.

Ashton, John W. "The Fall of Icarus." *Philological Quarterly,* XX, 3 (July 1941): 345–51.

Auden, W. H. "Musée des Beaux Arts" (1940). *The Collected Poetry of W. H. Auden.* New York: Random House, 1945; 3.

———. "The Problem of Nowness." *Mid-Century,* 19 (November 1960): 14.

Aycock, Wendell M., and Theodore M. Klein. *Classical Mythology in Twentieth-Century Thought and Literature.* Proceedings of Comparative Literature Symposium, Texas Technological University, vol. XI. Lubbock: Texas Tech Press, 1980.

Baatz, D. "Römische Wandmalereien aus dem Limeskastell Echzell, Kr. Budingen, Hessen." *Germania* 46 (1968): 40–52.

Baker, Herschel. *The Later Renaissance in England.* Boston: Houghton Mifflin, 1975.

Barasch, Moshe. *Gestures of Despair in Medieval and Early Renaissance Art.* New York: New York Univ. Press, 1976; esp. 39–56 (on the Minotaur in Dante and his early illuminators).

Barr, Alfred H., Jr. *Matisse: His Art and His Public.* New York: Museum of Modern Art, 1951.

Bartel, Roland. "Icarus Poems Since Auden's Musée des Beaux Arts." *Classical and Modern Literature,* 2 (1982): 95–99.

Beazley, J. D. "Icarus." *JHS,* 47 (1927): 222–33 and pl. XXI.

———. *Attic Black-Figure Vase-Painters.* Oxford: Clarendon Press, 1956; 80.

———. *Attic Red-Figure Vase Painters.* 2nd ed. Oxford: Clarendon Press, 1963; I, 696 and 700.

———. *Paralipomena.* Oxford: Clarendon Press, 1971; 30.

Becatti, G. "La leggenda di Dedalo." *Mitteilungen des Deutschen Archäologischen Instituts, Römische Abteilung,* 60–61 (1953–1954): 22–36.

Belli, Angela. *Ancient Greek Myths and Modern Drama: A Study in Continuity.* New York: New York Univ. Press, 1969.

Bens, John H., and Douglas R. Baugh. *Icarus: An Anthology of Literature.* New York: Macmillan, 1970.

Bérard, C. "Une représentation de la chute d'Icare à Lousonna." *Zeitschrift für Schweizerische Archäologie und Kunstgeschichte,* 23 (1963): 1–9.

Bérard, C., and M. Hofstetter. "Dédale et Icare: tradition ou renouveau?" *Bronzes hellénistiques et romains,* edited by Claude Bérard, Pierre Ducrey, and Antoinette Altherr-Charon. Lausanne: Diffusion de Boccard, 1979; 121–26.

Beschi, Luigi. "Il Monumento di Telemachos, Fondatore dell' Asklepieion Ateniese." *Annuario della Scuola Archeologica de Atene,* 45–46, n.s. 29–30 (1967–1968): 381–436.

Biddle, George. Letter to the author, dated *September 27, 1970.*

Bieber, Margarete. *Laocoön: The Influence of the Group Since Its Rediscovery.* Rev. ed. Detroit: Wayne State Univ. Press, 1967.

Bloch, Georges. *Pablo Picasso: Catalogue de L'oeuvre gravé et lithographie, 1904–1969.* 2 vols. Bern: Kornfeld and Klipstein, 1968–1971.

Bluestone, Max. "The Iconographic Sources of Auden's 'Musée des Beaux Arts.'" *Modern Language Notes,* 76 (April 1961): 331–36.

Bonnefoy, Yves. *Greek and Egyptian Mythologies.* Trans. Dorothy Figuiera, under the direction of Wendy Doniger. Chicago: Univ. of Chicago Press, 1992.

Bord, Janet. "Designed to Amaze." *Illustrated London News,* 263, 6928 (November, 1975): 76–77.

———. *Mazes and Labyrinths of the World.* London: Latimer New Dimensions, 1976.

Borges, Jorge Luis. *Labyrinths: Selected Stories and Other Writings.* Ed. Donald A. Yates and James E. Irby. Preface by André Maurois. New York: New Directions, 1962; rpt. Penguin Books, 1970.

Borsook, Eve. "Carlo Saraceni: His Life and Works." Master's thesis, New York University, 1953.

Brann, Eva T. H. *The World of the Imagination: Sum and Substance.* Lanham, MD: Rowan and Littlefield, 1991.

Brommer, Frank. *Beiträge zur griechischen Bildhauergeschicte. Mitteilungen des Deutschen Archäologischen Instituts, Römische Abteilung,* 3 (1950): 80–98.

———. *Denkmälerlisten zur griechischen Heldensage.* With the assistance of Anneliese Peschlow-Bindokat. Marburg: Elwert, 1971–1976; III, 59–64.

———. *Theseus: die Taten des griechischen Helden in der antiken Kunst und Literatur.* Darmstadt: Wissenschaftliche Buchgesellschaft, 1982.

Burness, Donald B. "Pieter Bruegel: Painter for Poets." *Art Journal,* 32 (1972): 157–62.

Burton-Christie, Douglas. "Into the Labyrinth: Walking the Way of Wisdom." *Weavings* XII, 4 (July–August 1997): 19–28.

Bush, Douglas. *Mythology and the Romantic Tradition.* Cambridge, MA: Harvard Univ. Press, 1937; rpt. New York: W. W. Norton, 1963.

———. *Pagan Myth and Christian Tradition in English Poetry.* Jayne Lectures for 1967. Philadelphia: American Philosophical Society, 1968.

Campbell, Joseph. *Hero With a Thousand Faces.* New York: Meridian Books, 1956.

———, ed. *Myths, Dreams, and Religion.* New York: E. P. Dutton, 1970.

Camps, W. A. *An Introduction to Virgil's Aeneid.* Oxford: Oxford Univ. Press, 1969.

Cantarella, R. *Euripide: I Cretesi.* Milan: Istituto Editoriale Italiano, 1963.

Cantini, Lorenzo. Letter to the author, dated *October 2, 1970.*

Casali, Sergio. "Aeneas and the Doors of the Temple of Apollo." *Classical Journal* 91, 1 (October–November 1995): 1–10.

Cassirer, Ernst. *Language and Myth.* Trans. Susan K. Langer. New York: Harper and Brothers, 1946.

Castleden, Rodney. *The Knossos Labyrinth: A New View of the 'Palace of Minos' at Knossos.* London: Routledge, 1990.

Cavina, A. Ottani. *Carlo Saraceni.* Milan, 1968.

Caws, Mary Ann. "A Double Reading by Design: Brueghel, Auden, and Williams." *Journal of Aesthetics and Art Criticism,* 41 (1983): 323–30.

Chilvers, Ian, and Harold Osborne. *The Oxford Dictionary of Art.* Oxford: Oxford Univ. Press, 1988.

Chipp, Herschel B. *Picasso's Guernica: History, Transformations, Meanings.* Berkeley: Univ. of California Press, 1988.

Clark, Sir Kenneth. *Landscape into Art.* Boston: Beacon Press, 1961. [Rpt. of *Landscape Painting.* New York: Scribner's, 1950.]

———. *The Nude: A Study in Ideal Form.* Bollingen Series No. 35.2. New York: Pantheon Books, 1956.

Connor, W. R. "Theseus in Classical Athens." In Ward, ed., *Quest for Theseus,* 143–74.

Cook, A. B. *Zeus: A Study in Ancient Religion.* Vol. I. Cambridge: Cambridge Univ. Press, 1914.

Coutts-Smith, Kenneth. *The Dream of Icarus: Art and Society in the Twentieth Century.* New York: George Braziller, 1970.

Cowart, Jack, et al. *Henri Matisse Paper Cut-Outs.* St. Louis Art Museum and Detroit Institute of Arts, 1977.

Cowling, Elizabeth, and Jennifer Mundy. *On Classic Ground: Picasso, Leger, de Chirico and the New Classicism 1910–1930.* London: Tate Gallery, 1990.

Cronin, Vincent. *Golden Honeycomb.* New York: E. P. Dutton, 1954; 2nd ed., London: Granada, 1980.

Crosby, Margaret. "Greek Inscriptions: A Poletai Record of the Year 367/6 B.C." *Hesperia,* 10 (1941): 14–27.

Cruttwell, Robert W. *Virgil's Mind at Work: An Analysis of the Symbolism of the Aeneid.* Oxford: Basil Blackwell, 1947; rpt. Westport, CT: Greenwood Press, 1971.

Cust, Lionel. *Anthony Van Dyck: An Historical Study of His Life and Works.* London: G. Bell, 1900.

Darr, William. "Images of Eros and Thanatos in Picasso's Guernica." *Art Journal,* 35 (Summer 1966): 338–46.

Davaras, Costas. *Die Statue aus Astritsi.* Bern: Francke, 1972 (= *Antike Kunst,* Beih. 8); 41.

Dawson, Christopher M. "Romano Campanian Mythological Landscape Painting." *Yale Classical Studies* 9 (1944).

———. "Postscript to *Yale Classical Studies,* Vol. IX." *Yale Classical Studies* 11 (1950): 299–303.

De Bosis, Lauro. *Icaro.* Trans. Ruth Draper; preface by Gilbert Murray. New York: Oxford Univ. Press, 1933.

De Franciscis, A. "Dedalo." *EAA,* III (1960): 16–17.

———. "Icaro." *EAA,* IV (1961): 82–83.

De Tolnay, Charles. *Pierre Bruegel l'Ancien.* Brussels: Nouvelle société d'éditions, 1935.

Diodorus Siculus. Trans. C. H. Oldfather. Vols. I–III, VII. Cambridge, MA: Harvard Univ. Press (Loeb Classical Library), 1963–1970.

Dionysius of Halicarnassus. *Dionysii Halicarnasei Opuscula.* Ed. Hermann Usener and Ludwig Radermacher. Leipzig: B. G. Teubner, 1899–1929.

———. *Three Literary Letters.* New York: Garland, 1987.

Donald, Sydney G. "Of Mazes, Men and Minotaurs: Friedrich Dürrenmatt and the Myth of the Labyrinth." *New German Studies,* 14, 3 (1986–1987): 187–231.

Doob, Penelope Reed. *The Idea of the Labyrinth: From Classical Antiquity through the Middle Ages.* Ithaca, NY: Cornell Univ. Press, 1990.

Dorsey, Gary. *The Fullness of Wings: The Making of a New Daedalus.* New York: Viking Penguin, 1990.

Dunbabin, T. J. "Minos and Daidalos in Sicily." *BSR,* 16 (1948): 5.

Edmonds, John Maxwell. *The Fragments of Attic Comedy.* Vols. I–III A. Leiden: E. J. Brill, 1957, 1959, 1961.

Ellmann, Richard. *James Joyce.* New York: Oxford Univ. Press, 1959.

Elsen, Albert. "Lipton's Sculpture as Portrait of the Artist." *Art Journal,* 24, 2 (Winter 1964–1965): 113–18.

Enciclopedia dell'Arte Antica. Roma: Instituto della enciclopedia Italiana, IV (1961); 81, pl. 104.

Fagles, Robert. *Bacchylides: Complete Poems.* New Haven: Yale Univ. Press, 1961.

Faris, Wendy B. *Labyrinths of Language: Symbolic Landscape and Narrative Design in Modern Fiction.* Baltimore: Johns Hopkins Univ. Press, 1988.

Feder, Lillian. *Ancient Myth in Modern Poetry.* Princeton: Princeton Univ. Press, 1971.

Feehan, Joseph, ed. *Dedalus on Crete: Essays on the Implications of Joyce's Portrait.* Los Angeles: St. Thomas More Guild, Immaculate Heart College, 1956.

Finn, David. *How to Look at Sculpture.* New York: Harry N. Abrams, 1989.

Fisher, Adrian, Randoll Coate, and Graham Burgess. *A Celebration of Mazes.* 3rd ed. Saint Alban's, Hertfordshire: Minotaur Designs, 1984.

Fisher, Adrian, and Georg Gerster. *Labyrinth: Solving the Riddle of the Maze.* New York: Harmony Books, 1990.

Fisher, Adrian, and Diana Kingham. *Mazes.* Princes Risborough, Buckinghamshire: Shire Publications, 1991.

Fitzgerald, W. "Aeneas, Daedalus and the Labyrinth." *Arethusa,* XVII (1984): 51–65.

Flacelière, Robert. *Greek Oracles.* Trans. Douglas Garman. London: Elek Books, 1965.

Fletcher, G. Review of *The Journey: Odes and Sonnets* by Gerald Gould. *Freeman,* 4 (28 December 1921): 379.

Frank, Joseph. *The Doomed Astronaut.* Cambridge, MA: Winthrop Publishers, 1972.

Freud, Sigmund. *Civilization and Its Discontents.* Trans. Joan Riviere. London: Hogarth Press, 1930; rpt. New York: Dover Publications, 1994.

Frontisi, Françoise. "Gods and Artisans: Hephaestus, Athena, Daedalus." In *Greek and Egyptian Mythologies.* Compiled by Yves Bonnefoy, trans. Dorothy Figuiera under the direction of Wendy Doniger. Chicago: Univ. of Chicago Press, 84–90.

Frover, A. "I mosaici romani di Cremona." *Bollettino d'Arte del Ministero della Publica Istruzione,* 2 (1957): 325–34.

Frye, Northrop. *Myth and Metaphor: Selected Essays, 1974–1988.* Ed. Robert D. Denham. Charlottesville: Univ. Press of Virginia, 1990.

Furtwängler, Adolf. *Beschreibung der Geschnittenen Steine im Antiquarium.* Berlin: W. Spemann, 1896.

———. *Die Antike Gemmen,* I–III. Leipzig: Giesecke and Devrient, 1900.

Galinsky, G. Karl. *The Herakles Theme: The Adaptations of the Hero in Literature from Homer to the Twentieth Century.* Oxford: Basil Blackwell, [1972].

García Márquez, Gabriel. *The General in His Labyrinth.* New York: Penguin Books, 1990.

Gardner's Art through the Ages. 7th ed., rev. Horst de la Croix and Richard G. Tansey. New York: Harcourt Brace Jovanovich, 1980.

Gibson, Michael. *Symbolism.* Köln: Taschen, 1999.

Gide, André. *Two Legends: Oedipus and Theseus.* Trans. John Russell. New York, 1950; rpt. New York: Random House (Vintage Books), 1958.

Gombrich, E. H. *The Story of Art.* 11th ed. London: Phaidon, 1966.

Gouldner, Alvin W. "Anti-Minotaur: The Myth of a Value-Free Sociology." *Social Problems,* (1961): 199–213.

Graves, Robert. *The Greek Myths.* 2 vols. Baltimore: Penguin Books, 1955.

Greece: A Bulletin of Record and Analysis. Washington, DC: Information Service of the Royal Greek Embassy III, 3 (April 1967): 196–97.

Green, P. "The Flight-plan of Daedalus." *Échos du Monde classique* XXII (1979): 30–35.

Gregory, J. C. "Myth and the Dream of Flying." *Contemporary Review,* 193 (April, 1958): 197–201.

Guichard-Meili, Jean, ed. *Bruegel: la chute d'Icare.* Fribourg: Office du Livre, 1974.

Haldane, Lord. *Daedalus, or Science and the Future.* London: K. Paul, Trench, Trubner, 1924.

Hall, Donald. *Henry Moore: The Life and Work of a Great Sculptor.* New York: Harper and Row, 1965–1966.

———. *Life Work.* Boston: Beacon Press, 1993.

Hampe, M. R. "Dädalus und Icarus auf spätrömischer Sigillatakane." *Mélanges Mansel,* 1 (1974): 25–30 and pls. 17–18.

Hanfmann, George M. A. "Daidalos in Etruria." *AJA,* 39 (1935): 189–94 and pl. XXV.

Harries, Karsten. *The Meaning of Modern Art: A Philosophical Interpretation.* Evanston, IL: Northwestern Univ. Press, 1968.

Harris, Stephen L., and Gloria Platzner. *Classical Mythology: Images and Insights.* Mountain View, CA: Mayfield Publishing, 1995.

Harrison, Regina. "Mythopoesis: The Monster in the Labyrinth according to Supervielle, Gide, Borges, and Cortazar." *Kentucky Romance Quarterly,* 32, 2 (1985): 127–37.

Hart, Clive. *The Prehistory of Flight.* Berkeley: Univ. of California Press, 1985.

Hartt, Frederick. *History of Italian Renaissance Art: Painting, Sculpture, Architecture.* 2nd ed. Englewood Cliffs, NJ: Prentice-Hall, 1979.

Hathorn, Richmond Y. *Greek Mythology.* Lebanon: American Univ. of Beirut, 1977.

Hauser, Arnold. *The Social History of Art.* Vol. 2. New York: Knopf, 1951.

Hayward, Thomas A. "The Fall of Icarus: Ovid, Brueghel, Auden, et al." *New England Classical Newsletter,* XIV, 1 (October 1986): 19–24.

Hedgecoe, John, and Henry Moore. *Henry Moore.* New York: Simon and Schuster, 1968.

Helbig, Wolfgang. *Wandgemälde der vom Vesuv verschütteten Städte Campaniens.* Leipzig: Von Breitkopf and Hartel, 1868.

———. *Führer* II, 2nd ed. Leipzig: B. G. Teubner, 1899. 4th ed., rev. Hermine Speier. Tübingen: Ernst Wasmuth, 1966.

Heller, John L. "A Labyrinth from Pylos." *AJA,* 65 (1961): 57–62 and pl. 33.

Henle, Jane. *A Vase Painter's Notebook.* Bloomington: Indiana Univ. Press, 1973.

Herberger, Charles F. *The Thread of Ariadne: The Labyrinth of the Calendar of Minos.* New York: Philosophical Library, 1972.

Herbert, Kevin. "The Theseus Theme: Some Recent Versions." *Classical Journal,* 55, 4 (January 1960): 175–85.

Herrera, Hayden. *Matisse: A Portrait.* New York: Harcourt Brace, 1993.

Hinks, R. P. *Catalogue of the Greek, Etruscan and Roman Paintings and Mosaics in the British Museum.* London: British Museum, 1933; see 15–16 (pl. 28 "Daedalus and Icarus").

Holland, Richard. *Die Sage von Daidalos und Ikaros.* Leipzig: A. Edelmann, 1902.

Hollis, A. S. *Ovid Metamorphoses Book VIII.* Oxford: Clarendon Press, 1970.

Holmes, Oliver Wendell. "The Chambered Nautilus." In *Poetry of the New England Renaissance 1790–1890.* Ed. George F. Whicher. New York: Holt, Rinehart and Winston, 1950; 293f.

Hopper, Stanley Romaine. "Myth, Dream, and Imagination." In *Myths, Dreams, and Religion.* Ed. Joseph Campbell. New York: E. P. Dutton, 1970; 111–37.

Hughes, Randolph. Introduction to *Pasiphaë: A Poem by A. C. Swinburne.* London: Golden Cockerel Press, 1950.

Huttar, Charles A. "*Paradise Regained,* the Hermeneutical Circle, and Christian Anticipations of Post-Modern Theory." *Religion and Literature,* 19, 3 (Autumn 1987): 15–26.

Immerwahr, Sara Anderson. *The Neolithic and Bronze Ages.* Princeton: American School of Classical Studies at Athens, 1971 (= *Athenian Agora,* vol. 13); see 107, 156, 192, and pl. 41.

Jackson, Sidney. "Tricephalic Heads from Greetland, Yorks." *Antiquity,* 42, 168 (December 1968): 314–15 and backpiece.

Jacoby, Felix. *Die Fragmente der griechischen Historiker.* Vol. I. Berlin: Weidmann, 1923.

Jaffe, Irma B. *The Sculpture of Leonard Baskin.* New York: The Viking Press, 1980.

Johnson, Arnold. *Of Earth and Darkness: The Novels of William Golding.* Columbia: Univ. of Missouri Press, 1980.

Jones, H. Stuart. *Select Passages from Ancient Writers Illustrative of the History of Greek Sculpture.* London: Macmillan, 1895.

Jonson, Ben. *Pleasure Reconciled to Virtue.* London, 1618.

Johnson, R. Stanley. *Pablo Picasso: Suite Vollard, A Selection.* Chicago: R. S. Johnson-International Gallery, 1979.

Joyce, James. *A Portrait of the Artist as a Young Man.* Serially in the *Egoist* (1914–1915), then London: Egoist, 1916; rpt. New York: Viking Press (Compass Books), 1956.

Judeich, Walter. *Topographie von Athen.* 2nd ed. Munich: C. H. Beck, 1931; 316.

Jung, C. G. *Two Essays on Analytical Psychology.* Trans. R. F. C. Hull. New York: Pantheon Books for Bollingen Foundation, 1953; New York: Meridian Books, 1956.

Jung, C. G., and C. Kerényi. *Essays on a Science of Mythology: The Myths of the Divine Child and the Divine Maiden.* Rev. ed., trans. R. F. C. Hull. New York: Pantheon Books, 1949; rpt. New York: Harper and Row (Harper Torchbook), 1963.

Jung, Carl G., et al. *Man and His Symbols.* Garden City, NY: Doubleday, 1964.

Kantor, R. E. "Art, Ambiguity and Schizophrenia." *Art Journal,* 24, 3 (Spring 1965): 234–39.

Karo, Georg. *Die Schachtgräber von Mykenai.* Munich: F. Bruckmann, 1930–1933.

Kaye, Julian B. "Who Is Betty Byrne?" *Modern Language Notes,* 71 (February 1956): 93–95.

Kelleher, John V. "The Perceptions of James Joyce." *Atlantic Monthly,* 201 (March 1958): 82ff.

Kenner, Hugh. *Dublin's Joyce.* Bloomington: Indiana Univ. Press, 1956.

Kern, Hermann. "Labyrinths: Tradition and Contemporary Works." *Artforum* 19, 9 (May 1981): 60–68.

———. *Through the Labyrinth: Designs and Meanings over 5,000 Years.* Munich: Prestel, 2000.

Kilinski, Karl II. *Classical Myth in Western Art: Ancient through Modern.* Dallas, TX: Meadows Museum and Gallery, Southern Methodist Univ., 1985.

Knight, W. F. Jackson. *Cumaean Gates: A Reference of the Sixth Aeneid to the Initiation Pattern.* Oxford: Basil Blackwell, 1936.

———. *Vergil: Epic and Anthropology.* Ed. John D. Christie. London: George Allen and Unwin, 1967.

Knossos Tablets B.I.C.S., Suppl. 2 (January 1956): 49; Suppl. 7 (1959): 49; Suppl. 15 (1964): 94–95.

Krause, Ernst. *Die Trojaburgen Europas.* Glogau, 1893.

Lactantius. *The Divine Institutes,* books I–VII. Washington, DC: Catholic Univ. of America Press, [1964].

———. *Institutiones divinae.* Paris: Editions du Cerf, 1973–1992.

Langford, John S. "DAEDALUS: The Making of the Legend." *Technology Review,* 91, 7 (October 1988): 24–35.

———. "Afterword." In *The Fullness of Wings,* by Gary Dorsey. New York: Viking Penguin, 1990; 347–50.

Lavin, Irving. "Picasso's Bull(s): Art History in Reverse." *Art in America* 81, 3 (March 1993): 76–93, 121, 123.

Law, Helen H. *Bibliography of Greek Myth in English Poetry.* American Classical League Service Bureau, Bulletin XXVII. Oxford, OH: Miami University, 1955.

Leeming, David Adams. *Flights: Readings in Magic, Mysticism, Fantasy, and Flight.* New York: Harcourt Brace Jovanovich, 1974.

Levin, Harry. *James Joyce: A Critical Introduction.* Norfolk, CT: New Directions, 1941.

———. *The Overreacher: A Study of Christopher Marlowe.* Cambridge, MA: Harvard Univ. Press, 1952.

Licht, Fred, and David Finn. *Canova.* New York: Abbeville Press, 1983; see 26–27 (color plates), 156–62, and 274; pls. 137, 138, 140, 141, 143, and 144.

Lockridge, Ross F. *The Labyrinth: A History of the New Harmony Labyrinth, Including Some Special Study of the Spiritual and Mystical Life of Its Builders, the Rappites, and a Brief Survey of Labyrinths Generally.* New Harmony, IN: New Harmony Memorial Commission, 1941.

MacLeish, Archibald. "Hypocrite Auteur." *Collected Poems 1917–1952.* Boston: Houghton Mifflin, 1952; 173–74.

Madden, Charles F. "The Fall of Icarus (*From Brueghel's Painting*)." *Northwest Review* [Univ. of Oregon], III, 3 (Summer 1960): 87.

Maiuri, Amedeo. *Roman Painting.* Geneva: Albert Skira, 1953.

Malinowski, Bronislaw. *Myth in Primitive Psychology.* New York: W. W. Norton, 1926.

Malville, Kim. *A Feather for Daedalus: Explorations in Science and Myth.* Menlo Park, CA: Cummings Publishing, 1975.

Martin, John Rupert. *Baroque.* New York: Harper and Row, 1977.

Martin, J. R. *The Farnese Gallery.* Princeton: Princeton Univ. Press, 1965.

Matthews, William Henry. *Mazes and Labyrinths: Their History and Development.* London: Longmans, Green, 1922; rpt. New York: Dover Books, 1970.

Mau, A. "Scavi de Pompei." *MDAI (R),* 5 (1890): 261–64, and 11 (1896): 49–51.

Mayerson, Philip. *Classical Mythology in Literature, Art, and Music.* Lexington, MA: Xerox College Publishing, 1971.

Meltzer, Françoise, ed. *The Trial(s) of Psychoanalysis.* Chicago: Univ. of Chicago Press, 1988.

Meyer, Bernhard C. "Notes on Flying and Dying." *Psychoanalytic Review,* 52 (1983): 327–52.

Miller, J. Hillis. *Ariadne's Thread.* New Haven: Yale Univ. Press, 1992.

Miller, Whee Kim. "Milet Andrejevic: Iconography of the Past and Present Tenses." *Arts Magazine,* 47, 1 (September–October 1972): 38–41.

Möbius, Hans. "Ein hellenistischer Daidalos." *Jahrbuch des Deutschen Archäologischen Institut,* 68 (1953): 96–101 and pls. 1–3.

Morford, Mark P. O. "Bruegel and the First *Georgic.*" *Greece and Rome,* ser. 2, vol. 13 (1966): 50–53.

Morford, Mark, and Robert J. Lenardon. *Classical Mythology.* 3rd. ed. New York: Longman, 1985.

Morgan, Anne Barclay. "Maze and Labyrinth." *Sculpture* 14 (July–August 1995): 28–33.

Morris, Sarah P. *Daidalos and the Origins of Greek Art.* Princeton: Princeton Univ. Press, 1992.

Murray, Henry A. "American Icarus." *Clinical Studies of Personality.* Ed. Arthur Burton and Robert E. Harris. Vol. II of *Case Histories in Clinical and Abnormal Psychology.* New York: Harper, 1955; 615–41.

———, ed. *Myth and Mythmaking.* New York: George Braziller, 1960.

Myers, David G. *Psychology.* 6th ed. New York: Worth Publishers, 2001.

Mylonas, George E. *Ancient Mycenae: The Capital City of Agamemnon.* Princeton: Princeton Univ. Press, 1957.

Nauck, August. *Tragicorum Graecorum Fragmenta.* 2nd ed. Bruno Snell. *Tragica Adespota.* Göttingen: Vandenhoeck and Ruprecht, [1971]–1985.

Neumann, Erich. *The Archetypal World of Henry Moore.* Trans. R. F. C. Hull. New York: Bollingen Foundation, 1959. New York: Harper Torchbook, 1965 (references are from this edition).

Nims, John Frederick. "Dedalus in Crete." In *Dedalus on Crete: Essays on the Implication of Joyce's Portrait.* Ed. Joseph Feehan. Los Angeles: St. Thomas More Guild, Immaculate Heart College, 1956; 75–88.

Norden, Eduard. *P. Vergilius Maro Aeneis Buch VI.* Darmstadt: Wissenschaftliche Buchgesellschaft, 1957.

Nyenhuis, Jacob E. "Daedalus and Icarus: A Symbol for our Time?" *Graduate Comment* (Wayne State Univ.), 10, 4 (1967), 223–38.

———. "Daidalos et Ikaros." In *Lexikon Iconographicum Mythologiae Classicae.* Ed. Lilly Kahil. Zurich: Artemis, 1986. III. 1, 313–21; III. 2, pls. 237–42.

———. "The Flight of Daedalus: From Myth to Reality." In *Silver Bells over Two Campuses.* Tokyo: Meiji Gakuin University, June 1990; 58–73.

Obregón, Mauricio. "Magic of Discovery Lures Astronauts as It Did Argonauts." *Smithsonian,* 7, 1 (April 1976): 80–85.

O'Brien, Justin. *Portrait of André Gide: A Critical Biography.* New York: Knopf, 1953.

O'Brien, Martin. "Garden-Variety Puzzles." *European Travel and Life,* 8, 2 (March 1992): 70–79.

Ogilvie, Daniel M. "The Icarus Complex." *Psychology Today* 2, 7 (December 1968): 30–35 and 67.

Otis, Brooks. *Virgil: A Study in Civilized Poetry.* Oxford: Clarendon Press, 1963.

Overbeck, J. *Die Antiken Schriftquellen.* Leipzig: Wilhelm Engelmann, 1868.

Palmer, Leonard R. *The Interpretation of Mycenaean Greek Texts.* Oxford: Clarendon Press, 1963.

———. *Mycenaeans and Minoans: Aegean Prehistory in the Light of the Linear B Tablets.* 2nd rev. ed. London: Faber and Faber, 1965; esp. 130–42.

Panofsky, Erwin. *Studies in Iconology: Humanistic Themes in the Art of the Renaissance.* Oxford: Oxford Univ. Press, 1936; rpt. New York: Harper and Row (Icon Editions), 1972.

PARABOLA: *The Magazine of Myth and Tradition,* XIX, 2, (May 1994).

Parke, H. W. *A History of the Delphic Oracle.* Oxford: Basil Blackwell, 1939.

Parke, H. W., and D. E. W. Wormell. *The Delphic Oracle.* Oxford: Basil Blackwell, 1956.

Paschalis, M. "The Unifying Theme of Daedalus' Sculptures on the Temple of Apollo Cumanus (Aen. 6.20–33)." *Vergilius,* XXII (1986): 33–41.

Patris, A. "La légende de Dédale dans l'antiquité classique." Diss. Belgium, date unknown. Cf. *Revue Belge de Philologie et d'Histoire,* 24 (1945): 512.

Pausanias. *Guide to Greece.* 2 vols. Trans. Peter Levi, S.J. Harmondsworth, Middlesex: Penguin Books, 1971.

———. *Pausaniae Graeciae descriptio.* Leipzig: Teubner, 1973–1981; rev. ed., 1989–1990.

Paz, Ocatavio. *The Labyrinth of Solitude: Life and Thought in Mexico.* Trans. Lysander Kemp. New York: Grove Press, 1961.

Pearson, A. C. *The Fragments of Sophocles.* Cambridge: Cambridge Univ. Press, 1917.

Pearson, D'Orsay W. "Spenser's Labyrinth—Again." *Studies in Iconography,* 3 (1977): 70–88.

Pennick, Nigel. *Mazes and Labyrinths.* London: Robert Hale, 1990.

Peters, W. J. T. *Landscape in Romano-Campanian Mural Painting.* Assen, the Netherlands: Van Gorcum, 1963.

Peyre, Henri. *What Is Romanticism?* Trans. Roda Roberts. University: Univ. of Alabama Press, 1977.

Pliny the Elder. *Natural History.* Cambridge, MA: Harvard Univ. Press (Loeb Classical Library), 1961.

Plutarch. *Parallel Lives: Theseus.* Trans. B. Perrin. Cambridge, MA: Harvard Univ. Press (Loeb Classical Library), 1914–1926.

Pollak, Ludwig. "Dédale et Pasiphaé." *Revue archéologique,* 33 (July–December 1898): 12–14 and pl. X.

Pope-Hennessy, John. *The Drawings of Domenichino in the Collection of His Majesty the King at Windsor Castle.* New York: Phaidon (distr. Oxford Univ. Press), 1948.

Praz, Mario. *Mnemosyne: The Parallel between Literature and the Visual Arts.* Princeton: Princeton Univ. Press, 1970; esp. 75–78.

Price, Eluned F. "The Eternal Maze." *House Beautiful,* 137, 12 (Dec. 1, 1995): 76–81.

Proweller, William. "The Meaning of the Bull and Horse in Guernica." *Art Journal,* 34 (Winter 1964–1965): 106–12.

Putnam, Michael C. J. "Daedalus, Virgil and the End of Art." *American Journal of Philology,* CVIII (1987): 173–98.

Read, Herbert. *A Concise History of Modern Painting.* New York: Frederick A. Praeger, 1959.

———. *Contemporary British Art.* Rev. ed. Harmondsworth, Middlesex: Penguin Books, 1964. [1964a]

———. *A Concise History of Modern Sculpture.* New York: Frederick A. Praeger, 1964. [1964c]

———. *The Philosophy of Modern Art.* London: Faber and Faber, 1964. [1964b]

———. *Art Now: An Introduction to the Theory of Modern Painting and Sculpture.* 5th ed. London: Faber and Faber, 1968. [1968]

Redford, Grant H. "The Role of Structure in Joyce's 'Portrait.'" *Modern Fiction Studies,* 4 (Spring 1958): 21–23.

Reed, John R. "Esthetic Directions in the Labyrinth." *Western Humanities Review,* XXIII, 1 (Winter 1969): 49–55.

Reinach, Salomon. *Répertoire de Peintures grecques et romaines.* Paris. Ernest Leroux, 1922; esp. 183 84 and 236.

Richter, Gisela M. A. *Kouroi: Archaic Greek Youths.* London: Phaidon Press, 1960.

———. *Engraved Gems of the Greeks and the Etruscans.* London: Phaidon Press, 1968.

Robbe-Grillet, Alain. *In the Labyrinth.* Trans. Christine Brooke-Rose. London: Calder and Boyars, 1967.

Robert, Carl. "Daidalos und Ikaros. Pompejanisches Wandgemälde." *Archaeologische Zeitung,* 35 (1877): 1–8 and pls. 1–2.

———. *Der Pasiphae-Sarkophag.* Halle: Max Niemeyer, 1890. (= *Hallische Winkelmannsprogramm* XIV.)

———. *Die griechische Heldensage,* vol. I. 4th ed. Berlin: Weidmann, 1920 (= L. Preller. *Griechische Mythologie,* vol. II, part 1); esp. 364ff.

Robinson, F. N., ed. *The Works of Geoffrey Chaucer.* 2nd ed. London, 1957.

Rocquet, Claude-Henri. *Bruegel, or The Workshop of Dreams. A Novel.* Chicago: Univ. of Chicago Press, 1991.

Rodman, Selden. *The Airmen: A Poem in Four Parts.* New York: Random House, 1941.

Rogers, Fred B. Letter to the author, dated *September 28, 1970.*

Roscher, W. H. *Ausführliches Lexikon der griechischen und römischen Mythologie,* vol. 2. 2. Leipzig: B. G. Teubner, 1894–1897, 3004–11; vol. 5. Leipzig: B. G. Teubner, 1916–1924.

Rosenberg, Alfons. *Die christliche Bildmeditation.* Munich: Otto-Wilhelm-Barth, 1955; esp. 257–88.

Rubin, William, ed. *Pablo Picasso: A Retrospective.* New York: Museum of Modern Art, 1980.

Rudd, Niall. "Daedalus and Icarus (i) From Rome to the End of the Middle Ages; (ii) From the Renaissance to the Present Day;" and "Daedalus and Icarus in Art." In *Ovid Renewed: Ovidian Influences on Literature and Art from the Middle Ages to the Twentieth Century,* ed. Charles Martindale. Cambridge: Cambridge Univ. Press, 1988; 21–53 and 247–53.

Russell, Bertrand. *Icarus, or The Future of Science.* London: K. Paul, Trench, Trubner and Co., 1924.

Rutledge, Henry C. "Vergil's Daedalus." *Classical Journal,* 62 (1967): 309–11.

Ryf, Robert G. *A New Approach to Joyce.* "Perspectives in Criticism" No. 8. Berkeley: Univ. of California Press, 1962.

Santarcangeli, Paolo. *Il Libro dei Labirinti.* Florence, 1967.

Schefold, Karl. *Pompejanische Malerei: Sinn und Ideengeschichte.* Basel: Benno Schwabe, 1952; esp. 106ff., 187ff., and 198.

———. *Die Wände Pompejis.* Berlin: Walter de Gruyter, 1957.

———. *Vergessenes Pompeji: Unveröffentlichte Bilder römischer Wanddekorationen in geschichtlicher Folge herausgegeben.* Bern: Francke, 1962; esp. 82–89, 140–63, 186–96, 205, and 208.

Schnabel, Ernst. *Story for Icarus: Projects, Incidents, and Conclusions from the Life of D., Engineer.* Trans. J. J. Dunbar. New York: Harcourt, Brace, 1961.

Schneider, Daniel E. *The Psychoanalyst and the Artist.* New York: Mentor Books, 1962; rpt., with new introductory material, Easthampton, NY: Alexa Press, 1979.

Schoder, Raymond V., S.J. "Ancient Cumae." *Scientific American,* 209, 6 (December 1963): 108–18.

Scholes, Robert E., and Richard M. Kain. *The Workshop of Daedalus: James Joyce and the Raw Materials for A Portrait of the Artist as a Young Man.* Evanston, IL: Northwestern University Press, 1965.

Schorer, Mark. "The Necessity of Myth." *Myth and Mythmaking.* Ed. Henry A. Murray. New York: George Braziller, 1960; 354–58.

Schweitzer, B. *Daidalos und die Daidaliden in der Überlieferung, Schriften der Königsberger Gelehrten Gesellschaft, Geisteswiss. Kl.* 9, I (1932) (= *Zur Kunst der Antike, Ausgewählte Schriften* I [1963]): 127ff.

Sebeok, Thomas A. *Myth: A Symposium.* Bloomington: Indiana Univ. Press, 1955.

Seznec, Jean. *The Survival of the Pagan Gods: The Mythological Tradition and Its Place in Renaissance Humanism and Art.* Trans. Barbara F. Sessions. New York: Pantheon Books, 1953; rpt. Princeton: Princeton Univ. Press, 1972.

Shames, Germaine W. "The Maze Craze: Taking a New Turn." *Rotarian,* 163, 6 (December 1993): 32–35.

Sharpless, F. Parvin. *Symbol and Myth in Modern Literature.* Rochelle Park, NJ: Hayden, 1976.

Shelburne, Walter A. *Mythos and Logos in the Thought of Carl Jung: The Theory of the Collective Unconscious in Scientific Perspective.* Albany: State Univ. of New York Press, 1988.

Shroder, Maurice Z. *Icarus: The Image of the Artist in French Romanticism.* Cambridge, MA: Harvard Univ. Press, 1961.

Silius Italicus. *Punica.* Trans. J. D. Duff. 2 vols. Cambridge, MA: Harvard Univ. Press (Loeb Classical Library), 1950–1961.

Simon, Erika. "Early Images of Daidalos in Flight." *The Ages of Homer: A Tribute to Emily Townsend Vermeule.* Ed. Jane B. Carter and Sarah P. Morris. Austin: Univ. of Texas Press, 1995; 407–13.

Skira, Albert. *Labyrinthe: Journal Mensuel des Lettres et des Arts.* Authorized reprint edition complete in one volume, including a specially prepared cumulative index. Intro. Albert Skira. Original Nos. 1–23 (October 1944–December 1946). New York: Arno Press, 1968.

Smith, A. H. *A Catalogue of Sculpture in the Department of Greek and Roman Antiquities, British Museum.* London: British Museum, 1904.

Smith, Cecil H. *Catalogue of the Greek and Etruscan Vases in the British Museum.* Vol. III, *Vases of the Finest Period.* London: British Museum, 1896.

Smith, Evans Lansing. "The Mythical Method of Descent into Hell." *Mythlore,* 76 (Spring 1994): 10–14.

Stanford, W. B., and J. V. Luce. *The Quest for Ulysses.* New York: Praeger, 1974.

Steele, Robert S. *Freud and Jung: Conflicts of Interpretation.* London: Routledge and Kegan Paul, 1982.

Stevens, Wallace. *William Carlos Williams: A Collection of Critical Essays.* Ed. J. Hillis Miller. Englewood Cliffs, NJ: Prentice-Hall, 1966.

Swain, Kathleen M. "The Art of the Maze in Book IX of *Paradise Lost.*" *Studies in English Literature 1500–1900,* 12 (1972): 129–40.

Swinburne, A. C. *Pasiphaë: A Poem by A. C. Swinburne.* Intro. Randolph Hughes. London: Golden Cockerel Press, 1950.

Tindall, William York. *The Literary Symbol.* New York: Columbia University Press, 1955.

Turner, John H. *The Myth of Icarus in Spanish Renaissance Poetry.* London: Tamesis Books, 1976.

Tuve, Rosemond. *A Reading of George Herbert.* Chicago: Univ. of Chicago Press, 1952.

Varro, Marcus Terentius. *Res Divinae.* Ancient Religion and Mythology. Bks. I, XIV, XV, XVI. New York: Arno Press, 1975.

Ventris, Michael, and John Chadwick. *Documents in Mycenaean Greek.* Cambridge: Cambridge Univ. Press, 1956.

Vickery, John B., ed. *Myth and Literature: Contemporary Theory and Practice.* Lincoln: Univ. of Nebraska Press, 1966; rpt. Bison Book, 1969.

Vilain, Jacques. "French Painting 1774–1830: The Age of Revolution." Catalogue of an exhibition held at the Grand Palais, Paris, the Detroit Institute of Arts, and the Metropolitan Museum of Art, New York, 1974–1975.

Von Blankenhagen, Peter Heinrich. "Daedalus and Icarus on Pompeian Walls." *Mitteilungen des Deutschen Archäologischen Instituts, Römische Abteilung,* 75 (1968): 106–43 and pls. 27–47.

Walters, H. B. *Catalogue of the Greek and Etruscan Vases in the British Museum.* Vol. II, *Black Figured Vases.* London: British Museum, 1893.

———. *Catalogue of the Bronzes, Greek, Roman, and Etruscan, in the Department of Greek and Roman Antiquities, British Museum.* London: British Museum, 1899.

———. *Catalogue of the Terracottas in the Department of Greek and Roman Antiquities, British Museum.* London: British Museum, 1903.

———. *Catalogue of the Engraved Gems and Cameos, Greek, Etruscan and Roman, in the British Museum.* London: British Museum, 1926. Part II, *Engraved Gems of the Romans.* London: Phaidon,

Ward, Anne G., ed. *The Quest for Theseus.* London: Pall Mall Press, 1970.

Warncke, Carsten-Peter. *Pablo Picasso: 1881–1973.* Köln: Taschen, 1998.

Watson-Williams, Helen. *André Gide and the Greek Myth: A Critical Study.* Oxford: Clarendon Press, 1967.

Webster, T. B. L., ed. *The Tragedies of Euripides.* London: Methuen, 1967.

Wheelock, Carter. *The Mythmaker.* Austin: Univ. of Texas Press, 1969.

Whicher, George F., ed. *Poetry of the New England Renaissance: 1790–1890.* New York: Rinehart, 1950.

White, John E. C. T. *Pieter Bruegel and the Fall of the Art Historian.* Newcastle upon Tyne: Univ. of Newcastle upon Tyne, 1980.

Williams, Phyllis Lehmann. "The Meander Door: A Labyrinthine Symbol." In *Studi in Onore di Luisa Banti.* Ed. Giovanni Becatti, et al. Rome: Bretschneider, 1965.

Williams, R. D. *P. Vergilius Maronis Aeneidos Liber Quintus.* Oxford: Clarendon Press, 1960.

Williams, William Carlos. "Pictures from Brueghel II: Landscape with the Fall of Icarus." *Pictures from Brueghel and Other Poems.* New York: New Directions, 1962; 4.

Wise, V. M. "Flight Myths in Ovid's Metamorphoses." *Ramus,* VI (1977): 44–59.

Wittkower, Rudolf. *Art and Architecture in Italy 1600–1750.* 3rd ed. London: Penguin Books (Pelican History of Art), 1973 and 1991.

Wolkomir, Richard. "It Is Easy to Get Bushed When You're Threading a Maze." *Smithsonian,* 18, 9 (December 1987): 108–19.

Woodward, Kenneth L. "On the Road Again: Americans Love the Search So Much That the Idea of a Destination Is Lost." *Newsweek,* 28 November 1994, 61f.

Zarker, John W. "Aeneas and Theseus in *Aeneid* 6." *Classical Journal,* 65, (1967): 220–26.

Zervos, Christian. *Pablo Picasso.* 33 vols. Paris: Cahiers d'Art, 1932–1978.

Photography Credits

Permission to reproduce the following photographs is gratefully acknowledged. The identity of the photographers for the remaining figures and plates could not be established. Anyone knowing the identity of the photographer for any uncredited photograph is urged to write the publisher so that correction can be made in any future edition of this book. Photographs known to be copyrighted are so designated.

Artists Rights Society (ARS), New York/© 2002 Estate of Pablo Picasso: Figures 12 and 13
Artists Rights Society (ARS), New York/© 2002 Succession H. Matisse, Paris: Plate 5
Artists Rights Society (ARS), New York/ADAGP, Paris, © 2002: Plate 14
BBC Information and Archives: Figure 1
British Museum: Plate 1; Figures 5 and 254
Central Photographic Service Ltd., the Broseley Studio: Figure 30
Cooper, A. C.: Figures 17, 18, 19, 23, 25, 26, 32, 33, 34, 35, 36, 40, 41, 42, 45, 46, 51, 54, 55, 57, 59, 60, 61, 69, 74, 99, 101, 108, 112, 133, 139, and 145
Courtauld Institute of Art, University of London: Figure 256
Eaden Lilley Photographers (copyright W. Eaden Lilley & Co., Ltd.), Cambridge: Figures 27, 39, 44, 53, 64, 68, 97, 100, 113, and 114
© Estate of Ben Shahn/Licensed by VAGA, New York, NY: Plate 6
© Estate of Leonard Baskin: Figures 14, 15, 16, and 66
Faiers, Gordon F., Sible Headingham, Halstead, Essex: Figures 31, 58, 126, 137, 158–176, 177 (?), 180, 181, 184–189, 191–204, 206, 208, 209, 211–215, 227, 229–231, 234, 235, 240–244, 247–249, and 253
Fineberg, Steve: Plates 8 and 9
Iverson, Brad, Detroit, MI: Figures 85 and 117
Korab, Balthazar, Troy, MI: Figures 236–239
Leeser, Paulus: Figures 149–151
Lewinski, J. S., London (copyrighted photographs): Figures 24, 84, 88–91, 94–96, 102, 107, 125, 128–130, 138, 140–144, 146, 147, 152, 153, 155, 156, 207, and 210
Library of Congress, Washington, DC: Figure 15
Martelli, Marina, Rome/Viterbo: Figure 3
Morgan, Henry, Yeovil, Somerset: Figures 20, 28, 183, 205, 228, 232, 233, 245, and 250–252
Museés royaux des Beaux-Arts de Belgique, Bruxelles: Plate 4 and Figure 9
Museo Correr, Venice: Figure 10
Museo Nacional Centro de Arte Reina Sofia Photographic Archive, Madrid: Figure 13
National Archaeological Museum, Athens: Figure 4
Nyenhuis, Jacob E.: Plates 2, 3, 7, 10–13, 15–53; Figures 6, 7, 49, and 121
Ontario, Canada, Art Gallery: Figure 8
Rykwert, Joseph: Figures 79, 111, and 118
Stearn & Sons (Cambridge) Ltd. (copyrighted photographs): Figures 47, 67, 70–72, 75–78, 80–82, 103, and 179
Vickers, John, London: Figures 21, 22, and 37
Webb, John, Brompton Studio, London: Frontispiece and Figures 38, 43, 50, 178, 182, and 190
Wong, Manyi, New York: Figure 66

Index

Colophon

Managing Editor
Kathryn Wildfong,
Wayne State University Press

Production and Design Manager
Alice Nigoghosian,
Wayne State University Press

Book Design
Savitski Design,
Ann Arbor, Michigan

Printing
University Lithoprinters, Inc.,
Ann Arbor, Michigan

Bindery
John H. Dekker & Sons Bookbinding,
Grand Rapids, Michigan.